THE HISTORY OF THE ROYAL W[illegible]
FRONTIER FORCE

Her Majesty Queen Elizabeth II
Colonel-in-Chief The Royal West African Frontier Force 1953-1960

Frontispiece

THE HISTORY OF THE
ROYAL WEST AFRICAN FRONTIER FORCE

BY

COLONEL A. HAYWOOD
C.M.G., C.B.E., D.S.O.

AND

BRIGADIER F. A. S. CLARKE
D.S.O., *p.s.c.*†

The Naval & Military Press Ltd

Published by

The Naval & Military Press Ltd
Unit 10 Ridgewood Industrial Park,
Uckfield, East Sussex,
TN22 5QE England

Tel: +44 (0) 1825 749494
Fax: +44 (0) 1825 765701

www.naval-military-press.com
www.nmarchive.com

TO THE WEST AFRICAN SOLDIER

FOREWORD

By General Sir Lashmer Whistler, G.C.B., K.B.E., D.S.O., D.L.
Late Colonel Commandant, The Royal West African Frontier Force

This is the History of a fine Force which has recently been dissolved. It records the story of sixty years' honourable service in peace, and of courage, loyalty, tenacity, cheerfulness and magnificent endurance in war.

The "Waffs" have displayed these qualities in the orchard bush and tropical forests of Africa, on the scorching deserts of Northern Kenya and Somaliland, as well as on the wet hills of Abyssinia. But, as the narrative unfolds, it will be seen that their sternest test was against two enemies in Burma. First, the Japanese, fanatically brave and skilful adversaries; and, secondly, the Arakan with its torrential rain, steep hills covered with bush or bamboo, often pathless, and paddy fields infested by tidal streams. Nevertheless, the West African Divisions, supplied by air and supported by their stout-hearted carriers of head-loads, could traverse the worst of this terrain and successfully undertake tasks which other formations could not attempt. They were, in effect, the "Special Force" of the 11th Army Group in the Arakan.

The R.W.A.F.F. is no more, but its regular units, except the Gambia Company, are incorporated in the Military Forces of Nigeria, Ghana, and Sierra Leone. These units have a fine record and great traditions which the authors of the History have striven to portray.

In conclusion, I wish to express my gratitude to all who have helped to produce this History and especially to the R.W.A.F.F. History Committee which consists of the two main authors Colonel A. H. W. Haywood, C.M.G., C.B.E., D.S.O., of Part I, and Brigadier F. A. S. Clarke, D.S.O., of Part II, under the Chairmanship of Major-General K. G. Exham, C.B., D.S.O.

ADDENDUM TO FOREWORD

By Major-General J. Y. Whitfield, C.B., D.S.O., O.B.E.
Chairman R.W.A.F.F. Officers Association

To the very deep regret of us all, General Sir Lashmer Whistler died at the Cambridge Hospital, Aldershot, on 4th July 1963, after a severe and protracted illness. It is sad indeed that he did not live to see the publication of the History, which owes its inception to his initiative, enthusiasm and determination.

During General Whistler's period of Command in West Africa, he did much to further the efficiency and well being of the R.W.A.F.F., and he was immensely proud when he was appointed its Colonel Commandant.

After the West African Territories had become independent, he continued to give unstintingly of his time and energy to the many tasks and problems which confronted the various emergent West African Armies; and the several governments showed their recognition of his services by inviting him to become Honorary Colonel of the new units, which were and are the direct lineal descendants of the R.W.A.F.F.

Not only did the last Colonel Commandant serve the R.W.A.F.F. with honour and distinction, but also with unswerving loyalty and devotion, and this history may in some true sense be regarded as a memorial to a faithful servant of the force.

Chiddingfold,
Surrey. April 1964.

CONTENTS

Foreword by General Sir Lashmer Whistler, G.C.B., K.B.E., D.S.O., D.L., and Addendum to Foreword by Major-General J. Y. Whitfield, C.B., D.S.O., O.B.E. vii

PART I

PAGE

AUTHOR'S FOREWORD . 3

CHAP.

1 ORIGINS OF THE WEST AFRICAN FRONTIER FORCE . . 5
Historical Background—Topography, Physical and Other Features—Distribution of Races, Characteristics and History—Competition with Foreign Powers—Early Tribal Campaigns to 1900.

2 THE FORMATION OF THE W.A.F.F. 31
The Early Years 1897–1901—Consolidation, 1902–5—Ashanti Campaign, 1900—Tribal Campaigns and Minor Operations, 1900–5.

3 THE YEARS OF PROGRESS 81
Further Consolidation, 1906–14—Tribal Campaigns, 1906–14—Tactics in West African Savage Warfare.

4 TOGOLAND AND THE CAMEROONS CAMPAIGNS: 1914–16 . 97
Togoland, 5th–26th August 1914—Cameroons, 1914–16.

5 THE EAST AFRICAN CAMPAIGN: 1915–18 . 176

6 THE YEARS OF ACHIEVEMENT: 1914–19. 251
Arrangements for Internal Security and Reinforcements—Egba Rising, 1918—Post-War Considerations and Afterthoughts—The Story of the Mounted Infantry—Some Account of the W.A.F.F. Artillery, 1898–1916.

APPENDICES

I Titles of W.A.F.F. and Battle Honours 283
II List of Inspector-Generals and Colonels 284
III Terms of Selborne Committee 288
IV List of Uniform: Officers and Other Ranks, 1903 289
V Recipients of the Victoria Cross 290
VI Description of Medals issued to W.A.F.F. 291
VII Honours: East African Campaign 292
VIII Casualties East African Campaign 300
IX Honours (Officers only): Cameroons and Togoland Campaigns . . 303
X Order of Battle: Cameroons 305
XI Dispositions of W.A.F.F., 1919 307
XII Bibliography 308
XIII Glossary Part I 310

PART II

AUTHOR'S PREFACE . 313

ACKNOWLEDGMENTS . . . 313

CHAP. PAGE

7 THE YEARS BETWEEN THE WARS 315
Conditions in West Africa—Peacetime Soldiering—Preparations for War.

8 THE CAMPAIGN IN EAST AFRICA 328
The Situation in the Middle East—Events in Kenya up to January 1941—Across the Juba to Mogadishu—On to Addis Ababa—Destruction of the Italian Forces in the South-West—Chronological Table of Main Events in the Middle East and East Africa, June 1940 to November 1941.

9 THE FALL OF FRANCE AND THE EXPANSION OF THE R.W.A.F.F. 363
The Situation in West Africa—Preparations for Defence and Expansion—Expansion First Stage—Administrative Problems—Some Defence Problems—Completion of Expansion and Events, 1941–2—Formation of 81 and 82 (W.A.) Divisions.

10 THE CAMPAIGN IN BURMA: 1943–4 376
The Situation in November 1943—The Two Enemies—Plans and Preparations for the Dry Season, 1943–4—Outline of Operations in Arakan, 1944—81 (W.A.) Division in the Kaladan Valley—The Withdrawal from Kyauktaw—81 (W.A.) Division ordered to the Kalapanzin Valley—The Move to the Kalapanzin and Subsequent Events—Withdrawal of Hub Force from the Kaladan—Chronological Table of Events in Burma: November 1943 to October 1944

11 'CHINDITS' (WINGATE'S W.A.F.F.) 411
Plans and Preparations for the Second Chindit Operation—Outline of Events—6 Battalion The Nigeria Regiment—12 Battalion The Nigeria Regiment and the Defence of White City—7 Battalion The Nigeria Regiment—3 (W.A.) Brigade in the Final Phase

12 THE CAMPAIGN IN BURMA: 1944–5 429
Plans for Dry Weather Operations: 1944–5—Outline of Operations in Arakan: November 1944 to May 1945—81 (W.A.) Division Advances down the Kaladan Valley—82 (W.A.) Division in the Mayu Offensive Myohaung, January 1945.

13 OPERATIONS IN SOUTH ARAKAN: 1945 453
82 (W.A.) Division in the pursuit from Myohaung—Operations by 82 (W.A.) Division on the Tamandu–An Road—The Last Phase: 82 (W.A.) Division Clears South Arakan—Chronological Table of Events in Burma from November 1944 to September 1945

14 THE POST-WAR YEARS 473
Return to Peacetime Soldiering—Events in the Fifties—Epilogue.

ANNEXURES

I *Commandants Nigeria and Gold Coast Regiments and Inspectors-General R.W.A.F.F.* 487

II *Honours and Awards Granted to the R.W.A.F.F. during the Second World War* 488

APPENDICES

I Notes on Regimental Customs, etc. 495

II Method Used for Advancing Through Thick Tropical Forest . . . 498

III The Aba Riots or the Woman's War. (i) The Incident at Opobo. (ii) Extracts from the Report of a Commission of Inquiry 499

IV Army Rifle Association Decentralized Matches won by the R.W.A.F.F. between the wars 501

V Hon. Captain Chari Maigumeri, M.M. 502

APPENDICES PAGE

VI Organization and Establishment of a Battalion and Battery, R.W.A.F.F., 1938 . . . 503

VII Distribution of Troops in West Africa, July 1941 (With details of R.W.A.F.F. units) . . . 504

VIII Dispositions in West Africa, October–November 1942 (R.W.A.F.F. units shown in detail) . . . 505

IX Order of Battle 81 and 82 (W.A.) Divisions, 1943, and List of Units remaining in West Africa . . . 506

X Congratulatory Orders and Message to 81 and 82 (W.A.) Divisions . 507

XI Casualties in XV Corps during the campaign of 1944–5 509

XII Order of Battle of the West African Divisions as organized in Burma, 1943–5, including Full Titles of A.C.F. Units . . . 510

XIII Primitive Soldiers of the Auxiliary Groups: An Anecdote . . . 511

XIV 81 (W.A.) Recce Regiment on the Main Arakan Front, 1944 . . 512

XV Chindits: Problems of Intercommunication . . . 514

XVI Scale of Clothing and Necessaries (1920–39) . . . 515

XVII Disturbances in the Gold Coast, 1948 . . . 516

XVIII The Return of the Flag of Sultan Attahiru Ahamadu to Sokoto . . 518

XIX Operations in the Southern Cameroons, 1959–60 . . . 520

XX Glossary. Part II . . . 521

List of Subscribers . 523

Indices . 527

ILLUSTRATIONS

Her Majesty Queen Elizabeth II, Colonel-in-Chief, The Royal West African Frontier Force, 1953–1960 . . . . *frontispiece*

PLATE		FACING PAGE
1	Lord Lugard of Abinger, P.C., G.C.M.G., C.B., D.S.O.	33
2	General Sir Thomas Lethbridge Napier Morland, K.C.B., K.C.M.G., D.S.O., Inspector-General W.A.F.F., 1905–9. Served throughout 1914–18 War, during which he commanded the X and XIII Corps .	34
3	The walls of Kano, 1903	64
	Kano from inside the walls	64
4	Yams galore	65
	Clearing bush for roadmaking	65
5	Marshal of the R.A.F. Viscount Trenchard, G.C.B., O.M., G.C.V.O., D.S.O. He was Commandant, Southern Nigeria Regiment W.A.F.F., 1908–10, and is here portrayed as the Colonel of the Royal Scots Fusiliers in 1916	80
6	Trenchard's interpreter haranguing a tribe; B.O.H. Expedition, 1906 .	81
	Fording a river; Niger–Cross River Expedition	81
7	The N.H.E. Expedition reaches its goal—the border of Southern/ Northern Nigeria	112
	A column making camp in a market-place	112
8	S.Y. *Ivy* entering Lagos Lagoon with troops	113
	The C.O.'s house on Lagos Lagoon	113
9	Regimental Sergeant-Major Belo Akure, D.C.M., M.M., Nigeria Regiment	128
10	Column arriving at Sanchu, Cameroons, 1915	129
	Troops crossing a bush bridge	129
11	1 Battery, Nigeria Regiment, in action, Cameroons, 1915	192
	1 Battery, Nigeria Regiment, in action, Cameroons, 1915	192
12	A machine-gun detachment in action	193
	Volta River ferry, Northern Territories, Gold Coast	193
13	Mounted Infantry: Company Sergeant Major in Marching Order; Private in Dismounted Review Order	208
14	Mounted infantryman on service, Cameroons, 1914	209
	Gun-carriers with cradle of 2·95 in. gun, Gold Coast Battery, 1905 .	209
15	A gun-carrier in full marching order	304
	Battery Sergeant-Major Maida Musa, D.C.M., M.M., Nigeria Regiment	304
16	Officer's Mess, Zaria	305
	Officer's bush house, Ibadan	305
17	African N.C.O.s in full dress	320
	Guard of honour, Kaduna, 1936	320
18	Hausa soldier of the Nigeria Regiment in full marching order, 1937 .	321
19	Gold Coast Troops marching into a town in Italian Somaliland . .	352
	Guard of honour for the Emperor Haile Selassie, Addis Ababa, 5th May 1941.	352
20	A British officer studying Italian positions across the River Omo .	353

PLATE		FACING PAGE
21	General Sir George Gifford, G.C.B., D.S.O.	368
22	The Kaladan Valley	369
23	Carriers on the march in bush	448
	Carriers on the march in paddy country	448
24	Hurri-Bombers attack Japanese position at Paletwa	449
	Supply drop	449
25	The Taungup–Prome Road	464
26	H.M. Queen Elizabeth II, Colonel-in-Chief, Royal West African Frontier Force, inspecting a Guard of Honour formed by the 3rd Battalion The Nigeria Regiment on 5th February 1956, during the Royal Tour in Nigeria	480
27	General Sir Lashmer Whistler, G.C.B., K.B.E., D.S.O., D.L.	481

ACKNOWLEDGMENTS

ACKNOWLEDGMENTS and thanks are due for permission to publish the following:

To the Imperial War Museum for photographs on Plates 19 (top) 20, 24 (both) and 25; and to the *Daily Telegraph* for 19 (bottom).

Acknowledgments and thanks are also due to the following for the loan of photographs; 22 and 23 (both) by Major-General C. G. Woolner, C.B., M.C.; 16 (bottom) and 17 (top) by Lieutenant-Colonel P. F. Pritchard, O.B.E., M.C.; 17 (bottom) and 19 (bottom) by Mrs. Colthurst.

The author of Part II also expresses his appreciation of the help given by the Editor, *African World*, in obtaining the picture for 26.

LIST OF MAPS

MAP NO.			PAGE
1	General map of West Africa	FACING	5
2	Tribal map of Nigeria	FACING	15
3	Ashanti, 1900		54
4	South Nigeria (Niger/Cross River Section) Operations of Aro Field Force, December 1901–March 1902		64
5	Column of 1 Gun and 3 Coys. in bush warfare		95
6	Togoland	FACING	97
7	The Cameroons (1914)	FACING	105
8	Duala and hinterland		128
9	The Muyuka–Chang Area		132
10	The Edea–Yaunde Area		144
11	Garua		152
12	The Mora Mountain		156
13	The Campo–Ambam Area		162
14	Strategic situation January 1916		170
15	Tanganyika	FACING	177
16	The action at Kikarungu Hill, 4th–6th September 1916		178
17	Operations around Kibata, November 1916–January 1917		186
18	Strategic situation, 20th December 1916		190
19	The advance to the Rufiji		192
20	The Rufiji Area		194
21	The pursuit of Wintgens and Naumann, May–June 1917		202
22	The Battle of Narungombe, 19th July 1916		208
23	Narungombe/Mihambia/Bweho–Chini/Ndessa Area, 19th–22nd September 1917		210
24	Battle of Bweho–Chini, 22nd September 1917		218
25	Strategic situation, October 1917		228
26	Battle of Nyangao (or Mahiwa) 15th–18th October 1917 (Robert's operations)		232
	Mann's operations at Mahiwa, 15th–18th October 1917		232
27	Action at Mkwera, 6th–7th November 1917		240
28	The Egba Rising, 1918		256
29	The campaign in East Africa		330
30	The Juba crossing		334
31	The pursuit to Jijiga		340
32	Marda Pass		342
33	Jijiga to Harar		344
34	South-West Abyssinia		348
35	Battle of Wadara, April–May 1941		352
36	Omo River, 31st May–6th June 1941		356
37	General map of Burma	FACING	375
38	Burma—Arakan and Akyab Area	FACING	381
39	Kaladan Valley		384
40	81 Division in the Kaladan		388
41	81 Division in the Kaladan		390
42	The Chindit fly-in Operations around Mawlu		412
43	Chindits—Final phase		422
44	81 Division advances down the Kaladan, December 1944–January 1945		434
45	82 (W.A.) Division in the Mayu Offensive		440
46	The Approach to Myohaung		446
47	Battle of Myohaung		448
48	Pursuit from Myohaung		452
49	Operations on the Tamandu–An Road	FACING	457
50	Operations in South Arakan		468

PART I

By

COLONEL A. HAYWOOD

C.M.G., C.B.E., D.S.O.

AUTHOR'S FOREWORD TO PART I

OWING to the lapse of more than half a century since the West African Frontier Force was raised, very few of those prominent in the events described in its early years are still with us. Consequently it has been exceedingly difficult to collect information other than that available from official sources.

The spelling of names often varies from that used in earlier writings, but, as far as possible, it follows the ruling of the Permanent Committee of the Royal Geographical Society on Geographical Names.

For simplicity an officer's rank is only given the first time his name is mentioned, thereafter he is merely referred to by his surname.

Chapter 1 (The Origins of the W.A.F.F.) has been read by Sir Alan Burns. In Chapters 2 and 3, under the title of 'Consolidation' will be found a diary of events for the year, which always begins with Gambia. In this diary tribal campaigns are briefly mentioned, but a fuller account of them is given under the title of 'Tribal Campaigns' in a later section of these chapters.

For Chapter 4 (The Togoland and Cameroons Campaigns) I have relied principally on the Official History (Brigadier-General F. J. Moberly, who was able to consult those who played a leading part in the operations, but nearly all of whom are now dead).

General Sir George Giffard, Brigadier H. B. Latham and Colonel R. A. de B. Rose, have read Chapter 5 (The East African Campaign).

The comments made in each of these readings are greatly valued.

The Colonial Office has given the author all possible assistance by allowing his access to its Library and documents in the Public Record Office, where he is especially indebted to Mr. B. Cheesman, Mr. H. Hannan and Mr. Blakiston.

The Governments and Military Staffs of Nigeria, Ghana, Sierra Leone and Gambia have freely placed relevant documents at the author's disposal. While in Nigeria, Major S. F. B. Francis, The Queen's Own Nigeria Regiment, carried out the duties of liaison officer with the utmost zeal.

In conclusion I must thank all those who contributed, with material or photographs. For the Section dealing with the Mounted Infantry I am greatly indebted to Brigadier J. G. Browne (14th Hussars) and Lieut-Colonel Lord Dorchester (9th Lancers), two of the small band of survivors from the early days of the Unit. The Section on the Artillery has been entirely compiled by Major R. J. Waller (R.A.)

WESTERN SAHARA
UPPER SENEG
SENEGAL
FRENCH GUINEA
PORT. GUINEA
SIERRA LEONE
LIBERIA
IVORY COAST
NORTHERN TERRITORIE
ASHANTI
GOLD COAST COLONY
Grain Coast
Ivory Coast
Gold
LEGEND
Railways
" under Const
" Proposed
Motor Roads Completed
" " Doubtful
BRITISH
FRENCH
GERMAN
PORTUGUESE
LIBERIA
SPANISH
GENERAL MAP OF
WEST AFRICA
SCALE
MLS. 100 50 0 100 200

1. General ma

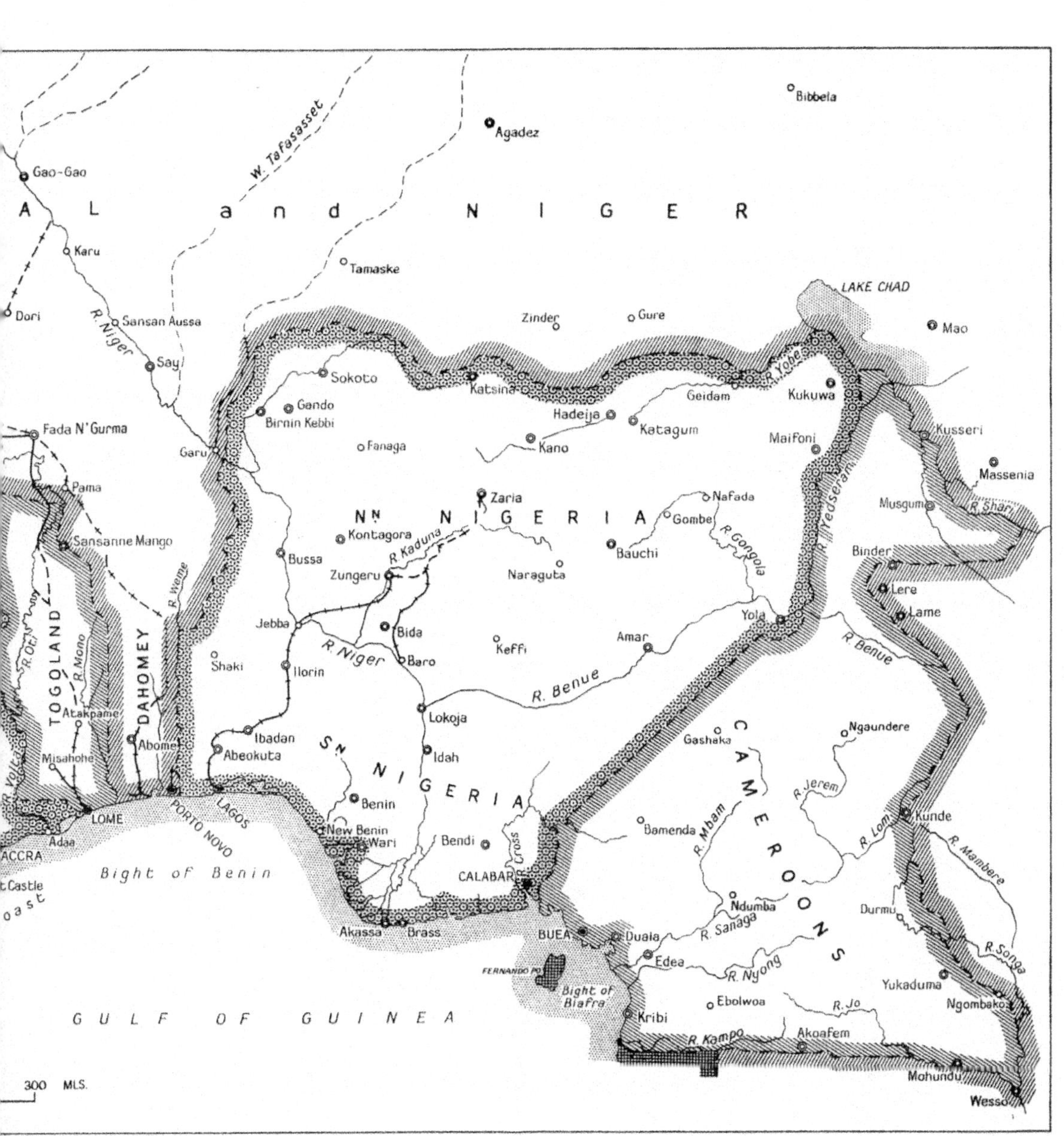

Bibbela
Agadez
W. Tafasasset
Gao-Gao
A L and NIGER
Karu
Tamaske
Dori
R. Niger
Sansan Aussa
LAKE CHAD
Zinder
Gure
Mao
Say
Sokoto
Katsina
R. Yobe
Geidam
Kukuwa
Gando
Birnin Kebbi
Hadeija
Katagum
Fada N'Gurma
Garu
Fanaga
Kano
Maifoni
Kusseri
Massenia
Pama
Zaria
Nafada
N^N NIGERIA
Gombe
Musgum
R. Shari
Sansanne Mango
Kontagora
R. Kaduna
R. Gongola
Bauchi
R. Yedseram
Binder
Bussa
Naraguta
Lere
Zungeru
Lame
R. Oti
TOGOLAND
DAHOMEY
R. Weme
Jebba
Bida
Yola
Keffi
Amar
R. Benue
R. Mono
Shaki
R. Niger
Baro
Ilorin
R. Benue
Lokoja
Atakpame
Abome
Ibadan
Gashaka
CAMEROONS
Ngaundere
Misahohe
Abeokuta
S^N NIGERIA
Idah
R. Volta
R. Jerem
Benin
Bamenda
R. Mbam
Kunde
LOME
PORTO NOVO
LAGOS
New Benin
Wari
Bendi
R. Cross
R. Lom
R. Mambere
Adaa
ACCRA
Bight of Benin
CALABAR
Ndumba
Durmu
Castle
oast
Akassa
Brass
BUEA
Duala
R. Sanaga
R. Songa
Edea
FERNANDO PO
R. Nyong
Yukaduma
Bight of Biafra
Ebolwoa
R. Jo
Ngombako
GULF OF GUINEA
Kribi
R. Kampo
AkoaFem
Mohundu
300 MLS.
Wesso

' West Africa

CHAPTER 1

Origins of the West African Frontier Force

(A) HISTORICAL BACKGROUND

ALTHOUGH the West African Frontier Force (commonly known as the W.A.F.F.) was not actually formed until 1897, its origins may be said to have had their beginning much earlier than this.

The story is told of a weary and exhausted traveller, riding a jaded horse across the uplands of Yorubaland in the middle of last century, surrounded by tribes making war upon each other for the purpose of capturing and selling slaves.

Lagos Battalion

As this man went through the country slaves ran away from their masters, seeking his protection. He reached Lagos in safety, and, on his return journey, these free slaves, organized and armed by him, gave him protection and encouraged others to join him.

This man was Lieutenant Glover, R.N., later Sir John Glover, Governor of Lagos. He had been on a voyage of exploration on the Niger with Dr. Baikie when their vessel the *Dayspring* was wrecked at Jebba, and was returning overland. The slaves he had freed formed the Lagos Constabulary and were known as 'Glover's Hausas'. The year was 1863.

At this time the garrison of Lagos was found by the West India Regiment. However, on the urgent representations of Glover, who had great faith in the loyalty and courage of these Hausa freed slaves, approval was given by the Imperial Government for their formation into a force for the defence of Lagos. A start was made with some 40 men, increased that June to 100. They were reported on as being 'very proud of being soldiers who fight faithfully and well, and are apt at their drill'.

In October of the same year sanction was given to increase the force to 600, to be called up for two months' training in batches of 100 during the year, while in 1865 the British Government authorized its constitution as a regular force, to be named 'Hausa Constabulary'. It was liable for police as well as military duties, the title being altered later to 'Lagos' Constabulary', which it retained until its incorporation into the West African Frontier Force as the Lagos Battalion in 1901.

Embryo of the W.A.F.F.

There is, however, an earlier force which may perhaps be considered as the embryo of the W.A.F.F. This originated when the British trading companies were granted Royal Charters in West Africa. The first charter was granted by Queen Elizabeth to trade with Senegal, Sierra Leone and the Gambia. But it was not till 1662 that trading to any extent materialized in West Africa, and this was started under a charter given by Charles II to 'The Company of Royal Adventurers', for the purpose of trading from Gibraltar to the Cape of Good Hope. This Company was succeeded by 'The Royal Africa Company' on the 27th September 1672.

It was on the Gold Coast that certain forts were built by this Company, and garrisons maintained, recruited from West Africans, with a small proportion of Europeans, for their defence against hostile natives.

The Gold Coast may, therefore, perhaps claim the honour of being the embryo of the W.A.F.F. It is interesting, too, to note that the badge of the Royal Africa Company, and subsequently that of the Gold Coast Constabulary, was an elephant. Moreover, the first golden guineas struck at the Mint were made from gold exported from the Gulf of Guinea, stamped with the elephant and issued to the Company.

The Royal Africa Company was succeeded by the 'African Company of Merchants'. Meanwhile in 1807 slavery was abolished by international agreement, and this led to the Crown taking over control of the Gold Coast settlements from that Company in 1822.

We now find Sierra Leone coming into the picture consequent upon its establishment as a home for freed slaves.

Origin of the Gold Coast Regiment

One of its early Governors was Sir Charles MacCarthy, whose duty it was to pay an annual visit to the Gold Coast. Upon the Crown taking control Sir Charles reorganized its force into a regiment of three companies, called the 'Royal African Colonial Corps of Light Infantry', and about the same time Militia and Volunteer Corps were formed mainly for the object of preventing raids by the Ashantis.

In 1823 the Corps was increased to five companies by recruits from England. In 1824 Sir Charles, while campaigning with a strong escort, was surprised by an Ashanti force and defeated at the battle of Isamankow, where he was killed. Here the Royal African Colonial Corps was practically annihilated, though acquitted itself well in spite of being heavily outnumbered. This defeat was avenged in 1826 at Dodowa.

From 1828 to 1843 the defence was in the hands of the Militia. In 1843 a company of the West India Regiment was stationed in the Gold Coast, and in the latter year an artillery corps was raised, but this was disbanded in 1863.

Between 1803 and this date there had been no less than five Ashanti wars. These were in the main caused by jealousy between that country and the Fantis, since Ashanti had no access to the sea, except through an alliance with Elmina, and was thus dependent on the Fantis for its trade routes thereto. The Fantis, however, denied freedom of these in order to maintain a complete monopoly of trade to the coast. Events culminated in 1872, when the Dutch settlements, Elmina, Accra, Dixcove and Sekondi were transferred to the United Kingdom, as we were anxious to acquire a Protectorate over the whole Gold Coast in order to prevent Ashanti encroachments.

Wolseley's Ashanti Campaign, 1873–4

Thus 1873 saw the opening of the sixth Ashanti War, when the invasion of an army from Kumasi, which threatened to capture Elima, caused the British Government to declare war in favour of the Fantis. In this campaign some 12,000 British troops, 500–700 W.I.R. and a few hundred Lagos Hausas (Lagos Constabulary) were employed under the command of Major-General Wolseley. There were also a few Mendes from Sierra Leone and some Gambia native levies. This point is of interest as being the earliest date when formed bodies of pre-W.A.F.F. tribes took part together in a campaign outside their own territory.

In the advance on Kumasi the Lagos Hausas actually fought under Glover, forming the Eastern Column based on the Volta River. After the Campaign about 300 remained behind to form the nucleus of the Gold Coast Constabulary, which was raised in 1879 with an establishment of 16 European officers and 1,203 Africans. It retained this designation until its incorporation in the W.A.F.F. as the Gold Coast Regiment in 1901.

Origin of the Sierra Leone Battalion

In 1829, after the Crown had taken over the administration of Sierra Leone, it was decided to form a Sierra Leone Police Corps for the defence of the country. Its establishment was 17 officers, 23 N.C.O.s and 300 African Creoles, Mendes and Timinis. This body became the forerunner of the Sierra Leone Frontier Police, which was established by Ordinance on 15th January 1890, for the maintenance of peace, in the hinterland now being developed, and to safeguard the Anglo-French borders.

The title of Sierra Leone Frontier Police (popularly known as 'The Frontiers') was retained until its incorporation into the W.A.F.F. as the Sierra Leone Battalion in 1901.

Origin of the Gambia Company

In the early part of the nineteenth century Gambia was a dependency of Sierra Leone, coming under the jurisdiction of the latter's Governor.

Sir Charles MacCarthy was the Governor responsible for suppressing the slave trade here in the years 1815–16. On 23rd April 1816 he established a garrison of the Royal African Colonial Corps for that purpose on the island of Banjol at the mouth of the Gambia River, which later became the site of the present capital Bathurst. The garrison was commanded by Captain Alexander Grant and may perhaps be considered as the forerunner of the W.A.F.F. in that colony.

In 1888 Gambia was separated from Sierra Leone and was given its own Governor. Its garrison was now found by a company of the W.I.R. until the end of 1901, when the Gambia Company W.A.F.F. was raised from a nucleus of 75 Mendes of the Sierra Leone Battalion.

Origin of the Northern Nigeria Regiment

In the first half of the nineteenth century McGregor Laird formed the 'Society of Merchants' to settle trade disputes on the Niger. At this time

Dr. Baikie was British Consul at Fernando Po and was instructed by the Government to co-operate with Laird in order to establish trade on the Niger and Benue Rivers. Baikie then visited Bida, Zaria and Kano. In 1864 he died, about the same year as McGregor Laird. Meanwhile a warship was detailed to show the flag each year in support of our trade, and to protect shipping from attacks by the natives. These visits continued until 1871. In 1879, George Goldie Taubman, who had succeeded Laird, formed a combination of all British firms, which he called the 'National Company of Africa'.

The scramble for Africa had now begun, and the French 'Cie. Française de l'Afrique Equatoriale' started operating on the Niger with a capital of £60,000. The National Africa Company at once increased its capital to £1,000,000, thereby qualifying for a Royal Charter, which was granted on 10th July 1886. This meant that the Company accepted responsibility for administering its territory north of the Niger.

On the same date the Royal Niger Company's Constabulary came into being for the protection of the area, as from which date the Niger Company's charter was revoked and a Protectorate of Northern Nigeria established. Eleven years later, in 1897–8, it formed the nucleus of the 1 and 2 Special Service Corps Battalions West African Frontier Force, subsequently named 1 and 2 Battalions Northern Nigeria Regiment, on 1st January 1900. At the same time the Constabulary was disbanded.

Origin of the Southern Nigeria Regiment

Turning now to the situation south of the Niger, that is on the Lower Niger. In 1885 the Government had made treaties with the chiefs on both banks and declared the 'Oil Rivers Protectorate' (subsequently changed to 'Niger Coast Protectorate') over the country extending south of Lokoja to Rio del Rey, with H.Q. at Fernando Po and Calabar.

The protection of this area demanded the raising of a force, called the 'Oil Rivers Irregulars' (nicknamed the 'Forty Thieves'). In 1891 it was renamed 'Niger Coast Constabulary', with H.Q. at Calabar. In 1893, by Order in Council, the Protectorate was extended definitely into the hinterland.

In 1898–9 the Niger Coast Constabulary became the nucleus of the 3 Battalion W.A.F.F., which in turn became the Southern Nigeria Regiment, W.A.F.F. in 1900.

(B) TOPOGRAPHY, PHYSICAL AND OTHER FEATURES

Zone of Responsibility

The countries for whose well-being the West African Frontier Force was responsible consisted of the British West African Colonies and Protectorates which at the close of the last century were as follows, starting from the north: Gambia (capital Bathurst), Sierra Leone (capital Freetown), The Gold Coast (capital Accra), Lagos (capital Lagos), Southern and Northern Nigeria (capitals Calabar and Lokoja, respectively). From the port of Bathurst to Calabar was a distance of 2,000 miles' steaming approximately.

Sandwiched between these territories in the main were French possessions, with, however, the German colonies of Togoland on the eastern boundary of the Gold Coast, and the Cameroons along the whole length of the eastern border of Nigeria. In addition Liberia formed the eastern border of Sierra Leone.

The area with which we have to deal extends from the southern fringe of the Saharan Plateau as far as the Atlantic seaboard, roughly from 13 degrees North latitude (Chad, Sokoto and Gambia) to 5 degrees North at the mouth of the Cross River in the Bight of Benin, and thence back to Gambia.

Area and Population

In considering the relative sizes of the countries forming British West Africa, for convenience, Lagos and the two Nigerias are taken as one unit. At the turn of last century their combined area was some 335,000 sq. miles, and population 18,000,000. The Gold Coast, with its Northern Territories, covered 90,000 sq. miles and had a population of 4,000,000. Lastly, the smallest were Sierra Leone and Gambia with areas of 30,000 and 4,000 sq. miles and populations of 2,000,000 and 200,000 respectively.

Physical and Other Features

In the north is the Futa Jallon Massif, the hydrographic centre of West Africa, which rises to 5,000 ft. and continues down to the Sierra Leone frontier and the sea. From its northern slopes rises the Gambia River.

In the Northern Territories of the Gold Coast, south of the Niger Bend, stretch grassy spurs of the great West African Plateau, between which flow the Black and White Volta Rivers, while farther south, between Accra and Kumasi, the Kwahu Plateau rises to some 2,000 ft.

In the north of Nigeria is a tableland, part of the main plateau of North Africa, varying from 1,200 to 800 ft high (at Chad). The water-parting between the Niger and Lake Chad runs north-west to south-east from Katsena to Bauchi. The Bauchi plateau is itself 4,000 ft. high, falling southward to the Niger basin and the sea.

Speaking generally the whole area comprises a belt of heavy forest and swampy bush extending from seaboard up to 100 miles inland. This is succeeded by a region of grassland and orchard bush for several hundred miles, merging into semi-desert country in the extreme interior of Nigeria where it borders on the Sahara.

Waterways

Freetown possessed the only deep-water harbour. Elsewhere bars and surf impeded navigation by other than shallow-draught vessels. Elder Dempster and the German Woermann lines accounted for practically all the ocean trade. The voyage from Liverpool to Lagos took about three weeks in a passenger ship of 4,000 tons. The longest rivers are the Niger, Volta, Gambia and Cross Rivers. The coast is permeated with numerous lesser rivers and creeks, which, however, were only navigable for launches and small craft for short distances. The Volta was navigable for barely 80 miles, while the Gambia and Cross Rivers could at certain times of the year take small vessels 250 and 150 miles up from their mouths respectively.

The Niger

As a matter of historical interest it will be remembered that the celebrated West African explorer, Mungo Park, started both his journeys from the Gambia River, for the exploration of the Niger.

His point of departure was a place called Pisania,[1] 200 miles from the sea, and the farthest British inland trading station at that time. On the first occasion he reached the Niger at Segu and followed its course to Sansanding (for about 50 miles). From that point he had to abandon the enterprise owing to sickness and deaths. This was in 1796. His second journey, in 1805, followed the same route and ended at Bussa in Northern Nigeria, where he was attacked by natives and either killed or more probably, drowned in the rapids when trying to escape.

This waterway, the Niger, dominates the scene of our present history, and, with its tributary the Benue, is the area from which the tribes composing the West African Frontier Force are recruited. In its upper reaches it is called 'Joliba' (hence the name Park gave to the craft he built for its exploration), while in Nigeria it is known to the natives as 'Quorra' (or 'Kworra').

The Niger is the third largest river of Africa. Its total length is 2,600 miles. Rising at an altitude of 2,800 ft. at Tembikunda on the Sierra Leone/French Guinea frontier, it flows though a mainly flat alluvial plain until south of Timbuktu, where rapids occur at intervals till Bussa is reached some 500 miles from its outlet to the sea at the port of Forcados.

Its basin drains, in its upper reaches, the habitat of the Mandingos and Temnes (Timinis), recruited into the Gambia Company and Sierra Leone Battalion respectively, while such tribes as the Moshis and Grunshis in its 'Bend', have always formed the backbone of the Gold Coast Regiment. As for the Northern Nigerian, Southern Nigerian and Lagos Units, the Hausa and Pagan states of the Middle and Lower Niger have been from the earliest days a highly fruitful source of recruits.

Clapperton and Lander Complete Mungo Park's Exploration of the Niger

It was given to Captain Clapperton, and his servant Richard Lander, to continue the work begun by Park. In 1826 they travelled from Badagry, through Yorubaland to Bussa, going on to Sokoto, where the former died in 1827. Lander then returned to England but led a second expedition to Bussa, whence he floated in canoes down to the Niger estuary, so finally proving the exit of the river (which had for so many years been in doubt) to be in the Atlantic Ocean, in 1830.

Roads and Railways

At the turn of last century metalled roads were almost non-existent, but a good road led from Cape Coast Castle to Kumasi, 141 miles long, in 1898. Elsewhere bushtracks had been widened and straightened to make

[1] A memorial stone was erected here by the Governor, Sir George Denton, to commemorate the event (1908–12).

them fairly good in the dry season between administrative centres. In the rains conditions were often very bad.

A start was being made at building railways, in Sierra Leone from Freetown to the eastern hinterland, in the Gold Coast from Sekondi to the Ashanti goldfields, from Lagos to Ibadan and from Baro towards Kano, but little progress was made before 1901–3.

Telegraph lines were in their infancy, but the capitals were generally connected with main administrative centres. Otherwise messages had to be sent by runners.

(c) RACIAL DISTRIBUTION

Tribal Composition of the West African Races in the W.A.F.F.

The West African people may be broadly divided into Negro, or debased races, and the finer types. As a rough guide it may be said that the former inhabited the country south of 9 degrees North latitude, while the latter were located north of this, the dividing line being drawn approximately through Yola, Keffi, Jebba, Tamale and the northern frontier of Sierra Leone.

Prior to the tenth century negroes inhabited a zone extending as far as 200 miles north of the Niger Bend, but were driven south by the Moorish invasion and conquest, and in the course of years retreated still farther southward. Herodotus quotes pigmies on the middle Niger, whereas now they are located about the Congo Forest, say 7 degrees latitude North of the Equator.

The W.A.F.F. units of each colony were recruited from the tribes in their own territories generally speaking, and these tribes varied a good deal in appearance and characteristics. They had, however, the useful attributes of cheerfulness and loyalty in common. A sprinkling of Hausas and Fulanis were to be found elsewhere then in Northern Nigeria.

In the earliest days of the Force pidgin English and interpreters were the usual method of communication, although in Northern Nigeria a few keen officers quickly picked up Hausa, the language most widely spoken there, and one easily acquired.

Gambia

The Gambia Company started with a nucleus of Mendes from the Sierra Leone Battalion in 1901. But gradually its composition was changed in favour of locally recruited tribes with warlike traditions. These were mainly Mandingos and Jollofs with a sprinkling of Fulas (called Fulanis in Nigeria) and Bambaras; the latter have a great reputation as soldiers and form the backbone of the French Senegalese tirailleurs, their country being really in Senegal.

Mandingos and the Melle Empire[1]

The Mandingos are among the earliest people of whom there is a record in Western Africa. The Mandingo invasion of Africa is supposed

[1] The Melle Empire rose on the ruins of Ghana in the thirtheenth century. At one time it reached from the Atlantic to the Niger in Hausaland and stretched in the north from the 20th parallel 200 miles beyond Timbuktu to the pagan country about the 9th parallel, south of the Niger Bend.

to have come from the East. In the fourteenth century the great Mandingo Kingdom of Melle, or Mali, was already established south of the Gambia River Basin. Its ruler Mansa Musa, known as the 'Great Emperor of the Blacks'; his capital was Manding. He made a pilgrimage to Mecca in 1324 thereby introducing Islam to his people. They are now located mainly in the Upper Niger Valley about Bafing.

Jollofs

They and the Jollofs are the most powerful tribes of the Gambia River. The Mandingos are less black than the Jollofs and have finer features. In the old days the Jollofs were called Felops, or Floops. Now they are often known as Wollofs.

Fulas

The Fulas are said to have come from Asia, or Lower Egypt. Their main habitat is Futa Jallon. In the early nineteenth century they raided eastward for about 70 years, scattering settlements as far as Nigeria, about which we shall read later when dealing with that country. They are serious-faced, melancholy-looking people with fine features of a reddish colour. The Fula name for Mandingo is Malinke, the Hausas call them Wongaras, supposedly owing to a kingdom of that name they established south of the Niger Bend.

SIERRA LEONE

Timinis

The Sierra Leone Battalion was recruited mainly from the Timinis and Mendes, who occupy the greater portion of the country. The Timinis were the original inhabitants, and now occupy the western region, viz. the Kwai area, around Port Lokkoh and the Skarcies River. They are pure negro, sturdily built and make excellent scouts in the bush, being also first-rate carriers. In the last century they were turbulent and the cause of much unrest due to raiding for slaves and their fetish practices. The Timinis conquered the Mendes and Susus in the sixteenth century.

Mendes

The Mendes, or Kussus, inhabit the Sherbro and Gallinas districts. They also are of pure negro origin, and their past history is similar to that of the Timinis, having much the same attributes and traditions.

In the Ashanti Campaign of 1900 both Mendes and Timinis earned the highest praise from Sir James Willcocks for their scouting prowess during the severe fighting through the thick Ashanti bush and forest on the way to Kumasi.

Susus

Besides the tribes mentioned the Battalion recruited a sprinkling of Susus, who come from the western border of the country. They are Mahomedans belonging to the Mandingo family described above, having the finer type of features in contrast to the negroid type of the Timinis and Mendes.

THE GOLD COAST

The men of the Gold Coast Regiment were almost entirely recruited from the Northern Territories, comprising Moshis, Grunshis and Mamprussis (including Fra-Fras).

Ghana Empire

However, before discussing these tribes it is necessary to give a brief account of the history of the ancient kingdom or Empire of Ghana, from whence they are supposed to have originated.

Ghana was the earliest known West African Empire. The inhabitants claimed origin from the Assyrians, or Babylonians, coming from the valleys of the Euphrates and Tigris. Fulanis may have been its first rulers about A.D. 300. They, or light-coloured, rulers continued to reign for 22 generations before being succeeded by 'black' kings.

Ghana was also known as Ain Walata, and was situated between the 17th and 18th parallel of North latitude, to the north-west of Timbuktu. In A.D. 750 it did a flourishing trade with Morocco and the Berber country to the east.

In 1076 the Almoravides from Morocco, led by Abu Bekr, sacked Audoghast, the capital of the Berber kingdom some 200 miles to the east, and partially conquered Ghana. Thereafter it was divided into two kingdoms, one being ruled by a Berber Mahomedan and the other by a Pagan. The two were only six miles apart. At this time the Ghana empire extended into Senegal and Gambia, with its southern capital at Jenne, in the Niger Valley 300 miles south-west of Timbuktu.

Conquest of Ghana by Moors and Melles

The conquest of Ghana was completed by the Melles (or Mandingos) about the year 1250. These people created an Empire, called Mellestine, which was at the height of its fame under Mansa Musa, in the early fourteenth century, until about 1333. Soon after, it began to decline, being finally conquered by the Songhay Empire in the fifteenth century and driven from Timbuktu. Askia the Great was the most famous Songhay ruler, taking his conquests farther east into Hausaland.

It may perhaps be concluded from the above account of ancient Ghana that the tribes of the Northern Territories at the present time are descended, partly or wholly, from people who were driven south by the remorseless process of invasion and conquest. Generally speaking, they are tough fighters, keen on bearing arms and proud of enlisting in the Gold Coast Regiment.

To bring their history down to modern times the following brief account will be of interest:

Moshis. Although this tribe is now located in the French territory of the Upper Volta it came partially into the British sphere of influence until the Anglo-French Boundary was defined in 1902–3, and fixed on 11 degrees North latitude. For 500 years, until the French conquest in 1895, they ruled the tribes of the Northern Territories and to some extent those of the Niger Bend. They were mainly of peasant pagan stock originally, but ruled by warrior bands of Mahomedan persuasion, from about 1400.

Mamprussis (and Fra-Fras). These people inhabit the extreme north of the territories, coming there previously from the Niger Bend.

Dagombas. Farther south we have the Dagombas, in the vicinity of Tamale and Yendi. They were for many years in a state of chronic warfare with their western neighbours, the Gonjas, whom they eventually defeated, being themselves overcome by the Moshis.

NIGERIA, INCLUDING NORTHERN AND SOUTHERN NIGERIA AND LAGOS

Although these three territories were separate units at the end of the last century, they are being treated under one heading with three subheads, in view of their subsequent amalgamation in 1914.

(I) NORTHERN NIGERIA

At the end of 1897 when the Royal Niger Company's forces were in process of being dissolved and the 1 and 2 Battalions of the West African Frontier Force were being raised, the nucleus of the latter was formed by transferring men from the former. The tribes thus recruited were practically all Hausa, Nupe and Yoruba. In order to fill the ranks more of these men were enlisted, as, generally speaking, they had proved good material, although gradually the Nupe element was eliminated in preference to the two others; a little later Kanuris and Shuas crept in. As time went on Hausa and Pagan tribes from Northern Nigeria excluded the Yoruba element, resulting in all recruiting being done north of the Niger, leaving Yorubas to Southern Nigeria and Lagos as being their natural habitat.

Under this subhead it is therefore intended only to give a brief description of the Hausas, and Pagans, of the north, at the same time touching lightly on the Kanuris and Shuas.

HAUSAS

They are a long-headed race as opposed to the pure negro with a short head, and are of mixed blood. Lady Lugard in her book on Nigeria, *A Tropical Dependency*, says they probably came from the Nile Valley before the eleventh century and occupied the seven states in the north of the country, Gober, Gando, Sokoto, Katsena, Kano, Zaria and Nupe; they then intermarried with Pagans from Adamawa and Bauchi. About A.D. 1200 they became Mahomedan. In 1400 the Fulanis spread to Hausaland and were given land in Zaria and Gazawa, gradually acquiring more and more influence there.

In 1550 Bornu became very powerful, overcoming the Hausas and Fulanis. But prior to this the Songhay Empire had gained the upper hand in the Western Sudan and, about 1512, had conquered Katsena, Zaria, Zamfara and Kano.

About 1590 the Moors, being defeated by the Turks and Christians, were driven south to the Niger, destroying the prosperous Songhay Empire and invading Hausaland up to Zaria. It was not till the seventeenth

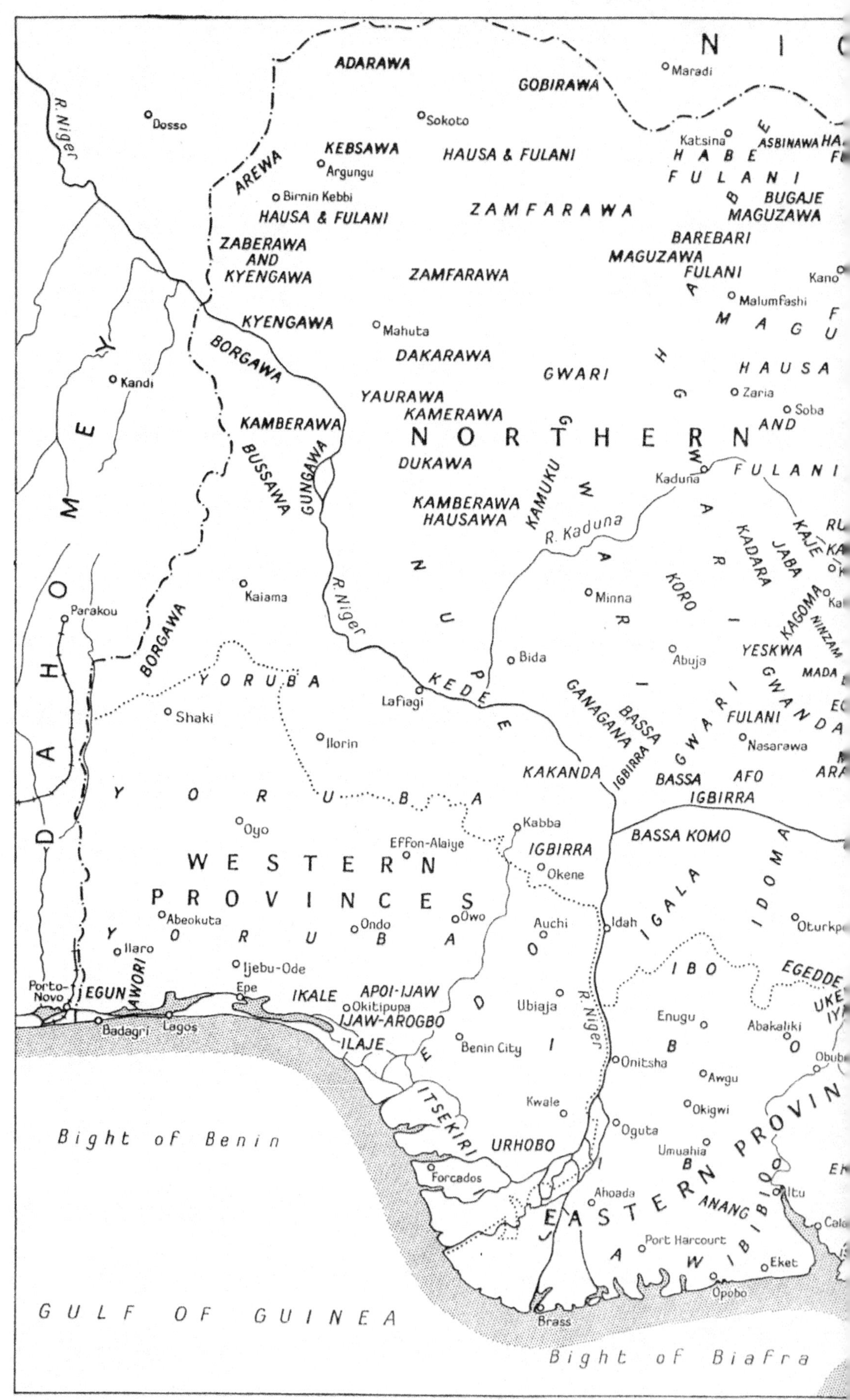
ADARAWA
GOBIRAWA
Maradi
R. Niger
Dosso
Sokoto
AREWA
KEBSAWA
Argungu
HAUSA & FULANI
Katsina
ASBINAWA
HABE
FULANI
Birnin Kebbi
HAUSA & FULANI
ZAMFARAWA
BUGAJE
MAGUZAWA
ZABERAWA AND KYENGAWA
BAREBARI
MAGUZAWA
FULANI
ZAMFARAWA
Kano
Malumfashi
KYENGAWA
Mahuta
BORGAWA
DAKARAWA
HAUSA
GWARI
Kandi
Zaria
YAURAWA
Soba
KAMERAWA
AND
KAMBERAWA
NORTHERN
BUSSAWA
GUNGAWA
DUKAWA
Kaduna
FULANI
KAMBERAWA
HAUSAWA
KAMUKU
R. Kaduna
KADARA
JABA
KAJE
KORO
Parakou
Kaiama
R. Niger
Minna
BORGAWA
KAGOMA
NINZAM
YESKWA
Bida
Abuja
MADA
YORUBA
KEDE
GANAGANA
BASSA
GWANDARA
Lafiagi
Shaki
FULANI
Ilorin
Nasarawa
KAKANDA
IGBIRRA
BASSA
AFO
YORUBA
IGBIRRA
Kabba
Oyo
BASSA KOMO
Effon-Alaiye
IGBIRRA
WESTERN
Okene
PROVINCES
IGALA
IDOMA
Abeokuta
Owo
Auchi
Idah
Ondo
YORUBA
Ilaro
Oturkpo
Ijebu-Ode
IBO
EGEDDE
Porto-Novo
EGUN
AWORI
Epe
IKALE
APOI-IJAW
Okitipupa
Ubiaja
IJAW-AROGBO
Enugu
Abakaliki
Badagri
Lagos
ILAJE
Benin City
EDO
R. Niger
IBO
Onitsha
Awgu
ITSEKIRI
Kwale
Okigwi
Bight of Benin
Oguta
URHOBO
Umuahia
Forcados
IBO
PROVIN
Ahoada
ANANG
IBIBIO
Itu
EASTERN
Port Harcourt
IJAW
Eket
GULF OF GUINEA
Opobo
Brass
Bight of Biafra

2. Tribal map

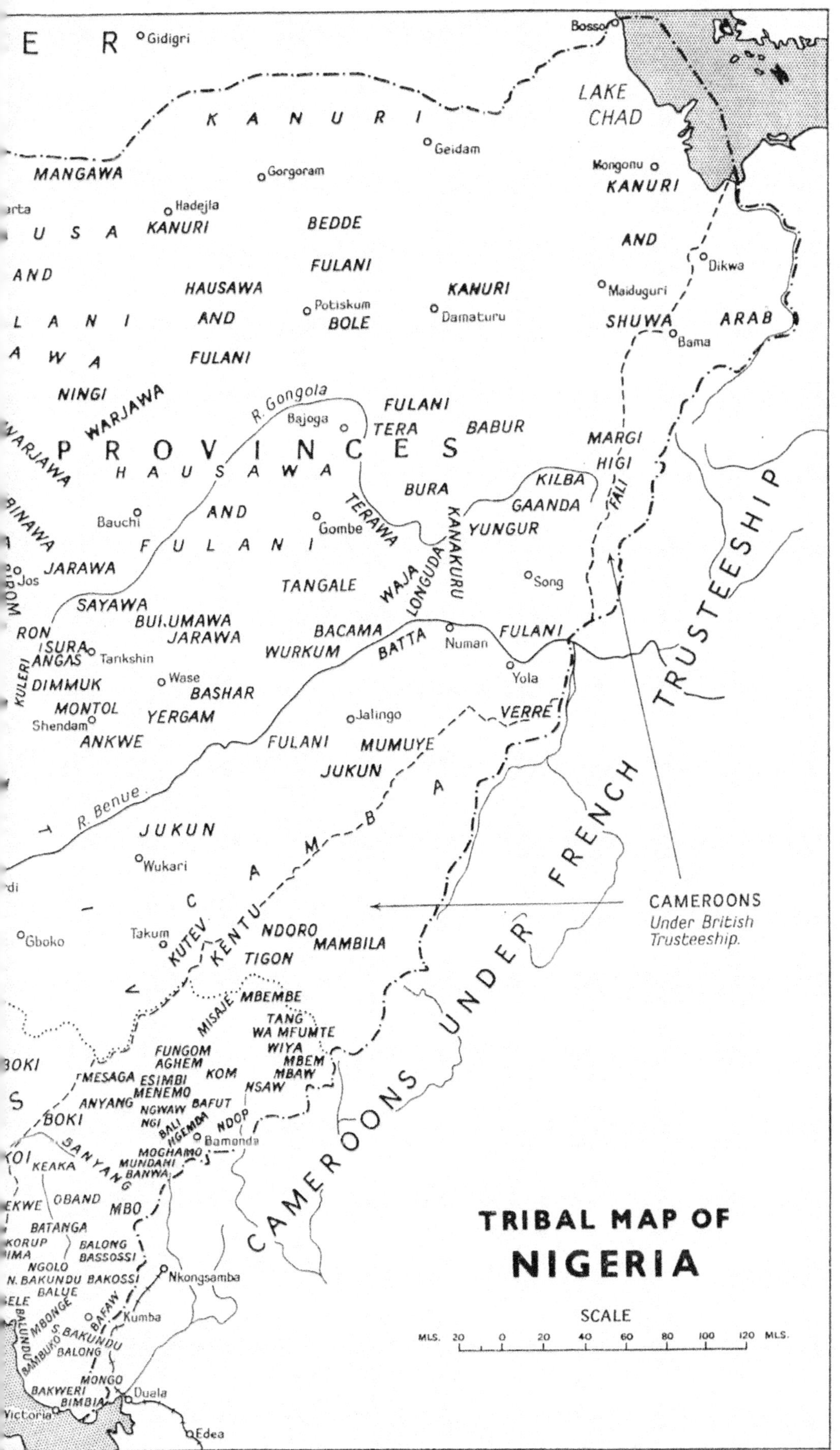
TRIBAL MAP OF
NIGERIA
SCALE
MLS. 20 0 20 40 60 80 100 120 MLS.
LAKE CHAD
KANURI
KANURI AND SHUWA ARAB
MANGAWA
BEDDE
FULANI
HAUSAWA AND FULANI
BOLE
PROVINCES
HAUSAWA AND FULANI
FULANI
TERA
BABUR
MARGI
HIGI
KILBA
GAANDA
BURA
YUNGUR
TERAWA
KANAKURU
WAJA
LONGUDA
TANGALE
JARAWA
SAYAWA
BULUMAWA
JARAWA
BACAMA
BATTA
WURKUM
FULANI
ISURA
ANGAS
DIMMUK
MONTOL
BASHAR
YERGAM
ANKWE
VERRE
FULANI
MUMUYE
JUKUN
JUKUN
NINGI
WARJAWA
KANURI
CAMEROONS
Under British
Trusteeship.
CAMEROONS UNDER FRENCH TRUSTEESHIP
NDORO
MAMBILA
TIGON
KUTEV
KENTU
MBEMBE
MISAJE
TANG
WA MFUMTE
WIYA
MBEM
MBAW
NSAW
FUNGOM
AGHEM
KOM
MESAGA
ESIMBI
MENEMO
ANYANG
NGWAW
BAFUT
BOKI
NGI
BALI
NGEMBA
NDOP
SANYANG
MOGHAMO
MUNDAHI
BANWA
KEAKA
OBAND
MBO
BATANGA
KORUP
BALONG
BASSOSSI
NGOLO
N. BAKUNDU
BAKOSSI
BALUE
MBONGE
BAFAW
S. BAKUNDU
BAMBUKO
BALONG
MONGO
BAKWERI
BIMBIA
KULERI
Gidigri
Bosso
Geidam
Gorgoram
Mongonu
Hadejia
Dikwa
Maiduguri
Potiskum
Damaturu
Bama
Bajoga
Bauchi
Gombe
Song
Jos
Tankshin
Numan
Yola
Wase
Shendam
Jalingo
Wukari
Gboko
Takum
Bamenda
Nkongsamba
Kumba
Duala
Victoria
Edea
R. Gongola
R. Benue

century that the Fulanis and Hausas succeeded in ejecting them and causing their withdrawal back to Morocco.

According to Sir Frederick Lugard (see his Annual Report for 1904–5) the Habe Dynasty had ruled in Hausaland for seventeen generations until 1750, when it was ousted by the Fulanis. Under both the country had prospered greatly and Kano thrived as the great emporium of Western Sudan.

In 1802 Othman dan Fodio, Fulani-born Sultan of Sokoto, was declared a Sheikh, and made a jehad against infidels. He conquered Hausaland as far as Bornu. He was succeeded by his son, Mohamed Bello, who completed the conquest at the battle of Dagh, where the combatants lost a total of 25,000 men.

From this time the Fulani Emirs governed Hausaland with an oppressive rule of extortionate taxes, bribery and corruption. In 1900, however, when a Protectorate was declared over Northern Nigeria, Lugard, as High Commissioner, had the W.A.F.F. available to enforce his authority and proceeded to deal with the tyrannical Emirs each in his turn.

In spite of, or because of, his development in an atmosphere of warfare and oppression, the Hausa took kindly to service in the Force, displaying many characteristics necessary to turn him into a valuable soldier.

The Hausa is usually a well-built and lithely figure, many of them average nearly 6 ft in height. He is hardy and active, and of a cheerful disposition. The Hausa is essentially a trader; he ranges from east to west and north to south wherever trade takes him. He is to be found in the Nile Valley, in Senegal and Tripoli, as well as on the Guinea Coast. For these reasons his language is the most widely spoken in Western Sudan.

He is both Mahomedan and animistic by religion.

PAGANS

Generally speaking, the tribes along the valleys of the Niger and Benue are Pagans of negro origin with short heads, thick lips and woolly hair. They were mainly recruited from Bauchi Province. As there are said to be more than 60 tribes, each speaking a different language in the Province, it became natural for recruits to acquire Hausa as their common mode of speech very quickly. Pagans were not usually so intelligent as Hausas, nor had they the same cheerful character, but they developed into good soldiers.

Up to this time there had existed a state of continual warfare between the Hausa states and the Pagans of Bauchi, slave raiding and looting of caravans was almost a normal practice; consequently the supply of recruits from Bauchi was very uncertain until more peaceful conditions had been created.

KANURI AND SHUA ARABS

In the extreme north-east of the country is the kingdom of Bornu, inhabited by the Kanuris. It forms the remains of a vast empire which extended at one time to Egypt and the hinterland of Tripoli. The King of Bornu was of Libyan origin, that is to say he was a Berber. Bornu was first heard of in the tenth century, when it ranged east and north-east of Lake Chad. The people are of reddish light complexion.

About 1080 Islam was introduced from Egypt, and Bornu extended its border from the Niger to the Nile and into Fezzan. Towards the end of the sixteenth century its power began to wane and it had difficulty in holding its own with the Fulani Empire; when the British came there were two empires in Northern Nigeria, namely Sokoto and Bornu. An element of Shua Arabs is mixed up with the Kanuris in the vicinity of Lake Chad; they are nomads and their origin is obscure.

Some Kanuris and Shuas were recruited later as Bornu became subjugated.

(II) SOUTHERN NIGERIA

In 1893 the Niger Coast Constabulary had been raised by Oil Rivers Protectorate for the defence of its territory, later to become Southern Nigeria. The Constabulary recruited chiefly from Yorubas and Ibos, so these tribes supplied the ranks of the Southern Nigeria Regiment W.A.F.F. as it was called eventually.

Yorubas. These people are worshippers of the dead, consequently venerating their ancestors. Originally they were wholly pagan, but many were converted to Islam at the end of the eighteenth century.

They are generally of sturdy physique; more stolid than Hausas, and essentially farmers rather than traders.

The Yoruba race are said to have descended from a king of Mecca, called Lamurudu. He had three sons who were driven by religious persecution out of Arabia into Upper Egypt. They founded races which settled in West Africa—one in Bornu, another in the Hausa States and the third at Ife, now the spiritual capital of Yorubaland, the actual capital being Oyo, and its king is called the Alafin. The tribal marks of Yorubas, Kanuris and Gojobiris are identical, which seems to indicate a common origin in the past due to the three brothers.

Yorubaland includes Egbaland and Jebuode and comprises most of the country south and west of the Niger, having, however, the Ibo and Beni people on the east and south-east. In 1897 the Yoruba nation numbered about 3,000,000. By treaties signed in 1893 and 1914 they formed part of the British Empire.

The Yoruba people lived in a constant state of slave raiding and warfare. At one time their influence is said to have extended as far west as Ashanti. It was only about the end of last century that Lagos Protectorate was declared and peace came to Yorubaland.

Ibos. The Ibo-speaking people consist of a large number of groups and tribes without owning allegiance to any one king. There are no traditions as to their origin. At the turn of the century the interior of their country was barely under administration, so it was in a perpetual condition of unrest. The bush native was much addicted to witchcraft and spirit worship, but in the towns Christianity had started to make considerable headway. The total population was around 3,000,000.

Ibos cover a wide area between the Niger and X Rivers, extending even some distance west of the Niger. Recruits were intelligent, training on to become signallers and technicians. Their physique is not as sturdy as that of the Yoruba.

(III) LAGOS

At the beginning of this chapter we described how the Lagos Battalion developed from the Lagos Hausas raised by Lieutenant Glover, R.N., in 1863. Hausas continued to be enlisted from traders who percolated to the port of Lagos, but the Battalion was chiefly composed of Yorubas and a few Ibos. Yoruba recruits were the best type of their race from Ibadan and farther north. There had been 12 years of rivalry between the Ibadans and Egbas from 1870 to 1882. The Ibadans then turned to expansion in Dahomey until 1890, when the French conquest of that country caused them to withdraw homewards.

Meanwhile the Governor of Lagos, Sir Gilbert Carter, continuing Glover's policy, declared a Protectorate over the hinterland, including Ibadan, but excluding Abeokuta.

(D) COMPETITION WITH FOREIGN POWERS

Although competition for acquiring territory in West Africa did not start before the end of last century, yet competition amongst European Powers for its trade had begun some 500 years earlier.

The earliest traders were the Portuguese. Prince Henry of Portugal sent a young Venetian, Cadomosto, and two others in a 70-ton caravel to explore the Gambia about the middle of the fifteenth century. He wrote an interesting account of his travels published by the Hakluyt Society. The surf was the subject of great amazement, it being thought that this was steam caused by contact of the sea with hot sand. By 1587–8 the English and French had ousted Portugal from the Gambia trade.

Portuguese as Earliest Traders Fifteenth Century

Meanwhile the Portuguese established themselves on the Gold Coast, where they built Elmina Castle in 1482. During the next century the slave trade grew to big proportions, Portugal, Spain, and then England, followed by the Dutch, competed in this market to supply labour for their colonies. But in 1642 the Portuguese resigned their claims on the West Coast in favour of Holland in exchange for the latter's withdrawal from Brazil.

British Influence Paramount in 1872

It was not till 1872 that the Dutch withdrew from the Gold Coast, when they transferred their settlements at Elmina, Accra, Dixcove and Sekondi to the British Government, which was anxious to proclaim a Protectorate over the whole Gold Coast in order to prevent further Ashanti encroachments. Incidentally this was one of the causes of the sixth Ashanti War, as will be described later in this chapter.

Throughout the eighteenth century the slave trade swelled to enormous proportions. The number of slaves exported annually amounted to some 20,000 for the West Indies alone.

The Slave Trade and its Suppressions: Eighteenth and Nineteenth Centuries

However, in 1807, owing to a revulsion of feeling throughout the Christian world, our Parliament passed an Act making the slave trade illegal for British subjects, although it continued to be surreptitiously carried on in some cases for a good many years later. Sierra Leone had been declared a Government Protectorate in order to accommodate slaves freed from our late North American Colonies and later from the West Indies. In 1823 the Gold Coast and Gambia were annexed to Sierra Leone, owing to the suspicion of slave trading being still carried on there, and were not separated again until a number of years after.

In 1865 a Government Committee declared that 'Extension of Government (in West Africa) and new treaties were inexpedient'. However, soon after the Franco-Prussian War of 1870 France's active policy in that region was probably the cause of a change of policy on the part of the British. Thus was initiated the competition of territorial aggrandisement between the European Powers.

Franco-British Agreement in the Gold Coast, 1898

France pushed forward into the hinterland of Senegal and French Guinea, occupying Bamako in 1883 and Futa Jallon in 1887; Timbuktu was reached in 1893–4 and Wagadugu (Upper Volta Province) in 1896. About this time the Ashanti campaign of 1896 had been successfully concluded by the banishment of King Prempeh, and it was decided to send a political mission into the Northern Territories with a view to making treaties with the chiefs there and so combating French influence in the neighbouring Upper Volta Province.

Consequently Lieutenant Henderson, R.N., with an escort of one officer and 100 Hausas of the Gold Coast Constabulary, left Accra on 21st November 1896 to carry out this mission. In spite of complications due to the ravages of a rebel called Samory, particulars of which are narrated in the next section of this chapter, agreement with the French was successfully reached by which the boundary was fixed in 1898 along the 11th parallel North latitude. In the following year competition with Germany in the Gold Coast was also settled by fixing the boundary with Togoland.

By 1895 French penetration from Futa Jallon south-eastward was approaching the hinterland of Sierra Leone and in order to avoid frontier disputes it was agreed to fix the boundaries between Great Britain and France. This was accordingly done under a treaty dated 21st January 1895.

Anglo-French Agreements with Sierra Leone and Gambia, 1896

Up to that date a Protectorate over Sierra Leone had never been declared, although treaties had been made with various chiefs with a view to stopping the sale of slaves and carrying on legitimate trade. On 31st August 1896 a Protectorate was declared to conform with the Anglo-French Boundary. Five companies of Frontier Police were distributed among the border districts to assist the administration in carrying out treaty terms with the chiefs and putting to an end the ever-recurrent inter-tribal warfare, as well as preventing slave raiding from across the border.

In the case of Gambia, England and France had come to an amicable agreement whereby the navigable course of that river was left entirely in British hands, with, however, the exception of a place called Yarbutenda, 200 miles from the sea, which was intended as a French port enabling their merchandise to have a maritime outlet. In actual fact this port has scarcely been used, trade being diverted to Dakar, in Senegal.

Anglo-French Friction on the Nigerian Border

It was in Northern Nigeria, however, that an extreme state of tension with France had developed between the years 1894 and 1897, mainly in the areas of Borgu and Sokoto. Here it became imperative to maintain a strong force to protect our interests. This resulted in the creation of the 1 and 2 Special Service Battalions West African Frontier Force, which later became the Northern Nigeria Regiment.

Prior to this there had been constant friction with the French on the Benue, as well as on the western frontier of Lagos hinterland from 1890.

About this time a French officer, Lieutenant Mizon, ascended the Benue and made a treaty with the Emir of Muri. This clashed with our interests in that region which had developed in the following manner.

Position on the Benue, 1854 Onwards

In 1854 the British Government had built the 'Pleiad' for the purpose of exploring the confluence of the Niger and Benue Rivers. This expedition was led by our Consul at Fernando Po, Mr. Beecroft, on whose death the command was taken over by Captain Baikie, who established the connection between the rivers, which up to that date had been uncertain. Baikie made treaties securing trading rights with the chiefs on the Benue. These we claimed gave us priority over the agreement made in the region by the French Government.

Position in Borgu, 1890–4

Meanwhile France had advanced south of the Niger Bend, declaring a Protectorate over Dahomey and occupying Porto Novo close to the south-western borders of Lagos, at the same time attempting to extend north-eastward to include Borgu country.

Here the British position was that the Royal Niger Company, whose chairman was Sir George (Taubman) Goldie, had concluded agreements with the Chief of Bussa and the Emir of Sokoto for trading rights in Borgu and Sokoto kingdoms. The French, however, repudiated our Borgu claim, maintaining that Bussa was merely a vassal of the King of Nikki, who was the former's overlord. At the same time the British Government agreed to recognize a French sphere of influence from Say on the Niger to Barewa on Lake Chad, excluding a 100 miles radius around Sokoto.

British and French Missions to Nikki, 1894

This state of affairs now led to the despatch from each Power of missions to Nikki. The British mission, led by Captain F. D. Lugard, with a small escort of Royal Niger Company's troops, concluded a treaty with Nikki on 10th November 1894, five days before the arrival of Captain Decoeur with an escort of 500 Tirailleurs.

From this moment a very critical situation was created, a conflict between the two Powers being narrowly averted until an agreement defining the boundaries on the north and west of Nigeria was finally reached in September 1898.

The part played by the West African Frontier Force in checkmating French aggressive action in Borgu is described in some detail in Section (E) of this chapter.

In the Benue region exclusive trading rights were conceded to Britain.

The Position on the Cameroon/Nigerian Border

Between the years 1885 and 1893 Germany had been establishing her position in West Africa. But even earlier than this German explorers had penetrated from Tripoli across the Sahara to Chad and Bornu. In 1869 the King of Prussia sent Dr. Nachtigall on a mission to the Shehu of Bornu. Nachtigall is said to have transported a golden throne and a musical instrument of considerable weight as gifts to this potentate, which represents no mean effort, bearing in mind the hazards of such a journey.

Nachtigall's second expedition to West Africa was, however, politically of far greater importance. In the penultimate decade of last century he was commissioned by Bismarck to visit Togoland and the Cameroons, for Germany, spurred on by French and British penetrations in West Africa, was determined to secure her share of trading rights and possessions in that undeveloped area. There never seems to have been any friction between England and Germany about the boundaries dividing Togoland and the Gold Coast on the one hand or the Cameroons and Nigeria on the other hand. Agreements for settling these boundaries were drawn up in 1899 amicably.

Boundary commissions were appointed during the early years of this century as between ourselves, France and Germany, thus eliminating further causes for friction.

So finally ended the competition between the European Powers for acquiring a monopoly of trade and territory in West Africa. From now on Great Britain, France and Germany proceeded to consolidate and develop their possessions in harmony until the First World War eliminated Germany as a Colonial Power.

(E) EARLY TRIBAL CAMPAIGNS AND MINOR OPERATIONS

SIERRA LEONE AND GAMBIA

At the beginning of this chapter, under the heading (A) Historical Background, it was shown how the Sierra Leone Battalion had its origin in the Sierra Leone Police, which was raised in 1829 and did not become the Sierra Leone Frontier Police until the beginning of 1890, at which date the Government assumed responsibility over the hinterland which hitherto had not been effectively administered.

Between these two dates the Sierra Leone Police participated in a number of small affairs in the hinterland, mainly necessitated by the lack of firm control above referred to. It is not here proposed to describe these, but merely to refer to them by name; anyone interested can find an account of each one in the *History of the Sierra Leone Battalion of the Royal West African Frontier Force*, compiled by Lieutenant R. P. M. Davis, published in 1932. They are: Aku, 1832; Malaghea, 1855; Jong, 1882; Bum-Kittam, 1883; Gallinas, 1884; Yonni, 1887; Largo, 1888; Wendeh, 1889.

On its formation in 1890 the Sierra Leone Frontier Police became responsible for the south-eastern portion of the hinterland, with detachments stationed along a frontage of some 200 miles, stretching from Kambia on the Skarcies River in the north to the Mano River in the south-east, with the duty of ensuring peace and safe transit in this troubled area. Its establishment at this time was four British and four Native officers with 280 N.C.O.s and men.

The Tambi Expedition, April 1892

However, between 1890 and 1892 a notorious freebooter called Karimu led bands of war-boys belonging to a chief named Bari Bureh, against the inhabitants of Upper Sands, a district near the Limba/Susu border. The enemy's H.Q. were in the stockaded town of Tambi. Two successive punitive expeditions were repulsed. Ultimately a stronger force consisting of some 500 troops of the W.I.R., including a detachment of 126 officers and men of the Frontier Police, under Major Moore, was despatched from Freetown and reached its objective on 7th April. Breaches were made with 7-pounder guns and the place was captured and destroyed with few British casualties, though the enemy had 200 killed. The West African Medal with clasp Tambi 1892 was granted for this operation.

During this year an interesting Regimental custom was introduced by Major Moore. It was the singing of the National Anthem, accompanied by the Lord's Prayer, after Tattoo Roll Call. This custom has been observed ever since.

Samory and the Sofas, 1892–4

In 1892 Alimami Samory, an important Mandingo chief, who belonged to the Sofa chiefdom, on the banks of the Upper Niger, began a series of savage raids into the north-eastern parts of the hinterland of Sierra Leone. His objects were slave raiding, combined with raping, which were devastating Susu, Limba, Koranko, Konno and Upper Mende districts. He also wanted to keep the routes to the coast at Port Loko open for his supplies. But before we describe his activities in this region some account of his career is opportune.

Alimami Samory raised himself into notoriety as a fanatical Mahomedan prophet and rapidly gathered a large following who acquired enough military cohesion to constitute a serious menace to the French forces on the Upper Niger. His sovereignty held sway over the countries on the right bank of the Niger. He even raided as far as the Northern Territories of the Gold Coast in 1897, and was finally defeated by the French in the Ivory Coast, dying in captivity in 1900.

The Waiima Disaster, 23rd December 1893

Though Samory had not visited Sierra Leone since 1892, he kept a very warlike and capable general, Kerneo Bilali, in Koranko province. It was decided to send an expedition against him in May 1893. In October the Sofas advanced into Mende country and seized the town of Kawea. Thereupon the Government hastened their plans of action.

A force of about 600 officers and men, consisting of W.I.R. and Frontier Police, was assembled under Colonel Ellis against the Sofas, who were at Kaiema and Yadu. He decided to march through Yadu on Waiima in order to cut the enemy off from French and Liberian country. Both these places were captured with only 15 casualties.

On 23rd December the British were encamped at Waiima when they were attacked by a French force of 1,200 tiralleurs under Lieutenant Maritz, who mistook them for Sofas. One officer and two privates of the Frontiers were killed in addition to seven W.I.R. casualties.

The Waiima disaster was avenged shortly after by a force of 40 Frontiers under a Native officer who completely routed a large band of Sofas near Panguma. This N.O., Sub-Inspector Taylor, subsequently received the D.C.M. for his gallantry. Again on 2nd January 1894 the Sofas were taken by surprise at Bagwema, losing 347 killed and captured, and the release of 673 slaves was effected. This ended the Sofa incursions into Sierra Leone.

The Sofa Expedition in Gambia, February–March 1894

In Gambia also the Sofas had been creating trouble. Chief Fodi Silah, one of Samory's lieutenants, had for some time been slave raiding and terrorizing the inhabitants of British Combo, a District west of Cape St. Mary. A naval expedition was despatched to subdue him, but ended in retreat and disaster. To avenge this and defeat the malefactors a military force, supported by ships of the Royal Navy, was equipped at Freetown, consisting of a few companies W.I.R. Fodi Silah's stronghold was captured while he himself fled to French territory. Actually only one officer, Captain Campbell, with a maxim and two rocket trough detachments of the Frontiers accompanied the British Force.

In August 1894 the Frontier Police were increased by 300 native ranks, and Captain Tarbett of the South Lancs Militia was appointed Inspector-General and seven other officers were shown on the strength.

In 1895 a small detachment under Lieutenant Boileau was sent to quell a Timini rising. No casulaties occurred, the trouble was suppressed, and the big drum now hanging in the Mess between the Regimental Colours was captured.

Declaration of Protectorate, 31st August 1896

On 31st August 1896 a Protectorate was declared in the territory adjacent to the Colony over which jurisdiction had been acquired. On 14th May in the following year 15 Frontiers under Captain Blakeney took part in the Queen Victoria's Diamond Jubilee.

Further Trouble with the Sofas, 1897

Late in 1897 the Sofas, and Kissis, who had been causing trouble in the Liberian border near Kailahun, were scattered with very heavy loss. This episode finally quelled further trouble from the Sofas in the region of Sierra Leone. Captains Fairtlough and Blakeney distinguished themselves leading the Frontiers here.

At this period the Force had a strength of 11 officers and 505 other ranks, and was organized in five companies distributed at Panguma, Bandajuma, Karene, Falaba and near Freetown, where the depot was stationed. This distribution was maintained until 1903.

The 1898 Rising, or 'Hut Tax' War

In 1896, on the declaration of a Protectorate, the Governor, Sir Frederick Cardew, decided to introduce a tax of 10/- for every four-roomed house, and one of 5/- for smaller houses, in order to pay for the administration of the districts concerned. The tax was to be imposed from the 1st January 1898.

The Protectorate was divided into five districts, viz. Karene, Ronieta, Bandajuma, Panguma and Koinadugu. The two latter were not included in the tax, being very undeveloped. Timinis and Limbas predominated in Karene, while Mendes formed the bulk of the population in Ronieta and Bandajuma.

Throughout 1897 meetings were held by the district commissioners to explain the reason for the tax. Towards the end of that year it became evident that imposition of the tax was going to be strongly opposed. Certain measures were therefore taken to reinforce the Frontier Police at key points.

In January 1898, when the tax came into force, a number of chiefs in Ronieta and Bandajuma were arrested owing to refusal to pay. Matters then rapidly came to a head. Hostile elements proclaimed a state of war by sending out runners bearing a burnt leaf to other disaffected areas.

Chief Bai Bureh of Kasse, Karene district, obtained a strong following of Timinis, and Major Tarbett of the Frontier Police was despatched from Freetown with a force to assist the District Commissioner, Captain Sharpe and 75 Frontiers. Bai Bureh's country was penetrated and his stockaded towns were destroyed, but he himself was not found there. Tarbett then decided to march on Karene. Soon after three companies W.I.R. were sent from Freetown to keep open the communications between Port Loko and Karene, which was practically surrounded by the enemy.

Bai Bureh's success encouraged the other tribes and a general outbreak occurred on 26th April. Once the rebellion started it spread apace and in a very short time a large number of English-speaking people in Bandajuma were murdered.

Operations in Karene

Lieut.-Colonel Marshall, W.I.R., now took command here, and succeeded in clearing the road to Port Loko and causing the withdrawal of Bai Bureh, who was finally captured in October by the newly formed

West African Regiment, commanded by Colonel E. R. P. Woodgate. In this area our forces had suffered 140 casualties by July, mostly W.I.R.

Operations in Ronieta

Here Captain Fairtlough was the District Commissioner. He had served for some time with the Frontiers and had 70 of them in his garrison at Kwellu. In April the chiefs on the Rokelle openly declared war. Thereupon Fairtlough with 50 Frontiers patrolled the area, and, in spite of severe opposition, thoroughly cowed the insurgents. In May, Colonel Woodgate with a column of W.I.R. and W.A.R. advanced on Kwellu, which in the meantime had been heavily attacked, but had repulsed the Mendes with severe loss. Woodgate then patrolled the north-east of the district and succeeded in compelling the subjugation of recalcitrant chiefs.

Operations in Bandajuma

The position here was that District H.Q. with Captain Eames and 50 Frontiers, was at Bandajuma in the centre of the Mende country, while there was a detachment of 28 Frontiers under Captain C. B. Wallis at Kambia on the Small Bum River some 50 miles to the south-west. On 27th April communication with Bandajuma was cut and Wallis' post was attacked by a large party of war-boys. The post was held all day, but at nightfall Wallis decided to withdraw, as his ammunition was exhausted. He reached Bonthe, near the mouth of the Sherbro River, where there was a garrison of 70 W.I.R. and Police.

Colonel Cunningham, commanding the W.I.R., arrived at Bonthe with reinforcements on 2nd May. He then proceeded up the Jong River to Mafwe, about 50 miles distant, where there was an important trading and missionary station. Mafwe was about half-way between Bonthe and Bandajuma.

He reached Mafwe on 17th, leaving a small garrison at Pepo *en route*. Mafwe had been devastated and most of the Europeans killed as well as Sierra Leone traders. Two days were spent in reconnaissance and cleaning the town up, when on the night of 19th/20th May a force of about 1,000 Mendes made a most determined attack on the camp. The attack was eventually driven off, the enemy leaving 130 dead and retiring to Bumpe, 25 miles north. During the attack another party of Mendes fell on the rear of the camp, but were repulsed with 40 killed. Communication with Bandajuma was then restored.

Next day at dawn a column advanced on Bumpe, where two stockades were captured. The rains now intervened, preventing further operations against Bumpe itself, which was not captured till later. It was afterwards burnt to the ground and caused the surrender of a large number of chiefs, effectually ending the opposition in Bandajuma district.

March Through the Protectorate. November '98 to March '99

To conclude the campaign it was decided to make a demonstration in force through the whole Protectorate. The only serious opposition met with was by the Kissis in Panguma District. The resistance shown by them was far greater than had been expected. It was supposed that this was due to the bad influence of certain deported Mende chiefs.

Casualties

During the whole of the operations from January 1898 to March 1899 the Frontiers lost 46 Africans killed, while four officers and 72 Africans were wounded. The Imperial troops had four officers and 17 men killed, and 16 officers with 94 men wounded. Some 4,000 officers and men had been employed with the expedition.

In his despatch to the War Office (dated 29/11/99) at the end of the operations the Secretary of State expressed his satisfaction at the conduct of all ranks of the Sierra Leone Frontier Police.

The West African Medal was awarded with clasp Sierra Leone 1898–9, and Major Tarbett, Captain Sharpe and Captain Fairtlough received the C.M.G., while Captain Fergusson was granted the D.S.O.

Comments

The massacres of English-speaking and loyal Natives in Bandajuma District at Mafwe were particularly savage and brutal. The same thing had occurred in Ronieta District at Rotifunk, although not quite so savagely.

The large proportion of Frontier Police made casualties as compared with the Imperial Troops was remarkable, but this was probably mainly due to the Frontiers often being isolated in small groups of a few men, owing to their duties in posts scattered over large areas. In his despatch the Governor gave special praise to the devoted behaviour of the Force, which, he said, was worthy of the highest traditions of the Sierra Leone Frontier Police.

The Navy played a considerable and distinguished part in the operations, transporting troops and supplies besides taking part in the fighting, particularly on the waterways.

THE GOLD COAST

At the beginning of this chapter the events leading up to the formation of the Gold Coast Constabulary have been described. It was seen how overwhelming had been the influence of the warlike Ashantis in creating the need for some military body to protect the country from invasion.

6th Ashanti War, 1873

In Wolseley's Campaign his success was largely due to the efficient organization of supply and transport which enabled him to march rapidly by moving in three columns. The main one was directed along the Prahsu–Bekwai road, with one column on either flank, Glovers Hausas being on the right. Although he beat the Ashantis decisively at the battle of Amoaful, his casualties, particularly in the Black Watch, had been very heavy, about 10 per cent of 2,000 combatants. At the same time the enemy's losses were extremely high, ending in the complete defeat of his army, the flight of the King and the occupation of Kumasi in February 1873.

In April 1888 Prempeh was King of Ashanti. His policy was to restore the country's prestige, which led him to invade Nkoranza on its northern frontier in August 1892. The town was burnt, people massacred and the countryside laid waste. Prempeh was then reported to be threatening Atabubu, just west of Krachi on the Volta. This decided the Government to act. A force of 300 Constabularly, under Sir Francis Scott, was despatched there and Nkoranza was put under British protection. At the same time the people asked that a British Resident might be stationed at Kumasi. This request was not supported by Prempeh, and a situation developed leading to the 1895–6 Ashanti Campaign.

Ashanti Campaign, 1895–6

A field force composed of 2 West Yorkshire Regiment, 2 W.I.R., 1,000 Gold Coast Constabulary Hausas and a few levies under Major Baden-Powell,[1] was organized to advance, under Scott, on Kumasi. The dispositions of the force were similar to those in 1873. Prempeh submitted without opposition. As he was unable to comply with the terms of the indemnity imposed he and his family were banished to the Seychelle Islands.

Consolidation in the Northern Territories

Now that Prempeh's influence north of Kumasi had been overcome it was decided to consolidate our position in the Northern Territories. This was all the more necessary to combat French and German influence in the region. In this connection Lieutenant Henderson's mission has already been alluded to in Section (D) of this chapter.

Lieutenant Henderson's Mission Encounters the Sofas, December 1896

On Henderson's arrival in the area in question he learnt that a Sofa force, led by a son of Samory, the fanatical Mahdi, had captured and burnt the town of Bona. Thereupon Henderson tried to open up negotiations with the Sofas by occupying Wa with 50 Constabulary and sending a message to say that if raids continued reprisals would be made. The Sofas replied by attacking him with 8,000 men. Henderson was forced to evacuate Wa, but went by himself to the hostile camp to negotiate. In this he was successful and the enemy withdrew to the Ivory Coast.

For this and several small expeditions in the Northern Territories between November 1896 and 14th June 1898 the West African Medal with appropriate clasp was granted.

LAGOS

As mentioned in Section (C) of this chapter there had been a constant state of inter-tribal warfare between Ibadan and Egbaland, as well as in Jebu-Ode, notwithstanding the efforts of the Governor of Lagos Colony and the Alafin of Oyo to bring about peace.

In 1895 the Government decided to declare a Protectorate over the hinterland of Yoruba country with the object of bringing it under effective

[1] Major (later Major-General) Baden Powell, of Scout fame, organized the scouts and has left an interesting diary which is now in the Regimental Museum at Kumasi.

administration. A force of 100 Lagos Constabulary was sent to Ibadan under Captain Bower for the purpose of stopping Ilorin raiding south for slaves in March 1896. However, the power of Ilorin was already being crushed by the Royal Niger Company's Constabulary from Northern Nigeria, ending in the surrender of its army and capital.

When the Protectorate was formed Egbaland was specially excluded in consideration of the right to build a railway through Egba territory. This railway was to be an important strategic link connecting the Niger at Jebba with Lagos Port. The exclusion of Abeokuta, the Egba capital, was to prove a thorn in the flesh of Lagos Administration, and it was only by the presence of a garrison of Constabulary at near-by Ibadan that a veiled peace endured between the two provinces.

To cover operations in the hinterland and Jebu-Ode during 1896–7 the West African Medal with clasp was awarded.

SOUTHERN NIGERIA

The Niger Coast Constabulary was only formed in 1893, as we have seen, but it was not long in going into action.

Operations Against Nana, 1894

In 1894 Chief Nana, Governor of Benin, misused his position to carry out slave raids. About 250 Constabulary, supported by ships of the Royal Navy under Admiral Bedford were used in the operations to capture his stronghold at Brohemie in the Benin River, ending in his defeat and flight. He subsequently surrendered and was deported. The casualties here included Captain Lalor of the Constabulary (*London Gazette*, 25/9/94).

Benin was then ruled by Chief Overami, who continued his practices of human sacrifice and slave dealing in spite of Government warnings. The situation had become too serious to be dealt with without strong reinforcements. These were asked for by Consul Phillips, but none were available in 1897.

Benin Massacre, 1897

Phillips, therefore, decided to attempt to handle it by marching to Benin himself with his small Constabulary escort. It ended in disaster. His small party was overwhelmed and all except two of the Europeans were killed. The two survivors, Captains Locke and Boisragon, the latter of the Constabulary, escaped only after suffering great hardships while making their way through dense bush to the coast.

Benin City Operations, February–March, 1897

(W.A. Medal; Clasp Benin 1897)

Admiral Rawson, commanding the Fleet on the West Coast, then proceeded to attack Benin with a force of 250 sailors and 500 Constabulary under Lieut.-Colonel Bruce Hamilton. There was some heavy bush fighting in which we had eight Naval officers and 32 ratings casualties, while the constabulary lost 40 killed and 23 wounded. The chief ringleaders escaped.

Benin Territories Expedition, April–May 1899

(W.A. Medal and Clasp S. Nigeria 1899)

This Expedition, led by Captain and Brevet-Major C. H. P. Carter, was to finalize the last operations. The ringleaders had set up war camps, which Carter captured and destroyed. The main leader Ologbosheri, responsible for the massacres, was tried and hanged. Our casualties were light, owing to damp powder used by the Benis. The Constabulary lost nine killed and wounded including two officers. Carter was awarded the C.M.G. (*London Gazette*, 31/1/1900).

NORTHERN NIGERIA

We recorded earlier that the Northern Nigeria Regiment was formed in 1900 from the 1 and 2 Battalions of the West African Frontier Force, which in their turn were composed of elements of the Royal Niger Constabulary on the disbandment of the latter.

The Royal Niger Constabulary appears to have been continually engaged overcoming opposition from the local tribes in the Niger Valley. The handbook of the Regimental Museum contains the following paragraph:

'There is in the museum a remarkable report of the activities of the Royal Niger Constabulary, the armed force of Goldie's trading company, later to become the North Nigeria Regiment, entitled Punitive Expeditions of the R.N.C. 1886–1899; it reports 57 actions, including all casualties, starting with the Beaufort Island and Robin Tree land expeditions and the two 1887 Patani Gunboat actions . . . and a report on the 1897 North Sudan Campaign addressed to Most Honble. the Marquess of Salisbury, K.G., Foreign Office.'

NORTH SUDAN

Bida/Ilorin Campaign, January–February 1897

(W. Africa Medal and Clasp granted)

It is not proposed to deal here with the 57 minor actions above referred to, but the North Sudan Campaign of 1897 mentioned is worthy of special description, for it was the first trial of strength against the Fulani rule.

The Emir of Bida, which is the capital of Nupe, had persisted in raiding for slaves, attacking and pillaging trading caravans, and threatening Lokoja, the Niger Company's main base. Sir George (Taubman) Goldie, the R.N.C.'s able director, determined to make an end to Nupe's misdeeds. He got War Office permission for seconding a number of special service officers to supplement the cadres of the Constabulary and secretly mobilized some 500 officers and men for the campaign. Captain Arnold was in command and on his staff was Lieutenant Vandeleur, Scots Guards, who wrote an interesting account of the operations, entitled 'Campaigning on the Upper Nile and Niger'. The Force was well equipped with rockets, field guns and maxims. Two mallams accompanied the expedition to prevent the Fulanis from enticing men by preaching a Jehad against the British.

Several thousand Nupes were known to be concentrated at Kabba with a view to raiding towards Lokoja. The British force endeavoured to cut them off, but they withdrew north-west towards the Niger. Goldie now declared the freedom of Kabba from Fulani rule and the abolition of slave dealing.

Meanwhile (later Sir) William Wallace, Goldie's second director, had prevented the enemy crossing the river with a flotilla. The British force now reorganized and followed up the retreating Nupes, who disputed its advance stubbornly with hordes of horsemen over ideal undulated ground right up to the walls of Bida. Vandeleur says: 'Emirs and chiefs in their brilliant robes trotted about at the head of their troops and horsemen, and bands of footmen armed with guns and spears. The air resounded with the horns and drums of dense multitudes ready to give battle.'

Square was formed, volley after volley was poured into the waves of horsemen galloping to the attack. The guns were brought up and did great execution. The enemy withdrew behind the walls of the town. Next morning the town was heavily shelled and the walls battered until the Nupes fled in panic; their losses being extremely heavy, while ours only amounted to eight killed, including one officer, Lieutenant Thomson, and nine wounded. It was estimated that the Fulani horsemen were about 20,000 strong, thus outnumbering the R.N.C. by 40 to 1. This was a crushing defeat indeed, which raised the prestige of the Constabulary immensely by showing it had nothing to fear from the Fulani horse whose prowess had been so much extolled.

The Borgu Incident

(W. Africa Medal and Clasp 1898 granted)

In his despatch to the Secretary of State for Colonies of May, 1898 and again of 10th March 1899 Lugard reports that an extremely difficult and delicate situation had arisen in May 1898 in the Borgu Province in the south-west of Nigerian hinterland.

The French from Dahomey had been extending their posts into territory held by the British Government. In consequence an expeditionary force, under Colonel Willcocks, assisted by Royal Niger Constabulary under Major Arnold, D.S.O., was despatched to deal with the danger.

By the time Willcocks's force arrived in the Kaiama neighbourhood his firm attitude checked any further advance by the French. Although no actual fighting took place, a collision, which would probably have resulted in a conflagration, was only averted by the firmness of the Commander, and the patience and tact of his officers on the spot.

Willcocks's expeditionary force was composed of the 1 and 2 Battalions W.A.F.F. (and a battery) commanded by Lieut.-Colonels Pilcher and Fitzgerald respectively.

It must be understood that these events occurred at the time of the French expedition to the Nile at Fashoda, known as the Marchand incident, and consequently tempers between ourselves and France were very inflamed. As a result of diplomatic negotiations agreement was reached between the two countries, whereby a convention was signed in Paris in

September 1898 recognizing the British rights in Borgu and the withdrawal of the French posts occupied there.

Illoh, Argungu and Lapai Operations

(W. Africa Medal and Clasp 1898 granted)

About this time the 1 and 2 Battalions were engaged in other operations. In the Illoh district a truculent chief of Helo Island was resisting the authorities. Lieutenant Keating, 1 Battalion, was sent with 30 men to effect his arrest, but was ambushed and his party massacred. To avenge this a very rapid and well-managed expedition was organized under Major Morland.

The Emirs of Lapai and Argungu had been raiding towns down to the banks of the Niger between 8th and 27th June 1898, unofficially aided by the Emir of Bida. To deal with this Pilcher with 300 men 1 Battalion, assisted by 100 Royal Niger Company and three maxims by a forced march surprised the enemy, consisting of 600 horse and 3,000 foot, and completely routed them. Their camps and strongholds were destroyed and their power completely broken. Pilcher says: 'The behaviour of my recruits was good, their volleys perfect and their conduct was soldierlike.'

Lugard reports that 'In each of these affairs our soldiers behaved admirably. Their fire discipline and steadiness were particularly noticeable, as was the control by their officers.'

CHAPTER 2

The Formation of the W.A.F.F.

(A) THE EARLY YEARS, 1897–1901

1897

IT was in 1897 that Mr. Joseph Chamberlain, Secretary of State for Colonies, ordered a military force to be raised, called the West African Frontier Force (familiarly known as the W.A.F.F. pronounced 'WOFF'). The title of 'Royal' was not conferred on it till 1928, by King George V.

The W.A.F.F. was a regular military force, recruited from a nucleus of officers and men of the Royal Nigerian Constabulary, supplemented by Regular Army officers and newly enlisted Hausas, Yorubas and Nupes.

Officers and British N.C.O.s were seconded from their British regiments for short periods. The first Commandant was Captain and Brevet-Major (local Colonel) Frederick Dealtry Lugard, C.B., D.S.O.,[1] gazetted on 26th August 1897.

It was decided to raise two Infantry Battalions, called 1 and 2, Special Service Corps Battalions, and three Batteries West African Frontier Force.

The 1 Battalion was formed under Major (local Lieut.-Colonel) T. D. Pilcher, Northumberland Fusiliers, in November 1897 at Lokoja, while in March 1898 the 2 Battalion, commanded by Major (local Lieut.-Colonel) H. S. Fitzgerald, Durham Light Infantry, came into being at Ibadan. The respective adjutants were Captains P. S. Wilkinson and A. W. Booth, both of the Northumberland Fusiliers.

On 8th November 1897 Lugard set up his headquarters at Jebba, appointing Lieut.-Colonel James Willcocks, Leinster Regiment, his Assistant Commandant on the 27th of that month (granted local rank of Colonel on 1st September 1898).

The Artillery consisted of two four-gun 7-pounder R.M.L. batteries and one six-gun 75 mm. reserve battery. The C.R.A. was Captain (local Major) W. A. Robinson, R.A. It is to be noted that in the early days there was some confusion between the use of the terms 'local' and 'temporary' where applied to an officer's rank. Later when an officer was granted a higher rank than his Army rank it was invariably called 'temporary'.

[1] In 1894 Sir George Goldie, Chairman of the Royal Niger Company, secured the services of Captain Lugard to make a treaty with the King of Borgu for trading rights. This he successfully accomplished in the face of French competition.

Owing to Lugard's reputation in East and West Africa, Mr. Joseph Chamberlain selected him as the best officer with Nigerian experience to raise a regular military force to counteract French influence in Niger territories. At the time, July 1897, Lugard was in the service of the South Africa Company. His intention had been to give up soldiering, so his first inclination was to refuse, but after further consideration, he decided to accept the appointment and returned to England to confer with the Colonial Office on measures required to implement it.

1898

On 9th March an Engineer Unit of 20 Madras sappers was formed. Also Telegraph, Transport, Medical and Accounts Sections were added later. The first Regular Royal Engineer officer to command it was Lieutenant J. R. E. Charles some months later.

On 10th March 10 officers and 11 N.C.O.s left Lagos for Epe by the lagoon, marching thence to Ibadan via Jebu-Ode. This was the nucleus of 2 Battalion. At Ibadan they took over 428 Yoruba recruits, who had arrived from 1 Battalion at Lokoja on the 16th; these were followed by seven officers and seven B.N.C.O.s. Here the Battalion was inspected by Lieut.-Colonel H. McCallum, C.M.G., the Governor of Lagos who commented on their soldierly bearing. The unit then marched via Ilorin to Jebba arriving there on the 9th May.

On 12th May Lieutenant T. E. Headlam (2 Battalion), R.M.L.I., was drowned in the Niger. Corporal W. Taylor, Scots Guards, had made a gallant attempt to save him by jumping into the river undeterred by the presence of alligators. For this action Taylor was awarded the bronze Humane Society's medal.

The 2 Battalion had barely established itself when the Borgu incident with the French arose (see Chapter 1 (E).) Lugard put Willcocks in command of the operations; he assembled his force at Fort Goldie, on the Niger between Jebba and Bussa. On 17th May Lieutenants H. M. Blair, Seaforth Highlanders, and H. A. Porter, 19th Hussars, with two maxims proceeded to join him there.

In June Pilcher's 1 Battalion was engaged in punishing the murderers of Lieutenant Keating in the Illoh District, as well as the Emirs of Argungu and Lapai, who had been raiding Niger towns for slaves. For further details see Chapter 1 (E).

Raising a M.I. Unit

During this month a start was made to raise a Mounted Infantry Unit which would have an establishment of 300 men and 100 horses.

The first officers appointed were: Lieutenants Beauclerck, 60th Rifles; Hawker, 3 Coldstream Guards, and H. C. Keating, Leinster Regiment. In effect the M.I. was superimposed on a unit known as 'Carroll's Horse', originated in 1898 for the R.N.C. by Lieutenant (temporary Captain) J. W. V. Carroll. It did not finally expand to a M.I. Battalion until the 5th February 1903, when its first commander was Major Eustace Crawley, 12th Royal Lancers. A full account of the history of the Mounted Infantry is given in Chapter 6 (D).

On 2nd August an order was promulgated approving the air 'Father O'Flynn' as the Regimental March. The marches of the 1 and 2 Battalions were respectively 'La Paloma' and 'The Lancashire Poacher'.

During this month Booth, Adjutant 2 Battalion, was appointed Staff Officer W.A.F.F. his place being taken by Captain Hon. Fitzroy Somerset, Grenadier Guards.

Lieutenant E. B. Macnaghten, R.A., reported the gallantry of Lance-Corporal Sambur, 1 Battalion, in saving three men from drowning in the

LORD LUGARD OF ABINGER, P.C., G.C.M.G., C.B., D.S.O.

Frederick Dealtry Lugard, distinguished soldier, explorer, and colonial administrator was born in India in 1858 and commissioned in the East Norfolk Regiment at the age of 20. There followed some ten years of campaigning in Burma, Sudan and East Africa, after which he led a memorable expedition forestalling the French occupation of Borgu in 1894–5. In 1897 he was appointed Commissioner for the Nigerian and Lagos Hinterland, as well as the first Commandant of the West African Frontier Force which he raised. He carried out the difficult and delicate task of deploying this force so as to check the French advance in the Niger Valley. From 1900–06 he was High Commissioner in Northern Nigeria; Governor of Hong Kong, 1907–12; Governor of both Northern and Southern Nigeria, 1912–13; Governor-General Nigeria, 1914–19. His work in pacifying, developing and consolidating the Niger Territories was outstanding. He died in 1945.

Face page 32

[*Photo: Topical Press*

General Sir Thomas Lethbridge Napier Morland, K.C.B., K.C.M.G., D.S.O. Inspector General W.A.F.F. 1905–1909. Served throughout 1914–1918 war during which he commanded the X and XIII Corps

Kaddera River, Bauchi, on the 21st August. For this he was awarded the Royal Humane Society's medal.

About this time Lugard recommended the introduction of a Higher and Lower Standard test in Hausa, stating that the system of using interpreters was to be discouraged.

In September the Sierra Leone Government requested the loan of the W.A.F.F. for employment in the rising there ('The Hut Tax War'). This had to be refused, owing to the local needs of Northern Nigeria.

On 18th November Lugard was appointed Governor and High Commissioner for Northern Nigeria. About this time his suggestion for creating a new Battalion (3 W.A.F.F.) was approved. The H.Q. would be at Calabar.

On his departure on leave at this time he published an order to express his high appreciation, in which he said: 'The really wonderful progress in the organization of the W.A.F.F. was owing to the untiring zeal and energy which had surmounted all obstacles.'

On 12th December Lowry-Cole, Royal Welch Fusiliers, succeeded Fitzgerald in command of the 2 Battalion (Fitzgerald did not return, as he was given command of his British regiment). On the 26th December Captain A. W. Baker, Durham Light Infantry, died of blackwater fever. This officer had formed the fifth company (of Hausas) in the 2 Battalion in July. A sixth followed in August, commanded by Captain A. McClintock, Seaforth Highlanders. It is to be noted that the intention had originally been for the 1 Battalion to be recruited from Hausas and the 2 Battalion from Yorubas entirely. The system had, however, broken down owing to shortage of Yorubas north of the Niger.

Although the Borgu operations[1] had come to an end in September on the conclusion of an Anglo-French Convention signed in Paris during that month, this had resulted in increasing the number of detachments, some of which had been previously taken over from the R.N.C. owing to disturbances in their ranks at Fort Goldie, Bussa, Kaiama, Leaba and Yangbassa (the last three in Borgu).

During the year H.Q. W.A.F.F. had moved to Zungeru, about 200 miles north-west of Lokoja and 150 miles north-east of Jebba. The 1 Battalion also moved from Lokoja, owing to its unhealthy climate, to Wushishi which was just south of Zungeru.

1899

On the 8th January, at a full-dress parade, C.S.M. J. Mackenzie, Seaforth Highlanders, was presented with the D.C.M. for gallant conduct on active service at the Offie River, a tributary of the Niger, in October 1898.

On 10th March, news being received from Liverpool of the death of Fitzroy Somerset, Adjutant of the 2 Battalion, Willcocks speaks of his 'zeal and devotion to duty'. His death was said to have been caused by repeated bouts of malaria.

Shortly after this, which was followed by the deaths of four B.N.C.O.s

[1] On the ratification of the Anglo-French convention the Government declared 'The defence should be taken over by the W.A.F.F. in lieu of the Royal Niger Constabulary, which would cease to be the Administrators.'

and the invaliding of two officers, the Acting Commandant strongly recommended no appointments should be made under the age of 25, and, in case of shortage of candidates, Militia and R.A. captains could be appointed, but as W.A.F.F. lieutenants.

On the 24th April Willcocks went on leave. Major Arthur Festing was made Acting Commandant in his place. This officer came from the Royal Irish Rifles and subsequently had a distinguished career in the W.A.F.F., his date of first appointment being 17th December 1898.

In May 900 Royal Niger Constabulary were transferred to the W.A.F.F., 500 to the 1 and 2 Battalions and 400 to the 3 Battalion. This brought the establishment of the north up to 2,600.

On 3rd June the Colonial Office issued a pamphlet about health: 'Africa, West No. 590, Hints to prevent relapses of malaria and blackwater fever, and other tropical diseases to be continued for at least six months after arrival in the U.K. (Dr. Patrick Manson).'

On the 20th June Morland was appointed to command the 1 Battalion in place of Pilcher, who had resigned.

During this month Lord Selborne's Committee recommended the integration of the W.A.F.F. by colonies. The details are set out in Appendix III. These recommendations did not actually come into force till August 1901 (C.O. Letter 322 of 17th June 1901); two of the consequences were the disbandment of the Royal Engineer Detachment and the abolishment of the C.R.A.

Major (Local Lieutenant-Colonel) G. V. Kemball, R.A.

On the 9th September Willcocks was appointed Commandant on Lugard's being made High Commissioner of Northern Nigeria. In consequence Kemball became Assistant Commandant. Major W. H. O'Neill became C.R.A. in place of W. A. Robinson.

In November Festing was invalided. He was instrumental in having a Paymaster appointed to each battalion, as the Adjutant's duties were too heavy to enable him to carry out the former's duties efficiently.

On 8th December Lieutenant A. B. Molesworth (Infantry) was made C.R.E.

1900

On 1st January Lugard was gazetted local Brigadier-General on appointment as High Commissioner for Northern Nigeria.

Incorporation of R.N.C. with the W.A.F.F.

On the same day he took over the Royal Niger Constabulary, incorporating it into the 1, 2 and 3 Battalions W.A.F.F., the 1 and 2 Battalions being the Northern Nigeria Regiment, while the 3 Battalion was designated Southern Nigeria Regiment. Major (temporary Lieutenant-Colonel) A. F. Montanaro, R.A., was appointed the latter's commander. Its Regimental March was 'Old Calabar'.

Brevet-Major C. H. P. Carter, C.M.G., Royal Scots Regiment, commandant of the Niger Coast Protectorate Constabulary (late Oil Rivers

Protectorate), was actually in command on 1st January 1900; Montanaro was appointed later, but did not assume command till 12th February 1901.

Operations in Northern Nigeria, 1900

During this year a number of military operations took place in Northern Nigeria in conformity with Lugard's plan for developing the country by abolishing slave trade and ensuring the safe passage of caravans:

In the South (Benue Valley)

(I) The Munshi Expedition, under Lowry-Cole, between January and March.

In the Centre (Kaduna Valley)

(II) Kaduna Surveys, under Morland, from February to May.

In the East

(III) Yola, under Morland between August and September.

In the South-West

(IV) Bida/Kontagora, under Kemball and O'Neill in December and January 1901.

Particulars of these are given in Section (D) of this chapter.

Ashanti Expedition, 1900

But the main operations undertaken by Nigerian troops were in Ashanti. In April Lugard was called upon to supply a large contingent for the expedition which covered the rest of the year. Willcocks was appointed Commander-in-Chief. The campaign is described in Section (C) of this chapter.

Lugard protested strongly against sending troops outside Nigeria, as it left companies very depleted; he also pointed out the domestic difficulties involved by long separation from the men's wives. Volunteers from India were called for to replenish the officers.

Incidence of blackwater fever was heavy during the year. In February Lieutenant E. B. Macnaghten (R.A.) was invalided; in April Captain Crutchley (Leinster Regiment) died, so also did Captain Kinsey in September, while Captain J. B. Cockburn (Royal Welch Fusiliers) was invalided home in October.

On 20th July Lugard received the following telegram from Willcocks: 'Carried out relief of Kumasi 15th July after Ashantis completely defeated. Hardest task I ever had. W.A.F.F. gallant behaviour. I never wish to see better soldiers, more especially Yorubas. Their conduct and also fire discipline were perfect. I am most proud to command such men. It is well worth two years spent training of troops. Congratulations to Y.E. This was first opportunity I had of taking command of them in action.'

On 19th April Wilkinson 2nd-in-Command of the 1 Battalion W.A.F.F., who was serving with his unit in Ashanti, was appointed Inspector-General of the Gold Coast Constabulary; on 17th May he was granted the local rank of Lieutenant-Colonel.

An event of much significance occurred in February this year when two columns entered Zaria, the most northerly point yet reached by the W.A.F.F. One consisted of troops of the 1 Battalion from Wushishi, and the other those of the 2 Battalion from the Benue, under Lowry-Cole. The Emir of Zaria turned out, though somewhat sullenly, to meet them.

In consequence of the experience gained during the Ashanti campaign it was evident that machine-gun carriers required to be much better trained. It was therefore decided to enlist them and give them better pay and status. With this in view enlistment was to be carried out from the same material as for soldiers, while their pay was put on a similar footing, and a khaki frock, knickers and puttees were adopted.

Keyes Incident, June 1901

On 21st June 1901 an unfortunate incident occurred when Captain C. V. Keyes, Q.O. Corps of Guides, was killed by a rifle bullet fired by a Frenchman at the village of Sonwa, 15 miles south of Argungu. Keyes was serving with the 2 Battalion N.N.R. at the time.

Three Frenchmen with seven armed natives had set up a trading post in the Argungu district. They had stolen some British Army rifles some time previously and Keyes had been sent from Illo with an escort to retrieve them. An altercation arose during which a member of the French party shot Keyes dead. The Frenchmen escaped in disguise, but were subsequently arrested and sent to Jebba for trial. After diplomatic negotiations they were repatriated to France. The late District Officer at Argungu, Mr. A. Warren, has recounted the incident and describes how there is a gravestone recording the burial of Keyes at Sonwa.

By the end of the year W.A.F.F. troops had been repatriated from Ashanti on the conclusion of hostilities.

For his services in Ashanti Willcocks received the Brevet of Colonel and the K.C.M.G. Moreover, the War Office decided to utilize his services elsewhere, thereby creating a vacancy for Commandant W.A.F.F.

1901

Lugard's Despatches, 1897–1900

Lugard's despatches for the period 1897–1900 were published during 1901 and were subsequently issued as Parliamentary Papers. They give an exhaustive account of the development of the W.A.F.F. during those years, the main items of which have been narrated above.

This was the year in which the integration of the W.A.F.F. by colonies came into force. The actual dates varied between July and the end of the year for different colonies.

Appointment of First Inspector-General and Consequent Other Promotions in Nigeria

Preparatory to this certain appointments and promotions in Nigeria became necessary. On 23rd July Kemball was gazetted Inspector-General W.A.F.F. and Morland Commandant Northern Nigeria Regiment, with

Lowry-Cole as 2 I.C., Beddoes taking over command of the 2 Battalion in the latter's place.

Meanwhile on 28th February McClintock had been given acting command of the 1 Battalion with Mellis as his 2.I.C.

Total of W.A.F.F. Personnel sent to Ashanti

Lugard reported that the duties of the W.A.F.F. had been severely restricted during the past year, in matters of controlling truculent tribesmen, maintaining escorts for political officers, etc., owing to the shortage of troops in the country. He said that 25 officers, 27 B.N.C.O.s and 1,229 other ranks had been sent to Ashanti, amounting to about half the strength of the Regiment. These had been accompanied by four Medical officers and two nursing sisters, as well as 300 carriers.

The following table shows the state of the W.A.F.F. at the time of its integration by colonies during the last half of 1901:

STATE OF W.A.F.F. (1901)

	Bn.	Coys.	Btys.	Guns	O.C.	2I.C.	Officers	O.R.s
N. Nigeria Regt.	1 (McClintock)	8	2	75 mm.	1	1	25	1,200
Commandant Morland								
2I.C. Lowry-Cole	2 (Beddoes)	8			1	1	25	1,200
S. Nigeria Regt. O.C. Montanaro	1	8	2	75 mm.	1	1	36	1,250
Gold Coast Regt. O. C. Wilkinson	1	12	2	75 mm.	1	1	33	1,657
Sierra Leone Bn. O.C. Blakeney	1	6			1	1	15	498
Lagos Bn. O.C. Applin	1	3			1	1	13	503
Gambia Coy. O.C. Graham	To be formed from Sierra Leone Bn.							

B.N.C.O.s. There were none in Sierra Leone. The numbers in other units varied.
Native Officers. Southern Nigeria and Lagos had one or two each. None elsewhere.
Headquarters. Respectively at: Zungeru, Calabar, Accra (moving to Kumasi), Freetown, Lagos.
Note: Both Northern Nigeria battalions, had a depot company each.

At the beginning of this chapter the purpose for which Mr. Chamberlain created the W.A.F.F. was related. Once the French menace to the territory of the Royal Niger Company had disappeared, however, to quote from Colonial Office Paper No. C.O.588 of June 1899, 'the question of the responsibility of the Imperial Government in connection with Niger Territory and the necessity for the relinquishment by the Royal Niger Company of the administration of those territories became apparent it became necessary to form the nucleus of a new military force for Imperial purposes on the Niger . . . this was chosen as a convenient moment to consider as a whole the position of the military forces of the Crown under the control of the Colonial Office throughout West Africa to make their forces mutually self-supporting . . . it was considered necessary the various constabularies and newly raised West African Frontier Force should be amalgamated into one organization and bear a military name'.

In order, therefore, to implement the principles laid down in the above

C.O. Paper a committee was set up under the chairmanship of Lord Selborne, Under Secretary of State for Colonies, and of which Lugard was a member. The decisions of this committee regarding the amalgamation of units is shown in Appendix III.

The actual integration of the W.A.F.F. by colonies did not take place until 1901, when Kemball was appointed as its first Inspector-General.

It may be opportune here to describe very briefly the conditions under which, in these early days, the Force lived in cantonments and on service. These conditions were such as made it essential to offer good pay and leave in order to attract suitable officers and British N.C.O.s. They generally lived in tents or bush huts. Fresh food was mostly not available, so diet had to be supplemented by tinned provisions, usually packed in 'chop-boxes', consisting of a 60-lb. load of shape and weight convenient to accommodate a native carrier.

The pay was, in consequence, very good, with special rates for 'bush' and 'horse' allowance. With care an officer could live on his allowances and save most of his pay. Polo and game shooting were available at many stations by way of recreation.

Troops were very mobile; they could generally live on the country; besides their pay they drew a 'chop' or ration allowance.

The climate was steamy in the coastal belt, while very hot and dry in the interior. In the rainy season tropical deluges descended in overwhelming torrents, conditions which were, however, relieved by the heralding of the 'harmattan', a cooling wind, blowing from the Sahara between October and March.

The natives were armed either with guns, or bows and arrows (often poisoned). The former were made like gaspipes, loaded with scrap metal capable of making a nasty wound at 40–50 yards.

(B) CONSOLIDATION, 1902–5

Although the Selborne Committee, appointed by the Secretary of State for Colonies, had recommended the integration of the West African Frontier Force by colonies in June 1899, this did not come into force till August 1901, *vide* C.O. letter 322 of that date.

In accordance with the terms of its recommendations an Inspector-General W.A.F.F., with rank of Brigadier-General,[1] was made responsible for putting the integration into effect, and thereafter for the efficiency of the Force. His H.Q. was located at the Colonial Office, from whence he would make a yearly tour of inspection to the W. African Colonies, visiting W.A.F.F. units as necessary, and submitting his despatches through the Governor concerned to the Secretary of State for Colonies.

The first Inspector-General was Major (local Lieutenant-Colonel) Brigadier G. V. Kemball, D.S.O., Royal Artillery, who had been Assistant Commandant Northern Nigeria Regiment till 1900. The I.G., as he was generally called, had on his staff a G.S.O.2 and a Staff Captain. In this case these were, Major F. Lyon, R.A., and Brevet-Major H. Bryan,

[1] When the rank of Brigadier-General was abolished in the Army the Inspector-General held his appointment as Colonel on the Staff until the rank of Brigadier was introduced.

Manchester Regiment, succeeded by Captain W. H. Maud, Somerset Light Infantry, who was known as 'Rosie' (owing to his chubby cheeks).

During his first tour, in 1902, Kemball took Lyon with him and was specially concerned with the following questions: (*a*) Standard of Officers; (*b*) Training; (*c*) Housing; (*d*) Health; (*e*) Arms; (*f*) Equipment; (*g*) Clothing.

(*a*) *Officers*

As the units of the W.A.F.F. had been largely created from Constabulary, a high proportion of the officers came from the Militia and had inadequate training in their profession. Commanding Officers were usually from the Regular Army.

(*b*) *Training*

Troops had been almost constantly engaged in tribal operations. Training had therefore been necessarily directed to 'bush' warfare, or fighting against primitively armed natives in open country.

(*c*) *Housing*

Although housing conditions were improving, they still left much to be desired and were having a serious effect on the health of Europeans. To quote the correspondent of the *Globe* when describing an officer's life in W. Africa: 'It is not difficult to appreciate the work officers are engaged on; in this climate, living in tents makes their lot pretty severe.'

(*d*) *Health*

Mortality and invaliding, especially from blackwater fever, was exceedingly high. (*c*) Naturally affected (*d*) materially. One battalion reported timber for hutting had to be used to a great extent for making coffins.

(*e*) *Arms*

Troops were armed with old carbines. Introduction of M.L.E. 303 magazine rifle and short bayonet to be urgently pressed for. Artillery 7-pounder guns useless, to be replaced with 2·95 in. mountain gun.

(*f*) *Equipment*

Brown leather equipment with a matchet was in use.

(*g*) *Clothing*

Rank and File. Up to the end of 1898 blue serge clothing was worn with a rolled fez. Lugard introduced a khaki frock flannel shirt and breeches, with cummerbund, and red blocked fez with tassel. A red zouave jacket was worn for review order. Some units wore sandals or chupplies, some were barefooted; all had puttees. Uniformity had to be established.

Officers. Khaki jacket (or bush shirt); khaki trousers (or shorts). Serge puttees khaki (or blue); brown ankle boots; Sam Browne belt; khaki helmet; cummerbund when wearing a bush shirt (colours varied); gilt buttons (or khaki) on jacket. In mess dress, some wore blue serge and some white drill, with cummerbund (colour varied); Wellington boots (patent or plain leather); forage cap (infantry pattern). Mounted officers generally wore khaki breeches. Swords were generally worn.

1902

GAMBIA

No constabulary existed in the colony as material for a W.A.F.F. unit prior to 1902. A company was therefore raised by Captain F. O. Graham, Royal Marines, who had already served with the W.A.F.F. in Northern Nigeria. It was first intended that the Gambia Company should form part of the Sierra Leone Battalion W.A.F.F., but later it was established with its own identity.

In December 1901 Graham, with Lieutenant Hoskyns, Lincolnshire Regiment, and Sergeant Noble, Coldstream Guards, proceeded to Sierra Leone with the object of recruiting there, while Lieutenant Morley, Manchester Regiment, and Colour Sergeant Wheatcroft, Worcester Regiment, with 30 men enlisted since 12th December, went up-river to a camp at Quinella.

By 2nd February 1902 the company had reached its full strength of 120 men. One-quarter of these were local natives and the balance from Sierra Leone.

In the first week of April the Company was inspected by the I.G., Brigadier-General Kemball, accompanied by his Staff Officer, Major H. Bryan, and very creditably reported on.

On 16th April, it supplied a detachment of two officers, one B.N.C.O. and 60 men and a maxim under Graham forming part of a force of the W.I.R. as escort to the Governor, Sir George Denton, to punish the natives of Bita (Foni) District.

On 10th June this place was again visited. No casualties occurred on either occasion. Captain E. H. Hopkinson, D.S.O., was the Medical Officer.

During the year Ordinance No. 20 separated the Company entirely from the Sierra Leone Battalion.

SIERRA LEONE

Nothing of consequence occurred, beyond handing over certain police duties on transforming the Sierra Leone Frontier Police into the Sierra Leone Battalion W.A.F.F. The Commanding Officer was Major Blakeney, 4 Essex Regiment.

THE GOLD COAST

At this time the Infantry of the Gold Coast Constabulary consisted of the 1 Battalion, about 1,600 strong, and the 2 (Northern Territories) Battalion, about 550 strong. Under the 'Selborne' Scheme it was intended to have only one Battalion of about 1,650 men.

Meanwhile the 2 Battalion continued to garrison the Northern Territories and act as constabulary. The complete reorganization would not take effect until the railway from Sekondi reached Kumasi, where H.Q., the Artillery and five companies were to be stationed, with three or four companies at outstations. Lieutenant-Colonels P. S. Wilkinson and A. H. Morris were the respective Battalion Commanders.

LAGOS

Major Aplin, C.M.G., 3 D.C.L.I., was commanding the Battalion, a Militia officer with much distinguished service in West Africa. His place was now taken by Major E. C. Tidswell, D.S.O., Lancashire Fusiliers, who had just returned from the South African War. On the I.G.'s report steps were being taken to build barracks for officers and men in order to remove them from the insanitary accommodation occupied in the town.

Consideration was also to be given towards reducing the number of detachments, as barrack accommodation at H.Q. become available. At present there were no less than six of these, viz. Meko, Jebu-Ode, Ibadan, Ilesha, Igbo-Bini and Saki, the last being over 200 miles distant.

During the year little had yet been accomplished to make the incorporation of the Battalion into an integral part of the W.A.F.F. effective, owing to the unit having been engaged in the Aro Expedition in Southern Nigeria. The troops had not returned to Lagos until April. Leave for officers and men then occupied the time until late autumn, while casualties and invaliding had depleted the ranks to a measurable extent.

SOUTHERN NIGERIA

Aro Exepdition, November 1901–March 1902

The Aro expedition, mentioned in the preceding paragraph, had occupied the activities of practically the whole of the Southern Nigeria Regiment from November 1901 to the end of March 1902. For particulars of these operations Section (D) (VI) should be referred to in this chapter. The Expedition was under the overall command of Lieutenant-Colonel A. F. Montanaro, Royal Artillery and Commandant of the Southern Nigeria Regiment, W.A.F.F. Its object was to bring a large area between the Niger and Cross Rivers under control by suppressing the fetish called the 'Long Juju'.[1] Besides the Lagos Battalion a contingent of the Northern Nigeria Regiment was employed.

The operations were successfully carried out in difficult bush country. Thirteen Europeans were wounded, while 167 native ranks became battle casualties, besides 70 died of disease.

Igarra and Uri Operations, February–May 1902

(Grant of Medal and Clasp)

Between February and May of this year Colonel A. F. Montanaro and Captain (Brevet-Major) W. G. C. Heneker, D.S.O., Connaught Rangers, carried out operations to finalize intertribal warfare in the Oguta area of Southern Nigeria. Details are given in Section (D) (VIII) of this chapter. Thirteen native ranks were killed, while six Europeans and 68 natives were wounded here.

[1] This Aro 'Long Juju' was concealed in a deep ravine with very steep sides in dense bush country. The Aro Priests pronounced doom on their victims from caves in which they were hidden inside the ravine. No dispute could be settled without judgment given by the Oracles (i.e. the Priest). Payments in wealth and slaves was exacted, while in many cases the loser in a dispute was sacrificed to the Juju. Montanaro's despatch relates the gruesome spectacle of mutilated corpses piled on the sacrificial altar.

The African General Service Medal, with appropriate clasp, was granted for both the above operations.

NORTHERN NIGERIA

In 1902 Lugard turned his attention to the north-eastern portion of the Protectorate. There he was much concerned about three matters:

(I) *In Bauchi* there existed an important centre of the slave trade. Strong protests and threats to the Emir of that province were unavailing. Lugard therefore decided to bring force to bear.

(II) *In Bornu* the position needed clarifying. Fad-el-Allah, a son of Rabeh (a notable leader of the Mahdi's Sudanese Army) had been making incursions into French territory around Lake Chad. The French had pursued him into Bornu, where he asked for British protection. In a battle between Chad and Gujba he was killed by the French, who by then had penetrated 150 miles into our country.

(III) *At Yola* the Emir was behaving in a very truculent manner, exporting slaves from Adamawa to the Hausa States, and defying Lugard's authority.

Bornu Expedition, February–May 1902

(Grant of Medal and Clasp)

In January 1902 Morland, with a section of artillery, four maxims, 20 Europeans and 515 rank and file, left Ibi for Bauchi *en route* for Bornu and Yola. He was accompanied by Wallace, acting High Commissioner. After the Emir of Bauchi had been dealt with and a company left to garrison the place, Morland had a surprise attack from a self-styled Mahdi, called Mallam Jibrella, whom he severely defeated, at Gujba.

Morland then came to an amicable arrangement with the French, who retired to east of the Shari and Dikwa. The Sheikh, Abubekr Gombai, was recognized and installed as Shehu of Bornu.

Morland then subjugated the Emir of Yola, traversing the frontier of Adamawa, and surveying a large stretch of that area. Altogether his operations had covered 60,000 sq. miles. A description of the activities of his column are given in Section (D) (V)) of this chapter.

Irgungu Escort, June–November 1902

(Grant of Medal and Clasp)

The object here was to ensure the safe passage of the Anglo-French Boundary Commission on the northern border of Nigeria. It consisted of another officer, Lieutenant McLachlan, 18th Hussars, and 50 rifles, under Captain G. C. Merrick, R.A. There were seven casualties.

Early during this year a garrison was stationed at Zaria on the Emir requesting support against the hostility of Kontagora.

A contingent of 300 rifles, 1 Battalion Northern Nigeria Regiment, under Lieutenant-Colonel A. Festing, was sent to join the Aro Field Force in Southern Nigeria between November 1901 and March 1902. (See Section (D) (VI) of this chapter.)

1903–4

GAMBIA

From 24th January to 1st July the Company, 96 strong, was in Camp at Sallikeni under Graham and Hoskyns. The remainder stayed at Bathurst for guard duties.

An African schoolmaster and a clerk were added to the establishment. The proportion of O.R.s was altered to one-third local and two-thirds Sierra Leone tribes.

In April 1904 the I.G. with his Staff Officer inspected the Company at its new camp, Cape St. Mary.

SIERRA LEONE

On 1st January 1903 the Battalion had completed its reorganization from Frontier Police to W.A.F.F. It was decided to move H.Q. out of Freetown, which in every way was most unsuitable. The choice lay between Moyamba and Daru. The latter was eventually selected. Outstations at this time were Kaballa, Mabanta, Panjuma and Bandajuma.

The men of the Battalion marched barefooted, as did those of the Lagos Battalion. However, the Aro Expeditionary Force had found casualties from cut feet extremely heavy in the Lagos contingent. The O.C. Sierra Leone Battalion (Major Blakeney) was therefore asked his views, but emphatically vetoed the suggestion of adopting footgear, saying 'it would be a great mistake and impair marching'.

During 1903 Captain C. E. Palmer, R.A., took over command from Blakeney with local rank of Major.

About this time Kissis from Liberia were raiding on a large scale into British territory. The despatch of a field force to suppress the menace was actively considered, and later decided upon.

In his report on the Battalion for 1904 the I.G. gave special praise to the high standard of intelligence and bushcraft throughout the men.

GOLD COAST

Major C. C. Watherston, R.E., was Chief Commissioner for the N.T., and now took over temporary command of the 2 Battalion from Morris. It was organized in six companies of 80 men. There was also a troop of 30 Moshi irregular cavalry. In December 1904 the I.G. recommended the reduction of the Gold Coast Battery from three to two sections (or four guns) so as to allow for extra permanent gun carriers needed for the 2·95 in. guns. His report also instructed that a Regimental Historical Record should be kept. (It is to be noted that such an historical record does not now seem to exist.)

The deaths from blackwater fever are recorded of Lieutenants H. A. Burgess at Odumassi on 3rd February 1904 and A. H. Hince while on leave on the 5th of the same month. In December Captain J. C. Ord (Cork R.G.A.) died at Kumasi.

LAGOS

In 1903 Captain and Brevet-Major P. Maclear, Dublin Fusiliers, was appointed 2I.C. to Tidswell. During this year and the next both these officers took energetic steps to improve the standard of training which had suffered from the number of detachments. These were now reduced from six to three, all being found from the company at Ibadan. This allowed of the concentration of H.Q. and two full companies at Lagos.

SOUTHERN NIGERIA

On 27th July Captain and Brevet-Major H. C. Moorhouse, R.A., was made 2I.C. On 23rd December Lieutenant K. Wilford died.

During 1903 and early 1904 a number of military operations took place for which the African G.S. Medal, with appropriate clasp, was awarded. These are described in Section (D) (XIII) and (XV) of this chapter. It is proposed here only to refer briefly to the most important of these.

On 8th July 1904 Captain H. P. Gordon died.

Between September and December 1903 the following operations were carried out:

(*a*) *Nun River*

To seize a pirate chief who had been terrorizing the area for many years. Montanaro, with a 2·95 in. gun, 13 officers and B.N.C.O.s, 300 rifles Southern Nigeria Regiment, assisted by a marine flotilla, successfully hunted out the whole district by the skilful co-operation of both services.

(*b*) *Eket*

Major A. M. N. Mackenzie was in command of a column of six Europeans and 185 rifles sent to punish the attempted murder of Captain Crewe-Read, the District Commissioner.

(*c*) *Mkpani*

A force, again under Mackenzie, comprised of 13 Europeans and 288 rifles, was occupied in the Obubra District of the Cross River in suppressing cannabalism.

Between January and April 1904 the most important punitive operations were: (*a*) N. Ibibio; (*b*) Asaba Hinterland; (*c*) Kwale; (*d*) River Imo; (*e*) Obokum.

These affairs ranged from the Niger to the Cross River and dealt with the suppression of secret societies, cannabalism and general defiance of authority. The first was composed of 440 officers and men, while the others were each about 200 strong.

NORTHERN NIGERIA

Early in 1903 there occurred the important Kano-Sokoto Expedition, as a sequence to which followed the Sokoto-Burmi Operations. For each of these the African G.S. Medal with clasp was awarded. For a detailed account Chapter 2, Sections D (XI) and (XII) should be referred to. But before giving a brief description of them here we have to record the deaths in March 1903 of Captain Carre, Royal Warwickshire Regiment, and Lieutenant A. J. R. Mackenzie, Royal Horse Guards.

Also in April 1903 the Sapper Company was disbanded in conformity with the 'Selborne' Committee's recommendations. In the same month the Mounted Infantry was expanded to a three-company battalion of 300 men (later increased to seven companies), the first Commanding Officer being Major Eustace Crawley, 12th Royal Lancers. In justification of the M.I., Lugard gives his opinion as to its value being double that of infantry, owing to its mobility for patrolling the Northern Frontier. See the 'Story of the M.I.', Chapter 6.

Kano–Sokoto Expedition, January–March 1903

A crisis had occurred in the Northern Hausa States owing to the Emir of Kano giving asylum to the Magaji of Keffi, murderer of Maloney,[1] the Resident. The Emir of Zaria was intriguing with Kano, while both were encouraged by Aburahman, Sultan of Sokoto.

Lugard decided on immediate action, despatching Morland with an expeditionary force from Zaria to Kano, where the city was stormed and the fleeing Emir pursued towards Sokoto. A hundred miles from Kano beside a waterless desert the hostile army was assembled. Here Wallace Wright with a small troop of M.I., having formed square, gallantly faced the enemy's charges. His action broke up the enemy's resistance, thereby gaining him the Victoria Cross. Our forces now commanded by Kemball, the Inspector-General W.A.F.F., then advanced to capture Sokoto with little opposition. The Sultan fled towards Bauchi.

Sokoto–Burmi, April–July 1903

Troops from Zaria, Bauchi and Gujba were sent in pursuit of Abdurahman, the fleeing Sultan. After a fierce battle at Burmi, his force was severely routed. He and several chiefs were killed. Major Marsh, who was in command, died from a poisoned-arrow wound, being succeeded by Major Barlow, Essex Regiment.

As a rallying-point for fanatical Mahomedans, Burmi held a special significance. Its occupants were the 'Tejani' sect, who, according to Lugard, as quoted in his annual report for 1903, were probably of Tuareg origin. It will be recollected that Morland in his 1902 Bornu expedition had been hotly attacked by Mallam Jibrella there, whom he defeated and killed. A new Mahdi had been elected to succeed Jibrella, so it was to him that Abdurahman fled for succour.

Flight and Capture of Aliyu, Emir of Kano, 25th February–12th March 1903

After the flight from Kano of Aliyu, the Emir, he put his brother, the Waziri, in command of the army he had assembled at Rawia behind the

[1] The circumstances leading to Maloney's murder were unfortunate. He had sent his Assistant Resident, Webster, to summon the Magaji to a conference. By some mistake, probably due to the wrong interpretation of a message, Webster was led to the harem and thereupon violently ejected. The Magaji's followers then set upon Maloney and killed him. These events inflamed Kano, whose Emir shouted defiance.

waterless desert already mentioned. He himself abandoned his army on the night of 25th–26th February, before the battle, fleeing northward towards a place called Tchiberi, or Gober, near the French frontier some 100 miles distant. The account of his capture is told by Major-General C. H. Foulkes, at that time a Sapper subaltern doing duty on the Anglo-French Boundary Commission in the area. He relates his story in the *West African Review* for June 1959 as follows:

'I was on detachment from the main body of the Commission at a small village called Illela with an escort of six Hausa soldiers, 95 miles due north of Sokoto. On the evening of March 9, 1903, two mounted men arrived in my camp. They had been sent by the chief of a town called Tchara to tell me that Kano had fallen and that the Emir was a fugitive. He was thought to have been sent by the Sultan of Sokoto towards Katsena to rally what was left of the Fulani empire to resist the British and was likely to pass near a town called Tchiberi on his way. Also that a great army was assembling at Sokoto, where a battle was imminent.'

Foulkes then goes on to say he decided to send word to the Seriki of Tchiberi the Emir must be held until he and his escort arrived. Setting out next morning, he journeyed 175 miles; after an almost non-stop ride of three days and two nights, he approached Tchiberi, which he now definitely located as Gober. Here he was met by the Seriki, Umoru, at the head of several hundred horsemen and some thousands of footmen armed with spears, swords, bows and arrows. Umoru was persuaded to surrender Aliyu, though not without reluctance. Before Foulke's departure he witnessed a display of military might, consisting of at least 10,000 armed men from Gober and Maradi (a near-by town). Aliyu's story was that he intended to make his way to Mecca and was bargaining with Umoru for equipment for his journey, in payment for which he would hand over half his treasure of 10 camels loaded with Maria Theresa dollars.

Lugard wrote to Foulkes later to congratulate him 'on his wonderful feat and on securing Aliyu'. Aliyu was banished first to Yola, and later to Lokoja.

Foulkes has something interesting to say about the location of the Battle of Dagh, where the Sultan of Sokoto, Bello, defeated and killed the Emir of Katsena and took prisoner the Emir of Gober in 1820. He says that near Tchara the Seriki of that place pointed out a large mound about 20 ft. high, saying it contains the remains of 20,000 men who had fallen in that battle.

Incident of the Sultan of Sokoto's Standard

Special interest attaches to the flag of the Sultan (or Emir Abdurahman) of Sokoto at the Battle of Sokoto in March 1903. An account of this is given in 'A short historical background of the Nigerian Military Forces', issued as a pamphlet for the Regimental Museum, pages 10–12.

The author, Captain H. A. J. W. Stacpoole, M.C., writes: 'The undoubted prize of the musuem is the Holy Standard lent by the 1 Battalion. This is alleged to be the original standard, green in colour, raised by Othman dan Fodio during his Jehad (Holy War). It was first captured at the Sokoto battle.'

The author goes on to quote Crozier, in his book *Five Years Hard*, as saying he himself found a green flag on the battlefield, but that someone stole it later.

On 27th July 1903, at the Battle of Burmi, Captain G. C. R. Mundy took a flag (presumed to be the same one) from beside the dead body of Abdurahman, the ex-Emir, and presented it to the officers of the 2 Battalion the Leicestershire Regiment in June 1904. The flag is now encased behind a glass panel with the donor's inscription on a silver plaque in the Officers' Mess of the 1 Battalion Queen's Own Nigeria Regiment.

Some doubt is thrown on the authenticity of the whole story by Lugard, who wrote in his Annual Report for 1902: 'It has been stated in the Press that the ex-Sultan (of Sokoto) had unfurled the ancient banner of dan Fodio (which though captured by us had unfortunately been misplaced and lost again during the action), and that it was to this standard that the people had flocked. There does not appear to be any grounds for this report, and the green flag has not again been heard of. The ex-Sultan found no appreciable aid in the country recently traversed by the Kano Expedition, and the newly appointed emirs and chiefs remained loyal.'

Again in the following year Lugard wrote: 'With regard to the so-called sacred banner of Otham dan Fodio, which was stated by the Press to have been used as the signal for rising, I am informed that it was lost in a fight with the Kebbawa some ten years ago.'

We learn that this flag was sent home to Messrs Hobson, the regimental tailors of Lexington Street, London, to be restored for the Independence Celebrations in Nigeria in 1960. It was in a very tattered and bloodstained condition when received by them, but was skilfully repaired and returned to Nigeria in time for the momentous and historic occasion.

Photographs of the Walls of Kano in the Regimental Album

The Regimental Museum pamphlet above referred to alludes to photographs of the walls at Kano, quoting Lugard's description of them given in his despatch on the 1903 Expedition. 'Unopposed, therefore, the force reached Kano, where the extent and formidable nature of the fortifications surpassed the best-informed anticipations of our officers. Needless to say, I have never seen, or imagined, anything like it in Africa. The wall was 11 miles in perimeter, with 13 gates, all newly built. Subsequent measurement at several points by the Public Works Department proved the walls to be from 30 to 50 ft. high and about 40 ft. thick at the base, with a double ditch in front.

'The loopholes, about 4 ft. from the crest of the wall (which was here 4 ft. thick), were served by a banquette and provided with mantlets at intervals, being crenellated between them. The ditch, or moat, is divided into two by a dwarf wall, triangular in section, which runs along its centre —the gates themselves were flimsy structures of cowhide, but the massive entrance tower in which they were fixed was generally about 50 ft. long, and tortuous so that they were impermeable to shell-fire. Some of them were most cleverly designed in a re-entrant angle, so that the access to them was enfiladed by fire from the walls on either side, while the ditch itself was full of live thorns and immensely deep.'

Lugard's Entry into Katsena, 15th–31st March 1903

After the capture of Sokoto and the flight of its ex-Sultan, Abdurahman, to Burmi, Lugard at once installed Atahiru (who was in the line of succession to the Sultanate and approved of by the local chiefs) in his place. He then proceeded by rapid marches to Katsena. The attitude of that Hausa State was uncertain. However, overawed by the fate of Kano and Sokoto, the Emir sent a messenger to meet him protesting he had no wish to fight and would welcome the British. Lugard comments that the Emir and his people were evidently in a state of panic, and reluctant to lead him into the town. On the 28th March he entered by the Yandaka Gate, where a plaque commemorates the event. Soon after he deposed the Emir, installing Alhaji Muhammadu Diko in his place. This man ruled in an exceptional manner for 37 years and was succeeded by his son, the present capable and enlightened Emir.

The deaths from blackwater fever are recorded of Lieutenants F. D. Adams, Leicestershire Regiment, on 11th April 1904 and C. E. Gallagher, 7th May 1904.

1904

Operations in Dakakeri, Wase, Semolika, Kilba, March–July 1904

(See also this chapter, Section (D) (XVI))

The disaffected areas were located in widely separated parts of Northern Nigeria, and the punitive force consisted of a small body of 100–200 rifles and a maxim gun. The fighting was with the wilder pagan tribes often in difficult mountainous country.

The Dakakeri and Semolika Operations took place in the Kontagora Province; *Wase* between the Benue and Bauchi was inhabited by the Yergam (Yerghum) people, who (with the Montols) were, and continued for several years later, to be a thorn in the side of the Government, murdering, pillaging and eating traders. *Kilba.*—These people inhabit a tract between Yola and Maiduguri. Their offences took the form of stopping and looting caravans.

The medal with clasp was given for each of these small affairs.

Okpoto Operations: December 1903–March 1904

(See also this chapter, Section (D) (XIV))

These operations were undertaken to punish and arrest the murderers of the Resident and Police Officer in the Bassa Province. They were successfully carried out by Captain (local Major) G. C. Merrick, R.A., with a force of one gun and 262 rank and file. Merrick received the D.S.O. and various other honours were given. There were over 40 casualties. The medal and clasp were awarded here.

On 2nd August 1904 Brevet-Major C. M. Dobell, Royal Welch Fusiliers, and Captain C. A. Wilkinson, Shropshire Light Infantry, were appointed majors in the 1 and 2 Battalion Northern Nigeria Regiment respectively.

Barracks at Zaria for M.I.

New barracks for the M.I. were completed at Zaria with accommodation for 10 officers, 10 B.N.C.O.s, 250 men and 250 horses early in 1904.

Kachia Detachment 1 N.R.

A station with detachment 1 N.R. was opened at Kachia to stop raiding.

GENERAL

Grant of African General Service Medal

This Medal was granted by Army Order 132 of 1902 to replace the 'West African Medal' current since the Ashanti War of 1873–4. (See Appendix VI.)

African D.C.M.

In 1903 the Inter-department Rewards Committee recommended the grant of an 'African' D.C.M. to Native personnel in lieu of the D.C.M. issued to the Army. It was not finally authorized till 1906.

Formation of a Reserve

In 1904 the I.G. recommended the formation of a W.A.F.F. Reserve. The terms approved were 14 days' annual training with pay and a retaining fee in addition to a grant of land. A musketry course was to be fired each year.

Issue of Green Cap and Chupplies

A green kilmarnock cap was approved to replace the fez in service dress. This cap became famous during the East African Campaign (1916–18). It was said of the W.A.F.F. that the 'Green Caps never retreat'.

About this time the adoption of a serviceable footgear to avoid cut feet was considered and agreed upon. Some units had bare feet even on active service, thereby suffering a high percentage of casualties. A stout chupplie was introduced.

Adoption of the Short Lee-Enfield ·303 Magazine Rifle and Bayonet

In 1903 the I.G. decided to rearm the W.A.F.F. with this rifle to replace the carbine in use, subject to a satisfactory report from the Northern Nigeria Regiment. Rearmament was completed by 1908.

The I.G. to be Qualified for Substantive Colonel's Rank

In September 1904 the War Office decided that the Inspector-General W.A.F.F. should qualify as Substantive Colonel.

Staff Captain to I.G.

On 16th December Captain W. H. Maud, Somerset Light Infantry, replaced Bryan, appointed Colonial Secretary for the Gold Coast.

1905

GAMBIA

New barracks, officers' mess and quarters were built at Bathurst. Some unrest occurred amongst married men living out while new lines were being built. This was settled by giving a monthly allowance of 3/-.

SIERRA LEONE

The Kissi Operations, March–June 1905

Continuous raiding by the Kissi tribe determined the Sierra Leone Government to undertake punitive measures. The operations were ably conducted by Major C. E. Palmer, R.A., commanding the Battalion, and are described in this chapter, Section (D) (XVII). The medal and clasp were granted here and Palmer received the D.S.O.

GOLD COAST

On 11th March Tidswell from Lagos took over command of the 1 Battalion, but he reverted to his British regiment in November on promotion. On 30th April Major C. C. Watherston took over command of the 2 Battalion from Morris, with rank of Lieutenant-Colonel. His Battalion in the N.T. was disposed as follows: H.Q. three companies and artillery at Gambaga, a company each at Kintampo, Yeji and Wa, with detachments at Bole and Salaga. It was now decided to stop recruiting Sierra Leone natives and Yorubas, as these men were inclined to desert. Local sources would be depended on.

Lieutenant L. H. T. Martin died at Sikassiko.

LAGOS

Maclear took over command from Tidswell. Two companies went as reinforcement to Kwale Operations mentioned in the next paragraph.

SOUTHERN NIGERIA

In October–November 1905 a patrol under Captain Vassall, Gloucester Regiment, while escorting the District Commissioner, got attacked and badly cut up. It was reinforced from Lagos by two companies under Maclear. The operations, named Kwale/Ishan Operations are described in this chapter, Section (D) (XVIII). The medal and clasp were granted here.

1905–6

Bende-Ohitsha Hinterland Operations, October 1905–April 1906

(See this chapter, Section (D) (XIX))

This covered a wide stretch of country from Oguta to Abakaliki and Bende to Owerri, where slave trading and human sacrifices had stopped trade. Trenchard was in overall command, operating with two columns. There were about 60 casualties, including five officers. Altogether over 500 rifles with two mountain guns were employed. Trenchard and Mair both received the D.S.O. The medal and clasp were given here.

Dispositions

At this time H.Q. and 2 companies were at Calabar, with one company each at Ikotekpene, Abakaliki, Okigwi, Agbor, Onitsha and Owerri.

NORTHERN NIGERIA

1905

On 30th May 1905 Cubitt took over command of the M.I. in place of Crawley, invalided. Hasler had been appointed, but held it for only a few weeks, as he was appointed Assistant Commandant. Julian Hasler was in the 'Buffs'. Owing to sickness at Zaria, H.Q. and three companies M.I. were moved to Gaza three miles from Kano, and the remaining companies were stationed at Katsena, Sokoto and Hadeija.

GENERAL

On 15th October Captain G. C. G. Craufurd, D.S.O., Gordon Highlanders, was appointed G.S.O.2 to the Inspector-General W.A.F.F., *vice* Lyon vacated. Meanwhile Morland had been appointed I.G. on 31st August in place of Kemball, who had proceeded on leave in January via Illo and Gambaga through French territory.

Kemball's term of office had been a strenuous and important one. He had made several drastic improvements in the quality of officers, in many cases substituting Regulars for Militiamen. Training had been conducted on up-to-date methods, musketry courses had been introduced on Regular Army lines. Accommodation for officers, B.N.C.O.s and men had been started in permanent houses. Health, though still far from good, had shown a slight reduction of mortality and invaliding. Rearmament with the magazine rifle was being pushed ahead. The 7-pounder gun was abolished, any replacements were to be made with the 2·95 in. mountain gun, adapted to carrier transport. Officer's uniform was standardized, and the soldier's clothing made more suited to service conditions. A pamphlet was published to cover the changes in uniform for all ranks (see Appendix IV). It was decided to adopt the Mk. VI/303 S.A.A. because of its greater stopping power than the Mk. V.; it did not violate the Geneva Convention.

(c) ASHANTI CAMPAIGN, 1900

(Battle Honour: Ashanti, 1900; Medal granted: Ashanti, 1900;

Clasp Kumasi; A.O.249, December 1901)

Ashanti Expedition, 1900

The operations can be divided into three phases:

Phase I. The encirclement of Kumasi Fort by the Ashantis, March–April 1900. Followed by the attempts to relieve the beleagured garrison by (*a*) Captain C. G. O. Aplin, C.M.G., with 250 Lagos Constabulary on 29th April, and (*b*) Major A. Morris, D.S.O., with 230 Gold Coast Constabulary from the Northern Territories, on 15th May. This was succeeded by the break-out from Kumasi to the Coast of the Governor with an escort of 600 men, led by Major A. Morris, D.S.O.

Phase II. The concentration of an Expeditionary Force at Prahsu, under Colonel James Willcocks, C.M.G., D.S.O., followed by the relief of Kumasi and the suppression of the Ashanti Rebellion.

Phase III. The completion of the subjugation of the Ashantis in the back areas of their kingdom.

However, before describing these operations some preliminary remarks are relevant. Subsequent to the 1895 Ashanti Expedition narrated in Chapter 1, Section (E), the sequence of events which led up to the 1900 Expedition may be briefly told. A strong small fort had been built to house a garrison at Kumasi. A Resident, Captain Donald Stewart, had been installed to initiate the policy of administering the country and keep the trade routes to the south open. The Ashantis, meanwhile, were very discontented and determined to get their king back. Moreover, during all this time they were pursuing their time-honoured practices of human sacrifice and bloodthirsty orgies. A European missionary, Mr. Ramseyer, who had been their captive for four years, has thus described the annual festival of Bantama, or death and wake.

'On this anniversary it was the custom for the king, or chiefs, to visit the burial-place of former kings of Ashanti. Here their skeletons reposed in richly ornamented coffins, placed in cells and fastened with gold wire. Each skeleton was offered food while the drums played and a human sacrifice was made. The victim to be sacrificed had a knife thrust through both cheeks and was then slain, the skeleton being washed with his blood. It was customary to slaughter some thirty in a day.'

PHASE I

With the object of putting an end to the state of unrest and fetish orgies, by adopting a very firm attitude, early in 1900 the Governor, Sir Frederick Hodgson, K.C.M.G., accompanied by Lady Hodgson, proceeded to Kumasi with an escort of 20 Gold Coast Constabulary commanded by Captain C. Armitage.

On 28th March he held a palaver at which he ordered the 1895 unpaid war indemnity to be paid, at the same time saying King Prempeh would never be allowed to return, and that, as the Golden Stool[1] was the emblem of Ashanti power it now rightly belonged to the representative of the Queen of England.

Siege of Kumasi

This pronouncement had the effect of incensing the Ashantis, who promptly laid siege to the fort with its small garrison of Constabulary and the Governor. For some time past the Ashantis had been laying up a big supply of guns and powder, so were both well armed, and numerous enough, to intercept all roads to the coast, thus effectively cutting off

[1] This stool was wrought about 1697, in the reign of King Osai Tutu. From that time it had been the throne of the Kings of Ashanti. It was never allowed to touch the ground, for legend said it had floated down from the heavens; it was therefore placed on a skin to prevent defilement.

communications. In spite of this, however, a runner conveying word of the desperate situation at Kumasi succeeded in reaching Government H.Q.

Concentration of Expeditionary Force

Early in April 1,400 troops began to concentrate under Colonel James Willcocks, C.M.G., D.S.O., the Commandant W.A.F.F. in Northern Nigeria. This force was ordered to rendezvous at Cape Coast Castle. Its composition was as follows:

1 and 2 Battalions W.A.F.F.: eight companies, under Colonel T. L. N. Morland.

3 (S/N) Battalion W.A.F.F.: two companies, under Lieutenant-Colonel H. Carter.

Gold Coast Constabulary, under Major P. S. Wilkinson.

250 Lagos Constabulary, under Captain Aplin, C.M.G.

50 Sierra Leone Frontier Police, under Lieutenant Edwards.

West African Regiment, under Major Burroughs.

Central African Rifles, under Lieutenant-Colonel C. J. Brake.

West India Regiment, detachment.

Total strength about 2,800 with two 75 mm. guns.

First Attempt to Relieve Kumasi

On 29th April the Lagos Contingent, having been the first troops to arrive at Cape Coast Castle, fought their way into Kumasi after meeting heavy opposition and suffering severe casualties. All six officers were wounded, besides 139 rank and file killed and wounded.

Meanwhile the Governor had summoned all available Constabulary from the Northern Territories. These arrived at Kumasi on 15th May with only light opposition, under the command of Major A. Morris, D.S.O. The garrison now totalled 700 troops. It was, however, very short of food and ammunition.

Break-out from Kumasi, 23rd June

Meanwhile, with a view to relieving the food situation, which was becoming very serious, the Governor decided to cut his way down to the coast with Morris and an escort of 600 troops, leaving only 100 to hold the Fort at Kumasi. In this he was successful, greatly thanks to the resource of Armitage, who commanded the advanced guard and held off the enemy's onslaughts on the column which at times gave him some anxious moments. The total casualties suffered in the retreat were some 100 killed and wounded. Included in the former were Captains G. Marshall and P. H. A. Leggett, both of whom had been wounded in earlier operations.

On 8th May 450 W.A.F.F. with two maxims and one 75 mm. gun arrived, also 98 Lagos Constabulary, under Captains Anderson and Elgee, as well as 50 Sierra Leone Frontier Police, under Edwards. As senior officer Captain W. M. Hall 1 W.A.F.F. took command pending the arrival of Willcocks.

At this time the Adansis were wavering on which side to throw in their

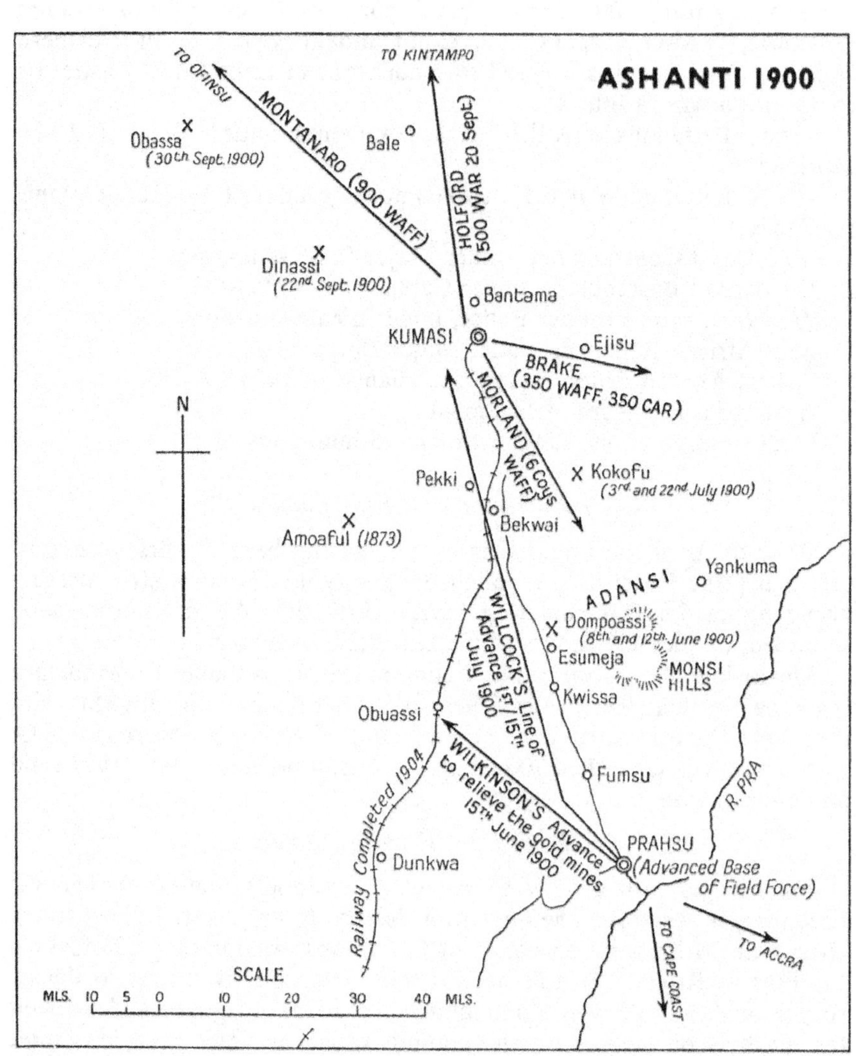

3. Ashanti, 1900

lot. So Hall, after putting a garrison under Elgee at Prahsu, and one at Obuassi to protect the gold-miners in the west, occupied Esumeja and Kwissa at the foot of the Monsi Hills, advancing north towards the Adansi country.

Engagement near Kokofu, 23rd May

With 200 rifles 1 W.A.F.F. he then made a reconnaissance towards Kokofu. Here he found the Ashantis in strength and was forced to retire on Esumeja. His foresight in occupying this place and Kwissa deserve great credit, as they formed valuable rallying-points in the subsequent operations. Fortunately, too, Bekwai remained loyal and controlled Pekki to the north, the more westerly of the two roads leading to Kumasi and the one later used by Willcocks in his advance to its relief.

About this time the garrison of Kwissa, comprising 20 Gold Coast Constabulary under Lieutenant Slater, was attacked unsuccessfully. In these actions three soldiers were killed and two Europeans with seven other ranks wounded.

PHASE II

Arrival of Willcocks, 26th May, and Concentration of Expeditionary Force

On his arrival at Cape Coast Castle on this date, Willcocks saw that operations had been conducted without any plan, but rather by unco-ordinated parties hastening towards the goal of Kumasi piecemeal, with consequent unsatisfactory results. He therefore determined to co-ordinate future operations.

Carter's Action and Retreat at Dompoassi, 6th June

On 2nd June Carter and Wilkinson of 3 W.A.F.F. and Gold Coast Constabulary respectively, who had reached Prahsu on 26th May left Fumsu via Kwissa for Bekwai with 380 rifles. At Dompoassi the enemy had built a stockade parallel to the road and 30 yards from it, hidden by thick bush. The column fell into an ambush which resulted in the loss of three killed and seven officers with 89 rank and file wounded.

Colour-Sergeant Mackenzie Wins the V.C.

Carter decided to retire on Kwissa, but Colour-Sergeant Mackenzie of the Seaforth Highlanders volunteered to charge the stockade with the bayonet with his Yoruba Company 1 W.A.F.F. This he accomplished, being followed up by other troops causing the Adansis to flee in panic. For his gallantry here Mackenzie was awarded the Victoria Cross.

Major Mellis and 150 men 1 W.A.F.F. were now sent by Willcocks to reinforce Carter at Kwissa, where they were attacked by the enemy on 12th June; the combined column then withdrew to Fumsu.

Wilkinson was now detached from Carter's force at Fumsu with 300 rifles and reserve ammunition to succour the manager of the Obuassi Mines and proceed thence to Bekwai.

Second Engagement at Dompoassi

On 12th June Captain Wilson with the Nupe Company 1 W.A.F.F. was ordered to Kwissa to support Carter, Willcocks not knowing that it had been evacuated. Wilson was attacked at Dompoassi by Ashantis and Adansis, he and six soldiers being killed, also one B.N.C.O. and 25 men were wounded, besides 16 carriers. The Company, commanded by Colour-Sergeant Humphries, then marched to Fumsu.

Third Engagement at Dompoassi, 30th June

On 22nd June Burroughs, with 400 W.A.R. one 75 mm. gun and four Maxims reached Prahsu, marching thence via the Monsi Hills to Dompoassi, where he surprised an enemy camp just after dark. He killed 30 enemy, captured many guns and kegs of powder and destroyed a number of new stockades. This was the first lesson taught to the Ashantis.

Attack on Kokofu, 3rd July

Contrary to Willcocks's instructions, which had the object of enticing the enemy to withdraw men from Kumasi to defend Kokofu, Burroughs, being flushed with success, decided to attack Kokofu. The force was assailed on all sides; failing to attempt a charge with the bayonet, he was forced to beat an ignominious retreat. His casualties were Lieutenant Browlie, 3 W.I.R., attached W.A.R., and three men killed; six officers, one B.N.C.O. and 72 natives wounded.

Advance to Kumasi, 13th July

Having organized his transport, Willcocks left Prahsu on 1st July and arrived at Bekwai on the 9th. He had now deceived the Ashantis into expecting him to advance on Kumasi via Kokofu, instead of via Pekki to the west, as he, in fact, did. He left a garrison of 200 at Bekwai, marching with every available man and gun. His column consisted of:

Two 75 mm. guns, four 7-pounders and six maxims.
700 W.A.F.F., Gold Coast and Lagos Constabulary.
200 W.A.R.
50 Sierra Leone Frontier Police.
1,000 troops; 60 Europeans and 1,700 carriers.

Willcocks in his despatch says: 'The cumbrous march through this country of such a large number of men is an experience one does not wish to repeat.'

On 14th July the column commanded by Wilkinson was attacked at Treda. Captain Eden, with a company W.A.F.F., and Edwards with the Sierra Leone Frontiers, rushed the place at the point of the bayonet. Subsequently a good deal of hostile fire was subdued by the maxims.

On 15th July the rearguard, under Captain Beddoes, was attacked beyond Ekwanta, but the enemy was repulsed. At 4.30 p.m., a mile from Kumasi, the advanced guard was attacked from stockades built across the road and flanked by others. A hot fire was first poured from our guns.

This was followed by 'cease fire', then by a charge of the whole extended infantry line. This was too much for the Ashantis, who fled, leaving many dead on the ground.

Relief of Kumasi, 15th July

The relief of Kumasi was an accomplished fact. To quote from Willcocks: 'No sound came from the direction of the Fort, which you cannot see till quite close. For a moment the hideous desolation and silence, the headless bodies lying everywhere, the sickening smell, etc., almost made one shudder to think what no one dared to utter—"Has Kumasi fallen? Are we too late?" Then a bugle sound caught the ears—the General Salute—white and black broke into cheers long sustained.'

Willcocks's Fine Performance

Our casualties in the final stage had been remarkably light. Willcocks's performance was outstanding for this type of bush warfare. He actually relieved Kumasi with less than half the men Wolseley had employed.

Here only African troops were used as against Wolseley's three British and a Naval brigade. Furthermore this time the Adansis were hostile and Obuassi needed protection. Wolseley had roads made by the Sappers, in this case only bush-paths were available. He was handicapped by Carter's retreat and Burroughs's disastrous attack on Kokofu. While in 1873 the campaign was carried out in the dry season, this time the operation had to be done at the unhealthiest time of year. Willcocks virtually marched without a line of communications (except for Bekwai and Esumeja). Officers were restricted to two loads and the men were on half rations. Supplies only allowed for a speedy operation, the provisioning of Kumasi garrison and one day's halt there.

Honours and Awards

On the capture of Kumasi Willcocks was awarded a Brevet-Colonelcy. At the conclusion of the Campaign he was given the K.C.M.G. Other honours awarded (*London Gazette*, 15th January 1901) were as follows:

D.S.O.

Lieutenant W. D. Wright, Royal West Surrey Regiment and 1 Battalion W.A.F.F.

Major P. S. Wilkinson, 5th Fusiliers, late 1 W.A.F.F.

Captain (local Major) C. J. Mellis, I.S.C. and 1 Battalion, W.A.F.F.

Brevet-Major

Captains H. M. Hall, W. Yorkshire Regiment and 1 Battalion W.A.F.F.; A. J. L. Eden, Oxfordshire Light Infantry and 2 Battalion W.A.F.F.; W. E. Edwards, R.A. and Artillery W.A.F.F.; H. R. Beddoes, Royal Dublin Fusiliers and 2 Battalion W.A.F.F.; H. Bryan, Manchester Regiment and 1 Battalion W.A.F.F.; Willans, Army Service Corps.

D.C.M.

Sergeants A. Major, Blair, and Foster.

Bugler Moma and Private Ojo Oyo.

Victoria Cross

Captain (local Major) C. J. Melliss, Indian Staff Corps and 1 Battalion W.A.F.F.

Sergeant J. Mackenzie, Seaforth Highlanders and 1 Battalion W.A.F.F.

PHASE III

Willcocks's column left Kumasi on 17th July, arriving at Bekwai the 19th, on which day Morland with supplies also reached there. Here a halt of several days was made to rest and refit.

Capture of Kokofu

On 22nd July a column of six companies 1 W.A.F.F., three 75 mm. guns, two 7-pounders, and four maxims, under Morland, captured Kokofu after Mellis with F Company had charged a stockade.

Completion of Subjugation by Beddoes

Finally, to complete the subjugation of the Adansis, Beddoes with one 75 mm., one 7-pounder and 400 rifles of 1 W.A.F.F., assisted by levies from Akim defeated some 6,000 by an enveloping movement on either flank. The Adansis fought with courage, making several determined counter-attacks which were repulsed by the guns and the bravery of the Hausas. In this operation our losses were five Europeans and 35 other ranks.

Early in August half a battalion C.A.R. under Major Cobbe reinforced the Kumasi garrison, bringing it up to a strength of 10 officers and 300 O.R.s. Willcocks now felt the place was strong enough to be self-contained and could safely be left while he took measures for clearing up the situation in the north and east whither, the bulk of the Ashantis had withdrawn.

Mopping-up Operations in the North and North-West, September 1900

He therefore directed the following columns to accomplish his purpose on 20th September:

(*a*) Major Holford with one gun and 500 rifles, mainly W.A.R., to Kintampo.

(*b*) Colonel Montanaro with two guns and 900 rifles north-west towards Ofinsu.
These troops were mainly 1 W.A.F.F. and C.A.R. with 40 Sierra Leone Frontiers.

(*c*) Colonel Brake with 100 W.A.R., 350 2 W.A.F.F. and 350 C.A.R. as well as two guns to clear the eastern flank as far as Ejisu.

Column (*a*) met little opposition, burnt Kintampo and returned to Kumasi.

Column (*b*) was attacked at Dinassi on 22nd September. After meeting stubborn opposition Montanaro decided to turn both flanks. Mellis with two companies 1 W.A.F.F. on the right and Cobbe with the C.A.R. on the left, drove back the enemy with a loss of 35 found dead on the ground.

On 30th September Chief Kofi Kofia had assembled 5,000 Ashantis at Obassa, where he made a most determined stand. It was only after a most gallant charge made by Mellis that the enemy's hordes were broken up and fled in disorder. For his action at Obassa Mellis was awarded the Victoria Cross. The enemy lost 150 men and all his stores here.

Column (*c*) succeeded in clearing the whole eastern flank before returning to Kumasi. The casualties amounted to two officers (including Brake) and 29 O.R.s wounded.

These operations finished any further resistance, thus terminating a very strenuous campaign.

Commendation

Willcocks in his despatches stresses the important part played by the Sierra Leone Frontier Police in scouting at the head of the advanced guard, where they distinguished themselves by their skill in bushcraft. While of the W.A.F.F., the Gold Coast and Lagos Constabulary he says: 'If I had my choice once more, nowhere would I sooner serve than with my faithful Hausas and Yorubas whom I learnt to admire and whose reputation is very precious to me. The best memory of the campaign will ever be the cheerfulness of the West African soldier. He has earned the love and respect of his officers and has proved he is worthy to take his place in the ranks of Her Majesty's Army, and that there he will at least find none more loyal than himself'.

Casualties

There is some discrepancy in the figures given in the official return and those quoted by Beddoes in his Official History. The latter are shown in brackets:

	Officers	Native Officers	B.N.C.Os	Rank and File	Carriers
Killed	9	1	0	113	
					45
Wounded	43	3	9	680 (834)	
Died of disease	6		1	103	430

Gambia Expedition, January–March, 1901

(African G.S. Medal granted, with clasp, Gambia 1901

(A.O./32/June 1902)

A dangerous state of affairs had developed in the Gambia, the details of which are given in a Colonial Office report, issued as a Parliamentary Paper, 'Africa West', No. 643, dated October 1901.

On the 14th June 1900, Travelling Commissioners T. C. S. Sitwell and Silva had been murdered in the Kiang District. The local chief refused to surrender the responsible natives and adopted a very truculent attitude. Disaffection in the colony was spreading to an alarming extent and no troops existed in the colony to deal with the matter.

Fodi Kabba himself had taken refuge in French country at Medina and was harrying both sides of the border from there.

It happened that Lieutenant-Colonel Brake, D.S.O., R.A., was returning with his battalion of Central African Rifles from the Ashanti Campaign in January 1901. His ship was therefore diverted to Bathurst to take command of the operations. Brevet-Major H. Bryan, of the 2 Battalion W.A.F.F. (Nigeria) was on board and acted as Brake's Staff Officer.

The operations were successfully carried out with the co-operation of the French. Fodi Kabba and the murderers were captured and a heavy fine imposed on the towns responsible.

It is not on record that any other member of the W.A.F.F. than Bryan was present, or could have received the medal, or clasp.

Besides the Central African Rifles four companies W.I.R. and the Navy took part in the operation.

(D) TRIBAL CAMPAIGNS

1900–1906

(I) *Munshi Expedition, February–March 1900*

(West Africa Medal granted, with clasp N. Nigeria 1900 (A.O./123/1903)

The object of the operations was to subdue the Munshi, who had been hindering the passage of caravans to and from Nassarawa and Keffi, and generally to bring peace to these regions. At first Captain Carroll with one company 1 W.A.F.F. attacked the town of Akwanagion on the Munshi border as a reprisal for the destruction of the telegraph line. It was surrounded by a ditch 8 ft. deep and 10 ft. wide with a stockade behind it. Carroll was opposed by heavy arrow fire which continued in skirmishes from 4th to 10th January. The town was then captured and burnt. Later Captain McClintock, R.E., having repaired the telegraph line, joined the force with 50 more rifles. Together they captured the strongly barricaded town of Gidan Barta on 27th January in spite of determined opposition.

With the object of thoroughly overawing the rest of Munshiland, Lieutenant-Colonel Lowry-Cole with a section of 7-pounders (under Captain Cubitt), 300 rifles and three maxims 2 W.A.F.F. marched to the Northern and Eastern Frontiers, effectually subduing several sections of the tribe *en route*. During these operations one B.N.C.O. was severely wounded by a poisoned arrow in the foot; three Native ranks were killed and 14 wounded.

The High Commissioner's despatch specially mentions Lowry-Cole, Cubitt and Carroll for their services.

(II) *Kaduna Surveys, February–May 1900*

(West Africa Medal granted with clasp N. Nigeria 1900 (A.O.128/1903)

The purpose of the operations was to survey a site for Government H.Q. in the vicinity of the Rivers Kaduna, Gurara and Okwa. In command was Colonel Morland, with a force of about 300 W.A.F.F. Here an opportunity occurred for dealing with big parties of slave raiders, some of whom offered stout resistance, particularly at the town of Lima, when Lowry-Cole was wounded by a poisoned arrow, as had been Lieutenant

Loder-Symonds shortly previously. Our total casualties amounted to about 20.

Lugard's covering despatch mentions the services of Captains Bryan, Abadie and McClintock, also Lieutenants Williams and Loder-Symonds.

(III) *Yola Expedition, August–September 1900*

(Africa G.S. Medal and clasp N. Nigeria 1900 granted (A.O.133/1902))

The object was to bring to heel the slave-raiding Emir of Yola. Colonel Morland was in command of a column of 365 W.A.F.F. with two 75 mm. guns. The troops proceeded up the Benue River from Lokoja transported by sternwheelers. Some 100 yards from Yola, Morland formed square at the edge of a lake, where he awaited attack. This only lasted 10 minutes; the enemy fleeing into the town in disorder.

The Emir's palace was 900 yards away; here and at the mosque a determined stand was made. Two French rifled guns were fired and caused several casualties to our troops; McClintock and Rose charged and captured them. Our guns then shelled the palace gates at close range. Captain Mayne and his Company worked round and cleared out pockets of resistance. The enemy fled, leaving much ammunition behind. Rifle-fire caused many enemy casualties; ours amounted to 39, excluding two officers wounded by poisoned arrows, of whom Morland was one. The Emir escaped; his brother was installed in his place.

The results gained were the effective occupation of British Adamawa, which put an end to the immense slave traffic from the south which for years had been the main source of supply for the Sokoto Empire.

The following were mentioned in the High Commissioner's despatch: Colonel Morland, Major A. McClintock, Seaforths (both awarded D.S.O.); Captains T. A. Rose, R.S.F., C. E. G. Mayne, H.L.I., E. M. Baker, Manchester Regiment; Lieutenants R. Henvey, R.A., D. A. McGregor, Goldstream Guards.

(IV) *Bida/Kontagora: 7 December 1900 and January–February 1901*

(Africa G.S. Medal and clasp N. Nigeria 1900 or 1901 (A.O.133/1902))

(*a*) At Bida the object was to avenge the death of Hon. D. Carnegie and to prevent repercussions by rapid action.

On 6–7 December 1900 Lieutenant-Colonel Lowry-Cole made a forced march with one company 1 W.A.F.F. to the village of Jawari concerned. It was found strongly fortified and difficult of access. After the gate had been blown in by gunfire little opposition was met with and the ringleaders were arrested.

(*b*) At Kontagora the Emir's slave-raiding bands were depopulating the country.

On 20th January 1900 Colonel G. V. Kemball, Assistant Commandant W.A.F.F. with 11 officers, three B.N.C.O.s, 433 infantry, two guns and three Maxims, advanced in square formation against some thousands of foot and horse who repeatedly charged, but our fire was held till they came to close quarters, excepting for a few picked marksmen.

The horsemen came on in a most intrepid manner, but were put to flight with heavy losses. In spite of heavy though ill-aimed arrow-fire, we had only one casualty.

The Emir was put to flight and the town was spared, but the effect of our attacks from the square were such as to destroy Kontagora's evil influence.

The behaviour of the men in holding their fire until the enemy were at such short range showed their remarkable steadiness and discipline.

In his despatch to the Secretary of State for Colonies Lugard mentions the good services of Colonel Kemball (given the D.S.O.), Captains T. A. Cubitt, R.A. (made a Brevet-Major), G. C. Merrick, R.A., E. H. Lewis, 21st Lancers; Lieutenants G. H. F. Abadie, Royal Scots (to be a Brevet-Major on promotion to Captain), and C. F. O. Graham, Royal Marines.

The Emir of Bida, who was known as the Sarikin Sudan or Nagwamachi (i.e. 'the Destroyer'), sent Lugard an insulting and defiant message:

'Come out, you fish. Can a cat cease mousing. When I die I will be found with a slave in my mouth.' Here he referred to the British as fish, meaning they could not live away from the Niger.

Although Nagwamachi was eventually captured in a war camp when he was surprised with some 12,000 Fulanis and Nupes in April 1902, he was subsequently reinstated as Emir by Lugard and proved a just ruler until his death.

Nagwamachi's capture was effected by a force of 37 M.I. and 135 infantry under Major H. C. Dickinson, Leinster Regiment, who was awarded the D.S.O.

(*c*) *Bida, June–December 1900* (*A.O.6/1902*). The Africa G.S. Medal, with clasp N. Nigeria 1900, was granted prior to (*a*) for the operations conducted by Major W. H. O'Neill, R.H.A., C.R.A., W.A.F.F., against Bida. The Emir had been slave raiding and making himself a terror in the country for a long time. O'Neill, with Lieutenant Porter, 19th Hussars and M.I. W.A.F.F., with only 13 mounted and 25 dismounted men, engaged the enemy in many skirmishes, particularly between 14th and 18th December, when O'Neill advanced towards the city driving large parties of Nupes before him, and inflicting heavy casualties. He pushed up to the walls of Bida, entering the town with a handful of men, where he engaged the Emir himself in a hand-to-hand encounter. O'Neill was badly wounded and only escaped through the opportune arrival of some of his men.

He had had positive orders not to approach too near the town, much less to enter it. A grave disaster was narrowly averted here; at the same time, the report stated that 'This most adventurous exploit created an immense impression on the people of Bida'. Porter was given a Brevet-Majority on promotion to Captain.

(V) *Ishan/Ulia Operations, March–May 1901*

(Africa G.S. Medal granted with clasp S. Nigeria 1901 (A.O.06/1902))

This was undertaken in order to bring into submission unfriendly tribes to the north-east of Benin City. The troops engaged were 255 officers and men of the Southern Nigeria Regiment, under the command of Captain (local Major) W. G. C. Heneker, Connaught Rangers.

He reported that 'very severe fighting' took place between 9th March and 8th May 1901. Twenty-five men were wounded of whom three died. The results were completely successful.

Sir Ralph Moor, High Commissioner Southern Nigeria, in his covering despatch to the Secretary of State for Colonies, mentions the good services of Major Heneker (made a Brevet-Major) and Captains A. M. N. Mackenzie, Royal Artillery, A. D. Lewes, Royal Scots Fusiliers, and G. E. Hewitt, West India Regiment.

(VI) *Aro Expedition, November 1901–March 1902*

(Africa G.S. Medal granted with clasp (ARO/1901–1902) (A.O.234/1904))

The objects were to suppress the slave trade actively carried on by the Aro section of the large Ibo family in the entire territory belonging to, or dominated by, them.

Further to abolish the fetish known as the 'Long Juju', which, by superstition and fraud, caused many evils amongst the Ibo tribe and all outlying tribes who constantly appealed against it.

It also had the object of opening up the whole Ibo country between the Niger and Cross Rivers to peaceful trade and freedom from bloody massacres.

The Field Force was commanded by Lieutenant-Colonel A. F. Montanaro, Royal Artillery. The troops engaged were 1,150 men of the Southern Nigeria Regiment, with some 300 each from the 1 N.R. and the Lagos Battalion, making about 1,750 troops all combined as W.A.F.F. for the first time in military operations. Altogether there were 11 companies of infantry and two four-gun batteries of 75 mm. guns. In addition there was a special corps of scouts. Some 2,300 carriers were required for transport.

These were the most important 'bush-fighting' operations undertaken since the Ashanti Campaign of 1900. The area to be covered stretched from the Niger to the Cross River, as far north as the head-waters of the latter: 90 miles from N. to S. and 120 from E. to W.

The Force was divided into four columns, commanded by:

No. I. Brevet-Major Festing, D.S.O., Royal Irish Rifles.
No. II. Brevet-Major Mackenzie, Royal Artillery (Heneker).
No. III. (Festing) Venour, Hampshire Regiment.
No. IV. Major W. G. C. Heneker, Connaught Rangers.

The operations were in three phases: (A) The Capture of Arochuku; (B) Mopping up the area around Arochuku; (C) Convergence of all columns on Bende.

Phase (*A*). Advancing by different routes the first to encounter severe opposition was No. I Column which had desultory fighting between 2nd and 4th December 1901 where stockaded towns and entrenchments were met and overcome with a loss of two officers and 40 men wounded.

On 7th–8th December the enemy was found entrenched in a ravine where he made a determined stand, near Okwogi, being eventually driven out by a charge with the bayonet.

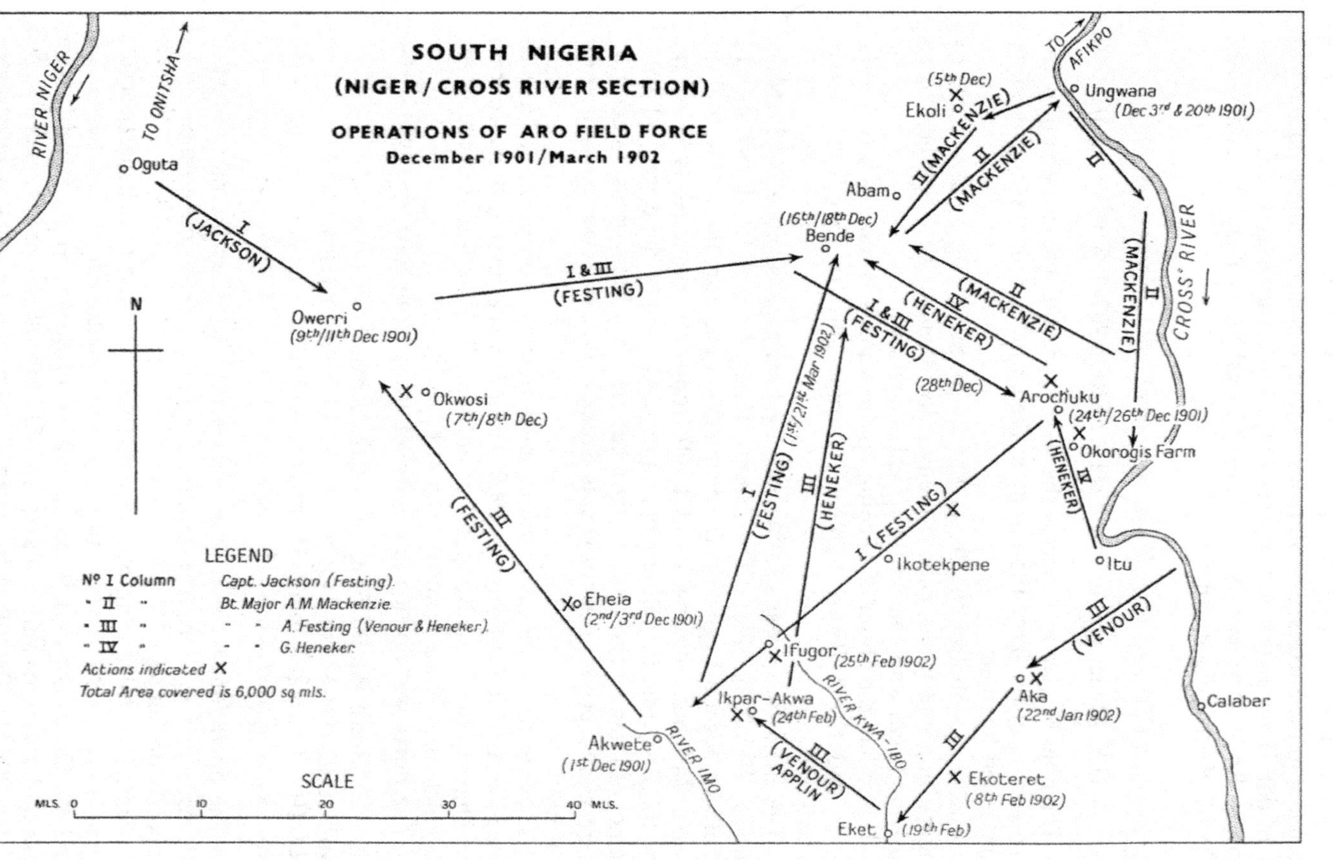

4. South Nigeria (Niger/Cross River Section) Operations of Aro Field Force, December 1901/March 1902

[*Photo: Topical Press*

The Walls of Kano, 1903

[*Photo: Topical Press*

Kano from inside the Walls

Face page 64

[Photo: Topical Press

Yams Galore

[Photo: Topical Press

Clearing bush for roadmaking

Face page 65

On 24th December Montanaro occupied Arochuku with Nos. II and IV Columns. They were attacked for 36 hours during the 26th–27th continuously, but on 28th Festing appeared with Nos. I and III Columns. This caused the enemy to surrender. The Long Juju was blown up and the war camp burnt down.

Phase (*B*). A big area around Arochuku was thoroughly patrolled and mopped up between 25th December and 13th February 1902 without meeting with opposition.

Phase (*C*). Between 15th January and 23rd March the country west of the Cross River was swept by all columns as far as Bende.

First converging on Akwete, then around Akwete and north of New Calabar, and finally north to converge on Bende.

Convergence on Akwete. Festing's No. I Column at the end of January had several severe engagements in the Kwa country, notably at Ifugor on 25th, where the enemy was strongly entrenched.

No. II Column (Heneker) met with stubborn resistance in the Kwa area from 20th–29th January, especially when the water picquet at Ikobbo was ambushed on 20th. Here Major Hodson dispersed the enemy by leading a charge.

No. III Column, under Venour, was heavily attacked on 8th February; when his troops debouched into some market-places surrounded by dense bush from which a heavy fire was opened.

North of Akwete and New Calabar. Between the 2nd and 27th February *Festing's Column* had much desultory fighting, particularly on 7th when advancing on Omo-Odo, where the path was defended by parallel trenches for a distance of 2½ miles. And again on 23rd–24th at the capture of the large town of Omuma.

Mackenzie's No. II Column, moving north of New Calabar, was opposed mainly by sniping tactics, but on 12th February at Ubele his advanced and rear guards were simultaneously engaged. Hollow square was formed, which was attacked with determination.

Heneker's No. III Column, on 7th February, operating in the Iga country, being held up by an hostile strongpoint in the market-place, was completely relieved by the charge of Captain Knowles's company. Again on 12th at Koreda his movements were badly hampered by hostile fire and misty weather.

Converging Movement on Bende. *Festing* had an uneventful march to Bende between 1st and 21st March. *Mackenzie*, marching from Elele, had only one serious engagement on 3rd March at Ikisi.

No. III Column, under Heneker, accompanied by Montanaro and Staff, marching via Obogu, captured two Aro chiefs responsible for massacres and executed them on 14th March. At Onor and Omoba there was strenuous resistance.

During this period Hodson with 50 men was sent to Sabagrega on the Lower Niger to settle the disturbed area there. Lieutenant-Commander D'Oyly, R.N., H.M.S. *Thrush*, co-operated by covering a landing force.

Casualties. Thirteen Europeans were wounded, and of W.A.F.F. other ranks 27 were killed and 140 wounded; 70 died of disease.

Honours (*London Gazette* 12/9/1902). The following honours were awarded for services in the Aro Expedition:

C.M.G. Brevet-Major (local Lieutenant-Colonel) A. H. Festing, D.S.O., Royal Irish Rifles.

D.S.O. Majors G. B. Hodson, India Staff Corps; H. D. Carleton, West India Regiment; Captains: Brevet-Major W. C. C. Heneker, Connaught Rangers; W. Gillman and M. L. Goldie, Royal Artillery; J. C. Grahame and C. R. G. Mayne, Highland Light Infantry; T. A. Rose, Royal Scots Fusiliers. Lieutenants G. Knowles, Indian Staff Corps; A. J. Campbell, 19th Hussars; R. H. D. Thompson, Royal Artillery.

Brevet to be Major. Captains W. J. Venour, D.S.O., Royal Dublin Fusiliers; H. C. Moorhouse and A. M. N. Mackenzie, Royal Artillery; R. E. P. Garbett, Royal Welsh Fusiliers.

D.C.M. Regimental Sergeant-Major H. E. Jordan, 1 Battalion Nigeria Regiment; Regimental Sergeant-Major J. Ambrose, Southern Nigeria Regiment; Colour-Sergeant C. Crowley, Southern Nigeria Regiment; Native Officer J. Daniels and Regimental Sergeant-Major Ojo Ibadan, Southern Nigeria Regiment; Native Officer Mama Nakuru, Lagos Battalion.

(VII) *Bornu: 1st February–16th May 1902*

(Africa G.S. Medal granted and clasp N. Nigeria 1902 (A.O.129/1903))

Objectives of Operations

The object of these operations was to march into Bornu via Bauchi, where a garrison was to be installed to stop slave raiding. In Bornu the position was to be clarified due to the recent incursions of Fad-el-Allah and his death at the hands of the French at Gujba. The expedition was to return along the Anglo-German frontier as far as Yola and to furnish Lugard with information on the geography and roads of that area.

Colonel Morland was in command. His force was composed of:

1 Battalion Northern Regiment W.A.F.F. 2 Battalions Nothern Nigeria Regiment W.A.F.F. 1 Section Battery Northern Nigeria Regiment W.A.F.F.	20 Europeans 515 rank and file.

4 maxims and 800 carriers.

Deposition of Emir of Bauchi

In January 1902 Morland, accompanied by Wallace, the Acting High Commissioner, left Ibi for Bauchi, where Wallace deposed the Emir who had fled. Here there was no opposition, but between 1st and 7th February, Lieutenant-Colonel Beddoes with 1 company 1 N.R. had a fight at Yerghum, whose villagers had been murdering traders. The Yerghums submitted. Morland left one company as garrison at Bauchi. He then marched via Gombe to Gujba in Bornu. On 29th February he was attacked by Mallam Jibrella, a self-styled Mahdi with 600 foot and 100 horse. The attack was met by steady fire from the infantry in line and kneeling. The guns fired Case shot. In spite of desperate efforts to get to close quarters and envelope our flanks, none got closer than 50 yards and they finally broke and fled, losing 60 killed and many wounded. We had two wounded.

The Mallam Jibrella Incident

A number of flying columns were sent in pursuit; finally on 15th March, after a 17-hour pursuit, by Lieutenant Dyer, the Mallam was captured near Burmi. Dyer had ridden 70 miles with 10 mounted infantry. Morland then marched on to Maidugari, which he reached on 23rd March. From there he went on to Kuka and back via Yola to Ibi.

Cubitt's Mission on Anglo-German Frontier

Meanwhile he sent Cubitt with one company, two maxims and a section of guns from Yola along the north bank of the Benue through the Bassama country and the Wurkum Hills to survey the Anglo-German boundary. Cubitt was attacked on 29th April, when Lieutenant Dyer was wounded.

In the whole of these operations a vast area was brought under control, involving a distance of some 1,000 miles, and an area of 60,000 sq. miles. One of Lugard's biographers says: 'Lugard and his envoys seem to dash about the country like Knights Errant, punishing wicked people, liberating the oppressed, overthrowing cruel kings and elevating new ones.'

Mentions

Lugard's despatch on the Bornu Operations gives great credit to Morland and Cubitt especially. Beddoes, commanding 2 N.R., Beamish and Dyer are also commended. Rank and file favourably reported on are: 717 Sergeant-Major Dowdu, 1 N.N.R.; 160 Sergeant Jinady Ikeram, 2 N.N.R.; R.A./43 Corporal Mama, No. 1 Battery N.N.R. (awarded D.C.M.).

In the case of Corporal Mama it is said: 'At Banjerum on 30th April one of the enemy threw a spear at Captain Cubitt, whereupon Mama pluckily seized the man by the throat, receiving a second poisoned spear in his ammunition pouch. The man fought like a fury, but Corporal Mama held on and disarmed him.'

(VIII) *Igarra and Uri, February–May 1902*

(Africa G.S. Medal granted and clasp S. Nigeria 1902 (A.O.4/1905))

The operations were undertaken to prevent and punish outbreaks of intertribal warfare, and to capture Chief Odukukukaiku, a bandit who was terrorizing the district.

Captain (Brevet-Major) W. G. C. Heneker, D.S.O., was in command of a force of about 200 rifles of the Southern Nigeria Regiment. On 22nd February the Igarra country was entered. On 24th the enemy resisted the attack on the stockaded town of Alede, which was captured after a stiff fight, by a double turning movement carried out by Lieutenant Ward's scouts. The only casualty was Sergeant Mama Juma.

The rest of the Igarra country lying between the Niger and Anambra Rivers was effectually cleared.

In the Uri Operations the object was to punish this tribe for raiding and stopping trade. Also to destroy the Igwe Juju, which was terrorizing the district.

For these purposes a force of about 350 rifles was assembled at Oguta under Colonel Montanaro on 3rd April. At Umbidi the water picquet was sharply attacked from trenches at Amokya and Omachima on 15th April. At the latter place Chief Islobi surrendered. On 25th–26th an entrenched camp was found at Omonoha: This was captured after a 4½ hours' engagement. From 27th to 15th May various towns which had collaborated in the disorders were punished and the Igwe Juju was destroyed.

On 16th May operations were concluded by the capture by surprise of the town of Elima which had abetted the offenders.

Casualties for the two operations of Igarra and Uri these were: Wounded: Europeans six, rank and file 68. Killed: rank and file 13. There were 22 casualties amongst the carriers.

Mentions. Colonel Montanaro, Brevet-Major Heneker, Captain I. G. Hogg, 4th Hussars; Lieutenant A. C. Ward, Lancashire Fusiliers; No. 729 Sergeant-Major Elisho Ondo.

Montanaro received a C.B., 28/10/04. Heneker was made a Brevet-Lieutenant-Colonel. Hogg and Ward were awarded the D.S.O. Colour-Sergeant A. Anderson was given the D.C.M. Sergeant-Major Ojo Ibadan was also granted the D.C.M. (African).

(IX) *Argungu, June–November 1902*

(Africa G.S. Medal granted clasp N. Nigeria 1902)

The object here was to ensure the safe passage of French convoys working with the Anglo-French Boundary Commission on the Nigerian border. It was also enjoined to avoid hostilities with Sokoto and Gando, which at that time would have caused great complications.

Captain G. C. Merrick, Royal Artillery, was in command. He had an escort of 50 rifles 1 N.N.R. under Lieutenant (local Captain) A. C. McLaclan, 18th Hussars.

The period covered the dates from 15th June to 30th November 1902. Except for one severe engagement at Giwazi no hostilities occurred. All convoys passed through successfully and a large area of new country was mapped. One soldier and three followers were killed and three rank and file were wounded.

(X) *Ten Minor Engagements in Southern Nigeria as Listed Below*

(*The details for these are not available, 1902–3*)

(Africa G.S. Medal granted and clasp S. Nigeria 1902 or 1903 (A.O.49/1906))

(*a*) Under the command of Captain P. K. Carre (now deceased), Royal Warwickshire Regiment, in the Niger country in July 1902.

(*b*) Under the command of Captain A. J. Campbell, D.S.O., 19th Hussars, in the Ebeku country, in September 1902.

(*c*) Under the command of Captain A. D. H. Grayson, Royal Artillery, in the Ikwe country in October 1902.

(*d*) Under the command of Brevet-Lieutenant-Colonel W. C. C. Heneker, D.S.O., Connaught Rangers, in the Ibeku Olokoro country, between the 26th October and 8th December 1902, both dates inclusive.

(*e*) Under the command of Captain and Brevet-Major I. G. Hogg, D.S.O., 4th Hussars, in the Ibekwe country, in October 1902.

(*f*) Under the command of Captain and Brevet-Major W. J. Venour, D.S.O., Royal Dublin Fusiliers, in the Nsit country, in December 1902.

(*g*) Under the command of Captain and Brevet-Major H. C. Moorhouse, Royal Artillery, in the Asaba Hinterland, in December 1902.

(*h*) Under the command of Brevet-Lieutenant-Colonel W. C. G. Heneker, D.S.O., Connaught Rangers, in the Afikpo District, in December 1902 and January 1903 (Clasp 1902/3).

(*i*) Under the command of Captain H. H. Sproule, 4th Cavalry, in the Ebegga country, in February 1903.

(*j*) Under the command of Captain E. L. Roddy, Cheshire Regiment, in the country west of Anan, in March 1903.

For the following operations these awards were made, no medal was issued.

Irua, 1904

D.C.M. Sergeant-Major A. E. Klee, Royal Artillery.

Onitsha Hinterland, November 1904–March 1905

D.S.O. Brevet-Major H. C. Moorhouse, Royal Artillery.

D.C.M. (*African*). Sergeant-Major Seberu Ilorin; Sergeant-Major Abubakare.

(XI) *Kano-Sokoto, January–March 1903*

(Africa G.S. Medal granted, clasp N. Nigeria 1903 (A.O.171/1903))

Causes of the Campaign

During the early years Lugard had made every effort to conciliate the Sultan of Sokoto (called 'Sarikin Mussulmi') and the other Emirs. Without their co-operation effective suzerainty could never be maintained, nor could there be any lasting freedom from warfare. The Emirs did not respond.

The Murder of Maloney 1902

A crisis occurred in 1902, when Kano received the murderer of Captain Maloney, Resident of Keffi, refusing to surrender him to the Government.

The Emir of Kano thus wrote to Lugard: 'I will never agree with you. I will have nothing to do with you. Between us and you there are no dealings except war. God Almighty has enjoined us.'

When Maloney was murdered at Keffi the ruler of that district, called the 'Magaji', fled to Kano to avoid arrest. At the same time Kano threatened to attack Zaria, the nearest W.A.F.F. garrison, but as the Emir of Katsena, Kano's nearest neighbour, refused to co-operate, Aliyu, Emir of Kano, held his hand.

Lugard realized that a showdown was inevitable. He therefore, without approval of the Secretary of State for Colonies, ordered the despatch of an expedition to subdue Kano, Katsena and Sokoto.

On 29th January 1903 Colonel Morland, Commandant N.N.R. W.A.F.F. left Zaria with all available Northern Nigerian troops, consisting of: 36 Europeans, 722 rank and file including 101 M.I. under Captains Porter and Wright; four 75 mm. guns and four maxims.

Captain Abadie, Resident of Zaria, was Political and Intelligence Officer.

Meanwhile, on hearing of the despatch of troops, the Colonial Office ordered up reserves from Southern Nigeria, Lagos and the Gold Coast and appointed the Inspector-General W.A.F.F. to take command of the whole Expeditionary Force.

The first opposition was at the town of Bebeji 50 miles south of Kano. When the gates were blown in and Lieutenant Mackenzie, V.C., scaled the walls with a storming-party the place surrendered (this was the Mackenzie who had gained his V.C. in Ashanti). The Fulanis fled to Kano, but most of the inhabitants, knowing they had nothing to fear, as many of the troops were their kinsmen, remained in the town.

Kano was reached on 3rd February. The fortifictions were formidable; walls with 11 miles perimeter and 30–50 ft. high and as wide; a double ditch in front; 13 gates cunningly loopholed protected these. In the I.N.R. Mess many interesting photographs are preserved of the fortifications.

After several hours of shelling without effect on the walls, a small breach was finally made at Zaria Gate. Lieutenant Dyer led a storming-party with ladders and axes, who charged to massed bugle calls. The defenders, 800 horse and 5,000 foot, fled. Shell-fire and pursuit by the M.I. turned this into a rout. Slight resistance at the palace was soon overcome. Our casualties were only 14 wounded, although the defenders had kept up a heavy fire from the walls. It was discovered that the Emir, Aliyu, had left with 1,000 horse and 2,000 foot for Sokoto on 2nd January.

Brigadier-General G. V. Kemball, D.S.O., I.G., W.A.F.F., had now arrived with reinforcements of 600 rifles from the S.N.R. and 300 from the Lagos Battalion W.A.F.F.

He and Morland left Kano for Sokoto on 16th February after disposing a garrison of 250 troops at the former place.

At Gusau, 100 miles from Kano, there stretches a waterless belt of 37 miles till Kaura is reached, where the army of Aliyu, fugitive Emir of Kano, was drawn up, threatening a surprise movement back to Kano, via Kamone or Duru.

In order to safeguard his force from such a movement, while the main column marched on Madamawa, Lieutenant Wallace Wright, the Queen's Regiment, with 45 M.I., was instructed to reconnoitre from Duru, Captain Porter carrying out the same role from Kamene with the balance of the M.I.

On 25th Wright was suddenly confronted with a large number of horse who charged his small troop at Kotokoroshi, on the road from Kaura. The attack was driven off with a loss of 40 to the enemy. Wright continued his advance, being again charged by 30 Fulanis, whom he repulsed. He camped for the night in a walled village.

Next day, 26th February, he continued his reconnaissance, located about 1,000 horse and 2,000 foot. He hurriedly formed square in a mimosa patch, placing his horses inside the square. He was repeatedly charged for two hours until 1000 hours, when the enemy withdrew, leaving 65 dead behind, amongst whom were 10 prominent Kano chiefs, including the Waziri, whom Aliyu had left in command while he himself had absconded.

Wright then advanced towards Rawia, where he located a considerable force of the enemy, but, having only 50 rounds per rifle left, he refrained from advancing farther, but kept in observation while the Fulanis filed away north to Kambarewa.

During these actions Wright was ably assisted by Lieutenant C. L. Wells, 3rd Hampshires. Wright himself was awarded the Victoria Cross.

Meanwhile Porter with his M.I. fortunately came on the scene and had struck the enemy at Kambarewa, charging a body of some 800 with great effect and dispersing them.

On 27th Morland's column reached Kaura, joining the M.I. from the Kotokoroshi road. During the following two days it was learnt that no organized bodies of Kano fighting men remained in the field. All were only too anxious to submit. A depot for our sick was formed at Kaura. Casualties in battle had been extremely slight, but many were ill from cold and thirst, while 52 had died from these causes.

On 10th March Morland arrived at Shagali, where Merrick joined him with two companies and a gun from the Anglo-French Boundary Commission in Argungu Province. A junction between the two forces had now become desirable, as it was evident that the Sultan of Sokoto had summoned all the chiefs with their fighting men to defend Sokoto.

On 13th Kemball ordered Morland to advance on Sokoto with his combined forces. Next day some thousands of the enemy were observed issuing from the gates on to the plain surrounding the town. The column then advanced in square formation to a ridge near by from which the guns, under Merrick, and the M.I. under Porter and Wallace Wright, scattered the enemy, who appeared to be without leaders. The whole Fulani army was then put to flight, pursued by the M.I.

The Sultan, Aburahman, fled eastward, whereupon Lugard installed Atahiru in his place.

Casualties. The enemy had suffered heavily at Kotokoroshi and Kamberawa on 26th February and further lost some 70 killed and 200 wounded at Sokoto on 14th March. Out total casualties amounted to three officers and 19 other ranks wounded. The officers wounded were Wallace Wright at Bebeji; Dyer and Farquhar at Kano.

Comments on the Campaign. The whole operation was well organized and the co-ordination of movements was well timed. On the fall of Bebeji the Emir of Kano began to lose heart and he very soon failed to have any influence on the direction of hostilities. His army relied on the power of its cavalry charges, which were often bravely pushed home, at Kotokoroshi and Kambarewa, for example, but could not stand up to the steady fire of our M.I., who held their ground firmly up to a range of 50 yards.

Lieutenant W. D. Wright's and then Captain Porter's gallant handling of their M.I. were the highlight of the expedition and undoubtedly broke the enemy's spirit.

Lugard was anxious to retain control of the operations by keeping the command in the hands of the Commandant Northern Nigeria Regiment (Morland), and was not therefore at all pleased when the Secretary of State decided to send supporting troops from Southern Nigeria and Lagos, since the W.A.F.F. Regulations provided that the Inspector-General should take command where the troops of more than one colony were involved.

Thus, Lugard became confronted with a situation he had wished to avoid, and resented. He further took the view that Morland had been superseded and seems to have said so in his correspondence with Mr. Chamberlain.

The Secretary of State in his despatch of 25th March 1903 says: 'The decision to place General Kemball in command was in accordance with the scheme of the W.A.F.F. and did not imply any want of confidence in you or Morland's ability to carry out the operations if the force was sufficient.' Again in his telegram of 25th April, Chamberlain says: 'There is no question of the supersession of Morland.'

It seems evident that Lugard was bent on terminating Kemball's command at the earliest possible moment, for in a letter to Morland dated 12th March 1903 he says: 'I have written to the General Officer Commanding that I see no reason why any action I may think it necessary to take in the direction of Sokoto should not be achieved by the Protectorate troops under their own officers in the normal way, and I have therefore desired him to terminate the existence of the Kano Expeditionary Force as soon as possible.' (Before this letter could have reached Kemball, Sokoto had been captured on 14th March.)

Lugard goes on to say he regrets the Force has gone to Sokoto, since he fears it may scare the Sultan into flight, also that 'he finds himself compelled to differ from one or two matters in Kemball's conduct of the operations and in his report'.

It is unfortunate that Lugard's attitude in the matter should have been so unco-operative; it might well have resulted in causing friction between Kemball and Morland, with unhappy consequences. Luckily their good sense prevented such a thing happening.

Honours

C.B. (*London Gazette*, 11/9/1903). Lieutenant-Colonel (Temporary Brigadier-General) C. V. Kemball, D.S.O.; Major and Brevet-Lieutenant-Colonel (local Colonel) T. N. Morland, D.S.O.

D.S.O. Captain and Brevet-Major T. A. Cubitt; Captain and Brevet-Major H. A. Porter, 19th Hussars; Lieutenant (local Captain) S. B. B. Dyer, Life Guards.

V.C. Lieutenant (now Captain) W. D. Wright, The Queens, Royal West Surrey Regiment. To date from 24th March 1903.

D.C.M. Staff-Sergeant G. C. W. King, R.A.M.C.; Colour-Sergeant J. H. Robinson, Royal Dublin Fusiliers; Lance-Corporal Dowdie Chicogo, Northern Nigeria Regiment, W.A.F.F.; Private Samari, Northern Nigeria

Regiment W.A.F.F.; Private Inomo Wurrikin, Northern Nigeria Regiment W.A.F.F.; Private Inomo Azair, Northern Nigeria Regiment.

(XII) *Sokoto/Burmi, April–July 1903*

(African G.S. Medal granted and clasp N. Nigeria 1903 (A.O.65/1905))

These operations were planned to effect the capture of the ex-Sultan of Sokoto, Abdurahman, and to suppress the rising led by him and his fanatical followers.

On 15th April 1903, at the request of the Resident of Sokoto, Major Burdon, Captain Goodwin 1 N.R. was detached with 60 men from that garrison to try to capture Abdurahman reported at Gusau, 100 miles east. He met with no success. Captain Sword was sent with 42 rank and file and a maxim from Kano in a south-easterly direction on 22nd. At the same time Major Crawley, O.C. M.I. at Zaria, despatched Lieutenant Crozier with 25 M.I. to Gimmi and Gala, where he inflicted much damage on the enemy's rearguard, but was forced to withdraw from lack of ammunition early in May.

On 9th May Major Plummer joined Sword with two officers and 70 rank and file from Bauchi, bringing his total strength to five Europeans and 130 rank and file with two maxims. At the same time Crawley sent Lieutenant Hon. D. Carleton with 15 M.I. south to capture a son of the ex-Sultan; in endeavouring to do so he defeated a party of 200 of his followers, and then returned to Kano, as the country appeared to have quietened.

On 10th May Sword was joined by 60 more M.I. With these further reinforcements he pursued Abdurahman along the banks of the Gongola River to Burmi. On 13th Sword tried to storm Burmi, but was repulsed with the loss of Plummer and Sergeant Hayes wounded, besides two rank and file killed and 54 wounded. He then retired to Bauchi.

On 1st June Major Barlow, with a few M.I. and 100 rank and file from Gujba garrison, reconnoitred Burmi and succeeded in luring out and killing a large number of the enemy. From 4th to 18th he continued to harrass Burmi. On that date he was attacked at night, but repulsed the foe.

On 19th Sword with 50 men from Bauchi, and Luttman-Johnson with 30 from Gujba, joined Barlow, making his force 270 and three maxims. Morland now ordered Major Marsh from Lokoja to reinforce and take command with a total strength of 445 infantry, one gun and three maxims. He reached Burmi from the south-west, joined by Barlow; meanwhile Sword was posted on the east. On 27th the attack began and after a fierce engagement Burmi was stormed and captured. Unhappily Marsh was hit by a poisoned arrow and died in 20 minutes. Our other casulaties were three men killed and three wounded. The enemy lost very heavily; amongst the killed were the ex-Sultan of Sokoto and the Magaji of Keffi.

Comments

Burmi was probably the hardest-fought engagement which had yet taken place in Northern Nigeria; the enemy fought desperately, not hesitating to take the offensive at a suitable moment. Our troops seem to have been sent up piecemeal until Morland ordered Marsh's force up from Lokoja. Had this been done after Sword's reverse on 13th May instead of a month later, no doubt the operation would have been finished much sooner. There was some disagreement between Sword and Plummer on the question of seniority which may have influenced the conduct of the fighting in its early phase.

Honours (*London Gazette*, 24/1/05)

D.S.O. Captain and Brevet-Major C. W. Barlow, Essex Regiment 2 Northern Nigeria Regiment; Lieutenant C. H. Christy, 20th Hussars, M.I. Northern Nigeria Regiment; Brevet-Major Captain R. H. Henvey, Royal Artillery.

D.C.M. Sergeant W. T. G. Williams, Royal Horse Artilley; Private Musa Katsena, 1 Nigeria Regiment.

(XIII) *Nun River, Eket, Mkpani: September/December 1903*

(Africa G.S. Medal and clasp S. Nigeria 1903 (A.O.I/1906))

(a) Nun River

These operations were undertaken in September 1903 to seize a pirate chief called Bibikala, who, from his stronghold on Wilberforce Island (on the Nun branch of the Niger) had for many years terrorized surrounding districts.

Colonel A. F. Montanaro, Commandant Southern Nigeria Regiment, with 326 rank and file Southern Nigeria Regiment, a 2·95 in. gun, six maxims, one Gardner Gun together with a number of river craft assembled at Akassa. Thirteen Europeans, Southern Nigeria Regiment, and nine Marine officers, with a Political and Medical Officer accompanied the force.

Bibikala was hunted from creek to creek till he was captured on 1st October and hanged.

There were no casualties mentioned in the despatch on the operations from the High Commissioner for Southern Nigeria, Mr. Walter Egerton. The success of the expedition was attributed to the close co-operation between the Marine department and the troops. The services of Lieutenants Cheetham and Child, R.N., and of Lieutenant G. A. S. Williams, Royal Fusiliers and Southern Nigeria Regiment, as Intelligence Officer, are highly commended by Montanaro.

(b) Eket

The purpose here was to punish several towns in the Eket District implicated in an attempt to murder Assistant District Commissioner E. C. Crewe-Read.

Major A. M. N. Mackenzie, Royal Artillery and Southern Nigeria Regiment was in command of a column of six Europeans and 185 infantry Southern Nigeria Regiment with two maxims. He was accompanied by a Political and a Medical Officer.

There were engagements at Efoi and Ekpa which were repelled by Captain E. L. Roddy, Cheshire Regiment, O.C. Advanced Guard, between 20th and 25th September when the towns involved submitted.

(*c*) *Mkpani*

The object in this case was to enforce the promises made by Mkpani, in the Obubra District of the Cross River, to keep their roads open to traffic and to give up cannibalism.

A force of 13 Europeans and 288 rank and file under Mackenzie was collected at Ugep on the Calabar River on 1st December. It was at once attacked on entering Mkpani country. During the engagement there were three casualties: Sergeant-Major A. E. Klee, Royal Artillery, Colour-Sergeant H. Pritchard, 3 Coldstream Guards, and No. 638 Sergeant Ali Bakare, all wounded.

On 5th December Mkpani submitted.

Honours

Major and Brevet-Colonel A. F. Montanaro was made a C.B. (28/10/04).

(XIV) *Okpoto, December 1903–March 1904*

(Africa G.S. Medal and clasp granted N. Nigeria 1903–1904 (A.O.1/1906))

The operations were necessitated by the urgency for punishing natives of Okpoto District in the Bassa Province of Northern Nigeria for the murder of a party with Captain O'Riordan (Resident) and Mr. Amyatt-Burney (Police) on 16th–17th December 1903.

Captain (local Major) G. C. Merrick, Royal Artillery, was in command with a force of 11 Europeans, 262 rank and file (I)—2·95 in. gun and two maxims. He had 307 carriers.

The country consisted of heavy forest and thick bush. On 24th–25th December a body of 100 infantry and the 2·95 in. gun were concentrated across the Niger at Dekina some 18 miles distant. By the 5th January 1904 the whole force had reached Ogwatcha, where Merrick organized a column (less two sections to guard ammunition and 300 carriers) with seven days' supplies.

This column left Ogwatcha on 5th and met opposition on 6th two hours' march away. Carefully covered by scouts unoccupied stockades were located and the enemy then started sniping from the bush.

Between 7th and 12th Merrick scoured an area of 20 by 15 miles. Altogether 10 villages were rushed and destroyed, two of O'Riordan's escort were rescued and a number of carbines recaptured. Our casualties so far were 11 killed and wounded. Merrick then returned to his base at Ogwatcha. Between 18th and 21st January he surprised and destroyed several towns in a sweep south, east and west from Giatu. He then marched north-west to Dekina wthout opposition; thence he moved south to Idah on the Niger, where he arrived 27th January.

Until 13th February he traversed the whole centre of the disaffected area locating some hostile parties after sharp fighting during which he had one killed and four wounded. On 15th some of Burney's clothing was found in a village which was then destroyed; operations were continued until the

12th March without much success, when Merrick left a garrison in the middle of the disaffected area and returned to Lokoja.

Casualties. The following is a summary of our casualties:

	Killed	*Wounded*
No. 1 Battery Northern Nigeria Regiment		6
1 Northern Nigeria Regiment	4	10
2 Northern Nigeria Regiment	2	19
Carriers, etc.	3	2

Mentions

Sir Frederick Lugard mentions the services of Major Merrick, Royal Artillery, Captain E. E. Williams, 5th Fusiliers, and Lieutenant R. D. F. Oldman, Norfolk Regiment.

Honours

The following awards were made:

D.S.O. Merrick, Williams, Maud, Oldman and Galloway.

W.A.F.F. D.C.M. No. 89 Corporal Edee (Artillery); Corporals 1 N.N.R. 422 Yatto Yola, 1111 Daday; 1331 Lance-Corporal Baba Duchi; 524 Private Lawani Kegi.

(XV) *Northern Ibibio, Asaba Hinterland, Kwale, January–April 1904*

(Africa G.S. Medal and clasp S. Nigeria 1904 (A.O.I. 1906))

(*a*) *Northern Ibibio*

The object was to bring under control the hostile Northern Ibibio District. Colonel A. F. Montanaro assembled a force of 15 officers, five B.N.C.O.s, two 2·95 in. guns and 428 rank and file Southern Nigeria Regiment W.A.F.F. at Mibakpan on 16th January 1904. On the right bank of the Cross River considerable opposition was met with. The whole area was traversed by two columns until the end of March, by which date all towns were disarmed.

One private was wounded and another missing was found half eaten. The services of Captain W. J. S. Hosley, Lieutenants C. A. S. Williams and H. A. Kirkby were favourably mentioned.

(*b*) *Asaba Hinterland*

This had the object of suppressing a rising instigated by the Secret Society called 'Ekumeku' (Silent Ones) which had destroyed several mission stations and murdered friendly natives.

Captain I. G. Hogg, 4th Hussars, was in command with 215 rank and file, and one 7-pounder. He left Asaba on 17th January 1904. There was severe fighting at the town of Ukunzu in which Colour-Sergeant Mendham was killed. On 11th February the force was increased by three Europeans, 90 rank and file and a 2·95 in. gun under Captain H. P. Gordon, 4 Connaught Rangers.

On 14th–15th February a final stand was made by the natives at Okuruku. They were routed and the place destroyed. By 25th April over

300 of the 'Ekumeku' Society had been captured and were eventually tried by the courts.

(*c*) *Kwale*

Here the Kwale people had carried on incessant warfare with their neighbours.

A force 288 strong with one 2·95 in. gun and two maxims commanded by Captain I. G. Hogg patrolled the country. Fighting took place at Atua, but by 26th March the opposition was crushed and six chiefs responsible for human sacrifices and tribal warfare surrendered. By 24th April trade was in full swing and the troops were withdrawn.

(*d*) *Owerri* (*right bank of River Imo*)

With the object of pacifying a portion of the Owerri district on the right bank of the River Imo a force of four officers, two B.N.C.O.s, 211 Infantry and two maxims, Southern Nigeria Regiment, under Captain and Brevet-Major H. M. Trenchard conducted a series of successful night operations during March 1904.

(*e*) *Obokum*

On 10th January 1904 the German station of Nsanakang, close to our frontier town of Obokum, was attacked and looted by rebellious natives. The German rebels overflowed into British territory and compelled our inhabitants to join them in an attack on Obokum between the 10th and 28th March.

A force of 267 rank and file Southern Nigeria Regiment W.A.F.F. concentrated at Okuni on 28th April and, in co-operation with Colonel Muller (the German commander) patrolled the country in a south-easterly direction from Aparabong to the Boundary. Between them they pacified the area, without firing a shot.

Lieutenant R. D. W. Wigham, Lancashire Fusiliers, and Captain H. H. Sproule, Indian Army, took part in this operation with a small detachment Southern Nigeria Regiment W.A.F.F.

Honours

The following officer was awarded a Brevet-Majority (*London Gazette* 25/8/05): Captain I. G. Hogg, D.S.O., 4th Hussars.

D.C.M. Sergeant Ali Bakare; 2197 Private Ojo Otan, Southern Nigeria Regiment.

(XVI) *Dakakeri, North of Wase, Semolika, Kilba, March–July 1904*

(Africa G.S. Medal and clasp granted N. Nigeria 1904 (A.O.I/1906)

(*a*) *Dakakeri*

The object here was to subdue the Dakakeri tribe owing to their lawless behaviour in attacking caravans in Kontagora Province.

Lieutenant (local Captain) Dyer, D.S.O., 2 Life Guards led a B.N.C.O. and 88 rank and file with a maxim and a 7-pounder in this operation. The town of Ebo was reached on 5th March 1904. The people refused to give up their weapons or pay a fine, so, after considerable resistance, the place was burnt.

(*b*) The wild pagan tribes in the country north of *Wase*, between the Benue and Bauchi, had murdered several traders and killed and eaten a messenger sent to warn them.

Lieutenant (local Captain) P. H. Short, Gloucester Regiment, with three Europeans, a section No. 1 Battery, 99 rank and file 2 Northern Nigeria Regiment and a maxim attacked the town of Gurkhwa on 26th March 1904. On 2nd April the village of Brett in Yerghum country was reached. The country was difficult and mountainous. By denying to the inhabitants the only water supply in the area Short forced them to submission. There was more desultory fighting between 2nd and 8th April, when the headmen of Yerghum submitted.

Between 11th and 18th April the Montoil country was entered; after desultory fighting these people submitted also.

(*c*) *Semolika*

Lieutenant Browne with 30 rank and file had been patrolling the southern frontier of Kontagora to prevent smuggling of gin and arms. On his way back to his H.Q. he attempted to ascend Semolika Hills, apparently not knowing the hostility of the tribesmen. He was attacked, having six men killed and 17 others besides himself wounded.

Major Merrick was thereupon sent to make reprisals. With a force of nine Europeans, 213 rank and file, two 2·95 in. guns and a maxim, he engaged the Semolikas, who fought in a very determined manner before submitting. Lieutenants Galloway and Burnett with nine rank and file were wounded on 21st April.

(*d*) *Kilba*

The Kilba tribe close to the German border north of Yola had closed the main roads by attacking caravans. Lieutenant I. G. Sewell, with four Europeans, 152 rank and file and two maxims, was sent to punish them in July. He had two casualties before they submitted.

(XVII) *Kissi* (*Sierra Leone*), *March–June 1905*

(Africa G.S. Medal granted and clasp Sierra Leone 1905 (A.O.277/1906))

Kissi Tribes at the instigation of Chief Kafura in the south, and chief Fassalokoh in the north, had been raiding British territory from Liberia and carrying off slaves. Those under Kafura had twice attacked the outpost at Korumba held by a Section Sierra Leone Battalion W.A.F.F. Liberia had consented to the despatch of an expedition to punish the aggressors.

Major C. E. Palmer was in command. A force of 14 officers, a Medical Officer, 359 rank and file and 600 carriers was concentrated at Karumba on 25th March with the town of Kenema, Kafura's H.Q., as its objective.

The stockaded camp of Boandu, the towns of Fankissi and Sefadu were occupied without much trouble. The last being now used as an advanced base. With two companies operating from there Kenema was rushed. Marching thence via Mina and Beredu, the column was attacked near Komendi. After two hours' fighting the Kissis withdrew on being counter-attacked by the rearguard under Captains Le Mesurier, Royal Dublin Fusiliers, and L. Murray (East Surrey Regiment). Komendi was burnt.

Desultory fighting went on till 15th April and many towns were burnt in the vicinity of Sefadu. It was then ascertained that Kafura had fled eastward outside our area of operations, being practically an exile. A number of his towns had been burnt and his vast stores of rice eaten by the troops. The column then returned to Korumba to refit.

On the 25th April Palmer left Korumba, marching north-east through very heavy rains towards Fassalokoh's country of Northern Kissi. On 7th May Kundama was reached and used as a base for operations against Fassalokoh. He and his truculent neighbour, Dimba, fled after their country was raided by Palmer. At the town of We, near the French frontier, on 17th May, the column met with serious opposition. Here Lieutenant Haseldine was wounded; the force camped at We and was attacked at intervals by day and night.

On 24th May Kundama was evacuated and the column marched south to Loma with a view to arranging the deportation of Kafura. Base was moved to Loma from Korumba. It was now found that eight out of the original 13 officers were unfit, leaving the force very short-handed. On 10th June Wulade was reached, where it had been decided to form a fortified post, and here a palaver was held appointing a new chief in Kafura's place. This brought the field force's activities to an end on 28th June.

The Battalion had proved themselves excellent bush-fighters, capable of undergoing great hardships. The campaign was carried out in wet weather with constant tornadoes. The bush was thick and food scanty. Major Palmer received the D.S.O. for his conduct of the operations.

(XVIII) *Kwale, October–November 1905*

(Africa G.S. Medal and clasp granted S. Nigeria 1905 (A.O.277/1906))

(*a*) *Kwale*

Early in October 1905 a certain amount of unrest in the Kwale District decided the District Commissioner, Mr. Davidson, to visit there with an escort of two officers, one B.N.C.O. and 70 rank and file Southern Nigeria Regiment W.A.F.F. The force met with an unexpected and serious reverse on 12th October at Ijonnema, where the enemy fought in a desperate manner. One man was killed and 21 wounded. Lieutenant Irvine, Captain Vassall and Mr. Davidson were also wounded.

The escort was compelled to retire. Thereupon a force of the Lagos Battalion W.A.F.F. under Brevet-Major Maclear was despatched as reinforcement. This consisted of one 2·95 in. gun (from Calabar) and 246 rank and file. This force patrolled the area around Ijonnema with only slight opposition until 10th November, arresting the chief responsible.

(*b*) *Ishan*

On 4th November, Captain E. C. Margesson, South Wales Borderers, entered the scene from the east with three officers, one B.N.C.O. and 135 rank and file Southern Nigeria Regiment W.A.F.F. The Lagos contingent left and Margesson was reinforced by three Europeans and 60 rank and file with two 2·95 in. guns. Until 12th December there was considerable opposition, but then all submitted. He then proceeded to Ishan to attempt the arrest of the murderers of a friendly chief of Egwaboi. The murderers were located at Ibiuru, where there was considerable fighting before they were surrendered. Margesson then left, arriving at Asaba on 27th January 1906.

(XIX) *Bende-Onitsha Hinterland, October 1905–April 1906*

(Africa G.S. Medal and clasp granted (A.O.277/1906))

The object was to bring under control the country lying to the south of latitude 6.30 N., bounded on the west by the Oka Oguta road, on the east by the line joining Afikpo and Ababkaliki, and on the south by the Bende/Owerri road, where slave trading and human sacrifices had closed trade.

Brevet-Major H. M. Trenchard, Royal Scots Fusiliers, was in command. There were two columns:

No 1 Commander, Trenchard, 10 Europeans, 325 rank and file, two 2·95 in. guns at Bende.

No. 2 Commander, Captain G. T. Mair, Royal Field Artillery, eight Europeans, 200 rank and file, and two maxims, at Oka.

Dr. Stewart had just been murdered in the Owerri district which provoked a general rising in that area. His murder called for prompt and drastic action. This Medical Officer was a new-comer in Nigeria, and as such unaccustomed to the hazards of travelling by himself in the bush. It appears that he was travelling on his bicycle alone along a bush-path when he lost his way. Being exhausted by nightfall he came across a native hut, where he lay down to rest. The occupant, said to be an old woman, alerted the tribe to his presence. He was probably killed while still asleep.

His body was cut up into small pieces and distributed by way of fetish, with the idea that those eating a portion would be protected from harm by any white man and be released from his domination. This resulted in a general rising in the district with severe fighting, which was not quelled before those responsible for the crime had been captured and hanged after summary trial.

The two columns joined up on 30th November. A base camp was made at the Imo River, after which Trenchard split his force into three or four sub-columns. In the southern sphere continuous resistance was encountered until the close of operations on 15th April.

In the west and north disarmament was thoroughly enforced and a new station established at Udi.

The columns marched over 1,100 miles of country, much of which had never previously been visited. Minor operations were carried out in Ikotekpene, under Captain Wayling, Canadian Militia, and in Abakaliki under Captain E. de H. Smith, Royal Field Artillery.

Nearly 3,000 guns were surrendered during the operations, which were the biggest since the Aro Expedition in 1902.

Casualties

Five officers wounded; one soldier killed, and 58 wounded. Major Trenchard and Captain Mair each received the D.S.O.

[Photo: Topical Press

Marshal of the R.A.F. Viscount Trenchard, G.C.B., O.M., G.C.V.O., D.S.O.
He was Commandant, Southern Nigeria Regiment W.A.F.F., 1908–1910, and is here portrayed as the Colonel of The Royal Scots Fusiliers in 1916

Face page 81

[*Photo: Topical Press*

Trenchard's interpreter haranguing a tribe; B.O.H. Expedition, 1906

[*Photo: Topical Press*

Fording a river; Niger-Cross River Expedition

CHAPTER 3

The Years of Progress

(A) FURTHER CONSOLIDATION, 1906–1914

1906

Gambia

CAPTAIN HASTINGS, D.S.O., Manchester Regiment, took over command from Graham, and Lieutenant Heeles, Royal Field Artillery, replaced Morley during the year.

Sierra Leone

The Kissi Operations had delayed the movement of H.Q. from Freetown, as well as any building projected at outstations.

On 6th October Lieutenant Crooke was drowned in the Mafessa River, near Wulade.

Gold Coast

During the year Carter, who had seen so much service in the Niger Coast Protectorate Force, in Southern Nigeria and in the Ashanti 1900 Campaign, was appointed Commandant of the Gold Coast Regiment, now reorganized as a battalion of eight companies and a battery. H.Q. and four companies as well as the battery were stationed at Kumasi, which point the railway from Sekondi had reached. The remaining companies were stationed at Accra, Mampong, Nkoranza and Odumasi. Soon after his arrival Carter advocated turning one infantry company into a pioneer company, but this was not put into effect until 1909.

On 6th August Captain J. H. C. Crane, 6 Worcester Regiment, died at Accra.

Lagos

On 17th May the amalgamation of the Lagos Battalion with the Southern Nigeria Regiment came into effect. The Lagos Battalion now joined with three companies of the Southern Nigeria Regiment and was designated the 2 Battalion Southern Nigeria Regiment.

On 13th June Captain F. R. Ewart, D.S.O., Adjutant and 2I.C. of the Battalion, died at sea on his way to England.

Southern Nigeria

On its amalgamation with Lagos the country west of the Niger became the Western Province; east of that river being the Eastern Province. H.Q. of the administration, of the Regiment and 2 Battalion, were at Lagos, 1 Battalion H.Q. being at Calabar. Company outstations remained as before amalgamation (see page 51).

The Owa operations encountered the stiffest bush fighting since the 1901–2 Aro Expedition. Apart from these during the year a punitive patrol in the Abakaliki District had a little fighting in which Captain E. de H. Smith, Royal Artillery, was unfortunately killed on 17th November. This officer had served about three years in the W.A.F.F. with distinction and was a severe loss to the Force.

Owa Operations, 9th June–3rd August 1906

(See this chapter, Section B (IV))

On 9th June 1906 the District Commissioner of the Asaba District was murdered. The people of Owa, near Agbor, west of the Niger, were adherents of the 'Ekumeku' Secret Society, known as the 'Silent Ones' and a frequent source of trouble.

At Asaba was the nearest military garrison of a company under Captain W. C. E. Rudkin, Royal Artillery, who, being apprised by survivors of the police escort, at once marched to the scene of action.

Stiff fighting occurred in dense bush for two months. Rudkin being eventually reinforced by two more companies and a 2·95 in. gun before he succeeded in overcoming all opposition and arresting the responsible chiefs.

There were over 200 casualties, including three officers.

Rudkin was awarded the D.S.O., and the medal with clasp was issued.

Northern Nigeria

The following promotions occurred on 8th September: Captains E. P. Strickland, D.S.O., Norfolk Regiment, and Skeffington-Smyth, Coldstream Guards, to be Majors, *vice* Dobell and Robinson, Dobell having been given a battalion. On 5th October the same year Strickland took command of Dobell's battalion on the latter going to the Staff College.

Munshi Affair, February–March 1906

Northern Nigeria was in a disturbed state this year. The Munshis, who inhabited the banks of the Benue, had burnt a Niger Company Store, which caused the despatch of a force 600 strong under Hasler to punish the offenders. The force was prematurely recalled owing to the Satiru rising early in March, although its objects had been nearly fulfilled. No medal was awarded in this case. A fuller account is given in this chapter, Section B (III).

Satiru Operations, February–March 1906

(See also this chapter, Section B (II))

A party of fanatical Mahomedans at Satiru, just south of Sokoto, had killed two political officers and routed a company of M.I. who were taken unawares when their commanding officer, Lieutenant Blackwood, was also killed.

A general Mahommedan rising was feared, with repercussions throughout the country. The Munshi force was recalled, but meanwhile every available man was collected, and Captain (temporary Major) R. H. Goodwin, Royal Artillery, advanced with over 500 troops on Satiru. His mounted infantry made a flank attack while the main body and guns poured in a withering fire from square formation. The result was a crushing defeat of the enemy. Goodwin received a Brevet-Majority, three D.S.O.s were granted, as well as four D.C.M.s. The medal and clasp were issued for Satiru.

Hadeija Operations, 16th–24th April 1906

(See this chapter, Section B (II))

These were undertaken to quell the aggressive attitude of the Emir of Hadeija, and to reassert the prestige of Government after Satiru. Lowry-Cole, Commandant Northern Nigeria Regiment, was in command. The total force available was 700 strong with a M.I. company and a section of guns. The Emir refused to surrender, charging repeatedly in spite of heavy losses. The town was entered and the Emir's palace stormed; he himself was killed when resistance ceased. Lowry-Cole received a C.B., and Dobell a Brevet-Lieutenant-Colonelcy.

For these operations the G.S. Medal and clasp were awarded.

Chibuk Operations, 12th November–4th December 1906, 22nd December 1906–17th February 1907

(See this chapter, Section B (V))

These were conducted against a truculent pagan tribe, who fought most tenaciously from their mountain foxholes and caverns. Lieutenant (Temporary Captain) P. Chapman, Suffolk Regiment, was in command and received the D.S.O. The G.S. Medal and clasp were awarded here.

Gambia

1907–8

Since the end of 1906 the men had been established in their new lines at Box Bar, Bathurst, while during the camping season the company left Bathurst for Cape St. Mary, where a new range had been built. During 1907 S.M.L.E. (part-worn but tested) rifles were issued in place of carbines. The 6-pounder guns were handed over to the Volunteers for coast defence.

In 1908 the Inspector-General (Brigadier-General Morland), accompanied by his Staff Officer, Captain Robinson, inspected the unit in camp. During May the Company proceeded to Fonis as escort to the Governor, where the people had adopted a defiant attitude. The trouble was quelled without any resistance, however.

On 9th November, at the King's Birthday Parade, Sergeant P. J. Webb was presented with the Long Service and Good Conduct Medal.

Sierra Leone

On 29th February 1907 Major Palmer vacated the command and was replaced by Major F. E. Le Mesurier, Dublin Fusiliers, while Captain

H. H. Bond was appointed 2I.C. and Adjutant. In 1908 Battalion H.Q. was established at Daru from Freetown. One company had been stationed at Wulade and one at Kanre-Lahun in the Kissi country since the expedition there. The former outstation was now handed over to the French, as coming into their sphere of influence.

In 1908 a proposal by Montanaro, now Commandant W.A.R., for the amalgamation of the Sierra Leone W.A.F.F. with the W.A.R. was vetoed.

Gold Coast

The question of enlisting Ashantis came up again during this year. It had before been hotly debated, for it was pointed out how bravely these people had always fought against us. The arguments against enlisting them, however, prevailed in the end, as it was thought they would not be amenable to discipline when away from their own chiefs.

On 21st November 1907 Lieutenant P. J. Partridge died at Navarro in the Northern Territories.

In 1907 Captain L. de lat Cockcraft, Royal Artillery, succeeded Stanley Clarke in command of the Gold Coast Battery.

During this period two enterprises, both at Kumasi, are worth recording. (1) All personnel were occupied several hours daily for several months in clearing a large area for a golf course, polo ground and tennis courts. The work entailed was considerable. It meant cutting back the heavy forest, clearing undergrowth and planting grass. The result was a noteworthy improvement in amenities and health. (2) Lieutenant Rich, Royal Artillery, was sent to the Northern Territories with a party of men to buy polo ponies. He returned with about 20 animals which he had got safely through the tsetse belt by saturating them with paraffin and clay. Polo was played for some years, but then had to be abandoned owing to recrudescence of the tsetse scourge. Polo flourished at Accra, however, where an annual tournament with Nigeria was played alternately.

Southern Nigeria

On 28th January 1907 Captain H. C. Fox, Royal Scots Fusiliers, was awarded the Royal Humane Society's Medal for saving Private Garuba from being drowned in the Niger.

On 1st June 1908 Trenchard was promoted to be Commandant *vice* Moorhouse, retired and transferred to the Political Service in Southern Nigeria. Major R. E. Power, the Buffs, became 2I.C. and on the 20th October Lieutenant A. Sherston, Rifle Brigade, was appointed Adjutant to Trenchard.

Northern Nigeria

The I.G. in his report on the Northern Nigeria Regiment for 15th April 1907 recommended the reduction of the M.I. to three companies each of 120 men, the abolishment of depot companies in the two infantry battalions and the increase of these battalions from eight companies each to nine. At this time the strength of the Northern Nigeria Regiment was 2,797. There were 1,738 Hausas, 361 Kanuris, and 362 Yorubas, also 215 Fulanis, besides 121 of various tribes.

On 25th September 1907 Hasler was appointed Commandant, with Cunliffe 2I.C. On 29th February 1908 Strickland replaced Cunliffe. On 6th April 1908 Sergeant Garuba Sokoto was awarded the D.C.M. for gallantry at Yo.

General

In October 1908 the despatch of W.A.F.F. reinforcements to Somaliland came under discussion between Morland and Gough, the I.G. King's African Rifles. But nothing conclusive was done before operations ended.

1907–8

The reduction of W.A.F.F. batteries from three sections of six guns to two sections of four guns was put into effect. At the same time an increase in permanent gun-carriers was authorized to improve the efficiency of gun teams.

On the recommendation of the I.G. the Secretary of State informed Governors that flogging would be abolished in time of peace, except for offences on the line of march against inhabitants of the country. It would be retained for offences on active service. An amending law to this effect would be brought in at once.

On conclusion of his tour of inspection in Northern Nigeria the I.G. (Morland), with his Staff Officer made a journey through French West Africa.

1908–9

Gambia

In March Captain R. D. F. Oldman, D.S.O., succeeded Hastings in command of the Gambia Company. Lieutenants Hasketh-Smith and J. A. Savage, Northants Regiment, joined the Company in July.

Sierra Leone

In June 1909 the Leopard Murder Society became very active in Timdale. Detachments of the Sierra Leone Battalion W.A.F.F. were consequently sent to Victoria in the Imperri District of the Mende country to suppress it, and were kept there till 1912. This secret murder society had been a grave menace in the hinterland for many years past and broke out in a violent form periodically. The following account is therefore of interest:

The Society has a close affinity with the 'Alligator Society', its rites and procedure being very similar. It is said to have originated about 1870 in the Sherbro and Mende countries in the south-east region of the Protectorate. Its object was to remove, by murder, any individual who stood in the path of ambitious chiefs, or other persons, desiring to retain power in their own hands. Its members were sworn to secrecy under pain of death, taking an oath to carry out its commands to the letter.

As the leopard is one of the most cunning of jungle animals and most deadly in attack, its form and methods were adopted as the model to be used by the human murderer on his victim.

The actual man selected to carry out the murder went through a very thorough training; dressed in a leopard skin, he copied the stealthy movements of that animal. He was armed with a vicious-looking knife having blades made to simulate a leopard's claws with which the victim was killed. The body was then cut up and certain fatty portions were removed. The fat was used to make a 'fetish' medicine, called 'bofina' (or 'bofimoor'). It was mixed with certain herbs having the reputation of being able to work potent spells. The concoction was supposed to act as a charm protecting the Society from punishment and enabling it to carry out its evil purpose in safety.

Note. This account is taken from the book *The Advance of Our West African Empire*, written by C. Braithwaite Wallis, a District Commissioner in Sierra Leone at the beginning of the present century.

Gold Coast

Nothing of consequence occurred in 1909.

Southern Nigeria

Niger Cross River and Northern Hinterland Expeditions. In 1908–9 the bulk of the Southern Nigeria Regiment, under Trenchard's command, was engaged in opening up an unexplored area of about 6,000 sq. miles, incorporating territory which extended northward to the border of Northern Nigeria, and included country inhabited by the Munshi tribe south of the Benue.

The plan of operations was briefly to divide the whole force into three columns based on Calabar, Onitsha and Bende, each of which would march on a compass bearing directed on a central (imaginery) point 'X', for which an elastic target date of arrival was given.

Careful mapping was to be done *en route*, and, as conveniently spaced areas were pentrated, Political Officers would be installed for their administration. Every endeavour was to be made to avoid hostilities.

The scheme was ambitious but it succeeded. There was little opposition, casualties occurring almost entirely from sickness only. Communication between columns was sometimes possible by firing star shell; otherwise it was non-existent to all intents and purposes.

As the outcome of these operations three new districts and stations were created at Udi, Ogoja and Obudu, each garrisoned by a company.

No medal was awarded for these expeditions.

During the year two punitive operations took place, both of which are described more fully in Sections B (VII) and (V) of this chapter.

Ogwashi-Oku Operations. These began in November 1909 and finished in May 1910. The people involved were members of the Ekumuku Society, which had been responsible for the Owa Operations in the Agbor District in 1906. They had stopped trade, destroyed Government buildings and defined authority. Major G. N. Sheffield was in command with a company and maxim gun. Strong opposition was met with until Major Bruce (Norfolk Regiment) brought another company as reinforcements and ended the resistance. We had 34 casualties, with one officer, Captain H. G. Chapman (Suffolks) killed.

Sonkwala Operations. These took place in December 1908 during the Anglo-German Boundary Survey in the north-east of Southern Nigeria in the Benue/Cross River area. The British escort was commanded by Captain C. E. Heathcote, King's Own Yorkshire Light Infantry. Both British and German escorts were attacked by little-known natives for some days on end before dispersing the hostile tribesmen and permitting the Commission to accomplish its task. There were about 20 British casualties.

For both operations the African G.S. Medal and clasp was granted.

Northern Nigeria

There were no events of importance to record.

General

On 30th July 1909 Brigadier-General P. S. Wilkinson, whose service with the Northern Nigeria Regiment and Gold Coast Regiment has been recorded, was appointed Inspector-General W.A.F.F. in place of Morland. On the 1st September in the same year Captain A. H. Ollivant, Royal Artillery, became Staff Officer, replacing Craufurd.

1910–11–12

Gambia

In January 1910, Lieutenant F. V. Manger, Durham Light Infantry, replaced Hasketh-Smith. In September that year Captain H. T. Dobbin, Duke of Cornwall's Light Infantry, took over command from Oldman, Captain V. B. Thurston of the Dorsets replacing Savage, and Freman, Royal Artillery, taking Manger's place on the transfer of the latter to the Sierra Leone Battalion.

In 1912 the Governor, Sir George Denton, was succeeded by Sir Henry Gallway. The former's term of Governorship is notable as the commemoration of Mungo Park's expeditions of exploration down the Niger at the beginning of the nineteenth century. This was marked by the erection of a pillar at Pisani 200 miles up the Gambia River, which was Park's point of departure on both of his expeditions.

Sierra Leone

The Company at Victoria was withdrawn to Bandajuma in 1912.

Gold Coast

The Coronation of George V was celebrated by a parade at Kumasi in 1910. During the proclamation the interpreter, being momentarily stumped for the Hausa equivalent of 'Lord High Admiral of England' got a brain wave and triumphantly declaimed 'Same like the headman for canoes at Yeji'! (Yeji being a place on the Volta.)

Southern Nigeria

Trenchard was in favour of reorganizing the Southern Nigeria Regiment from two battalions into a regiment of 12 companies, as he considered control would be easier. This was accordingly carried out in August 1911. At the same time three Majors completed the organization. R. E. Power of the Buffs as 2I.C., G. T. Mair and A. H. W. Haywood, both Royal Artillery, as O.C.s Calabar to be responsible for the Cross River area, the idea being that one Major would generally be on leave.

Northern Nigeria and General

In the north nothing of importance occurred. On the I.G.'s Staff, Major F. Jenkins, Coldstream Guards, was appointed from 7th August 1911 *vice* Ollivant.

1912–13

Gambia

Lieutenants O. C. R. Hill, Royal Artillery, and A. McC. Inglis, Gloucester Regiment, were appointed during 1913. The former died at Bathurst on 9th November.

Sierra Leone

The disposition of the Battalion was now H.Q. and three companies at Daru—one company each at Kanrelahun Obagbana and Teasani.

Southern and Northern Nigeria

In Northern Nigeria a Durbar was held at Kano in February 1913, including an inspection of the Regiment by the Governor and a Gymkhana, at both of which the regiment acquitted itself with distinction.

On the amalgamation of the two Colonies, Sir Frederick Lugard was made Governor-General, and the two Regiments were amalgamated, Colonel C. H. P. Carter, C.B., C.M.G., former Commandant in the Gold Coast, being appointed Commandant Nigeria Regiment from 24th November 1913, with Cunliffe as Assistant Commandant, Captain W. D. Wright, V.C., of Kano-Sokoto Campaign fame, being made G.S.O.2.

General

On 1st September 1913 Brevet-Colonel C. M. Dobell, D.S.O., who had previously served with distinction in Northern Nigeria, was appointed I.G. W.A.F.F., succeeding Wilkinson.

1914

General

The final reorganization of the W.A.F.F. had now been completed with the amalgamation of the Southern Nigeria Regiment and Northern Nigeria Regiment into the Nigeria Regiment. The Southern Nigeria Regiment had been divided into two battalions, i.e. 3 and 4 Battalions Nigeria Regiment, and the new organization had barely had time to settle down when war broke out in August 1914. The Battalion Commanders were: 1, Cockburn; 2, Maclear (formerly O.C. Lagos Battalion); 3, Mair; 4, Haywood; 5 (M.I.), Lord Henry Seymour, Grenadier Guards.

COMPOSITION OF THE W.A.F.F. IN 1914

Formation	(Batteries) Artillery	(Battalions) Infantry	(Battalion) Mounted Infantry
Nigeria Regt.	(2) 4-gun 29·5 in.	4 (30 coys.)	1 (3 coys.)
Gold Coast Regt.	(1) 2-gun 29·5 in.	1 (8 coys.)	—
Sierra Leone Bn.	—	1 (6 coys.)	—
Gambia Coy.	—	— (1 coy.)	—
Total	(3) 12 guns	6 (45 coys.)	1 (3 coys.)

(B) TRIBAL CAMPAIGNS AND MINOR OPERATIONS 1906–14

(I) *Satiru: 14th February–10th March 1906*

(Africa G.S. Medal and clasp granted, N. Nigeria 1906 (A.O.260/1906))

There existed at the village of Satiru, 14 miles south of Sokoto, early in 1906 a party of malcontents and fanatical Mahomedans, under the leadership of Mallam Isa (whose father declared himself to be a Mahdi) and one Dan Maikafo, who was an outlaw from French territory. They started a revolt by murdering some dozen persons and destroying the village of Tsomo, which had refused to join them.

The revolt was directed as much against the Emir of Sokoto as against the British, that is to say as much against the head of the Mussulmans as against the Government, inasmuch as the Emir was unaware of the movement.

On 14th February 1906 the Resident (Mr. H. R. P. Hillary) and his assistant (Mr. A. G. M. Scott) being anxious to settle the matter without bloodshed, moved towards Satiru with an escort commanded by Lieutenant F. E. Blackwood, of 69 mounted infantry and a maxim.

The Political Officers left the troops and rode towards the village shouting that they had not come to fight but to discuss the causes of the disturbance.

Blackwood, fearing for the safety of the civilians advanced at a gallop, then hurriedly halted and formed square. The rebels, paying no heed to Hillary's invitation for a discussion, charged the semi-organized square, killing Blackwood, Hillary and Scott, as well as 25 rank and file, also wounding the Medical Officer, Dr. Ellis. Privates Mama Wurrikin and Mama Zaria gallantly rescued Ellis and retired in good order, but the rest of the M.I. were panic-stricken.

Sergeant Slack, Royal Artillery, had been left in charge of the Fort at Sokoto. He at once put it in a state of defence, summoned the Emir and wired to Jega, the nearest garrison, for reinforcements. Some 3,000 of the Sultan's men collected at Sokoto, but dared not face the rebels, whose prestige had been enormously enhanced by their success.

This was the first reverse sustained by the W.A.F.F. since its formation by Lugard in 1897. Reinforcements of 75 infantry from Kontagora, 100 from Lokoja and 200 M.I. from Kano reached Sokoto by 8th March. Further, owing to the fear that a fanatical rising throughout the country might occur, Lugard asked for reinforcements from the Southern Nigeria Regiment and Lagos Battalion W.A.F.F., his country at this time having been denuded of troops by the despatch of an expedition to Munshiland.

On 10th March, a column commanded by Major R. H. Goodwin, Royal Artillery, with 21 Europeans, 517 rank and file, of whom one-half were M.I., one 2·95 in. gun, and two maxims Northern Nigeria Regiment, marched on Satiru preceded by a screen of M.I.

The first body of the enemy to approach was engaged by fire; the square then advanced on a second and larger formation, some of whom tried to outflank its left or western face, whereupon Sergeant Maynard with a few picked marksmen made a turning movement on that flank.

The square then moved to the east of the town, which by that time had been set in flames by gunfire. The M.I. now moved to the west end of Satiru while 'D' and 'B' Companys 1 Northern Nigeria Regiment charged the south end with the bayonet, doing great execution with that weapon, no less than with rifle-fire from the rest of the infantry.

The M.I. went in pursuit of the rebel force retreating to the east. Lieutenant Gallagher had been wounded leading the charge of the 1 Northern Nigeria Regiment companies. Captain D. H. Macdonell of the M.I. was also wounded.

The enemy did not exceed 1,500. The leader Mallam Dan Maikafo was taken prisoner, a large number were killed and the remainder scattered. Thus the revolt was effectually crushed.

Comments

Lieutenant Blackwood made a bad tactical mistake by being caught in a position when he was unable to open fire on the charging fanatics. Subsequent operations were well executed by Major Goodwin. The reinforcements from the Southern Nigeria Regiment and Lagos Battalion were halted at Zungeru until it was certain there would be no further fanatical repercussions in the rest of Northern Nigeria.

Honours (*London Gazette*, 2/7/1907)

Goodwin was given a Brevet-Majority, while D.S.O.s were granted to Macdonell, Galagher, and Lieutenant P. P. W. Fendall (Border Regiment) of the M.I.

Sergeants Slack and Maynard were rewarded with the Meritorious Medal, while four rank and file Northern Nigeria Regiment received the African D.C.M.: 2313 Company Sergeant-Major Alieu Arfam; 144 Sergeant Awudu Birnin Kano; 1569 Corporal Fajenyo; 3223 Private Nomad Bamba.

(II) *Hadeija: 16th–24th April 1906*

(Africa G.S. Medal with clasp granted, N. Nigeria 1906 (A.O.260/1907))

The object of the operations was to reassert the prestige of the Government after the Satiru incident, as well as to quell the aggressive attitude of the Emir of Hadeija and of a war faction among his chiefs.

Colonel Lowry-Cole, Commandant Northern Nigeria Regiment, was in charge of operations. The following troops took part:

Artillery—two Europeans, 33 rank and file and one section 2·95 in. guns; M.I.—10 Europeans, 100 rank and file; 1 Northern Nigeria Regiment—eight Europeans, 166 rank and file, one maxim gun; 2 Northern Nigeria Regiment—eight Europeans, 165 rank and file.

There was in addition a garrison of 250 infantry and 86 M.I. in Hadeija, bringing the total force available to some 700 strong.

On reaching a village about five miles from Hadeija Lowry-Cole was joined by a half-company of M.I. under Captain E. B. Macnaghten from the garrison, who scouted the approaches to the town. A message was then sent to the Emir to surrender his biggest chiefs. The Emir replied by striking the messenger and refusing. The whole ramparts were manned by enemy except at the Eastern Gate. The walls were immensely thick.

Lieutenant A. A. C. Fitzclarence, 1 Northern Nigeria Regiment, was sent with a company to occupy this gate while Lowry-Cole deployed his force inside the wall. He sent an interpreter to tell the people if they laid down their arms they had nothing to fear. This was repeated three times. Lowry-Cole then instructed the guns to be directed on the Emir's palace. Just then the enemy's mounted spearmen charged. Maxims and the fire of volleys swept them away. Repeated charges were made with the same result. It was decided reluctantly to enter the town. Lieutenant C. M. Leatham went to the right or north-east with one company while Lieutenant-Colonel Dobell, commanding the infantry, went to the east with two companies. The enemy held their compounds stubbornly and repeatedly charged down the streets. After one and half hours the Emir's palace was reached, the entrance rushed and most of the defenders were killed. The Emir and his son were killed charging gallantly. Many were frenzied with drink and drugs. The resistance then ended.

All leaders were captured or killed. Our casualties were negligible.

The following honours were granted (*London Gazette*, 2/7/1907): Brevet-Colonel A. W. Lowry-Cole, C.B.; Brevet-Major C. M. Dobell, Brevet-Lieutenant-Colonel; 4178 Private Katon, D.C.M.; 3626 Private Danan, D.C.M.

(III) *Operation in the Munshi Country, February–March 1906*

No medal or clasp was granted for this affair. The operations were planned because the Munshis had attacked and burnt a Niger Company store at Abinsi on the Benue River. A number of traders had been killed and others taken into captivity as slaves.

A force some 600 strong with a section of 2·95 in. guns was assembled at Lokoja at the end of January 1906 to punish the offenders.

Temporary Lieutenant-Colonel J. Hasler, The Buffs, acting Commandant, was in command. He divided his force into two columns. No. 1 under himself operated south-east and No. 2 under Lieutenant-Colonel C. M. Dobell, Royal Welsh Fusiliers, south-west.

The main purposes required by the operations were successfully achieved by the time the force was recalled early in March on account of the Satiru Rising.

The only casualty was Captain C. F. Thornton wounded. After leaving a small garrison of half a company at Abinsi, the whole force did a remarkable march to Zungeru, one column of one gun and two companies covering 312 miles in 12½ days.

Captain and Brevet-Major (Temporary Lieutenant-Colonel) Hasler was made a Brevet-Lieutenant-Colonel. Captain P. H. Short, the Gloucestershire Regiment, was awarded the D.S.O.

(IV) *Owa Operations, 9th June–3rd August 1906*

(Medal and clasp granted, West Africa 1906 (A.O.102/1908))

On 9th June 1906 Mr. O. S. Crewe-Read was murdered at Owa, near Agbor, west of the Niger. He was Assistant District Commissioner in the Asaba District. For some time past the members of a secret society, called the Ekumeku, or Silent Ones, had been very active and troublesome. It appeared that on that night they surrounded Crewe-Read's bush camp with the intention of attacking it. His police escort, however, gave him warning, enabling his party to get away in the dark.

Soon after leaving camp Crewe-Read found he had not got his dog, thereupon he went back to retrieve the animal. He was set upon and killed. The bulk of his small escort managed to get away to Asaba, the nearest military post where there was a garrison of a company of the Southern Nigeria Regiment, commanded by Captain W. C. E. Rudkin, who at once set off for the scene of action.

Rudkin found the whole area up in arms. The bush was very dense, and the enemy was well armed with dane guns, but difficult to locate. Severe fighting took place south/south-east of Agbor, particularly on 11th June, where the natives were in great force. By nightfall the column had reached a point some three miles from Agbor. Determined resistance continued until 2nd July, by which time about half his troops were casualties. Meanwhile he had been reinforced by a second company and one 2·95 in. gun on 19th June.

On 2nd July further reinforcements of three officers and 130 rank and file arrived. By this time the enemy had been driven back to their stronghold of Owa, which was assaulted and taken. This broke the rising, although some towns did not submit without more fighting until 3rd August.

The casualties had been very heavy and the enemy exceptionally tenacious. Lieutenants Walmisley-Dresser, H. C. Fox and M. C. Miers were wounded. While of the rank and file 12 had been killed and no less than 193 wounded.

Captain Rudkin was awarded the D.S.O. for his able conduct of the operations.

(V) *Chibuk Patrol, 12 November–4th December 1906, 22nd December–17th February 1907*

(Africa G.S. Medal and clasp granted, West Africa 1906 (A.O.102/1908))

Here a Northern Nigerian pagan tribe fought with great tenacity from caverns in their rocky mountains. Captain Chapman, Suffolk Regiment, was awarded the D.S.O. for his successful conducting of the affair.

No despatches can be traced.

The last half of the operations were ably conducted by Lieutenant Wolseley and at the conclusion the following African other ranks were awarded the African D.C.M.: 2547 Sergeant Dan Halide; 3464 Private Garuba Kofa; 1576 Company Sergeant-Major Amadu Yoruba; 3335 Lance-Corporal Danibebi Kano; 2128 Private Adetuna Ogbomosho.

(VI) *Sonkwala, December 1908*

(Medal and clasp granted, S. Nigeria 1908 (A.O.160/1910))

These operations arose from the circumstances attending an Anglo-German Boundary Commission surveying the frontier between Nigeria and the Cameroons in the Benue/Cross River region. The Sonkwala tribe inhabited the district and harassed the escort by blocking the roads and attacking it.

Lieutenant-Colonel G. F. A. Whitlock, Royal Engineers, and Ober-Leutenent V. Stephani were the respective Anglo-German Survey Commanders. Captain G. E. Heathcote and V. Stephani were respectively Escort Commanders. The British escort had 60 rifles and the German 40, with a machine-gun in each case.

The country was very hilly and wooded. While marching through the Sonkwala Valley on 25th December the dispositions of the escorts were—British marching south and Germans east. The Sonkwalas first attacked Heathcote by working round his flanks. Stephani was next attacked and surrounded, but beat off the enemy by machine-gun fire. Both he and his second-in-command were wounded and several of the escort became casualties. Heathcote, supported by Lieutenant Homan, who had been garrisoning Sonkwala station with 50 rank and file, drove the Sonkwala across a yam field into the hills and dispersed them.

A Section of 25 men F Company 1 Nigeria Regiment had joined Heathcote by this time and the pursuit continued until 27th December. The D.C.M. was awarded to Colour-Sergeant W. King, the Black Watch, and to three native rank and file.

Total British casualties were five killed and 18 wounded.

(VII) *Ogwashi-Oku, November 1909–May 1910*

(Medal and clasp granted, S. Nigeria 1909–10 (A.O.149/1911))

The object was to punish disaffected natives in the area who were stopping trade by blocking roads and had destroyed a rest house and Roman Catholic mission buildings.

The operations were in three phases:

First Phase, November 2nd–December 19th 1909

Captain G. N. Sheffield was in command of a company, with four officers, one B.N.C.O. and 131 rank and file and a maxim.

There was strong opposition in the town of Ogwashi-Oku for several days from 2nd November. The bush was very dense. Efforts to capture the ringleaders were unsuccessful. On 18th December the people were given three weeks grace to bring them in. Casualties here were one killed and five wounded.

Second Phase, 6th January–24th April 1910

During this period severe fighting continued, without resulting in the capture of the wanted chiefs. The casualties were seven killed and 15 wounded, besides 10 carriers. On 24th April the column returned to base, until reinforced by Major Bruce in Third Phase.

Third Phase, 25th April–27th May 1910

Major Bruce brought reinforcements of five officers, 160 rank and file and two maxims. During this period several enemy bush camps were surprised and a number killed. Our casualties were Major H. G. Chapman (Suffolk Regiment) and three soldiers killed, also three wounded.

(C) TACTICS IN SAVAGE WARFARE

As much of the early history of the W.A.F.F. relates to small and large military operations dealing with warfare against primitively armed tribes, it seems opportune to describe here the tactics employed by the W.A.F.F. in coping with their methods.

In Bush Warfare

Up to the beginning of this century our methods were for a column, preceeded by the advanced guard with its point, to advance in single file along the bush-path with no troops deployed in the bush. When opposition was encountered sections turned right and left, firing volleys by word of command into the bush. As no enemy was visible these volleys were fired 'blind'.

If the enemy did not give way he was probably entrenched behind stockades and would inflict heavy losses from the dane guns with which he was armed. Dense smoke, caused by the damp atmosphere of the thick undergrowth, and bush fires, made it impossible to see more than a few yards. The 7-pounder guns and maxims would open fire at the point from whence the greatest volume of noise proceeded. This generally caused the tribesmen to retire to another position, towards which the troops would then advance firing volleys. This procedure would continue until the enemy had had enough, but the result would mean severe losses on our side and comparatively few on his side, unless it might be for a lucky hit from our guns.

In these affairs the expenditure of ammunition was prodigious. In the 1898 Sierra Leone Rising, in the Benin City Operations of 1897 and the Benin Territories Expedition of 1899, when the same system was used, the supply of small-arms ammunition ran short, frequently causing a retirement of our troops with the resulting danger of envelopment. This occurred in 1899 when a reconnaissance was sent to Okemue, Chief Ologboshiri's town. The reconnaissance had to retire, reaching camp with only three rounds per man left out of 100 taken in the pouches.

Again in the 1900 Ashanti Campaign, a force of 250 Lagos Battalion with a 7-pounder and two maxims, was ordered up to the relief of Kumasi. The contingent fought its way most gallantly against heavy opposition all the way. All six officers were wounded and of the men the casualties amounted to 150, so although the Fort was reached its relief was impossible; 80,000 rounds of small-arms ammunition were expended and only 9,000 were left on arrival at Kumasi.

Stockades were often formidably built. In 1898 Colonel Marshall describes some Sierra Leone stockades as built of logs 6 ft. high backed with rocks and boulders between and from 3 to 4 ft. thick. In 1900 Willcocks reports the Kintampo stockade near Kumasi as being well designed and 300 yards long.

During the Ashanti Campaign bush-warfare tactics were vastly improved. From now on the columns were not entirely confined to the bush-path. A line of scouts from each company was deployed on each side of the path. Men worked in pairs, the leader of the file used his matchet to cut a path forward, while the rear man of the file kept his rifle with fixed bayonet ready loaded for mutual protection and attack. Pairs kept touch visually or by whistle. The column kept touch with the two files next to the path. Enemy's stockades were charged to a bugle call. Sometimes it was possible to locate camps or stockades by climbing trees and directing gunfire on the target by this means.

Long columns were slow moving and vulnerable. It was wiser to break

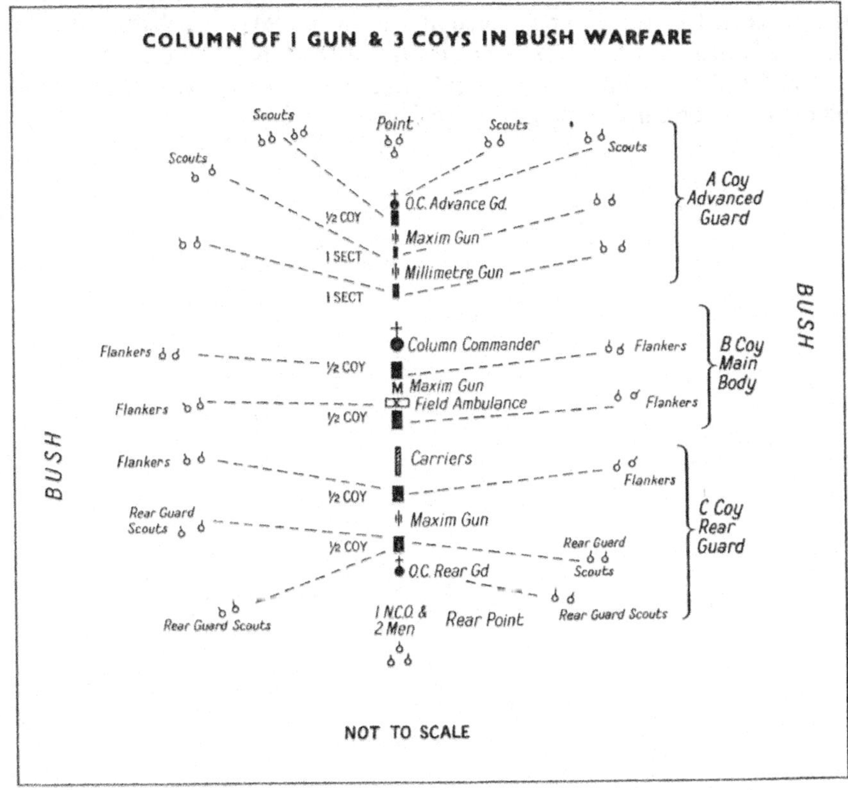

5. Column of 1 Gun and 3 Companies in bush warfare

into two and make each self-supporting. One of the chief axioms was to keep carrier's ranks closed up with a baggage guard distributed so as to ensure this being done.

In Open Country

In his despatch on the operations of the Aro Field Force (1901–2) Montanaro bears testimony to the efficacy of the new tactics, to which he attributes the small number of battle casualties and the low expenditure of small-arm ammunition.

There are not many instances of successful night operations. The chief drawbacks to undertaking these were the lack of reliable intelligence and the untrustworthiness of local native guides. If these difficulties could be surmounted and a clear moonlit night occurred the moral and physical results accruing paid very high dividends.

Targets for guns and maxims were seldom visible so that their power for effecting casualties was slight, but this was to some extent compensated for by the noise of their discharge, which shook the tribesmen's nerve considerably.

Particularly against Fulani horsemen in Northern Nigeria square formation was adopted, when similar tactics to those used in Egypt and the Sudan were necessary. Classic examples of advances in square formation are Arnold's Bida campaign in 1897: Kemball's operations at Kontagora in 1900; the Kano-Sokoto expedition when Wallace Wright withstood the onslaught of the Emir's Horse at Rawia in 1903; the disaster to the M.I. at Satiru, and the subsequent defeat of the rebels there in 1906.

For a fuller account of any operations mentioned here reference should be made to 'Tribal Campaigns' in their respective years.

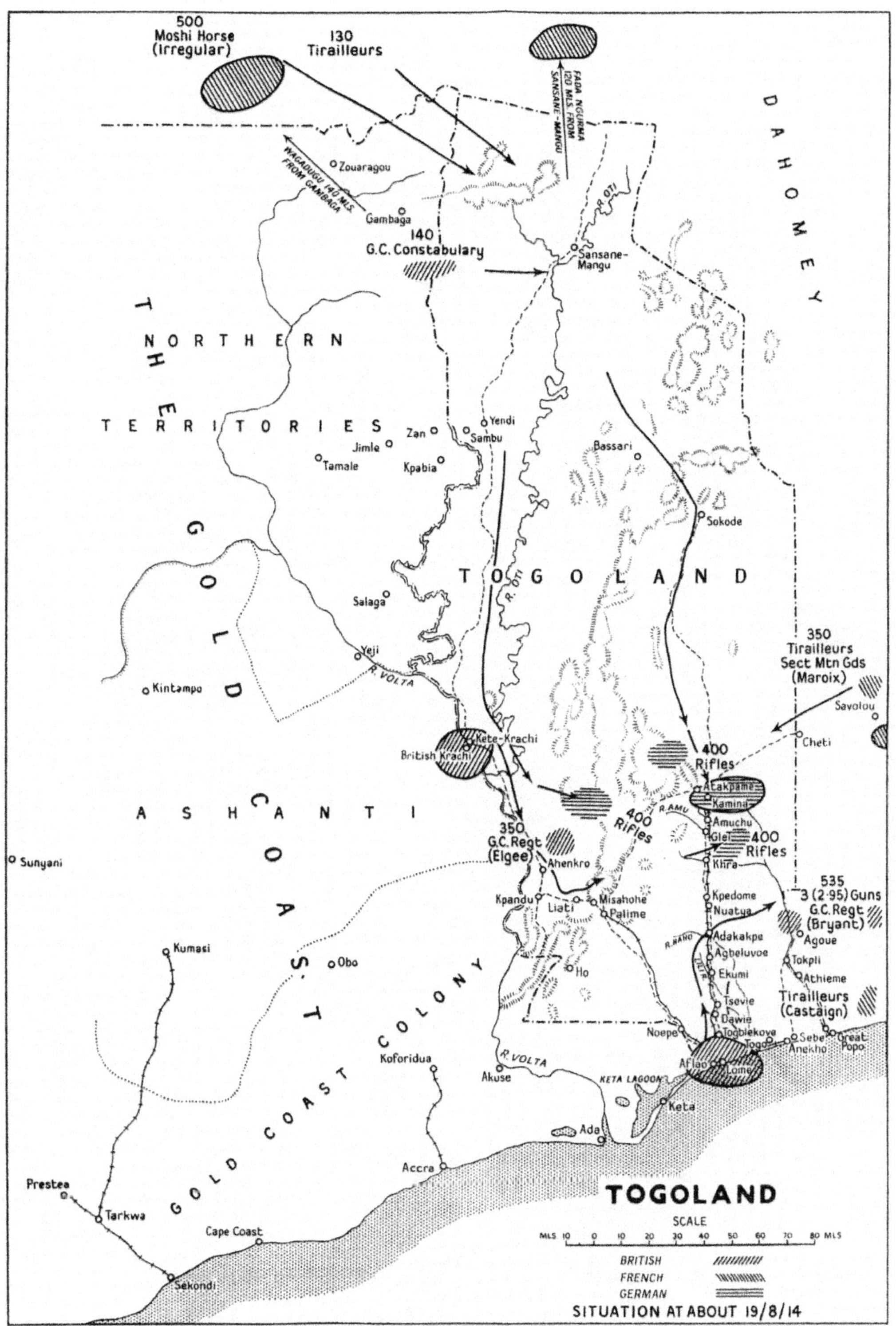

6. Togoland

Face page 97

CHAPTER 4

Togoland and the Cameroons Campaigns

In accordance with the principles laid down by the Imperial General Staff in 1911, the forces of each territory throughout the Empire maintained and equipped sufficient troops for self-defence for which local defence schemes were prepared. Yet it was certain that these arrangements would not suffice to meet the case of war with Germany, as the Navy would look to the Army for assistance in capturing places on land which menaced their main sea communications.

It was in these circumstances that on 5th August 1914, the British Government set up the Offensive Sub-Committee of the Committee of Imperial Defence to decide what combined Naval and Military Operations should be undertaken in foreign territories, it was agreed that the objectives must all be naval, and of these the most important were the enemy's foreign bases and centres of intelligence.

Togoland with its powerful wireless station at Kamina, and the Cameroons with its deep-water harbour at Duala, quite definitely fulfilled these requirements. For these reasons it was decided to invade Togoland and the Cameroons.

The Offensive Sub-Committee was composed of representatives of the Admiralty, the War, Foreign, Colonial and India Offices. The Chairman was Admiral Sir Henry Jackson, and Brigadier-General C. M. Dobell, Inspector-General West African Frontier Force, was one of its members.

TOGOLAND

Togoland was about the size of Ireland, a rectangle 400 miles from north to south and 100 to 150 miles wide, with a population estimated at a million. In 1884 Dr. Nachtigall, ostensibly sent to establish trade agreements, declared it to be a German Protectorate. In the next year both France and Great Britain signed agreements recognizing German influence. Administrators were given almost absolute powers, resented by the natives to such a degree that a steady emigration to the Gold Coast had been taking place for some years past.

The country is divided into approximately two halves by a range of mountains running from south-west to north-east, sometimes rising to 3,000 ft. South of this barrier were three 3-metre-gauge railways and good roads, but north of it the country was poorly developed. Kamina was on the Northern Railway 110 miles from the capital, Lome.

On the west was the Gold Coast, while on the northern and eastern frontiers were the French colonies of Upper Senegal and Dahomey. About half the length of the Anglo-German frontier was formed by the Volta River, but a strip of land 80 miles along its lower course was included in Gold Coast territory, the military value of which was lessened by swampy bush which covered its surface. A further notable factor of this frontier was that it divided the country of the Dagomba and Mamprussi tribes in the north, who were both very pro-British in their sympathies.

The Volta was navigable for launches from its mouth at Ada for 80 miles to Akuse. There were no navigable rivers in Togoland.

On the outbreak of war both the Governor and the Officer Commanding the Gold Coast Regiment were on leave. In their place were Mr. Robertson and Captain F. C. Bryant, Royal Artillery.

The general situation of the opposing forces was then:

Germans

About 200 Europeans and 800 native troops between Lome and Kamina. About 100 Europeans and 400 native troops in Northern and Western Togoland. Small detachments at Anacho, eastern railhead.

British

Half a company *en route* to Krachi. 'C' and 'G' Companies with one 2·95 in. gun *en route* to Ada. Half 'A', 'F', 'I' and 'D' Companies concentrating at Kumasi, 'B' Company at Gamabaga. Battery (less one gun) at Kumasi. These troops were all part of the Gold Coast Regiment W.A.F.F.

On 5th August 1914 a telegram from the Colonial Office announced the declaration of war; this was received a few hours after an intercepted wireless message from Kamina had given Mr. Robertson the news. Shortly after on the same day the Governor of Togoland, Major von Doering, sent a telegram to Robertson suggesting the advantages of declaring neutrality between the two Colonies. The suggestion was rejected after referring it to the Home Government.

On this date our preparations for an offensive were practically ready, thanks to the energy and initiative of Bryant and the Acting Governor. By 31st July reservists had been called up and mobilization completed. Bryant's request for calling on loyal chiefs to enlist partisans was vetoed by the Governor owing to the fear that it might re-create tribal warfare, which was always a latent danger.

On 6th August, unknown to Robertson, Bryant had sent the Officer Commanding at Ada under a flag of truce to Lome to demand the surrender of Togoland. It appeared that Bryant had learnt that the French in Dahomey and the North were anxious and ready to co-operate with us in an offensive; this had decided him to clear up the attitude of the Germans. Captain Barker, the O.C. Ada, was instructed to point out to the German Governor that we had three strong columns ready to invade from the east, while the French also had three columns ready to cross the German eastern and northern frontiers; furthermore two important Togoland chiefs were ready to support us, and that therefore any resistance was useless. The Governor was given twenty-fours hours to decide.

On hearing of Bryant's action Robertson asked the Colonial Office whether he was to be given a free hand in forward movements. A reply came that pending further instructions a forward movement could not be sanctioned.

While this had been happening General Dobell had drawn up an appreciation for the Offensive Sub-Committee based on the assumption that the invading force would require a reinforcement of three companies Sierra Leone W.A.F.F., which would need a naval escort, whose co-operation in the attack on Lome would be of great value. The timing of this offensive, he said, must be dependent on when the Navy could provide the necessary ships. Hence the instructions to await sanction for a forward movement.

On 7th August a wireless message in clear from the German Governor to Berlin was intercepted saying he was evacuating Lome and withdrawing towards Kamina to defend the wireless installation there. On receipt of this news the British Government instructed Bryant to move two companies and a section of guns by the quickest route to Ada, and if Lome surrendered, to occupy it as a base for a subsequent advance on Kamina.

At 1900 hours Barker, accompanied by Mr. Newlands, District Commissioner of Keta, and two orderlies, proceeded to Lome by Ford car, where they were met by Mr. Clausnitzer, to whom Major V. Doering had delegated full powers to surrender Lome and the coastline to Anecho with territory extending 120 miles inland, i.e. as far as Khra village.

At the same hour Major Maroix, commanding the French troops in Dahomey, occupied the frontier post of Agbanake without opposition and next morning Captain Marchand entered Anecho.

It having been ascertained that the French were ready to assist in an attack on Kamina, and that Bryant considered the Anglo-French force sufficient for the purpose, the Colonial Office sanctioned the operation, at the same time putting Bryant in command of the whole force with temporary rank of Lieutenant-Colonel on 9th August.

Meanwhile Barker and Newlands were spending an anxious time in Lome awaiting the arrival of the troops from Ada and Keta. They duly arrived on 9th, having marched over 50 miles in 50 hours, being consequently in a very exhausted state.

On 12th August[1] Bryant arrived at Lome. On that date the situation was as follows:

Germans

	Europeans	*Rank and File*
Northern Railway; at railhead and north of Khra River	200	800
Sansane Mangu, Yendi Kete Krachi and Palime Railway	100	400
	300	1,200

[1] On this date Regimental Sergeant-Major Alhaji Grunshi, D.C.M., M.M., fired the first shot in the Campaign. It is said to be the first shot fied by any British soldier in the 1914–18 War.

Allies

	Europeans	Rank and File
Gold Coast Regiment W.A.F.F.		
At Lome; 'C', 'G' and 'I' Companies; three machine-guns; Battery (less one sub-section)	23	535
At Kete Krachi; Captain Elgee and three companies ('A', 'D' and 'F')	20	350
En route from Gambaga to Sansanne, Mangu G.C. Constabulary	5	140
Total British (3 guns)	48	1,025
French		
En route from Wagadugu	7	130
At Anecho, under Captain Castaign	8	150
At Savalou and Cheti, under Major Maroix (one section mountain guns)	20	350
Total French (2 guns)	35	630

Kete Krachi had been found unoccupied when the detachment of 'A' Company Gold Coast Regiment had crossed the Volta from Krachi on 8th August. About the same time Robertson had heard from the French Governors of Dahomey and the Ivory Coast that 500 'Auxiliary Cavalry' (or Moshi Levies) with 50–60 *gardes cercles* were due at Sansane Mangu from Upper Senegal by 15th to guard the area from an attack.

On 13th Bryant, having heard the small wireless station and bridge at Togblekove had been destroyed, pushed two companies north to prevent further damage to the railway.

The advance to Kamina began on 14th August. 'I' Company, under Captain Potter, formed the advanced guard from Togblekove. The main body moved along the railway and road which ran parallel to it. No attempt was made to use motor-lorries, as the roadway had fallen into disrepair. Road and railway at times were a considerable distance apart, the intervening country being swampy and covered with dense bush and high grass. Mutual co-operation was generally difficult and frequently impossible therefore.

By the evening 'I' Company had reached Tsevie without opposition; advanced patrols under the Intelligence Officer, Mr. R. S. Rattray, reported all the country south of Agbeluvoe clear of the enemy. The main body had concentrated at Togblekove. At 2200 hours 'I' Company started to advance by the road.

The main body, leaving a section of infantry at Togblekove, moved from there at 0600 hours on 15th August. About 0830 hours, when Bryant's column was half-way to Tsevie, he learnt from local natives that a German train had come south and opened fire on Tsevie station about 0600 hours, retiring some two hours later. As Bryant had heard nothing from 'I' Company since the previous night, he pushed forward with all speed.

In the meantime 'I' Company at Ekuni, halted on the road, had heard the train pass south. Potter at once detached Lieutenant H. S. Collins with a section to try to cut it off, while he pushed on with the rest of the Company as fast as possible to Agbeluvoe. Reaching the railway by a bush track shown them by a local Hausa, Collins's section piled up a barrier of stones about 200 yards north of Ekuni bridge, and then took up a position in the bush by the bridge. Soon after a second train from the north arrived, but getting stopped at the barrier, withdrew before Collins's party could intercept it. Meanwhile Potter's company, having heard it pass, took up a position to ambush it. Although the train was riddled with bullets, it succeeded in escaping at full speed. Potter, who then had been rejoined by Collins, proceeded to Agbeluvoe Station, where he took up a defensive position across the railway and road (here about 80 yards apart) against attacks from north and south. Both German trains were still south of Agbeluvoe and for the last two hours the escort to 'I' Company's carriers had to defend themselves and their convoy against continuous enemy attacks, their safe arrival at Agbeluvoe being largely due to the courage of their commander, Colour-Sergeant Gethin.

At an early hour that evening the Germans in force attacked the British position from the south, but were beaten off, and further attacks during the night had no better success. Early on the 16th news of Bryant's advance caused the enemy to return to his train, where, after some further fighting, he surrendered to Potter. The gallant and skilful British defence, for which Bryant paid great credit to Potter and his company, had completely foiled the enemy's attempts at a breakthrough, and subsequently contributed in large measure to his final downfall.

According to an account given by a German Sergeant-Major their force consisted of two companies under Captain Pfaeler, who, with five other Europeans, was killed. The native troops became demoralized and fired wildly with little consequent result.

At 1500 hours Bryant encountered opposition at the Lili River, where the hostile force blew up the bridge and took up a position behind it. Here the British were delayed by difficult bush country until 1630 hours. He did not reach Ekuni until 1730 hours, consequently having to bivouac there for the night. Alarm was later caused by a few shots from enemy stragglers resulting in a stampede of 700 carriers, many of whom did not come into Ekuni until 1000 hours next day. On the 16th the main body resumed its march on Agbeluvoe, meeting little opposition, though the route was covered with abandoned equipment. On approaching Agbeluvoe heavy firing was heard, when it was found that most of the enemy who had come south by the two trains had surrendered. Some 30 Europeans were accounted for with most of 200 men. One of the most important results was that the demolarized flying remnants made no attempt to destroy the railway vehicles or line, which thus fell intact into our hands for a distance of 30 miles north of Agbeluvoe. Our military casualties had been slight, but included 34 preventive service and carriers killed or wounded.

Bryant now learnt that the Germans were compulsorily enlisting native levies. He therefore asked permission to do the same, but this was again refused. As the length of his communications made it necessary to get reinforcements, instructions were telegraphed from London to send two companies W.A.F.F. from Sierra Leone and one from Nigeria. It is to be noted that the latter reached Lome on 24th August, and the former three days later, but neither were required owing to operations having ended.

On 17th strong officer patrols secured the railway bridge over the Haho River, seven miles north. As they reported strong enemy forces advancing south, 'C' Company was despatched to join them. Meanwhile Castaing's detachment of eight Europeans and 150 *tirailleurs* on arrival from Anecho was also sent to reinforce the party.

On 18th half 'C' Company occupied Adakakpe, four miles farther up the line. On the same date a preventive-service detachment was pushed up the Western Railway to protect Bryant's flank and the railway was cut 30 miles from Lome.

By this time, thanks to the untiring efforts of the Gold Coast Railway engineers, the Northern line was repaired as far as Togblekove and the telegraph opened from Lome to Agbeluvoe. On 19th the advance was resumed to Nustya. That day Bryant notified Maroix at Cheti and Elgee at Kete Krachi that he intended to be on the Amuchu River on 26th, requesting them to be within two days' march of Kamina by that date.

Maroix's Cheti Column advanced on Kamina on 22nd, while Elgee's Kete Krachi Column, of 'A', 'B' and 'F' Companies Gold Coast Regiment W.A.F.F., left via the Kpandu road on 19th. His Staff Officer was Captain P. J. Mackesy and his Intelligence Officer was Lieutenant Kyngdon, Royal Artillery, of the Survey Department.

It should be noted that the Gold Coast Regiment had no telephone equipment, so messages had to be sent by runners. In this case both messages were delivered on time. This can largely be attributed to the dislike of the natives for the German rule and their anxiety to help the British in every way.

Advancing through Nustya, Bryant's patrols under Captain A. F. Redfern reported on 21st that the enemy was holding a very strongly entrenched position about 500 yards north of the railway bridge over the Khra River. This bridge and two mines on the railway were blown up as Redfern approached. The patrols also came under heavy machine-gun fire, but, being well and boldly handled, they were able to get enough information to enable Bryant to formulate a plan of attack.

Khra village stood across the road and just west of the railway. It was oval in shape, measuring about 400 by 150 yards from south-east to north-west; there was a railway cutting close to the village. Trenches had been dug close to, and around, the village as well as to the eastward of the railway cutting. Three or four machine-guns had been placed on the flanks, covering all approaches from the surrounding dense bush. The density of the bush made a co-ordinated attack out of the question, success must depend on the initiative of subordinate commanders. On the morning of 22nd August, covered by an advanced screen, Bryant's force moved forward in two columns. On the right, on the railway, were the Pioneer Company and half 'G' Company, Gold Coast Regiment, with Castaing's Senegalese detachment. The Pioneers were to hold the enemy in front while the rest turned his left flank.

The column on the road consisted of half 'C' Company, 'I' Company Gold Coast Regiment and its three guns. While half 'C' Company held the enemy in front, 'I' Company was to turn his right flank. The guns would give support as required.

Lieutenant Thompson only had 22 men in his half 'G' Company, so was given 17 of Castaing's *tirailleurs* to help him out. This combined party led the attack on the enemy's left flank, working their way through the bush. By 1100 hours they were held up by heavy machine-gun fire. They held their ground till about 1530 hours, when the machine-guns seemed to slacken owing to the British gun support. Thompson then led his men to the assault, ably supported by Castaing. But the attacking force was brought to a standstill within 50 yards of the German trenches. Both he and the French Lieutenant Guillemart were killed, besides many casualties in native ranks, making further progress impossible, and necessitating a retirement. The devotion of the 17 *tirailleurs* calls for special comment. All were killed or wounded and their bodies were found defending the British officer to the end.

'I' Company managed to work round the German right flank, but was held up 300 yards away by nightfall and heavy machine-gun fire.

British casualties here were one officer and five natives killed, two officers and 23 natives wounded. Combined allied casualties totalled 75. This was the first time the W.A.F.F. had faced machine-gun fire and its effects had been distinctly demoralizing.

Next morning the enemy had retired. He had been reinforced by one company, just when our attack on his left had seemed dangerous according to a German prisoner's report, making his total force some 60 Europeans and 400 men. His casualties were only three Europeans and ten natives, so his retirement seems to have been unnecessary.

On 23rd–24th Bryant remained at Khra to reorganize and evacuate his wounded.

In view of his depleted numbers Bryant ordered the Krachi Column to move at once via Palime to reinforce him, meanwhile he sent out officer's patrols towards Glei and the Amuchu River.

On the night of 24th–25th loud explosions were heard from the direction of Kamina, and in the morning the masts at Kamina were no longer visible. By 1030 hours on 25th Bryant's leading troops were on the Amu River, where they were met later in the day by two Germans carrying a white flag to submit terms of capitulation. Bryant informed them that the terms must be unconditional. At 1030 hours on 26th these terms were accepted.

Newlands was sent that afternoon to arrange the ceremony of surrender for the following day. He found the wireless installation completely wrecked. Although its destruction was a loss to us, to the Germans its importance was a great disaster; without its direct means of communication the German ships in the Southern Atlantic would be completely out of touch with current events and handicapped accordingly.

Maroix's column from Cheti arrived at Kamina on 27th, after meeting only slight opposition, while the Krachi Column had an uneventful march into Kamina on the same day.

Over 200 Germans surrendered with three machine-guns, 1,000 rifles and about 320,000 rounds of ammunition.

The rapid Allied success was due greatly to the wholehearted co-operation between French and English, both civil and military, inspired by the initiative and skill with which Bryant conducted the operations.

THE CAMEROONS CAMPAIGN

At the beginning of this chapter the necessity was explained for restricting the objectives of any joint naval and military operations in foreign territories to such as could be dealt with by local forces. The forces in the British West African possessions in 1914 consisted of the Imperial garrison of Sierra Leone and the units of the West African Frontier Force in those possessions. The sole representative of the Navy was the gunboat H.M.S. *Dwarf*.

The Imperial Garrison of Sierra Leone

The Imperial Garrison in Sierra Leone was maintained for the defence of the coaling station. It comprised the 50th Company Royal Garrison Artillery, the Sierra Leone Company Royal Garrison Artillery, the 36th Company Royal Engineers, the 1st West India Regiment, the West African Regiment, and detachments of Army Service Corps, Royal Army Medical Corps and Army Ordnance Corps. Of these the Sierra Leone Company Royal Garrison Artillery, half the Royal Engineers and the West African Regiment were composed of locally recruited Africans, trained and commanded by British officers and N.C.O.s.

Order of Battle

The constitution of the W.A.F.F. has been fully dealt with in Chapter 3 (A), while the Order of Battle for the Cameroons Campaign is set out in Appendix X.

Preparedness for War in the W.A.F.F.

As regards its preparedness for war, the W.A.F.F. had attained a highly satisfactory standard of efficiency for native troops, but, in the case of the Nigeria Regiment, it suffered under two handicaps. Firstly, its establishment was extremely small in relation to the area of the country over which it was distributed, namely about 5,000 troops scattered in detachments over 335,000 sq. miles where sporadic disturbances required constant supervision. And secondly the amalgamation of Southern with Northern Nigeria had only come into effect on the 1st January 1914, giving little time for the unified forces to settle down. Consequently an entirely new Defence Scheme had become necessary. When war broke out this was still in draft form; thus neither military nor civil authorities knew with any certainty what action was required by them.

Nigerian Police and Marine Services

Besides the Nigeria Regiment Nigeria had a police force of some 2,100 Africans under about 30 officers semi-militarily trained and armed

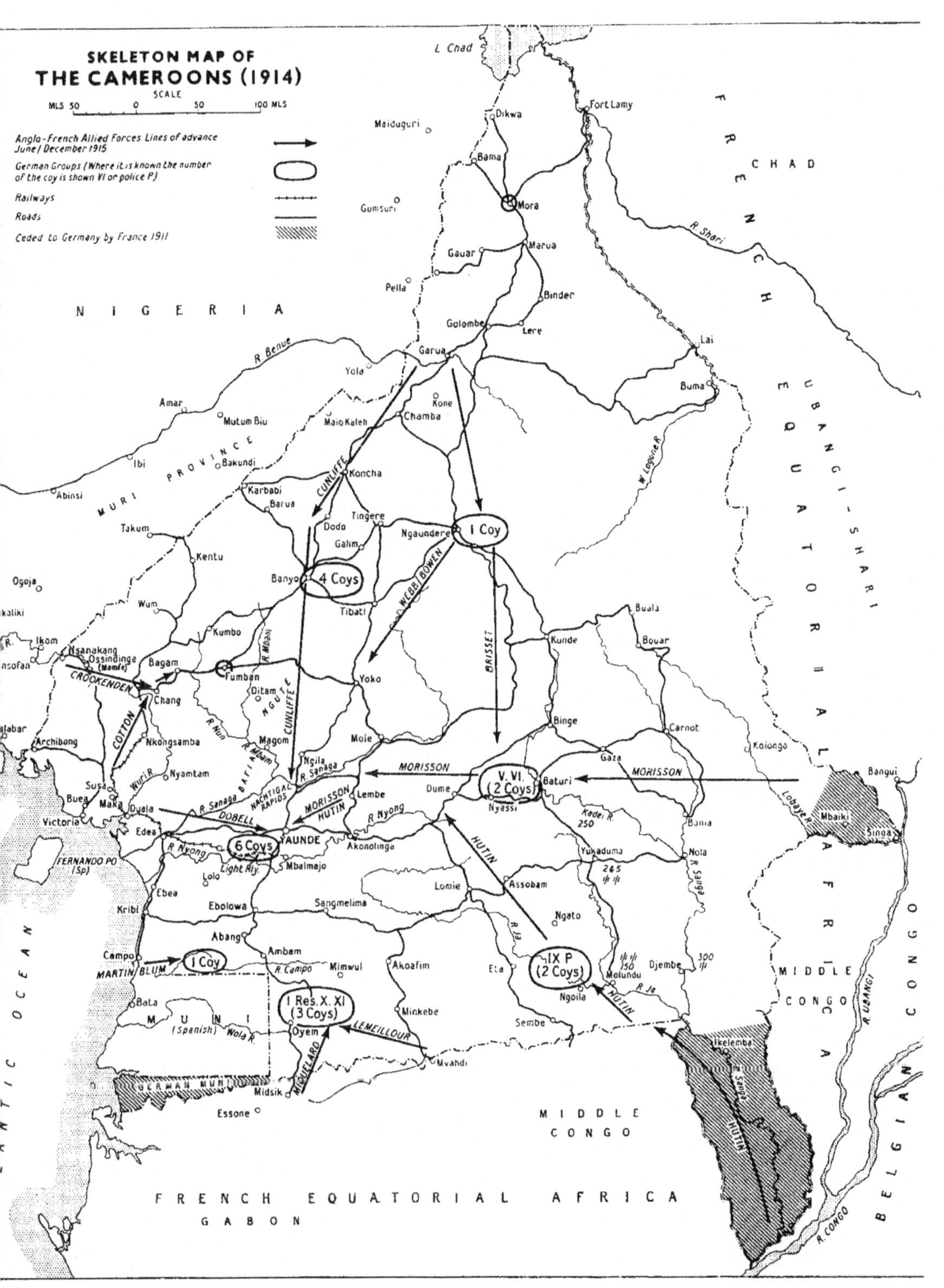

7. The Cameroons (1914)

Face page 105

with carbines. There was also a Marine department, about 1,000 strong, well trained by British ex-naval and R.N.V.R. officers, equipped with steamers and launches to operate over the inland waterways. These vessels could be, and were during the Campaign, fitted with light quick-firing and machine-gun armament.

German Forces in the Cameroons

In the German account of the Campaign included in Volume IV of *Der Grosse Krieg 1914/1918*, edited by Herr Schwartze, the total of troops and police is given as 200 Europeans and 3,200 Africans, with about a dozen guns and a plentiful supply of machine-guns. Rearmament with magazine rifles was in process of being completed. The troops were organized in 12 companies. At the conclusion of hostilities about 6,000 African and 500 European combatants were interned in Rio Muni, showing the extent of expansion of the German Forces during the campaign, without making allowance for casualties.

Topography

In 1884 Dr. Nachtigall was sent as Imperial Commissioner to promote German trade in West Africa; having first proclaimed a Protectorate over Togoland, he then did the same with the Cameroons. The territory acquired in the latter case covered an area of about 300,000 sq. miles, being bounded on the west by Nigeria and on the east by French Equatorial Africa and French Congo. The Nigerian frontier was nearly 1,000 miles long. The country is roughly triangular in shape, with its apex on Lake Chad in the north, and its base, some 600 miles long, on French territory (i.e. Gabon and Congo).

The capital, Duala, possesses one of the finest natural harbours on the west coast of Africa. Other prominent features are the Mandara Mountains in the north-west, the central Ngaundere plateau rising to 2,500 ft, and lastly in the extreme south-west the Cameroon Peak towering up to 13,000 ft., of which Hanno says 'a very loftie mountain, called the "Chariot of the Gods" is as a great fire reaching to the stars', meaning, of course, that it was a volcano in eruption at the time.

The southern belt of the country is heavy forest for 70–80 miles, with swamps and dense undergrowth limiting the vision often to a few yards; the country then opens up to a grass belt which gets thinner as one goes northward.

Communications

Roads were practically non-existent, except for a fine motor road from Kribi to Jaunde. Otherwise there were only narrow paths 10–12 ft. wide.

There were two railways, one from Duala to Eseka 120 miles, the other from Bonaberi to Nkongsamba 100 miles. Main centres were connected by telegraph, but lines were destroyed as the enemy retreated. Mostly rivers were only navigable for canoes; the Nyong and Sanaga could, however, take coastal steamers for short distances from their mouths, as could the Sanga in the south-east.

Plan Based on Dobell's Appreciation

In pursuance of an appreciation drawn up by General Dobell the Offensive Sub-Committee formulated the plan of making Duala, Victoria and Buea the first objectives. With a view to sweeping for mines and surveying the harbour at Duala, H.M.S. *Cumberland* and H.M.S. *Dwarf* with a flotilla of Nigerian Marine, under the orders of Captain Fuller, R.N., proceeded to Suellaba Point in the Cameroon Estuary, where a base was established on 10th September 1914. Meanwhile arrangements were made with the French for a contingent of Senegalese *tirailleurs* to join Dobell's Expeditionary Force, which was to be escorted by H.M.S. *Challenger* and the French cruiser *Bruix*. The total strength of the allied force for the capture of Duala was fixed at 3,500, of which more than half was British, with two and a half four-gun mountain batteries.

Situation in Nigeria 13–19th August 1914

We must now turn to the situation in Nigeria, where the following columns had been concentrated near the frontier of the Cameroons:

Maiduguri, Geidam and Nafada,

One company of mounted infantry and three companies of infantry.

Yola

One company of mounted infantry, a section of guns and four companies of infantry.

Ikom (or No. 2)

A four-gun battery and four companies of infantry.

Calabar (or No. 1)

A section of guns and two companies of infantry.

The above Columns were commanded by Captain R. W. Fox, Lieutenant-Colonels P. R. Maclear, G. T. Mair and A. H. W. Haywood respectively.

Reconnaissances by Columns

Colonel Carter, the Commandant Nigeria Regiment, had arrived at Kaduna from Lagos so as to be nearer Government Headquarters at Kaduna. On receipt of instructions from London on 14th he ordered special reconnaissances by the Maiduguri, Ikom and Calabar Columns. No reconnaissance was ordered from Yola, as the arrival from Garua was expected of Major A. H. Festing, a retired officer now employed with the Niger Company. He arrived at Yola on 15th and reported that when he left Garua on 11th nothing was known about the war, and the garrison consisted of about 70 rifles with 10 Europeans, and two machine guns.

As the result of the various reconnaissances Carter requested permission to attack Garua before reinforcements arrived there. The Colonial Office replied authorizing this, while he was to bear in mind the general plan, and to use his own discretion in the case of Garua and any other similar post.

Acting on the latitude given to him, Carter issued instructions on 20th August to the Maiduguri Column to attack Mora if Fox thought himself strong enough. Meanwhile Fox had left Maiduguri with 'A' Company 2 Nigeria Regiment on 9th August *en route* to Mora, some 85 miles distant across open park-like country.

Maiduguri Column 10–29th August 1914

On 10th August Fox reached Konduga just on the British side of the frontier, where he made an entrenched camp. He then pushed a small detachment forward, which got information that Mora was held by about 100 Africans and six Europeans. On 15th he received instructions from Carter to use 'C' Company M.I. which was *en route* to join him from Geidam (or Nafada) in a reconnaissance on Mora. On 19th his patrols came in contact with Von Raben's troops from Mora. The German commander thereupon decided to abandon the brick-built post there and withdraw to a strong position on the main ridge to the southward.

On 20th Fox advanced with his whole column across the frontier in order to make a thorough reconnaissance of the enemy's position. On 21st Captain Ferrandi with 15 Senegalese arrived at Maiduguri from Fort Lamy with the information that Colonel Largeau, commander in Chad, could not concentrate sufficient troops for an offensive before September; Ferrandi and his party left next day to join Fox.

By 26th the Maiduguri Column had moved round to the east of Mora Mountain and was encamped at Sava, about two miles from the German position, where it was joined by Ferrandi.

Meanwhile Von Raben, who in addition to commanding the 3rd Company at Mora, was Resident of the Province, ordered the Marua detachment of two Europeans and 34 Africans with a machine gun to join him. He also enlisted 60 recruits.

Von Raben's Position at Mora

The position he had taken up was on a ridge overlooking the town at the north-eastern extremity of the Mandara Range. It was about three miles long and one mile wide. Just south-east of the town is an under-feature called Wacheke, connected by a col with the main ridge on which the German trenches lay; they extended from Dabaskum spur south-east for about 1,500 yards, then turning southward to Molugve by gradually ascending ground. Thus Molugve overlooks Dabaskum, and is some 1,600 ft. above the plain. To the west of the crest is the Gauala Ridge, 1,200 yards away and somewhat lower. A steep valley separates the two ridges.

Leaving a small detachment of M.I. and a machine gun to defend the camp, Fox marched out at 2000 hours on 26th August. He had decided to make for Molugve, which he realized commanded the enemy's position. Guided by two natives, the allied troops reached Molugve after a strenuous climb. The Germans had manned their trenches and kept up a steady fire with two machine guns. The position was 1,500 yards away with a deep valley intervening. Surprise was out of the question and a British attack with one machine gun to support it gave little prospect of success. In any case transport of supplies and ammunition was impossible if a further stay had been desired.

Fox therefore gave the order to retire, but at this moment the whole top of the mountain became enveloped in a thick mist, and three small parties lost their way, one of which was the machine-gun crew, which ran into a German detachment sent to make a counter-attack. This resulted in the capture of the gun, while Dr. Fraser, two native soldiers and five gun-carriers were killed, also Sergeant Turner and one soldier were made prisoners.

Except for this unfortunate mishap the retirement was carried out unmolested. Fox then withdrew to Sava, situated on a rocky hill, where he made an entrenched camp while awaiting reinforcements from Lagos and Fort Lamy, which he said must include some guns. In this position he felt secure, was in touch with the enemy and able to get supplies easily from the natives.

Yola Column, 18th–22nd August 1914

The Yola Column, commanded by Lieutenant-Colonel P. R. Maclear, 2 Battalion Nigeria Regiment, consisted of H.Q. and 'B' Company M.I.; one section 1 Battery; H.Q., 'C', 'G' and 'H' Companies 2 Battalion, and 'H' Company 3 Battalion, totalling about 600 rifles, with five machine guns.

Maclear reached Yola on 18th August. On 19th he received instructions from Carter to advance to a position from which he could strike at Garua quickly as soon as sanction for an attack was given by the Colonial Office. It must be noted that Garua was 90 miles to the east on the north bank of the Benue, Yola being on the south bank, as the river's course here is very sinuous.

On 20th Maclear reported he proposed leaving Yola on 22nd; at the same time he sent information to H.Q. that German natives were actively patrolling the frontier and that many carriers were said to have left Garua with loads for Ngaundere. On receipt of this telegram Carter urged him to start before the 22nd, as he inferred the Germans were evacuating the post. Maclear's column, however, had not completed its concentration, also he was having difficulty in collecting the 1,400 carriers he required.

At 1300 hours on 22nd Maclear started to cross to the north side of the Benue; his mounted infantry moved off eastward that afternoon. 'H' Company 3 Battalion only reached Yola at noon and did not join the column till next day.

The Action at Tepe, 25th August

After two long marches on 23rd and 24th August the frontier was crossed on 25th and the enemy was encountered at Tepe, the German customs station on the Benue. Reports had placed a small observation post as being here, but the mounted infantry under Lord Henry Seymour, forming the column's right flank guard, met with strong opposition. Concealed by high grass, corn and thick scrub the Germans allowed the scouts to pass through and around the village, withholding their fire until the head of the advanced guard was within 50 yards. Under this sudden fire the

British fell back slightly, but were reinforced by the rest of the M.I., who had dismounted and carried the line slightly forward on both flanks.

A fire fight then ensued in which Captain T. S. Wickham was shot dead. Seymour, finding it very difficult to observe or control the fire, left Captain J. T. Gibbs to contain the enemy, moved to the more open country on his right with two sections and charged with great dash. Directly his troops were in the midst of the enemy Seymour[1] was severely wounded and shortly after Lieutenant G. L. S. Sherlock and a German officer were killed. The enemy then broke off the fight and retired on Garua, numbering apparently three Europeans and some 50 men.

The British lost four out of six officers killed or wounded, including Captain D. H. Macdonnell, who was in charge of the machine-gun detachment. The men had behaved admirably, but had only two casualties. The German casualties included two Europeans and two natives killed.

Gibbs reporting these casualties to Maclear asked for reinforcements. He was first sent one and a half companies, followed by the whole column, which subsequently established an advanced base at Tepe, to which supplies were brought by river.

On 26th August the advance was continued over a road made very slippery by rain. On 27th the column halted at Saratse to allow the transport to close up. On 28th it camped at Bulungo, four miles west of Garus. Little information had been obtained of the German strength at Garua, but, impressed by Carter's instructions to act with rapidity, Maclear decided to attack next day.

Maclear left Bulungo at 0600 hours 29th August, halting the column under cover of a low ridge, running roughly north and south about three miles west of Garua. As the M.I. on the left flank topped the ridge they came under accurate fire from three guns. Our guns replied, causing some casualties to a group of labourers working on the road short of the position.

Maclear then reconnoitred the position from a commanding point called Observation Hill, at the north end of the ridge. He obtained a good view of an entrenched position without locating the permanent post or native town. He now sent for his artillery and company commanders, pointing out three knolls separated by a few hundred yards on each of which was a detached fort, the centre one being the highest and largest commanding the two others. It may be noted that the permanent post was about half a mile south-east of the southern fort and overlooked the native town.

The country was open and parklike with grass about 2 ft. high. Between Observation Hill and the enemy's position the ground sloped south-west towards the river, while parallel to the position were two flat-topped low ridges about 500 and 1,200 yards from it.

[1] When Lord Henry Seymour was wounded Sergeant Chiroma and Private Awudu Sakadade very gallantly and devotedly remained with him, covering him with their bodies. In this action, too, Lance-Corporal Sanni Zozo and Private Sadieko stood over Lieutenant Sherlock, who was lying wounded within twenty yards of the enemy, and remained there firing until the end of the engagement. Sanni Zozo, though under a hot fire, killed one European and two rank and file. For their conspicuous gallantry on this occasion Sergeant Chiroma and Corporal Sanni Zozo were awarded the D.C.M.

Maclear decided to make a night attack and marched back to camp. That afternoon, accompanied by Major Puckle, 2I.C., Captains G. S. C. Adams and J. T. Gibbs, he proceeded to Observation Hill to make a further inspection of the position. The distance to the northern fort by range-finder was shown to be 4,300 yards. No close reconnaissance was made, probably to avoid disclosing intentions.

The Attack on Garua, 29th–30th August 1914

The plan of attack was to assemble the infantry and guns at Observation Hill at 2200 hours, three companies advancing directly against the northern fort, while the fourth company, all the machine guns and the artillery were to entrench on Observation Hill. The M.I. would take up a position on the right front, opening fire at midnight.

'H' Company 3 Battalion under Adams would lead the attack, while 'C' and 'H' Companies 2 Battalion followed; distances between companies to be 100 yards. 'C' Company with the machine guns arrived late, delaying the start till about 2300 hours. The three attacking companies advanced about 3,000 yards to the position of deployment, formed into line and extended to one pace interval. The further advance, which was to be carried out without a halt, then commenced, but had only proceeded a short distance when the M.I. on the right opened fire according to orders. In a moment all three forts opened a heavy fire and sent up numerous rockets lighting up the line of advance.

As soon as the firing commenced Maclear moved up to the leading line, which he ordered to halt and lie down. Some confusion ensued, but the men of the right section, under Lieutenant Bowyer-Smijth, not hearing the order, continued to advance steadily without firing. Finally with bayonets fixed they dashed up the slope and drove the enemy out of the northern fort, killing a German officer and seven men and capturing a machine gun; as, however, no support was forthcoming Bowyer-Smijth was forced to retire and had finally to withdraw to camp.

In the meantime, unaware of the success of the right section, the progress of the remainder had been very slow. On Maclear's orders halts were made frequently for considerable periods, causing the two companies following in rear to overtake and get mixed up. Eventually part of the force succeeded in occupying the northern fort. Here several officers repeatedly urged Maclear to advance against the centre fort while there was yet darkness to cover the movement, but he decided to rest the men and wait for dawn.

At dawn he sent a verbal message by Sergeant-Major Steed instructing the reserve at Observation Hill and the M.I. to move round by their left to the Demsa road near the captured fort. From this time his troops were subjected to a heavy concentrated fire from rifles, machine guns and guns at about 400 yards range.

Crowded in a confined space of 50 yards diameter, without covering fire to support them, and in too exposed a situation to reply effectively, when 0730 hours the enemy launched a heavy counter-attack with about 20 Europeans and 60 natives, the British troops broke and fled. All efforts of officers and N.C.O.s failed to rally them before they reached camp. The reserve saw what was happening, but was too far away to help.

On arrival in camp the officers found soldiers and carriers much demoralized. Maclear had been killed, the last seen of him was as he was staggering away into the bush. Adams, as senior surviving officer, decided to withdraw to Tepe. This retirement began at 1230 hours, the severely wounded being left behind in the care of Doctors W. A. Trumper and J. Lindsay, to be taken prisoner later by the Germans. Sergeant Salumi Yola here showed conspicuous fortitude; although severely wounded, he marched 40 miles back to Tepe.

Total British casualties were 63, including four officers killed,[1] one mortally wounded and captured and two wounded. The enemy, whose force appeared to have consisted of most of the 7th Company and a section of the 8th Company from Ngaundere, were said to have lost 21, including two Germans.

The result of this unfortunate affair cannot be satisfactorily explained, owing to the death of the commander. According to the surviving officers the native ranks behaved steadily and with courage in the initial stages of their first experience against modern-gun and machine-gun fire. The delay in starting the advance from Observation Hill, which led to the premature opening of fire by the M.I., seems to have led to a series of tactical errors which threw the plan of attack into confusion. When the northern fort was finally occupied, had a bolder course been adopted by an immediate assault on the central fort, the demoralizing effect of the enemy's concentrated fire would have been avoided, while there would have been a fair chance of success.

Lieutenant-Colonel Cunliffe, Assistant Commandant Nigeria Regiment, gave Adams great credit for the way he conducted the retirement.

Sir Frederick Lugard's Return to Nigeria

The Governor-General of Nigeria, Sir F. Lugard, returned from leave in England on 2nd September. The next day he received instructions from the Colonial Office that British troops were to be strictly confined to the frontier, in consequence of the disaster at Garua, and pending the major offensive planned at Duala.

Cunliffe Made Commandant in Place of Carter

On 6th September Carter was recalled to England and Cunliffe was appointed Commandant. He reorganized the Yola column, appointing Major W. I. Webb-Bowen to command it, and placing the Maiduguri column under his control.

Reorganization on German Bornu Front

The disposition of the troops on this front was now as follows: *At Yola:* One section 1 Battery; H.Q. and 'B' Company M.I.; H.Q., 'B', 'C',

[1] Killed: Lieut.-Colonel P. R. Maclear, Major T. N. Puckle, Captain A. C. Aubin, Lieutenant A. H. Stewart. Mortally wounded and captured: Lieutenant H. W. Brown. Wounded: Lieutenants R. Scott-Moncrieff and E. E. Loch.

'G' and 'H' Companies 2 Battalion; 'H' Company 3 Battalion. *At Sava:* 'A' Company M.I.; 'C' Company 1 Battalion. *At Mubi:* In reserve 'B' Company 1 Battalion (moved up from Nafada).

Affair at Takum, 17th September 1914

The news of the reverse at Garua caused considerable unrest among the tribes in the Benue valley, although the Emir of Yola remained our staunch ally. The effect of the reverse lessened substantially, however, when a German attack on the post of Takum was successfully repulsed. Takum, about 70 miles south of Ibi, was held by 57 Nigerian Police under a Political Officer, Lieutenant B. E. M. Waters, R.N. The German force of a company, their No. 3 Reserve Detachment, under Captain Adametz, with three Europeans, crossed the frontier from Kentu, but retreated hurriedly with a number of casualties.

Ikom Column, 10th August–6th September 1914

As stated earlier, Lieutenant-Colonel G. T. Mair, D.S.O., commanding 3 Battalion, was put in command of the Ikom Column, where he arrived on 10th August. His instructions were altered two or three times, but finally directed him to observe the frontier and ascertain all possible roads eastwards. It must be noted that the whole Cross River area was covered with dense forest and information about trans-frontier communications was extremely scanty.

In this area the Cross River was the main tactical feature. The principal German post was at Ossidinge (Mamfe), some 30 miles inside the frontier and about 50 miles south-east of Ikom. The Cross River rises 20 miles south of Ossidinge, thence flowing in a westerly direction to the German customs station at Nsanakang; across the river and a few miles west was our customs post of Obokum. At this point the river makes a wide U-shaped bend to Ikom, but across the arc of the U was a direct road, 17 miles long, from Ikom to Obokum. The Cross River in its upper reaches here is a swift-flowing, wide and unfordable stream.

On 16th August a telegram was received asking for information as to whether there was any movement of enemy troops in progress and in particular whether Ossidinge was occupied. Mair, having received news from Calabar that the Germans were concentrating 500 or 600 troops at Nsanakang, started to make active reconnaissances across the frontier. For this purpose Captain C. R. T. Hopkinson, with 'G' Company, and Captain J. Crookenden with 'A' Company, who had already been sent to Obokum, were directed to ascertain definitely if any German troops were in Nsanakang.

On 17th, under orders from Hopkinson, Crookenden with a detachment of rather more than his company crossed the river at night and occupied Nsanarati, half-way to Nsanakang, without opposition. Next morning an officer's patrol from Nsanarati reconnoitred to Nsanakang, finding no signs of German troops.

That evening Mair received a telegram from Lagos to say there was as yet no question of a general advance. This was communicated to Hop-

[Photo: Topical Press

The N.H.E. Expedition reaches its goal—the border of Southern/Northern Nigeria

[Photo: Topical Press

A Column making camp in a market place

[Photo: Topical Press

S.Y. 'Ivy' entering Lagos Lagoon with Troops

[Photo: Topical Press

The C.O.'s house on Lagos Lagoon

kinson, but gave him permission to make small reconnaissances from Nsanarati.

Late on 21st Mair had a telegram from Carter that two German companies had been reported at Old Ossidinge (west of Ossidinge), and that he was to do all he could to lead the enemy to believe that a main advance towards Ossidinge was to be undertaken. Meantime officers' patrols had reported a German concentration at Nsanakang and that two companies, each about 100 strong, were near Old Ossidinge.

On 22nd Mair instructed Hopkinson to obtain all possible information about the roads from Nsanarati to Nsanakang to create the impression that an advance on that place was imminent. At the same time he gave permission to reinforce Crookenden with another half-company if considered necessary.

British Occupy Nsanakang, 24th August 1914

On 24th Hopkinson reported to Mair that patrols from Nsanarati had been attacked the previous day and that Crookenden with two companies and three machine guns had occupied Nsanakang at 0630 hours at the cost of three wounded. A German detachment of three Europeans and forty men had been driven back to the Munaya River, where they were holding the bridge. Hopkinson himself had taken a detachment and one gun up the Cross River to support Crookenden, but had been heavily fired on and forced to retire.

That evening Mair wrote to Hopkinson that the advance to Nsanakang was scarcely justified by the order to confine his movements to reconnoitring patrols, but pending further instructions from H.Q. its occupation would continue. Mair then paid two visits to Nsanakang on 25th and 26th to investigate the situation there. He ordered Hopkinson to take command of the garrison and made certain redistributions whereby a section of 2 Battery and 'E' and 'G' Companies 3 Battalion were left there intact.

On Mair's return to Ikom he found a reply (to his telegram reporting the occupation of Nsanakang) to the effect that as the main British objective was elsewhere he must do his best to avoid casualties.

Milne-Home's Reconnaissance to Old Ossidinge, 30th August

In pursuance of the policy of carrying out demonstrations towards Old Ossidinge, Lieutenant Milne-Home carried one out on 20th August with one gun, two sections of infantry and a machine gun. The bridge over the Munaya was found destroyed, so the river was crossed by canoes at 0800 hours. On approaching Old Ossidinge a few shells were fired and the machine gun opened on a party of Germans. The return to Nsanakang was made next day without incident.

A few days previously Mair had been told that the Overseas Expeditionary Force for the main attack on Duala would consist of three Nigerian infantry battalions, each of four companies. He would be in command of No. 3 Battalion. On 3rd September he was informed the Battalion would probably embark at Calabar on 15th, and that after its departure, 'B' and 'D' Companies would be responsible for the defence of the frontier near Ikom.

On the evening of the 5th he received a telegram saying his Battalion for overseas was to leave Ikom on 10th September. He at once sent messages to Obokum and Nsanakang that he was coming up that day, 6th September, to superintend the withdrawal which was to be carried out by the morning of the 9th.

The dispositions of Mair's force on 6th September were as follows: *Ikom:* ½ 'B' Company and 'D' Company 3 Battalion; *Ava River junction:* ½ 'F' Company 3 Battalion; *Nsanarati:* ½ 'F' Company 3 Battalion; *Obokum:* 'A' Company 3 Battalion (less one section); *Abia:* One section 'A' Company 3 Battalion; *Abunorok:* ½ 'B' Company 3 Battalion; *Nsanakang:* Section 2 Battery, 'E' and 'G' Companies 3 Battalion and five machine guns.

Affair of Nsanakang, 6th September 1914

In the dense bush on the south bank of the Cross River, to the westward of Nsanakang village, were two small hills, the site of the German customs house and factory. The British position consisted of entrenchments on these two hills, which were 800 yards apart, separated by a creek with a canoe bridge. The westerly hill, called Customs Hill, was the higher and 60 ft. above the river-level, while Factory Hill was 40 ft. lower.

The garrison of Factory Hill was six infantry sections and four machine guns, their trenches faced east, south and south-west. Customs Hill was held by the artillery section, two infantry sections and one machine gun. It had only been possible to clear a field of fire of from 150 to 300 yards round these trenches.

The only communication of the garrison with their base was by the road from Factory Hill, or by the Cross River. The road to Ossidinge led from Factory Hill through Nsanakang village. On these two roads were picquets of six and 12 men, at Nsanakang village and about 600 yards south of Factory Hill respectively.

About 0200 hours on the 6th September, hearing a short sharp burst of fire in the vicinity of Nsanakang village, all British trenches were manned. Some three hours later a heavy rifle and machine-gun fire was opened by the enemy from the surrounding bush, at ranges of 200–300 yards, directed against Customs Hill and the southern trenches of Factory Hill.

The German force was about 500 strong, composed of three companies with six European-manned machine guns. Its first objective seems to have been the high ground west of Customs Hill. On the 5th two of these companies had moved to Eyomodyo, and the third, under Captain Sommerfeld, to the eastern bank of the Munaya River ferry. Sommerfeld's company crossed two miles above the ferry during the night, pushing forward two patrols which overwhelmed the picquet at Nsanakang village at about 0200 hours. The two companies from Eyomodyo appear to have accounted for the picquet on that road without giving it a chance of sending any warning, and by 0500 hours had reached the edge of the cleared ground with their right south of Factory Hill and their left near the bank of the Cross River. From here they gradually moved through the forest to the high ground on their left, whence they enfiladed and took in reverse many of the trenches on Customs Hill, and also, those on Factory Hill at long range.

The British on Customs Hill suffered severely, especially the guns' crews, who were poorly protected by the low parapets required for their guns. By about 0630 hours two successive attempts by the enemy to rush our right on Customs Hill had been repulsed by the section and machine gun under Lieutenant W. G. Yates; and Hopkinson apparently saw an opportunity to counter-attack, but the message he is said to have sent to Factory Hill for reinforcements to carry it out never reached its destination. Owing, too, to the configuration of the ground, Lieutenant A. C. Milne-Home, who was commanding there, could not see how the fight on Customs Hill was going.

The enemy then concentrated the fire of two machine guns on the trenches held by Yates's section, taking them in reverse. By this time all the gun ammunition had been expended—there had been only 30 rounds—rifle and machine-gun ammunition was running short, and many trenches had become untenable. Consequently, soon after 0700 hours Hopkinson gave orders to fall back on Factory Hill; during this movement he himself was killed and Yates was wounded. The enemy at once occupied Customs Hill.

Meanwhile, about 0615 hours Sommerfeld's company had come into action astride the Nasanakang road and engaged Factory Hill, whose garrison, however, easily held its own until Customs Hill was lost. Then surrounded closely on three sides, with most of their trenches under enfilade or reverse machine-gun fire, the British situation became desperate.

Considering further resistance hopeless, Milne-Home issued orders for his force to attempt a breakthrough and gain the shelter of the forest; 62 out of the original 220 succeeded in escaping. Of the rest of the garrison Hopkinson, Lieutenant A. C. Holme and Sergeant J. Dennis with 39 native ranks were killed; Yates and 24 natives were wounded and captured; Lieutenants O. G. Body, A. L. de C. Stretton and R. R. Taylor, and Sergeant J. Mannion and 36 natives were taken prisoner.

The Germans, who captured the two guns and five machine guns, had also lost heavily. It is understood that eight Europeans and 118 native ranks were killed or wounded, including Captain Rammstedt, commanding the force.

Both British and German accounts testify to the courageous behaviour of the Nigerian troops. After their gun ammunition was exhausted the gunners fought with their rifles to the last; the gallant conduct of Sergeant J. Dennis, Royal Artillery, who was in charge of one gun, being specially worthy of mention. He fought his gun to the end, though wounded in both thighs, and was eventually found bayoneted beside it.

At 1330 hours on the day Nsanakang was attacked, 6th September, Mair with 'D' Company 3 Battalion in the sternwheeler *Jackdaw*, and on his way to superintend the withdrawal from Nasnakang, met the *Sandfly* from Obokum with a message from Crookenden. In this he said that hearing heavy firing at an early hour he proceeded in the *Sandfly* to reconnoitre, anchoring some 500 yards below the Nsanakang position. After remaining in observation some time he had come under fire, and having no troops with him, had returned at once to Obokum, learning soon after that Nsanakang had been captured. He also attached a report from the commander of the Nsanarati detachment saying he was evacuating that place and returning to Ikom in the *Hornbill* after picking up the detachment at the Awa River junction.

The *Jackdaw* soon after met the *Hornbill* and both returned to Ikom. Next day Mair marched to Obokum with 'D' Company and reserve ammunition. On arrival there he received a letter from Sommerfeld requesting his presence under a flag of truce in order to discuss establishing a neutral zone for a joint Anglo-British hospital for treating the wounded. Accordingly a four-mile neutral zone was declared around Nsanakang until the cessation of hostilities.

On the 8th September Mair telegraphed to Lagos an account of what had occurred, giving his dispositions: half a company at Abia, one section each at Obokum and opposite Nsanarati, and the remainder of his column at Ikom. The advanced detachments had orders to fall back on Ikom in case of an attack in force. Headquarters replied that any reinforcements required must be found from Calabar.

Mair had never liked the Nsanakang position, as the configuration of the ground made a retirement on Nsanarati very difficult, and there were not sufficient river craft for a retirement by water. The retention of the position, he felt was only justifiable because of his instructions to do all he could to lead the enemy to believe that an advance on Ossidinge was about to be undertaken. On the 3rd September he had arranged with Hopkinson that, in case of attack, the main defence should be concentrated on Customs Hill and that Factory Hill should be abandoned, but on the evening of the 5th, on news of the German approach, Hopkinson decided not to abandon Factory Hill, though pressed to do so by Milne-Home. Milne-Home, at that time a subaltern in 'E' Company 3 Nigeria Regiment gives a graphic description of the Nsankang affair in his diary:

6th Sept. 1914: Firing heard at Nsanakang town, where we had a small post; all of us stayed in the trenches. At 5 a.m. it began and there was continuous war till 7 a.m.

We had just a bare 200 in defence with 10 white men. The Germans 500 and eight Europeans. For the first hour firing was frontal to me and right flank for rifles and machine guns and for the last 40 minutes in reverse. I have never known such hell and pray God I will never see or feel like it again. The men were magnificent.

The key of the position went at about 6.30, but we stuck it for about half an hour during which my sergeant-major, lance-corporal and two men were knocked out in my trench of about 15 rifles. At this point Holme appeared on my right and told me more or less what had happened. He suggested a rush at the village. I agreed, ordering the men to fix bayonets and charge.

This we did; it was a forlorn hope. Holme, Stretton, Colour-Sergeant Byrne and self went off with 20 or 30 men. Holme was shot almost at once.

Several men went down and I had a miraculous escape as a perfect blast of bullets whizzed past me and broke a hole in the roof of the shelter just behind the trench as I left it. One bullet cut a hole in my right sleeve!

I got up towards the village and ran against two German soldiers on the left of the road in the bush. One loosed off and I shot No. 2 with my revolver; missed No. 1 badly, who bolted. Then set out to collect stragglers.

I got about 12 and the Colour-Sergeant. We scouted about getting into a very deep swamp full of undergrowth out of one's depth. In crossing this one man was drowned and one hit in the wrist hanging on to a branch. An unpleasant number of bullets dollopped into the water. However, we got out at last, going to ground to consider the position.

There we spent day and night peering about to locate the German guards. Insects, mosquitoes and rain were awful, for there was no shelter, while we, Colour-Sergeant Byrne and myself, were in alarm kit. Self had trousers tucked into Wellingtons, vest and thin khaki shirt, small forage cap the flaps of which I turned over to keep the sun off. Rations of food and water nil.

At dawn moved to river bank and lay doggo. Picked up two hospital boys. Ration 1 slice of unripe pawpaw with a few drops of Cross River water! Stood by in the evening to knock a canoeman on the head, but none appeared. After dark scoured the bank of the X River up to the Munaya for canoes, but found only one with a hole in it and a log of wood which I thought was one. One of the hospital boys and a soldier said they knew there was one on the opposite bank, so I called for volunteers to swim the river with me and bring it over. One soldier agreed so we started. There was a very swift current and half-way the man funked it, starting to shout. I had a tussle in midstream, almost dragging him out by the hair! The current had in the meantime taken us so far down that we only got into the bank with 200 yards to spare from the German sentries. Behold then the picture of the least of the Homes as the Lord made him, leading a chattering savage about ¼ mile through the bush of West Africa up the bank of the X River about 11 p.m.! Very cold; my feet and most of myself cut to ribbons, being bitten by every bug in creation. Rejoined my squad and went to roost in pouring rain.

8th Sept.: A perfect nightmare, I gave up the river and decided to go on foot to Nsanarati. From 5 to 12 noon was chivvied in pelting rain by German patrols from pillar to post. I had to keep my temper, as one shot would give the show away and I was determined to get out.

By twelve noon I was temporarily fed up, sitting down to think. Considering that they were hunting the bush for us the rather mad idea occurred to me that they would leave the roads alone. I therefore ordered the four remaining men and Colour-Sergeant to throw away all ammunition, keeping only 10 rounds each magazine charged, so that if we ran into a snag we could give the snag ginger leaving a minimum number of rounds to be captured.

Off we went and marched to Nsanarati without seeing a single German! Upon my soul some extraordinary Providence seems to have been about for they had been at Nsanarati the day before and came again next day! I got to Tsouonenyong at 4.30 p.m., on our bank of the river, by canoe.

Here I nearly embraced Bostock (Manchester Regiment), with a section there. Byrne and I nearly finished a bottle of whisky. He, Bostock, was picnicking and had no bed or chop for more than 24 hours. But he played up well, sharing blankets, food and drink. Slept very badly.

9th Sept.: Back to Ikom by 4 p.m., where the Colonel and Salier killed the fatted calf; I have been recuperating ever since, collecting the fragments of 'G' and 'E' Companies into one.

Sixty out of 121 of my Company are killed or missing, and about 10 wounded. About 45 of 'G' have survived out of 100. I have raised about 95 in all and am busy rearming and equipping them. If we get at the Huns again, Heaven help them! Taylor made a great fight of it before being captured, while Sergeant Dennis (Gunner) was killed astride his trail, wounded and firing the last shot full in the face of his attackers.

Milne-Home goes on to say that there were 120 German wounded in hospital, while only 20 of our men. By this he implied that the enemy had killed most of our wounded in the trenches, but this evidence is not borne out from other sources. This was the more unfortunate as, at that stage of the war, neither he nor his officers realized that the trenches they had dug would prove ineffective against machine-gun fire likely to be brought against them.

The Calabar Column, 3rd August–6th September 1914

Early in August Haywood, accompanied by his adjutant, Lieutenant A. E. Beattie, was on tour, visiting his outstations between the Niger and the Cross River, when he received a telegram by runner informing him of the outbreak of war with Germany, and ordering him to proceed to Calabar to take command of a column being concentrated there for an overseas expeditionary force. He arrived there on the 13th August. Between that date and 6th September a number of instructions were received from Lagos by him as to the composition of his column, with the result that the actual units of which it was finally composed were not settled, or concentrated, before the latter date.

Meanwhile, in accordance with his instructions, Haywood made reconnaissances in the area between Calabar and Rio del Rey. On the 29th August, after slight opposition, the German post of Archibong was entered and Rio del Rey, which the Germans had apparently abandoned in some haste, was found evacuated.

On getting news of the Nsanakang disaster on the 8th September at Calabar Haywood left with reinforcements of one section 2 Battery and 'A' and 'D' Companies 4 Battalion for Ikom, arriving by the 10th. Next day information received at Lagos stated that a strong German force was marching on Calabar, probably joined by troops from Ossidinge. Headquarters thereupon issued instructions giving Mair and Haywood a free hand to deal with the situation. Accordingly Haywood left Ikom with the force he had just brought there and returned to Calabar. The alarm, however, proved to be false.

By 6th September 2 Battalion, which Haywood was to command for overseas service with Dobell's Expeditionary Force, was concentrated at

Calabar. It consisted of 'A', 'D', 'E', and 'F' Companies 4 Battalion Nigeria Regiment.

General Dobell's Progress, 31st August–17th September 1914

The transport *Appam*, with General Dobell and some of his staff, left Liverpool on the 31st August. On 7th September her escorting warship was relieved off Las Palmas by H.M.S. *Challenger*.

At Bathurst, on 10th September, the Gambia Company W.A.F.F. was embarked. Here Dobell received reports of the actions of the various Nigerian columns; he also heard that Carter, who was to have commanded the British land contingent of the Expeditionary Force had been recalled to England.

On reaching Sierra Leone on the 12th news of the Nsanakang disaster was received. Here four mountain guns, a detachment Royal Engineers, six companies West African Regiment, various administrative services and 1,275 carriers were taken on board with ammunition, stores and supplies. Colonel E. H. Gorges, Commandant West African Regiment, was appointed to command the British Contingent *vice* Carter.

At Lome, on the 16th, Lieutenant-Colonel R. A. de B. Rose, 'C' and 'E' Companies Sierra Leone Battalion W.A.F.F., one section Gold Coast Battery, the Pioneer Company Gold Coast Regiment and 800 carriers joined the convoy in the transport *Elmina*. Lagos was reached on the morning of the 17th September.

The distribution of the troops in Nigeria on that date was:

For the Overseas Expeditionary Force

Forcados: No. 1 Battalion (called 1 Nigeria Regiment) (O.C. Lieutenant-Colonel J. B. Cockburn), i.e. 'A' and 'F' Companies 1 Battalion and 'D' and 'F' Companies 2 Battalion.

Calabar: No. 2 Battalion (called 2 Nigeria Regiment) (O.C. Lieutenant-Colonel A. H. W. Haywood), i.e. 'A', 'D', 'E' and 'F' Companies 4 Battalion; No. 1 (Battery) (O.C. Captain C. F. S. Maclaverty), i.e. two sections 1 Battery four 2·95 in. Q.F. mountain guns).

For Service on the Eastern Frontier of Nigeria

Maiduguri Column: 'C' Company M.I. and 'A' Company 1 Battalion.

Nafada Detachment (at Mubi): 'B' Company 1 Battalion.

Yola Column: 'H' Company 1 Battalion; 'B', 'C', 'G' and 'H' Companies 2 Battalion; 'H' Company 3 Battalion; 'B' Company M.I.; one section 1 Battery.

Ikom Column: 'A', 'B', 'D', 'E', 'F' and 'G' Companies 3 Battalion; one section 2 Battery.

'E' and 'G' Companies and the artillery section were practically destroyed at Nsanakang.

Calabar: 2 Battery (less one section), i.e. two guns; 'C' Company 3 Battalion and 193 Reservists.

Lagos: 'C' Company 1 Battalion; 'B' Company 4 Battalion (less half company at Abeokuta); Depot 4 Battalion; Reserve section artillery two guns).

Internal Security

Birnin Kebbi: 'D' Company 1 Battalion.
Sokoto: 'E' Company 1 Battalion.
Lokoja: 'G' Company 1 Battalion.
Ogoja, Okwoja, Abakaliki: 'E' Company 2 Battalion.
Udi and Okigwi: 'C' Company 4 Battalion.
Kano: 'A' Company M.I.

SITUATION OF THE FRENCH FORCES ON THE CAMEROON FRONTIER

At this stage it is opportune to give a brief outline of the French dispositions in the area of operations. General Aymerich was the Commander-in-Chief of French Equatorial Africa, with headquarters at Brazzaville in Middle Congo. The other three territories included in his command, starting from the north, were Chad, Ubangi-Shari and Gabon.

Chad. Here the garrison comprised a calvary squadron, two camel companies (i.e. Meharistes), a mountain artillery section, a machine-gun section and the 4 (Chad) Regiment, altogether 220 French and 2,300 natives.

Ubangi-Shari. The 3/3rd Senegalese Tirailleurs of six companies, totalling 90 French and 1,160 natives. But without artillery or machine guns.

Middle Congo. The 2/2nd Senegalese Tirailleurs, with a strength of 115 French and 1,190 natives. A mountain gun, but no machine guns.

Gabon. The 1st (Gabon) Regiment organized in eight companies, but also without artillery or machine-guns, numbering 150 French and 1,370 natives.

Grand total: 575 French and 7,020 natives, which were barely sufficient for internal security.

Moreover, the troops were dispersed in small detachments over an enormous area, devoid of good communications, making any concentration of force for offensive operations a difficult proposition along a frontier of nearly 2,000 miles. In the south-eastern corner of the Middle Congo, however, the Sanga River valley formed a salient which provided a suitable line of advance from Mesaka, at its confluence with the river Congo to Wesso, 200 miles inside the Cameroons. The Sanga being navigable for steamers of 6 ft. draught as far as this point.

French Dispositions, August–September 1914

In Gabon: Libreville, and places on the coast, were put in a state of defence, while a column of three companies was concentrated at Midsik, near the south-western border of the Cameroons, and one at Mvahdi eastward.

Middle Congo: A column of 500–600 rifles had occupied Wesso.

Ubangi-Shari: Lieutenant-Colonel Morrison, advancing from Bangui, had reached the Lobaye River and established posts along its banks as far north as Kolongo. He was then directed to co-operate with the Wesso column with Nola on the Sanga River as their joint objective.

Chad: Colonel Largeau, commanding there, had on 24th–25th August made an abortive attack on Kusseri, situated on the opposite bank of the

Shari River to Fort Lamy (the French fortified post), but captured it on 20th September. He had also arranged for the concentration of 450 rifles and a mountain gun at Fort Lamy by the end of September. Further, as already noted, he had detached Captain Ferrandi with a small escort to co-operate with the Maiduguri Column.

THE CAPTURE OF DUALA

At Lagos, on 17th September, Dobell had a conference with Lugard, at which it was decided that as the Expeditionary Force was now losing 3 Battalion Nigeria Regiment, owing to the situation at Nsanakang, Sir Hugh Clifford should be asked to send two companies of the Gold Coast Regiment to enable a composite battalion to be formed with the two companies of the Sierra Leone Battalion that had joined the Force at Lome. To this Clifford agreed.

Cunliffe to Control Operations in North Cameroons

The control of the operations in Northern Cameroons was discussed. It was arranged that Dobell should assume responsibility for these, but actual command would be vested in Cunliffe. Before leaving Lagos, Dobell issued orders that Mair would take command of all troops on the Cross River, including Calabar, and was to remain on the defensive till he heard the Expeditionary Force had reached the Cameroons. The Yola Column, when joined by the Maiduguri Column, was to attack Garua with all possible strength.

On the 20th Dobell's convoy left Lagos, picking up the transports *Niger* and *Lokoja* carrying 1 Nigeria Regiment at Forcados, and 2 Nigeria Regiment in the transport *Boma* off Calabar. The whole flotilla entered the Cameroon estuary on the 23rd and anchored off Suelaba base.

The Order of Battle of the Allied Expeditionary Force is given in Appendix X.

On the 24th a reconnaissance was carried out on the north bank of the Dibamba River, where the maps showed a small road leading to Duala. An attempt to land a force there next day was a complete failure owing to the mangrove swamp and dense bush which covered the area.

Capture of Duala, 27th September 1914

Dobell had decided to call on the Germans to surrender Duala, failing which it would be bombarded. Early on the 27th the wireless station was blown up by the enemy and a white flag hoisted over Government House. Shortly after a German representative arrived to officially surrender Duala, Bonaberi and a prescribed area surrounding them.

On the 28th September 1 Nigeria Regiment (Lieutenant-Colonel J. B. Cockburn) disembarked at Duala. On the 29th General Dobell established his headquarters at Government House and 2 Nigeria Regiment (Lieutenant-Colonel A. H. W. Haywood) and the Nigerian Battery disembarked at Bonaberi.

On the 30th a reconnaissance of the 2 Nigeria Regiment up the Northern

Railway towards Maka found the Bapele Bridge damaged but passable. An enemy detachment of about 50 men with a machine gun in an armoured truck was strongly entrenched at the far end. Haywood also learnt from native reports that Maka was held by 150 Germans.

FIRST OPERATIONS UP THE NORTHERN RAILWAY: 1ST–10TH OCTOBER 1914

Action at Bapele Bridge, 1st October 1914

Haywood was now reinforced with two companies of the Composite W.A.F.F. Battalion and given orders to attack Maka.

On the 1st October he moved out of Bonaberi with a column consisting of one gun Nigerian Battery, 'D' and 'E' Companies 2 Nigeria Regiment, 'B' Company Gold Coast Regiment, 'E' Company Sierra Leone Battalion, and 470 carriers. He made a personal reconnaissance of Bapele Bridge and posted his gun in a good covered position. Meanwhile, to create a diversion, Captain Sargent with a party of 15 men and a machine gun, 'A' Company 2 Nigeria Regiment, in a launch accompanied by a section in canoes, proceeded up the Bomono creek towards the bridge.

At 1500 hours when the sound of firing against Sargent's party was heard, the gun opened fire at a range of about 1,000 yards. Twenty minutes later the enemy retired. The British troops then advanced, crossed the bridge and entrenched at the northern end, by 1615 hours.

Captain J. P. D. Underwood, commanding 'D' Company 2 Nigeria Regiment, was then sent forward to reconnoitre. He reported that about 1,000 yards short of the town of Maka he could see a white flag displayed. Haywood ordered firing to cease and went forward with Underwood and half his company to take over the town from which two white flags were now flying. When reaching a point some 400 yards away fire was suddenly opened from three sides of the bush and swampy country which completely concealed the enemy. As it was getting dark, Haywood decided to withdraw his troops, who fortunately had suffered only two casualties. The column then bivouacked by the bridge in great discomfort owing to a torrential downpour.

Capture of Maka, 2nd October

Next morning after a bombardment of the enemy's position, the British advanced and occupied the town without further opposition. The Germans —apparently No. 4 (Expeditionary) Company—retired northward. In this area information acquired during the day indicated there was a force of about 50 Europeans and 450 natives around Susa and Mbonjo.

Maka was tactically a strong position, and Dobell approved Haywood's proposal to leave two companies and a gun to hold it, returning with the rest of his column to Bonaberi on the 4th October. On the 3rd there was a patrol encounter six miles north of Maka.

Capture of Susa, 8th October

Headquarters now issued instructions for the attack on Susa with as strong a force as possible. As the General was anxious to secure some rolling stock, a small party of engineers was sent to accompany the column, in order to cut the railway behind the enemy. While another party was to cut it near Kake. This was accomplished on the 8th, but the enemy had already passed northward.

Leaving half a company Composite Battalion at Bonaberi and a company 2 Nigerian Regiment at Maka, Haywood concentrated the Nigerian Battery, three companies 2 Nigeria Regiment and one and a half companies Composite Battalion[1] at Kake on the 7th October. An armoured train was reported to be south of Ndale, so the engineers with an escort were sent out that evening to cut the line north of Ndale. This they successfully did, but the train had unfortunately already retired.

On the 8th October, advancing in two columns, along the railway and by a bush-path west of it, Susa was occupied with practically no opposition. There it was learnt that the Germans, with three armoured trains, two or three guns, and 200 or 300 rifles, had just retired to Kake. Haywood therefore pushed on at once, reaching Kake at 1730 hours, but there was no sign of the enemy, who had evacuated a strongly entrenched position. The column bivouacked for the night at Kake railway station.

Reconnaissances on the 9th showed the country was clear as far as Miang, Muyuka and Mpundu on the Mungo River; Mbonjo had been burnt.

Haywood left 'F' Company and half 'D' Company 2 Nigeria Regiment at Susa, also a small detachment at Maka, returning with the rest of his column to Bonaberi. On the 15th he received a telephone message from Susa saying that German parties were in the vicinity of Kake. He sent half 'D' Company with a machine gun to reinforce Susa. On the 17th the O.C. Susa reported German troops in some strength at Kake, where they had driven out British patrols. On getting a free hand to deal with the situation, Haywood left Bonaberi at 2300 hours with a section of the Nigerian Battery and 'A' and 'E' Companies 2 Nigeria Regiment. Rain and darkness delayed the column, which did not reach Susa till 0800 hours. He pushed forward with a gun and two companies, driving back the enemy from Kake Bridge after a brisk engagement. The Germans, estimated at about a company, retired rapidly down a bush-path west of the railway.

Next morning before daylight Lieutenant E. B. Wesché, with half 'F' Company and a machine gun, was sent to reconnoitre this path with a view to laying an ambush for the enemy's armoured train. The Germans attacked Susa that morning with a force about 300 strong, which included the 4th Company. The attack was made from the north and west, but after about four hours' fighting it was driven back with some loss.

Attack on Susa, 19th October 1914

In the meantime Wesché's detachment emerged on the railway three miles north of Kake station, where they were passed by an empty armoured train going north. His machine gun opened fire on it before his party started to return to camp. This firing evidently betrayed his presence to the enemy at Susa, who laid an ambush about a mile north of Kake. Faced

[1] The two Gold Coast Regiment companies and the two Sierra Leone companies had been made a Composite Battalion under Rose.

here by superior numbers the Nigerians displayed great gallantry, their machine gun being particularly boldly handed by the native in charge. Wesché was killed, a number of casualties occurred, and ammunition gave out. After three gallant bayonet charges the men were forced to scatter. Several hours later Lieutenant K. S. Grove with about half the detachment succeeded in rejoining at Susa. The machine gun was abandoned, but the spare parts were rescued. Total British casualties during the 19th October amounted to 29. German casualties this day were about 50.

OPERATIONS UP THE WURI RIVER TO YABASI: 6TH–16TH OCTOBER 1914

North of Duala a German force of about 60 Europeans and 300 natives was reported to be concentrated on the Wuri River about Yabasi and Nyamtam. In order to widen his area of manoeuvre Dobell decided to assemble a column under Gorges to attack Yabasi. This was to consist of two mountain artillery sections (Sierra Leone and Gold Coast), the West African Regiment, two companies 1 Nigeria Regiment, half the Pioneers and 680 carriers transported by launches with a naval escort. It is not proposed to deal in detail with this operation, as the W.A.F.F. portion was mainly in reserve and the result was a failure. The whole force returned to Duala on the 10th October.

A fresh expedition under Gorges' command was organized and left Duala on the 12th. The military portion this time was composed of 1 Nigeria Regiment, the Composite Battalion, the Nigerian Battery (less one section), the Gold Coast Artillery section and 450 carriers.

Advancing on the 13th, and profiting by previous experience, the bulk of the Composite Battalion was landed at Nsake on both banks of the river. By 1000 hours Rose had two and a half companies on the left bank and one on the right bank. Officers' patrols got within two miles of Yabasi, finding the enemy holding positions on both banks and that there was dense bush on the left bank.

Second Attack on Yabasi, 12th–16th October 1914

That evening Rose's force on the left bank, half a mile north of Nsaka, had been stopped by an impassable creek. Before daybreak on the 14th, therefore, this portion was transferred by launches to the northern side of the creek, and at 0530 hours, covered by the detachments on either bank, the flotilla, in which Gorges had his headquarters, proceeded slowly upstream.

At 0920 hours 1 Nigeria Regiment (less one company), one section of Pioneers, the Nigerian Artillery section and a Naval 12-pounder, landed on the right bank. A section of infantry and the Gold Coast Artillery section were left to guard the flotilla. A reserve of one company 1 Nigeria Regiment, half a company Composite Battalion and the balance of the Pioneer Company were retained in three vessels to reinforce either bank as necessary.

Gorges then issued his orders for the attack. On the left bank Rose was to assault two factories the enemy was said to be holding. The main attack was to be made on the right bank. Cockburn, with the 1 Nigerian Regiment, the Nigerian Artillery and Pioneers, was to make a turning movement to his left and come in from the west on to the heights above Yabasi. His rear and right flank would be protected by the Company Composite Battalion and the naval 12-pounder on a hill near the river.

At 1100 hours the troops on both banks moved forward covered by a 6-in. gun mounted on one of the vessels. Little opposition was encountered and both banks were cleared before dark at a cost of only two men wounded. Ten Germans were taken prisoner by Cockburn's column.

Reconnaissances on the 15th October, accompanied by some skirmishing in the bush, indicated that the enemy was retreating towards Nyamtam. On the 16th, leaving 1 Nigeria Regiment to garrison Yabasi, the remainder of the Force returned to Duala.

OPERATIONS BY THE FRENCH AGAINST YAPOMA BRIDGE AND EDEA: 1ST–26TH OCTOBER 1914

When Duala was captured it was evident that the principal German force had retired along the Eastern Railway, where it was reported to be based on Edea with an advance detachment at Yapoma Bridge on the Dibamba River. Colonel Mayer with his French Contingent was entrusted with operations in this area. By the evening of the 30th September a Senegalese detachment had established itself on the right bank, near the bridge and in touch with the enemy.

Capture of Yapoma Bridge, 6th October

On the 1st and 2nd October the French detachment near Yapoma Bridge was increased to a total of one battery (six mountain guns) and one battalion (2nd Senegalese), also the Sierra Leone Section Royal Engineers. British naval co-operation up the Dibamba River with 12-pounders mounted on river craft was arranged for. By nightfall on the 5th preparation for the attack on the bridge was completed. At 0500 hours on the 6th the French infantry, under cover of French and British gunfire, moving with great coolness and courage, carried the bridge by a frontal attack under a heavy fusillade. The Germans retired slowly, supported by machine-gun fire from an armoured railway truck. French casualties had been surprisingly small, totalling only 14.

Leaving a strong French garrison at Yapoma Bridge, the remainder of the Force was withdrawn to Duala. Meanwhile preparations for a further advance to Edea were put in hand. On the 18th October the G.O.C. issued orders for the operation; at this date his information led him to locate the enemy's total forces as follows.

Enemy's Dispositions, 18th October 1914

(i) *In the north, about Mora, Garua, etc.:*
Four regular companies (Nos. 3, 7, 8 and 12).

(ii) *Southward towards Ossidinge:*
One regular company (No. 2), a reserve detachment (No. 3), and one and three-quarters police companies.

(iii) *Victoria—Buea—Muyuka—Yabasi area:*

A European detachment, two regular companies (Nos. 1 and 4), and two police companies.

(iv) *On the railway east of Yapoma:*

A reserve detachment (No. 2) and a section of a police company.

(v) *At Edea:*

Military headquarters and police company with a detachment at Lobetal on the Sanaga River.

(vi) *At Yaunde:*

Government Headquarters, a police company and recruits.

(vii) *In the Kribi-Lolodorf-Ebolowa area:*

A reserve detachment (No. 4) and two police companies.

(viii) *Engaged with the French in South and South-East Cameroons:*

Five regular companies (Nos. 4, 6, 9, 10 and 11), a reserve detachment (No. 1) and a police company.

Plan for the Advance on Edea, and Operations there, 20th–26th October 1914

The enemy was evidently prepared for an allied advance on Edea by the railway, or by the Sanaga River, but not for one by the Nyong River, which was deemed unnavigable. Our naval reconnaissance, however, showed that it would be possible to reach Dehane, some 30 miles from the mouth and about the same distance south of Edea, subject to careful navigation at high water for three miles in the lower reaches.

The G.O.C. decided, after discussion with Captain Fuller, the Senior Naval Officer, to send the main column of the attacking force by sea from Duala, to move up the Nyong River, disembarking at Dehane, while two simultaneous advances would divert the enemy's attention along the railway and up the Sanaga River respectively.

Colonel Mayer, of the French Contingent, was to command the main column, totalling about 1,000 rifles (all French except for one and a half companies West African Regiment) and two French artillery sections. Commandant Mathieu, with two companies Senegalese Tirailleurs and a small West African Regiment detachment, with a French artillery and machine-gun section, was to command the railway column, while the naval flotilla for the Sanaga River would have a small West African Regiment escort and some naval guns.

As this operation was one in which no W.A.F.F. troops were engaged, it is not proposed to describe it in further detail. Suffice it to say that after a good deal of opposition met with by all three forces Edea was finally captured on the 26th October by the main column with comparatively light casualties. It appeared that the landing of Mayer's column from Dehane took the enemy by surprise, as no landing up the Nyong River had been expected.

Mayer with his French Contingent was detailed to hold Edea, the main enemy force having retreated towards Eseka on the railway. The remainder of the Allied force was withdrawn to Duala. Since landing at Duala the total casualties had amounted to 23 deaths from disease and 170 killed and wounded. (There is some doubt about the accuracy of these figures.)

OPERATIONS FOR CLEARING THE FLANKS SOUTH OF EDEA AND WEST OF THE NORTHERN RAILWAY: NOVEMBER 1914

(A) *South of Edea, 20th November–2nd December 1914*

By this date the French Sanaga Column had captured Wesso, and the Oyem Column was advancing on that place from Midsik.

With a view to extending his hold on the Nyong valley and towards Kribi, where he would be better able to co-operate with the French Oyem Column, the G.O.C., in conjunction with Mayer at Edea, planned a Franco-British (Naval) expedition for the purpose.

Owing, however, to serious losses incurred in a heavy engagement with the enemy just north of Dehane, it was decided to abandon any further operations other than the occupation of Kribi, which was effected by a French detachment under Commandant Mathieu on the 2nd December. Subsequent events seem to show that the Germans, encouraged by the abandonment of this attempt, greatly increased their activity in this area and sent forces there to cover their communications with Spanish Muni.

(B) *Buea and West of the Northern Railway, 1st–15th November 1914*

At this time, in the area under consideration, the dispositions of the enemy were as follows:

On the Northern Railway, opposing Haywood, who held Susa with three companies 2 Nigeria Regiment and an advanced detachment at Kake Bridge, was a force of about 60 Europeans and 400 natives, with several machine guns and an armoured train.

Guarding the approaches to Buea, with outposts at Victoria, Tiko and Mpundu, was a force of about 50 Europeans and 300 natives, with five or six machine guns.

The object of the operations here was to attempt to encircle the German force in the Buea area. The General's plan was to use Naval forces for a demonstration against Bibundi, on the west side of the Cameroon Mountain, combined with the occupation of Victoria. At the same time an attack was to be made on Buea by two columns of troops advancing via Tiko, and Mpundu. A third column was to advance up the Northern Railway from Susa to Muyuka, with the aim of cutting off any retreat.

Preliminary to these operations Haywood was instructed to carry out a reconnaissance along both banks of the Mungo River as far as Mpundu. Headquarters and two companies Composite Battalion were to reinforce him on the 4th November. At the time there was a company 2 Nigeria Regiment at Mbonjo.[1] Haywood therefore directed Rose to carry out the

[1] *Gallant conduct of Company Sergeant-Major Belo Akure, 4th November 1914.*
Company Sergeant-Major Belo Akure, 'A' Company 2 N.R., had before the outbreak of war, been awarded the W.A.F.F. D.C.M. for bravery in the field, when bugler to Major Trenchard, who was at the time commanding a column in operations in the

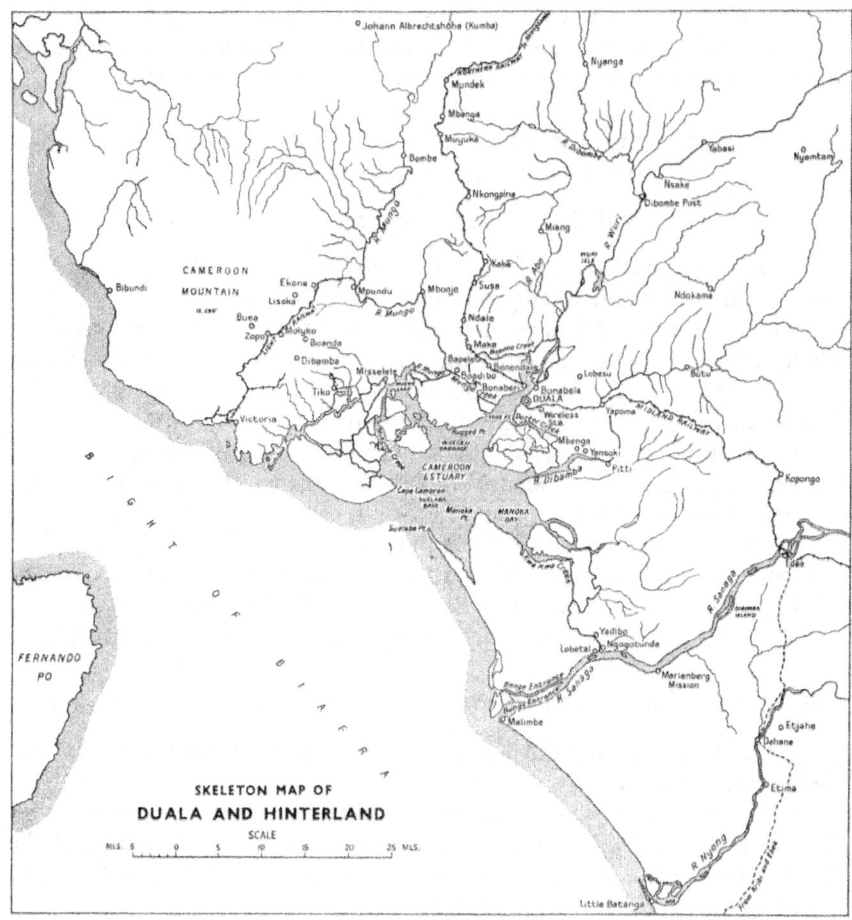

8. Duala and Hinterland

reconnaissance with this company and one of the Composite Battalion, while he himself made a reconnaissance in force towards Muyuka, between the 5th and 8th November. Both reconnaissances were successfully carried out, without serious opposition. Rose found the path to Mpundu practicable and estimated the German detachment there about 100 strong. One

Cross River area in which the Southern Nigeria Regiment was engaged. On this occasion he received a clasp to his D.C.M. with the following citation:

'On the Mungo River on the 4th November 1914, his behaviour was particularly cool and courageous. He received orders to conduct the retirement of an advanced post which was being heavily attacked. The post was separated from the main body by an unfordable river 35 yards in width. Sergeant-Major Belo Akure got his men into the only available canoe, and, finding it would founder if he entered it himself, with great self-devotion he lay on the bank and covered its retirment, being all the time submitted to a heavy fire, one bullet penetrating his sleeve. When the canoe reached the farther bank he ordered the men into their trenches and swam the river to join them.' Later in the campaign he was commended for his coolness and sound judgment in the attack on Fongdonera. After yet another display of coolness and gallantry the G.O.C. told Haywood the next time this N.C.O.'s conduct in action was brought to favourable notice he would be recommended for the Victoria Cross.

of his patrols had the unusual experience of being scattered by an elephant, of which there were a number in the district.

In the case of the Muyuka reconnaissance a detachment of about a company was driven out of the railway station in an armoured train. The main force here was located in an entrenched position on a hill some 1,500 yards to the north-west of Muyuka.

Gorges was the overall commander of the military operations and personally commanded the Tiko Column, which consisted of two Naval 12-pounders, the Nigerian Battery 1 Nigeria Regiment, half the Pioneer Company and one company of Senegalese Tirailleurs, numbering 70 Europeans, 1,077 natives and 1,015 carriers. (Yabasi had been evacuated, owing to the fall of water in the Wuri River, thus enabling the 1 Nigeria Regiment to complete the strength of this column.)

The Mpundu Column, commanded by Rose, consisted of the Composite Battalion, Gold Coast Artillery and half the Pioneer Company, with 550 carriers; it concentrated at Mbonjo on the 11th November. Here it was joined next day by a flotilla under Lieutenant-Commander Sneyd, R.N., which had successfully negotiated the Mungo River, overcoming considerable navigational difficulties.

Haywood's Northern Railway Column consisted of 2 Nigeria Regiment, a section of the Sierra Leone Battery, Royal Engineers and Telegraph details, the garrisons of Susa and Bonaberi having been taken over by the West African Regiment to relieve the 2 Nigeria Regiment.

The demonstration at Bibundi, and the attacks on Victoria, Tiko, Mpundu and Muyuka were to take place simultaneously on the 13th November.

At Bibundi the *Dwarf*, with the transport *Boma*, pretending to put ashore a number of Krooboys, succeeded in making the enemy believe that a considerable force had actually been landed. Off Victoria on the same day the *Ivy*, with some small vessels and the transport *Niemen*, carrying a company of Marines, attended by the French cruiser *Bruix* to cover the landing, arrived at an early hour. The German commander refused a summons to surrender, so under cover of a short bombardment, the Marines landed well to the west of the town, occupying it after a slight resistance about 1130 hours.

For the attack on Tiko Gorges' column and a flotilla of small steamers under the command of Captain Beatty-Pownall, arrived at dawn and covered the landing force from the 6-in. guns of the Dreadnought, enabling it to disembark and bivouac for the night at Tiko.

Rose's column, supported by fire from Sneyd's flotilla, advanced along both banks of the Mungo River, forced the enemy to evacuate a strong position on the right bank resulting in the occupation of Mpundu, by 1130 hours. Leaving a half-company to guard stores there, Rose pushed on for three miles before bivouacking for the night; his advance being hampered by the nature of the country and slight opposition.

Haywood's column occupied Muyuka with slight opposition at the cost of only two casualties. Reconnoitring patrols located the main enemy forces entrenched still 1,500 yards north-west of the station, and learnt that there were reserves of unknown strength at Mbanga and Mundek.

14th November

On this day Gorges advanced towards Buea by the main road with a right flank guard of a company and two guns, through Dibamba. At this place about 0930 hours his advanced guard met with opposition which was overcome with vigour and dash supported by the fire of a section of mountain guns. It proceeded to carry a series of entrenchments held by about 50 rifles with four Europeans, of whom the latter were eventually captured. About 1530 hours the men began to show signs of fatigue after nine hours of ascent through dense forest against opposition. Gorges therefore called in his flank guard, which had reached Boanda with slight opposition, and bivouacked for the night near Molyko.

Rose's column reached Ekona the same day, having been lightly opposed by some 30 rifles with one or two Europeans, but being hampered mainly by the intricate light railways which intersected the numerous plantations. Nine Germans surrendered to his column at Ekona. He detached a small party to hold Lisoka.

Haywood's column occupied the strong position north-west of Muyuka which was surprisingly evacuated during the night of 13th–14th. This was fortunate, as its capture would have been no easy matter.

Capture of Buea, 15th November 1914

Gorges entered Buea at 1345 hours unopposed, where the German District Commissioner handed over the keys of Government House. On the 16th Rose joined Gorges at Buea, having left a detachment of 50 men with a machine gun under Lieutenant J. E. P. Butler at Lisoka to try and capture some enemy parties reported sheltering in the district.

An episode near Lisoka next day deserves special mention. Butler, with Dr. D'Amico and a party of 13 soldiers, surprised the rear guard of a German detachment some 50 strong with a machine gun, causing it to retreat hurriedly, abandoning stores and ammunition. Following the enemy up so rapidly that about half his party got left behind, Butler suddenly came under fire of the machine gun at 30 yards' range. He, however, was not to be denied, and with D'Amico, taking cover on either side of the path, shouting 'Fix bayonets and charge', caused the enemy to retire again, with the loss of three Germans killed.

In the meantime Haywood's column reconnoitred north and west of Muyuka on the 15th and 16th with two companies and a gun, occupying Bombe on the Mungo River after a slight skirmish.

During the next few days parties from here and Buea searched the intervening country, bringing in a number of prisoners. The total killed, wounded and captured in the whole operations amounted to about 1,200, including 68 European women.

Communications with Buea, Muyuka and Mpundu were quickly established by telephone, and thence via Susa with Duala. Traffic on the light railway from Victoria to Zopo was restored by the 18th. This well-laid line ascended to an altitude of nearly 3,000 ft. from sea-level and covered the whole plantation area. Most of the rolling stock was undamaged.

The sojourn at Buea was welcomed by the troops. The atmosphere was cool and pleasant. Fresh milk, butter and good meat were available; also European vegetables and fruit. The natives here had been well treated, in contrast to the severity shown them round Duala and elsewhere.

At the end of November, Dobell, accompanied by Lugard, who had arrived on a short visit to Duala, spent a short while at Buea, with a view to investigating German complaints of their women being harshly treated. These allegations were proved to be without foundation, however, many of the German ladies expressing gratitude for their treatment in the strongest terms.

FINAL OPERATIONS UP THE NORTHERN RAILWAY AND THE ADVANCE TO CHANG: 3RD DECEMBER 1914 TO 12TH JANUARY 1915

The G.O.C.'s intention now was to clear the Northern Railway, thereby facilitating co-operation with the Cross River Column based on Ikom under Mair, which would advance via Ossidinge from the west.

The operation was put under the command of Gorges. The striking force concentrated at Muyuka on the 2nd December. It was composed of a Naval 12-pounder from the *Challenger* and two machine guns manned by seamen; the Nigerian Battery, a section Gold Coast Artillery, Field Section Royal Engineers, 1 Nigeria Regiment, 2 Nigeria Regiment, and half the Pioneer Company, with administrative details. The Line of Communication Troops, from Bonaberi inclusive, consisted of two companies Composite Battalion, one company West African Regiment, and one gun Sierra Leone Battery. The train service was reinforced by another engine from French Guinea.

To cover a possible attack from the south-east and protect Gorges's right flank a detachment West African Regiment was sent via the Wuri River up its tributary the Dibombe in two armed motor-launches, to Nyanga from which the enemy had been driven.

Gorges's instructions were to advance along the railway with all speed to railhead, attacking the enemy wherever found, and endeavouring to gain communication with Mair. Little information was available about the enemy, other than that he intended to fight at Lum and to blow up the Nlohe Bridge.

The main column advanced by the railway, while two small parties covered the left flank, one on each bank of the Mungo River; on the west bank, 'E' Company 2 Nigeria Regiment, a section Pioneers and a Gold Coast gun, under Captain C. Gibb; on the east bank a company 2 Nigeria Regiment and a section Pioneers under Lieutenant R. H. Poyntz.

3rd–4th December

The Mungo River and Nyanga detachment advanced without special incident, while the main column camped at Penja station.

5th December

A company 1 Nigeria Regiment, moving by a path east of the railway, tried to surprise an armoured train reported at Lum station. After five

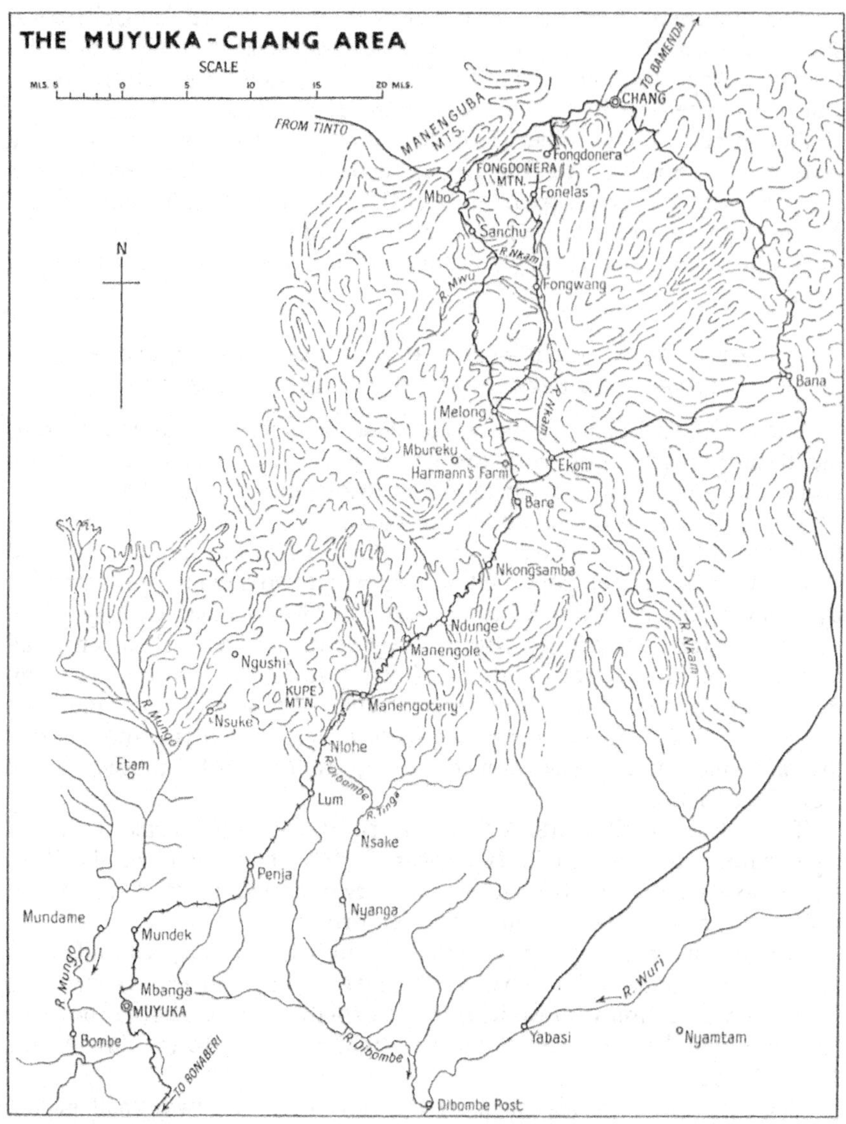

9. The Muyuka-Chang Area

hours' march through dense bush an enemy detachment was dispersed, but the train escaped. At 1030 hours the main column bivouacked at Lum; at midday a company 1 Nigeria Regiment under Captain J. W. Chamley, with a party of Royal Engineers under Lieutenant H. H. Schneider, was sent to reconnoitre the Nlohe Bridge over the Dibombe River; the river appeared unfordable and the bridge was found destroyed. In the course of his reconnaissance Chamley's company fell into an ambush, which had been skilfully covered by machine guns on the farther bank of the river. By good leadership Chamley extricated his men with the loss of two killed, including Schneider, and nine wounded, including Lieutenant C.

Luxford. He was reinforced by a second company 1 Nigeria Regiment and bivouacked for the night without being followed up by the enemy. On the Mungo River only slight opposition was encountered, the detachment reaching Etam and Nauke respectively. The Nyanga party moved up to Nsake.

6th–9th December 1914

During this period the main column crossed the Dibombe by temporary bridges below Nlohe, reaching Manengole after a trying and very hot march, hampered nearly all the way by snipers, having derailed a dynamite-filled truck and exploded it before it could do any damage. The retiring Germans had left behind rolling stock and telephone equipment, which seemed to indicate they were getting demoralized. Meanwhile the Nyanga party had fulfilled its mission on reaching the junction of the Tinga and Dibombe Rivers, and the Mungo River detachments had united under Gibb at Ngushi, proceeding over difficult country in the Kupe Mountain to within four miles of the railway, near Ndunge. At this place, while the camp was being entrenched on the 9th, the enemy opened fire from the surrounding hills, but was soon dispersed by gunfire.

10th December

On this day the column met slight opposition; its advance was however assisted by Gibb's left-flank column, and about 1030 hours a German officer came in under a white flag with a message from Lieutenant von Englebrechten surrendering Nkongsamba and the surrounding country as far as, and including, Bare. Gorges then occupied Nkongsamba, where he was joined by Gibb's column. A quantity of rolling stock and stores were found here. Twenty-three Germans fell into our hands. The Nlohe Bridge was soon repaired and a train service to Bonaberi was opened by the 3rd January.

Occupation of Bare, 11th December 1914

On the 11th December Gorges, taking with him one section Nigerian Battery 2 Nigerian Regiment and a party of Royal Engineers, entered Bare. Here about 40 Germans fell into our hands, also many stores and two aeroplanes—the first to reach West Africa, though as yet unpacked.

Bare was the headquarters of a German District. It lay in open country in a healthy position on a hill, and north of the forest-covered tropical belt. It is within two days' march of the central plateau towards which the hills rise steeply with their summits often enveloped in mists and enjoying a cool breeze except during the midday hours.

Owing to the light opposition offered the total British casualties had been less than 20. But, although there had been little fighting, the nine days' advance had entailed much exhausting work inseparable from the 'blind' operations due to the forest.

Congratulating him on the way the advance had been carried out, the G.O.C. instructed Gorges to pursue the enemy northward vigorously when in a position to do so. Mair was informed of these orders, being told to co-operate as far as possible.

Meantime it was necessary to collect supplies, a slow business owing to the break at Nlohe Bridge. Gorges thereupon occupied Melong, a road junction 14 miles north of Nkongsamba, establishing supply depots there and at Bare, and making defended posts at all three places.

Advance on Chang, 25th December 1914

By the 25th December Gorges had filled up his depots with supplies and concentrated sufficient carriers for his advance on Bare. His main column moved up the Nkam valley, while a left-flank column under Haywood, composed of two and a half companies 2 Nigeria Regiment and a section of the Gold Coast Battery, advanced up the alternative and much steeper road, leading between rugged and thickly wooded heights, via Mbo Fort to Chang. Both columns were to reunite at the road junction some seven miles south-west of Chang.

26th December

After some skirmishing through thick grass the main column bivouacked for the night near Fongwang. On the left flank Haywood's column had met with serious opposition, but had driven the enemy back at a cost to the British of 12 casualties, including Colour-Sergeant J. J. Winter, 2 Nigeria Regiment, killed. On the right flank Lieutenant J. E. P. Butler of the Gold Coast Pioneer Company, who had been sent out with a patrol to disperse a hostile detachment which had been harassing the main column on the previous day, returned, having successfully accomplished his task. Two of his men had been wounded and he himself by his coolness and gallantry in swimming an unfordable river under fire, single-handed, here performed another of the feats which gained him the Victoria Cross. He was later to be killed in East Africa.

27th–31st December

During this period the enemy was forced out of a series of entrenched positions by both columns[1] without severe opposition, but the country was steep and often heavily wooded, entailing arduous scouting and the picqueting of innumerable hills. Road repairs and damaged telephone lines (caused by elephants) caused further delays. On 1st January Gorges reached the road junction just south of Chang, where he was joined by Haywood early on the 2nd, the latter having occupied Mbo Fort without opposition the previous day.

Capture of Chang, 2nd January 1915

Gorges decided to push on to Chang at once. The road lay up a narrow valley, though the country was more open than it had been hitherto. On approaching Chang the column was fired on from neighbouring hills, but after a few rounds had been fired from the Naval 12-pounder and the Nigerian guns, a white flag was hoisted on the fort. In spite of this, how-

[1] While skilfully handling his vanguard at one of these Lieutenant D. H. S. O'Brien, 1 N.R., was severely wounded.

ever, intermittent firing by the enemy continued until the town was occupied by 1700 hours.

The sudden evacuation of Chang was most unexpected. The enemy had apparently been surprised by the skill with which Gorges had overcome the physical difficulties of the advance.

Dobell had urged on Gorges the necessity of withdrawing to Bare as speedily as possible after destroying the fort. The G.O.C. felt some anxiety for his long line of communications and shortage of reserves. Cockburn was therefore despatched with a column to disperse the enemy, who was retiring towards Bamenda; he returned to Chang on the 5th. On the 6th Haywood with 2 Nigeria Regiment and a section of the Nigerian Battery moved south, escorting sick and prisoners. Next day the whole force withdrew unmolested, arriving at Nkongsamba on the 10th.

1 Nigeria Regiment was left to garrison Bare and Nkongsamba, 2 Nigeria Regiment held the line of communications down the railway to Bonaberi inclusive, while the rest of the Force withdrew to Duala.

Operations of the Cross River and Ibi Columns, December 1914–January 1915

During this period, and with a view to co-ordinating operations with the advance of Gorges's column up the Northern Railway and to Chang, forward movements were made by Mair's Cross River Column (*a*) and Mann's Ibi Column (*b*).

(*a*) *Cross River Column*

On the 25th December Mair crossed the frontier with the object of first occupying Ossidinge. He marched south via Araru, crossing the Munaya River on the 27th, bivouacking there till the 28th, when he was joined by Major J. Fane with the supply column. On the 29th the whole column moved north towards Ajunde, 'B' Company 4 Battalion Nigeria Regiment driving back an enemy party across the Bakori River, where the far bank was held by about a company of Germans with two machine guns. Supported by fire from the main body, the advanced guard made good the crossing and enabled the rest of the column to follow unmolested. Our casualties numbered six and the enemy's were about the same.

Continuing his advance against lessening opposition, Mair reached Ossidinge on the 1st January 1915, finding it unoccupied. He now changed his line of communications to the main road via Nsanarati, ordering the Obokum and Nkami garrisons to join him. Leaving a small garrison at Ossidinge, he occupied Tinto without further opposition on the 8th January. On the 12th the G.O.C. instructed him to withdraw to Ossidinge, Chang having been captured and the fort destroyed.

(*b*) *Ibi Column*

Mann's headquarters were at Takum, whence he had been actively patrolling the frontier of the Muri Province during December and January. It had been intended that he should seize Kentu and gain touch with Mair in the Tinto area, but supply and transport difficulties caused the idea to be abandoned.

GERMAN OFFENSIVE IN THE EDEA/KRIBI AREA: DECEMBER–JANUARY 1915

The German forces in the Edea area, within a radius of 40 miles of Edea, were estimated at about 800 rifles and eight machine guns. Learning of the despatch of a large number of allied troops up the Northern Railway, the enemy concluded that the Edea garrison had been greatly depleted to assist the movement, thereby creating a favourable opportunity for a counterstroke in the Edea area. Between the 2nd and 4th January two consecutive attacks were made on Kribi, but both were easily repulsed.

On the 5th January both Kopongo and Edea were heavily attacked. The attack on Kopongo lasted from 0445 to 1730 hours, but was defeated with a loss to the garrison of 10 men and double that number to the enemy. Edea was a scattered area to defend; inequalities of the ground and the close proximity of the forest made this no easy matter. However, Colonel Mayer showed great skill in laying out his line of defence and the enemy's attack was defeated with heavy losses to himself. The German onslaught was carried out with great determination from 0515 to 0830 hours, but was everywhere repulsed with a loss of 20 Europeans and about 80 natives killed, while quantities of arms and equipment were captured. The French had displayed great courage and tenacity; their total losses were 15.

The defeat had been the heaviest the Allies had yet been able to inflict and was a matter of great satisfaction to the G.O.C. The Germans on the other hand, claimed that the attack, though tactically defeated, had gained its object strategically by causing the Allies to abandon Chang, the key to the Central Plateau of Ngaundere.

GENERAL SITUATION: JANUARY 1915

The general situation towards the end of January 1915 was:

Northern Cameroons

The French had captured Kusseri during September, but failed to prevent Lieutenant Kallmeyer with about half the garrison from escaping to reinforce the Mora garrison under von Crailsheim.

Investment of Mora

Lieutenant-Colonel Brisset, who had assumed command of the Allied forces on the Benue, decided after a further attempt to capture Mora, that the place was impregnable and the only course open to him was to invest it closely. Captain R. W. Fox was therefore left to undertake the task with his Maiduguri column.

Brisset then marched south, joining Webb-Bowen's Yola Column for an advance on Garua. The German defences had by this time been made very strong. To hold them they had a garrison of 40 Europeans, 537 natives, four guns and 10 machine guns. Brisset could see little chance of capturing the position by a speedy assault. He decided to keep it under close observation.

He established the French Contingent, consisting of a cavalry squadron, two guns and three companies of infantry at Nassarao, while Webb-Bowen's force of 'B' Company M.I., a section 1 Battery 'H' Company 1 Nigeria Regiment, 'B' Company 2 Nigeria Regiment, and 'H' Company 3 Nigeria Regiment occupied the entrenched camp at Bogole, south of Nassarao and the Benue River. The French had the duty of watching the approaches northwards towards Mora, while the British observed those between Garua and Ngaundere. Further steps were now taken to ensure better control over the operations in the Northern Cameroons, by delegating the command there to Cunliffe entirely and sending Major W. D. Wright from the staff of the British Contingent at Duala to assist Cunliffe, who was now a brigadier-general. A Naval 12-pounder gun detachment under Lieutenant Hamilton, R.N., was sent with Wright to strengthen the forces in the Northern Cameroons.

Ibi Column

The Germans had various small posts in the Kentu area. Mann with two and a half companies and a gun based on Takum was watching the frontier here.

Cross River Column

This consisted of six companies of infantry ('A', 'C', 'E', 'F' and 'G' 3 Battalion, and 'B' 4 Battalion) and one section 2 Battery Nigeria Regiment. The two latter companies left for Yola shortly after; at the same time Crookendan relieved Mair, who was invalided to the United Kingdom. This column was at Ossidinge, holding in check some 300 Germans in the Tinto area.

Bare and Railway, including Buea area

The German force dispersed from Chang, and probably based on Bamenda, was estimated to be about 300 strong. At Bare and Nkongsamba, Cockburn had the Nigerian Battery and 1 Nigeria Regiment. On the railway to Bonaberi Haywood had the 2 Nigeria Regiment; Rose's Composite Battalion was in and about Buea; also the Gold Coast Artillery.

Duala

G.H.Q., H.Q. British Contingent and the West African Regiment with the Sierra Leone Artillery were at Duala.

Kribi Edea Area

The whole of the French Contingent under Mayer was facing some 600 enemy rifles based on Yaunde, with posts at Eseka and southward towards Kribi.

AYMERICH'S FORCES IN EASTERN AND SOUTHERN CAMEROONS

About this time the Council of Defence of French Equatorial Africa had decided that, pending co-operation with Dobell's Force, Aymerich's objective should be limited to the line Oyem, Akoafim, Lomie, Dume. It was not considered safe to advance beyond this line owing to the strain on Aymerich's extended line of communications.

Lobaye Column

Morisson's Lobaye Column was opposed by the 5th and 6th Companies; he had by this date advanced as far east as Bertua-Nyassi, but had been obliged by heavy pressure to withdraw to the Kadei River; his column was about 1,000 strong, but his line of communications absorbed a large part of his strength.

Sanga Column

Lieutenant-Colonel Hutin was commanding here. He had detachments at Sembe, Molundu, Ngoila and Yukaduma, comprising about 1,000 rifles and five mountain guns. The 9th and 1st Reserve Companies had been opposing him. There had been some severe fighting on the Ja River before Hutin finally occupied Molundu with the help of 225 Belgian reinforcements.

Nvahdi Column

This column had taken a long time to concentrate owing to the distances to be covered. It had, however, got as far as Minkebe, where heavy rains made a further advance impossibe. Le Meillour was the commander. He had about 250 rifles and had met with no opposition.

Oyem Column

This column had been split up into small detachments before Major Miquelard took command. The German 10th, 11th and No. 1 Reserve Companies had been actively engaged in driving them back from German Muni across the frontier into Gabon. Miquelard with 680 rifles now concentrated his column and succeeded in repulsing the enemy and finally occupying Oyem.

From the foregoing it will be seen that the various Allied columns, with a total strength of about double their adversaries, were operating over a vast area and were widely separated from one another by large tracts of difficult and frequently roadless country. Co-ordination of their movements was precluded by poor communications. Supply and transport difficulties limited the extent of any advance, and the nature of the country necessitated the maintenance of strong garrisons to ensure the retention of important positions gained. Reliable intelligence was difficult to obtain, owing to the severity with which natives were punished for giving information. Moreover, the enemy's guerilla tactics and his knowledge of the country enabled him to cope successfully with the Allies' superior numbers while escaping severe losses.

A dominant factor was his superiority in machine guns—these were lighter and of better type than our own, and were especially useful in the close country where so many of our engagements took place, while for the same reason the Allies were seldom able to use their mountain guns effectively. The dense nature of the terrain, too, made arduous turning movements often necessary, as well as exhausting to our troops; all of which had a serious effect on the health of officers and men.

The G.O.C. had more than once asked for reinforcements on account of the serious toll taken by casualties and sickness in the Expeditionary Force. Towards the end of January two companies of the Gold Coast Regiment, four companies of the Sierra Leone Battalion and half the Gambia Company arrived. The companies forming the Composite Battalion were then transferred to their own separate units and the Composite Battalion ceased to exist.

GERMAN ACTIVITY NORTH OF NKONGSAMBA: AFFAIRS OF MBUREKU AND HARMANN'S FARM: FEBRUARY–MARCH 1915

At the beginning of February parties of the enemy were showing great activity in the region north of the railway. Reports indicated that their forces were encamped along the line of Mbureku-Harmann's Farm-Ekom, with headquarters at Melong. It seemed they were collecting supplies and carriers. Their strength was computed as about 50 Europeans and 500 natives, with four machine guns.

British Attack with Two Columns, 3rd February 1915

To clear up the situation and free the railway posts from raids, Cockburn issued orders on the 2nd February for an offensive against the enemy's main force. His plan was to carry out simultaneous attacks next morning by a column from Nkongsamba on Mbureku, and another column from Bare on Harmann's Farm.

The first column, commanded by Cockburn, composed of a section Nigerian Artillery and 400 rifles 1 Nigeria Regiment, marched by moonlight, hoping to be within striking distance of Mbureku by daybreak on the 3rd February. About 0330 hours, supposing he was some four miles south of the enemy's position, Cockburn was on the point of halting to rest his men, when a rifle shot rang out killing the leading man of the 'point'. A concentrated fire from three machine guns and rifles caught the British front and left flank at close range from the enemy's main position.

For a short while there was confusion in the column, much enhanced by carriers dropping their loads and stampeding through the ranks to the rear. High grass and hilly country added to the British difficulties. But the officers, under Cockburn's resolute leadership, rose well to the occasion and quickly rallied their men. At this critical stage many distinguished themselves, but Cockburn gives special praise to Captain A. H. Giles, commanding the advanced guard, also to Sergeant-Major Shearing, whom he sent up with a machine gun to reinforce the advanced guard.

Casualties at Mbureku

As day broke the enemy abandoned his position, in which was found a quantity of dynamite, ammunition and equipment. He left 11 dead behind. On the other hand, the British were in no condition to pursue; their casualties totalled 65, including Colour-Sergeant H. R. G. Hooker killed.

While the column was in process of reorganizing heavy firing was heard from Harmann's Farm direction. Cockburn decided to march there by the quickest route, via Bare, where he arrived at 1815 hours, having detached a company to escort the wounded back to Nkongsamba.

Capture of Harmann's Farm by the Sierra Leone Battalion

Lieutenant-Colonel G. P. Newstead, O.C. Sierra Leone Battalion had moved out from Bare with three and a quarter companies and one sub-section Nigerian Artillery at 0600 hours on the 3rd February. He had three days previously reconnoitred Harmann's Farm, where he found the enemy entrenched, and in unexpected strength, behind a field of fire cleared for 600 yards. Newstead's troops advanced under cover of the fire of his mountain gun and captured the position by 0930 hours with little loss.

Germans Counter-attack on Harmann's Farm

An hour later the enemy, reinforced from Melong, launched a vigorous counter-attack supported by the fire of two or three machine guns. This attack was met by the Sierra Leone men with steadiness and courage, but they were in an exposed situation and had no machine guns. Consequently, after suffering considerable casualties, they were forced to evacuate the position they had won. The retirement was carried out in good order at noon, but was not followed up by the enemy. Newstead received two messages from Cockburn. The first sent off seven hours previously, arrived at 1120 hours, asked for assistance. The second received about noon announced his success. Newstead was unable to get into communication with Cockburn and decided to return to Bare, starting at 1530 hours. His total casualties were 55, including Lieutenant M. J. Parker, severely wounded and made prisoner.

Gallant Attempt to Rescue Lieutenant Parker by Lieutenant G. Dawes and Private Monde

Gallant attempts were made by Lieutenant G. Dawes and some of his men to carry Parker out of action. But these were abandoned after Parker had been twice again wounded (apparently mortally), and Private Monde Yeraia, one of his rescuers, had been severely wounded. For their gallantry Davies and Monde were awarded the M.C. and D.C.M. respectively.

Cockburn had difficulties in reorganizing. The rain was incessant; he had lost all his permanent company commanders in the 1 Nigeria Regiment; a large proportion of his men were lame from 'jiggers'.

On receiving reports of these operations Dobell at once sent reinforcements to Nkongsamba, also sending Gorges to assume control. In the meantime Cockburn was instructed to keep on the defensive.

Reorganization of British Troops

Dobell now withdrew the 1 Nigeria Regiment to quieter areas. Two companies going to Buea, Victoria and Zopo, and two to Kribi. A section

Gold Coast Battery and two companies West African Regiment reached Nkongsamba on the 6th and 8th February respectively. By the 15th February the troops at Bare and Nkongsamba consisted of: 1st Nigerian Battery (less one section), section Gold Coast Battery, section Sierra Leone Battery, H.Q. and four companies West African Regiment, H.Q. and five companies Sierra Leone Battalion, Pioneer Company (six guns; 900 rifles).

The strength of the German forces based on Melong and their apparent anxiety to prevent an advance of our columns northward of the line Ekom, Harmann's Farm, Mbureku, seemed to indicate their anxiety to safeguard the line of retreat to Ngaundere, which at this time was thought to be the focal point towards which many of their columns would be ultimately directed.

Dobell was of the opinion that the enemy should be attacked and driven away from Melong; he therefore arranged to reinforce Gorges for this purpose. But before these reinforcements arrived Gorges concluded that the growing concentration at Mbureku threatened Bare, and he decided to strike at once.

Gorges Attacks Mbureku, 27th February 1915

A column—consisting of a sub-section each of the Sierra Leone and Gold Coast Batteries, two companies and the machine-gun section West Africa Regiment, and a company Sierra Leone Battalion—under Lieutenant-colonel Vaughan, West African Regiment, left Nkongsamba at 0500 hours to attack Mbureku from the south, while from the east Newstead, with two companies Sierra Leone Battalion and a machine gun, left Bare at 0600 hours. To distract the enemy's attention a company West African Regiment was also despatched from Nkongsamba through Bare towards Harmann's Farm and Ekom. Newstead was instructed to leave a a half-company and a machine gun at Bare itself.

Vaughan Captures the Position, but is Driven Off by a Counter-attack

Vaughan came into action at 1115 hours south of Mbureku. The enemy fought tenaciously, supported by three machine guns, and his men did not capture the position until 1345 hours; it lay along a razor-backed ridge covering Mbureku from the south. Soon after its capture Newstead's and Vaughan's patrols met. About 1430 hours, however, the enemy, apparently reinforced from Melong, made a counter-attack against Newstead's right flank. At the same time communication between the two British Commanders was broken; this prevented Vaughan from getting any indication of the direction in which to shell the enemy attacking Newstead; he, however, sent a company to try to make contact, but this was stopped by German enfilade fire. At this stage our gun ammunition gave out, and the enemy, having worked round Vaughan's left flank and rear, caused him to order a general retirement. This was carried out in good order; the two columns met about 1800 hours and returned together to Nkongsamba. Total British casualties were 18, including 2nd Lieutenant F. E. Andrew killed.

Gorges is Reinforced by a section Sierra Leone Battery and Gold Coast Battalion

Gorges continued his preparations for an advance on Melong, being reinforced by the 3rd March by a section Sierra Leone Battery and Rose's Gold Coast Battalion. On the 4th March the main column under Gorges, composed of a section Nigeria Battery, 550 rifles and four machine guns, advanced by the main road from Bare to a position called Gun Hill which gave a clear view of the enemy entrenchments about Harmann's and Stoebel's Farms, both close to the road and respectively west and east of it. A Sierra Leone gun was posted on Gun Hill with orders to bring a cross fire on Harmann's Farm in conjunction with the Nigerian guns when they opened fire. It seems that through some misapprehension this gun returned to Bare at 1030 hours.

A detachment West African Regiment guarded the right flank, while Rose's column occupied Mbureku.

At 1130 hours Newstead (O.C. advanced guard) reported he had occupied Stoebel's Farm and that the nearest enemy seen was about 1,000 yards north of Harmann's Farm. Gorges sent orders to Newstead to make good his position at Stoebel's Farm and to clear Harmann's Farm, sending a Nigerian gun under Captain C. F. S. Maclaverty forward to help him, and moving himself with the main body to about 600 yards south of Stoebel's Farm, where a wooded gully offered a covered reserve position.

The Repulse at Harmann's Farm, 4th March 1915

At 12 noon the advanced guard came under a heavy and concentrated fire from positions about 500 yards north and 900 yards west of Harmann's Farm, and a few minutes later Gorges received a request from Newstead for reinforcements; thereupon a company of the Sierra Leone Battalion from the main body was sent by the least exposed direction to reinforce the right flank of the advanced guard. No clear account of what happened is available; the two officers most concerned were killed or wounded (Newstead and his adjutant Finch). It seems, however, that the enemy had previous notice of the projected attack. A German European detachment was skilfully posted behind a deep and densely wooded gully with at least three machine guns. Covering the position was a screen of native riflemen who fell back as the British approached.

When a heavy fire was opened, though the vanguard held its ground, part of the advanced guard became unsteady and the machine-gun carriers discarded their loads. We now quote from the Official History page 241 (this statement seems to be erroneous, the explanation being that the shell used at the time were double common and not shrapnel): 'To add to the difficulties many of the shells from Maclaverty's gun failed to explode'.

Influenced by the unsteadiness in front, the reinforcing company on the right began to retire. Officers and British N.C.O.s made gallant, but unavailing, efforts to stem the tide of the retreating troops. Gorges pushed out a half-company of the Sierra Leone Battalion under Lieutenant de Miremont, while he and his staff on the road on the northern bank of the gully exposed themselves trying to check the retreat, with the result that

Captain C. H. Dinnen (Staff Captain) was killed. While firing double common shell at short range Maclaverty had been severely wounded, but the gunners continued to serve their gun with courage and devotion until forced to abandon it.

To retrieve the situation and to secure the gun, and machine gun which had been dropped by their carriers, Gorges sent forward part of the West African Regiment to Stoebel's Farm. This was accomplished with steadiness, assisted, too, by a slackening of hostile fire. By this time, thanks to the strenuous efforts of Lieutenant-Colonel A. J. Turner (who had been lent from G.H.Q. for the operation), backed by the coolness of other officers, confidence had been restored and the British retirement was carried out free from molestation at 1315 hours, Bare being reached at 1500 hours.

From Bare Gorges sent orders to Rose at Mbureku and to the Ekom detachment to return to Nkongsamba. Neither had suffered any casualties, but those of his main column amounted to 27, mostly in the Sierra Leone Battalion, and included two officers killed and two wounded.

Redistribution of Troops, March 1915

The following redistribution of troops was now made: *Nkongsamba:* Gorge's H.Q.; four companies West African Regiment, one company Gold Coast Regiment, section Sierra Leone Battery. *Northern Railway posts:* Sierra Leone Battalion. *Bonaberi:* Two companies 1 Nigeria Regiment from Kribi. *Bare:* H.Q. and two companies Gold Coast Battalion. *Duala:* Section Nigerian Battery.

Gorge's patrols continued to be very active north of Bare, locating a force estimated at 80–100 Europeans and 600 native troops north of Melong, also a body of 400 men on the Ban-Yabassi road. Reports indicated that the enemy had been severely shaken by the continuous fighting north of the railway and was very short of ammunition. It seemed a second attack on Chang had been expected.

During the month of March a French Commission had come to Duala to arrange with Dobell for co-operation, if possible, for an advance on Yaunde. This place, the temporary seat of the German Government, was regarded by the authorities in French Equatorial Africa as the most important objective they could aim at. Since the enemy would almost certainly endeavour to defend it, he must lay himself open to defeat, and this, with its capture, was calculated to hasten the end of the campaign. The French delegates informed Dobell that French troops would probably have occupied Lomie and Dumie by the end of March, and that co-operation by the British was desired in their intended advance on Yaunde from these localities.

As we now know, this estimate of French future achievement in this quarter was unduly optimistic. At the time, however, Dobell had no grounds for questioning the accuracy of the French forecast, while he fully realized the importance of Yaunde. But he foresaw other difficulties. It took a month for telegrams from the Lobaye column to reach Edea, so that close co-operation was impossible; Mayer's contingent was in no condition to supply a force to advance 120 miles; the rainy season would shortly set in, while the strength and physical condition of the British

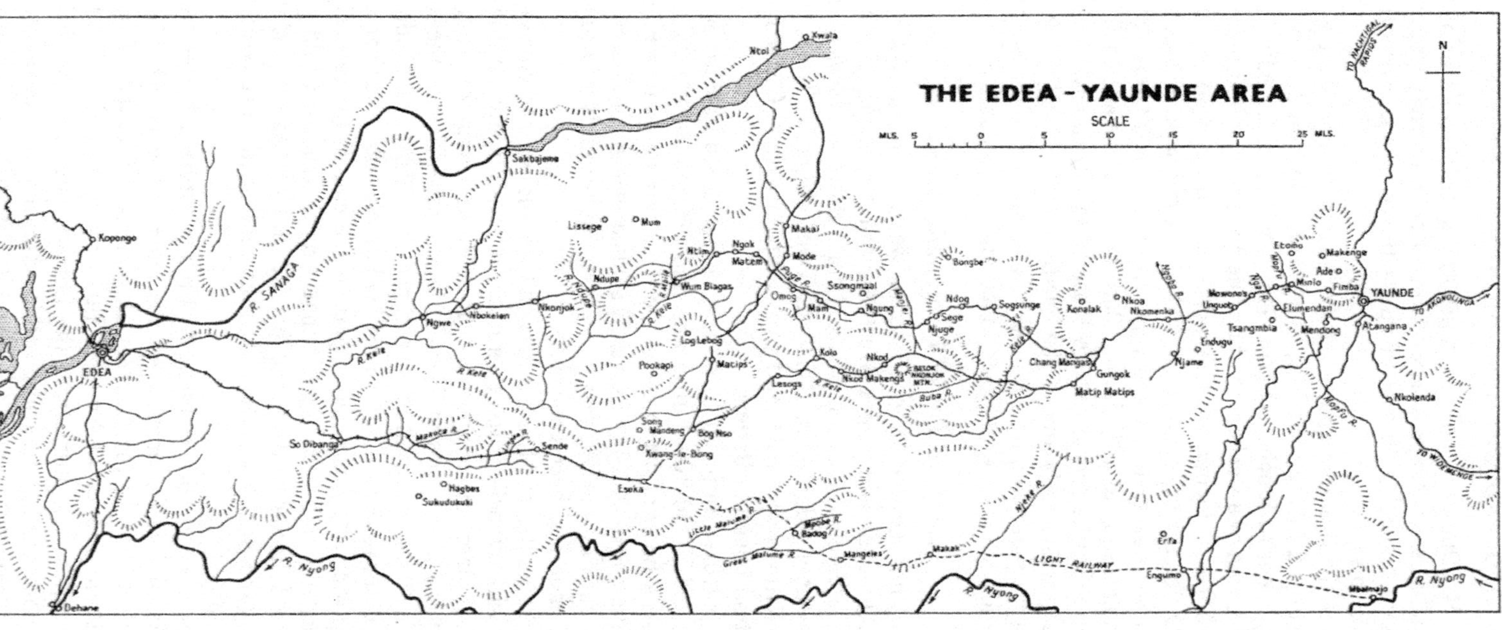

10. The Edea-Yaunde Area

Contingent rendered it difficult for it to assist by protecting Mayer's line of communication. In deference, however, to the representations of the French Commission, Dobell agreed that if reinforcements for Mayer were forthcoming he would co-operate in the French advance from the south-east by despatching a force of 1,000 rifles from Edea to move against Eseka; otherwise his forces would only display local activity. It was understood that the role of the force from Edea would be to prevent the enemy transferring troops from the west to the east.

Reinforcements from Senegal, Gold Coast and Nigeria, April 1915

On the 18th March Dobell heard from Dakar that two Senegalese companies with two machine guns were leaving to reinforce Edea at once. As the arrival of these troops would bring Mayer's column up to the required strength, it was arranged that the combined advance should start on the 20th April. On the 19th March Dobell telegraphed to the Governor-General at Brazzaville that he was prepared to co-operate in the operation with a force of 1,000 French and 600 British troops, including line-of-communication troops. Dobell's ability to furnish the British troops for the purpose was due to hearing that a strong draft from the Gold Coast[1] and a smaller one from Nigeria would shortly reach Duala, and also to hearing from Gorges that the enemy's main forces had retired to about 30 miles north of Nkongsamba.

War Office Takes Control 1st April 1915

On the 19th March the French Government made it clear to our own that it now had in mind the conquest of the whole German colony, a question upon which there had been some doubt previously. In consequence the magnitude of the task in the Cameroons assumed greater proportions and the War Office took control of the military operations from the Colonial Office on 1st April.

During the third week of March it was reported that a force of some 200 Germans had occupied Yabassi. This led the G.O.C. to despatch two small columns under Haywood to advance from Dibombe Post and Penja on the Northern Railway to clarify the situation. These columns gained touch with each other on the 19th but found next day that Yabassi had been evacuated. After patrolling the district for two days, without encountering any enemy, both columns withdrew downstream.

With the object of strengthening Dobell's hand during the forthcoming Yaunde offensive operations the Naval and Garua blockades were tightened up.

Tightening of Blockade on Muni and Garua, April 1915

Blockade of Spanish Muni

During March and April the Navy had been very active patrolling the trade routes adjoining the Cameroon Coast. Armed Naval craft had also

[1] The Gold Coast draft was 160 strong, and was formed into a fourth (D) Company to complete the Gold Coast Battalion under Rose. The Nigerian draft consisted of 30 Reservists. The latter was supplemented by two further drafts in succession of 100 each.

been creating diversions by raiding parties of Marines landed at Kribi and in the Nyong River, as well as at Campo, where blockhouses had been built to accommodate large numbers of refugees gathered there.

From midnight 23rd–24th April a formal blockade was declared of the whole Cameroon coast, except the entrance to the Cameroon River (Duala having previously been declared an open port), and the coast of the territory to the south of Spanish Muni. This was fully justified by the clear evidence that, during the past few months, German agents and their sympathizers in Fernando Po and Spanish Muni had established a system of regular convoys for food supplies and ammunition.

On the 21st April the cruiser *Astreaca* arrived off Duala to relieve the *Challenger*, it being arranged that Captain Fuller should exchange commands with *Astraea's* captain to enable the former's retention as Senior Naval Officer for the Expedition.

Investment of Garua

The situation in the Northern Cameroons had been most unsatisfactory for months past. The Allied troops had effected nothing, as attacks on either Mora or Garua had not been considered feasible. Shortly, however, nearly 2,000 troops with the Naval 12-pounder would be concentrated in the Yola Garua area and it was hoped to effect the capture of Garua in a few weeks.

The Allied blockade of this German post had been so far ineffective. Cunliffe therefore, after consultation with Brisset and Webb-Bowen, started on the 20th April to move troops south-westwards from Bogole to close the road to Koncha and Ngaundere. He established his headquarters at Bilonde, being the best observation-point near Garua. He also contemplated moving the French Contingent westward from Nassarao, but Brisset asked for time to first withdraw some outlying detachments.

Von Crailsheim's Attack on Gurin

While these movements were in progress Crailsheim, the Commander at Garua, succeeded in eluding the investing forces and raided the British post of Gurin 47 miles to the south at daybreak 29th April. The garrison consisted of 42 soldiers and police under Lieutenant D. W. Pawle, Nigeria Regiment. Crailsheim's force, 300 strong with five machine guns, caused a number of casualties, including Pawle, who was killed, and Colour-Sergeant J. H. Fraser wounded. The command then devolved on Lieutenant J. Fitzpatrick, who put up a stout resistance. Crailsheim suffered 30 casualties and withdrew at midday on 29th April. Crailsheim managed by skilful manoeuvring to get back to Garua unobserved, after what must be considered a very daring, if hazardous, episode.

The gallant defence put up by the garrison of Gurin was not the only noteworthy feature of this affair. On getting notice of Crailsheim's raiding force Cunliffe at once despatched a company of M.I. and one and a half companies of infantry under Webb-Bowen to Gurin. The M.I. covered the distance in 16 hours, and the infantry in 21 hours—a particularly fine performance.

THE FIRST AND UNSUCCESSFUL ADVANCE ON YAUNDE: 1ST MAY–30TH JUNE 1915

As a preliminary to the Allied advance on Yaunde the G.O.C. put a column of two guns with six machine guns and 600 rifles, commanded by Haywood, at Mayer's disposal, i.e. one section Nigerian Battery, one company 1 Nigeria Regiment, H.Q. and three companies 2 Nigeria Regiment, one company Sierra Leone Battalion, the Gambia Detachment.

Capture of So-Dibanga, 13th April

Mayer decided first to advance to the line of the Kele River, with a French column under Commandant Mathieu along the railway, while the British marched by the Yaunde road. Supply depots were to be established on the Kele River, at So-Dibanga and Ngwe respectively.

Both columns started on the 10th April. The French column forced the passage of the Kele on the 13th after incurring 15 casualties.

Haywood's column encountered continuous opposition and was much hampered by the thickness of the forest. On the 13th he bivouacked about 1,000 yards from the Ngwe, where he found the bridge still intact. The enemy was entrenched on the other side in a well-concealed position. It consisted of trenches and a redoubt with overhead cover, wire entanglements and abattis, having a field of fire cleared for 300 yards, on all sides except the north, where there was dense bush.

In his attack at daybreak on the 14th Haywood's movements were screened by a thick mist. Three companies 2 Nigeria Regiment formed the main attack, supported by the section of guns, while the company 1 Nigeria Regiment moved southward to cross the river two miles downstream and fall on the enemy's rear.

Capture of Ngwe, 14th April

By 0700 hours the main attack was hotly engaged, having drawn the fire of a machine gun on each flank. Progress was delayed while a suitable place for the guns to come into action was found with difficulty. By about noon a hill on the west bank of the river was occupied and from this the guns were able to bring fire to bear on the enemy's redoubt just as the effect of the 1 Nigeria Regiment's turning movement was making itself felt. The enemy began to retire and shortly after the position was taken at the point of the bayonet. The British casualties were 14, including Colour-Sergeant R. Dokes wounded. The enemy's losses were believed to have been slight. The German force consisted of No. 2 Reserve Detachment, 150 strong, and No. 1 Depot Company on the Sakbajeme road. In order to clear his left flank Haywood sent a column of 200 rifles to Sakbajeme on the 16th to reconnoitre the vicinity. This was done with little opposition being encountered.

Supply Difficulties Delay Aymerich

On the 24th April Dobell received a telegram from Brazzaville saying supply difficulties would cause delay in the advance of Aymerich's troops.

In reply he said his own plans would not be affected as a halt would be necessary on the line Eseka-Wumbiagas till the 10th May, in order to organize for the further advance.

On the 1st May the French column, now under Commandant Mechet, and the British, continued their advance to Eseka and Wumbiagas respectively. It poured with rain incessantly throughout the next few days. On the 1st and 2nd Haywood's column brushed aside the opposition without difficulty, but on the 3rd he found the enemy holding the crossing over the Mbila River at Wumbiagas in a position more formidable than any he had yet encountered.

The bridge had been destroyed; the waist-deep stream was filled with stakes and abbatis and a field of fire for 300 yards had been cleared. Skilfully constructed trenches had been dug on a frontage of 1,600 yards on the eastern bank. These were connected with the rear by an ample system of covered approach trenches. Both flanks were strong. The right rested on a steep forest ridge about 800 ft. high, and the left on the unfordable Kele River, here 120 ft. wide and running south of, and parallel to, the road. From a personal reconnaissance Haywood concluded that a purely frontal attack would be costly and that the enemy's right flank would be the least difficult to turn. He accordingly decided to make a strong holding attack in front, while sending Gibb with two companies (less two sections) 2 Nigeria Regiment to turn the enemy's right.

In face of heavy hostile fire, the frontal attack, supported by the guns, succeeded before long in advancing to within 200 yards of the enemy's line and established a distinct fire superiority. About 1400 hours Gibb reported he was heavily engaged, and, two hours later, that strong opposition and the steep ascent in front would prevent him completing his task in daylight. Gibb was therefore ordered to draw his men out of action before dark. This was successfully accomplished by 1745 hours and the whole British force was withdrawn behind a screen of outposts.

During the night there was a good deal of firing by the outposts and at an early hour on the 4th Haywood sent a company to reconnoitre for a crossing over the Kele River. By 0800 hours the enemy's fire had slackened so much that he called for volunteers to cross the Mbila and reconnoitre up to the enemy's trenches, with the result that the enemy was found to have retired.

Capture of Wumbiagas, 4th May 1915

The British had sustained 22 casualties, including Lieutenant K. Markham-Rose, Gambia Company killed, and Lieutenants J. F. Warren and A. E. Beattie, and Sergeant O'Dwyer, all of 2 Nigeria Regiment, wounded. The enemy's losses were unknown. His strength was some 350 men, consisting of Major Haedicke's No. 1 Depot Company with three machine guns. His failure to offer a longer resistance in such a strong position seemed to indicate his policy of avoiding battle.

The Gold Coast Company had been left to garrison Ngwe; with the rest of his column Haywood now built a defensible post at Wumbiagas and started to collect a reserve of supplies. In accordance with his instructions to assist the French in their advance on Eseka he sent out reconnaissances in that direction without getting any news from that quarter. As, however, he understood Machet would be in front of Eseka by the 7th–8th, he despatched a column of 200 rifles with three days' supplies to threaten the German position.

It transpired that Mechet had been held up at Sende, but had occupied it on the 6th. On the 9th the British column returned with information from Mechet that he expected to attack Eseka on the 13th, and would hope for co-operation then from the Wumbiagas Detachment. Eseka was, however, captured on the 11th with considerable loss to the enemy. Mechet's casualties during his advance from Edea totalled 39, largely due to the inexperience of the Senegalese in the bush, although they fought with great gallantry. A quantity of rolling stock was found at Eseka, but for some time it was unusable owing to the destruction of the railway line and bridges.

On the 18th the G.O.C. issued instructions to Mayer to advance as rapidly as possible, pointing out the urgency of gaining early possession of Yaunde. By the 23rd the whole of Mayer's force had concentrated at Wumbiagas, including a Naval 12-pounder which he had especially asked for. During this time Haywood's camp had been twice attacked at night in a somewhat half-hearted fashion. Despite every precaution malaria and dysentry were rife and the general health of the troops was far from good. Dobell therefore lent Mayer the services of Lieutenant-Colonel Statham, his Director of Medical Services, for the coming operations.

After detaching about 300 rifles for the line of communications, Mayer now had available one Naval gun, four mountain guns (two British Nigeria Regiment and two French), with about 750 French, and 540 British, rifles.

The Engineers had repaired all the bridges on the main road and railway except for the bridge over the Kele River, which still precluded the use of trains.

Advance from Wumbiagas to the Puge River, 25th May–13th June 1915

On the 25th May the advance commenced, the British, who were leading, encountered strong opposition from the outset. Along the main road were many strong defensive positions, too costly for frontal assault, thus favouring delaying tactics, as turning movements meant cutting a way through the dense forest. From this date till the 12th June successive strong positions were met with, the principal ones being the affairs at Ngok, 27th–30th May, Matem, 21st May–4th June, and the Puge River, 7th–12th June. The effect of these arduous operations, sickness, and incessant rains, had by now so worn out the troops that Mayer, after consultation with Haywood and Mechet, decided to advise Dobell to order a retirement to Wumbiagas, or Ngwe. This became all the more urgent as the French had lost two food convoys and were dependent on the British for supplies. Moreover, the latest information from Brazzaville indicated that Aymerich's columns had remained practically stationary since the end of April.

Having received the G.O.C.'s sanction to a withdrawal, the whole Force retired to Wumbiagas on the 14th June, without molestation; the distance of 12 miles, laboriously gained in the last 19 days, being covered without difficulty in five hours.

On the 16th the retirement was continued to Ngwe, but was harassed by the enemy about Nkonjok and Ndupe. Meanwhile Dobell had pushed up what reinforcements he could make available under Cockburn from Duala, leaving him to garrison Ngwe, with seven companies and three mountain guns and a machine-gun section. The remainder of Mayer's Force dispersed to Edea and Duala.

In these abortive operations directed towards Yaunde the Allied Force under Dobell had incurred 301 battle casualties and at least 600 from sickness.

German Attacks on Outposts and Communications

Between the 18th and 22nd June the enemy displayed great activity in attacking the outpost line at Ngwe as well as the communications between Ngwe and Edea. Cockburn sent a French detachment through the bush north of the road to Nbokelen to surprise a post the Germans had established there. This party met with considerable success, inflicting serious casualties and capturing supplies of ammunition and important documents.

In clearing the road to Edea, Rose, with 300 rifles (company each from the 1 Nigeria Regiment, Gold Coast Regiment and the French Contingent), encountered a force of about the same strength, which he dispersed after a lively action in which Lieutenant Earle and 16 men of a Gold Coast Company were made casualties.

By the 26th June the enemy, who had suffered severely during the past two months' fighting, withdrew from the Ngwe/Edea area, and, on Mayer's strong recommendation, the British troops left for Edea while the French troops took over Ngwe garrison.

Distribution of British Troops under Dobell, at the Beginning of July 1915

Northern Railway and Bare: Sierra Leone Battery, section Gold Coast Battery, West African Regiment, Gold Coast Battalion (less one company).

Buea, Victoria, Zopo: Sierra Leone Battalion H.Q., and two companies Nigeria Battery, 1 Nigeria Regiment, 2 Nigeria Regiment, one company Gold Coast Regiment, two companies Sierra Leone Battalion, Gambia Detachment.

Dibombe Post: Two companies Sierra Leone Battalion.

The effective rifles strength of Dobell's British troops was as under:

	Effective	Sick	Total	Number of companies
Gambia Detachment	34	27	61	
Sierra Leone Battalion	514	65	579	6
Gold Coast Battalion	789	87	876	5
1 Nigeria Regiment	437	224	661	4
2 Nigeria Regiment	291	286	577	4
West African Regiment	682	34	716	6
	2,747	723	3,470	

These figures show how depleted by sickness the two Nigerian battalions in particular had become. A lull in the operations at this time provided a suitable moment for Dobell to request the War Office's guidance on the future policy to be adopted, bearing in mind the incidence of sickness in the Expeditionary Force.

Dobell pointed out that the rainy season, now in full progress, precluded extensive operations till November; that few experienced European officers were capable of sustained effort at the moment; and that the Nigerian troops in particular were suffering from dysentery and unfit for hard work, having borne the brunt of the operations since the start of the campaign. He said unless Europeans and Africans were sent on leave to their homes to recuperate he considered few would be fit for active service in November.

He further expressed grave doubts as to whether, having regard to the difficulties he was experiencing, Aymerich would be able to reach Yaunde. For a successful advance on Yaunde, independent of Aymerich, Dobell said he would require a reinforcement of at least 1,000 men, as well as the improvement and repair of the road and railway leading thereto. The provision of motor vehicles and a large number of carriers was essential. The War Office expressed their agreement generally and promised to do what was possible to carry out his suggestions.

Dobell thereupon replied his main efforts would be directed to maintaining a strict blockade on Muni during the rainy season, provided a sufficient supply of officers could be sent from England to relieve those being sent to recuperate.

We must now turn to the operations in the Northern Cameroons, leading up to the capture of Garua.

THE GERMAN DEFENSIVE POSITION OF GARUA AND DISPOSITIONS FOR ITS CAPTURE

The German position is shown on the sketch map. It consisted of a series of seven redoubts, marked A to G at heights from 230 to 80 ft. above the Benue, covering an area of about 2,000 yards by 1,000. Each redoubt was self-contained and mutually supported each other by flanking fire. Each was surrounded by deep pits protected by an outer ring of wire entanglements and abattis. From the position the ground sloped down in all directions, giving a good field of fire up to some 5,000 yards range. A tremendous amount of work had been done to strengthen the position since Maclear's attack was repulsed in August 1914. The garrison was estimated to be about 500 of all ranks, armed with four guns, 10 machine guns and some 250 rifles.

Cunliffe started making his preparations in April in order to coincide with the Allied Advance on Yaunde. A French 95 mm. gun was brought from Dakar to make the artillery bombardment more effective. The transportation of this heavy gun from the railway at Baro (on the Niger) to Garua on the Benue, up 750 miles of river fallen almost below canoe draught, had been a fine feat, which reflected the greatest credit on the Nigerian Marine.

Composition and Strength of Allied Forces at Garua, 31st May 1915

British (78 Europeans, 1,130 Natives): One Naval 12-pounder, 1 Nigerian Battery (three guns), 10 machine guns, 'B' Company M.I., 'B'

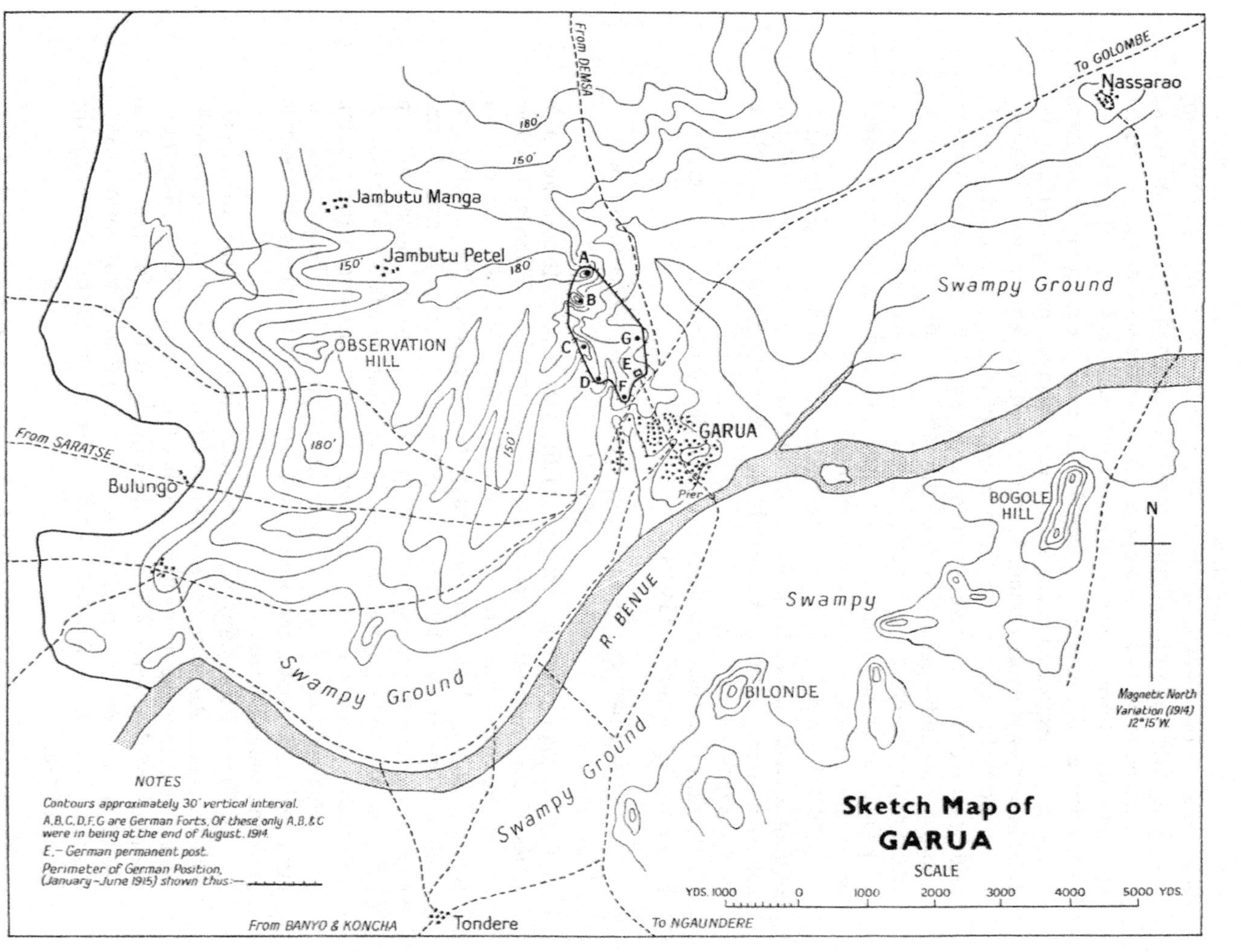

Sketch Map of
GARUA
SCALE
YDS. 1000
0
1000
2000
3000
4000
5000 YDS.
N
Magnetic North
Variation (1914)
12°15′W.
To GOLOMBE
Nassarao
From DEMSA
180′
150′
Jambutu Manga
Jambutu Petel
A
B
C
D
E
F
G
OBSERVATION
HILL
GARUA
Pier
Swampy Ground
Swampy
BOGOLE
HILL
BILONDE
R. BENUE
From SARATSE
Bulungo
Swampy Ground
Swampy Ground
From BANYO & KONCHA
Tondere
To NGAUNDERE
NOTES
Contours approximately 30′ vertical interval.
A, B, C, D, F, G are German Forts. Of these only A, B, & C were in being at the end of August. 1914.
E.– German permanent post.
Perimeter of German Position, (January–June 1915) shown thus:–

11. Garua

(less one section) and 'H' Companies, 1 Battalion Nigeria Regiment, 'H' Company 2 Battalion Nigeria Regiment, 'B' 'D' and 'H' Companies 3 Battalion Nigeria Regiment, 'B' Coy 4 Battalion Nigeria Regiment.

French: (46 Europeans, 580 Natives): One heavy, two Hotchkiss, two mountain guns, one squadron cavalry, three infantry companies, two detachments Gardes Régionnaux.

Dispositions of Attacking Force

Cunliffe, in consultation with Brisset, had decided to concentrate the whole British Force, except for one company 'B' 4 Battalion left to cover the main crossing over the Benue at Bilande, at Jambutu Manga north-west of the Garua position. The movement had to be carried out at night to escape attention; it started on the 15th May and was completed by the 25th. The attacking force was divided into H.Q. troops and two columns, the latter commanded by Webb-Bowen and Uniacke respectively. Till then the Germans had no idea such a movement was in progress. In fact, Crailsheim had intended to evacuate the position next day, with the object of marching south and joining hands with the main German forces opposing Dobell.

While Cunliffe concentrated his British troops north-west of Garua, Brisset was to guard the exits at Nassarao and Bogole, to the eastward.

At daybreak on the 31st May the enemy discovered the Allied firing line was entrenched some 3,000–3,500 yards north of Fort A, and opened fire with their artillery. Four hours later the Allies replied with their heavy guns and soon silenced the enemy. Little damage had been done by the German fire, as our men were well entrenched. On the other hand, native reports said the enemy had suffered some casualties and a quantity of ammunition blown up in Fort A.

The artillery duel continued on the 1st June, but the German volume of fire was considerably reduced. By the 2nd the Allies had advanced 1,000 yards, but Cunliffe decided the strength of the position precluded any further advance without sapping. This he proceeded to do and by the 6th June the Allies had made considerable progress, completely cutting off all sources of supply from outside. By the 10th our trenches had reached to within 1,000 yards of Fort A.

Cunliffe now learnt that Crailsheim had, the previous night, attempted to cross the Benue with his whole force. However, the river was in flood and his attempt failed with the loss of 15 men drowned. Cunliffe at once ordered the bombardment to be intensified and his troops to close in.

Suddenly, about 1530 hours, white flags were run up and a German mounted officer, Captain Wanka, was seen approaching. Major Wright and Captain Ferrandi were sent to meet him. Terms of unconditional surrender were finally arranged. It eventually was ascertained that Crailsheim's real reason for surrendering so easily was that the Native troops had mutinied, having become demoralized by the bombardment of the Allies' heavy guns.

The prisoners numbered 37 Europeans and 212 native combatants. More than half the original native garrison had either become casualties or deserted. A quantity of stores, including four guns and 10 machine guns fell into our hands.

The fugitives from Garua had apparently fled to Ngaundere. To keep them on the run and to secure a good base for operations south, besides anticipating any enemy concentration, Cunliffe decided to send a column (one gun and two companies Nigeria Regiment) under Webb-Bowen to secure the northern fringe of the plateau there.

Occupation of Ngaundere, 29th June 1915

Leaving Garua on the 17th June, Webb-Bowen reached the very steep ascent to the plateau on the 28th without incident. Here he found the German outposts strongly posted, but under cover of a tropical rainstorm Captain C. H. Fowle's advanced guard surprised these and uncovered their strong positions in rear. The French cavalry squadron pursued the fleeing Germans for several miles and next morning the main body occupied the forts without opposition, the enemy retiring on Tibati. Our casualties had been only nine.

Brisset at Ngaundere, 7th July 1915

Meanwhile, Brisset, who considered himself now independent of Cunliffe, proceeded with his French troops to Ngaundere with a view to getting in touch with Morisson's column on the Kadei River from that base. By the 7th July he had reached Ngaundere. On the 19th July Fowle, with 'H' Company 2 Battalion Nigeria Regiment and a French cavalry troop, occupied Tingere to the west in order to gain touch with the British post at Koncha.

Tingere Affair, 23rd July 1915

Fowle's garrison was attacked on the 23rd by the former German garrison reinforced from Tibati, of a strength estimated at four Europeans and 150 rifles. But they met with such a hot reception that they were soon put to headlong flight by a bayonet charge initiated by a native section commander. Shortly after, the garrison of Tingere was reinforced by the other British company and mountain gun under Webb-Bowen.

From Ngaundere Brisset established communications with the Lobaye Column under Morisson at Kunde, to the south-east.

Ibi Column

The leading company of the Ibi Column ('H' Company 3 Battalion), hearing the enemy was holding a river crossing two miles from Gashiga, made a wide turning movement across very difficult country over hills and rivers, completely surprising the party there and securing a quantity of canoes and equipment. This dashing little enterprise was carried out by Captain C. G. Bowyer-Smith.

Cross River Column

The Cross River Column was immobilized by the rains, having met with no incidents of note since May.

Progress of Aymerich's Columns in July 1915

During July Dobell received more reassuring news of the French columns comprising Aymerich's Force. Lomie had been occupied by Hutin's Sanga Column, the Lobaye Column (Morisson) was in contact with it at Abong Mbang, and had reached Bertua-Dumie farther north. The Oyem Column, now commanded by Le Meillour and designated South Cameroons Force, had occupied Bitam.

Hopeful Prospects for Terminating the Campaign

Thus, by the end of July, the capture of Garua and Ngaundere in the north, Aymerich's progress in the south and south-east, and the blockade measures along the coast, had brought about a hopeful prospect of drawing a net round Yaunde which would compel the Germans either to fight a pitched battle or surrender.

Operations at Campo and on the Nyong River, July 1915

A mission of the Pioneer Company, under Captain N. Goodwin, was directed in July to clear small hostile detachments in the Campo area, and ascertain if convoys were plying between Spanish Muni and the Cameroons. There was little opposition, two or three enemy camps were found deserted and destroyed, while it was ascertained that no convoys of any significance were leaving Muni.

The Germans had organized small parties of levies to harass the vessels of the Nyong Flotilla. Captain M. E. Fell with a company 1 Nigeria Regiment was sent to this area and later Major R. G. Coles took command, reinforced by 120 rifles (1 Nigeria Regiment and Gold Coast Battalion), also by a French company. The whole force concentrated at Dehane and successfully broke up the hostile detachments, leaving a half-company of the Gold Coast Battalion to garrison the Nyong base before returning to Duala.

Operations Against Mora Mountain, August and September, 1915

While there was a lull in major operations Cunliffe decided to make another attempt to reduce Mora, having come to the conclusion that the best chance of success lay in attacking Dabaskum from Wacheke by night. His dispositions were as follows: *Wacheke:* H.Q.; two mountain guns; 'H' Company 1 Battalion, 'D' and 'G' Companies 3 Battalion Nigeria Regiment; a French company (Captain Remond), for the main assault. *Padiko:* 95 mm. gun. *Gauala Ridge:* 'A' Company 2 Battalion. *Vami:* A French company (Captain Popp). *Sava:* 'C' Company M.I.

Between the 1st and 8th September no less than three attempts to capture Mora failed. 'H' Company 1 Battalion gained a footing on Dabaskum and advanced to within 60 yards of the German breastworks before being stopped. Raben, the German commander, pays tribute to the gallantry of these Nigerians. Captain R. N. Pike was shot dead while leading the attacking force, which incurred 38 casualties, including Captain A. Gardner and Lieutenant A. J. L. Cary wounded.

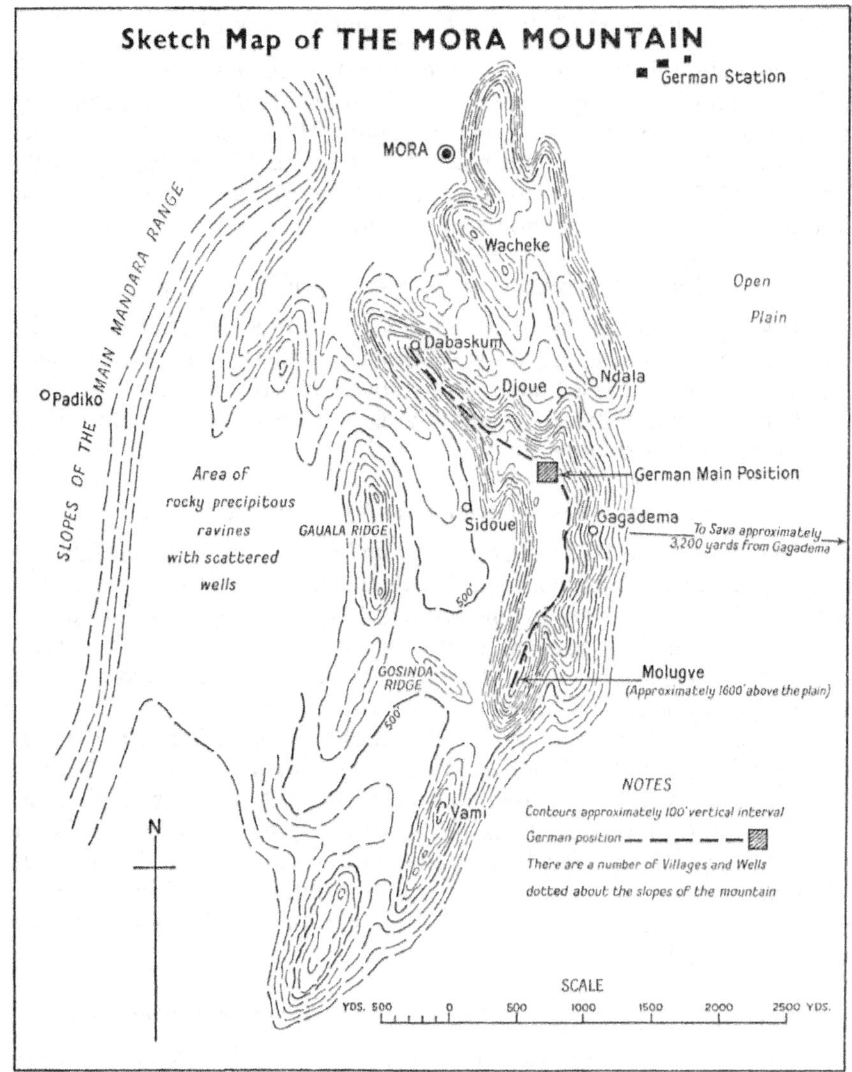

12. The Mora Mountain

On the 9th Cunliffe decided to withdraw and reorganize; however, on receipt of a telegram from the Governor at Lagos, giving the information that Dobell was preparing for an advance on Yaunde in October and wanted Cunliffe's co-operation, he decided to abandon Mora and return to Yola. The force left to invest Mora was 'C' Company M.I., 'G' Company 3 Battalion and two French companies.

Cunliffe, who had been promoted Brigadier-General on the 26th July, had little enough time to make his preparations. By the 2nd October he had decided to march against Bamenda, Banyo and Tibati, threatening the enemy simultaneously from every direction. The main objective was Banyo, on which all columns were to converge; Webb-Bowen was to act independently of Brisset, but also to be a connecting link between the latter and Cunliffe.

OPERATIONS LEADING UP TO THE INVESTMENT OF BANYO MOUNTAIN: OCTOBER–NOVEMBER 1915

Ossidinge Column (Crookenden)

On the 12th October Crookenden with four companies 3 Battalion Nigeria Regiment, a section 2 Battery Nigeria Regiment and eight machine guns, advanced via Bamenda to Bagam, 20 miles north of Chang, where he expected to make contact with a column from Bare, composed of the 5th Indian Light Infantry,[1] and the West India Regiment, under Lieutenant-Colonel Cotton, but failed to do so. His difficulties had been due rather to the rains and mountainous bush-covered terrain than to opposition from the enemy. He returned to Bamenda on the 30th, Captain C. N. Heathcote and three men being the only casualties

Minor Operations at Gandua and Kentu

Towards the end of September and during October certain minor movements were taking place north of the Ossidinge Column. Captain F. J. H. Pring with three sections 'C' Coy 1 Battalion carried out a skilfully planned surprise attack from Gashiga on the German outpost at Gandua, killing two Europeans and six natives, with trifling loss to the British. This affair caused the Commander at Banyo to weaken his post at the important pass in the Genderu Mountains, thereby much facilitating the subsequent advance of Cunliffe's columns in the attack on Banyo Mountain. On the 12th October the Company at Takum under Captain B. C. Parr advanced towards Kentu which he occupied after slight opposition on the 17th, the enemy withdrawing to a precipitous hill commanding the Bamenda road, which Parr subsequently occupied after sustaining 13 casualties.

Concentration of Cunliffe's Main Force at Koncha

By the 14th October Cunliffe had concentrated his main column at Koncha, consisting of 'B' Company M.I., one section 1 Battery, one gun 2 Battery, 'B' and 'H' Companies 1 Battalion 'A' 2 Battalion, and 'D' 3 Battalion, (half 'B' Company 3 Battalion was left to garrison Koncha).

By the evening of the 22nd Mann's Ibi Column of two and a half infantry companies ('C' 1 Battalion, half 'C' 2 Battalion, and 'H' 3 Battalion) was at Gandua, Cunliffe's main column at Mba and the M.I. at Mbamti.

The spirit animating the Nigerian troops was well illustrated by the exploit of five sick M.I. left at Dodo with remounts. These men, hearing there was a small German detachment near Mbanti, surprised it, killing two and putting the rest to flight.

[1] The 5th Indian Light Infantry and a section of machine-guns West India Regiment had come to reinforce Dobell in August.

Advance to Banyo, 23rd–24th October 1915

On the 23rd the combined advance from Gandua and Mba began. Major Porter's M.I. were directed to cut the Banyo–Tibati and Banyo–Fumban roads. The converging movement caused the enemy to evacuate his covering position and withdraw to Banyo Mountain. Next morning Mann occupied the European cantonment at Banyo an hour before Cunliffe arrived there. British casualties had only amounted to 13, while the Germans were known to have lost 28, including two Europeans. The country traversed had been mountainous, covered with elephant grass and intersected by rivers and streams. Protective duties had in consequence been arduous and Cunliffe had good reason to congratulate all ranks on their fine efforts, and especially that portion of his force which had covered 445 miles in the past five weeks (including halts) between Mora and Banyo.

Occupation of Tibati, 3rd November 1915

The occupation of Tibati was successfully accomplished on the 3rd November. Webb-Bowen's column advanced from the north, which enabled Brisset to surprise the garrison by advancing from the south-east. A short bombardment by the French guns sufficed to cause the enemy to beat a hurried retreat in the direction of Yoko to the south. The garrison was computed at 150 rifles; the Allies suffered no casualties.

Cunliffe was faced with a formidable obstacle at Banyo Mountain, which seemed likely to involve heavy casualties. However, he decided that the risk of these must be taken if his force was to advance farther south and co-operate effectively with Dobell. He transferred his base to Ibi from Yola and with a view to eventually making his advanced base at Banyo, asked Lugard to consider constructing a field telegraph line from Ibi so as to shorten his line of communication.

Attack on Banyo Mountain, 4th–6th November 1915

Banyo Mountain rises as a single feature about 1,200 ft. above the surrounding area of broken country. Its slopes are very steep and covered with large boulders, many of which the enemy had linked together in stone breastworks. Altogether some 300 of these had been constructed. In all immense preparations had been made for a prolonged defence. On the summit cement reservoirs had been built; brick houses had been made for Europeans, equipped with heavy furniture; cattle and grain had been stored in quantities. It was evident that the place had been intended as a rallying-point for the garrisons of Banyo, Bamenda and Chang. There was complete confidence that it could be held till the end of the war.

Cunliffe made careful preparations for his attack. By the 2nd November his four and a half infantry companies with 10 machine guns were established on the under-features round the mountain; in the plain behind them the M.I. were disposed in a wide circle to give early information of any attempt to break through.

Orders were issued for a general attack at dawn on the 4th, the three mountain guns were disposed north-east, south-west and south. Four companies attacked in a converging movement as follows: 'H' Company 1 Battalion from the north-east; 'B' Company 3 Battalion from the west, with half 'G' Company 2 Battalion' as a connecting link; 'H' Company 3 Battalion from the south-west and 'C' Company 1 Battalion from the south. Companies had orders to act independently, as communication would be difficult, moving steadily and advancing in depth, making full use of cover.

A thick mist enabled progress to be considerable. 'H' Company 3 Battalion, in fact, almost reached the summit before being seen by the enemy. It then came under fire from all directions at short range. Bowyer-Smijth, its commander, and one of the most fearless and dashing officers, was killed and the company forced back some distance. By midday the rest of the attacking infantry had got half-way up the mountain and, in many places, were within 30 yards of the breastworks. While daylight lasted they could do no more than hold their ground. At nightfall the enemy began throwing bombs, a missile to which our troops were unaccustomed. For a time the position was critical. Then, extricating themselves, and reorganizing, the Nigerians made a further slight advance.

During the 5th steady progress was made, one breastwork after another being outflanked, till by dusk all four companies had reached to within 100 yards of the summit. At 1900 hours a violent thunderstorm intervened and at daybreak on 6th November the summit was carried. The white flag was hoisted but the enemy had fled.

It appears that the German commander, realizing the position was hopeless, at 1700 hours on 5th November had issued orders for the garrison to break away in small parties and rendezvous at Ngambe. Not many escaped, however. Out of a total of 23 Europeans and 200 natives, 13 Europeans and 103 natives were killed, wounded or captured. The commander, Captain Schipper, was killed. A quantity of stores and material were also taken.

The capture of this formidable position was a feat of which Cunliffe and all ranks had every reason to be proud. Skilful planning, resolute and gallant leadership, endurance and courage all contributed to the success. Considering the nature of the position the casualties were not excessive, totalling 60, and including Captains C. G. Bowyer-Smijth and L. N. A. Mackinnon and Colour-Sergeant W. King killed; Captain G. Seccombe and Lieutenant J. Chartres wounded.

Extract from a letter from Captain C. P. L. Marwood, written to a Political Officer in Nigeria, dated 13/11/1915:

'We took Banyo after 11 days "hate", the last two days of which we stormed a mountain 1,200 ft. high, and the men had their first taste of hand grenades—nasty things—but they did splendidly, and we got in at dawn on 6th November. Our casualties Bowyer-Smijth, Mackinnon, Colour-Sergeant King killed, Seccombe, Chartres wounded; 50 rank and file killed and wounded. We rounded up nine Germans (white men) and killed three or four.

'Since then we have been pursuing. Our men have got their tails up and the Huns have got theirs down. I would never have believed before the War that the men would advance within 30 yards of an entrenched position and stay there two days, and then rush—it was raining all the time, too.'

Cunliffe then decided to advance to the line Ditam-Ngambe-Yoko.

We must now turn to the operations of Dobell's and Aymerich's forces in the Southern and Eastern Cameroons.

OPERATIONS IN THE SOUTHERN CAMEROONS: JULY–OCTOBER 1915

The lull in active operations from July to October was of great benefit to Dobell's troops. It enabled both officers and men to be sent to their homes for a much-needed rest. It also released troops to help the Navy in tightening the blockade where German supply columns had been active in the Campo area. During July and August Rose (Gold Coast Battalion) and Hastings (Sierra Leone Battalion) carried out a combined operation in the valley of the Campo River with a Naval gun detachment, one sub-section Nigerian Battery, 1 company 1 Nigeria Regiment, two companies Gold Coast Battalion and half company Seirra Leone Battalion. This operation was also valuable in assisting the advance of the Oyem Column, now commanded by Lieutenant-Colonel Le Meillour, by helping to clear his left flank.

DISPOSITION OF FORCES PREPARATORY TO ADVANCE ON YAUNDE: OCTOBER–NOVEMBER 1915

(*a*) *Dobell's Forces*

The advance from Edea was to be carried out on two distinct lines, each with its own line of supply, and under Dobell's personal direction.

A British column under Gorges would advance along the main road, while a French column under Mayer would follow the railway.

(1) *Gorges's Column*

On the 4th October this was disposed as follows:

At Ngwe (Haywood): One section Nigerian Battery; one gun Gold Coast Battery; one field section Sierra Leone Royal Engineers; 2 Nigeria Regiment; two companies Sierra Leone Battalion; Gambia Company.

At Sakbajeme (Rose): One gun Gold Coast Battery; machine-gun section West India Regiment; three companies Gold Coast Battalion.

Edea-Ngwe line of communication: One company Sierra Leone Battalion.

Duala (in reserve): One section Nigerian Battery; 1 Nigeria Regiment; two companies Gold Coast Battalion.

(2) *Mayer's Column*

At Edea and Eseka: One battery of six mountain guns; three battalions of Senegalese Tirailleurs; one section of Engineers; medical and transport details.

Totalling approximately, 3,000 all ranks.

(*b*) *Aymerich's Forces* (*South and East Cameroons*)

(i) *At Bitem:* South Cameroon Column (Le Meillour); three guns; seven companies (940 rifles); two machine-gun sections.

(ii) *About Tina* (*West bank of Long River*)*:* Right column, Eastern Cameroon Force (Morisson); four guns; eight companies (1,000 rifles).

(iii) *Dume Area—Abong Mbang:* Left column, Eastern Cameroon Force (Hutin); two guns; 1,100 rifles (including 600 line of communication troops).

The plan was for all three of Aymerich's columns to converge on the Yoko–Yaunde road, and then advance on Yaunde from the north, if possible in co-operation with Cunliffe's Force, while Dobell's column attacked from the west.

As it is no part of our purpose to follow in detail the operations of Aymerich's forces, we will now turn to the forces operating directly under Dobell's command.

DOBELL'S FORCES ADVANCE ON YAUNDE: OCTOBER–DECEMBER 1915

Orders for the Advance Issued, 22nd September 1915

On the 22nd September 1915 Dobell issued orders for the advance on Yaunde. In accordance with these orders Gorges sent instructions to Haywood and Rose to the following effect. The enemy was believed to be holding strong positions astride the Ndupe and Mbila Rivers. On the 6th October Haywood was to advance from Ngwe against Wumbiagas with one section Nigerian Battery and 2 Nigeria Regiment. On the same day Rose, leaving a company to garrison Sakbajeme, was to advance with the rest of his detachment and co-operate with Haywood. Rose was to be prepared to assist in Haywood's attack on the Ndupe position as well as turning the enemy's right flank at Wumbiagas, acting under Haywood's orders as soon as a junction was effected.

Haywood moved out of Ngwe on the morning of the 6th October, leaving a garrison there of a sub-section Gold Coast Battery, the Gambia Company and two companies Sierra Leone Battalion. He camped for the night about four miles west of Ndupe, having met with only slight opposition; learning early next day that the enemy had evacuated the Ndupe position, he pushed on through pouring rain. The bridge over the Ndupe was broken and the river was shoulder-deep and flowing swiftly. By 1400 hours the bridge had been mended and the baggage was across. As all attempts at communicating with Rose had failed, camp was made here. During the night a message arrived saying Rose had reached Lissage after negotiating difficult country.

Capture of Wumbiagas, 9th October 1915

Haywood then sent Rose instructions to try to reach the right rear of the Wumbiagas position by 1600 hours on the 8th October. Owing to delays caused by the state of the terrain this proved impossible and the attack was postponed till next day. Meanwhile a careful personal reconnaissance showed the enemy's position lay about 100 yards behind the east bank of the Mbila River, extending for some 1,600 yards from a high ridge on its right to the Kele River, 600 yards south of the road, on its left. The ground had been cleared of thick bush for about 500 yards to afford a good field of fire. The whole position was strongly entrenched.

At 0530 hours next day the attack started. After feeling for a 'soft spot'

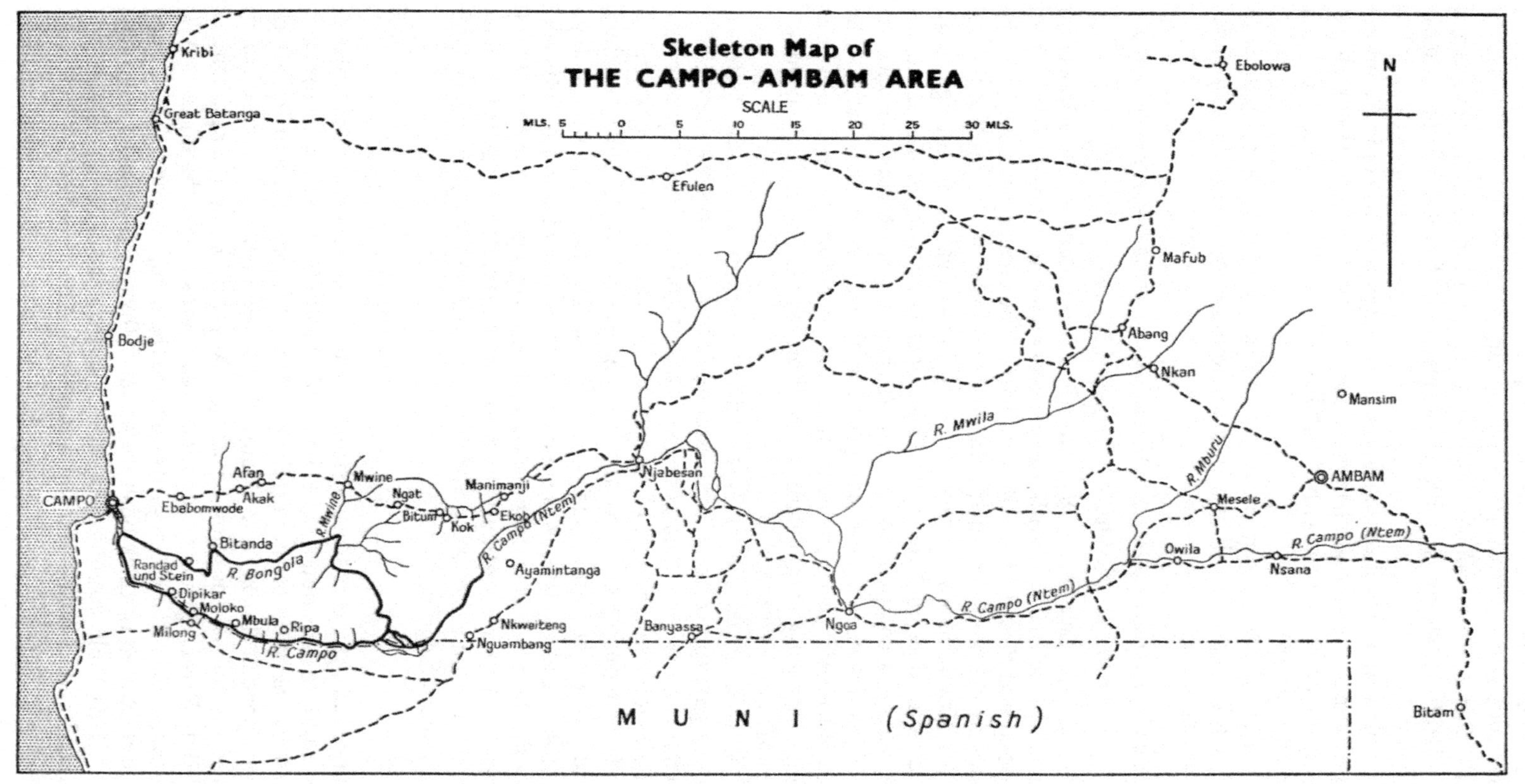

13. The Campo-Ambam Area

all along the front, Haywood decided on reinforcing his left while containing the rest of the line. The guns had come into action first on our right, but were then switched to the centre and left to support the main attack. About 1500 hours Rose's gun was heard; a heavy bombardment was then concentrated on our left, followed by an assault by the whole of Haywood's column. By 1600 hours the enemy's fire was mastered to a great extent and a portion of the British centre had managed to wade across the waist-deep Mbila (the bridge having been destroyed). This body was quickly supported and the trenches rushed. The enemy had, however, made good his retreat and the British, who pursued till dusk, only encountered small hostile parties.

Rose had been much delayed by the difficulties of the ground. Reaching the Mbila at 0930 hours he sent his baggage and supplies under escort to Ndupe and pushed on as rapidly as possible through the hilly country lying to the north of the Wumbiagas position. Here about noon he encountered parties of Germans retreating. Having sent a message to Haywood he bivouacked for the night about 1615 hours.

Total British casualties were 31, of which 11 were in Rose's column. The 20 in Haywood's column included Lieutenant W. H. Cathie, 2 Nigeria Regiment, killed; Lieutenants H. N. Steptoe and R. V. Trengrouse (2 Nigeria Regiment), Lieutenant T. Vise (Nigerian Battery) and Dr. K. K. Grieve (West African Medical Service) wounded. The enemy's losses were not known; his strength appeared to have been Nos. 1 Depot, 3 and 4 Reserve Companies, with three machine guns totalling about 450 rifles.

Haywood now organized the advanced base at Wumbiagas, allotting to the line of communications under Rose's command a sub-section Gold Coast Battery, two companies Gold Coast Battalion, and the machine-gun section (West India Regiment).

Operations of the French Column, 6th–13th October

On the 6th October a column of 750 rifles and four machine guns under Mechet marched out from So-Dibanga, encountering heavy opposition until he reached a point 10 miles along the railway from his starting-place. Mechet expected to attack Sende on the 14th October and then advance to Eseka.

Dobell therefore instructed Haywood to co-operate by despatching a detachment to cut off the enemy's retreat towards Eseka; to assist him 'B' Company Gold Coast Battalion was sent from Duala as a reinforcement. Putting Rose in command of the operation and making up his column with a Gold Coast gun and 'A' Company 2 Nigeria Regiment, Haywood despatched the Sierra Leone field section Royal Engineers to instal a flying bridge over the Kele River, to hold the crossing. On the 18th Rose reached the crossing after a night's torrential rain to find the bridge had been washed away by the flood. After several attempts Rose finally got his column over the river.

Capture of Sende and Eseka

By the 24th Rose's threat to the enemy's line of retreat caused him to evacuate Sende and then to evacuate Eseka without a fight. Here the

French captured a lot of railway material and rolling stock on 30th October. Rose's column marched off next day to rejoin Haywood at Wumbiagas. The French had suffered 116 casualties since leaving So-Dibanga, practically the whole of which occurred before reaching Sende. Rose's casualties had been very light and had occurred mainly in the Gambia Company, which had been sent from Wumbiagas to reinforce him under Captain Thurston's command. The whole of the area in which Mechet and Rose had been operating was exceptionally thick and difficult to penetrate. The enemy's resistance to the French until the capture of Sende had been particularly stubborn, making Mechet's progress very slow. He was hampered, too, by the lack of experience in bush warfare of his Senegalese troops, although this was to some extent compensated for by their conspicuous gallantry.

Appreciation of the Position in November 1915

As soon as Eseka was captured Dobell ascertained that the French would not have collected sufficient supplies there for a further advance till the 23rd November, which date was provisionally fixed therefore for the final stage of the Yaunde operations.

In some ways the delay was beneficial. The rains had not yet ceased; in consequence the motor road under construction for the 50 miles from Edea to Wumbiagas had not been completed up to standard. But by the 23rd November this was accomplished, and in addition 24 days' supplies and a body of 3,500 carriers had been collected at the latter place.

The enemy's strength is difficult to estimate, as the Intelligence diary maintained at Dobell's Headquarters is missing from the records and the German official account in *Der Grosse Krieg* gives us no assistance. On the other hand, reports received at the end of hostilities, and from the Spanish authorities in Rio Muni, give the total number of Europeans at 600, and 6,000 of native ranks. The British estimated that not more than about 5,000 of these could have had rifles, and that they were organized in 23 companies, excluding the garrison of Mora.

These companies varied greatly in strength. Approximately an equal number of each were opposing Cunliffe, Aymerich and Dobell's Forces, while towards the end of November greater weight was brought to bear against the two latter as opposed to Cunliffe.

While Gorges's column would continue to move along the main Edea–Yaunde road, Mayer's objective would be Erfa on the Yaunde–Kribi road towards which he would follow the direction of the light railway from Eseka. Both columns were to be responsible for guarding their own flanks, and, with this in view they were directed to advance on as broad a front as possible, by utilizing parallel tracks to the north and southward.

During the month Gorges concentrated his whole force about Wumbiagas, inclusive of the reserve at Duala, now reinforced by a 4·5 in howitzer from England. He reduced the Sakbajeme Garrison and established posts at Mum (60 rifles, Gold Coast Battalion, under Captain G. A. E. Poole) and at Ngok ('F' Company 2 Nigeria Regiment under Major G. N. Sheffield).

From Wumbiagas to Yaunde was about 65 miles. The first 40 miles lay through dense forest, consisting of high trees and nearly impenetrable undergrowth, making movement difficult and slow. Added to this the country was intersected with deep valleys, numerous streams, and swamps, on either side of which loomed precipitous rocky hills. It was a terrain ideally adapted to the siting of strong defensive positions in which machine guns could play a decisive part. From the attacker's point of view machine-gun posts and the flanks of the positions were extremely difficult to locate, making the fighting very blind, and artillery targets consequently seldom visible.

At Chang Mangas, 25 miles from Yaunde, the forest gave way to more open and less broken country in which the scales became much more evenly balanced in favour of the attackers.

The first objective was therefore to be Chang Mangas, where a halt would be made to reorganize for the final assault on Yaunde, which was reported to be strongly fortified.

The method to be adopted in the advance was for the main column to follow the direct road to Yaunde, while strong flanking detachments would operate on either side of it in order to minimize the danger of hostile turning movements.

The Puge River Position, 23rd–30th November 1915

On 23rd November Gorges's force left Wumbiagas, its right flank covered by one sub-section Gold Coast Battery, a detachment Sierra Leone Royal Engineers and 1 Nigeria Regiment (less 'I' Company), under Cockburn's command, while the left flank detachment, under Rose, was composed of one company 1 Nigeria Regiment and one and a half companies Gold Coast Battalion.

Cockburn's flank guard bore the brunt of the fighting, coming up against a well-sited position at Lesogs, covering the Kele River bridge. On the 29th he asked Gorges for reinforcements, which were directed from Mam on Kolo consisting of 'A' and 'B' Companies 2 Nigeria Regiment under Sargent. The threat of this movement towards the enemy's right caused him to break off the engagement. Cockburn suffered severely during these six days' fighting. His casualties amounted to 64, including Captain A. W. Balders, Lieutenants E. R. Hills and G. Walker killed and Captain the Hon. R. Craven, Sergeants J. Hutchinson (Royal Army Medical Corps) and W. Chadwick wounded.

Rose's left flank detachment advanced through Makai and Mode on Ngung, which was captured by a fine assault by Biddulph's half company. Rose had maintained communication well with the main column, whose successful attack on the Puge position was thereby much assisted, with only three (2 Nigeria Regiment) casualties on 28th November. Rose's casualties were eight, including Captain M. E. Fell wounded.

The exceptionally strong Puge River position captured by Gorges's main column consisted of a system of carefully sited trenches along two successive ranges of hills which must have taken a great deal of labour and time to prepare. It was afterwards learnt that its capture was a grievous disappointment to the Germans and had a serious effect on the morale of their troops, who had thought it was almost impregnable. The position was defended by No. 1 Depot, 2, 3, 5 and 3 Reserve Companies (total five) under Major Haedicke.

Mayer's Force, 24th November–6th December

During this time the French had advanced only about half-way to Mangeles, which was 23 miles from Eseka. The dense forest was much accidented and the light railway followed an extremely tortuous course. The area was, in fact, admirably adapted to delaying tactics. The French had incurred 120 casualties after driving the enemy from five or six entrenched positions. On the 25th November Lieutenant-Colonel Faucon took over command from Mayer, who was invalided to Edea. He informed Dobell that he would halt for 10 days at Mangeles and his date of arrival there was very uncertain.

Upon hearing this, Dobell ordered Gorges to push on as rapidly as possible to Yaunde. He informed him that the Germans opposing Faucon's force were expected to retire on Ebolowa; that the enemy was reported to be getting demoralized so that speed was the essence of the problem, and Gorges's movements must in future be independent of the French.

Belok Nkonjok/Manjei River Position, 7th–16th December 1915

On 7th December the advance to Chang Mangas was continued. The right flank column, now commanded by Haywood, was composed of one sub-section Nigerian Battery and 2 Nigeria Regiment (less one company). On the left flank was a detachment of one machine gun West India Regiment and two companies Gold Coast Battalion, under Captain Butler.

The enemy here occupied a strongly entrenched position dominated on our right flank by the Belok Nkonjok massif some 2,500 ft. high. From trenches and fire pits constructed behind cleared fields of fire at every point of vantage the enemy contested Haywood's advance stubbornly. Here our gunfire, directed skilfully by Captain R. J. R. Waller, was most effective in helping to eject him, thus saving heavy casualties. It was also reported that the German ammunition was inferior, possibly because some had been manufactured at Yaunde.

Butler's detachment successfully surprised a hostile camp at Sege, gaining possession of a machine gun and a quantity of ammunition. He was counter-attacked in a half-hearted fashion, but drove off the enemy without suffering any casualties.

On the 17th December Haywood's column struck the main road about one mile east of Chang Mangas, where it was followed by the main column with Butler's left flank detachment in occupation of the high ground four miles north-east at Konalak. The casualties during the past 10 days had been as follows: 1 Nigeria Regiment, 32, including Sergeant R. Macleod wounded; 2 Nigeria Regiment, 25, including Lieutenants D. M. Crowe and B. T. B. Dillon and Sergeants Kennedy, Flanagan and Elliott wounded; Gambia Company, 12, including Lieutenant A. E. Coombs wounded.

At Chang Mangas itself were a fort and blockhouses, in addition to stores, magazines and a hospital, which gives every indication of the enemy's intention to put up a determined resistance, and consequently reflects highly on the successful tactics employed by Gorges as well as the gallantry and endurance displayed by the W.A.F.F. throughout the operations.

Faucon's Advance to Mangeles, 7th–21st December

Faucon's French Force, advancing along the light railway, reached Badog on the 7th December without much difficulty. Thenceforth it met with stubborn opposition, occupying Mangeles on the 21st. He had incurred 175 casualties during this period; it being evident that the enemy was determined to safeguard his line of retreat southwards.

At Mangeles Faucon halted awhile to bring up supplies and form an advanced base. The Midland Railway was now open as far as Eseka and enough rolling stock had been reconditioned for through traffic.

Capture of Yaunde by Dobell's Forces, 23rd December, 1915–1st January 1916

Between the 7th December and the 22nd the arrival of additional troops from Duala enabled Gorges to reinforce his main column and reorganize his line of communications. It was significant that the local natives were now returning in large numbers to their villages, contributing guides and supplies freely. All this assisted in no small measure to ensuring the safety of the back areas connecting Gorges's and Faucon's columns with their base at Duala.

For the final advance on Yaunde Gorges disposed of his Force as follows:

Right Flank Detachment (Rose): One sub-section Gold Coast Battery (at Gungok); H.Q. and three companies Gold Coast Battalion (just east of Chang Mangas).

Centre Column (Haywood): Howizer detachment; one section Nigerian Battery; field section Royal Engineers; 2 Nigeria Regiment (just east of Chang Mangas).

Left Flank Detachment (Major F. Anderson): Two companies Gold Coast Battalion (at Konolak).

General Reserve (Gorges and H.Q.): One sub-section Nigeria Regiment Battery; one sub-section Gold Coast Battery; machine-gun section West India Regiment; 1 Nigeria Regiment; Gambia Company.

The enemy was reported to have seven companies under Haedicke holding entrenched positions on both banks of the river Mopfu about 10 miles west of Yaunde.

On the 23rd the right and centre drove the enemy out of two successive positions for four or five miles, with slight casualties. The left was forced back after incurring 14 casualties, including Lieutenant H. E. Corner, and had to be reinforced by a gun and a company from the General Reserve.

On the 26th the Ngoa River position was taken without serious loss, mainly due to the wild firing of the German troops, who showed signs of demoralization. On the 27th Cockburn, with 1 Nigeria Regiment and the Gambia Company, relieved Haywood and 2 Nigeria Regiment in the centre column, reaching Unguot. On the 29th and 30th an extensive and strongly entrenched position about the Mopfu River was encountered along the whole line of advance, but this again was poorly defended with bursts of wild firing. On the 31st Rose's right flank detachment occupied Mendong astride the Yaunde-Kribi road.

On the 1st January 1916 Haywood's centre column, having relieved Cockburn, occupied Yaunde Fort without opposition, while Rose's right flank troops entered the Catholic Mission Station, which stood on a commanding ridge south of the Fort covering the roads to Kribi and Widemenge. It appeared the Germans had retired towards Widemenge and Ebolowa, the Governor, Ebermaier, having left with 20 women four days previously, accompanied by a large supply convoy. The Germans had, in fact, carried out their evacuation with complete success.

From subsequent information it was ascertained that Ebermaier had made an urgent appeal to the troops to hold out longer as peace in Europe was imminent, but their morale could not be sustained and by the 25th December the government was transferred to Ebolowa, while a retirement of all troops to an area south of the Nyong River was decided upon.

During the whole operation from the 6th October 1915 to the 1st January 1916 British casualties had been less than 200.

MEASURES FOR THE PURSUIT FROM YAUNDE: 5TH JANUARY–22ND FEBRUARY 1916

At the occupation of Yaunde the position of the Allied forces in the north and east was as follows:

Cunliffe (having advanced from Ditam–Ngembe–Yoko) was on the line Ndenge–Ngila, where Brisset was in touch with Morisson. His striking force was about 1,600 rifles and eight guns.

Aymerich: Morisson's and Hutin's Columns were respectively west and east of Lembe; Le Meillour's Southern Cameroons Column occupying Ambam; Captain Martin's Campo Column just east of Akak.

There had been very little opposition to Cunliffe, while all Aymerich's commanders had been held up considerably by opposition and supply troubles.

Dobell now ordered his Allied Forces under Gorges and Mayer (or Faucon) to take up the pursuit by directing a column from Yaunde on Widemenge and one from Mangeles on Ebolowa via Olama. The former, consisting of one section Nigerian Battery, one field section Sierra Leone Royal Engineers, 2 Nigeria Regiment and two companies Gold Coast Battalion, under Haywood, left Yaunde on the 5th January. The latter consisted of Faucon's French troops. It was later decided to send a column of one sub-section Nigerian Battery, 1 Nigeria Regiment and the Gambia Company, under Coles, to converge on Ebolowa via the Kribi road.

As Morisson's and Brisset's columns had reached Yaunde on the 9th and 10th January, it was arranged that Aymerich should control the final operations for attempting to cut off the retreat of the German Forces into

Spanish Muni, while also directing Hutin's column now arriving at Akonolinga (east of Yaunde) on Sangmelima.

We will now follow the movements of Haywood's column which was the one to keep in closest touch with the enemy.

On the capture of Yaunde, Cunliffe's Force (except for Webb-Bowen's column sent to Duala) was withdrawn to Fumban, where the supply situation was easier. Gorges himself was summoned to Duala, leaving Cockburn in command of the British troops at Yaunde, which also became Aymerich's Headquarters.

On the 8th January Haywood, unopposed, reached the Nyong River at Widemenge. Here he received a letter under a flag of truce from Hauptmann von Stein saying he had orders to hand over 34 European and 180 African prisoners of war. These were taken over at noon next day, under an armistice.

Haywood obtained the following information. Between the 23rd December and the 7th January the Germans had crossed the Nyong at three points a few miles above and below Kolmaka, beginning with part of the force opposing Aymerich. On the 8th the whole force some 2,500 strong was moving on Sabade and Ebolowa. Its rearguard was at Bidegambala, about 10 miles away, while a detachment was marching on Sangmelima. South of Ebolowa, Hagen had a force of some 2,000 rifles. The total strength of the enemy was about 500–600 Europeans and 6,000 native troops. Their objective was definitely Spanish Muni. They appeared to be very tired, short of food, and distinctly demoralized, while their supply of ammunition, especially for machine guns, was limited. One of the released British officers who gave this information offered the opinion, from conversation he had had with Germans, that their prolonged resistance had been due to uninterrupted communication with Spanish Muni, to Ebermaier's strong personality, and the influence and example of their few Regular officers. It should be noted that the staff both at Yaunde and Duala considered the estimate of German troops given above was much too high.

Reconnaissances were pushed out by Haywood's column from Kolmaka while waiting for supplies and for a company of the West African Regiment to take over his line of communications and enable the concentration of his whole six companies for operations. As the supplies had not arrived, his column had to go on half rations.

On the 15th Aymerich issued his operation orders. These directed the pursuit to be pushed on rapidly to Ebolowa, which had already been assigned as Faucon's objective. At the same time Aymerich reinforced Haywood with five Franco/Belgian companies and four guns under Captain Schmoll.

These combined columns were now placed under Morisson's direction, Faucon's column totalling three guns and 13 companies, and Haywood's six guns and 11 companies.

On the 16th Haywood pushed Gibb forward with a gun and two companies to secure the crossing of the Sao River, which he did by skilful manoeuvring, surprising the enemy. On the 19th, having covered 46 miles by rapid marching, he reached Ngulamakong, protected on both flanks by

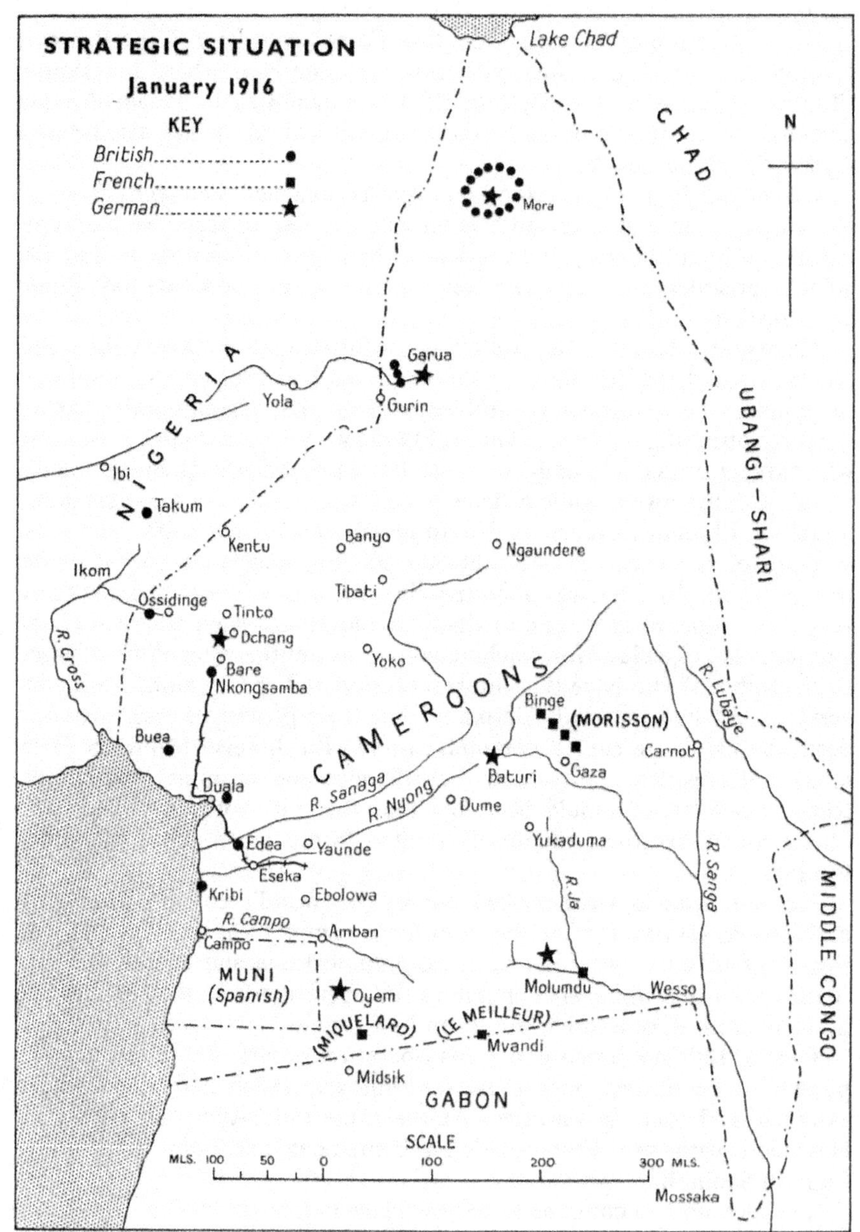

14. Strategic situation January 1916

detachments marching by parallel roads. Here contact was made with Coles at Elabe and news was obtained that Faucon had arrived at Ebolowa, but was immobilized there for lack of supplies.

Being without further instructions from Morisson and considering it imperative to hustle the enemy and co-operate with Hutin, Haywood pushed on from Ebolowa on the 23rd with three guns and 900 rifles. His left flank detachment under Captain Mésegué had not yet rejoined him. After a long march of 18 miles that day he caught up with the German rearguard which was holding a position at Mafub, covering the main body's retirement to Ngoa.

Next day he encountered severe opposition from a force about 100 strong.

Affair at Mafub, 24th January 1916

The lack of suitable paths for a turning movement on either flank made a frontal attack unavoidable, and the British suffered rather heavily in spite of the fact that the enemy had no machine guns. After some hours' fighting the position was captured. This fighting and further obstinate resistance beyond Mafub limited the progress to four miles that day, causing 22 British and one French casualties, including Lieutenant G. A. Anthony killed and Lieutenant K. McIver mortally wounded. The stubbornness of the resistance was explained by the capture of an order from Zimmermann to Buhler, the commander, directing him to hold on all day at whatever cost.

Natives reported Nkan strongly held and Le Meillour's column to be south of the Mburu River on the Ambam road. Accordingly Haywood detached Schmoll's companies to co-operate in an attack on Nkan and to get a letter to Le Meillour.

That evening instructions were received from Morisson, who had reached Ebolowa on the 23rd, to continue his movement towards Nkan and Ngoa, withdrawing when opportune to Kribi via Efulen. A reinforcement of one and a half French companies was being sent from Mechet's column (Mechet having relieved Faucon), said Morisson.

Affair South of Abang, 26th–27th January 1916

On the 25th Haywood continued his advance, occupying Abang in face of slight opposition. However, immediately south of this place he met with stubborn resistance from two successive positions, from which the enemy was only ejected at dusk. This result was largely due to the fire of the Nigerian guns under Waller, whose effect was so demoralizing, that in spite of a very large expenditure of hostile ammunition, we only had four men wounded.

Le Meillour is still Held Up at Mburu River, 28th January 1916

Pressure was kept up on the enemy pending a reply from Le Meillour which arrived on the 28th saying he was still held up on the Mburu River. On receipt of this information Morisson concluded there was no chance of immediate effective co-operation between the two columns, so he sent Haywood orders to withdraw with his British troops to Kribi, which was accomplished by the 31st January 1916.

Final Operations by Aymerich, February 1916

Subsequently Schmoll with a gun and three companies, advanced on Ngoa from Nkan, while Mathieu (of Mechet's column) took a more westerly route to the same objective with a similar force. The enemy disputed the crossing of the Ntem River on the 10th–11th February and every yard of the way to Banyass, the point where he finally crossed into Spanish Muni on the 15th February 1916. On the 12th Morisson, with the rest of Mechet's column, and Le Meillour's column had also met at Ngoa. During this final phase the French had incurred 48 casualties. The German official account in *Der Grosse Krieg*, Col. IV, says that a final defensive position was taken up in the great northerly bend of the Ntem (or Campo) River, where after fighting from the 5th to the 15th February, being short of supplies and ammunition, they were forced to retire in faultless order across the frontier.

Capitulation of Mora, 18th February 1916

When Cunliffe left Duala for Lagos on the 5th February Captain Von Raben was still holding out at Mora. After discussing the matter with Sir Frederick Lugard it was decided to send him a message stating that the other German Forces had taken refuge in Muni, and if he was prepared to surrender he and his officers would be allowed to retain their swords, though all other prisoners would be sent to England. These terms were accepted and the garrison of 11 Germans and 145 native ranks surrendered on the 18th February, with four machine guns and 183 rifles.

This ended the campaign, and to mark its conclusion H.M. The King sent the following telegram on the 22nd February to General Dobell:

'I heartily congratulate you and the naval and military forces under your command on the successful termination of the operations in the Cameroons, and the occupation, in conjunction with our Allies, of that country.'

Dobell's Order of the Day, March 1916

On the 13th March 1916 General Dobell issued to his Force the following order of the day:

'With the departure of the troops, beginning on the 16th March, the Allied Force which I have had the honour to command during the last nineteen months commences to be broken up. I therefore take the opportunity of bidding farewell to all those who have taken part in the camapign which has terminated so successfully. I desire to express my thanks to all officers, non-commissioned officers and men of the Allied Force, both European and native, who have rendered me such loyal and unswerving assistance in achieving the arduous task which has lain before us.

'I desire also to place on record the invaluable help which has been rendered to the Allied cause by the Force commanded by General Aymerich, Brigadier-General Cunliffe, Colonel Brisset, and all under their respective commands, who have borne the brunt of much fighting and marching in difficult country.

'To all officers, petty and non-commissioned officers and men of the Allied Navies I wish to express my deepest thanks for the share which they have taken in the operations both by sea and land. Finally, I wish all those who have served under me, or who have been associated with me, the best of good fortune in whatever adventure may lie before them.'

Conclusion

The Allied Operations in the Cameroons very naturally appeared of insignificant importance to the nation at large when compared with the vast operations being conducted in the main theatres of war at this time. The respective forces engaged were relatively small and the battle casualties in no way comparable with those incurred on the major fronts.

Yet the conditions of service, the climate, and the extent of the operations covering a territory about one and a half times the size of the German Empire, almost entirely lacking in good communications, made the undertaking one of considerable magnitude.

One of the chief factors contributing to the success of the campaign was the skilfully planned stretegy of the Allied Higher Command and their international co-operation. The results of these were apparent in the timing whereby the various columns, starting from points several hundred miles apart, converged on Yaunde within a few days of one another. An equally important factor was the fine spirit which animated the Europeans in face of all difficulties and adversities. The example set by them inspired the African soldiers they led to deeds of devoted gallantry and endurance. Nor must we forget the cheerfulness and good humour—a characteristic feature of the W.A.F.F. soldier and carrier—which at all times was of inestimable value in making the best of his misfortunes.

It has been no part of our task to follow in detail the operations of our Navy and the Nigerian Marine, but as Dobell pointed out in his despatches, without their assistance the military forces could not have accomplished the task by which they were confronted.

No complete casualties are available for the W.A.F.F., but in the figures given below showing the total British casualties in the campaign only a small percentage can be allotted to other units.

	Europeans	*Africans*
Killed, or died of wounds	24	192
Wounded	30	557
Died of disease	6	84

Out of a total of 864 British Europeans and 5,927 combatant Africans, 151 Europeans and 434 Africans had been invalided. Of approximately 20,000 carriers imported to Duala 574 became casualties in battle or from disease. The French casualties amongst combatants approximated closely to those of the British.

Mentions

Of the W.A.F.F. officers brought to notice by Dobell and Cunliffe, apart from Column Commanders, prominence is given to Lieutenant-Colonels A. J. Turner, J. Brough, W. D. Wright of the General Staff; while of regimental officers these are specially noted:

Nigeria Regiment: 1 Battalion or 1 Nigeria Regiment, Captains M. H. S. Willis, F. J. H. Pring, and A. H. Giles; 2 Battalion, or 2 Nigeria Regiment, Captains C. Gibb, J. Sargeant, J. P. D. Underwood, C. H. Fowle and M. E. Fell; 3 Battalion, Captain G. C. Bowyer-Smijth; Nigerian Artillery, Captain R. J. R. Waller.

Gold Coast Regiment: Captains J. F. P. Butler, V.C., and C. G. Hornby.

Sierra Leone Battalion: Captain F. Anderson, Lieutenant G. Dawes.

Comments

Brigadier Gorges, in his book, *The Great War in West Africa*, makes the comment 'that perhaps at times there was a tendency to set too high a value on the enemy's fighting qualities and to overestimate his strength'. This is thought to be a fair comment in cases where the fighting was in bush country. Rushing tactics and a bayonet charge usually succeeded here. On the other hand, it must be borne in mind that to charge a totally concealed enemy supported by machine-gun fire needs a high standard of resolution on the part of officers and men.

Artillery

In the open country of the north this was most effective, but in the southern bush country it was very difficult to site and targets were nearly always invisible. Waller, however, was often successful in overcoming the difficulty by the methods he adopted in thick bush and which are explained in Chapter VI (E)

Wireless

In the forest it appeared to be useless, so results were most disappointing.

Motor Transport

In the final advance on Yaunde a motor road was opened to Wumbiagas and motor transport was available, thereby improving the supply problem enormously.

Importance of the Campo-Ntem Area

It may be thought that the failure to cut off the enemy's retreat into Spanish Muni was due to a miscalculation of his strength in the Campo-Ntem River area, and that much greater support should have been given much earlier from Campo to Le Meillour's column. On the other hand, Dobell never had a big reserve in hand and might not have felt justified in denuding other parts of the front. But there seems to be no doubt, that in spite of the Naval blockade, for a long period of the campaign supplies of all kinds were getting over the Spanish border and materially helping the

Germans to hold out, so that the most strenuous efforts to prevent this leakage were of the first importance.

Tribute to the Enemy

We cannot bring this narrative to a close without giving full credit to the German foes. They were fighting against overwhelming odds with no hope of succour. Their pluck and resourcefulness in keeping the Allies at bay were beyond praise. They were, however, well supplied with machine guns, which, particularly in bush country, were of outstanding value, and being generally well-sited, these did much to redress the balance of numbers. Still, when all is said and done, it must be admitted that their defence of the Cameroons during the period of nineteen months deserves the highest praise. Their native soldiers stuck to their officers in a most surprising way until the position became hopeless. The pick of their troops were the Yaundes, who were certainly every bit as good as our W.A.F.F. soldiers. Their Commander-in-Chief was Colonel Zimmermann, but the Governor, Ebermaier, seems to have been the dominant personality in the campaign.

CHAPTER 5

The East African Campaign: 1915–18

THE GOLD COAST REGIMENT

FROM the outbreak of the First World War until the conclusion of the Campaign in the Cameroons, in April 1916, the Gold Coast Regiment had been continuously on active service for some 30 months. During this time it had won a high reputation for courage and endurance against African troops armed with modern weapons and skilfully led by Europeans.

It was only after enjoying a few weeks' rest in cantonments at Kumasi that instructions were received to prepare for service in East Africa.

Apart from the personnel of the Regiment now proceeding on active service, details of which are given below, its military responsibilities further involved the garrisoning of the Gold Coast and Togoland, as well as providing for the training of recruits and reinforcements for overseas; for these purposes 750 rank and file were needed. As the campaign proceeded these numbers were considerably exceeded in order to cope with the expansion of training units.

From the first to last five drafts, totalling 2,602 men, were sent to reinforce the Expeditionary Contingent, although the total effectives in the field at any one time never much exceeded 900 rifles.

By the 5th July the Regiment had assembled at the port of Sekondi. It consisted of four Double Companies, 'A', 'B', 'G', and 'I' with a Pioneer Company and a Battery of two 2·95 in. guns, also 12 machine guns and a complement of carriers. Its strength was 36 British officers, 15 British N.C.O.s, 11 native clerks, 980 rank and file, 177 gun carriers, one storeman, 204 other carriers, and four officers of the Royal Army Medical Corps, making a total of 1,423. Their Commanding Officer was Lieutenant-Colonel R. A. de B. Rose, D.S.O.

The Governor of the Gold Coast and its Dependencies—Ashanti and the Northern Territories—had come from Accra to inspect them and wish them God-speed. Sir Hugh Clifford records that the Regiment presented a most smart and workmanlike appearance on the occasion, having the look of thoroughly seasoned troops with achievements already to their credit which filled the Colony to which they belonged with pride.

Embarkation was completed and the transport *Aeneas* sailed about 1400 hours on the 6th July. On 26th, after a journey round the Cape devoid of incident, the vessel arrived at Kilindini, the port of Mombasa, where disembarkation was made by lighters. Although there had been no rain for weeks, a sudden tornado speedily soaked all ranks to the skin. Two trains conveyed them to Ngombezi, some 40 miles from Tanga, where they went into camp. The men had suffered from severe cold on the journey, and owing to their damp clothing were further chilled by the low

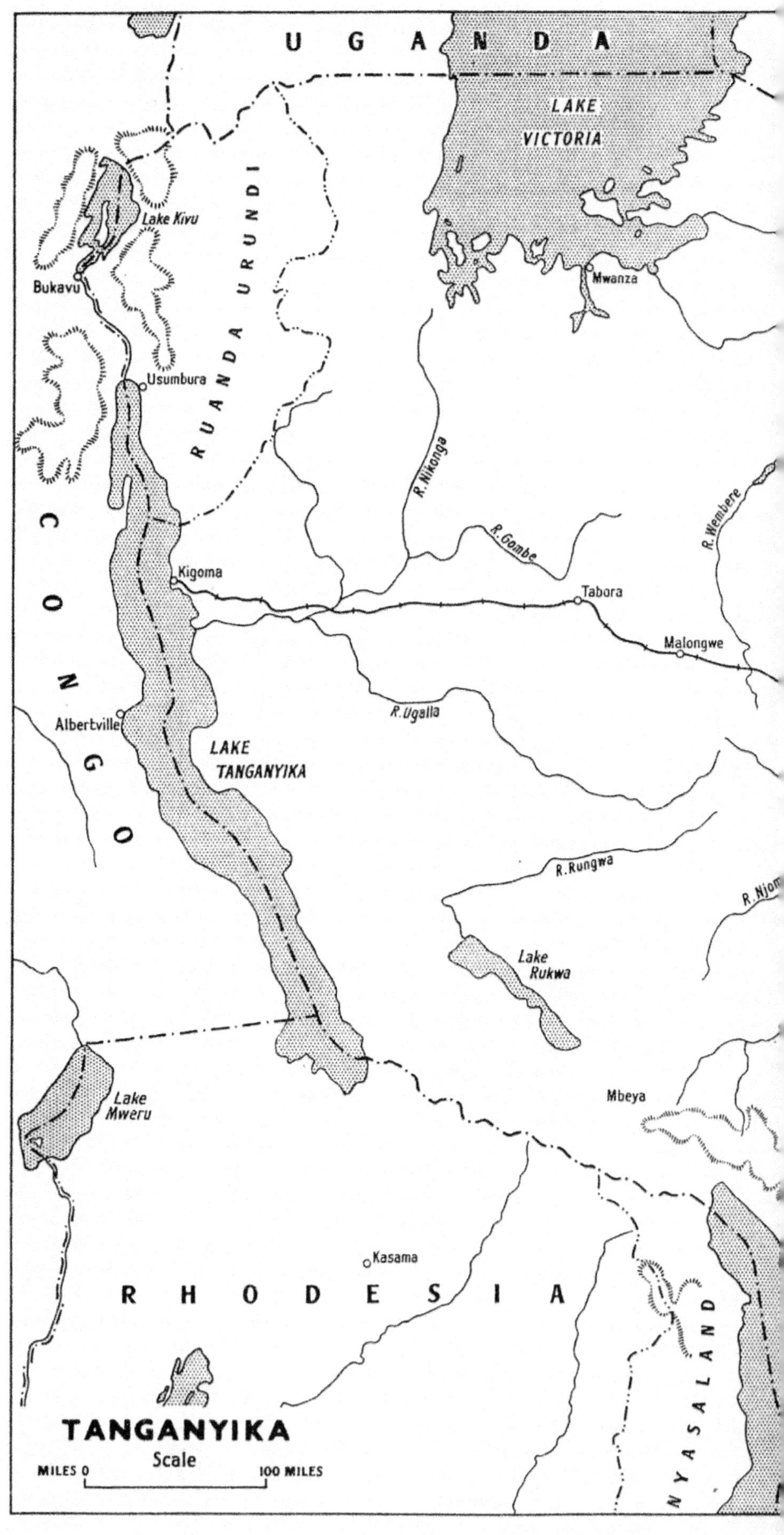

U G A N D A
LAKE
VICTORIA
Lake Kivu
Bukavu
Mwanza
R U A N D A U R U N D I
Usumbura
R. Nikonga
R. Wembere
R. Gombe
C O N G O
Kigoma
Tabora
Malongwe
Albertville
R. Ugalla
LAKE
TANGANYIKA
R. Rungwa
R. Njom
Lake
Rukwa
Lake
Mweru
Mbeya
Kasama
R H O D E S I A
N Y A S A L A N D
TANGANYIKA
Scale
MILES 0
100 MILES

15. T

NAIROBI
K E N Y A
Lake Natron
Moshi
Arusha
Lake Eyasi
Lake Manyara
MOMBASA
Kondoa
Korogwe
Tanga
Ruvu or Pangani R.
PEMBA I.
ZANZIBAR I.
Zanzibar
I N D I A N O C E A N
Dodoma
R. Wami
R. Ngerengere
R. Kingoni
DAR ES SALAAM
Kilosa
Morogoro
ULUGURU MTS.
Dutumi
R. Ruvu
R. Mgeta
Gt. Ruaha R.
Iringa
R. Rufiji
Mkindu
Ngwembe
Utete
MAFIA I.
R. Kilombero
Kibata
Kilwa Kivinje
R. Matandu
Migeregere
Narungombe
Mihambia
Mpingo
Bweho Chini
Mawerenye
R. Liwale
R. Nakiu
Nahungo
Liwale
R. Luwegu
R. Mbarangandu
R. Depate
R. Angai
R. Mbemkuru
Lindi
Ruponda
Mtua
R. Lukuledi
Mahiwa
Nyangao
MAKONDE PLATEAU
Masasi
Songea
Tunduru
R. Ruvuma
Port Amelia
M O Ç A M B I Q U E

nyika

temperature experienced at altitudes of some 6,000 ft. where the line crossed the lower spur of Mount Kilimanjaro. In a number of cases this caused pneumonia.

On 30th July the Regiment was inspected by Brigadier-General Edwards, Inspector-General of Communications, who was much impressed by their physique and soldierly appearance, and emphasized the fact that no other unit he had inspected had arrived so well equipped. He consequently wired to the Commander-in-Chief that the Regiment was fit to take the field at once.

The military situation at this time on the Eastern Section was approximately as follows. General Smuts, the Commander-in-Chief, had his Headquarters 60 miles north of Morogoro on the main railway. Here also was the 1st Division (Hoskins), composed of the 1 and 2 East African Brigades, under Sheppard and Hanyngton respectively. Both were composed of native troops, except for a machine-gun detachment of the Loyal North Lancashire Regiment, attached to the 2nd Brigade. The Gold Coast Regiment was to form its Divisional Reserve.

On the right was the 2nd Division, entirely South African, infantry and mounted troops, under Van Deventer, based on Kondo-Irangi. Between the two divisions was a force of mounted troops under Brits, operating independently, while on the extreme left was a column of Indian troops moving down the coast towards Dar es Salaam.

The plan was to attack the German railway simultaneously at Dar es Salaam, Morogoro, Kilosssa and Dodoma, depriving the enemy of its use and driving him south towards the Rufiji River.

On 4th August, leaving the Depot Company at Korogwe, the Regiment left for the 1st Divisional Headquarters at Mziha. This was a very trying march over an unmetalled track along which motor-lorries had been ploughing their way for several weeks, reducing the surface to six inches of fine red powder. Eyes, nose and mouth became filled with the stuff, causing acute thirst, which could only be relieved by recourse to a few holes of foul, brackish water. The transport consisted of cape wagons of 16 oxen, many of which were infected with trypanosomae and were on their last legs, but had, however, to be driven as long as they could stand owing to the exigencies of the situation. For eight days the men endured one of the worst marches of their experience in East Africa, plodding, parched and choking, along that interminable road. They had become unrecognizable. Usually cheerful and light-hearted, they were now sullen and suspicious. For the first time their officers could not get a grin out of them; a thing they had never failed to do before.

On the 12th, Divisional Headquarters was reached, where a river of running water was found and where the luxury of bathing and a rest restored the men to their usual good spirits. On the following day the advance of the Division was resumed and proceeded without much incident, driving small German rearguards before it until the mission station at Matombo was reached, where the enemy had left a hospital of sick and wounded together with a number of old men, women and children. This place was at the entrance to the Uluguru Mountains, which the British were now engaged in forcing.

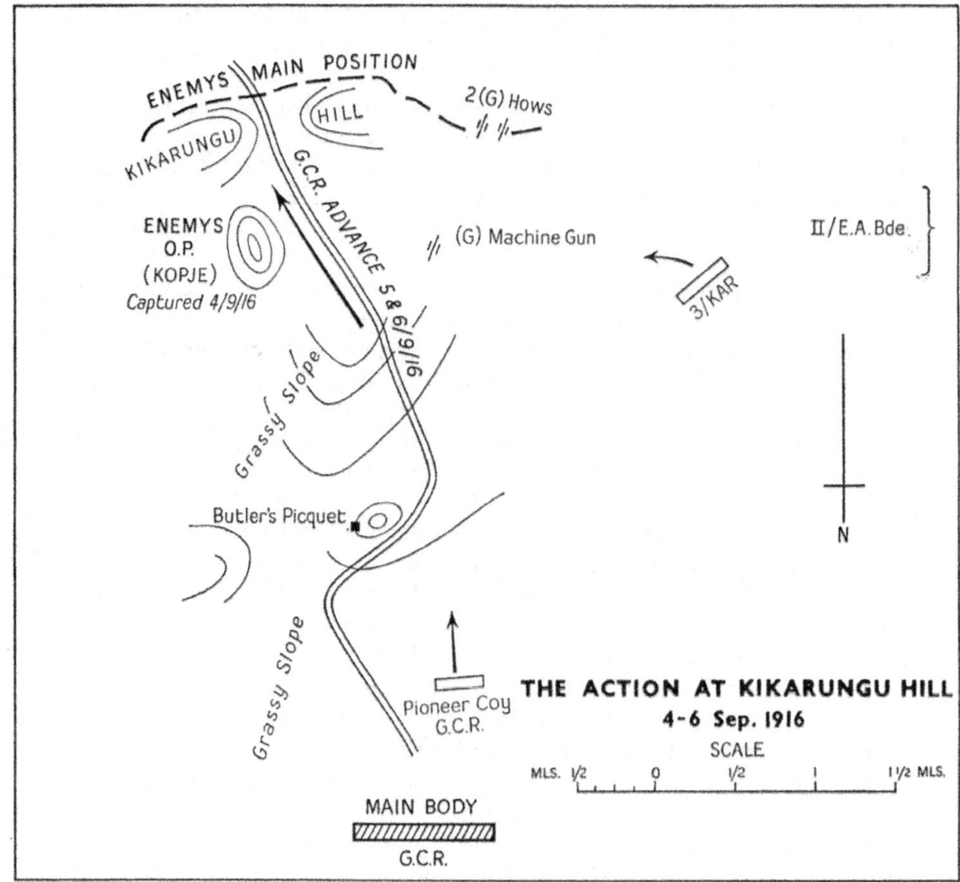

16. The action at Kikarungu Hill, 4th–6th September 1916

General Smuts had now crossed the main railway from Dar es Salaam to Lake Tanganyika and the 1st Division was faced with a mountainous area of some 100 sq. miles between the railway and the low-lying Rufiji valley. The principal highway, where the main battle was proceeding lay some miles to the east of Matomba, when the Regiment left its camp on 4th September on its first serious engagement in East Africa.

Action at Kikarungu Hill, 4th–6th September 1916

Facing our line of advance the enemy had taken up a strong position with Kikarungu Hill, a sugar-loafed mountain some 300 ft. high, as an observation point. The Regiment's task was to expel him from this hill. About 0900 hours two German howitzers opened fire upon the road by which it was advancing. No casualties occurred; the troops were moved off the road to a sheltered position on right of it between the gut of two hills. This road led up a winding valley with kopjes on either side, at the top of which on the left is Kikarungu Hill, and beyond lies a pass leading into the Uluguru Mountains.

Captain J. Butler, V.C., D.S.O. (who had won both distinctions in the Cameroons), was sent forward to reconnoitre the enemy's position. Having occupied one of these kopjes about one and a half miles from where the Regiment was halted, he sent a picquet of the Pioneers to a point where the road took a U-shaped bend towards the left. Beyond the U bend, on the right, was another kopje, from the crest of which the enemy opened fire with a machine gun.

About 1700 hours the Pioneer Company became heavily engaged. Butler went forward to the picquet to see how they fared. While he was lying there, beside his men, a sudden burst of machine-gun fire from the kopje in front wounded him and several of his party. In all 12 of the Pioneers were wounded that afternoon, but they held firm until later reinforced by 'B' Company under Captain Shaw, who made the ground won secure for the night.

The wounded were safely evacuated, though Butler died the same evening. This young officer possessed a charming and forceful personality combined with an absolutely fearless nature and more than usual ability. He had won the devotion and affection of his men in a very special degree. His death, in this first action in which the Regiment had been engaged in East Africa was felt to be a malignant stroke of ill fortune and was mourned as a personal loss by his comrades of all ranks.

Shaw received orders to push on at the earliest opportunity. Under cover of darkness he crept forward until dawn gave enough light to continue up the grass slope towards the German position on the kopje. Here the charge was sounded, and, with bayonets fixed, the men rushed up the hill, capturing it successfully. In this charge Acting Sergeant Bukari of 'B' Company displayed conspicuous bravery, subsequently rewarded by a bar to the D.C.M. he had already won in the Cameroons. His subsequent history was, however, a sad one; he was evacuated with a slight wound which had become septic, and he died in hospital at the base.

During the rest of the day Shaw continued to fight his way up the road from kopje to kopje, the Pioneers under Lieutenant Bray and 'B' under Shaw advancing alternately until a point about 400 yards from the head of the pass was secured.

By this time the whole of the 2nd East African Brigade was in action, the 3rd King's African Rifles moving well out to the right with the object of turning the enemy's left flank. A gun of the Gold Coast Battery came up in support, but owing to the strength of the enemy's position and the lateness of the hour no great progress was made. Next day Captain Wheeler with 'A' Company relieved 'B'; throughout the 6th the Regiment pressed their attack supported by the Battery, while the flank attack progressed, accompanied by heavy shelling from the 5th South African Mountain Battery. In spite of violent machine-gun fire upon their advanced positions, the Gold Coast succeeded with 'G' Company (Poyntz) in effecting a junction with the King's African Rifles by 1400 hours, while the enemy, pressed in front and flank, began to retire and Kikarungu Hill was captured that evening.

The Regiment's casualties during these two and a half days numbered 42, of whom one officer and six rank and file were killed, whilst Colour-

Sergeant Beattie was wounded. The enemy's casualties, as is usual in this type of engagement, were hard to estimate. Three each Europeans and Askaris were definitely killed, while a good deal of arms and equipment were picked up. The enemy had, however, succeeded in holding up our troops for two and a half days and withdrawing without being cut off. In this type of warfare the defence has a considerable advantage, usually being able to break off the engagement at the moment when his retreat is in danger of being held up.

The following telegram was received by Colonel Rose from the Brigade Commander on the evening of the 6th September. 'Please tell your Regiment that I think they worked splendidly today, and I wish to thank them for their good work.'

On the 7th the Regiment rested and reorganized. Next day it pushed forward along the road under the lee of Kikarungu, making its way into the heart of the Uluguru Mountains, which consist of clumps of high hills covered with grassy scrub and strewn with boulders. Having caught up with the King's African Rifles, the march was continued until the main road connecting Tulo with Kisaki was reached on the 10th. Here the 2 East African Brigade was met and the Regiment rejoined the reserve.

Action at the Dutumi River, 10th–12th September

Close touch had been kept from Kikarungu, until the enemy now showed a disposition to stand. Here a wide plain stretched towards the Dutumi, which flowed south from the Ulugurus, to join the Mgeta River. There the enemy was entrenched about 2,200 strong with 24 machine guns concealed in bush and elephant grass, prepared to dispute the crossing. The 3rd Kashmir Rifles with machine guns of the Loyals and one section of the mountain battery attempted a frontal attack which made little progress owing to dense bush, while 57th Wildes Rifles were ordered to secure Kitoho Hill which overlooked the position on the north of the road. At 1400 3 King's African Rifles got orders to turn the enemy's right by making a wide sweep round Kitoho Hill, crossing the Dutumi and threatening the enemy's retreat downstream.

At dawn on 11th Fitzgerald sent half his battalion down the right bank of the Dutumi, but they were driven back by enemy reinforcements from Kisaki, who had already checked the South Africans near the place. Meanwhile the other two companies of the King's African Rifles, moving down the left bank, were held up by machine-gun fire from a spur of Kitoho Hill, as were Wildes Rifles.

Early next morning the Gold Coast Pioneers, 'I' Company and the Battery under Poyntz reinforced the King's African Rifles. At 1430 hours the Gold Coast Contingent, supported by 'C' Company, crossed to the right bank of the Dutumi, while the King's African Rifles, moved down the left bank, establishing themselves, with Wildes Rifles, on the lower slopes of Kitoho Hill. The enemy's position opposite Poyntz lay across the Tulo road, and at right-angles to it. The country was mostly thick scrub and high grass. From a salient in his line very heavy fire was opened which held Poyntz up, forcing him to retire and dig in, the 29th Baluchis being sent to his support.

Meanwhile on the other (right) flank of the British, Major Goodwin had sent 'A' and 'B' Companies to occupy two hills overlooking Nkessa, the edge of which was strongly held by the enemy. Progress was slow against determined opposition and by 1800 hours an outpost position was taken up on these hills where rifle pits had been dug.

On 13th patrols discovered the enemy had retired. A general advance was made throughout the day opposed by strong counter-attacks on Poyntz's flank which was now reinforced by 'B' and three sections of 'A' Company. Night coming on, the troops dug in. The country throughout these operations was covered with thick elephant grass, making the exact location of the hostile position very difficult.

On 14th it was found that the enemy had withdrawn, and the Gold Coast Regiment, having been relieved by the King's African Rifles, marched to the Brigade camp at Nkessa.

The casualties between the 11th and 13th numbered four killed and 33 wounded. The latter included Captain Greene, Lieutenants Bray and Arnold and Colour-Sergeant May. Arnold died in Tulo Hospital from wounds received on the 12th. Lieutenant Isaacs was captured by an enemy patrol.

Although Smuts had failed to envelop von Lettow's forces in the Uluguru Mountains he was still fairly confident that one more determined effort might end the war before the advent of the rainy season bogged down his troops in the Mgeta valley, which is a branch of the Ruvu. This country, into which the enemy had disappeared, is a tropical, swampy, jungle of a fever-laden steamy character. Immediate action was therefore imperative.

Consequently the 2 East African Brigade was ordered to advance south from Nkessa to the Mgeta with a view to locating the enemy's right flank.

On the evening of 18th, 3 King's African Rifles left Nkessa, reaching the Mgeta and wading across it on 19th. By 2330 hours the enemy's picquets were met, screened by heavy bush. Progress was slow and strongly opposed. The battalion consolidated its position, but was unable to advance further, being reinforced by the Gold Coast Regiment on 20th. During this time rain fell in torrents and no progress was made for the next five days, when the position was taken over by the Regiment and the King's African Rifles marched back to Nkessa. Operations were confined to patrol and outpost encounters; these, however, caused the Regiment a good many casualties.

After being relieved by 130th Baluchis the Gold Coast Regiment was moved to Nkessa on 2nd October, as an attack on that place was expected. Here encounters between patrols were frequent, without much damage on either side. On 16th the Kisaki road was found to be mined by a four-inch shell embedded a few feet in the ground, but no casualties occurred.

On 17th the Battalion moved to Tulo, where it remained till 7th November, upon which date the 2 Brigade broke camp and began a march to Dar es Salaam. The way led by the Ruvu River to Mafisi along a green and fertile valley, perhaps the most attractive area seen during the campaign. At Mafisi the Ruvu valley was quitted and the march continued in an easterly direction parallel to the railway, reaching Dar es Salaam on 17th November, where the Regiment embarked for Kilwa Kisiwani, 150 miles down the coast.

The reason for the move to Kilwa was that the advent of the rainy season had made operations north of the Rufiji valley impracticable owing to the low-lying, swampy and unhealthy character of the terrain there.

It was evident, too, that the enemy would endeavour to establish himself in the higher, and more salubrious, country to the south of that river. It was with a view to frustrating his plan that Brigadier-General Hanyngton with his Brigade had been sent some weeks earlier to conduct operations in the area described, and for this purpose the Gold Coast Regiment was being despatched to act as his reserve. A further, and dominating, factor in the situation was the difficulty of supplying the troops north of the Rufiji during the rainy season and the consequent necessity of reducing their numbers to a minimum consistent with a safety margin. It was the lot of the Nigeria Brigade (due to arrive from West Africa) to fill the latter role.

On 19th the Regiment disembarked at Kilwa Kisiwani, encamping at Mpara the same afternoon. Here it was joined by the Depot Company, which had hitherto remained at Kotogwe, on the Tanga–Moshi Railway under Major Read. On 24th it moved to Bloss Hill near Kilwa, where 'G' Company was broken up and its men posted to other companies.

While the operations south of the Uluguru Mountains were in progress the coastal columns, assisted by the Royal Navy, had occupied the ports as far as, and including, Dar es Salaam, with little opposition, G.H.Q. moving thence from Kotogwe and Tanga. The 2nd Division was directed on the railway towards Malongwe. Advanced G.H.Q. remained at Morogoro and began work to establish railway connection between them. Practically every bridge and culvert had been destroyed, but the first train got through on 24th November.

Invasion from the West and South

During this time in the Western Sector two columns were advancing on Tabora, the capital of Tanganyika, an important base of supplies. These consisted of a Belgian force of 11,000 men under General Tombeur, and a British one of some 2,000 under Brigadier-General Crewe. On 19th September Tabora fell and with its capture the Belgians were not inclined to go farther.

The main German force (Major Wahle's) had withdrawn south under Captain Wintgens, while another column of 400 rifles proceeded east along the railway, both finally joining up at Iringa, leaving the whole railway in Smuts' hands. This ended the role of Crewe's force, the irregular units of which were disbanded, and 4th King's African Rifles joined van Deventer's 2nd Division at Malongwe station early in October.

In the Southern Sector Brigadier-General Northey disposed of some 3,500 combatant troops, based on Lake Nyassa. By September 1916 they were scattered along a front stretching between the Great Ruaha and Rufiji rivers, with the object of intercepting the German line of retreat towards the Mahenge plateau, 150 miles distant. Northey reported the disposition of his columns as follows:

Commander	*Rifles*	*Machine Guns*	*Area*
Hawthorn	800	18	Lupembe to Mfrika
Murray	905	16	Ubena
Rodoes	320	10	Ubena
Bryon	1,150	12	Songea
Line of Communication	500		
	3,675	56	

He was therefore much perturbed to hear of the rapid approach of the enemy's Tabora Force, commanded by Major Wahle, who had some 2,000 Askaris at his disposal. These were marching eastwards in three columns which broke through his communications between Iringa and Lake Nyassa in the latter half of October.

It is not part of my task to follow the operations in this area any further, as they were not undertaken by West African Frontier Force troops. Suffice it to say that the pressure of our main forces from the north during the early days of 1917 gradually led to the withdrawal of Wahle's Contingent until they united with von Lettow in the south-east of Tanganyika near the Portuguese border.

On 25th November the Gold Coast Regiment began its march in a westerly direction via Mitole to Chemara, which was reached on 28th. This march had been a very trying one, largely across an arid plain scorched by the tropical sun, and bereft of water. The Gold Coast soldier is a tough individual, not generally affected by great heat, but the absence of drinking water is a great privation to him, as, like all Africans, he is blessed with very open pores. More than forty of them fell out on the first day, sinking exhausted on the line of march; many of them, as well as eight officers, had to be sent to hospital as the result.

At Chemara the Regiment relieved the 2/2 King's African Rifles and on this being effected 'I' Company (185 all ranks) took up an outpost position at Namaranje.

The breaking up of 'C' Company had been necessitated by the very serious reduction in the Regiment's strength. On 28th November the field-state showed only 19 British officers, as against 36 who had embarked from the Gold Coast in July, while B.N.C.O.s had fallen from 15 to 10 and rank and file from 980 to 715. Although battle casualties had been severe, far greater loss had been occasioned by ill health due to exposure, overexertion and shortage of food and water, both of which were often of bad quality.

During this period von Lettow had been steadily withdrawing his forces from the swampy Rufiji valley to his main supply centre in the high Utete area, north of Kilwa. Kibata fort lay in the middle of this region. Kibata had been occupied by the King's African Rifles on 14th October with slight opposition, but during November the enemy were reported to be threatening its recapture. By the middle of November Headquarters 1st Division (Hoskins) and the 2 Infantry Brigade (Brigadier-General D. de C. O'Grady) had landed at Kilwa. Reinforcements were hurried to Kibata to counter the threat. O'Grady, in whose Brigade was the Gold Coast Regiment, now took command of these operations. He proved himself in these operations, as well as subsequently, to be an outstanding Brigade Commander.

Action of Kibata, 6th–15th December

The garrison of Kibata was about 800 strong, composed mainly of King's African Rifles and 130th Baluchia. About 1300 hours on 6th the German columns attacked and drove in Kibata's outposts, on the north about Ambush Hill and Coconut village, firing continuing till nightfall. Next morning a determined onslaught was made on Picquet Hill, the key to the position on the west side. A 4·1 in. gun from the Konigsberg bombarded the defences heavily, demolishing a redoubt here. The Germans continued to press the defences by every means, while O'Grady massed his Brigade and advanced from Chamara to reinforce the fort. The role allotted to the Gold Coast Regiment was to turn the enemy's right flank. At dawn on 15th December Poyntz led the advance with the Pioneer Company. When he had passed a post occupied by Captain Harman with half of 'A' Company and a machine gun, he came under fire from an outlying spur, called Banda Hill, on his right. At this point Captain Biddulph, O.C. vanguard, was dangerously wounded and Lieutenant Duncan was killed; the vanguard then withdrew while the Battery came into action and started shelling Banda Hill. About 0800 hours Poyntz continued his advance, working round some small hills on his left and reaching his objective, Gold Coast Hill. During his advance he occupied Banda Hill, where he left a small detachment.

While this was in progress the enemy opened fire with his 4·1 in. gun on the main road south of the Battery. Here one of the shells burst almost at Rose's feet where he was sitting with his Adjutant, Captain Pye, and an orderly beside him. Both the latter were killed instantaneously and Rose was flung back some distance, but was otherwise unharmed.

At 1300 hours a heavy counter-attack opened on Gold Coast Hill as well as on a small ridge in front of it which was held by Lieutenant Shields with 30 rifles and a machine gun. Heavy shelling with machine-gun and rifle fire was concentrated upon these places, quickly causing many casualties.

By this time the rest of the Regiment, under Major Goodwin's command, had come up in support on Banda Hill and a small eminence some 500 yards north-west of it. Captain Wheeler with half 'A' Company advanced to reinforce the Pioneers on Gold Coast Hill, while Lieutenant Piggott with a machine gun of 'B' Company took up a position on his right flank. Piggott was almost immediately wounded, but nevertheless continued in the firing line.

At 1430 hours Poyntz was dangerously, and Wheeler severely, wounded. Harman, himself slightly wounded, took over command on Gold Coast

Hill, with Shields on the ridge in front and Piggott on the right flank of the crest.

Shortly after Lieutenants Kinley and Taylor with the rest of 'A' Company and a machine gun came up in support, but Taylor was at once severely wounded.

About 1500 hours the enemy again opened heavy shell fire causing more casualties; Goodwin then went forward with the remainder of his reserves, some 50 rifles under Shaw of 'B' Company, who took up a position on Piggott's right.

For two and a half hours longer the Regiment clung tenaciously to its position, but at 1730 it was relieved by the 40th Pathans when it took up outpost positions between Gold Coast Hill and the main road from Mtumbei Juu to Kibata.

It was estimated that the German Naval gun had fired some 180 shells between 1100 and 1730 hours. The men had been terribly exposed to concentrated shell, machine-gun and rifle fire during these six and a half hours, being unable to dig themselves in. Their behaviour had been magnificent, while their supports had moved forward without any show of wavering. It was their severest test so far, as can be judged from the following casualty list.

No less than 140 casualties had been suffered on this day, 15th December. Two officers were killed and seven wounded. One B.N.C.O. was wounded. Of the rank and file 26 were killed and 87 wounded, while five gun- and ammunition-carriers were killed and 12 wounded—approximately 50 per cent of officers and 15 per cent of the men.

On 16th the Regiment went into camp to rest and reorganize its shattered forces. On the west it took up positions on a semicircular ridge north-east of Mtumbei Juu Mission, where it remained some days, using the Battery to support the 40th Pathans on Harman's Kopje, and sending out patrols.

On 24th it was learned that Military Crosses had been awarded to Captains Shaw and O'Brien, Royal Army Medical Corp (Medical Staff), for gallantry at Kikirungu Hill. On 27th Kelton with 80 rank and file relieved the Pathans at Harman's Kopje. On 29th the Battery opened fire on a German camp located behind Gold Coast Hill; the enemy retaliated so strongly that Foley was driven back to another prepared position.

On the same day Captain Wray and Lieutenant Downer arrived with welcome reinforcements from Kumasi and Volunteers from Accra. The reinforcements consisted of 180 Fulanis and 90 Jaundis, who had been recruited in the Cameroons. The Volunteers were under Captain Hollis, as were 200 Sierra Leone carriers.

That day, too, Captain Biddulph died of wounds received on the 15th December, when commanding the vanguard near Kibata. On 30th December the Regiment's strength, after receiving its reinforcements amounted to 19 officers, 14 B.N.C.O.s, 10 clerks and dressers, 860 rank and file, 444 gun and other carriers, 34 servants and 48 stretcher-bearers—a total of 1,429.

During the first week in January the Regiment continued to occupy

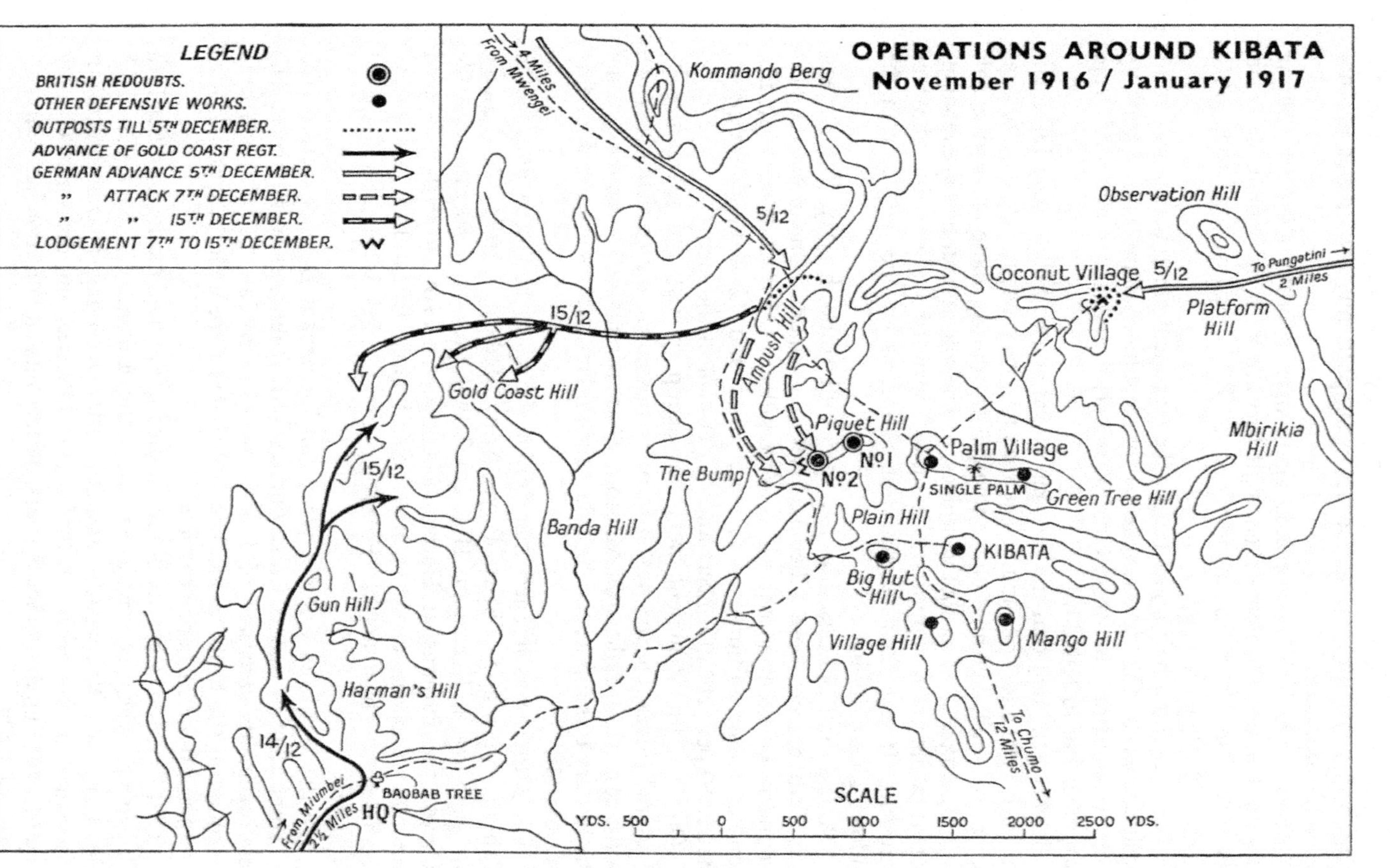

17. Operations around Kibata, November 1916—January 1917

the position between Mtumbei Juu and Kibata, while O'Grady had dealt the enemy a severe blow on the latter's extreme left flank.

On 8th and 9th Rose pushed a strong reconnaissance force of 'A' and 'B' Companies with the Gold Coast Battery and 24 Mountain Battery, in an easterly direction in order to confirm reports that the enemy was withdrawing north-west by the Mwengei road. This was duly confirmed and touch was gained with the 29th Baluchis and the 2nd King's African Rifles, who had been operating from Kibata.

On 10th the reconnaissance returned to headquarters and active patrolling of the Kibata-Mwengei road began. On the same day notice was received that Poyntz had been awarded the M.C., Colour-Sergeant Campbell the D.C.M., and Lance-Corporal Sully Ibadan the M.M. for their gallant services on 15th December.

During the next few days two German prisoners were captured by the Pathans: these included a Major von Bompkin, who had been second-in-command to von Lettow. It appeared that von Bompkin had headed a deputation to von Lettow representing that enough had been done to satisfy honour, that further resistance was useless and the only sensible course was to surrender. Von Lettow's reply was to degrade him to the rank of Patrol Commander, which was his position when he was captured.

The Kibata engagement had been fought under conditions which tried the African troops highly. Rain was incessant; the opposing sides were often engaged in trench warfare at a range of some 80 yards with grenades, while being bombarded with gun- and machine-gun fire. The German attack at Kibata was notable for hard fighting. The fine King's African Rifles units were decimated here before they had had time to assimilate their raw recruits. Only the Gold Coast Regiment and best Indian battalions were able to meet the veteran Askaris on equal terms. The Gold Coast Regiment bore a considerable share in these operations, out of which they came most creditably.

Before retiring the Germans destroyed their Konigsberg gun. This was the last action fought before they evacuated the Mtumbei Hills.

The British occupation of the Matumbei highlands in the Kibata area had to some extent the strategic result of barring the road south of the main German forces in the Rufiji basin, thus giving an opening for the far-reaching plan which Smuts was maturing for the next stage in the campaign.

On 20th January the Regiment moved down the mountains to Kitambi. Rose was appointed temporarily to command the 3 East African Brigade, while Goodwin took over command of the Gold Coast unit. On 26th the latter left for Kiyombo, where the Brigade Camp was established. From 29th to 6th February 'A' and 'B' Companies were detached to a place on the Lugomaya River, which became known as Greene's Post. From all these points the work of patrolling was regularly carried out. On 3rd February a patrol under Shields, with Colour-Sergeant Nelson, 50 rank and file and a machine gun, was sent on a road leading to Utete, 11 miles north of Kiyombo, with orders to meet a patrol of the King's African Rifles coming from Kiwambi. When he had proceeded only about one and a half miles his point reported it had seen a group of about 10 Germans. Shortly after a white man dressed in King's African Rifles uniform made his appearance, saying: 'Don't fire; we are King's African Rifles.' Shields, who was very shortsighted, thought he had made a mistake as to the identity of the group he had glimpsed. He thereupon bade his men not to fire; a large body of enemy, estimated to be some 200 strong, at once poured in a heavy volley and charged Shield's patrol. As a result of this unlucky episode Shields, Nelson and nine other ranks were killed and several carriers were wounded, but the remainder managed to save the machine gun, whose corporal had been shot, and make good their retreat.

George Hilliard Shields was headmaster of the Boys School at Accra, in the Government Education Department. He had volunteered for service with the Gold Coast Regiment and had already distinguished himself by gallant behaviour on the ridge beyond Gold Coast Hill on 15th December.

Arrival of the Nigerian Brigade

The Nigerian Contingent from the West African Frontier Force must now come into our picture. After the Cameroons campaign a considerable number of the rank and file of the Nigeria Regiment had been dispersed owing to demobilization and discharge due to invaliding, as well as furlough, while others were unfit; moreover, the difficulties of reassembling them because of the remoteness of many of their homes was greater than in the Gold Coast.

It followed that the Nigerians did not reach East Africa until four and a half months later than their comrades from the Gold Coast.

They were organized in a Brigade of four infantry battalions and a four-gun battery of 2·95 in. guns, under the command of Brigadier-General Cunliffe. Between 11th and 14th December 1916 three battalions arrived at Dar es Salaam, while on 19th Headquarters, the Battery and 2 Battalion reached that port. Incorporated in the Brigade was the Gambia Company. This small unit, some 120 strong, was composed mainly of Mandingos, Fulanis and Bambaras, whose habitat was, generally speaking, in Senegal; they were of a similar type to the Hausa from Nigeria.

Sierra Leone had formed a Carrier Corps, which was allotted to the Nigerian Brigade and the Gold Coast Regiment for head transport. The corps was recruited chiefly from the Mendi and Timini tribes consisting of men of sturdy physique well used to carrying a 60-lb. load on a 15-mile march. Experience had shown that the carrier played a most important, indeed one might almost say vital, part in an African campaign where wheeled transport could not be used owing to the absence of roads. The local carrier in East Africa, unless specially recruited from those tribes accustomed to the work, was hopelessly unfitted for the job physically. Moreover, his immediate reaction on the sound of rifle or gun fire was to discard his load and bolt.

The King's African Rifles 'Porter' was specially enlisted in consequence, while the German carriers were recruited from the same tribes as their Askaris, carried out a certain amount of military training, and even formed a reserve for taking their place in the fighting line when required.

Before dealing with events from the time the Brigade disembarked in East Africa certain factors affecting the state of training achieved must be considered. When instructions for raising the Nigerian Contingent were issued at the end of August 1916 it was expressly stipulated that every man should be a volunteer. In some companies they did so *en bloc*, but it had been decided that the number of trained soldiers should be restricted to 52, with an equal number of recruits, and in addition 26 reservists, making a total of 130 rank and file. The companies were then linked in pairs, forming four double companies per battalion, or 16 for the whole brigade. When this was completed companies were re-numbered 1 to 16. The objection to this organization was that men took some time to get used to their new (in some cases) officers and N.C.O.s.

Mobilization was completed by the end of October. Up to this date a number of companies were still armed with the long rifle; the rest of the short rifles did not arrive until the transports for the voyage to East Africa reached Lagos. The result was that a great many of the other ranks had to be instructed in their use while at sea. Some 40 per cent had actually never seen the sea before and in consequence took some time to get their sea-legs. Incidentally both ship and sea were a source of great wonderment; for instance, it was thought that the log-line was the 'wire' by which communication with Lagos was maintained!

Much time was spent on musketry. Empty barrels were thrown astern to act as targets for rifle and machine-gun practice, while the exercising of battalion buglers added to the din which was created, making any office work a distracting task until the staff got used to the noise.

The work of training young officers and B.N.C.O.s was actively pursued throughout the voyage. Many of these had never served with native troops before, so had much to learn, all of which had to be crammed into the space of four weeks.

1 and 4 Battalions, commanded respectively by Lieutenant-Colonels Feneran and Sargent, sailed from Lagos on 15th November in H.M.S. *Berwick Castle*. The 2 Battalion two reserve companies, and the Battery gun-carriers followed on 16th in the *Seangbee*, while the *Mendi* left for Calabar on 27th with Brigade Headquarters and the Battery. At Calabar she picked up the 3 Battalion. The 2 and 3 Battalions were commanded by Lieutenant-Colonels West and Archer, while the Battery Commander was Major Waller, D.S.O.

All four ships made a halt at Durham, making a welcome relaxation, and where the people received the Nigerians most hospitably. A route march and a visit to the picture palace gave officers and men both exercise and pleasure during their brief stay.

On arrival at Dar es Salaam the Brigade was entrained for Mikese, about 100 miles inland. Owing to the damage done by the retreating enemy, practically every culvert and bridge had to be approached with caution, making the journey slow and tedious. At Mikese the railway was left behind and the 1, 2 and 4 Battalions went forward by road to Tulo, which was reached on 23rd December. On 29th they were joined by 3 Battalion and Battery, who had been the last troops to arrive in port.

18. Strategic situation, 20th December 1916

Mgeta River Action, 1st–4th January 1917

At this time the enemy were holding an entrenched position on both banks of the Mgeta River, while a force, commanded by Cunliffe, was concentrating at Duthumi, seven miles from Tulo. Here the 1 and 4 Battalions and Battery arrived by 30th December; 2 Battalion joined a column commanded by Colonel Lyle of the Kashmiri Battalion on a special mission (details of which are given below), while 3 Battalion remained in reserve at Tulo.

On 31st 4 Battalion moved forward to a camp known as 'Old Baluchi camp', which was the most advanced position we held at the time. Between the opposing forces lay a belt of swampy ground. On 1st January 1917 1 Battalion took over 4 Battalion's trenches and the 4th advanced 1,000 yards and dug in.

At 1030 hours our howitzers and Naval guns opened fire on the enemy trenches on the north bank of the Mgeta; at 1130 hours the 4th advanced to the attack with three companies in the firing line and one in support; progress was slow, as the enemy were able to concentrate heavy rifle and machine-gun fire on the open ground at the near side of the river. However at 1500 hours the Germans retired some 600 yards south of the Mgeta. Our guns then shelled their new position heavily, whereupon a general withdrawal took place.

During the 4 Battalion's advance a German machine gun had been particularly troublesome and could not be silenced by our artillery until Lance-Corporal Suli Bagarimi of 16 Company volunteered to point out its exact position to the G.P.O. In spite of being heavily fired on he carried out his mission successfully. The machine gun was put out of action and the infantry advance continued. This N.C.O. was afterwards awarded the M.M. for gallantry.

Turning now to the action of Lyle's column on 1st January, it became engaged with the enemy retiring from the Mgeta River. 2nd Nigerians formed the advance guard, who became sharply engaged; however, they handled the enemy so roughly that he beat a hurried retreat, leaving behind a quantity of ammunition and stores. A party under the personal leadership of Captain Gardner charged the escort to the 4 in. howitzer, resulting in its capture together with three Europeans and some Askaris. Near by lay one European and a number of Askari casualties. For this action Gardner won the M.C.

The advance guard of the 2 Nigerian Regiment was then reinforced by a third company, and, while digging themselves in, they were attacked at 1530 hours by a strong enemy force with the object of recovering the howitzer. Being unsuccessful it retired at dusk. In spite of these two sharp engagements the Nigerians had only four casualties; Lieutenant Dyer and one man wounded and two other ranks killed. On the following day more than twenty Askaris were found to have been killed. Many others lay unburied in the bush, according to the evidence of the column's nostrils.

On 2nd January 1 and 4 Battalions advanced from Kiderengwa to Tsimbe, where Lyle's column was met with, returning to Baluch camp on 3rd, owing to shortage of supplies and transport. On the same day Lyle

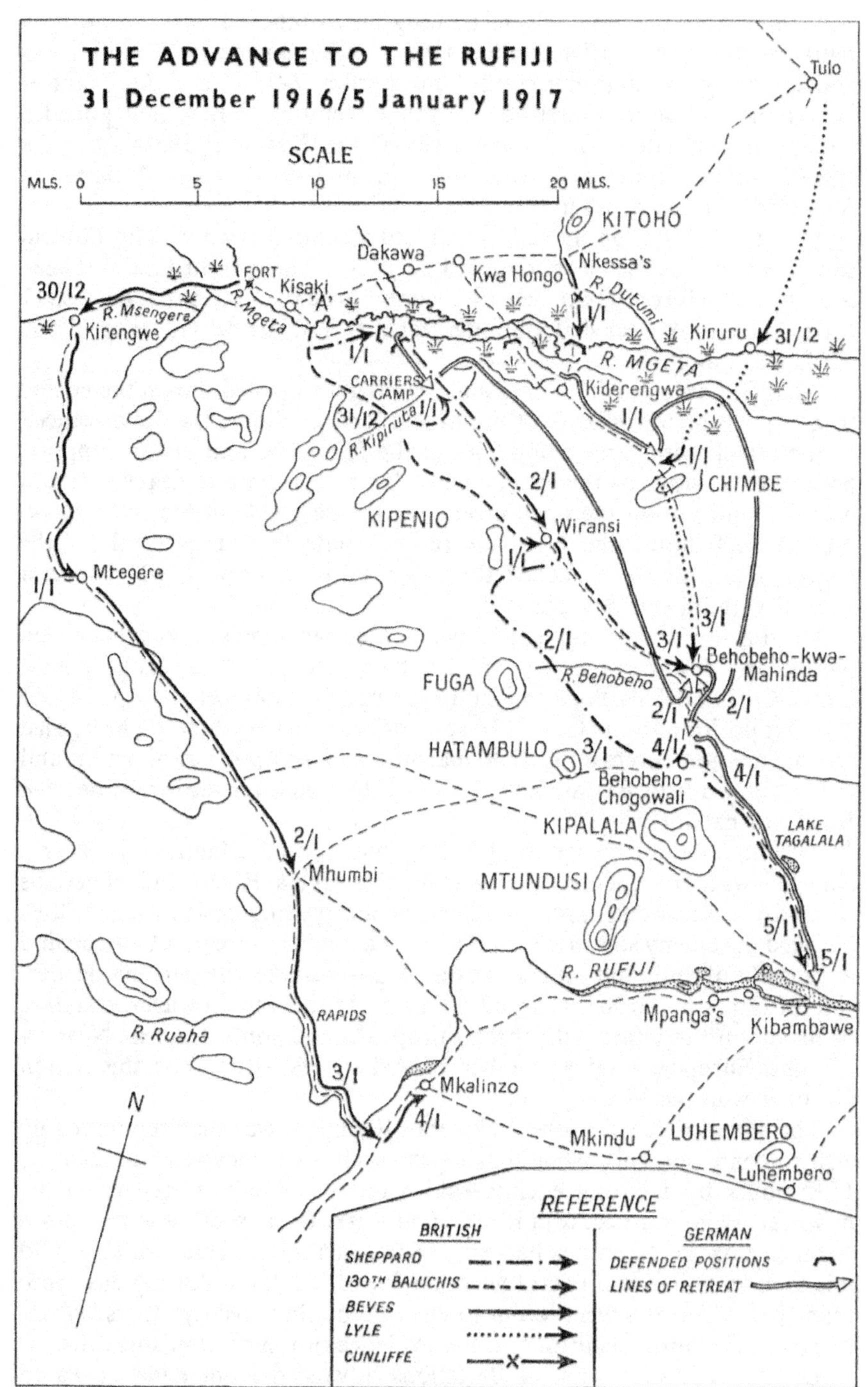

19. The advance to the Rufiji

[*Photo: Topical Press*

1st Battery, Nigeria Regiment in action, Cameroons, 1915

[*Photo: Topical Press*

1st Battery, Nigeria Regiment in action, Cameroons, 1915

[Photo: Topical Press

A Machine Gun Detachment in action

[Photo: Topical Press

Volta River Ferry, Northern Territories, Gold Coast

Face page 193

joined Sheppard's Brigade at Beho-Beho after the latter had been heavily engaged by strong German forces covering their retreat across the Rufiji.

On the 4th the 1 and 4 Battalions and the Nigerian Battery were withdrawn to Duthumi. During these four days' action the Brigade had suffered comparatively lightly considering the results achieved. In addition to the casualties already mentioned, 29 other ranks had been killed and 49 wounded.

On the 6th and 7th Lyle pushed a reconnaissance across the Rufiji under cover of our gunfire. Meanwhile Beves's South African Brigade, part of the 2nd Division securing our right flank in the Mgeta River fighting, had been making a wide detour to the east with the object of crossing the Rufiji 30 miles farther up. He succeeded in doing so at Kipenio without opposition. He was then followed by Cunliffe from Duthumi with 1 and 3 Battalions, who crossed the river on 15th January at night. At the end of the dry season the river here is about 300 yards wide. The crossing was made by a swing bridge built by Indian Sappers and Miners. Here Private Awudu Eloof the 3 Battalion gained the Meritorious Service Medal for gallantry in saving life.

The march of 1 and 3 Battalion from Duthumi had been particularly trying. No water was available at Kissengwe camp, so that light Ford cars had to be sent with relays of canvas water bags nine miles to Kisaki, with the result that many companies were without water till late in the evening.

Between the 14th and 18th 2 Battalion crossed the Rufiji near Kimbabwe; during this operation a difference of opinion as to how the crossing was to be executed arose between West and the Brigadier. As the result of this West was ordered to hand over the command of his battalion to Major Uniacke. West returned to England, while Uniacke remained in command until the end of the campaign.

On 17th January the Nigerians at Kipenio got orders to drive the enemy from a strong position they held on the flat-topped hill of Mkindu. This feature has a sharp escarpment on three sides, whilst sloping away gently towards the south. The hill itself was covered with bush and trees, affording excellent cover from view. The Mkindu stream flows round the north and west sides. Badham with two companies 1 Nigeria Regiment was ordered to turn the enemy's right flank by crossing the stream higher up. This threat to their line of retreat forced the Germans to retire without offering much opposition. The Kimbabwe force had no option than to conform likewise. Our casualties here were one killed and nine wounded, including two officers.

On 19th 2 Battalion the Cape Corps and two guns Kashmiri Battery reached Mkindu, under the command of Lieutenant-Colonel Morris (Cape Corps).

The Germans had now fallen back to Kibonji, where they were reported to be 13 companies strong, having beein reinforced. Feneran's 1 Battalion with a section of the Battery, was ordered to attack the enemy's left flank, while Morris engaged him in front. These tactics were completely successful. Kibongo was occupied, the enemy retiring south and south-east towards Ngwembe.

1 Battalion now remained at Kibonji; 2 Battalion with Cape Corps

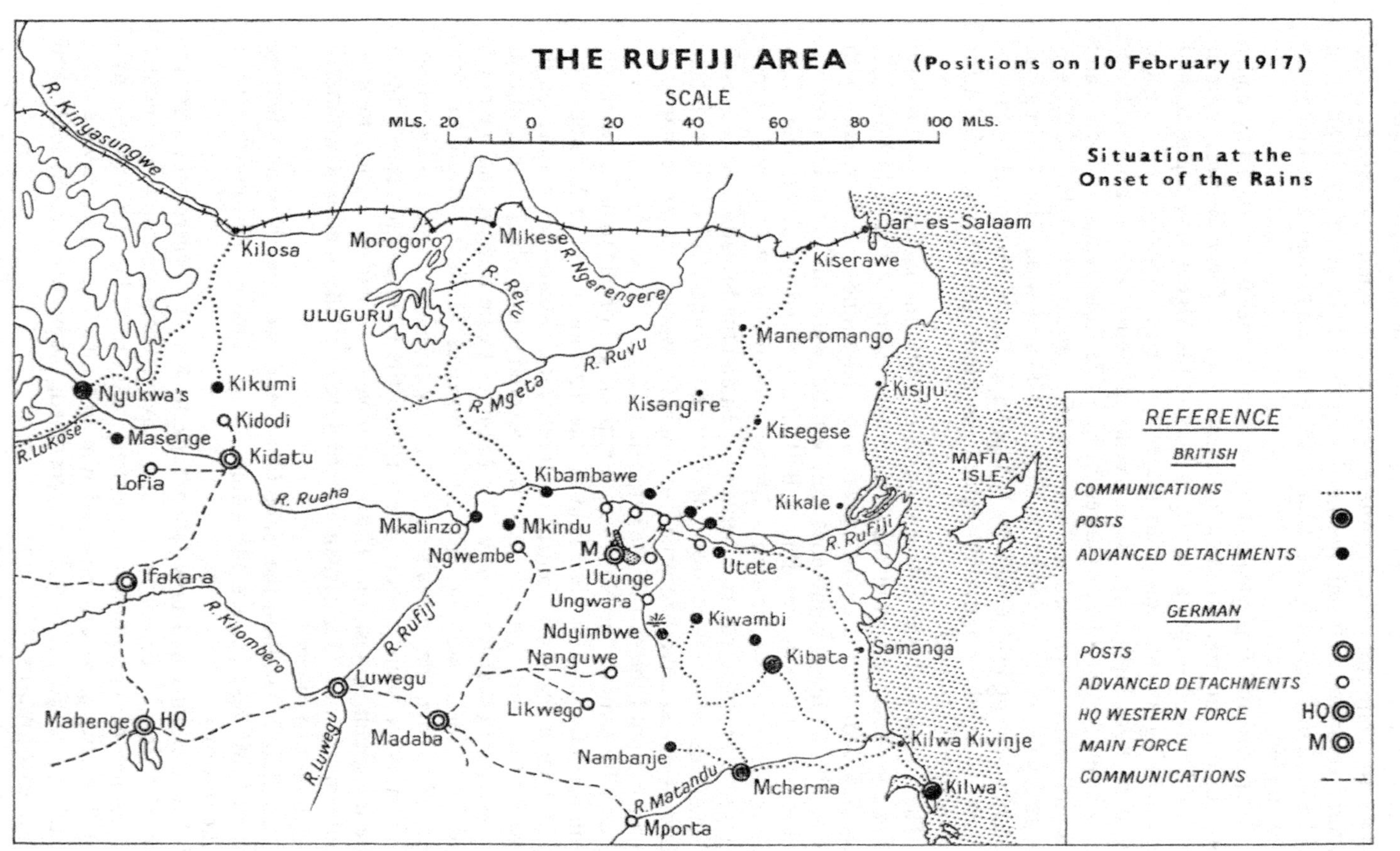

20. The Rufiji Area

and all artillery returned to Mkindu; 3 Battalion patrolled towards Ngwembe, where Colour-Sergeant Russell gained the D.C.M.; 4 Battalion from Duthumi arrived at Kibambawe, marching via Beho-Beho. During this march the weather was terribly hot, the path bad and dusty, and water very scarce. The carriers, who were of extremely poor physique, fell out in considerable numbers, and each day added to the number unfit to carry a load. On 21st 4 Battalion reached Kibonji.

On 24th Captain Green handed over his company to Captain Barclay and took over second-in-command 2 Battalion *vice* Uniacke. The same day a section of Nigerian Battery arrived at Kibonji from Mkindu. On their arrival a force of 3 Battalion with the guns escorted by 16 Company 4 Battalion, the whole under Archer's command, set out to attack the German position at Ngwembe, which was reported to be held by only two companies.

Action of Ngwembe, 24th–25th January 1917

About seven miles from Kibonji the enemy was encountered in some strength. This was about a mile from the water holes, which were the objective of the force. Major Gardner, commanding the advanced guard, was ordered to turn the German right with two companies. About 1100 hours Captain Milne-Home's company was leading; having deployed and reached within 50 yards of the water holes, it was driven back about 200 yards on to the supporting company. A vigorous fight continued for about an hour, during which two machine guns were captured and the bodies of some 30 Askaris were counted lying between them.

The enemy then put in a heavy counter-attack on Gardner's force, during which Captains Cooke and Dudley were killed, as were Lieutenants Ewen and Harrison. Gardner himself was wounded and three of his machine guns were captured. The two companies became disorganized and retired through the bush, not emerging until some distance behind Archer's main body.

In the meantime Archer had wired for reinforcements. 15 Company 4 Battalion was despatched at 1345 hours, not arriving till 1615 hours. By this time Archer had begun to retire and Captain Maxwell, commanding this company, was ordered to withdraw and dig in at a small stream three miles farther back. Some 10 minutes later Maxwell met Sargent with 4 Battalion headquarters, 13 Company, and the Battalion baggage, coming to reinforce Archer's Battalion from Kibonji. At this time 15 Company's carriers were in front of the Company. It is supposed they mistook the reinforcement for Askaris, causing them to panic and bolt; they were not seen again that day.

About 1630 hours Sargent met Archer; the latter is reported to have agreed to dig in with 3 Battalion at the stream aforementioned, but this he did not do, continuing his retreat to Kibonji. On this understanding Sargent ordered 15 Company to rejoin 4 Battalion; he then put Major Roberts in command of half 13 and 15 Companies with instructions to cover the retirement of 3 Battalion.

By 1700 hours these six sections were in position and the whole of Archer's force, except his rearguard of No. 10 Company, had passed through them. At this juncture the enemy counter-attacked, supported by concentrated rifle and machine-gun fire; thereupon the carriers of both battalions stampeded. To add to the confusion and the carriers' demoralization a few snipers had worked round both flanks, causing further casualties among them.

No. 10 Company now joined Roberts's detachment. A firing line was built up on each side of the road and continued to hold the position for half an hour when he was forced to retire, as his right flank was enveloped. Captain Barclay was killed at this moment; he had only taken command of 13 Company a few hours earlier. Colour-Sergeant Lamb of this company had been killed directly the 1700 hours counter-attack began; this B.N.C.O. had greatly distinguished himself at Gallipoli, where he won the D.C.M. and bar. By his death the brigade lost one of its best N.C.O.s.

On Barclay's death Lieutenant Hilton took command of the two sections of 13 Company, whose behaviour in carrying out the difficult retirement was beyond praise, as the denseness of the bush and the heavy fire to which they were subjected made it most difficult to see their enemy. This retirement, had, however, left 10 Company 'in the air', so Sargent in person advanced with 15 and half 16 Companies to their support. It was now 1815 hours and the enemy withdrew, Sargent now learnt that Archer had withdrawn to Kibonji. He thereupon retired to camp himself, leaving 15 and half 16 Companies to hold an outpost position that night, collect what wounded they could and as much baggage as possible, under Roberts.

At 2030 hours Sargent arrived at Kibonji; at 0015 hours the 25th January, Badham with a company from each 1 and 4 Battalions left to recover all loads. His column had a difficult march of seven miles on a pitch-dark night through almost trackless bush. At 0230 hours a tropical deluge made the foothold so greasy that one slipped back half the distance as each step was taken. It was in a great measure due to Company Sergeant-Major Morakinyo Ibadan, acting Regimental Sergeant-Major 4 Battalion that the way was found to Roberts's position. For his services he was awarded the D.C.M.

It was estimated that the enemy's force (commanded by Otto with 3, 23 and 24 Ks and 14 Res. K) in this engagement numbered some 600 rifles and many machine-guns. Their casualties were reported as 12 killed, 14 wounded and 20 missing. British casualties, besides those mentioned, included Lieutenants Pomeroy and Thompson and Sergeants Speak, Rowe and Woolley captured and wounded. Also Lieutenant Jeffries captured with Gardner while helping to dress the latter's wound. Forty-three other ranks were wounded and eight captured.

The action of gun-carrier Awudu Katsena, by birth a Munshi, must be recorded as an example of loyalty and extreme gallantry. He was carrying Barclay's haversack, etc., when the latter fell mortally wounded. Awudu was completely isolated by the rapid advance of the enemy. He picked up the rifle of a dead soldier, kneeling over his officer he opened rapid fire upon the Germans. This was so effective that the enemy were checked long enough to enable a stretcher party to get Barclay away. This brave act was rewarded by the Military Medal.

There is no doubt that Sargent's part in the affair was outstanding. He probably saved 3 Battalion and the guns from disaster. For this he was awarded the D.S.O. The M.C. was gained in the engagement by Robinson, O.C. 10 Company, also by Captains Armstrong, 3 Battalion, and Winter, 4 Battalion.

In criticizing the Ngwembe action it would seem that faulty intelligence at Brigade Headquarters led to a grave underestimate of the enemy's strength, while the reserve companies at Kibonji, seven miles distant, were obviously too far away to avert a crisis. At the same time Archer does not appear to have shown much initiative throughout the action. It was unfortunate that the artillery was unable to affect the situation. This was said to be due to poor visibility and the enemy's heavy and accurate machine-gun fire.

On the other hand, the enemy's tactical handling of his force was most effective. He seems to have only broken off the action owing to the exhaustion of his troops in the fighting line, although he can hardly have called on his reserve at the time.

On 27th January the Nigerian Brigade was concentrated at Mkindu, leaving only a post at Kibonji. The rains had now set in in earnest. February, March and April were comparatively inactive months in consequence. However, the brigade passed through a period of great hardship, due to shortage of rations and sickness. On 30th January half rations were officially ordered, as carrier transport for supplies over some 130 miles of flooded roads and tracks became wellnigh impossible. River transport by the Rufiji was out of the question; it had become a raging torrent.

The C.-in-C., who was now Hoskins, decided that all troops other than Nigerians were to be withdrawn from the Rufiji, leaving that Brigade to hold this area during the rains. On 13th March Headquarters moved to Mpangas, 3 and 4 Battalions being left to garrison Mkindu, under Sargent.

So nearly had the two British forces joined hands that at the limit of their advance their foremost troops were within three days' march, and from the hills near Kibonji the signallers of 2/2 King's African Rifles were able to pick up the flash of the Nigerians' helio on Mkindu, the intervening country being virtually trackless bush and hill for 50 miles, save for the all-important road from Utenge Lake to Mbaba, Madaba and south.

Von Lettow's line of retreat here was secure, while he garnered in supplies to furnish his depots southwards. The British staff realized this, but could do nothing to affect it, for it was not now possible to renew the offensive until the rainy season had passed. For the third time the difficulties of movement and supply had proved more baffling than the resistance of the enemy.

The hard fighting at Kibata, and again at Ngwembe, had proved the German Askaris, now veterans of three years' warfare, were still a match for the best. Equal valour had been displayed by the two Baluchi battalions, and 30th Punjabis, by the Gold Coast Regiment around Kibata, and by the Nigerians, but the new King's African Rifles Battalions had yet to prove themselves, whilst many South African and Indian battalions were unfit for further service in this theatre of war. To the Staff of G.H.Q. it was evident there must be a complete reorganization and the decisive struggle had yet to come.

Attack on Convoy, Mkindu, 14th February 1917

On 14th February one section of the battery, the signalling section, a number of stretcher cases and 700 carriers left Mkindu for headquarters. The escort was very small, being only three officers, 49 other ranks and two machine guns, all of 3 Battalion. About 0730 hours the convoy was attacked. The vanguard all became casualties almost immediately; the convoy was halted, and Milne-Home, who was escorting the guns, formed his men in a crescent around them with one of the machine guns. Firing became heavy both in front and on the right, where the machine gun did good execution. Waller was dangerously wounded, so command of the guns devolved on Lieutenant Vise, who then fired two rounds with fuses set at zero. After this the enemy drew off, the affair having lasted an hour. Besides Waller his native Battery Sergeant-Major and nine other ranks were wounded, while three were killed. Buchanan-Smith handled his advance guard with gallantry and skill, while Vise's initiative saved the guns. Both were awarded the M.C. Lance-Corporal Awudu Kaduna got the D.C.M. for his conduct with the advance guard.

There seems to be some doubt of the purpose with which this attack was made. It was not driven home with the usual vigour expected in such cases. It therefore was suggested that, instead of an attack on the convoy, a raid was intended to try and capture the General and his staff, who had planned to leave Mkindu that day, but whose plans had luckily been altered. The reason given for the smallness of the escort to such a big convoy was that for some weeks no enemy activity had been shown in the area.

Until the middle of April incessant rain, shortage of rations and dismal conditions were the order of the day. Constant patrol work relieved the monotony without showing much evidence of the enemy's activity in this area. Two incidents, both relating to Company Sergeant-Major Belo Akure of the 4 Battalion are, however, worthy of note. This N.C.O. had already distinguished himself in the Cameroons, as has been related in the account of that campaign.

On the first occasion Belo Akure was leading a patrol of three men near Kibonji on the 16th March when he saw a party of the enemy approaching, led by two white men. He ordered his patrol to lie down and on no account fire until he himself had accounted for one of the Europeans. When the Germans were within some 100 yards he took careful aim at the fatter of the two, who was seen to throw up his arms and succumb to the shot. Thereupon Belo's party opened rapid fire on the remainder before beating a hasty retreat to camp covered by another round of magazine fire from Belo, before himself withdrawing.

Again on 25th March Lieutenant Travers of 4 Battalion led a patrol of 24 other ranks, including Belo. Travers's object was to lay an ambush for small parties of the enemy which had lately been harassing the Kibonji vicinity. He distributed small groups well hidden in the bush near certain paths much used by the Germans. One group consisted of himself, Belo and two other men. Soon a German patrol was heard approaching, led by a European. As soon as the latter presented a good target Belo fired, wounding him in the leg. The rest of the group immediately took up the fire, which was returned by the Askaris, who, however, seemed unable to locate their opponents and retreated a short distance. Thereupon Belo crept forward and succeeded in bringing the wounded German back a prisoner. For the two above actions Belo was awarded the M.M.

On 16th April the question of supplying the Nigerian Brigade became so acute that the Battery and 4 Battalion were ordered to withdraw to Morogoro on the Central Railway. This was most heartening news, as can be well imagined. On 30th 1 Battalion was also evacuated to the railway.

On 18th while 14 Company was crossing the Rufiji in the ferry a tragic accident occurred. The last party of 11 men were nearly across when to the horror of those standing on the bank the ferry was seen to capsize, only one Nigerian being saved. The river was running like a millrace at the time. This was the first accident which had ever occurred, although many thousand troops had been ferried across safely during the past months.

The following extract from an officer's diary gives a picture of the state of the road back to Morogoro: 'On 24th April we left Duthumi at 0630 hours for Tulo. It is doubtful if there could be a worse piece of road in the country or even in the whole of Africa. The distance is not more than 12 miles, but for nearly the whole of the way the road led through the worst sort of black stinking mud, it was knee-deep in water, and sometimes the water was above the waist. To make matters worse large numbers of cattle and donkeys had died in the swamp, and having rotted, the stink was too bad for words. Two weeks before 80 head of cattle had died in this swamp, together with several natives. The party arrived at Tulo at 1500 hours after the worst trek up to date.'

Donkeys had been used in an attempt to economize the number of carriers.

In order to feed 3,000 persons at least 12,000 carriers had to be employed. Mechanical transport drivers fell sick so frequently that in one month there was nearly a complete turnover amongst them. They had to work seven days a week without rest, and with insufficient time to get their food. Their work began before daylight and was not finished till after dark. Their lot was indeed a hard one.

On 2nd May 4 Battalion was concentrated at Morogoro together with the Battery, where it remained until 23rd, when orders were received for 4 Battalion to hold itself in readiness to operate with the Belgians at Tabora. Here we must leave 4 Battalion in order to complete the narrative of the Rufiji Valley operations.

The 2 and 3 Battalions continued to patrol south of the Rufiji, but without any incident of note until the end of May, when active operations became possible as the rains ceased, but until the road from the Central Railway via Duthumi could be made fit for motor transport the supply situation precluded a general advance south.

In June and July two enemy camps were captured, the first some 35 miles south of the Rufiji, and the second at Mswega, some 20 miles farther south. In both these engagements a great deal of equipment was taken, though casualties on either side were light: the enemy retired on his main position at Kitope. This can be said to have concluded the operations in the Rufiji Valley area. The 2 Battalion was now ordered back to Morogoro to rejoin the Brigade, while 3 Battalion did not leave the Rufiji area till 18th September.

Wintgens Raid North Towards Tabora

On page 182 it was mentioned that Major Wahle's German Contingent had withdrawn south to Iringa towards the Portuguese border. Early in 1917 Wintgens had decided, without von Lettow's authority, to act independently and carry out a series of raids on British posts, cutting himself free from any lines of communication and living on the country where his fancy took him. He left Gumbiro, about 120 miles north-east of Wiedhaven on Lake Nyassa, with some 500 combatants, 13 machine guns and three small guns, making towards Neu Utengelein in a north-westerly direction and foraging on either flank at will. The speed of Wintgen's column made it impossible for Northey's forces to catch up with him. Northey thereupon appealed to Hoskins for help: meantime Wintgens was heading for the Central Railway. By 17th March Belgian co-operation had been promised and a column of 300 ex-German Askaris formed under Major H. G. Montgomerie (Special Reserve).

Montgomerie left Tabora on 23rd of that month, his march being much delayed through transport difficulties; he did not reach Kipembawe, about 300 miles south, till 1st May, to find Wintgens had long since left, heading for Tabora. By this time the Belgian IVth Battalion was in the field, and Brigadier General Edwards, O.C. Lines of Communication, had been put in command of operations against Wintgens. By the middle of May Wintgens, worn down by hardship and fever, handed over command to Ober-Leutenant Naumann, himself surrendering to the British. Naumann decided to strike northwards across the railway and exploit his nuisance value by devastating the country there.

Pursuit of Naumann

Naumann's force consisted of three companies and a machine-gun company, with 50 Europeans, 450 Askaris, 12 machine guns and two 3·7 cm. guns. He was accompanied by a big drove of cattle. On 26th May he reached Km. 744, which was 7 kilometres west of Malongwe. He took the greatest precautions to conceal his movements, posting picquets east and west along the railway, and even muffling the feet of the cattle. At about noon he crossed by a deep culvert. It was most unfortunate that, owing to a combination of circumstances, there were no troops on the spot to bring him to battle.

The victims of these circumstances were the 4 Nigeria Regiment, who, as already narrated, were at Morogoro, under orders to co-operate with the Belgians in intercepting Naumann.

Owing to shortage of rolling stock the battalion, temporarily under the command of Major Webb, was divided into two portions. The first, having been delayed some 24 hours owing to a mistake in the transmission of orders, left at 2100 hours on the 24th May; its strength was 200 rifles and eight machine guns. The second half, leaving next morning, composed of 150 rifles and four machine guns, with the reserve ammunition, arrived on the scene too late to affect the issue.

Webb reached Tura, Km. 714, that is 30 kilometres east of the point at which Naumann was crossing, at 1000 hours on the 26th May. The rate of travel was only about eight kilometres an hour, which was said to be due to a heavy train and poor wood fuel. In view of the fact that the Higher Command had issued instructions for the trains conveying 4 Nigeria Regiment to be given priority and that arrival at their destination was obviously very urgent, the impression gained was that the whole movement was unduly dilatory.

On arrival at Tura, Webb expected that detonators would be encountered to blow up his train. He therefore loaded two trucks with ballast to precede the train, and halted there for a cooked meal for the troops, leaving again at 0030 hours.

From subsequent information it seems that Naumann crossed the line only an hour or two before Webb's train passed Km. 744, so he was missed by a very narrow margin of time. Actually Naumann crossed the railway about 1300 hours, while Webb must have passed the same point between 1500 and 1530 hours, if we reckon the speed of the latter's train at eight kilometres per hour.

At the same time it must be noted that Webb had only 200 rifles and eight machine guns at his disposal, while Naumann's strength was considerably greater, being more than double at 450 rifles and 12 machine guns with two guns of 3·7 in. calibre. So that the result of an engagement must be considered doubtful, with the advantages of surprise being in favour of the Germans, even admitting the hampering effect of his big herd of cattle. As the second train, under Captain Downes's command, did not reach Malongwe, Km. 737, until early the next day, 27th May, the weight of his numbers together with Webb's reserve ammunition, would not have been available.

After Webb's train left Tura his orders were to proceed to Nyahua, Km. 772, instead of to Tabora. On arrival there he was instructed to return immediately to Malongwe, as in the meantime Headquarters had had news of Naumann's presence in the vicinity of that place. Webb did not reach there till daybreak next morning, by which time Naumann was heading north for Mkalama.

1 Nigeria Regiment had been detailed to join Colonel Dyke's (30th Baluchis) column in the endeavour to trap Naumann before he recrossed the railway in August. The plan was to block the vital Chenene Gap here. On 4th Pring with 3 Company 1 Nigeria Regiment arrived there. He found about 100 de Jager's scouts, with some King's African Rifles M.I. holding the northern end of the gap, and bivouacked himself about a mile farther south. During the night of 4th–5th August considerable commotion was heard and the de Jager Scouts came fleeing in confusion through Pring's company. It was discovered that Naumann had broken through the north

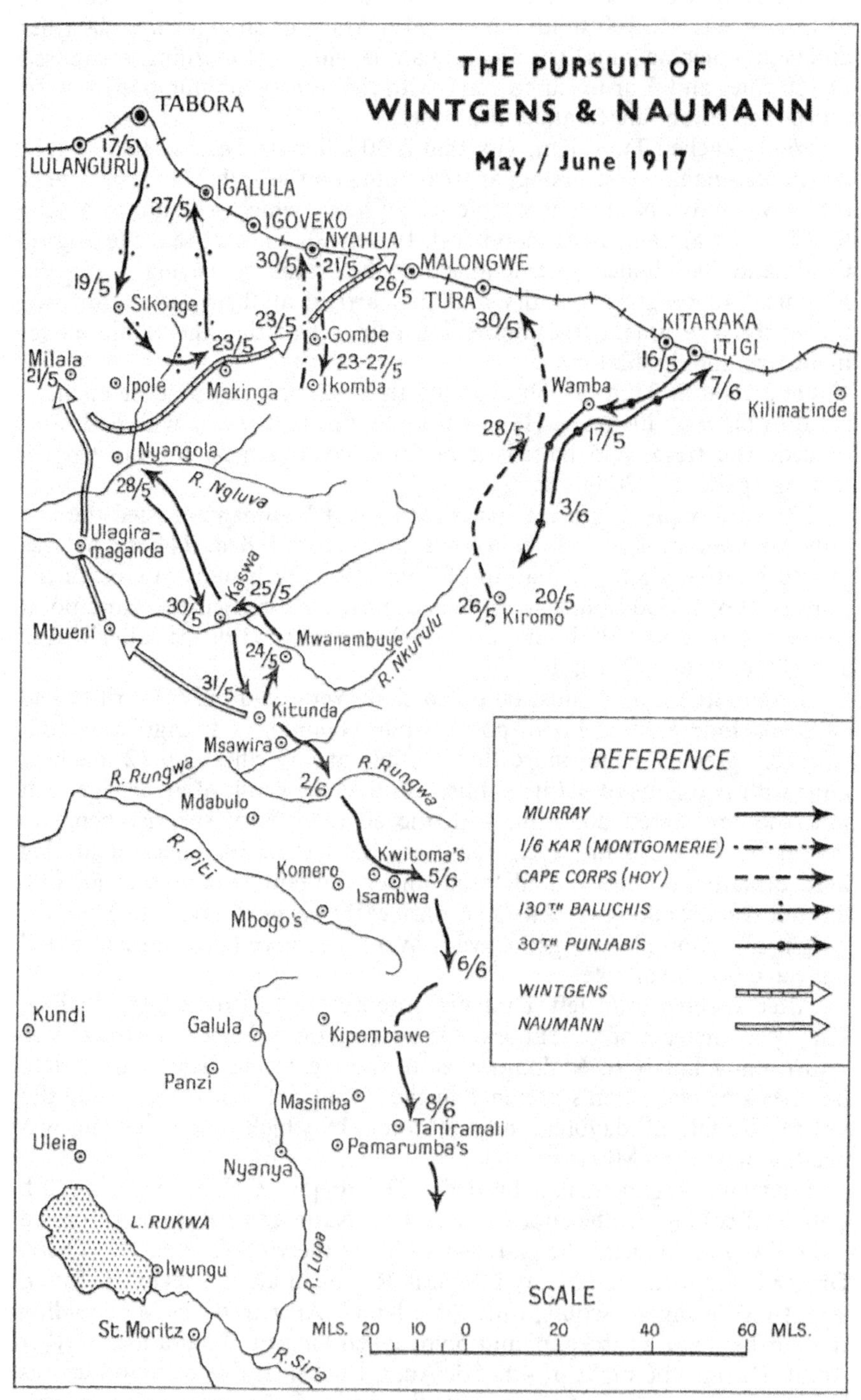

21. The Pursuit of Wintgens and Naumann, May-June 1917

end of the gap without any resistance, or any warning being received by Pring. This unfortunate episode was to result in Naumann's raids being prolonged a further two months until his surrender in October.

On 28th XIII Belgian Battalion arrived. The Malongwe Column was then formed to take up the pursuit vigorously, for by then it had been ascertained that Naumann's objective was ultimately Mkalama Fort, held by only a small garrison of six whites and 30 soldiers distant 170 miles east of north. On 29th Sargent returned from leave and took command of the column. In spite of extremely hard marching the Malongwe column never overtook Naumann until it reached Mkalama on 8th June. By this date the fort had been under siege for four days and very little ammunition was left, so Sargent's arrival was timely. Naumann abandoned the siege and hastened farther north, still hotly pursued, to a place called Tirimo about 50 miles short of Lake Victoria Nyanza. Here the 4th Nigerians were recalled to Tabora, having covered 500 miles on foot in 36 marching days, which must be reckoned as a remarkable performance. There had been little fighting beyond a few skirmishes with patrols. Needless to say the battalion was in need of a period of well-earned rest on its return to Morogoro after seven weeks of such strenuous efforts.

It was not till 2nd October that Naumann surrendered with 14 Europeans and 165 Askaris. Since touching Nyanza region he had threatened Lake Magadi, Moshi and Arusha and was finally encircled near Kondoa Irangi. He had kept the field for eight months, deflecting about 1,700 troops from other operations and covered some 2,000 miles. His original strength was estimated to be 500 Askaris, well-seasoned troops but indifferently armed with the old rifle.

Turning once more to the Gold Coast Regiment, after the disaster to Shield's patrol, it moved to Njimbwe five miles north of Kiyombo. Here it was joined by the 40th Pathans and together they sent out small daily patrols. On 5th February the Pioneers and Battery left camp in support of the 2/2 King's African Rifles in order to deliver an attack on two German camps overlooking the Ngarambi–Utete road. After a small post had been dislodged and the King's African Rifles contacted it was found the enemy had abandoned his camps. Here the troops went into bivouac, under depressing conditions, lying out all night with no shelter other than the men could improvise, with the rain pouring down relentlessly in a steady tropical deluge. The detachment had hardly got back to Njimbwe next day when it was attacked from the south-east by a party of Germans who, however, hurriedly withdrew on discovering the strength of their opponents. In this encounter, owing to its surprise effect, the Regiment suffered 10 casualties; while the Pathans had twice this number. The known enemy losses were 10 wounded including one European.

On 9th February a patrol discovered the bodies of Shields and Nelson together with eight soldiers who had been killed on the 3rd February. The bodies were brought back to camp, where the Rev. Captain Nicholl read a burial service over them.

For some weeks past the supply of food, as well as its quality, had been causing the Regiment acute suffering. Many of the men were terribly emaciated and some 80 had to be sent to hospital due to starvation. Many officers, too, had to live on nothing but mealie porridge, which only satisfied their hunger for a few hours.

Under this prolonged ordeal the discipline of the men was beyond all praise. The rainy season had set in in earnest, the country was waterlogged in all directions, patrols at times found themselves cut off by a more than usually heavy downpour flooding the swampy, low-lying ground. Yet never once was there a murmur of complaint against their officers. Our patrols had several skirmishes with enemy foraging parties, during which a few casualties were incurred. In one of these, on Valentine's day, Machine-gun Corporal Tinbela Busanga behaved with great gallantry, working his gun after being badly wounded, until too faint to carry on. On another occasion Corporal Amandu Fulani was ambushed with his patrol of six men when, after a gallant fight, all were killed to a man. Here there were evident signs that the patrol had sold their lives dearly.

On 23rd the Regiment marched out of Njimbwe to Namatewa, a good 20 miles, which was a tough day's work for a body of half-trained men. Finally Mitole was reached on 27th February, where the men went into camp to rest and reorganize. They had been continuously on the march, or fighting, ever since their arrival at Kilindini seven months previously.

News was received that Rose, who had been in command of the Regiment since August 1914, and had served in the Cameroon Campaign before bringing it to East Africa, was made a Brevet-Lieutenant-Colonel. An announcement which gave great satisfaction to all ranks.

Operations South of Kilwa, February–August 1917

Lieutenant-General Hoskins had now taken over command from Smuts. He had been Inspector-General of the King's African Rifles at the outbreak of war and no one had a wider knowledge of East Africa or the East African Askari than himself. Although Smuts had given the impression that the East African Campaign was nearly over, Hoskins stated plainly that a formidable enemy was still in the field. Von Lettow had control of a vast area of practically unknown country, where he would be difficult to reach and where his escape into Portuguese East Africa might prove impossible to prevent. No quick end to the campaign could be expected, nor was the task likely to prove an easy one.

The King's African Rifles were now being rapidly expanded from six to some twenty-odd battalions but meanwhile it was imperative that Indian units should continue to serve in East Africa, especially as more South African troops were denied him. Hoskins also asked for more transport, artillery, Stokes mortars and Lewis guns.

Patrols during the rains confirmed that von Lettow's main forces were leaving the Rufiji Valley. Hoskins's plan was to penetrate the German front from five directions and drive it south. For this purpose the Nigerian Brigade was to advance from the Rufiji; the 1 Division from Dilwa Kivinje towards Liwale; O'Grady with a Brigade due south towards Massasi; the Iringa Column towards Mahenge and Northey from Songea also towards Liwale. Before Hoskins's plans could be put into action the War Office had decided to relieve him, transferring him to the command of the 3 Lahore Division in Mesopotamia. He was succeeded by van Deventer, who reached Dar es Salaam from South Africa on 29th May, meanwhile in April an unusually prolonged rainy season postponed all prospects of serious operations. The Germans, however, having reached higher ground, found movement was feasible.

As soon as it was realized that von Lettow was concentrating south-west of Kilwa the 1 Division was re-deployed, the Brigade formation being temporarily suspended, and two columns formed. One north of the River Matandu under Lieutenant-Colonel Grant of 2 Brigade, and the other under Rose of 3 Brigade.

Rose set up his headquarters at Mnasi, some 20 miles from Kilwa Kivinje and on the main road to Liwale. On 3rd April the Regiment left Mitole, arriving at Mnasi next day. 'B' Company was detached to Kirongo, a few miles west.

Ambush at Makangaga by Lieutenant Kinley, 11th April

Early on 11th April a report was received that two companies of the enemy were advancing on Makangaga, which place is only some four miles south-east of Mnasi. Lieutenant Kinley, with 75 men and a machine gun, were at once despatched to lay an ambush. The party passed through Makangaga into a patch of flat country broken by gentle undulations and covered with tall, very thick, grass. Here he drew his men up in a compact line, securely hidden, some 60 yards parallel to the road with the machine gun set up ready for action.

Soon the sound of a large body of men marching was heard; Kinley held his fire until he judged them to be opposite his position when he let fly with everything he had in the way of rifles and gun. Taken completely by surprise, the Germans panicked, then charged into the bush on a wide front.

Fearing to be enveloped by a superior force, Kinley ceased fire then rapidly withdrew to a flank where he repeated his previous tactics. This game of hide and seek was continued with great success for some quarter of an hour. Having done as much damage as he considered possible with due regard to the safety of his small force, he extricated it skilfully and led it back to camp. In this brilliant little encounter the Regiment had six men killed and six wounded. On the other hand the enemy's losses were three white men and 15 Askaris killed and over 30 wounded. For this daring exploit Kinley was recommended for the D.S.O.

On 15th April the Regiment made a nine-mile march to Migere-gere, where a new camp was formed. On 17th Lieutenant Beech with a patrol of 50 men had a brush with some Germans cutting the telegraph wire, losing one killed and one wounded. On the 18th the Battery and its escort of 30 men came into action to cover the advance of the 40th Pathans near Rungo. Foley was commanding the Battery. The country was dense bush and the guns were shelling an enemy concealed completely from view. After this had been going on for some time the Battery trumpeter reported the enemy were creeping close up to the guns; suddenly the bush became alive with them, but the gallant action of both gunners and escort extricated the guns from capture and Foley's initiative secured an orderly retreat to camp. The details of this incident are narrated in the chapter on 'R.W.A.F.F. Artillery'. During the course of the day Shaw with 'A' and 'B' Companies marched to the support of the Pathans, who had been heavily engaged and had suffered severe losses. The following day the rest of the Regiment relieved the Pathans; during the night the enemy withdrew. Rose's headquarters were established at Rungo, the defences of which were considerably strengthened.

For the rest of April and May the Regiment continued in camp at Rungo. Only minor incidents were reported during routine patrol work. Captain Macpherson was engaged on 18th and 20th April near Beaumont's Post, when he had eight casualties including Company Sergeant-Major Hassan Bazaberimi and three other ranks killed. Also during this period von Lettow-Vorbeck made a small raid on Kilwa Kisiwani harbour. Having got a gun on to a hill in the vicinity he opened fire on three transports; this unexpected attack caused a certain apprehension for the safety of the sea base so that even the Depot Company was mobilized at Mpara and posted along the northern shore of the harbour. However the Germans were not strong enough to stage a serious attack, and quickly withdrew when a British cruiser steamed on the scene.

On 1st May the combatant strength had fallen to nine officers, six B.N.C.O.s, 786 other ranks in spite of the reinforcements received on 27th December, but by the end of June four officers rejoined for duty, though Rose and Goodwin had been invalided to the base, the former with dysentery.

On 29th May half the Pioneers, under Lieutenant Bray, went to reinforce the garrison of Migere-gere. During May news came of the award of Military Crosses to Kinley and Foley for services rendered in April at Makangaga and Rungo respectively. A D.C.M. and four M.M.s were also awarded to the Battery and its escort of 'A' Company on the latter occasion. On 1st June Goodwin was appointed Acting Lieutenant-Colonel and awarded the French Croix de Guerre, while Piggott received the silver medal of the Italian Order of San Maurice. On 11th June Goodwin and Harman received the D.S.O. and Piggott the M.C., while Sergeant-Major Medlock received the D.C.M.

On 12th June Macpherson with three sections of 'I' Company rejoined at Rungo from Beaumont's Post. Next day Lieutenant Biltcliffe also rejoined with the remaining section of 'I' Company from Beaumont's Post. On 15th 987 men of the Sierra Leone Carrier Corps were attached to the Regiment, replacing the far less efficient local porters.

On 16th Shaw was appointed second-in-command and Acting Major, while on 28th he was appointed Acting Lieutenant-Colonel *vice* Goodwin invalided. Colonel Orr had now taken command of 3 Brigade, and Beves had succeeded Hannyngton in command of the 1 Division.

On 28th a camp on Linguala Ridge, a few miles south of Rungo, which had been evacuated by the enemy, was occupied by Bray with 'I' Company. On the same day the Regiment reconnoitred Ukuli, south-east of Rungo, where enemy activity had been reported, returning to Rungo on the 30th.

The end of June showed the dry season as fairly established, and the Regiment looking forward to a resumption of more active campaigning after six months of harassing patrol work.

The military situation now was that the enemy was roaming at large over an area devoid of railways, intersected by bush tracks and with no line of communications which could be severed. Instead, his supply depots, mainly in the Liwale-Masasi region, were stocked and replenished locally from well-cultivated farmlands.

Speed was of primary importance if von Lettow was to be attacked and overcome before the advent of the next rains. Between Kilwa and the Rovuma River, here forming the boundary of Portuguese East Africa, lay a high table-land intersected by the valleys of the Mbemkuru and Lukuledi Rivers, the important harbour of Lindi lying at the mouth of the latter. This was to be the main theatre of operations as far as the West African troops were concerned. The War Office promised several hundred lorries, got permission from the Portuguese to recruit carriers, and instructed van Deventer to hasten the conclusion of the campaign.

Kilwa and Lindi were to be the main bases for the autumn offensive. The Division was re-consituted in two columns, No. 1, which included the Gold Coast Regiment, was under Orr, while No. 2 was under Grant. Van Deventer had not yet received enough transport to equip the Kilwa Force, but had built a light railway as far as Migeregere, which was half-way to Mnasi. The British held a line from Kilwa towards Liwale with No. 2 Column on the right. The Germans held the high ground to the south, in positions well concealed by thick bush.

Lindi was the most important port in the southern part of German territory; it possessed a stone fort, barracks and other buildings, with a number of European estates in the vicinity. It was first garrisoned by two companies of the West India Regiment, who were watched by small German patrols. When the Rufiji offensive died down Hoskins decided to reinforce Lindi, as a base for offensive operations. O'Grady was put in command of a brigade of King's African Rifles and other units with orders to draw off and contain as many of the hostile troops from Kilwa as possible.

On 4th July Beves was ready to advance. To protect his left flank he formed an extra column of two battalions (Pathans and King's African Rifles) under Colonel Taylor to advance down the coast. There was no fighting of note until 7th July, when No. 2 Column had a serious engagement involving many casualties on each side. Next day the Gold Coast Regiment was transferred as support to No. 2 Column at Mnindi.

Meanwhile 'B' Company, under Eglon, which had been left behind at Lingaula Ridge, had carried out its task brilliantly by deceiving the enemy as to the main thrust. On 7th July, having located three German companies, he promptly attacked and succeeded in driving them from three successive positions, evidently creating the idea that they were about to be attacked in force. During this affair Lieutenant Scott was seriously wounded, while Sergeant Awudu Argungu, who had previous long service with the Northern Nigeria Regiment, was killed and eight other ranks were wounded. Having effected his purpose, Eglon rejoined the Regiment

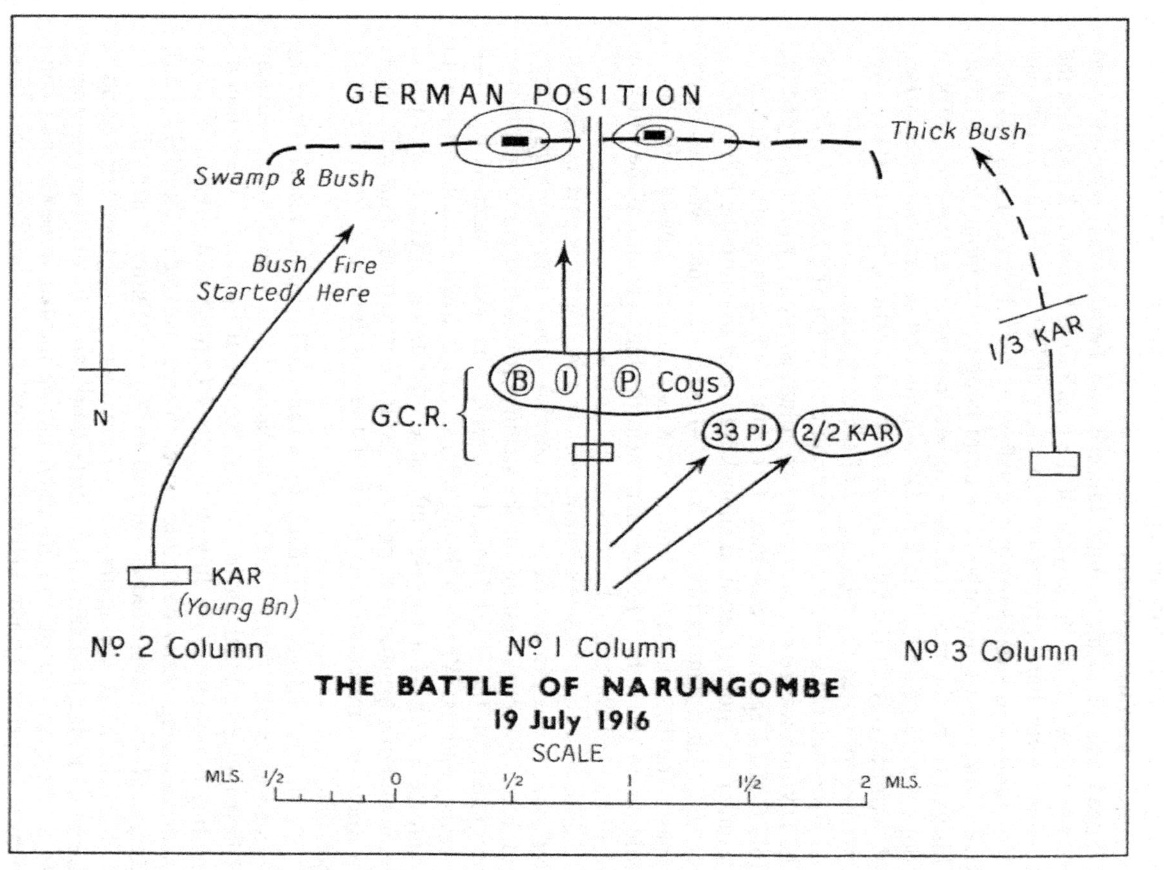

22. The Battle of Narungombe, 19th July 1916

MOUNTED INFANTRY
The Company Sergeant Major in Marching Order, a "Zeberma" from North-West of Timbuctoo, talking to a "Fulani" Private in Dismounted "Review Order" from Gombi, on the Border of the Cameroons.

Face page 208

[Photo: Topical Press

Mounted Infantryman on Service, Cameroons, 1914

[Photo: Topical Press

Gun-carriers with Cradle of 2·95 in. Gun, Gold Coast Battery, 1905

Face page 209

on 9th at Makengaga. Until 17th the column continued in a southerly direction with occasional brushes with enemy rearguards. On this day junction was made with No. 1 Column and the Regiment was then re-transferred. Here also No. 3 Column joined forces, having carried out a wide sweeping movement very successfully, thereby causing the enemy to evacuate a formidable position at Mikikama. It so happened this junction of the columns, though unintended, was timely, for the enemy were holding a strongly entrenched position at Narungombe.

Battle of Narungombe, 19th July 1917

The importance of Narungombe lay in its water holes, and as the existing supply of water for the force was very limited the capture of this ample supply became a matter of urgency. Little was known of the strength and dispositions of the German force, but a combined attack was ordered for this day. The position proved to be a strongly entrenched one, consisting of a series of redoubts lying on the upper slopes of two hills, one on either side of the road. These redoubts were connected by breastworks two and a half feet high built of earth stoutly faced with sticks driven deeply into the ground. The right flank rested on a swamp and the left on very thick bush; the whole extending about two and a half miles. The whole front was covered with open forest and long grass. The enemy had four companies in the firing line and four in Reserve with two 3-in. guns and 48 machine guns.

The frontal assault was allotted to No. 1 Column, with Nos. 2 and 3 attacking the enemy's right and left respectively. At daybreak No. 1 Column advanced with the Gold Coast Regiment leading; simultaneously No. 3 Column moved forward on our left. An advance in extended order through long grass is a slow operation, and, while the Regiment was working its way forward a company of King's African Rifles from Reserve was sent to occupy a ridge on their right flank to protect it. Although it had been reported that no enemy was within 100 yards of their camp, the enemy opened fire at 300 yards before they had deployed, inflicting five casualties. At 0815 hours they became heavily engaged within a short distance of the strongly entrenched position. Here Eglon, leading 'B' Company, was killed and many casualties were suffered. Eglon was the gallant young officer who had done so well when attacking the Lingaula ridge a few days earlier.

Shaw had taken up a position on the road behind a mound from which he was able to observe the operations he was conducting; and he now sent 'I' Company to prolong the line on the right of the attack. A few minutes later the Pioneer Company was also sent forward farther to the right; and at 0930 hours the 33rd Punjabis were sent to still further prolong the line to the right, while the 7th South African Infantry deployed on the left of the Gold Coast Regiment.

At this juncture No. 3 Column was ordered to execute a wide turning movement on the right of the enemy's position with certain water holes as their objective. All this time No. 2 Column had been steadily advancing towards the German left flank. By 1015 hours it was in a position to attack

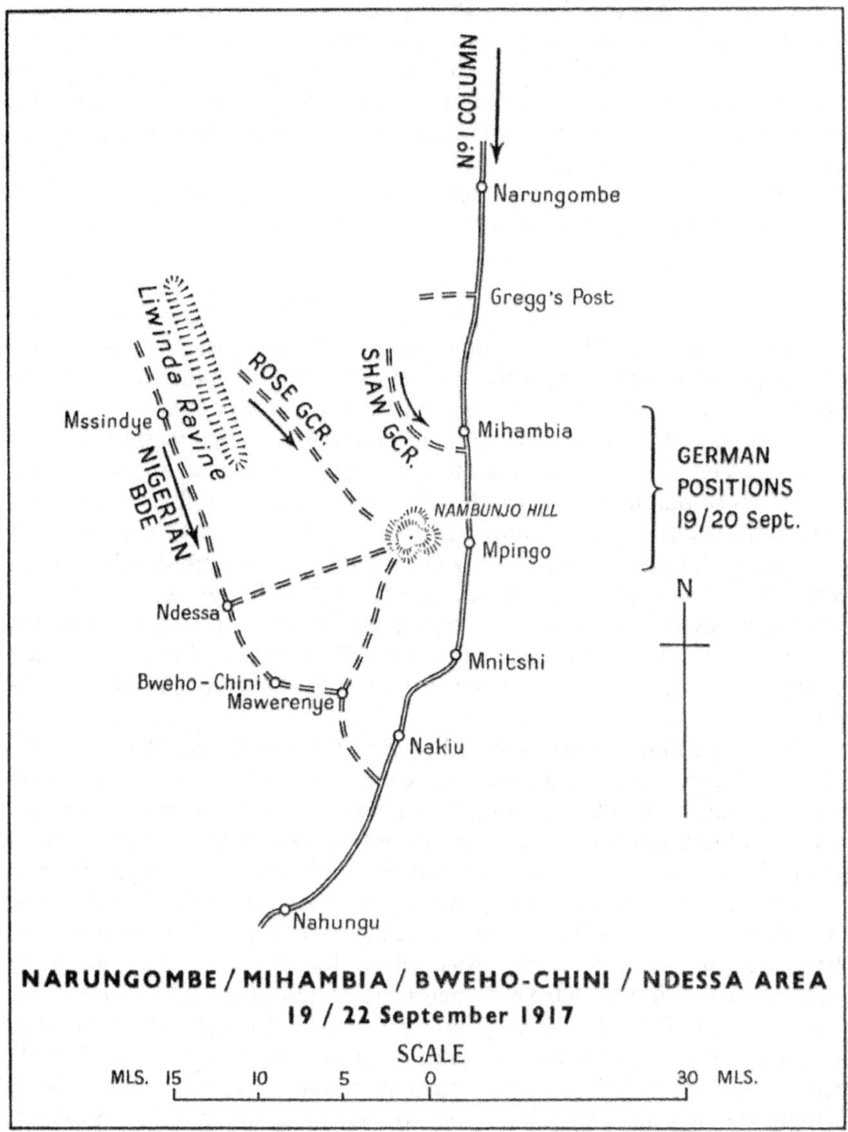

23. Narungombe/Mihambia/Bweho-Chini/Ndessa Area, 19th/22nd September 1917

and by noon had got in touch with the enemy in very thick bush. Meantime No. 3 Column had become heavily engaged, suffering severely. Most of the men of 3/3 King's African Rifles were in action for the first time, and their difficulties were increased by the fires that raged through the long grass and which had been started by the Stokes Mortars; their Commanding Officer had been badly wounded and the young Askaris were very shaken. This failure on the left placed the Gold Coast Regiment in a perilous position; the men, however, remained steady, showing no signs of giving way in spite of the heavy fire to which they were exposed.

About 1530 hours, when our left flank (No. 3 Column) was giving way, the enemy mounted a fierce counter-attack against 1/3 King's African Rifles, who were leading the advance of No. 2 Column on our right. His troops charged the line to the accompaniment of much cheering and bugle blowing; all available men were collected and the attack was held. The 1/3 King's African Rifles fixed bayonets and charged, driving the enemy out of his trenches and scattering them in all directions. The position thus gained was consolidated by the occupation of the enemy's trenches.

All this time the troops of No. 1 Column were being very hard pressed to maintain the frontal attack, so several companies of 2/2 King's African Rifles were called up from Reserve, and one company was sent to support the 33rd Punjabis, on the right of the Gold Coast Regiment. At 1600 hours orders were sent not to attempt any further advance here. These orders arrived too late, as by this time the Regiment with the Punjabis and 2/2 King's African Rifles had charged, taking a certain number of enemy trenches. Owing, however, to their ammunition running out and their left being unsupported, they were compelled to retire about 100 yards to more favourable ground, where they dug in for the night.

At dawn next day it was found the enemy had retired, beating a hasty retreat southwards before he could be enveloped. After the occupation of Narungombe no major movements took place until September. Sickness and casualties had greatly reduced the strength of Kilwa Force and all units were in need of a rest.

The casualties suffered by the Regiment had been very heavy in relation to its strength. One officer killed (Eglon) and three wounded. Also two B.N.C.O.s wounded. Of the other ranks 37 were killed and 114 wounded. Amongst the killed was 'B' Company's Sergeant-Major, Awudu Bakano, a very fine soldier. The German losses had been heavy.

The climax to the battle was undoubtedly the action of the King's African Rifles on our right. At the same time the firm stand taken by the Gold Coast Regiment and Punjabis was a substantial contribution to their effort, as it prevented the Germans from reinforcing their left flank. Von Lettow was greatly annoyed at the position being abandoned, for he was already hurrying north from the Lindi area with reinforcements.

Never had the men of the Gold Coast Regiment shown more grit than at Narungombe. They went into action early in the morning of 19th July, after having been marching, or cutting paths through bush for motor traffic, for two weeks almost unceasingly. They were hotly engaged from 0800 hours until nightfall at short range with gun, rifle and machine-gun fire. In addition they had constantly to fight the blazing grass, which rendered their position even more exposed. In spite of all this these Africans stubbornly continued to hold their position, though in some cases companies had been robbed of all their European leaders and were commanded solely by their native N.C.O.s. This performance was indeed a striking proof of the Regiment's high qualities as a fighting unit.

For his services in command of the Regiment this day Shaw was awarded a bar to his Military Cross.

The Combined Offensive from Kilwa and Lindi, September–November 1917

Reverting to the Nigerians, in order to bring the story up to date, when the 4 Battalion returned to Morogoro from the pursuit of Naumann in July, a draft of 150 men under the command of Major Gibb had arrived via Dar es Salaam from Nigeria. This draft was composed of excellent material which afterwards did very good work in the heavy fighting around Kilwa and Lindi. At the same time the Gambia Company commanded by Captain Law, M.C., arrived with a large number of carriers from Nigeria and Sierra Leone.

While at Morogoro all ranks were put through courses of machine gun, as well as Lewis, Stokes gun and bombing. It was soon found that the W.A.F.F. soldier made a remarkably good bomb thrower.

During the second week of August the Nigerian Brigade, less the 3 Battalion, was given orders to concentrate at Kilwa. In conformity with these instructions 2 Battalion left Mpangas, south of the Rufiji, for Morogoro, having completed eight months in this unpopular area. For a few days the Brigade (less 3 Battalion) had a cheerful gathering at Dar es Salaam, where they savoured the delights of shopping and picture-seeing.

It was in the last week of August that Brigade Headquarters, the Battery, the 4 Battalion, together with the Gambia Company, the W.A.F. Ambulance and a section of the 300 Field Ambulance, embarked on the S.S. *Hong Wan I* at Dar es Salaam. This vessel had, some 40 years earlier, been the pride of the City Line, known as the *City of Edinburgh*. She was now commonly called the '*One Lung*', a term which fairly described her steaming powers, for she took three days to cover the 120 miles to Kilwa-Kisiwani, the port of Kilwa Township.

On 26th August the troops arrived at Redhill or Saingo camp near to Kilwa. A few days later they were joined by 1 Battalion, while 2 Battalion completed the concentration of the Nigerian Brigade (less 3 Battalion) on 3rd September. Here the first week of September was devoted to field training in the open, undulating country which is found in that area. At this time the Nigerians first met the King's African Rifles, whom they affectionately named the 'Hapanas', a Swahili term meaning 'No'. The other ranks of the Corps soon became fast friends, when they learnt to appreciate each other's fighting qualities and rely on each other's support in a tight corner.

By 17th September the aforementioned troops, together with the Nigerian Pioneer Section, Stokes Gun Section, and Supply and Ammunition Column, had concentrated at Masindyi. Here van Deventer, the Commander-in-Chief, had set up his headquarters. Here, too, Hanyngton, the Commander of the Force, had arrived. This place was reached after a hot and dusty march of 80 miles along a newly cut motor road.

On the 12th September a draft of 1,800 recruits had arrived from Nigeria; of these 1,000 were ordered to join the brigade at once to act as carriers temporarily for the forthcoming operations. On the 17th the Commander-in-Chief inspected the Brigade, while next day the advance commenced.

Since the battle of Narungombe the Gold Coast Regiment, with the rest of Beves's column, established a large fortified camp and aerodrome at that place, where they were able to refit and recuperate. Moreover, a long delay of two months was necessary to give the Nigerian Brigade time to reach the Kilwa area in order to co-operate in the larger plan decided on by the Commander-in-Chief. This delay, unfortunately unavoidable, gave the enemy time to reorganize his forces, to accumulate supplies at his depots, and generally to prepare for further strong resistance.

At this time the military situation was as follows:

In the north-east Naumann with a small force was still raiding near Kondea Irangi, followed by the Belgians. In the central region of the fertile Mahenge plateau, whence von Lettow drew a large portion of his supplies, von Tafel was still in possession, though being threatened by the advance of Northey's columns under Hawthorn and Shorthose, and by the Belgians. Von Tafel had some 1,700 Askaris under his command. Hawthorn and Shorthose, with a combined strength of some 2,000 rifles, much strung out in detached posts, and still based on Songea and Tunduru, were the best part of 100 miles distant from their objective, Liwale, which was at the southern extremity of Mahenge.

Von Lettow's main forces had been driven south-east into the Kilwa Plateau Lindi region. He was known to hold strong positions at Mihambia and Ndessa, a few miles south of Narungombe. Captain Looff of the Konigsberg, who had driven the Portuguese from Newala, was ordered by von Lettow to take command of the troops defending the southern approaches to Lindi.

The British Commander-in-Chief's plan, alluded to above, was to drive the enemy southward from Narungombe with Hanyngton's force, whose right, or western, flank would be protected by the Nigerian Brigade. At the same time his retreat was to be cut off by a large force concentrated in the Lindi area, of which the 3 Battalion Nigeria Regiment formed part. This force, called Linforce, was commanded by O'Grady and divided into Nos. 3 and 4 Columns.

This time there were to be no limited objectives, but a continuous advance designed to envelop the enemy's main forces by linking up the Kilwa and Lindi groups. A big problem for the Kilwa group had been, and continued to be, the supply of water. Until the capture of the water holes at Narungombe the troops had suffered greatly from thirst. The enemy's position at Mihambia covered the water holes immediately south of Narungombe, while farther south again lay their supply depots of Mnitshi, 10 miles from Mihambia, Mawerenye, Ndessa and Mombonya.

After the engagement at Narungombe, Rose returned and took over command of the Gold Coast Regiment. He was accompanied by Captain Hornby; both of them had been sick for some time. Hornby will be remembered as the Regiment's Adjutant in the Cameroons. Four new officers joined about this time, Captains McElligot and Methven, M.C., and Lieutenants Lamont and S. B. Smith. On 28th Captains Briscoe, Hartland and Brady, and Lieutenants Bail, Willoughby and Maxwell joined with reinforcements of 354 other ranks and seven machine-gun carriers from the Gold Coast. A supply of Lewis guns arrived for the first time, and the work of training the teams was forthwith put in hand. During August no incident of note occurred other than routine patrolling, which was vigorously carried out. The Regiment was nearly up to strength on 31st August, with 29 officers, 17 B.N.C.O.s, 957 other ranks and 133 enlisted gun- and ammunition-carriers.

On the 7th September Methven, with 70 rifles of 'B' Company, was sent to Liwinda Ravine to reconnoitre for water, with instructions to take every precaution to prevent his movements being known to the enemy. He dropped a picquet of 1 B.N.C.O. and 20 men at Kitiia *en route* and had orders to reconnoitre all paths leading to Mihambia and Mnitshi. Liwinda Ravine is a peculiar feature in the district, lying some 10 miles west of Mihambia. It consists of a trough 200 ft. deep and 350 yards wide running from north-west to south-east, concealed by orchard bush with good cover for a camp. It proved, however, to be waterless. This necessitated the laborious conveying of water to the site, which met with only qualified success.

During the next week Methven's patrols learnt from deserters that there were five companies at Ndessa and 150 rifles with two machine guns at Mbombonya water holes. Also that Mnitshi had been reinforced by nine Europeans with 200 Askaris and four machine guns. The enemy were also reported to be short of food.

On 18th certain movements forward of Hanyngton's columns took place with a view to attacking the Mihambia position next day. The Gold Coast Regiment marched out of Narungombe to Liwinda Ravine Camp. No. 1 Column's main body, consisting of 2/2 King's African Rifles, one and a half companies of the Regiment, the 27th Mountain Battery and the Stokes Battery, were to make a frontal attack, while Rose's force less one and a half companies of the Regiment would threaten the German retreat and prevent any reinforcement from Ndessa and Mbombonya to the westward.

On the same day the Nigerian Brigade marched out of Masindye and concentrated at Nsuras Fort. Meanwhile a small patrol under Griffiths reported a moderate supply of water at Luale, some 20 miles south.

Engagement at Mihambia, 19th September 1917

At dawn on 19th September Shaw, who was covering the right flank of No. 1 Column's main attack, with 'A' Company, half the Pioneers, and the 27th Mountain Battery, moved out to Kitiia, which place lies five miles east of the Liwinda Camp and three miles west of Mihambia. Having gained touch with the 2/2 King's African Rifles, which was advancing along the main road, he worked through the bush on a compass bearing with the intention of striking the enemy's left flank. However, he missed his objective, as can so easily happen in bush warfare, and found himself in front of the position. He attacked forthwith, bringing the Battery into action. Simultaneously the King's African Rifles joined in the attack.

In front of the British lay a valley in which were the water holes, while the enemy's trenches were drawn along the crest of the hill, which sloped up from them, astride the main road from Narungombe. On Shaw's left there rose an isolated hill which appeared to be unoccupied, and commanded the main road.

The water holes were captured without offering a very stout resistance. Shaw then proceeded to advance on the isolated hill, which, however, was found to be held in great strength. Repeated attacks were repulsed and the British advance was definitely held up until nightfall, when the troops were compelled to dig in. By dawn on the 20th September the enemy was found to have retreated south down the main road.

Meanwhile Rose with the rest of the Gold Coast Regiment had moved out of the Liwinda Ravine Camp to Nambunjo Hill, which dominated the main road between Mpingo and Mnitshi and some two and a half miles west of it. At 1445 hours the hill was reached, while in the interval two officers' patrols had been detached, one under Woods to protect the Regiment's right flank and rear down a path leading to the water holes at Mbombomya, and the other under S. B. Smith to attempt to secure the enemy's Signal Station at Npingo. Both these patrols were held up during the day, having to dig in.

At 1430 hours Methven with 90 rifles of 'B' Company was sent to support Woods near Mpingo, with instructions to advance towards Mihambia, where No. 1 Column reported being held up in their attack on the isolated hill before mentioned.

At 1700 hours Methven became heavily engaged, while at 1730 Smith, who had been almost surrounded, managed to join Methven at a spot about one and a half miles from Mihambia. Any further advance in the direction of Mihambia was now impossible owing to the fall of darkness and the thick bush. Moreover, the whole of Rose's command had long since exhausted their water and were suffering acutely from thirst.

At 1815 hours Woods's patrol on the Mbombonya road was vigorously attacked by a full company with two machine guns, and was compelled to fall back. His men had been fighting all day and were much exhausted for want of water. McElligot was sent with a section of 'I' Company to his support with instructions to hold on at all costs in order to protect the Regiment's rear and right flank on Nambunjo Hill.

Rose's troops were now in a desperate state for supplies, and particularly for water; in spite of urgent requests to No. 1 Column nothing had arrived. However, their despatch was notified at dawn and they arrived at 1120 hours on the 20th September. Meanwhile patrols sent out at dawn reported the enemy had evacuated his trenches at Mihambia and was covering his retreat by fighting rearguard actions with his machine guns.

At 0800 hours Wray with another section of 'I' Company was sent to reinforce McElligot and take over command of the post. About 0930 hours he became heavily engaged, but his men continued to put up a stout resistance until reinforced by Methven with three sections of 'B' Company about noon, when the enemy withdrew. This post had been without water for 24 hours; the men were terribly exhausted, while in the course of the fight Wray had been severely wounded and Corporal Issaka Kipalsi had shown great pluck and coolness while in charge of a bombing party.

The supply of water received on the 20th was very inadequate; on the next day a further small supply arrived with the Pioneers from No. 1

Column. After being watered the Regiment left its camp on Nambunjo Hill for some high ground north of Mombonya village. Methven with 'B' Company was then sent to occupy the water holes one and a half miles to the west. To everyone's intense disappointment the supply was pitifully small.

Owing to the shortage of water the Regiment was forced to remain at Mombombomya on the 22nd until some 1,000 gallons arrived that evening from Mihambia. At long last the men's thirst was able to be sensibly relieved after patiently enduring such a prolonged agony of thirst during the past four days. It says much for the discipline of the Regiment that no man had strayed away in an insane quest for water. On this day the Nigerian Brigade was reported to have been in action at Bweho Chini, 10 miles north of Nahungo in the valley of the Mbemkuru River, where the enemy were known to have a position of great strength. Between the 22nd and 25th the Regiment marched via Ndessa Juu, where large water holes were found, to Bweho Chini, where it joined up again with No. 1 Column. On 26th the Column advanced to Beka and camped there preparatory to attacking Mahungo next day. Since attacking Mihambia on the 19th September the Gold Coast Regiment had sustained the following casualties: Two officers wounded (Wray and Percy), eight other ranks and one carrier killed, with 22 other ranks and three carriers wounded.

The Battle of Bweho Chini, 22nd September 1917

We must now turn to the operations of the Nigerian Brigade, which, as has already been related, had the task of turning the enemy's left flank, thereby intercepting his retreat towards the Lindi area. On the 19th September Brigade Headquarters 1 and 2 Battalions with the Signalling Section marched out of Msuras *en route* for Luale, camping on the night of 21st/22nd at Luale Chini, in a wild and desolate country, with every effort being made to avoid detection. The 4 Battalion with the Battery and baggage columns followed a day in rear.

At 0830 hours next morning, when about two miles from Bweho Chini, the leading company of the 1 Battalion drove in an enemy picquet and entered the village. As the field telegraph had been cut during the night the Brigadier had received no news of the whereabouts of the other British Columns, nor had he any information of the enemy's position. The country was unknown and the guides unreliable, making his task no easy one.

The whole column concentrated at Bweho Chini, forming a perimeter camp with lying trenches, while patrols were sent out to the south and east, Lieutenant Hobson moving out with both battalions' baggage to be handed over to the 4 Battalion on its arrival here. About noon the patrols returned to camp with definite information obtained from European prisoners, that the enemy were at Mawerenye, four miles to the east.

In order to clear up the situation, which seemed to indicate that Bweho Chini was on the enemy's direct line of retreat southward, two companies 1 Battalion, under Captains Pring and Stretton, were ordered to make a reconnaissance towards Mawerenye.

Nigerian Brigade War Diary

Cunliffe's appreciation of the situation was that there were only two lines of retreat open to the enemy. Firstly south-west through Bweho Chini, and secondly due south via Makiu; the former was the shorter. His plan therefore was to make a strong reconnaissance towards Mawerenye, while he prepared an entrenched position at Bweho Chini.

The reconnaissance was forced to retire in the face of heavy opposition. Captain Higgins and Lieutenant Stevenson were left behind wounded, their bodies being later recovered shockingly mutilated. The Germans kept up continuous heavy attacks on the position all day and during the night. At dawn, being threatened by No. 2 Column from Mawerenye, they split into small groups and retreated through the bush.

Nigerian casualties amounted to Higgins, Stevenson, Oliver and Joseland killed; Feneran, Budgen, Colour-Sergeant Booth and Sergeant Nass wounded. Among the Africans 13 other ranks were killed, and 104 wounded, while of the carriers seven were killed and 29 wounded, one being missing. Of the enemy 16 Europeans and 87 Askaris were buried.

(The above extracts are quoted from the Nigerian Brigade War Diary for October; the November War Diary is completely missing, so that the record of subsequent operations leading to the pursuit along the Makonde Plateau is not on record.)

Soon after the reconnaissance had left an aeroplane flew over the camp dropping a message on Brigade Headquarters. At the same time Pring and Stretton became heavily engaged at some 700 yards from the camp. The volume of fire indicated that they were being opposed by a very strong force; in fact, it was afterwards learnt that the Germans had about 1,000 Askaris with over 100 Europeans and at least 20 machine guns.

The enemy sounded the charge, almost enveloping our two companies. It was thought at the time that the Germans had no idea that these companies were covering a bigger body of troops.

Nothing daunted, the Nigerian companies fixed bayonets and met the assault with a heavy burst of fire, momentarily checking it. The fight was too one-sided however, and, fighting doggedly, they gradually fell back on to the main position, eventually regaining their place in the perimeter, though not without heavy losses. Downes in his book *With the Nigerians in East Africa* (page 172) says: 'This action of these two isolated companies was one of the finest pieces of fighting that ever occurred in the Brigade throughout the whole of the campaign.'

The enemy followed up their advantage by pressing their attack against the 1 Battalion upon the east face of the perimeter, gradually working round to No. 7 Company (2 Battalion), which was on 1 Battalion's right or southern flank.

Within half an hour No. 8 Company (2 Battalion) under Fowle, on the 1 Battalion's left, was very heavily engaged. Its left flank was completely open and in danger of being turned; half of No. 5 Company from Reserve, under Gardner, therefore came up to prolong it. Meanwhile the O.C. 2 Battalion had ordered the remaining half of No. 5 Company under Studley, with a Lewis gun and a machine gun, to dig in on the unguarded

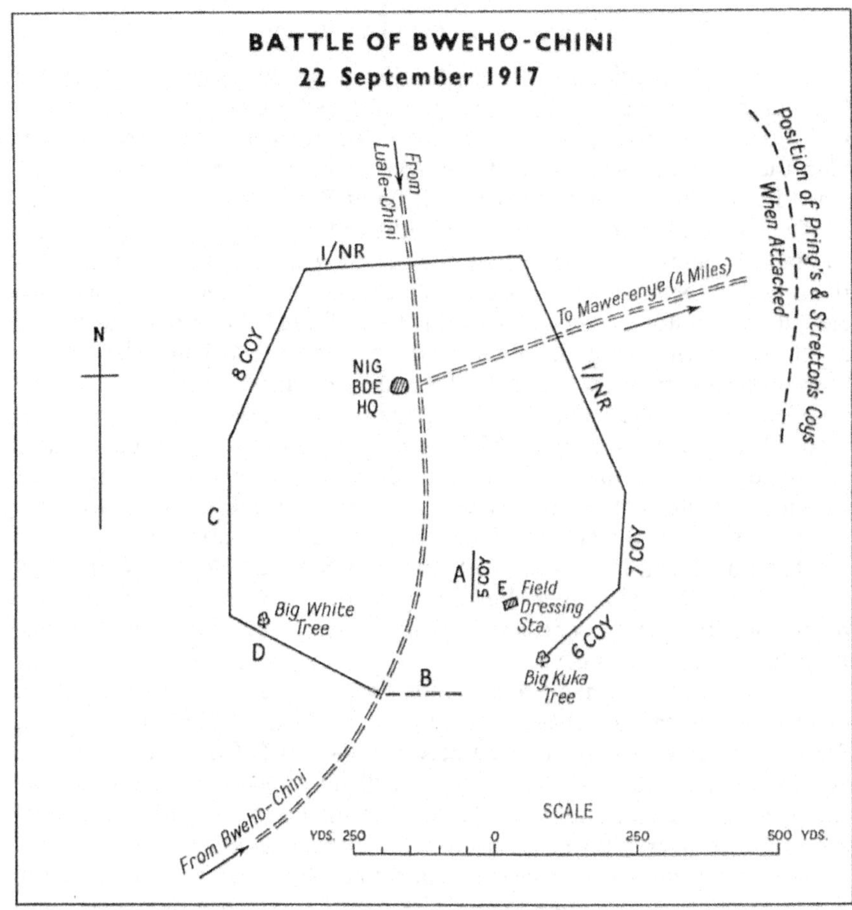

24. Battle of Bweho-Chini, 22nd September 1917

southern face at position 'B' on the sketch. No sooner was this completed than Studley was ordered to position 'D' on Fowle's left. This again left the southern face with an ugly gap in it. From the account given in Downes's book it would seem that Brigade Headquarters must have given Studley his last orders, and that there was some doubt as to whether the Reserve was under it or under 2 Battalion.

By 1500 hours the Germans were attacking furiously on the north, north-west, and east, and had begun to feel round the rest of the perimeter for a weak spot. At 1530 hours Sergeant Maifundi Shua, a section commander of No. 5 Company, gallantly led a charge against a party of the enemy under two Europeans, who were in the act of turning the Company's flank. In this charge the sergeant was severely wounded, but not before he had bayoneted one of the Europeans. Maifundi Shua had several times shown the greatest devotion to duty and was now awarded a well-earned Military Medal.

By 1600 hours the perimeter was completely encircled, with the main effort directed on the weak southern face. This attack was supported with three machine guns, chiefly on 'D' and concentrated mainly on the big white tree marked in the sketch. By this time Studley had again been moved with one section and a machine gun, with orders to deploy in the open, there being no trenches here. In order to cover his last position at 'B' Gardner brought up his half company from 'A'. This resulted in the whole of No. 5 Company (less one section) facing south.

The Germans kept on reinforcing their attack on the south, hoping, no doubt, to break through here. This they were just too late to accomplish owing to No. 5 Company having filled the gap in time. Finding it now impossible to break through, the enemy concentrated a very heavy fire on the troops lying in the open at 'D', searching the ground right and left of the white tree. No. 5 Company now had 33 casualties, of whom one European was killed and one wounded. No. 6 Company also suffered severely from an attack on the south-east, losing 18 men in half an hour.

After dusk fighting continued with varying intensity until 2350 hours, with a lull of about an hour at 2000 hours which was utilized to improve the defences. The dressing station at 'E' had suffered very severely, being in an exposed position, an attempt was therefore made to improve its cover.

The rest of the night passed quietly except for some sniping. Hanyngton's columns were now threatening the German line of retreat, so they broke up into small parties and made good their escape to Nahungo.

The troops on both sides had fought with great dash and courage. The Germans pushed their attacks on the perimeter regardless of casualties, and it was only the determination of the Nigerians which saved the day. Our casualties totalled 10 Europeans and 124 other ranks, while the enemy's losses were estimated at some 40 Europeans and 300 Askaris.

For this battle Uniacke, commanding the 2 Battalion, was given the D.S.O., Gardner had a bar added to his M.C., while Waters, Studley and Burney received the Military Cross. Sergeants Tanti and Badger were awarded the D.C.M., and four other ranks were given the Military Medal. Bweho Chini counts as a Battle Honour on the Regiment's Colours.

It may be thought that the opportunity of converting the battle into a decisive defeat was missed by the failure of the Nigerian Brigade to pursue; on the other hand, it must be remembered that the troops had very little ammunition left, were in urgent need of food and water, and had barely enough carriers available to deal with the wounded.

As regards the tactical siting of the camp a smaller perimeter would have been more suitable for the size of the force; the 2 Battalion had to cover nearly double the frontage of the 1 Battalion, while the Reserve was probably too small to be effective. Further the trenches were not deep enough to allow for a parados; this resulted in many casualties occurring from reverse fire. Two hours were available between arrival at Bweho Chini and the despatch of the reconnaissance towards Mawerenye, viz. from 1000 hours till noon; it is thought that better use might have been made of it by better planning on the part of Brigade Headquarters.

On the 24th September telegraphic communication was reopened, and a Nigerian patrol made contact with one from the King's African Rifles of Hanyngton's columns. On the same day the wounded were evacuated to

Mawerenye, then occupied by the Gold Coast Regiment. That evening Cunliffe's force moved to Bweho Ju, where they were joined by the 4 Battalion, with baggage and supply columns, who had cut a motor track through the bush direct from Luale.

Engagement at Nahungo, 27th September 1917

The German position at Nahungo was conspicuous and exposed to artillery fire. The attack was carried out in three columns. On the right were the 2 Battalion Nigeria Regiment, a battalion of the King's African Rifles, the Nigerian Pioneers and Brigade Headquarters under Cunliffe; in the centre Sargent commanded the 1 and 4 Battalions, and a section of the Nigerian Battery, while on the left Orr led the Gold Coast Regiment, a battalion of the King's African Rifles, a section of the 27th Mountain Battery and a section of Stokes guns.

The attack was carried out simultaneously on three converging roads. The left met with most opposition. During the afternoon the Germans brought two guns into action, against Orr; one was quickly silenced by the 27th Battery. About 1830 hours the enemy delivered a strong counter-attack against Orr's column which was repelled by the Gold Coast Regiment. The action continued all along the front till 2000 hours, when firing died down. During the night the enemy evacuated their position at Nahungo. It seemed that he was much shaken by the severity of the fighting at Bweho Chini and was anxious about his line of retreat.

The brunt of the fighting at Nahungo Hill was borne by the Gold Coast Regiment on the left. It was nearly dusk when the Germans opened their attack on this flank, which was first opposed by a picquet of 20 men of 'B' Company posted on the Mbemkuru River. The rest of Methven's Company, together with a company under Shaw, were in reserve some 200 yards in rear. Methven had gone forward to tell the picquet they would have to stay out all night, when the enemy appeared and opened fire on him with a machine gun. The picquet at once started rapid fire to avoid being overwhelmed. Meanwhile 'B' Company joined in, shooting over their heads. Firing became intense and somewhat wild owing to the darkness, causing ammunition to run out. Methven crawled back to secure a further supply, and this gallant act probably saved the picquet from being overwhelmed.

Shaw now brought up 'A' Company on the left of 'B' and this definitely turned the tide in our favour, preventing what might have been an enemy success of some importance.

On this occasion Corporal Bila Busanga especially distinguished himself by his steadiness and courage with the picquet, while the steadiness of 'B' Company and the prompt action of Shaw deserve to be recorded.

Considering the confused nature of the fighting in the dusk the casualties were light, amounting to 23 other ranks with 15 carriers.

At dawn on the 28th the enemy was reported to have retired. Pori Hill, the commanding position on our left, whence the German counter-attack had been launched, was at once occupied by a patrol from the Regiment, while the King's African Rifles took up a position on Nahungo Hill.

During the day a party of Nigerians visited the Regiment, this being their first mutual contact since coming to East Africa. In the Officers Mess the greatest cordiality prevailed and the incidents of the battle of Bweho Chini were eagerly discussed; among the rank and file this encounter created the greatest excitement and delight. Many men of the Regiment spoke Hausa, while in some cases Gold Coast men had been recruited from Northern Nigerian tribes.

Action at Kihende and Mitonono, 30th September–1st October 1917

No. 1 Column had now been reinforced by the 129th Baluchis and a battalion King's African Rifles. Meanwhile No. 2 Column had reached Nakiu, some 10 miles lower down the Mbemkuru Valley. On the 29th Goodwin with 'A', 'B' and 'I' Companies was instructed to follow up the enemy along the north bank of the Mbemkuru River; at the same time an officer's patrol of 20 men was to keep in touch with this force proceeding along the south bank. Goodwin, who was in command, got in touch with the enemy about eight miles from Nahungo, where he dug in for the night. In front of him was a strongly entrenched position dominated by Kihende Hill and Mitonono on opposite sides of the river.

On the 30th No. 1 Column reached Goodwin's camp. Next morning, while a battalion King's African Rifles, supported by the 27th Mountain Battery, made a frontal attack on the position, the rest of the column attempted to envelop both flanks. The Gold Coast Regiment crossed to the south bank to carry out its part in the operation. Fighting continued all day without the enemy being dislodged, but next morning the position was found evacuated, the enemy having withdrawn down the right, or southern bank of the Mbemkuru River. During the fighting on the 1st October the Regiment had 58 casualties, including three officers wounded.

Until the 8th October the enemy followed the Mbemkuru Valley covered by light rearguards, which by skilfully chosen tactical positions succeeded in keeping the troops of No. 1 Column at bay. Up to this point the route followed by No. 1 Column had been in a south-westerly direction. At Mbemba, some 30 miles from Nahungo, the pursuit left the Mbemkuru River turning nearly due south towards the Lukuledi Valley.

On the 9th the Column crossed the main Liwale/Masasi road, a first-class lateral highway, which was followed for about nine miles to Mnero Mission, where camp was made. Next day the Column reached Ruponda, with little resistance. Here lay a big supply dump, which fell into our hands. Until 16th the troops were encamped at Ruponda.

By the capture of Ruponda a wedge had been driven between von Tafel's force retiring from Mahenge and von Lettow's main army in the east, which by this time had been joined by von Wahle and Kraut with some 1,700 Askaris. On the 2nd October Naumann had surrendered near Mgera in the north-east.

It is now opportune to fill in the story of the 3 Battalion's activities since it joined Linforce on the 20th September. During this time the German forces in the Lindi area, under Wahle, consisting of about nine companies, had been resisting the British advance stubbornly where it had been held up at Nrunyu, barely 20 miles from Lindi. Linforce was divided into Nos. 3 and 4 Columns, respectively commanded by O'Grady and Taylor. The 3 Battalion (Nigerians) was allotted to Taylor's column. On the night of 25th–26th September the volume and accuracy of our artilley fire caused the enemy to evacuate his Narunyu position. Mtua was occupied that evening and next day the 3 Battalion camped at the Nongo stream.

On the 28th No. 4 Column was in reserve, while O'Grady's column became heavily engaged against a crescent-shaped hill which covered the enemy's position defending the Nengidi River. After a hard fight and a good many casualties, O'Grady had gained the crest, but was unable to advance along the level ground beyond. The 3 Battalion was then called up from reserve to prolong the line to our right and search for the enemy's left flank with a view to turning it.

The bush here was extremely dense, making it difficult for Badham, who commanded the Battalion, to keep his direction. The two leading companies, under Armstrong and Buchanan-Smith, were in the act of deploying when they were attacked from the right rear at close quarters. Buchanan-Smith thereupon right-formed his company to meet the situation. The two companies thus became at right-angles to each other. The movement was well executed, taking the enemy by surprise and throwing him into confusion. Dusk now overtook the combatants, preventing any continuance of operations. In the engagement five officers were wounded, including Armstrong and Buchanan-Smith, while there were 25 casualties amongst the men.

The troops dug in on the ground won and no move on either side took place till 0630 hours on the 30th September.

Engagement at Nyengedi, 30th September 1917

The enemy next made a determined stand at the Nyengedi River, to which he held all the approaches. The country consisted of open patches of farmland interspersed throughout with thick bush. The 3/2 King's African Rifles of No. 3 (O'Grady's) Column was to follow the southern track along the trolley line, while the 3 Battalion was to advance by a track on their right. The only map was (as so often happened) a map made by missionaries, of very doubtful accuracy. Partly owing to this, and partly to delay caused by a guide, touch between the two battalions was lost and the King's African Rifles came into action before the Nigerians could co-operate.

The 3 Battalion was working on a compass bearing through the bush until it struck the road. No. 10 Company (Robinson) was advance guard, Nos. 12 and 9 Companies (Ambrose and Southby respectively) were main body, while No. 11 Company was divided between the duties of camp guard and occupying Chirumaka Hill to protect the right flank.

At 1000 hours the advance guard made contact with the enemy's patrols and deployed, but open order formation was difficult to maintain owing to the nature of the country. About a mile and a half farther on resistance stiffened and a hasty line of entrenchments was dug, to which half No. 12 Company was sent as reinforcement. In the meantime the main body dug a strong defensive line in rear. The firing now became very heavy and the advance guard suffered severely. Robinson was reporting the situation by telephone to the C.O. when he was hit. Owing to shortage of ammunition, and the enemy's shelling, combined with a threat to Robinson's right flank, he ordered a retirement.

This retirement had to be carried out in single file because of the denseness of the bush. In spite of casualties from sniping occurring all the time it was executed with praiseworthy steadiness, the last to retire being Robinson, sitting on the back of his orderly, Private Afolabi Ibadan, while the Company Bugler and Sergeant-Major were in rear. The latter was hit when shielding his Captain's body, and the bugler stayed to assist him. Afolabi was decorated with the Military Medal and Sergeant-Major Sumanu received a mention in despatches. The men themselves were full of fight, and of the Europeans all but one were casualties.

The remnants of No. 10 Company were now rallied at the trenches occupied by the main body and supplied with what ammunition could be spared. The enemy, after making two determined efforts to turn the right flank of this position, broke off the action at dusk, but not before one officer had been killed and two others, including Captain Collins, the Adjutant, wounded. On checking the ammunition remaining it was found there was left only an average of 15 rounds per man, with two belts per machine gun and four drums per Lewis gun.

This action had been remarkable for several cases of individual initiative as well as conspicuous gallantry, one of which deserves to be specially recorded. Enlisted gun-carrier Abudu Dinga had spent the whole morning passing backwards and forwards to the advance guard through a bullet-swept zone with water and ammunition. In the evening, when food and water had to be conveyed to a detachment four miles distant on Chirumaka Hill, Abudu Dinga volunteered for the job in spite of the fact that he had been working hard all day in the extreme heat and constantly under fire.

3 Nigeria Regiment's Conspicuous Part in Actions of Nengidi and Nyengedi

At both Nengidi and Nyengedi the enemy had been driven from a strongly defended position, at each of which the 3rd Nigerians had played a conspicuous part. Their casualties at the latter place were regrettably high, amounting to three officers killed, nine Europeans wounded, and 98 other ranks killed and wounded. The strength of the whole battalion was barely 400 men. On 2nd October the Battalion rejoined No. 4 Column at a congested camp near Nengidi.

Nigerian Brigade March to Join Linforce, 3rd–18th October

Meanwhile the Nigerian Brigade had orders to march across country to strengthen Linforce (commanded by O'Grady) in the neighbourhood of Nyangao, a distance of about 80 miles in a direct line over the hills in a south-easterly direction. The utmost secrecy was to be observed throughout the march, the object of the movement being to crush the enemy's forces in the Lukuledi valley between the Nigerians and Linforce, which had by this time advanced close to Mtama, some 40 miles from Lindi. O'Grady was to start his movement on the 8th, the Nigerians being due at Nyangao about the 10th.

Mann had taken command of the Brigade, owing to Cunliffe being on the sick list. His force was composed of the 1, 2 and 4 Battalions, the Gambia Company, the Pioneer Section, Stokes Gun Section, Signalling Section, 300th Field Ambulance, a Section West African Field Ambulance and Supply and Ammunition Columns.

Major Pretorius, who knew this difficult stretch of country well, was to act as Chief Intelligence Officer. His task of guiding an unwieldy column in secrecy across a bush-covered area of badly mapped country, frequently intersected by deep ravines, along winding tracks was no easy one.

Mann's chief problems were supply and transport. Rations had to be carried for eight days, no local supplies of food were to be found on the route taken, while the march passed through a district scantily supplied with water, which consisted of some indifferent water holes and a very few small streams. A column of about 2,000 combatants and as many non-combatants would require several thousand carriers, making it extremely unwieldy, slow-moving and conspicuous. The difficulty was met to some extent by substituting 1,000 donkeys for a large number of carriers; this course, however, had the objection that an increased supply of water would be needed.

On the 3rd the 4 Battalion advanced to Mhulu, nine miles away, and the place at which the motor road would be left behind. Here the Pioneer Section dug extra water holes to improve the supply for the rest of the Brigade. On the 5th the whole force was assembled at Lihero, seven miles away. Next day the march led through a waterless tract 14 miles off at Nahanga, where information was received of two German posts being on the projected route south. In order to avoid contact with these the line of march was diverted via the Tschipwadwa stream to the Nyengedi stream. On the 7th Narumbego was reached, some 12 miles distant by a circular route through very hilly country, the last four miles of which followed the Tschipwadwa stream in a deep valley.

Dense bush and long grass had greatly hampered the movements of the column, so that the rearguard did not reach camp until dusk after a most trying march resulting in a number of casualties. Narumbego lay at the bottom of a deep valley with almost precipitous sides, in which the main body camped covered by a strong line of outposts.

On the 8th the advance guard left camp at 0400 hours; after an hour's hard climb it reached the plateau above the Mirola stream. Although its valley was only 13½ miles from the Tschipwadwa River the rearguard did not arrive there till after 1000 hours on the 9th. Much of the delay was caused by getting the donkeys up the very steep hills; many of them died on the way, necessitating the despatch of 500 carriers to help carry their loads. During the previous day's march the heat had tried both Europeans and men severely, but it was even greater on this day, causing heavier casualties.

Early on the 8th heavy gunfire was heard far away to the south-east, being the first indications of the activities of Linforce. On this day, too, a patrol sent out from Nahanga succeeded in rushing one of the German posts at Mtete and capturing three Europeans. They evidently had no idea British troops were in the neighbourhood and were astonished to see this huge column winding its way through the hills.

On the 9th and 10th orders were received from Beves, under whose direction the Brigade had now been placed, that every possible effort was to be made to fall upon the rear of the enemy's forces at Mahiwa. Therefore after a much-needed halt on the 9th the column resumed its march at 0530 hours on the 10th, arriving at the Tshitshiti stream at 1600 hours, although the ammunition and supply train did not get into camp until midnight. The crow-fly distance was only five miles, but the actual length of the march was no less than 13, owing to the tangled mass of hills around which the column had to wind its way. This day had been almost as severe a test on the troops as had that of the 8th; to add to its trials the ration situation had become acute, while the country was totally devoid of supplies.

On the 11th all the donkeys were sent back to Lindi via Lake Lutimba, as the country had become quite impracticable for them. At the same time 130 loads of ammunition, for which there were no carriers, were dispensed with. As supplies were exhausted the rest of the ammunition was transferred to the supply porters. This day the way led up to Rupiagine on the summit of the Rondo plateau. Water had to be fetched from Lake Lutimba, 1,200 ft. below. However, the wonderful view across the lake compensated to some extent for this hot climb.

On the 12th the Brigade crossed the Rondo plateau and reached Nyengedi, where two days' rations were awaiting its arrival in charge of two companies of the 2 Battalion, but the 300 carriers who had brought them had been sent back by mistake.

Beves's Headquarters sent orders for the advance to be continued as soon as possible, but a short halt was essential to rest the exhausted column. Baggage was cut down to the barest necessities, allowing only one personal load per European; 283 sick were evacuated to Mtua, of whom 11 Europeans and 38 natives were stretcher cases, which was striking evidence of the hardships the Brigade had undergone in these nine days. The strength of the three battalions did not now number much more than 1,000 rifles.

On the 13th at 1300 hours the march was resumed, first making a steep descent into the valley of the Nyengedi, followed by a stiff climb along a bad road to Ngedi on the Rondo plateau. Owing to the slow pace of the carriers, due to the difficult descent into the valley, the rearguard was unable to leave Nyengedi Camp until after dusk, and it was late at night before it arrived at Ngedi, yet the column was under orders to march again at 0430 hours next morning. It camped at Namupa Mission on the 14th, three and a half miles north of Mahiwa.

Mahiwa was the enemy's central supply depot. Intelligence reports from G.H.Q. stated it was lightly held; these, however, conflicted with the information obtained by Pretorius locally. This was that von Wahle, who had replaced Looff, had about 1,000 rifles opposing Linforce: 600 in reserve, and 600 were marching south under von Lettow.

Small patrol engagements on the 12th and 13th made it evident that the enemy now was well aware of the presence of the Nigerian Brigade on their flank. It seemed, therefore, only reasonable to anticipate energetic measures being taken to oppose it; this clearly indicated the likelihood of Mahiwa being strongly, and not weakly, held.

In fact, according to von Lettow's account (see page 200 of his *Reminiscences*) on the 15th von Wahle was holding a position astride the Nyangao–Mahiwa road with eight companies, a 70 mm. and a 4 in. gun, with one company in reserve behind his left flank. By the evening of the 15th he had been joined by von Lettow with five companies, alongside the reserve company.

(See Strategic Map of Situation 15th–18th October 1917.)

Battle of Mahiwa (Nyangao), 15th, 16th, 17th October 1917

Orders had been received from Beves for the Brigade to detach one battalion and send it to Nyangao, four miles to the south-east, with the object of blocking the road from that place to Mahiwa, by which it was thought the enemy might retreat. The 1 Battalion the Gambia Company and a section of the Battery were consequently detailed for this duty, leaving camp early on the 15th.

Brigade Headquarters, the 2 and 4 Battalions, the rest of the Battery and the Stokes Gun Section left at 0530 hours to make the attack on Mahiwa, while company 1 Battalion and the Pioneers remained at the Mission with the baggage, ammunition column and ambulances.

The main column's advance guard was composed of 15 and 14 Companies, in that order, under Gibb. Maxwell's company was leading and got in touch with the enemy very soon after leaving camp. At 0820 hours Mann received orders to press forward in spite of all opposition. Gibb accordingly instructed Maxwell to push on regardless of casualties. The opposition gradually increased until the vanguard finally got held up when approaching the Mahiwa River; here Sergeant Spratt was killed and the company suffered a number of casualties. It was first reinforced by 14 Company, and later by half 16 Company. At this juncture a three-sided perimeter camp was formed, which was presently strengthened by the addition of a company of the 2 Battalion at noon. Kneeling and standing trenches were then dug.

At 1615 hours Beves again sent orders to push on. Mann therefore decided to search for, and turn, the German right flank. For this purpose Hetley's 16 Company was detailed, moving due east at 1645 hours. After proceeding about a mile through the bush a path was met leading south, which was followed by Hetley. A screen of scouts covered the movement, and this was held up about half a mile farther on. Hetley then deployed on both sides of the path with his flanks thrown back.

While this deployment was being executed heavy fire was opened on the right and left front when Corporal Abdulai, who had been leading the scouts with great skill and gallantry, was killed. Two Lewis guns were now pushed up with a reinforcing section to build up the firepower in front. Within the next 10 minutes the enemy was enveloping Hetley's left; to meet the situation a section under Lieutenant Kellock with two machine guns, under Sergeants Element and Hervey, were brought into action facing left. The consequent volume of fire was too much for the unenlisted carriers, who bolted to a man, taking with them most of the reserve ammunition and entrenching tools. The company was now nearly surrounded and in danger of being overwhelmed.

Although the enemy was checked by the hot fire brought to bear on him, the lack of ammunition was beginning to make itself felt, which soon put both machine—and Lewis—guns out of action. Hetley then carried out a very skilful retirement by alternate sections, ably assisted by Sergeants Element, Hervey and Trollop. The gallant conduct of Company Sergeant-Major Tukeru Bouchi and Sergeant Awudu Katsena deserves to be specially recorded for the way in which they controlled their men during a most difficult retirement. Twice the enemy charged in overwhelming numbers, and twice they were beaten back. During this period Kellock was hit and the faithful Tukeru Bouchi was mortally wounded; earlier in the fighting Lieutenant Mulholland, and Sergeants Riley and Eley had been hit.

By this time there was only enough ammunition left to fill the pouches of a dozen men and feed one Lewis gun; this little band formed the rear-guard which covered the retirement of the company with all their killed and wounded. It was first led by Lieutenant Fox, who had borne the brunt of the fighting and displayed great gallantry throughout. He was hit when working the Lewis gun, and was succeeded by Corporal Sali Bagirimi, to whom the credit is due of safely covering the retreat of the unit to the shelter of its trenches at Mahiwa.

The casualties of 16 Company amounted to no less than three officers, two B.N.C.O.s and 58 other ranks, killed or wounded, or 40 per cent of the strength. The conduct of this company had been beyond praise throughout an engagement where it had been outnumbered by a far superior force and been severely handicapped by an almost total lack of ammunition, calling for skilful leadership on the part of the commander and high fighting qualities on the part of the men. Hetley was awarded the Military Cross for this action.

At the same time as 16 Company was engaged a most determined attack was delivered against the front and right of the Nigerian main position. This was continued until 1930 hours. The total casualties this day in the 4 Battalion were about 80 of all ranks. The night passed quietly except for casual sniping. A message from the 1 Battalion stated it had been held up by a strong force at Nyangao.

Patrols sent out at dawn on the 16th reported the enemy in strength on the south-east and west, while a Linforce message stated von Lettow with four companies and two field guns was advancing to reinforce the askaris attacking Mahiwa. The morning was occupied improving our defences to the depth of standing trenches. Water parties were unable to reach the Mahiwa River owing to machine-gun fire.

At this time the ammunition situation became serious owing to the heavy drain on it during the previous day's fighting. Reconnaissance showed the enemy were now intercepting communication with the 1

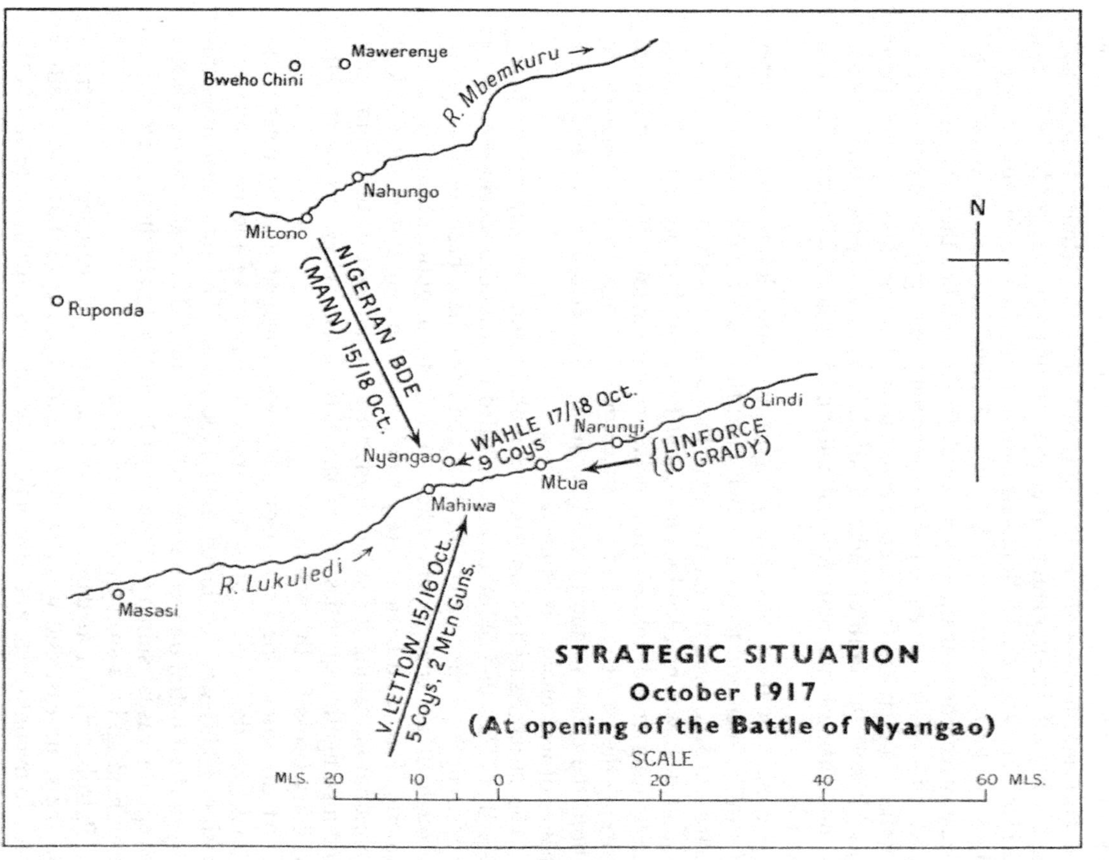

25. Strategic situation, October 1917

Battalion at Namupa Mission, precluding the arrival of any reserve ammunition; during the night the telephone lines between Brigade Headquarters and Roberts had been cut.

Throughout the morning there was desultory firing only, but at 1430 hours the Nigerians experienced what was to be their severest trial of the campaign. From the south-west a Naval 4·1 in. gun started to shell the position without, however, doing any serious damage. But at 1530 hours a 70 mm. quick-firing gun came into action on Mremba Hill. This hill was barely a mile away on the south-west, behind the Mahiwa River. Retaliation by the small guns of the Nigerian Battery was quite useless, and, in any case precluded by the shortage of ammunition.

By 1600 hours the 70 mm. began to get the range of the 4 Battalion trenches, mainly concentrating on the left of 14 Company with disastrous results. Rounds were falling at the rate of one a minute on a position totally unprepared for artillery fire, for there were no traverses and no dugouts, or alternative trenches, to which the troops could retire. 'Every direct hit found a human target; the trees above this trench were dripping with blood for two days afterwards from limbs and trunks of men that had been blown up and been wedged between the branches. It was a ghastly quarter of an hour. Nigerian troops before this had never been exposed to heavy shell-fire either in the Cameroons or in East Africa.' Thus quotes Downes in his book.

This heavy bombardment, without any means of effective retaliation, was more than the most seasoned troops could be expected to endure. Casualties were piling up and the morale of the men was visibly shaken. Sargent therefore ordered the company to withdraw to a position 100 yards in rear of their trenches. Here sections were re-formed and the men made to lie down. Sergeant Evans and a number of men had been killed, while this part of the line was scattered with wounded limping, or crawling, to the dressing station.

It was only a few minutes after 14 Company had evacuated their trenches that the bombardment suddenly ceased and was immediately followed by a determined infantry assault. The Company Commander at once called for the remanning of their trenches. This was led by the Europeans and energetically supported by the rank and file, who opened rapid fire on the advancing enemy. Downes records how he found his orderly, machine-gun carrier Awudu Katesna, sitting on the parapet blazing off his private ·333 Jeffreys rifle with the greatest unconcern. This man had been awarded the Military Medal on the 24th January at Ngwembe in the Rufiji Valley, for a previous act of gallantry.

In this attack, about 1630 hours, the Germans must have lost very heavily. Confident that the spirit of the Nigerians had been broken by the heavy bombardment, they attacked in close formation, being mown down by the machine-gun and rifle fire at close range, by 14 and 15 Companies, reinforced by a section from the 2 Battalion.

During the day the German 70 mm. gun had put a number of our machine and Lewis guns out of action, especially in 14 and 15 Companies. It had been a dominating factor in the German battle tactics. At the same time the courage and dash shown by the enemy's askaris deserves the fullest admiration; they attacked the Nigerian trenches at the double under a hail of fire to within 150 yards, when they hesitated and finally retreated in disorder.

That night the enemy lit hundreds of small fires about 1,000 yards to the south, the object of this ruse being apparently to draw the British fire, but this it failed to do. The troops were worn out with fatigue; they had eaten their emergency rations; they were desperately short of ammunition, and only too thankful to be left undisturbed.

Patrols, sent out at dawn on the 17th reported the position was entirely surrounded except on the east, and that the enemy was entrenched. At 1000 hours news came through that Roberts's column from Namupa had suffered a reverse on the 16th, losing a gun in an attempt to break through to Mahiwa. At 1030 hours heavy firing to the south-east indicated the approach of Linforce. Shortage of ammunition precluded any attempt at a sortie to co-operate with O'Grady's troops, while the only exit still open lay towards Nyangao. Beves therefore ordered Mann to retire to that place, to be covered by a company of the 3 Battalion. This movement was duly carried out with no further fighting, and the evacuated trenches were taken over by the 3 Battalion.

The Action South of Namupa Mission, 15th–16th October 1917

As already stated, 1 Battalion, the Gambia Company and a section of the Nigerian Battery had been instructed to block the Nyangao/Mahiwa road. This column, under command of Roberts, left Namupa Mission at 0700 hours. The advance guard proceeded with great caution in the face of gradually strengthening opposition. By about 0930 hours it became heavily engaged and could advance no further without suffering severe casualties. It was then some two miles from Namupa and had reached a knoll, marked Z on the sketch, which commanded a track leading to Mremba Hill, half a mile north-west of Mahiwa and two miles north-west of the main Nyangao/Mahiwa road. Roberts ordered a perimeter entrenchment to be prepared at Z.

Early on the 16th the column received orders to return to Namupa and then to reinforce Mann's force at Mahiwa. No opposition was encountered on the return march, and the Mission was reached about 1100 hours. After rations had been consumed the march to Mahiwa was continued. At 1300 hours the whole column, less one company escort to the reserve ammunition, supplies and baggage, set out with Stretton's No. 1 Company as advance guard. At this time it would appear that Roberts had no idea that the Brigade was surrounded, nor was he aware that von Lettow with five companies and two mountain guns had arrived at Mremba Hill, on the previous evening (*vide My Reminiscences of East Africa*, by von Lettow, p. 200).

Mremba Hill, where there already was at least one German company, was a commanding position, giving good observation on to the road by which Roberts was advancing and as far north-east as the Makadi River valley. At this time, about 1400 hours, Captain V. Goering, who was commanding two companies of von Lettow's force and was engaged in leading an attack against the eastern side of the Mahiwa position, had discerned the advance guard of 1 Battalion, just south of Namupa Mission. He at once switched his troops to the left and occupied the high ground between the second and third streams shown on the sketch, where he fell on Stretton's company, which narrowly escaped annihilation.

To account for the fact that Stretton was taken by surprise, he is reported to have calculated he could fall on the rear of the enemy who were engaged with Mann's column by hastening his pace and advancing without the precautions he had previously been taking. It was most unfortunate, too, that he failed to inform Roberts of the action he was about to take, thus giving him no chance to appreciate the situation before the advance guard was almost irretrievably committed.

In this disaster Stretton and Lieutenant Stirling-Miller were killed, and the rank and file suffered most heavy losses. The remnants of the company managed to force their way back to the main body by rushing the enemy at the point of the bayonet. By the death of their gallant commander the Brigade lost one of its best officers who had endeared himself to all who knew him. It will be recollected that he had fought at Nsanakang in the Cameroon Campaign, and been unlucky enough to be kept a prisoner of war till the end of hostilities there.

Tactically, however, the results of this unfortunate affair were more far-reaching, and indeed most serious, for it had the effect of immobilizing the whole of 1 Battalion and their supporting guns, thus preventing the reserve ammunition and supplies from coming to the help of the Brigade at Mahiwa, where these things were so desperately needed. Finally it paralysed Mann's force from co-operating with the columns of Linforce attacking from the east and, eventually, from attempting any pursuit of the enemy when he retreated from Mahiwa.

Directly it became apparent that the advance guard had met with a disaster Roberts took energetic steps to remedy the situation. Nos. 2 and 3 Companies were sent to the left and right of the road, with half the Gambia Company between them, forming a front to withstand the German assault, the other half of the Gambia Company being despatched to the extreme right of No. 3 Company, where the section of guns came into action. No. 4 Company remained on the left of the road behind the second stream.

By 1500 hours the whole column, except the rearguard, was heavily engaged. The remnants of No. 1 Company had fallen back and got integrated in the firing line. Soon after a number of the carriers, who were lying down beside their loads, were hit, causing them to stampede, until they were met and turned back by No. 4 Company, who checked them with fixed bayonets.

By 1600 hours the firing was at its greatest intensity, the enemy's weight being mainly thrown against our right, or western flank. At this stage the guns were firing with fuses set at zero and matters had become critical. The half Gambia Company acting as escort to the guns were hopelessly outnumbered, suffering terrible casualties and falling back in disorder. Both guns were put out of action by having their buffers perforated, while the entire team of one gun were either killed or wounded, resulting in its gun

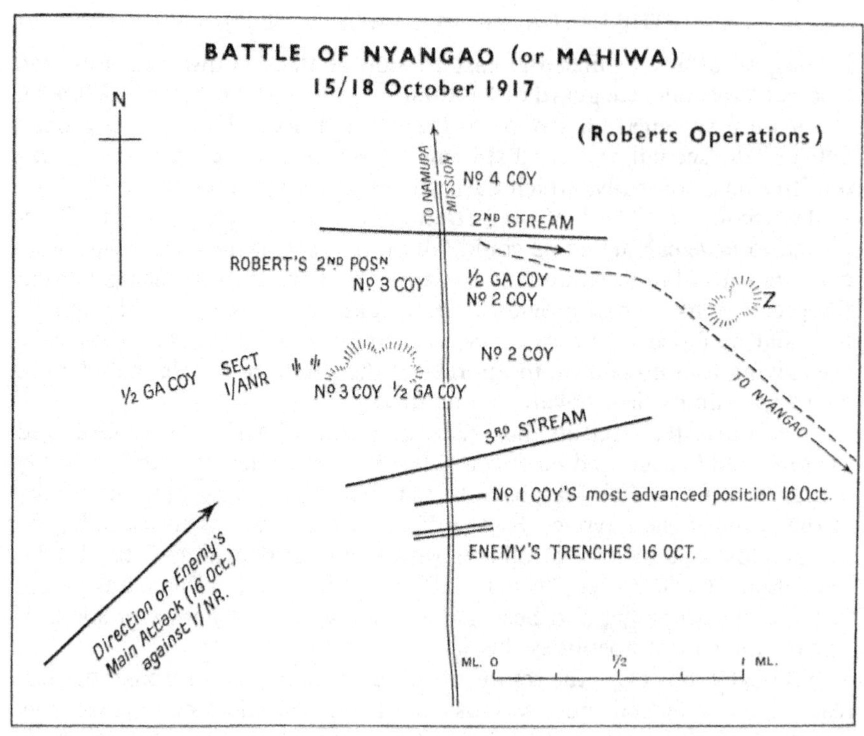

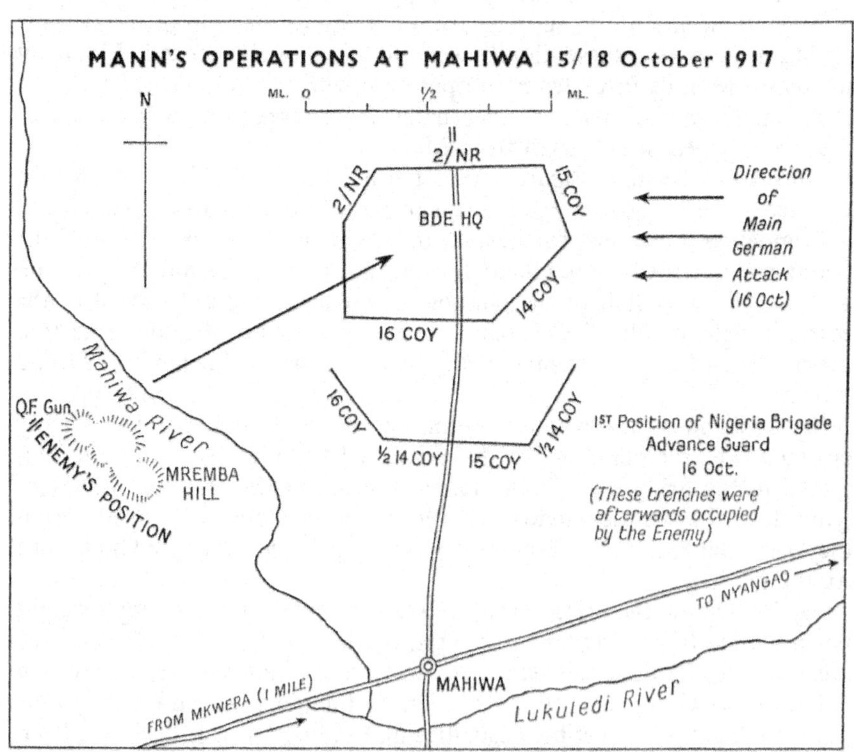

26. Battle of Nyangao (or Mahiwa) 15th/18th October 1917 (Robert's operations) Mann's operations at Mahiwa, 15th/18th October 1917

being captured. The second gun was only saved by the gallantry of Sergeant Tasker, who drove the rapidly advancing askaris back with Lewis-gun fire.

Roberts now ordered No. 2 Company to retire gradually for about 250 yards on his left flank, with instructions to dig in there, with half Gambia Company. In front of them was practically the whole baggage column with the ammunition; a very dangerous state of affairs. Von Lettow claims to have captured 150,000 rounds in this engagement, as well as the gun, although the former claim is not corroborated by Downes's account. In conformity with the movement of No. 2 Company, No. 3 Company took up its position on the right, or western, flank. Shortly after, a number of carriers were sent up to the front and gradually most of the loads were withdrawn to No. 4 Company's perimeter.

It was not very long, however, before Roberts's second position became untenable, necessitating a general withdrawl to the Mission, which was reached about 1900 hours. Luckily for the Nigerians the enemy broke off the fight at dusk. Whether this was done because he was exhausted, or, as von Lettow states, because he wished to reinforce Wahle's front against Linforce, seems a debatable point.

3 Nigeria Regiment Reinforce Roberts at Namupa Mission

The 1 Battalion passed a fairly quiet night, and at dawn on the 17th patrols reported there was no possibility of getting in touch with the Brigade at Mahiwa entrenched camp. However, later in the day heavy firing was heard from the south-east, and about 1300 hours 3 Battalion arrived at the Mission with instructions to escort Roberts's column with all the Brigade's baggage back to Nyangao from which the Germans had been driven.

Linforce Prepare for the Attack on Nyangao, 3rd–15th October 1917

Reverting now to the activities of Linforce, commanded by O'Grady, as previously narrated the 3 Nigerian Battalion had rejoined No. 4 Column of that Force at a camp near Nengidi, preparatory to the latter's concentration for attacking the Nyangao position.

3 Nigeria Regiment Relieve 1 Nigeria Regiment at Namupa Mission, 17th October

Screening Nyangao were the entrenchments of Mtama. On 12th and 13th the artillery of both sides carried out bombardments without very decisive effect. The enemy then fell back on Nyangao, while the British occupied Mtama on the 14th/15th. Here 3 Nigeria Regiment was detached to relieve 1 Nigeria Regiment at Namupa Mission, reaching it on 17th under orders from O'Grady.

Position of Night of 16th–17th

The position on the night of 16th–17th was that the main force of the enemy had evacuated Nyangao and retired to a ridge behind the Nakadi

River two miles south-west of the former place and about the same distance south-east of the Nigerian entrenched camp at Mahiwa. Column 4 (Tyler) was at Nyangao, while No. 3 (O'Grady) was on its right, or northern flank.

Battle of Nyangao, 17th–18th October 1917

At dawn on the 17th Column 4 advanced towards the ridge held by the enemy and carried part of it by 1300 hours, meanwhile Column 3 was also attacking the northern end of the enemy's ridge by this hour, led by the 1/2 King's African Rifles, who were supported later by the 3/2 King's African Rifles. The savage nature of the fighting is described in the following words by Moyse-Bartlett, in his history *The King's African Rifles*. 'Few actions of the campaign exceeded in fury the fighting at Nyangao. Attack and counter-attack succeeded each other without respite and casualties mounted. Early in the action all the light machine guns of 1/2 King's African Rifles were disabled and practically all the gun teams were wiped out. "A" and "B" Companies had been first committed to battle and when they were forced to fall back "C" Company went through them at the double with bayonets fixed. Lieutenant-Colonel Giffard, who at great personal risk was rallying his troops in the forward line, brought up "D" Company, while "A" and "B" were being re-formed. By early afternoon his whole battalion was again committed, and in answer to his representations the column commander sent forward two companies of 3/2 King's African Rifles in support and the whole force remained on the defensive until the enemy broke off the attack about 2000 hours. 1/2 King's African Rifles had lost over half its European and over a third of its African personnel.'

The 3rd Nigerians, having accomplished their mission of escorting their 1 Battalion back from Namupa Mission to Nyangao on the 17th, now received orders from O'Grady to rejoin his No. 3 Column in the attack on the northern end of the ridge mentioned in the last paragraph. Having gained touch with this column early on the 18th, Badham, who commanded the Battalion, was instructed to fill the gap on the column's left which existed between itself and Column 4. This was done by two companies, while the other two had orders to protect the right, or northern, flank of the column. The Gambia Company, having just arrived helped to fill the gap.

At 1500 hours Column 3 was withdrawn to the high ground just north of Nyangao, while 3rd Nigerians (less one company) covered the movement. This one company was entrenched on the Mahiwa–Nyangao road. The battalion had scarcely got into position at about 1715 hours when it was heavily attacked by the enemy until 1830 hours but the rest of the night passed quietly. Its casualties during the 18th were Lieutenant Ryan and Sergeant Tomlin killed and about six Europeans wounded, also 15 other ranks killed and 50 wounded.

On 18th, while at Nyangao in camp, the 1 Battalion, and the Gambia Company, also took a smaller part in this battle; that taken by the latter has already been mentioned. As regards the former it was called up to support a King's African Rifles battalion in difficulties, but never really got seriously into action, although Captain Waters, who was in command of its advance companies was mortally wounded and received a posthumous bar to his M.C., for his services in that connection.

It is clear that the results of the battles at Mahiwa and Nyangao had a decisive effect on the campaign by shattering the strength of von Lettow's main force, although neither side could claim a tactical victory, for the German Commander had made the British pay heavily in the losses he had inflicted upon them, while he had skilfully prevented their efforts at encircling him.

The Nigerian losses between the 15th and 18th amounted to 328 of all ranks, 38 being Europeans, while it was estimated that the total losses on our side were about 2,700, and those of the enemy about 800. The courage displayed on both sides by the African soldier, be he Nigerian, King's African Rifles, or German askari, was remarkable, showing what first rate material could be fashioned from such raw material under European leadership.

Comparison of Adversaries Strength and Casualties. Quote: War Office Official Narrative; Chapter XVIII

'So ended this complex and desperate action; the largest and most severe of the whole campaign, in which the opposing forces lost one-third of their fighting strength and in which both the Germans and British came near to achieving a great success. The pluck and endurance of our fighting troops averted the defeat in detail of four separate bodies without effective co-ordination. The high spirit of Mann's two Nigerian battalions enabled them to hold out for three days, encircled, without food or reserve ammunition, while the plucky resistance of 1 Nigeria Regiment south of Namupa Mission saved the reserve ammunition and stores. On the other hand the Commanders (of the operations of Linforce) in their anxiety to extricate the Nigerians missed the chance of a great tactical success.'

Von Lettow, on the other hand, used all his reserves to reinforce Wahle's fighting line instead of advancing to envelop the open north flank of O'Grady's column. To sum up the tactical effect of Nyangao (called Mahiwa by the Germans) was equal, but strategically it was a success for von Lettow, since it effectively threw out the whole plan of Van Deventer, delaying for several weeks the concentration of forces he had planned. Linforce was paralysed by its losses during the past three weeks, whereas von Lettow, leaving Wahle to reorganize and watch their equally stricken opponents at Nyangao, marched swiftly westwards on 19th October with his best troops to assist Kraut at Lukuledi. Von Lettow took his six best companies, leaving 13, much depleted ones, under Wahle at Mahiwa.

The strength of the British at Nyangao had been:

	Rifles	Machine-guns	Lewis guns	Guns	Mortars
No. 3 Column	1,200	18	20	2	—
No. 4 Column	1,000	21	21	6	—
Nigerian Brigade	1,000 (approx.)	33	34	4	4

CASUALTIES

Nyangac-Mahiwa	British Officers	British N.C.O.s	Indian Officers	Indian O.R.s	African O.R.s	Carriers
		KILLED				
No. 3 Column	3	7	—	36	45	14
No. 4 Column	5	35	6	53	45	183
Nigerian Brigade	7	6	—	—	135	—
Total			(383)			
		WOUNDED				
No. 3 Column	13	16	3	94	257	76
No. 4 Column	13	46	2	139	161	79
Nigerian Brigade	11	13	—	—	304	?
Total			(1,072)			
Grand Total			(1,455)			

The Engagement at Lukuledi Mission, 18th October 1917

We had left the narrative of the Gold Coast Regiment at the point where they had reached Ruponda as part of No. 1 Column, No. 2 Column being some 10 miles to the east. Ruponda is about 30 miles north-east of Nyangao, and the same distance north of Lukuledi, which was No. 1 Column's next objective. On the 16th October the Gold Coast Pioneers, with a battalion King's African Rifles, marched 15 miles south of Chingwea to prepare a camp and develop the water supply there. On 17th the rest of the column followed. Next morning at 0530 hours the whole column started for Lukuledi Mission, preceded by the Gold Coast Regiment as advance guard.

'B' Coy (Methven) was the vanguard; it was not quite 160 strong. The other Europeans were Lieutenants Woods, Baillie and S. B. Smith, with Colour-Sergeant Cuneen. It was accompanied by Captain Gush, of the West African Medical Staff. With it was the 7th Light Armoured Car Battery, consisting of two Rolls-Royce cars, each having one machine gun manned by an officer and two men. The machine guns were placed in armour-plated turrets; the driver and bonnet were also protected by armour. The vanguard was some two miles ahead of the main body.

About three miles from camp the 1/3 King's African Rifles had instructions to leave the road by a path on the right and carry out a wide turning movement with the object of outflanking the German position at Lukuledi Mission. Methven now searched the paths on either flank as he advanced until he had proceeded a few miles farther. He then deployed his company, keeping the armoured cars on the road. Soon after this it was learnt from a native that the Lukuledi position was still occupied with an advanced post on the river.

Two miles from the Mission station the road climbs up a fairly steep hill for half a mile, from the summit of which it descends in a long slope to the Lukuledi River, during this season quite dry. On the hill above the Mission is situated. The country here consisted of low scrub and patches of short grass, but the slope up to the Mission from the river had been burnt quite bare, while that leading down to the river valley gave very little cover from view. Methven descended the hill with his men deployed on either side, and the armoured cars on the roads.

Wood's section led the advance, crossing the river and ascending the hill until a thorn zareba was reached which blocked the road. Woods reported to Methven that he thought the Mission was unoccupied, but had sent forward a small party to confirm this.

At this time 'B' Company was deployed along the base of the hill; on the left was S. B. Smith's section, next to it Baillie's section; astride the road the machine gun was posted with Methven and Cuneen, while Woods's section was on the extreme right; the left and right flanks were both advanced. The whole terrain covered by the company was devoid of any cover for a distance of about 100 yards in all directions. Suddenly there was a violent outburst of machine-gun fire from both flanks, combined with a heavy fusillade of rifle fire from the Mission. Shortly after a party of the enemy was seen endeavouring to outflank 'B' Company's left.

Methven's machine gun was quickly put out of action, Cuneen, who was working it being killed, and his successor, Sergeant-Major Mawa Juma, being wounded and the whole gun detachment becoming casualties. 'B' Company manfully held their ground, though be it with heavy losses. Early in the fight Woods was killed, while Methven had been hit three times, in a leg previously wounded in France. Both armoured cars had their tyres shot to ribbons and were quite unable to retaliate effectively.

On Methven's left Baillie had been shot in both feet; farther to the left still S. B. Smith alone survived unhurt, but his position was being outflanked by the enemy. It was evident that the firing line could not be withdrawn save at the risk of total annihilation. The fire continued to be so hot that many of the dead and wounded were hit over and over again.

When Woods was killed Sergeant Mamprussi took command of his section, steadying his men and directing their fire with great coolness. The Pioneer Company, under Goodwin, had now come up to relieve the situation. After discussion with Methven it was decided to reinforce Yesufu Mamprussi on the extreme right, Lieutenant Sanderson being sent on this mission. Shortly after his arrival he attempted a desperate charge loyally followed by his men. This gallant feat was, however, impossible of achievement, and was stopped within a yard of the Zareba, where his body fell riddled with bullets. Yesufu Mamprussi, after taking part in the charge, led the survivors back to their former position, and continued to exhibit great courage to the end of the day, though wounded in three places.

Meanwhile Lieutenant Foster, of the 27th Mountain Battery, had joined Goodwin on the northern slope of the hill leading to the river, and from the crest of which his battery had come into action. This was the only relief afforded to the unfortunate 'B' Company during this trying afternoon. Soon after the enemy's fire slackened, and about the same time a detachment of 1/3 King's African Rifles appeared on our right, which probably decided the Germans in the end to abandon the position after dusk.

Before breaking off the fight the enemy had made a determined attack on the left flank of the Gold Coast Regiment, which by this time had dug itself in above the river. The attack was beaten off, however, by 'A' Company and three sections of 'I' Company, which had been posted to guard against such a threat.

The account of this engagement would not be complete without mention of the gallant action of Foster (27th Mountain Battery), who learnt that Baillie's body was lying in a small patch of bush near what remained of his section. To reach this spot about 100 yards of burnt stubble had to be crossed devoid of any cover. This area had been swept all the afternoon by rifle and machine-gun fire, showing that the range was known to a nicety. Although Methven warned Foster that he risked almost certain death by attempting to reach Baillie, he refused to be deterred and actually succeeded in bringing Baillie back to the dressing station without either of them being hit. Foster was awarded the Military Cross for this signal action of bravery. Methven, who had already gained this decoration on the Western Front, was now awarded a bar to be added to it.

The casualties sustained that afternoon were two officers and one B.N.C.O. with 12 other ranks killed, and three officers, including Gush, the M.O., with 32 other ranks wounded.

This action illustrates forcibly the difficulty of co-ordinating movement in bush country. Methven deployed on Mission Hill about 1430 hours, whereas the 1/3 King's African Rifles did not arrive on the scene till about 1700 hours, during which time 'B' Company of the Regiment bore the whole weight of the enemy's attack at Lukuledi Mission, which he was reported to be holding with three companies and a number of machine guns.

On 22nd October No. 1 Column started to fall back on Ruponda. The retrograde movement was dictated by the necessity for shortening the communications of Hanforce; difficulties of supplying it any further than Ruponda became insuperable. It was still based on Kilwa Kisiwani, 150 miles distant, and it had been hoped that by this time Lindi could be used for the purpose, but the slow progress of Linforce had only opened the road from Lindi for some 35 miles, leaving an equal distance to be bridged before Lukuledi was reached. From the 23rd October to the 7th November therefore, the Gold Coast Regiment remained in standing camp at Ruponda, where patrols and training were the order of the day. The opportunity now was taken of instructing teams on the Stokes guns of which a battery had just been supplied.

The Action at Mkwera, 7th–8th November 1917

On 19th October the command of Linforce was taken over by Cunliffe; Mann continued temporarily in command of the Nigerian Brigade. Sargent was appointed G.S.O., and Milne-Home Staff Captain to Cunliffe, whose Headquarters were now at Mtama. On this day a big draft of 16 officers, eight B.N.C.O.s and 512 other ranks joined the Brigade, bringing battalions up to their original strength. Active patrolling and training exercises occupied the days until 6th November, when an advance was made along the Lukuledi Valley towards Mkwera, where the enemy had taken up a position a few miles south-west of Mahiwa. Between Mkwera and Nangoo lay a waterless stretch of 20 miles; it was imperative for the enemy to hold the Mkwera position to cover his retreat to Nangoo. The Nigerians were on the right just south of the Lukuledi River; No. 3 Column in the centre and No. 4 on its left. No. 2 Battalion was left at Mremba Hill, while No. 1 Battalion was still with No. 3 Column, but rejoined the Brigade later. On the 7th the enemy were forced to retire to Mkwera Hill. Next day Column 3 was held up in its advance towards Hatia. 3 Nigeria Regiment supported by the 4 Nigeria Regiment, both being under Badham's command, were ordered to clear up the situation. No. 10 Company was advance guard and had just extended when it was heavily attacked on its left. No. 12 Company was ordered to reinforce this flank, but lost direction in the bush, emerging well in front of No. 10 Company. It was immediately received with a heavy volume of fire from the German main position and suffered about 50 per cent losses before it could regain touch with the Battalion firing line.

No. 11 Company was now moved up to prolong the left of our line, leaving No. 9 Company with Badham in support. At this stage a temporary shortage of ammunition in the centre caused firing to die down. This misled the enemy, who at once directed a determined counter-attack against the centre, coming into the open at a distance of only 50 yards from the 3 Nigeria Regiment line, and supported on both flanks by machine-gun fire. At 1500 hours No. 14 Company was called up, opening fire with three machine guns, two Lewis guns and every available rifle, thus relieving the situation to some extent.

Hetley (16 Company) was then ordered to send half a company to either flank. No. 14 Company at this time was extended on both sides of the main road, and was now called on to demonstrate against the German position on the hill; this it did with all available weapons for three-quarters of an hour, which greatly relieved the pressure on 3 Nigeria Regiment; at the same time 16 Company moved up to 3 Nigeria Regiment Headquarters, sending half the company to support Badham's left and the other half to support his right.

The opposing forces were now within 100 yards of each other and casualties were mounting up. At 1600 hours a determined attack was made against our right flank, where the enemy gained a foothold from which a heavy enfilade fire was poured upon the whole Nigerian front. After some fierce fighting, however, the enemy were driven back.

At 1630 hours a company of 1 Nigeria Regiment, followed by two of 4 Nigeria Regiment, reinforced the firing line further. Fighting continued until dusk, when the Germans withdrew in disorder, leaving behind a quantity of rifles and equipment, and their retreat being accelerated by the Cape Corps falling on their right and capturing a machine gun with little opposition.

The enemy must have suffered very heavily, but so also did we. The 3 Battaion had 133 casualties, including Green, who died of wounds. The 4 Battalion also had 17 casualties in this action. This was a bitterly fought contest, and the last noteworthy stand made by the enemy before he crossed the Portuguese border. Next day a heavy artillery concentration drove the enemy out of the Hatia position, and the advance was continued via Ndanda and Nangoo to Chiwata.

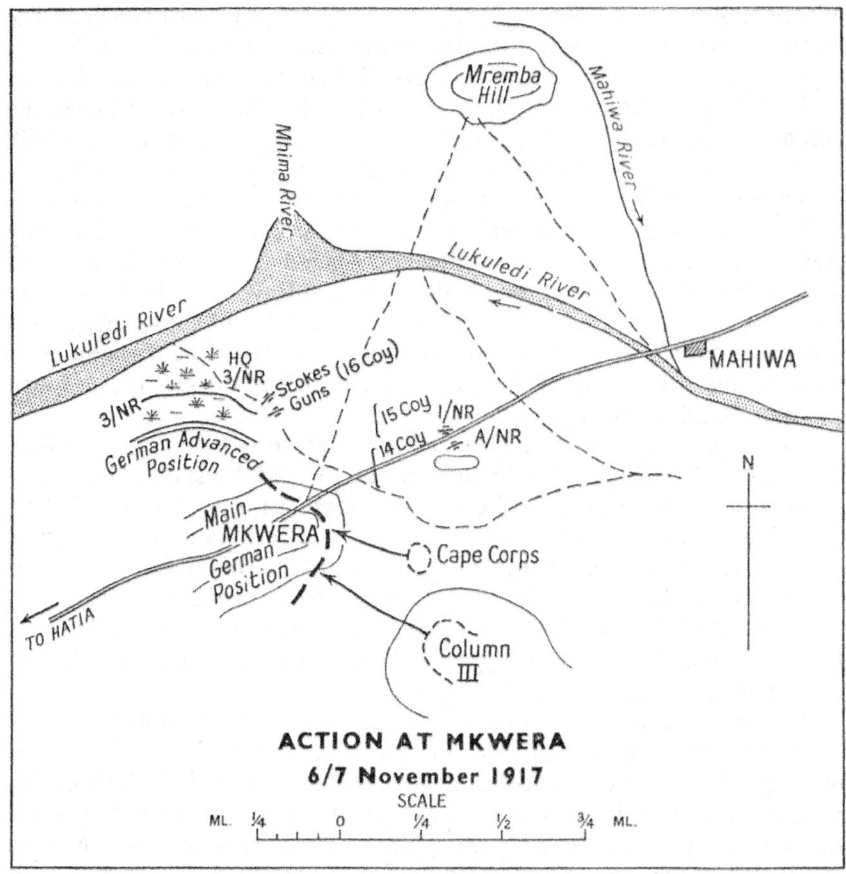

27. Action at Mkwera, 6th-7th November 1917

The Advance to the Makonde Plateau, and the Expulsion to Portuguese East Africa

We had last left No. 1 Column, which, it will be recollected, included the Gold Coast Regiment, encamped at Ruponda.

On the 7th November it continued its operations southward, reaching Chigugu next day; meanwhile Column 2 had crossed behind it and occupied Lukuledi, pushing reconnaissances up the valley of that river. On the 14th junction was effected with all columns in a concerted movement on Chiwata, where the Makonde plateau was reached. On the 16th during a minor rearguard action the Gold Coast Regiment sustained 16 casualties, including Captain Dawes wounded. Van Deventer now hastened on the pursuit with his whole forces without, however, trapping the elusive von Lettow, who escaped via Newala and Nakalala, crossing the Rovuma into Portuguese territory on 26th–27th November at Ngomano, with about 300 Europeans, 1,700 askaris and 3,000 followers.

During the last weeks von Tafel had been making his way south to join von Lettow; towards the end of November he was reported to be in the foodless and uninhabited district near the Bangalla valley. No. 1 Column was despatched to that area, No. 2 Column operating to the east, while a screen of the 25th Cavalry covered the front. Between the 27th and 28th Tafel, being very short of food and realizing there was little hope of effecting a junction with Lettow, surrendered to a detachment of the Gold Coast Pioneers through the medium of his Chief Staff Officer, who was conducted to the Column Commander, Orr, where terms were arranged and approved. Altogether some 150 Europeans and 1,200 askaris with a few thousand followers were unconditionally surrendered.

From Chiwata the Nigerian Brigade was diverted south-west through Massassi, down the Bangalla valley to the Rovuna, and was actually the nearest column to von Lettow when he crossed the latter river at Ngomano. Incidentally Ngomano had been a Portuguese post of consequence, which was attacked by surprise by von Lettow on the 25th November—Major Pinto, in command of the post, was killed, the place captured and a considerable quantity of ammunition, food and equipment secured. These supplies were a very welcome addition to the enemy's resources.

With the expulsion of the Germans to Portuguese territory and the onset of the rainy season, Van Deventer completely reorganized his forces. He decided to dispense with all troops other than Africans, and in addition to repatriate the Nigerian Brigade. In consequence two columns were formed, named Rosecol and Kartucol under the command of Rose and Giffard respectively.

The Nigerians embarked on the *Saxon*, *Briton* and *Kinfauns Castle* during February, arriving at Lagos on the 16th March, receiving a tremendous welcome wherever they went from both European and native inhabitants.

In the middle of December an advanced detachment of the Gold Coast Regiment, under Shaw, landed at Port Amelia. Rose and the remainder arrived there early in January, but for lack of transport were unable to move inland for some time.

In the meantime von Lettow had established his Headquarters 100 miles up the Lugenda River from its confluence with the Rovuma. Here he was in a fertile area, free from molestation whilst the rains lasted, and free from the anxieties of maintaining a number of detachments in the field. He had got rid of all but the pick of his war-hardened veterans, and with these he felt he could continue to lead the British a merry dance for many months to come, and so in the end he did until the declaration of the cessation of hostilities in Europe.

Towards the end of February Brigadier-General Edwards, who had been in command of the Lines of Communication during the campaign in German East Africa, was given command of Pamforce, as the combined Rosecol and Kartucol Columns were now named. Rosecol was composed of the Gold Coast Regiment, 4/4 King's African Rifles, 22nd Mountain Battery, and a body of King's African Rifles mounted infantry. Kartucol comprised 1/2 and 2/2 King's African Rifles.

It had been decided that the combined force should operate along the main road from Port Amelia to Medo, some 120 miles distant, where the enemy had fortified a strong position. Until the end of March, owing to the rains, progress had been slow, but an entrenched camp had been established at Meza, which was about half-way between the British base and Medo. As far as this place the road had been improved as much as the weather conditions permitted, and supplies of all sorts had been accumulated for the final advance on Medo.

On March 27th Rosecol began their advance on Medo, which continued steadily, with only minor patrol incidents, until a place, to which the name of Rock Camp was given, was reached on 9th April, about seven miles from Medo. Edwards and his staff reached the camp early on the 10th. And at 1330 hours the Gold Coast Regiment moved out towards Medo.

The German position occupied a site on rising ground astride the road; on the left, or south side, the prominent Chirimba Hill completely dominated the road, for about two miles. Major Kohl, who was in command and was one of the ablest of von Lettow's lieutenants, had a force of six companies, 12 machine guns and a field gun captured from the Portuguese. Along the bush-covered base of Chirimba Hill he had skilfully concealed two companies, holding four in reserve. Edwards's plan was to make a frontal attack with Rosecol and turn the enemy's right with Kartucol.

Action of Medo, 10th–12th April 1917

A strong reconnaissance of 50 rifles under Captain Harris was sent out that afternoon to try and establish itself on the eastern extremity of the hill. The eminence itself consists of a razor-edged ridge several hundred feet high, rising into three main peaks divided by deep ravines. In this broken ground, Harris ran into an ambush, losing Sergeant Flatman killed besides several other casualties. He was forced to retire, but eventually made good a post on the slopes of Chirimba.

It was evident that the hill must be occupied before the enemy could be evicted from their position. It also was clear that the ridge was quite unsuitable as a line of approach, on account of its sharp edge. The Regiment camped for the night two miles from Rock Camp with an advanced post a mile farther down the road. Twelve more casualties had occurred that afternoon.

On the morning of the 11th, Shaw, who was in command of the advance guard of the attacking force, consisting of 'I' and 'A' Companies Gold Coast Regiment, pushed forward to the post which had been established overnight; from here he deployed his force with his left on the eastern peak of Chirimba, down the northern slope, across the road as far north as a track called the 'telegraph line' which ran parallel to the road. The left of his line soon became engaged with the enemy posted in thick bush and low forest on the lower slopes of the hill. By the end of the day the eastern extremity had been cleared, while a post under a native N.C.O. had been established, about 400 yards in advance of the firing line, on the road. Late in the afternoon of the same day Kartucol set out for a night march preparatory to making their flank attack at dawn next day, and were in position by 0300 hours of the 12th.

On the 12th at 0600 hours Shaw's advance guard, now composed of

'B' Company and two Stokes guns, moved forward covered by the fire of the 22nd Mountain Battery directed against the bush-covered lower slopes of Chirimba, from which a galling machine-gun and rifle fire was proceeding. All this time the Stokes guns, under Foley and Lamont, were of the greatest assistance in neutralizing the enemy's machine guns by throwing their shells about 150 to 300 yards to the right and left on either side of the road. When our line halted to fire 15 minutes were allowed the Stokes guns to take up fresh positions, generally about 50 yards in rear of the firing line. This plan worked very well, and the advance, though slow, was practically continuous, until about 1230 hours, when the resistance became very stubborn.

At 1400 hours half 'A' Company (Wheeler) reinforced Shaw's right, soon followed by half 'I' Company under Harman. Goodwin then took over from Shaw; simultaneously the right flank was ordered to be prepared to swing round in order to enfilade the enemy as soon as the advance continued. About 1500 hours Kartucol on the southern side of the hill was heard to be heavily engaged, thereby causing a slackening to the opposition against the Regiment. Shaw, now in command of the firing line, was therefore able to work round the western extremity of Chirimba Hill and get in touch with the King's African Rifles, who were very hard pressed and hastily digging themselves in.

At the moment of Shaw's arrival the enemy was making a strong counter-attack on Kartucol; a sharp fight ensued which resulted in his being driven off with considerable loss. Meanwhile Harman, with 'I' Company's detachment, had been separated by swampy ground from the rest of the firing line, and did not regain contact with it till after dusk, having been attacked on his right flank and right rear with considerable persistence. His small party fought back gallantly, but was roughly handled by the fire of a machine gun captured from the Portuguese. Colour-Sergeant Thornett was killed, while three of his team and three carriers were hit. Just after this Sergeant Mudge and Lieutenant Barrett were hit, the former dying in a few minutes.

The total losses of the Regiment from the 10th to the 12th were four Europeans and 10 men killed, with one officer and 40 men wounded. Next morning patrols reported the enemy had withdrawn.

During these three days a great strain had been placed on O'Brien of the West African Medical Staff and his assistants. O'Brien, by no means for the first time, showed almost reckless courage while attending to the wounded under fire.

In the engagement at Medo Kartucol had been caught by heavy machine-gun fire while crossing a piece of swampy ground south-west of Chirimba Hill. The 2/2 King's African Rifles were leading and the advance guard had halted on the far side of the swamp when fire was opened as two companies were in the act of deploying to the left flank. Being caught on unfavourable ground in awkward formation, it was a fortunate chance which brought the Gold Coast Regiment on the scene at a critical moment in the action, resulting in the discomfiture of the enemy, though not before the King's African Rifles had suffered severe casualties.

Once again von Lettow had successfully achieved his object of delaying and wearing down his adversaries. It was now more than three months since the British had first landed at Port Amelia and we were no nearer to rounding up the enemy, who had remained practically invisible throughout the fighting at Medo.

On the 13th both columns encamped at Medo. On the 15th Rosecol advanced towards Mwalia, about 25 miles away, preceded by Kartucol, each column taking its turn at leading in this manner. Some 15 miles farther the road which Kohl was following branched south-west to Koronje, 40 miles away, where it was thought the enemy would make another determined stand, although he had put up only light resistance since quitting the Medo position.

The advance from Medo to Koronje had lain through difficult country, where the bamboo thickets and elephant grass grew so high that the tracks became mere swampy funnels through the bush. From here, however, more open ground was reached and the rate of progress became consequently greater. Koronje itself was reached on 1st May. Here, Kartucol, whose turn it was to lead, deployed for the attack on Koronje Hill, covered by the guns of the Mountain Battery, to which 50 rifles of 1 Company Gold Coast Regiment were doing escort, under Lieutenant Kay. About 1700 hours an enemy party of some 40 men, having worked its way through the bush to the rear, suddenly made an attack on the Battery as it was limbering up. For a moment the guns were in peril of capture, but Kay, acting with great coolness and promptitude, beat the attackers off while the mules and their loads were got away in safety. Throughout next day Kartucol was engaged without making much progress, but on 3rd May the position had been evacuated overnight.

On 4th May the British force came up against an enemy position on the Milinch Hills, which was quickly abandoned. From here the retreat followed a west-south-west direction to Msalu, where Rosecol remained till the 15th May. The country here is orchard bush, much infested by lions. At night these animals were particularly troublesome, causing widespread alarm amongst the carriers and actually killing two men of the King's African Rifles. On 20th May Rosecol crossed the Msalu River, camping next day three miles north of the road to Mahua, where Kohl was reported to be with five companies.

The situation at this time was as follows: Kohl's force was in the vicinity of Korewa-Wanakoti, 25 miles west of Narungo, where he was reported to be holding a strongly entrenched position in the hills astride the main road to Mahua. Kartucol had passed through Narungo, marching west along the main road, while Rosecol was following a parallel route just north of Giffard along the valley of the Msalu River. Meanwhile Northey's columns were closing in on the enemy from the north, south and west. The last, commanded by Lieutenant-Colonel Griffiths, consisting of one and a half battalions King's African Rifles, being the nearest, was advancing from Mahua, some 20 miles west of the German position.

At this juncture Edwards decided to attempt the encirclement of Kohl's force by using Griffith's column to co-operate with Pamforce. His plan was for Griffiths to strike the main road behind Kohl's position, while Kartucol made a frontal attack, and Rosecol turned his left flank.

On the 22nd May Kartucol was approaching a gorge 24 miles from Nanungo, and flanked by precipitous hills covered with dense bush, thus providing the enemy with an ideal defensive position along which small well-posted rifle and machine-gun parties could delay an advancing force for a considerable time. While Kartucol pressed their frontal attack Griffiths struck the main road west of the position, capturing Kohl's camp and much of his heavy baggage. The enemy shortly afterwards counter-attacked as soon as he had recovered from his surprise, causing the British severe losses. His action gave Kohl's main force time to scatter and get away before either Giffard or Rose could close the gap left open for retreat. The Germans here had 60 casualties, besides losing 100,000 rounds of ammunition and baggage.

Between the 23rd and 28th May Lieutenant Percy and Sergeant Kent were wounded when Rosecol was engaged in minor actions with the enemy's rearguards, which were covering the retreat of von Lettow's main force towards the Lurio River, southwards. This concluded the first phase of the operations in Portuguese East Africa. Rosecol was then broken up and on the 1st June the Gold Coast Regiment left Korewa Camp on its march back to Port Amelia.

The rest of June and July were occupied in refitting and collecting men who had been employed on the line of communications. On the 29th July Rose sailed for Durban, accompanied by the Quartermaster, Major Read. On the 13th August Hornby, with 37 officers, 17 B.N.C.O.s, 862 other ranks, 135 stretcher-bearers and gun-carriers, embarked on H.M.T. *Magdalena*, sailing next day for West Africa. Durban was reached on the 18th August, where Rose and Read rejoined the Regiment. At Cape Town, on the 27th, several officers, who were taking leave, were landed. Accra itself was reached without incident on the 5th September. On the next day the Governor came on board to welcome and inspect the troops, and to thank them on behalf of the Colony for the splendid manner in which, through all the trials and dangers of the campaign, they had upheld its reputation.

Rose and Read landed at Accra, but the Regiment sailed on the 6th for Sekondi, where it arrived next morning. From this port to Kumasi the train journey was a triumphal progress. At every halting-place crowds had assembled to load the men with food and gifts. Both Europeans and natives alike were eager to show the Regiment what pride they felt at the reputation it had won for itself and how deep was the popular sympathy for all they had suffered and endured. It was a royal homecoming when they arrived at Kumasi at dawn on the 8th of September. Here they were met by a clamorous mob of their women, who accompanied them to their cantonments with the songs and dances wherewith the warriors of their tribes have always been greeted on their return from a victorious campaign. But alas! There were wailings and lamentations, too, for many a poor fellow lying buried on the other side of the continent.

The casualties incurred in the campaign are shown in Appendix VIII. The strength in the field never numbered more than about 900 rifles, while from first to last the number of officers and men despatched was about 3,800. Bearing these facts in mind the table of casualties strikingly illustrates the severity of the fighting and the ravages of disease suffered by the Regiment.

Before concluding this account of the military effort of the Gold Coast during the East African Campaign, the story of the Gold Coast Mounted Infantry deserves to be briefly recorded, although this unit never served in the field with the rest of the Regiment. It was not fit for service until the Regiment was leaving Korewa for Port Amelia in June 1918.

At the end of February 1918, Lieutenant G. H. Parker, Royal Artillery, was picked out from the Gold Coast Battery to raise and train a small body of mounted infantry. Rose instructed him to select about 40 men from a newly arrived draft of recruits. Lieutenants Drummond and Saunders, with five B.N.C.O.s, were also attached to the unit.

The men chosen were from the Northern Hinterland Provinces of the Gold Coast, as they were familiar with horses, although their knowledge of horse-mastership and management was of the crudest.

Four riding schools were constructed near the camp at Port Amelia, where daily for hours at a time instruction was given by the European personnel. On the whole the men took kindly to their work and many of them became quite fearless riders; some, however, were incurably horse-shy and had to be relegated to being trained as infantry men. By the 30th May No. 1 Troop was passed as fit to take the field.

This troop, under the command of Drummond, consisting of 1 B.N.C.O., 41 other ranks, 51 horses, two mules and two camp followers, left Port Amelia on the date mentioned and rode up the Medo road to Wanakoti, Edwards's Headquarters. It is not our purpose here to follow in detail the activities of this mounted infantry unit, as this would involve a full account of the second phase of the campaign in the Province of Mozambique. A brief sketch of the career of the Gold Coast Mounted Infantry is all that is now contemplated.

After von Lettow had crossed the Lurio River from the Nyassa Province of Portuguese East Africa to the Mozambique Province, Drummond's troops had been scouting southward from Wanakoti for the columns operating in the pursuit of the enemy. At Namirrue, a place some 60 miles north of the mouth of the Ligonha River, it had just joined up with the garrison of a company of the 2/3 King's African Rifles, when the little force was surrounded. After a gallant resistance of three days, being cut off from their water supply, Bustard's company and Drummond's mounted infantry were compelled to surrender at the end of July.

Meanwhile the three remaining troops of the Gold Coast Mounted Infantry, having completed their training, had sailed from Port Amelia on the 1st July. They comprised eight officers, 10 B.N.C.O.s, 137 other ranks, 97 followers, 133 horses, 50 mules and 141 donkeys. Disembarking at Mussuril Bay, off the Island of Mozambique, they established their depot on 5th July at Monapo, 20 miles inland. On 11th Mamupla was reached, 80 miles farther west, where Edwards had his Headquarters.

On the following days Parker's squadron pushed on towards the Lighonha River with orders to locate the enemy and hold the fords across it, in the vicinity of Metil. On the 19th Metil was reached, where it was found that the Ligonha was quite shallow for a distance of 20 miles; by this time the unit had marched about 170 miles, averaging nearly 25 miles a day, which was good going for a newly formed body of mounted troops.

From Metil one troop under Lieutenant Poole was sent eastward to Napue; a second under Lieutenant Viney went five miles south-east towards Muligudge; and a third, under Lieutenant Saunders, was sent north towards Pekerri, which place was a few miles south-east of Namirrue. Headquarters with Lieutenant Broomfield and 20 men remained at Metil.

On 23rd July news of the investment of Namirrue garrison was received, and that an attempt by Fitzgerald with two battalions of the King's African Rifles to relieve it had failed. Parker was thereupon ordered to collect his unit in order to scout towards Namirrue. Poole's and Viney's troops were in consequence recalled, and on the 24th Parker moved up to Pekerri, and thence pushed through the bush to the banks of the Ligonha. From here Viney with 12 men went scouting towards Namirrue; Broomfield with 20 men was despatched to Lutete, while Parker and Saunders with the balance of 28 rifles moved up the left bank of the river.

At 1600 hours that day Parker surprised a small baggage train, at a spot where there was a trail which Saunders was left to watch; meanwhile Parker set off for Pekerri with his prisoners. He, however, unfortunately fell in with a superior force of enemy, lost his prisoners as well as a good many men and horses, and was himself reported missing for three days. At the end of that time, however, he contrived to rejoin with the remains of his troop. Saunders also came to grief, being wounded and losing several men and nearly all his horses, while Viney was surprised when off-saddled and was killed, though most of his men escaped through the bush.

It had been a disastrous time for the Gold Coast Mounted Infantry. In a matter of three weeks they were reduced from 165 to 65 men; these were left in the field under Broomfield, where they did some very useful scouting for the G.O.C., meanwhile Parker returned to the depot at Mnapu to train and re-equip drafts.

Although the enemy had succeeded in cutting off the British force at Namirrue, and had also had another success at Nhamaccura, where the Gold Coast troops did not figure, he was now compelled to concentrate all his detachments near Chalana owing to the rapid convergence of six King's African Rifles columns.

It was at this time that Broomfield and his small body of mounted infantry specially distinguished themselves by keeping in close touch with the enemy and reporting his exact movements to Edwards at a time when it was vital to ensure the correct disposition of his forces in order to close the net securely. At Liome von Lettow suffered the worst hammering he had experienced in the whole campaign, when on the 31st August and 1st September he lost some 50 Europeans and several hundred askaris, killed, wounded or captured. At this time, too, Drummond was able to make his escape.

Thereafter, as is well known, the German Commander crossed the Lurio River going northward, passing through the Nyassa Province, crossing the Rovuma at Ngomano, whence he re-entered German East Africa hotly pursued by the indefatigable King's African Rifles, but when he finally surrendered after the signing of the Armistice it happened in Northern Rhodesia.

The Gold Coast Mounted Infantry joined in the pursuit as far north as Ngomano, under Parker. On the 3rd October they received orders to return to the Gold Coast, where they were disbanded and rejoined the Gold Coast Regiment.

Conclusion

(*a*) *Troops*. When it is considered that von Lettow-Vorbeck, with his comparatively meagre resources, kept a vastly superior British army at bay for over four years, it must be acknowledged as a brilliant feat of arms. At the outbreak of hostilities the strength of the German askaris and the King's African Rifles was about equal, in the region of 2,500. On the other hand, the proportion of Europeans to natives was a good deal higher on the side of the enemy, averaging 9 per cent against 4 per cent approximately. This factor was of considerable importance, and made itself felt throughout the campaign. As time went on it was realized that white troops were far less well suited to the conditions prevailing in the tropical jungles and malaria-infested swamps of the country than were African troops; consequently the former were repatriated and complete reliance came to be placed on the latter. By the end of 1916 the West African Frontier Force, as represented first by the Gold Coast Regiment and then by the Nigeran Brigade, took the field. Meanwhile the King's African Rifles were being rapidly expanded from three to more than 20 battalions. But the proportion of Europeans to native ranks remained about the same as it had been at the beginning of the war. The Germans had always appreciated, even more than had we, that the African soldier makes admirable material, but needs the leadership of the European to develop his qualities to the full.

As regards numbers it is probable that von Lettow never mustered more than 4,000 rifles in the field, while on our side the maximum is unlikely to have exceeded 20,000 to 30,000 combatants.

(*b*) *Artillery*. Owing to the dense nature of the bush in which operations were frequently conducted, the artillery of either side was largely ineffective; targets could not be seen, so perforce shooting was blind. In a few cases where targets were well defined, such as the Nigerian trenches at Mahiwa, or the German position at Nahungu, however, the artillery support was proportionately most effective. In 1916–17 the German 4·1 in. Naval guns from the *Konigsberg* dominated our artillery, for instance, at Gold Coast Hill and Kibata; later we brought up heavy howitzers which redressed the balance.

(*c*) *Machine Guns*. At the outbreak of war each German company had an armament of three or four machine guns; whereas each King's African Rifles had only one. In the W.A.F.F. the establishment for the Gold Coast Regiment was three per company, while it was four in the Nigerian Brigade. The enemy made particularly skilful use of his machine guns with correspondingly effective results. Great care was taken in siting trenches for enfilade fire.

(*d*) *Stokes Guns*. On the British side Stokes guns did not come into the picture till the autumn offensive of 1917, when they proved their worth in close support of attacking infantry. The African soldier showed himself very adaptable as a bomb thrower; here again bombs were not available till late in 1917.

(*e*) *Aircraft.* It cannot be said that they had much material effect on the situation. In any case, when operating over bush country targets were not often visible.

(*f*) *Training.* The standard of training for bush warfare on both sides was high, though the enemy had the great advantage of knowing the terrain over which he was fighting. In the bush and forest country this was an asset of major importance, particularly as considerable areas were virtually unmapped.

(*g*) *Transport.* In tropical Africa the human carrier was the normal method, owing to lack of roads for wheels. In East Africa animals are affected by tsetse fly; moreover, black cotton soil is impassable in the rains. Motor transport cured this. Its value is decisively shown when it is calculated that to keep up a 3-lb. ration for ten stages calls for as many carriers as men in the force.

The enemy's transport was very efficiently organized. Each company was self-contained; 15 per cent of the carriers were trained and armed as a reserve to the fighting men. There were 322 porters per company of 120 askaris.

Until motor transport became available in 1917 carriers and donkeys had to be used. The mortality amongst these was extremely high, for instance in the Rufiji Valley and on the Nigerian Brigade's march to Mahiwa. This greatly delayed supply columns, resulting in shortness of rations and consequent rise in the rate of sickness. The enemy, having a well-established system of enlisted carriers, with well-furnished supply depots suitably sited for their operations, did not suffer much in this respect. Their movements were not restricted by lack of a smoothly running supply and transport organization.

(*h*) *Water* In some parts of the country the question of water supplies was of overriding tactical importance. For example, in the dry country between the Matandu and Mberuku Rivers the Germans fought very hard to prevent the capture of the water holes at Narungombe.

(*i*) *Tactics.* By reason of the enemy acting on the defensive they were often able to choose favourable sites for their camps and headquarters, leaving the swampy and unhealthy areas to be occupied by the British troops, as indeed occurred in the rainy season of 1916–17 in the case of the Nigerian Brigade during the Rufiji Valley Operations.

(*j*) *Strategy.* The strategy planned first by Smuts, then by Van Deventer, was to encircle the enemy's main forces and prevent reinforcements reaching them from outlying detachments. In this both Commanders failed mainly owing to von Lettow's superior mobility. For instance No. 1 Column of the Kilwa Force outran its supplies and had to withdraw to Ruponda, leaving a gap in the Lukuledi Valley by which the enemy could retreat. The retreat through Portuguese East Africa met with no better fortune on our side, so that in the end the German Commander could claim to have succeeded in fulfilling his mission by not surrendering until the Armistice was declared in Europe.

(*k*) *Casualties.* Our casualties, according to the figures given in Brigadier-General Fendall's book, *The East African Force, 1916–1919*: Killed, or died of wounds, 4,000 troops and followers; died of disease, 5,500 troops and many times more carriers.

Commendations

Finally what of the devoted band of officers, leaders of the gallant soldiers of the West African Frontier Force. Where so many distinguished themselves it would be an invidious task to discriminate. Surely, however, pride of place must be given to Rose, who commanded the Gold Coast Regiment, with such conspicuous success throughout the Campaign. Most prominent of others it may perhaps be fair to mention Shaw of the Gold Coast Regiment, also Sargent and Badham of the Nigerian Brigade.

CHAPTER 6

The Years of Achievement: 1914–19

(A) ARRANGEMENTS FOR INTERNAL SECURITY AND REINFORCEMENTS OVERSEAS: 1914–19

Gambia

ABOUT one-half of the Gambia Company had formed part of the Cameroon Anglo-French Expeditionary Force between September 1914 and April 1916, while the balance remained at Bathurst for Internal Security and training reinforcements.

In April 1917 a somewhat similar course was adopted when the Gambia Company embarked for the East African Campaign, in which it was commanded by Captain R. Law, who was decorated with the M.C. for his services there. The Company returned to Bathurst on 8th April 1918.

For the East African Campaign the Company had embarked at full strength, so it had been found necessary to call on a company of the West African Regiment to garrison Gambia. This company now returned to its permanent station in Sierra Leone.

In September of the same year a virulent epidemic of Spanish influenza broke out. Ninety-eight per cent of the company was attacked and seven deaths occurred.

It is recorded that a review was held at Bathurst on 22nd November to celebrate the signing of the Armistice, and for the first time in its history Gambia paraded two companies strong. The second company was disbanded next day, but 171 men transferred to the Reserve.

On 19th December the Governor presented medals as follows:

African D.C.M.: 300 Company Sergeant-Major Saisey; 309 Corporal George Thomas; 544 Corporal Dembah Krubali.

African M.S.M.: Interpreter Karifa Dembeli.

On 1st June 1919 Captain H. T. C. Stronge, M.C., took over command from Law. The former received the D.S.O. on 4th June for services on the Western Front.

Sierra Leone

Although the Sierra Leone Battalion W.A.F.F. did not take part in the East African Campaign the Colony played a highly important part by supplying an efficient Carrier Corps of between 3,000 and 4,000 men on the conclusion of hostilities in the Cameroons.

On 17th February 1918 Major J. Dawes was awarded the Croix de Guerre.

On 28th March, 1918 Lieutenant K. McIver was appointed Adjutant.

A training centre at Daru had dealt with reinforcements for the

Cameroons, while internal security was looked after by the West African Regiment.

In 1919 Major A. N. Ogilvie, North Staffordshire Regiment, was appointed to command the Sierra Leone Battalion. He had served with it as a captain in the Cameroons and had a well-deserved reputation for his wit and humour. One day his orderly reported Ogilvie's dog was 'sick with some juju'. To this Ogilvie replied without any hesitation: 'Which be dem witch which done witch him.'

Gold Coast

During the Cameroons and East African Campaigns recruiting had flourished. The main training centres were at Kumasi and Tamale. Major Elgee was first made Officer Commanding Troops, and was succeeded in February 1917 by Potter, who had so distinguished himself in Togoland.

The Regiment did not return from East Africa until September 1918. Shortly after it was decided to form a Gold Coast Brigade for service in Palestine, with Rose as Brigadier in command. But the cessation of hostilities in November 1918 deprived this gallant unit from adding a further chapter to its brilliant record.

The Brigade was to be called the 2nd West African Service Brigade; in it was to have been incorporated the Gambia Company as a Pioneer Company.

Nigeria

In Nigeria the question of internal security constituted a bigger problem than in the other West African Colonies. On the outbreak of the 1914–18 War it was not, however, the Mahomedan Emirates which seemed a matter of concern, but rather the Pagan tribes in the Plateau District. The policy adopted, therefore, was as far as possible, to avoid depleting garrisons of outstations in these more turbulent areas.

The Northern Emirs from the very start of War renewed their profession of loyalty to the Crown, and gave every assistance possible by collecting supplies of grain and cattle for rationing the troops, as well as encouraging recruiting. Even when the Tuareg Rising in 1916 might have been calculated to make them waver they retained their staunchness.

Tuareg Rising, December 1916–March 1917

This Tuareg Rising was led by a Senussi, called Kaossen, and was said to have been fomented under German and Turkish auspices. The oasis of Agadez, 300 miles north of the Nigerian Frontier in the Sahara, was a French outpost which had been invested in December 1916 by the Senussi leader. The French Government asked for our co-operation. Two columns of W.A.F.F., one from Sokoto and the other from Katsena, numbering in all 425 rifles with 37 Europeans, were accordingly held in readiness to reinforce the French if required. At the same time three companies West African Regiment were sent to Zaria from Sierra Leone. In March 1917 Agadez was relieved and the Tuaregs were dispersed.

Early in 1917 the Mada Hill Pagan tribes of the Bauchi Plateau, who had for many years shown a turbulent spirit, encouraged by the withdrawal of troops for the Cameroons, renewed their attacks on convoys, virtually stopping trade in the area. Captain Norton-Harper was dispatched from Wamba with a company to quash the trouble. The country was very hilly and the enemy mobile and elusive. Harper was later reinforced by another company, when Major Napier took over control and succeeded in arresting the ringleaders and bringing hostilities to a successful termination.

In Nigeria at the outbreak of war training centres had been established in the north for Hausas at Zaria, and in the south for Yorubas at Ibadan. These were the principal ones, although a few smaller ones existed. In February 1916 Major Jenkins, who had been Staff Officer to the I.G., was appointed Acting Assistant Commandant to Cunliffe and became O.C. Troops Nigeria when the Nigerian Brigade, under Cunliffe, sailed for East Africa later in that year.

After the return of the Nigerian Brigade from East Africa the War Office decided to mobilize the 1st West African Service Brigade for Palestine under Cunliffe's command. Mobilization was first delayed by a severe outbreak of Spanish influenza in September. Luckily the influenza epidemic did not start until the Egba Operations had been concluded, otherwise it would have been very difficult to assemble the troops required to quell the rising at Abeokuta, the capital of Egbaland.

An account of the Egba Operations is given in Section (B) below.

As we have already stated, the West African Service Brigades were never despatched owing to the conclusion of the 1914–18 War. During 1919 demobilization was proceeded with and peacetime routine again adopted. By the end of the year battalions and companies had settled down to their normal distribution; for details see Appendix XI.

In April of this year Captain P. T. Easton's death is recorded.

General

War-time Administrative Measures at the Colonial Office

While the appointment of Inspector-General was in 'suspended animation', owing to Dobell's nomination as G.O.C. Cameroon Expeditionary Force in August 1914, a Staff Officer remained at the Colonial Office to preserve the administrative W.A.F.F. link with the West African Colonies. Captain W. B. G. Barne, Royal Artillery, was appointed for this duty. He was relieved on 25th January 1916 by Captain A. E. Beattie, M.C., Royal West Surrey Regiment, who had been invalided from the Cameroons when severely wounded in the hand at Wumbiagas in 1915.

Termination of Dobell's Appointment 1916

On 9th June 1916, on the termination of Dobell's appointment as G.O.C. Cameroons Expeditionary Force, the appointment of Inspector-General W.A.F.F. was held in abeyance until the First World War ended, and was not again filled until the end of 1919, when Major and Brevet Lieutenant-Colonel A. H. W. Haywood, C.M.G., D.S.O., Royal Artillery, was nominated to it, with Beattie and Captain A. C. Milne-Home, M.C., Northumberland Fusiliers, as his Staff Officers.

Recruiting Mission to West Africa, November 1916

During 1916, when the shortage of manpower was being acutely felt, the steps taken by the War Office to remedy the state of affairs as far as West Africa was concerned were to appoint a mission to proceed there with a view to recommending what should be done to increase the flow of recruits. Haywood was therefore appointed Deputy Assistant Director of Recruiting, with the temporary rank of Colonel, on 30th November 1916. He took with him as Staff Officer Captain C. J. Blackburn, M.C., West Yorkshire Regiment, who had been present with the 3rd Battalion Nigeria Regiment at the fighting at Nsanakang in September 1914.

The West African Governments gave the mission their cordial support, whereby its success was greatly facilitated. In the case of the Gold Coast, the Acting Governor, Mr. Slater (later Sir Ransford Slater), made a special recruiting tour himself, in Haywood's company, to the principal chiefdoms in the country, where his active and moral assistance were of the greatest value.

On returning from his mission, Haywood's ship, the *Abosso*, was torpedoed off the coast of Ireland with the loss of about 60 lives. He, however, was among the survivors, and Blackburn also escaped, as he was in another ship.

While the recruiting mission was at work the Nigerian Brigade and the Gold Coast Regiment were both on active service in East Africa. Wastage was considerable both from sickness and casualties. However, on the whole the flow of recruits from this time till the end of the war continued at a satisfactory rate.

As a result of the mission's recommendations, amongst other things, certain new sources were tapped. One of these was Ashanti, but the experiment here proved a failure. The Pagan areas in Northern Nigeria, on the other hand, produced a useful and steadily expanding volume of material.

(B) EGBA RISING: JUNE–AUGUST 1918

(Medal and clasp granted, S. Nigeria/1918 (A.O. 460/1924))

In Chapter 1 (E) we mentioned that the Egba Kingdom had been specially excluded from the Protectorate established over the rest of Yorubaland in 1895. In 1914 this Treaty of Independence was terminated, and the British Government gradually introduced the system of indirect administration. A Native Court's Ordinance was applied and a Native Treasury established.

In 1914 troops were brought into the country on the occasion of the Ijemo trouble, brought about by the ending of the Treaty of Independence. Further resentment was caused by the introduction of a water rate.

In 1918 the old system of financing by tolls was abolished in favour of direct taxation. Clerks brought from Lagos in a number of cases proved to be dishonest. These and other matters led to a protest from the people to the Alake and Council. Direct taxation was resented.

This rising had its origin in the disaffected state of Egbaland, during the first half of the year 1918. Although at this time the 'Independent United Egbaland Government' nominally ruled the country through the Alake (or king) and his advisory Council, in actual fact Edun, the Council's Secretary, held the authority and seems to have been mainly responsible for many abuses, such as the illegal acquisition of lands and the exercise of power by a secret society, called 'Ogboni', whose rites were very suspect and wielded terrorism extensively.

Hearing mutterings of revolt, the British Resident at a mass meeting of chiefs and people made the mistake of threatening to send for troops. This alarmed the Egbas, who rebelled. The revolt was called the Adubi War.

On 11th June an officer and 50 W.A.F.F. 4 Nigeria Regiment, arrived at Abeokuta from Kaduna, also one company 1 Nigeria Regiment, was brought to repair and guard the railway which had been destroyed and looted by the insurgents. These troops were soon reinforced by 4th Service Battalion, under Lieutenant-Colonel Sargent, and 1st Service Battalion under Major Hawley, besides 250 men from Ibadan Training Centre.

Two companies under Captain Walker now attacked a rebel camp at Itori on the railway, where there was much fighting until 18th June.

Two companies attacked the rebel camp of Awba, 10 miles south of Abeokuta, where Chief Osile had been murdered on 18th June. Here there was considerable opposition.

Operations were now directed to encircling the insurgents by converging drives of five columns all directed on Iraw and Mawkawlawki on the Ogun River south of Awba: No. 1 Column (Captain Walker) from north; No. 2 Column (Captain Maxwell) from central; No. 3 Column (Captain Norman, M.C.) from south; No. 4 Column (Captain Johns) from east; No. 5 Column (Captain Evans) from Awba and Teppoma (each two companies).

On 4th July the movement was successfully completed, all guns were surrendered and the ringleaders were taken into custody. Between 11th and 23rd July 3,400 guns were surrendered at Lafenwa on the railway.

Our casualties were W.A.F.F., eight killed and 67 wounded; Police and others, two killed and 11 wounded. Four Europeans were also wounded.

The fighting had not been severe, though sniping was continuous.

Brigadier Cunliffe, Commanding the Service Brigade, first directed operations; when he and Lieutenant-Colonel Sargent went on leave Major Hawley took over.

(C) POST-WAR CONSIDERATIONS AND SOME AFTERTHOUGHTS

The experiences of the war had indicated the general lines on which rearmament and re-equipment of the W.A.F.F. should be modelled. Before these matters could be settled, however, the future size of the Force had to be determined. In view of the urgent need for economy, particularly in Nigeria, where the Governor said to the present writer 'they had not two sixpences to rub together' (admittedly an exaggeration!), this was a pressing question. The new Inspector-General's task, therefore, lay in this direction. Part II of the History will deal with this.

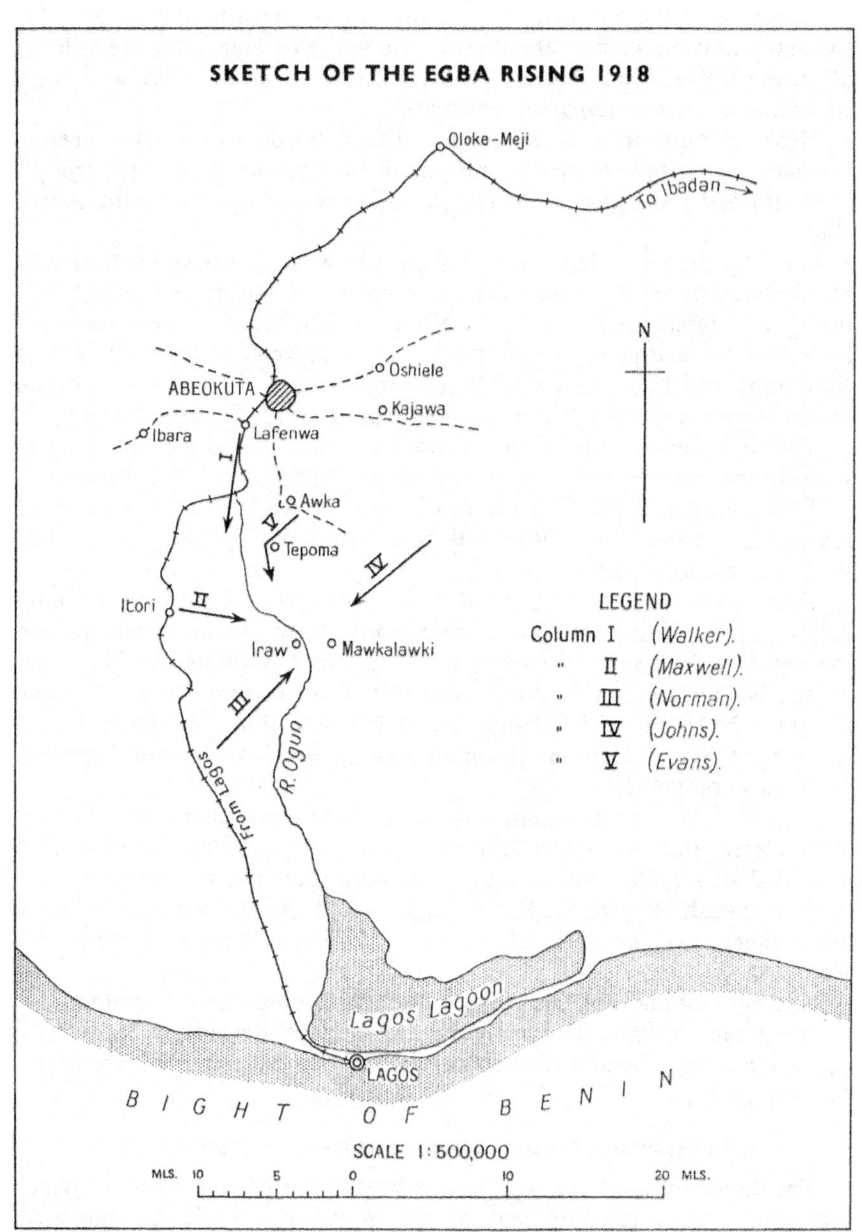

28. The Egba Rising, 1918

In 1897, when instructions for raising the W.A.F.F. were first issued by the Colonial Office, could anyone have foreseen that from such a small embryo there would develop so highly trained and efficient a fighting machine, well prepared to play its part alongside our other forces in the First World War?

Tribute to the West African Soldier

In speaking of the quality of the men, we cannot do better than quote from Major-General Sir Charles Dobell's despatch to the War Office on conclusion of the Cameroons Campaign:

'The troops of the West African Frontier Force, with whom I happily was closely connected in peace, have realized my fullest expectations. To them no day appears to be too long, no task too difficult. With a natural aptitude for soldiering they are endowed with a constitution which enures them to hardship; they share with their Senegalese brothers an inexhaustible fund of good humour.'

Of the officers and British non-commissioned officers, who trained, and often led, them in war, we may here mention a few of the officers who served with the W.A.F.F. in its early days and specially distinguished themselves in later years:

Lugard finished his active career as Governor-General of Nigeria.

Trenchard, the 'Father' of the Royal Air Force.

Willcocks, famous in Ashanti.

Morland became a Corps Commander on the Western Front.

Cubitt was a distinguished General and Governor of Bermuda.

Kemball became a major-general on the Staff in Mesopotamia.

Dobell was later a Lieutenant-General in the Egyptian Expeditionary Force.

The B.N.C.O.s were an important, and at times, vital, link in the chain of command of the Company. It not infrequently happened on active service that casualties amongst officers caused the B.N.C.O. to take over command of a platoon or company, when his first-hand knowledge of the men proved invaluable.

While each and every formation of the W.A.F.F. is deserving of the highest praise for sustaining a prolonged effort from the start to the finish of the 1914–18 War, yet, in fairness, pride of place must surely be given to the Gold Coast Regiment, which nobly acted up to its motto, 'Kulum Shiri' ('Always ready'). It claims to have fired the first shot in the war, on 5th August 1914, during the Togoland Campaign. From that date until September 1918, on its return from East Africa, it was continuously on service, except for four months occupied in refitting after the Cameroon Campaign, between March and July 1916.

Interrelation with the West African Political Service

From the nature of things there had always to be a very close connection between the W.A.F.F. and the Political Services for, when necessary, the Political Officer had to call on the Officer Commanding Troops in his territory for the means to enforce his authority. While touring his district the Commissioner in Charge had the right to ask for a military escort if he thought this desirable. Should hostilities occur, the O.C. escort would be given a free hand to deal with the situation.

Political Officers accompanied columns on military operations; their duties were to help in the collection of intelligence, supplies and labour.

The relations between civil and military, in peace and war, were generally speaking very cordial, ensuring close co-operation. It should be realized, too, that in a number of cases in the early days before a West African Political Service was firmly established, W.A.F.F. officers had to act in a dual capacity owing to shortage of civilians. A few years later many W.A.F.F. officers retired from the Army and transferred to the Political Service, in which some achieved noteworthy prominence. Names readily called to mind are, in Nigeria, McClintock, Festing and Moorhouse; in the Gold Coast, Armitage; in Sierra Leone, Blakeney, and in Gambia, Hopkinson.

Besides the R.W.A.F.F. Dinner Club we have a West African Dinner Club which makes it possible for both W.A.F.F. and civilian elements to foregather and exchange recollections of their West African days.

(D) THE STORY OF THE MOUNTED INFANTRY, NIGERIA REGIMENT, W.A.F.F.

Royal Niger Constabulary and 'Carroll's Horse' as Nucleus

The earliest records of the existence of any mounted infantry in Nigeria appear to show that the idea originated with the Royal Niger Constabulary, when Lieutenant (Temporary Captain) J. W. V. Carroll was commissioned to raise a unit of 300 in 1898. How far he got with organizing and training this body is not known. But, apparently, this was not very far. At the same time it may have formed, and probably did form, the nucleus of the Mounted Infantry Battalion of the W.A.F.F. in Northern Nigeria.

Lugard, in his despatch of 21st June 1900 to the Secretary of State for the Colonies, particularly mentions the services of Captain Carroll, Norfolk Regiment, with the mounted infantry on the occasion of his leaving Nigeria. Seemingly, then, Carroll's Horse, as it had been named, was still in being at that date.

Supply of Remounts

Starting on the 14th March 1898, there is correspondence with the Director of Remounts on where to buy horses for the M.I. Tripoli, Syria, Asia Minor and Argentine are suggested; the price varying from £10 in Asia Minor to £22 10s. in Argentine. In the end, however, it was probably wisely decided to purchase locally, and remounts are supposed to have come mainly from Asben in the Sahara.

Appointment of First W.A.F.F. Officers to M.I.

Soon after this the appointments of the 'first officers for the W.A.F.F. M.I.' are notified, which may be taken as some time in 1898. The names of these officers are given as Lieutenants Beauclerck, 60th Rifles; Hawker, Coldstream Guards, and H. C. Keating, Leinster Regiment. We think, therefore, it is a reasonable assumption that by 1899 Carroll's Horse had been merged with W.A.F.F. M.I., but its strength must have been far less than the 300 contemplated in 1898, for in 1902 it cannot have furnished more than a company for the Kano-Sokoto Expedition. This is corroborated by Captain H. C. Hall, in his book, *Bush and Barrack*, where he says: 'One company (of M.I.) had been in being some years previously to 1903.'

Arms

The M.I. were first armed with the Lee-Metford carbine, Martini action, carried in a bucket. The short Martini-Lee-Enfield with bayonet was not introduced until about 1909. A matchet was carried on the waist belt. After Kano-Sokoto, in 1903, Lieutenant MacDonnell introduced the hog-hunting spear for his troop, but in 1907, 6 ft. 8 in. spears, or lances, formed the equipment of one-third of each troop.

Clothing

At first the men wore a khaki blouse and breeches. Recruits, in the early days, were barelegged and barefooted, later they had puttees and boots. In 1907 the 'kulla' and 'lunghi' replaced the fez.

From about 1903 officers wore the Crown Bird Crest on their helmets. All ranks wore the khaki puggaree. Officers had it on the helmet, and other ranks around the waist. An attempt was made to introduce an old gold and blue puggaree for officers, but it is thought this was discontinued.

Recruiting

Recruits first of all came from the infantry; later the M.I. did their own recruiting chiefly from Bornu and Zaberma. A few Fulanis also were taken.

In his report for 1902 Lugard stresses the necessity for raising a battalion of M.I. in the words: 'Mounted troops are very necessary, now that we occupy the greater part of the Hausa States, and the Commandant fully concurs with me in the view that the additional battalion to be raised next year should consist of mounted infantry. The value of this arm was conclusively proved in the Kano operations.

'So long as our garrisons were confined to the banks of the Niger it was not found possible to maintain the mounted infantry establishment which formed part of my original organization of the Force, for practically the whole of the horses died in the rainy season. In the Northern States, however, they thrive well, and their mobility makes a small number equivalent in value to a large infantry garrison.'

The establishment was to be one lieutenant colonel; one major; one adjutant; two quartermasters; seven company commanders; 20 subalterns; two veterinary surgeons, 24 B.N.C.O.s (including two armourers and three farriers) 15 non-combatants, 700 rank and file and 96 grass-cutters and 400 horses. Its H.Q. was at Zaria, and its first C.O. was Brevet-Major Eustace Crawley, 12th Royal Lancers, appointed on 10th December 1902.

As we have seen at the time of the Kano-Sokoto Expedition, a small unit of about a company was in existence in 1902 and there took a memorable part in the operations which are fully described in Chapter 2, Section (D) (XI).

As far as can be traced from existing records the M.I. Company was commanded by Lieutenant (Local Captain) H. A. Porter, 19th Hussars. The subalterns were: Lieutenants F. P. Crozier, Royal Irish Fusiliers; J. Mackenzie, Royal Horse Guards; C. L. Wells, 3 Hampshire Regiment; and W. D. Wright, Royal West Surrey Regiment, the last of whom gained the V.C. for gallantry in withstanding the onslaught of masses of Fulani Horse against his troop of 45 men near Rawia on 26th February 1903.

'London Gazette', 31st July 1903

General Kemball's despatch on the Kano-Sokoto Expedition bears the highest testimony to the services of the M.I. on several occasions, and in particular to those of Porter in the following terms: 'The valuable services rendered by the 100 Mounted Infantry, raised, trained and led by Lieutenant (Local Captain) H. A. Porter', where he especially alludes to that officer's dashing charge on 800 Fulani Horse while they were watering their horses at Kamberawa.

To quote further from the despatch where it relates the capture of Kano: 'The Mounted Infantry guarded the flanks outside the walls, a proportion dismounting to keep the enemy's fire down', and again when the Fulanis tried to escape from the city: 'The vigour of the Mounted Infantry pursuit turned the defeat into a rout, and the pursuit continued until the enemy was dispersed in all directions.'

'Five Years Hard'

According to Crozier's account of the capture of Sokoto on 14th March 1903, the slaughter of the Sultan's fugitive army during its pursuit by the M.I. ran into several thousand. It is possible, however, that Crozier's account is too highly coloured, for he seems to have had a reputation amongst his brother officers for exaggerating. Crozier became a Brigadier-General in the First World War, and during the Irish Rebellion he held a responsible appointment in the Auxiliary Irish Constabulary, dying between the wars.

The M.I. then returned to their H.Q. at Zaria, where they were engaged in training and recruiting to gradually build up to battalion strength.

Pursuit of ex-Sultan Abdurahman, and the Operations at Burmi

About 22nd April the ex-Sultan of Sokoto, Aburahman, was reported to be between Kano and Zaria, making his way with a large following eastward. While Captain Sword with half company of infantry had been sent in pursuit from Kano, Crawley despatched Crozier and 12 M.I. to worry the enemy's rearguard. This he successfully accomplished, being forced to return a few days later through lack of ammunition.

Early in May Crawley sent Lieutenant Hon. D. Carleton (now Lord Dorchester) with 15 M.I. south to capture a son of Abdurahman; near

Gaya, in the neighbourhood of Birnin Fudu, he had an engagement with some 200 of the ex-Sultan's followers before returning to Zaria on instructions from the O.C. Bauchi. During the month Sword was reinforced with another half company infantry and 60 M.I. and later he was held up before the strong position of Burmi on the Gongola River. A description of this fierce engagement is given in Chapter 2, Section (D) (XII).

Distribution of M.I. Battalion and move of H.Q. from Zaria to Gaza

By the end of 1903 the M.I. had reached a strength of 22 officers, 18 B.N.C.O.s, 174 rank and file and 256 horses. During 1904 the Battalion was built up to an establishment of seven companies. H.Q. and three companies were at Gaza near Kano, whence they had been moved from Zaria owing to tsetse fly and bad watering at the latter place. Four companies were on outpost duty, stationed respectively at Sokoto, Katsena, Hadeija and Damjiri. They covered 620 miles of frontier, from a point 100 miles west of Sokoto to Lake Chad. Crawley was now a Lieutenant-Colonel (Temporary).

On 29th April 1904 Captain (Brevet-Major) T. A. Cubitt, D.S.O., Royal Artillery, was gazetted to command[1] with temporary rank of Lieutenant-Colonel, in place of Crawley, who had been invalided. During Crawley's tenure of command the M.I. had made a very good polo ground, steeplechase course and racecourse at Zaria, where they founded the 'Western Sudan Turf Club', where meetings were held annually for some years.

On 10th December 1904 Brevet-Major C. W. Barlow, Essex Regiment, succeeded Cubitt, who was restored to his British Regiment. Barlow held the command till 28th July 1905, being replaced by Captain A. D. Green, D.S.O., Worcester Regiment.

Reduction of M.I.

In 1906, with a view to cutting the W.A.F.F. Estimates in Northern Nigeria, a suggestion was put forward to reduce the M.I. from a battalion to three companies, consisting of a depot company and a service company attached to each infantry battalion. The I.G., Morland, finally decided to retain Battalion H.Q. and three companies of M.I. The O.C.'s rank was then reduced to Major. The new establishment provided for 120 men and 100 horses per company. H.Q. and outstations were at Kano, Sokoto and Geidam respectively. The reductions did not take effect till 1907.

On 15th November 1906 Captain H. F. Searight, 1st Dragoon Guards, was gazetted to the command. He was succeeded by Captain Lord J. S. Cavendish, 1st Life Guards, on 1st September 1909, who was himself followed by Major J. B. Orr, Norfolk Regiment, on 12th January 1913.

Satiru Disaster, February 1906

Meanwhile the Satiru disaster occurred early in 1906. For a full account see Chapter 3, Section (B) (I). Briefly, Lieutenant Blackwood with

[1] Julian Hasler of the 'Buffs' had been appointed, but was made Assistant Commandant.

a company of M.I. was charged by a fanatical mob while dismounted and before they had time to form square. He was killed and his company, nearly annihilated, fled in panic. An infantry column from Zungeru and a column of three companies of M.I. from Katsena and Kano, making forced marches, defeated the fanatics, then the M.I. carried out a 15-mile pursuit, routing the fugitives. This was in February and March.

Hadeija Operations, 16th–24th April 1906

In April 1906 Lowry-Cole attacked Hadeija with 700 men, including one M.I. company. The M.I. were used to guard the flanks outside the walled town and were in position to take up the pursuit of any fugitives later. (See also Chapter 3, Section (B) (II)).

Chibuk Affair, November 1906–February 1907

A company of M.I. from Maidugari, under Lieutenant Chapman, reinforced by a company 1 Northern Nigeria Regiment under Lieutenant Wolseley, were engaged here. At the end of December the M.I. were withdrawn. The account of this affair is in Chapter 3, Section (B) (V).

During the operations in 1906 related in the previous paragraphs the mounted infantry had been severely tested, and their state of efficiency had borne out the Commandant's annual report made at the end of 1905, when he particularly commented upon the stable management, riding and manoeuvring of the unit; he said, 'The condition of the horses is good and shows that pains have been taken with them.' It is to be noted that men and horses must have been in hard condition to have marched from Kano to Sokoto, a distance of 280 miles in five and a half days, followed by a 15-mile pursuit after the victory of Satiru.

Reduction to H.Q. and 3 Companies takes Effect in 1907

Owing to the reduction of the M.I. to a battalion of three companies the year 1907 saw the retrenchment of Lieutenant-Colonel C. W. Barlow, Essex Regiment, and Captains C. G. V. Wellesley and R. W. V. Bruce, of the Lincolns and 17th Lancers respectively.

1908–13

It has not been possible to trace the history of the M.I. in the succeeding years up to 1913, but is thought that there were no major incidents during this period. Locations of H.Q. and outstations appear to have remained the same.

1914

On 14th January 1914 Major S. J. B. Barnardiston was appointed to the command and was succeeded shortly before the 1914–18 War by Major Lord Henry Seymour, Grenadier Guards, who was wounded and invalided at the action of Tepe in the Cameroons in August at the start of the Campaign. When Seymour was invalided Captain J. T. Gibbs, 3rd Dragoon Guards, was appointed to the command dating from 13th November 1914, a position he held till the end of the Cameroons Campaign in 1916. During the subsequent operations the role of the M.I. was mainly one of reconnaissance. One company was detached to watch the German fortified post of Mora, while the two others acted on the flanks of Cunliffe's Northern Force in his 'mopping-up' actions between Garua, Banyo and Ngaundere towards Yaunde, covering a distance of about 600 miles from north to south.

In March 1916, on conclusion of the Cameroons Expedition, the M.I. returned to their former peace stations, not being required for the East African Campaign. Between December 1916 and March 1917 they were in a state of alert, actively patrolling the Saharan frontier while the French were conducting their operations against the Senussi at Agadez, but were not near any fighting.

It is thought that M.I. companies were administered by infantry battalions from 1916 to 1919, when Major Underwood, North Lancs Regiment was appointed to command the Battalion, before it was finally disbanded for reasons of economy in 1922.

When the amalgamation of the Southern and Northern Nigeria Regiments took place in 1914, the M.I. Battalion was renamed the 5th (M.I.) Battalion Nigeria Regiment. After the disbandment of the M.I. in 1922 the nomenclature of 5th Battalion disappeared, but was resuscitated in 1933 as an infantry battalion, formed at Maiduguri,

In 1908, when troops were required for a campaign against the Mad Mullah of Somaliland, as the result of a conference between the I.G.'s King's African Rifles and W.A.F.F., it was tentatively arranged for a W.A.F.F. contingent to form part of the Somaliland Expeditionary Force. In this contingent one company of M.I. was included. The idea was, however, ultimately dropped, probably owing to transport difficulties. No subsequent suggestions for using the M.I. of the Nigeria Regiment overseas were made. It is pertinent, however, to record that in the East African Campaign of the First World War a M.I. company of the Gold Coast Regiment was raised and trained in Tanganyika, where it did excellent service in the pursuit of von Lettow through Portuguese East Africa, being finally disbanded at the end of 1918.

A notable figure during 1903–4 in the Officers' Mess of the M.I. was their Medical Officer, Dr. E. C. Adams, affectionately called 'Adamu', best known in Nigeria for his ballads, *Lyrae Nigeriae*. In these a good deal of space is allotted to the M.I., to the welfare of which he was devoted. He is said to have been part author of the play *White Cargo*, which had a popular run in London some years later.

A correspondent, Captain (now Brigadier) J. G. Browne, 14th Hussars, who served with the M.I. at Satiru in 1906, gives us an amusing account of how one of his men accidentally wounded himself in the stomach with a knife and was brought to him with a part of his entrails hanging out. After some discussion, and as there was no M.O. available, it was decided to wash the protruding portion, grease the hole with cooking fat, and reinsert the intestine. This was done with some difficulty. The operators, Browne, Wellesley and Sergeant Topless, then took some hairs from a horse's tail, soaked them in Condy's fluid, and succeeded in sewing up the cavity. The patient seems to have made a good recovery, though liable to indigestion at times! Dr. Ellis, who was consulted later, said their only mistake was in pushing the intestine through only one layer of muscle instead of three!

Lord Dorchester has recounted rather a gruesome story of the time he was with the M.I. at Zaria in 1903 (he was Lieutenant Hon. D. Carleton, 9th Lancers, at the time). Lieutenant J. Mackenzie, Royal Horse Guards and M.I., died at Zaria, where he was buried by Carleton. Some time later his relatives wished to have the body sent to England. The remains had to be dissected to make them fit into ammunition boxes, suitable in size and weight to be transported on carrier's heads to the coast for embarkation to the United Kingdom.

We will now conclude 'The Story of the Mounted Infantry, Nigeria Regiment', with the following apt quotation from Adamu's *Lyrae Nigeriae*.

The Old M.I.

I saw a man sitting beside the road, and by him a horse lay dead,
'What's the matter? The show bust up?' said I,
But he laughed and shook his head.
'No, I shot the old doki to save its life;
I reckon he'd tsetse fly.
And now the old cripple has gone to rest,
I'm the last of the old M.I.'

LIST OF OFFICERS WHO SERVED WITH THE M.I.
COMPILED TO 1919

Name and rank	Unit in Army	Period with M.I.N.N.R.	Notes
Adams, Dr. E. C.		1904–7	Doctor to M.I.N.N.R. (nickname 'Adamu', author of *Lyrae Nigerae*
Ambrose, Lt. W. J.	Gen. List	1918–19	
Badham, Capt. J. F.	Worcester Regt.	1916–	
Barlow, Maj. C. W.	Essex Regt.	1903–6	
Browne, Capt. J. G.	14th King's Hussars	1906–7	Went to 2 Bn. N.N.R. in 1907
Blackwood, Capt. F. E.	E. Surrey Regt.	1904–6	Killed at Sarturu 1906
Brocklebank, Capt. J. J.	1st K.D.G.s	1905–7	Went to civil side
Brodie, Maj. L. C.	Essex Regt.	1918–19	
Bruce, Capt. R. W. V.	17th Lancers	1903–6	
Browning, Sgt.			
Campbell, Lt. J.	Argyll & S. Highlanders	1903–4	
Carr, Capt.	R.A.V.C.		Went to Sudan
Carleton, Capt. Hon. D.	9th Lancers	1902–	Now Lord Dorchester
Cavendish, Capt.	R. Horse Guards	1906–7	Killed in 1914–18 War
Church, Capt.		1904–6	Left in 1906
Chapman, Capt.	Suffolk Reg.	1905–7	Commanded column at Chibuk Operations
Christy, Lt. S. H.	20th Hussars	1903–4	
Chartres, Dr.	R.A.M.C.	1906–7	
Cockburn, Capt. J. B.	R. Welch Fus.	1906–7	Severely wounded in 1914–18 War
Condon, Capt. G.		1904–5	
Crawley, Lt.-Col. E.	12th Lancers	1902–	Killed in 1914–18 War

Name and Rank	Unit in Army	Period with M.I.N.N.R.	Notes
Crozier, Capt. F. P.	R. Irish Fus.	1902–5	Died between the Wars. Got Brigade in 1914–18 War
Creswick, Lt. B. C.	9 London Regt.	1918–19	
Cubitt, Lt.-Col. T. A.	R.A.	1904–5	
Ellis, Dr. M. F.	R.A.M.C.	1905–9	Wounded at Sarturu. Died later
Farmer, Capt.	4th Hussars	1905–7	Believe he died in Nigeria
Fendell, Capt.		1905–7	Killed out hunting at Aldershot
Festing, Lt.-Col.	R. Irish Rifles	1903–4	Killed in 1914–18 War and got posthumous V.C.
Foster, Lt. A.		1904–7	Killed in 1914–18 War
Gallagher, Lt. C. E.		1902–4	
Gascoyne, Lt. F. K.	20th Hussars	1902–3	
Gibbs, Lt. J. T.	3rd Dragoon Guards	1906–7 1914–16	
Gosling, Sgt.		1905–6	
Graham, Tpr. S. M.			
Greene, Maj.	Worcester Regt.	1904–6	Killed in 1914–18 War
Hall, Lt. C.	Imp. Yeomanry	1903–4	
Hall, Lt. H. C.	W. Yorkshire Regt.	1903	Went to civil side
Hasler, Lt.-Col. J.	The Buffs	1902–7	Killed in 1914–18 War
Hebden, Lt. H. H.	R. Fusiliers	1918–19	
Herbert, Capt. W. N.	5th Northumberland Fus.	1905–7	Died after 1914–18 War
Hides, Capt. M.		1905–8	
Higgins, Capt. T. C. R.	Was in Navy, Army and R.A.F.	1905–8	Died between the Wars. Air Commodore R.A.F.
Huddlestone, Lt. H. J.	Dorest Regt.	1903–4	Went to Sudan after 1914–18 War. Sirdar in Egypt
Blakiston-Houston, Lt. J.	11th Hussars 12 Lancers	1905–6	Died 1959
Knapp, Capt. A. F. P.	N. Lancs. Regt.	1916	
Lowry-Cole, Col. A. W.	R. Welsh Fus.	1904–6	
McCulloch, Capt. B. J.	16th Lancers	1904–6	Went to Southern Nigeria
McDonnell, Capt. D. H.	City of London 1 Yeomanry	1906–7	In H.L.I. 16 Bn 1914–18 War
Mackenzie, Capt. J.	R. Horse Guards	1902–3	Died at Zaria
MacLachlan, Capt. C.	18th Hussars	1903–5	Adjutant M.I. 1904. Left 1905
Martin, Lt. F. S.	Gen. List	1918–19	
Manuk, Dr.	R.A.M.C.	1903–4	
Morland, Col. T. L.	60th Rifles	1902–7	Inspector-Gen. in 1907
Moberly, Lt. V. Essen	11th Hussars	1903–4	
Anwyl-Passingham, Capt. A. M. O. A.	Middlexex Regt.	1904–7	Died 1958
Porter, Lt. H. A.	19th Hussars	1901–2	
Romilly, Lt. F. W.	Welsh Regt.	1902–4	
Searight, Capt. H. F.	1st K.D.G.s	1904–8	O.C. M.I.N.N.R. 1907–8
Secker, Capt. V. H.	14th King's Hussars	1904–7	Rejoined Regiment 1907

Name and rank	Unit in Army	Period with M.I.N.N.R.	Notes
Smyth, Lt. H. H. G.	3rd Munsters	1918–19	
Sparkes, Lt. F.	16th Lancers	1918–19	
Spender, Capt. J. T.	12th Lancers	1918–19	
Tudor, Lt. H. O.	Gen. List	1918–19	
Venour, Capt. C. M. H.	Hants Regt.	1918–19	
Villiers, Lt. R. H., D.S.O.	12th Lancers	1902–3	
Wright, Capt. Wallace D.	Queen's W. Surrey Regt.	1901–4	V.C. in action near Sokoto
Wellesley, Capt. C. J. V.	Lincolnshire Regt.	1905–7	Killed in 1914–18 War
Welch, Capt.	R.A.V.C.	1905–7	Veterinary Officer, M.I.N.N.R.
Wells, Capt.		1901–4	
Wickham, Capt. T.	Manchester Regt.	1905–7	Killed at N. Garua 1914–18 War
Topless, Sgt. T.	16th Lancers	1905–7	
Stuart-Wortley, Lt. J.	Scottish Rifles	1903–4	

(E) THE ROYAL ARTILLERY IN THE WEST AFRICAN FRONTIER FORCE

(Compiled by Major R. J. R. Waller, D.S.O., Royal Artillery)

In 1899 the Interdepartmental Committee of the War Office amalgamated the Colonial Military Forces in West Africa. It was held under the chairmanship of Lord Selborne. The battalion to be the unit of organization. The artillery to consist of: Northern Nigeria—two batteries formed from the Nigeria Constabulary; Southen Nigeria—two batteries formed from the Nigeria Constabulary; Gold Coast—two batteries formed from the Gold Coast Constabulary.

At first the armament consisted mainly of 75 mm. and 7 R.M.L. guns. The gunners carried Martini Metford and Martini Enfield carbines.

Dress: Khaki uniform with the letters W.A.F.F. on the shoulder straps.

Later the armament of the batteries was the 2·95 in. quick firing mountain gun. The gun was carried on the heads of gun-carriers.

In the short History of the Nigeria Regiment W.A.F.F. by Colonel C. S. Taylor, the artillery used in the Kano-Sokoto Expedition in 1903 is not definitely named as a battery, the account only reports the blowing in of the gate at Bebeji by a gun on the way to Kano and later that of Kano itself which caused the city to surrender without casualties to our forces.

1903

The expedition against the Sultan of Sokoto is mentioned by Colonel Taylor; the Sultan with some irreconcilable chiefs had gone on a pilgrimage to Mecca. He was pursued by troops as far as Burmi in Bornu. The troops attacked the town, but without a gun were unable to make a breach in the walls and were repulsed with loss. A larger force having been collected, the town was eventually taken. The enemy lost 600, including the Sultan. Our losses were 10 killed and three officers and 69 men wounded.

Satiru Expedition 1906

To retrieve the position after the disaster of Satiru, a force was collected and at once despatched, including a gun and several maxims. These were formed up in line with the 30 Europeans and 570 rank and file, in front being a screen of M.I. They were charged by about 2,000 rebels. The M.I. wheeled aside to allow the infantry and guns to pour in a very heavy fire which destroyed the attack. The rebels were pursued by the M.I.

It may be said that in the period from the raising of the W.A.F.F. to the Great War there were few forces who saw so much fighting as the Nigerian Regiment.

The Great War 1914

The W.A.F.F. artillery at this time consisted of three guns in the Gold Coast. In Nigeria the W.A.F.F. artillery at this time consisted of two batteries each of six guns.

The guns were 2·95 in. mountain guns, all carried on the heads of gun-carriers.

The German forces in the Cameroons were known to be superior in numbers to our forces; but an expeditionary force was collected to capture Duala and Kamina in Togoland—the latter place being forced to be surrendered by some brilliant work by Lieutenant-Colonel F. C. Bryant, Royal Artillery. The action by the Navy caused the vacation of Victoria by the Germans. The Navy also caused the surrender of Duala and Bonaberi.

Yola Column, Tepe, Garua, Ikom, 5th August

Lieutenant-Colonel Maclear, having with him two guns Nigerian Artillery, marched on Garua; but a night attack failed and was a severe repulse. The guns were out of range (over 4,000 yards) and did not come into the action and the force retired on Tepe.

Lieutenant-Colonel Mair, Royal Artillery, arrived at Ikom on the Cross River on 10th August where his force was joined by two guns of No. 2 Battery.

Captain Crookenden occupied Nsanakang and took up a position on Customs Hill and Factory Hill. He had with him two guns of No. 2 Nigerian Battery, which took up a position on Customs Hill on the banks of the Cross River, the bank of which here was very steep; also here were posted two infantry sections and a machine gun. The line of retreat to Nsanarati, six miles away, was to the right front of Customs Hill, as the Cross River was behind the position. Captain Hopkinson was in command of the position when the Germans attacked very strongly. Fire was poured into the gun position at 200 yards range. The guns had only 30 rounds each of ammunition and as long as these held out the enemy were kept at bay; but at length the trenches were taken more or less in reverse, and in spite of the gallantry of the native gunners, and especially Sergeant J. Dennis, Royal Artillery, the two guns were captured with the position. Sergeant Dennis, though wounded through both thighs, retained charge of his gun to the end and was eventually found bayoneted beside it. The Germans at first threw the two guns into the Cross River, but recovered one which was used by them but eventually recaptured by our troops. The other gun was retrieved from the river by us later and now surmounts the War Memorial at Calabar.

In the order of battle of the Anglo-French Expeditionary Force against the Cameroons, the following Royal Artillery units of the W.A.F.F. appear: No. 1 Battery (less one section) Nigeria Regiment, Captain C. F. S. Maclaverty and three officers, two British N.C.O.s (all Royal Artillery); Gold Coast Battery—one section, Lieutenant W. L. St. Clair, Royal Artillery. (Note: One section No. 1 Battery accompanied Lieutenant-Colonel Cunliffe's force in the Northern Cameroons Campaign.)

Lieutenant-Colonel A. J. Turner, Royal Artillery, was G.S.O.1 to General Dobell. Captain H. G. Howell, Royal Artillery, was on Colonel Gorges's staff as Chief Intelligence Officer. Lieutenant-Colonel A. H. W. Haywood, Royal Artillery, commanded the 4th Battalion Nigeria Regiment.

28th September

The 1st Battalion Nigerians (Lieutenant-Colonel J. B. Cockburn) disembarked at Duala at 0800 hours and sent a company to occupy Bonaberi across the creek. This company was relieved by Colonel A. H. W. Haywood's[1] 4th Battalion Nigerians with the 1st Nigerian Battery (hereafter referred to as 1 A.N.R.) under Captain C. F. S. Maclaverty, Royal Artillery.

1st October

Colonel Haywood moved out from Bonaberi with his Battalion and one section 1 A.N.R. Captain Maclaverty chose a covered position for his guns, by the side of the railway, and opened fire on the Bepele Bridge at 1,000 yards. After 20 minutes the enemy retired and the British troops crossed the bridge without casualties; but when Colonel Haywood approached Maka on the far side of the creek some miles farther on, fire was opened by the enemy and the troops bivouacked by the bridge in torrents of rain.

2nd October

Next morning Maka was bombarded by the guns and occupied, two companies and one gun being left to hold the place while the remaining troops returned to Bonaberi.

12th–13th October

A second attack was made on Yabassi up the Wuri River by Colonel Gorges—1 A.N.R. (one section) and the Gold Coast Battery less one section took part and shelled the town, which was occupied with small loss. The 1st Nigerians remained in occupation, the remainder of the troops returning to Bonaberi, 1 A.N.R. being sent up the Northern Railway to assist Colonel Haywood in capturing Susa. Colonel Haywood was then ordered to send back to Bonaberi two guns of the 1 A.N.R.

19th October

The Germans attacked Susa, but were repulsed with some loss to the enemy. After this the 2nd Nigerians and the section 1 A.N.R. were allowed some rest by the enemy.

[1] Colonel Haywood's battalion (the 4th) was named the 2nd Nigerians in the Cameroon Campaign.

In addition to the Germans, two other enemies sometimes were encountered—one small but numerous and one large. The latter—elephants—sometimes attacked the troops, and during one encounter between the British and the Germans a herd of some 60 elephants dashed amongst the combatants, who retired hastily on either side.

A section of 1 A.N.R. moving up to Yabassi along the Wuri River were attacked by thousands of bees. Fortunately this occurred whilst the gunners were near elephant grass. Most of the men (and officers) who knew a good deal about such attacks made for the shelter of the grass and so escaped what can be a serious danger. But two British sergeants of the escort, not being so skilled, plunged into the river, where the bees, following them, stung them whenever they put their heads up to breathe. The battery's trumpeter was so badly stung that he could not perform on his trumpet for several days! Sunset caused an easing of the situation and the march could be safely resumed.

Northern Railway, 6th November

By a skilful use of his small force, Colonel Haywood advanced on Muyuka station, on to which he drove the enemy. He had placed a gun in position and fixed the bearing of the station by map. Three rounds were fired on the station, which caused the enemy, about 100 in strength, to retreat in their waiting train, and the British occupied the station. In the whole of this operation only one man was wounded.

9th November

Operations on the Cameroon Mountain District. In command Colonel Gorges.

1 A.N.R., 1st Nigerians, half Gold Coast Pioneer Company, one company Senegalese left Duala in small steamers towing lighters on 12th November, anchoring for the night in the Bimbia River, which flows out just south of Victoria—the port of Buea; the flotilla arrived off the Tiko island pier, where they disembarked the troops on the 15th November.

The column advancing from Mpungo on the Mungo River, at 0940 hours, near Dibemba, encountered resistance to its advanced guard from an entrenched position that could be clearly seen from the position of our main body.

It was one of the few positions that could be called a good artillery target, and the two guns of 1 A.N.R. made good practice at it, and the enemy were soon cleared out of the position with a loss of only two British casualties.

Buea, 15th November

Buea was surrendered on 15th November—Major G. D. Mann, Royal Artillery, by a long and difficult march with his force at Obudu, including one gun, reached Takum and took over command there in order to stop raiding parties of Germans from creating disturbances in Nigeria. He entered Cameroon territory and shelled the enemy fort at Karbabi dispersing their troops in the vicinity. The situation in Nigeria was greatly improved by this action.

14th November–January 1915

Colonel Gorges began his advance up the Northern Railway on 3rd December and reached Mundek without opposition. He had been joined by the 1 A.N.R. marching across the difficult mountainous country of the Great Mountain, which took them nearly three days; this was good timing, considering that the section had no water the last two days.

In the advance Colonel Gorges had an engine and trucks as transport along the Northern Railway; but the bridge over the river at Nlohe having been destroyed, transport from thence forward was restricted to carriers.

The column reached Manegoteng on 7th December. That night the Germans sent down the railway a truck loaded with dynamite timed to explode at the British bivouac. But some rails had been removed as a precaution north of the camp and the truck was derailed and exploded harmlessly.

9th December

Colonel Gorges's column reached Ndunge in mountainous and difficult country; the camp was shelled and the 1 A.N.R. battery came into action, also the Naval 12-pounder. These drove the enemy out of his position and Nkongsamba, the railhead, was occupied on 10th December, the Germans surrendering it and the country to the north as far as Bare some six miles farther north. Bare was occupied by the 2nd Nigerians and one section 1 A.N.R. It lies in fairly open country and a good road runs through it from Nkongsamba to Chang.

25th December

The advance on Chang was commenced—Colonel Haywood's battalion plus the section Gold Coast Artillery on the left through Mbo—the road winding between rugged and thickly timbered heights, Mbo itself being on a high ridge. The main column (1st Nigerians) had a difficult terrain along the Nkam River; the two columns eventually joined up before Chang, which was surrendered. The Fort was blown up and the British retired to Bare and Nkongsamba on General Dobell's orders, the lines of communications having become too greatly extended for the number of troops in the Cameroons at that time.

January 1915

Bare was attacked several times in January by about 150 of the enemy and two machine guns. One of the 1 A.N.R. guns and part of the 1st Nigerians held Bare. The gun was in a small stone emplacement, rather exposed, on the topmost peak of the Bare hill (hereafter called Bare Fort). But the gun had a first-rate field of fire to front and rear, where some German huts stood, and to the flanks, where, however, the bush was only some 70 yards distant, though on the front and rear there was about 300–400 yards of cleared ground. Concentrated enemy machine-gun fire on this gun luckily caused it no damage or casualties to the detachment, and gunfire plus machine-gun and rifle fire caused the attackers not to press into hand-to-hand fighting.

23rd February

The Nigerian companies were withdrawn from Bare, their place being taken by Lieutenant-Colonel Newstead and three and a quarter companies of the Sierra Leone Battalion, but the 1 A.N.R. gun remained at Bare.

3rd February 1915

Lieutenant-Colonel G. P. Newstead and three and a quarter companies of Sierra Leone Battalion and one gun 1 A.N.R. moved out from Bare to attack Harmann's farm. The infantry, covered at a distance of 1,800 yards by the gun which was on a hill well above and clearly in view of Harmann's Farm, occupied it with little loss, the gun under Lieutenant Waller shelling both Harmann's Farm and Stoebels Farm, which lay several hundred yards to the south-east.

The Germans counter-attacked at about 1030 hours, and threw the Sierra Leone troops violently back on to the gun position. Our troops lost 55 men, including one officer. The Germans did not follow up their success and after remaining in observation for about four hours, the troops retired back to Bare Fort. The 1 A.N.R. section was sent back to Duala, as it had been decided at H.Q. that the Battery deserved a rest, as they had been hard at it ever since landing. But Colonel Turner, the G.S.O.1, interviewed Captain Maclaverty, D.S.O., who had brought the section of 1 A.N.R. back from the railhead on 2nd March and asked him to take a section of 1 A.N.R. back to Bare, because they had decided to launch an attack on Harmann's and Stoebel's Farm next day. But Colonel Turner stressed that the guns would have to give absolutely close support, as the Sierra Leone troops had been badly shaken on the 3rd February. This Captain Maclaverty agreed to do, and he entrained his other section of guns on the Northern Railway and returned to railhead.

Colonel Turner and Colonel Statham, who had come up with Captain Maclaverty, reconnoitred the country and the position of the guns was fixed. Captain Maclaverty asked that the Sierra Leone Battery should take up a position near Bare to help guard the flank, and this was agreed to.

4th March

On the day of the attack Captain Maclaverty took up the position that had been decided upon. Very soon he received a message to take a gun right up in close support, so he took one gun up to where Colonel Newstead and his Adjutant had placed themselves, leaving his subaltern, Lieutenant H. J. J. Peele, in charge of the other gun. Practically at once the Germans opened a heavy fire, but somewhat badly aimed on the British position with three machine guns in bushes not very far away. The Colonel and Adjutant retired and both were hit as they went, the Colonel fatally wounded; and then almost at once all the Sierra Leone troops came back in panic, having thrown away their machine guns. Captain Maclaverty could not fire, as the infantry masked his gun, so with the help of some of his gun-carriers he managed to halt some of the infantry and made them open fire; but he had to go back almost immediately to his gun, as it was no longer masked. He put some spare gunners to protect the gun by rifle fire and opened fire with the gun.

The story in the official history that the situation was made worse because some of the shells fired from this advanced gun did not burst is an entire fabrication. What happened was that the Germans got cold feet and retired to a hill which they had entrenched, and Captain Maclaverty resorted to using double common, which does not burst in the air like shrapnel. In doing this he was doing what was done in France against trenches, if not in 1914 certainly very early in the fighting against trenches. He sent a written message back to his other gun under Lieutenant Peele by Bombadier Ango, asking him to open fire on the hill trenches which the bombadier would point out.

Shortly after that Captain Maclaverty was dangerously wounded, the bullet grazing his spine as it passed through his neck and paralysing him. The gunners under Corporal Awdu Kano, who had all behaved most gallantly, continued firing—they kept on saying, 'The infantry are coming—no, they are going back.' It appears that Colonel Turner tried to bring them up again, but was unable to get them to move. As his gun ammunition was getting very short, Captain Maclaverty told his detachment to fire off what was left, remove the breech block rendering the gun useless and retire; they refused to retire and leave him, however. Colonel Statham and Major Booth very gallantly came up with some gunners and a stretcher under heavy enemy fire to get Captain Maclaverty away.

The Germans behaved very well and ceased fire whilst they were getting Captain Maclaverty away. He ordered Corporal Awdu Kano to take away the breech block and bring all the gunners with him. This was done. He thinks that had the Germans got to the gun position they would have wiped out the entire column, which was now in a dip, and if they had retired from this dip they would have been in full view of the enemy, and, as they retired up the hill, would have been subjected to merciless machine-gun and rifle fire at pretty close range. After the rescue party had got back the Battery, Sergeant-Major Maida Musa formed up the party of gunners and gun-carriers and brought the gun away. For this he was awarded the D.C.M., and Captain Maclaverty received a mention, as did Colonel Statham and Major Booth.

In writing up the part the Royal Artillery took in the Cameroons, it is necessary to qualify remarks made in the Official History of the War—Cameroons and Togoland volume.

At page 212, line 30 *et seq.*, it says, 'they were seldom able to use their mountain guns effectively'. This is obviously erroneous for the open country in the Northern Territory; and also for the jungle country where the following tactics in Colonel Gorges's advance on Yaunde and in the pursuit of the enemy into Spanish Muni were used. These tactics were as follows as used by 1 A.N.R.

The Battery Commander had a good portable telephone and plenty of telephone cable coiled on drums. He placed himself just behind the point of the advanced guard, and made an accurate road sketch as he advanced. Telephone cable was unrolled behind him back to where the guns were marching. The officer with the guns saw to the rolling up of the telephone cable as he advanced and by frequent check saw that he was in constant communication with his Battery Commander. The latter whenever he came to a suitable position for his guns to come into action placed a picquet in the ground with a label such as, Position 'A', 'B', 'C', etc. Positions were obtainable, it was found by experience, on the average every 1,000 to 2,000 yards along the path of the advance. What was necessary was a short clearance of 100 yards towards the enemy from the gun position.

As the Battery advanced he made the necessary corrections for line of fire by compass bearing and phoned these with the range obtained off his sketch to the Battery Leader at the gun position chosen. By this means it was *never* found impossible to open fire by indirect method on the ground immediately in front of the point, where the Battery Commander stood on any local 'point of vantage' to observe the fire of his battery.

It is admitted that there were for the Battery Commander a few breathless moments whilst awaiting the first round from his guns; but it is satisfactory to relate that there were no untoward incidents of our fire causing casualties to our advanced guard. Shell-fire thus reaching the enemy from an unknown source seems to have had a discouraging effect on the enemy and on quite a good many occasions obtained a direct hit on the enemy's trenches and on occasion wiped out a machine gun, or their crew anyway.

The mountain gun used (2·95 in. quick firing) had two shells—(1) a 12 lb. shrapnel, and (2) an 18 lb. double common. This last necessitated a separate range table and made the little gun almost a howitzer, the trajectory being a high-angle one. Thus premature bursts due to intervening trees were avoided. When Colonel Gorges's advance on Yaunde commenced it was found that to get the guns into the firing line caused a very unwelcome concentration of fire on the troops in the vicinity of the guns which, being carried on the heads of gun-carriers, made a wonderful mark for the enemy. One of Colonel Haywood's Company Commanders (a most capable one, incidentally) told the Battery Commander that he wished the latter would take his '. . . ironmongery' elsewhere!

Turning to the advance on Yaunde east of Edea under Colonel Mayer, French Commander and French Contingent in April 1915. He had with him a British Contingent consisting of: one section 1 A.N.R.; one company 1 Nigeria Regiment; H.Q. and three companies, 2nd Nigerians; one company, Sierra Leone Battalion; the Gambia Detachment (all under Colonel Haywood).

11th April

Colonel Haywood's column's advance was by the northern bank of the Kele River, and left Edea on 11th April, meeting constant opposition in dense forest. He bivouacked on the night of the 13th April 1,000 yards west of Ngwe Bridge, which had been left intact, but with a clear field of fire west of the bridge of some 500–600 yards.

On the far bank of the Ngwe Bridge was a strongly entrenched position with overhead cover in parts.

Colonel Haywood had sent his company of the 1st Nigerians under Captain Balders to move southwards about two miles, parallel to his own advance, in order to turn the enemy position. Captain Balders with great skill got his men to the required position to the left rear of the enemy and charged home. Captain Waller's two guns bombarded the position and the Germans were forced out, Colonel Haywood's troops getting in with little difficulty.

3rd May

Advancing to Wumbiagas on the Mbila River, Colonel Haywood came up against a very strong and skilfully sited position on the river. All cover had been removed on Colonel Haywood's (the west) side of the river. The enemy position rested on its left on the unfordable Kele River, his right rested on a high hill with impenetrable jungle. The river, too, had been staked with the timber cleared by the Germans, who resisted all Colonel Haywood's efforts to storm across the river, assisted by gunfire from the 1 A.N.R. But next day it was found that the enemy had retired and Colonel Haywood occupied his trenches. The advance was continued after a few days' rest for the troops. On the 26th May Colonel Haywood, advancing from his bivouac at 0545 hours, encountered strong opposition which was not finally overcome for two and a half hours, helped by fire (by indirect method already described) from the 1 A.N.R. guns. The Germans, however, took up another position a mile east of Ntim, from which they were not turned out till 1630 hours.

The advance continued very slowly; and, chiefly due to the destruction of two convoys on the line of communications, it was decided to retire to Ngwe. To make up for the loss of carriers due to the convoy's destruction, the Naval gun, which had been unable to fire owing to its flat trajectory, fired off all its ammunition—over 100 rounds—from the top of a hill, Captain Waller observing the shoot from the top of a very tall tree to which he was hoisted by a tackle made by the Sappers.

12th June

This shoot took place on 12th June in the evening, and with the carriers made available by shooting off the Naval guns' ammunition the British commenced their retirement that night.

At first the retirement was peaceful, but before two days had passed the Germans were pressing the column hard behind.

Owing to total lack of news from Colonel Mayer due to the cutting of his communications, General Dobell ordered up every available man from Duala and Edea. Colonel Cockburn and two of his companies arrived at Ngwe at a critical moment, and their presence enabled the much-harassed Yaunde column to reach Ngwe. On this day the 1 A.N.R. was in the advanced guard and encountered very strong enemy resistance in its effort to force a way through the enemy troops who had got round to the road between Ngwe and where the column had reached, but the arrival of the leading 1st Nigerian Company caused the collapse of the German efforts and the march into Ngwe was made without further enemy resistance.

It was fortunate, too, that on the 17th June Colonel Haywood had taken the precaution of sending a company of his Nigerians to occupy the Ndupe Bridge some six miles east of Nkonjok on the road to Ngwe. Had the enemy, who had been getting round in front of the British retirement, seized this crossing of the Ndupe River, the consequences might have been most serious for the whole force.

Most of the troops who had advanced up the Yaunde road were evacuated to Duala for rest, their place being largely taken by the 1st Nigerians and some French troops, all under Colonel Cockburn, who had with him one gun 1 A.N.R. and two French guns.

Garua, 10th June

Garua was at length captured, the W.A.F.F. guns assisting, though the chief weapon was the French 95 mm. gun, which actually caused the Germans to surrender.

6th October

General Gorges's forces remained inactive during the rainy season. This was not over when the advance on Yaunde recommenced on 6th October, Colonel Rose advancing on his left from Sakbajame on the Sanaga River towards Lissege, which he reached without opposition.

9th October

Colonel Haywood began his assault of the Wumbiagas position at 0530 hours. Assisted by Colonel Rose's column coming in on the left of the attack, the German trenches across the Mbila River were carried with a total loss of 31, amongst whom were five British officers in Colonel Haywood's troops. Wumbiagas was now made into an advanced base, more bush being cleared and gun positions taken up within the perimeter.

Colonel Gorges arrived at Wumbiagas from Duala on 17th November, accompanied by Major H. G. Howell, Royal Artillery, who was now the senior General Staff Officer in place of Colonel Turner, Royal Artillery, invalided. The advance on Yaunde was resumed on the 27th November, though the rains had far from ceased; Colonel Gorges's column along the Wumbiagas-Yaunde road, Colonel Mayer and the French to the south from Eseka. Colonel Gorges's column included a howitzer detachment Royal Artillery which had to move on wheels, not being of the mountain artillery description. Also one section Nigerian Battery (1 A.N.R.) under Captain Waller and one section Gold Coast Artillery under Lieutenant St. Clair, a field section Royal Engineers, machine-gun section, West India Regiment, 1st and 2nd Nigerians, H.Q., and three companies Gold Coast Battalion, Gambia Detachment, Field Telegraph Detachment. The general plan was to march up the road with flanking detachments on either side.

21st November

General Dobell arrived at Colonel Gorges's camp and awarded medals. Those receiving them in 1 A.N.R. were: Sergeant-Major Maida Musa, Corporal Awdu Kano, Corporal Ossumen II, Bombadier Awdu Keffi. Gun-carrier Momma Kano IV had already received his at Duala.

23rd November

Colonel Cockburn's right flanking column with one gun Gold Coast Regiment started.

24th November

Main column (Colonel Rose's column on the left flanking movement) started. The main column reached the Puge River about 1100 hours. The Germans had a strong position here, about 700 yards of the British side of the river and 500 yards up the other side having been cleared. Captain Waller worked his way down to the river to get a near observation point to the enemy trenches and fired some double common on them. The Germans, hearing Colonel Rose's attack on their right rear, soon cleared out; the shelling seems to have helped Lieutenant Biddulph's Gold Coast Company, which charged the German trenches most gallantly and took them on 28th November. Later the 1 A.N.R. fired some rounds of shrapnel to help Lieutenant Fell (1st Nigerians), who was coming in from the enemy's right. Ngung was occupied by the section 1 A.N.R.

Colonel Cockburn's troops had suffered the loss of Captains Balders and Walker killed and Captain the Hon. R. Craven and Sergeant J. Hutchinson, Royal Army Medical Corps, wounded, but after more severe fighting by 0300 p.m. they were holding positions on the amphitheatre of hills round Lesogs.

9th December

The advance from Ngung was resumed, Colonel Haywood and three companies of his Battalion with one gun 1 A.N.R., Captain Waller in command being on the right flank.

The main column, Colonel Gorges, howitzer, section Gold Coast Battery, one gun 1 A.N.R.

Left flank Captain J. H. Butler and two companies Gold Coast Regiment. Colonel Haywood launched his attack at daybreak up the steep precipitous slopes of the Belok Nkojok mountain.

1 A.N.R. by indirect fire shelled the German trenches at 1,200 yards range and secured direct hits on the German emplacements where two machine guns were stationed and caused them to be evacuated. The observation point on this occasion was only 150 yards from the enemy trench, so observation was easy. Later shrapnel was tried with good results, and the column advanced with only 6 casualties—the fewness of which may be partly due to the enemy's poor ammunition and the British effective gunfire.

On the main road fighting was not so successful, attempts to eject the enemy from their position on the Mangei River having to be abandoned on the approach of night.

10th December

But next day Captain Butler on the left flank continued his advance to take the enemy in the rear, which he did so successfully that he took by surprise the German camp at Sege, where he captured 4,000 rounds of enemy ammunition and some rifles, stores and food. His good work cleared the way for the main column, whose advanced detachment under Colonel Cockburn and two companies 1st Nigerians and the second gun 1 A.N.R. suffered 15 casualties.

Colonel Haywood advanced with no opposition for the first mile, but was then held up by the enemy, who had one machine gun, but a shell from the gun of the 1 A.N.R. struck this gun's emplacement (and it is thought the gun itself), and the enemy withdrew to another position a mile farther on, and here he maintained a stubborn resistance till dusk, when fighting broke off. The column sustained four casualties, including Lieutenant B. T. R. Dillon wounded.

11th December

Next day a turning movement in the morning forced the enemy to evacuate his position; but Colonel Haywood found the country so broken and densely wooded that it was impossible to continue the advance immediately. However, in the next two or three days he encountered little opposition in the next few miles up to the Buba River, where he was checked on the 13th December. Next day, however, by a turning movement and effective assistance from his gun he took the enemy position without loss. On the 15th he carried the carrier road over the Kele River by a dash which put the enemy to flight and caused the British only one casualty.

17th December

On 17th December Colonel Haywood's column struck the main road four and a half miles east of Changmangas, and the main column marched in there unopposed. Here a fort and blockhouses were constructed in addition to stores magazines and a clearing hospital.

To the British it appeared that both on the main column and the right flank the more open country had made the gunfire exercise a demoralizing effect on the German forces.

It was decided to give the British forces a much needed rest till the 23rd December.

General Gorges organized his columns for the final advance on Yaunde:

Right Flank Detachment (Lieutenant-Colonel Rose), one gun of the Gold Coast Battery and three companies Gold Coast Battalion.

Centre Column (Colonel Haywood), Howitzer Detachment Royal Garrison Artillery, one section Nigerian Battery (1 A.N.R.), 2nd Nigerians, Field Section 36th (Sierra Leone) Company Royal Engineers.

Left Flank Detachment (Major F. Anderson), two companies Gold Coast Battalion.

General Reserve (Colonel Gorges and his H.Q.), one gun 1 A.R.N., one gun Gold Coast Battery, machine-gun section, West India Regiment, 1st Nigerians, and Gambia Company.

23rd December

The advance on Yaunde was resumed by Colonel Gorges. Compared to previous fighting, little resistance was encountered. The howitzer assisted on three occasions. Intricate trenches were encountered, but had been vacated, so there was little work for the artillery to do. Yaunde was entered unopposed on the 31st. According to the account in *Der Grosse Krieg, 1914–18*, it attributes the decision to retire into neutral territory to various causes, such as desire to avoid the acceptance of humiliating terms, and it says that in the severe fighting that led up to the fall of Yaunde the Allies owed much of their success to their artillery.

See page 418 of the War Official History: It transpired after the fighting, on the evidence of a British officer, prisoner of war with the Germans, that the Germans had a special respect for Colonel Haywood's military abilities and that even their native troops talked of him, saying that he had war juju and that it was no use fighting him.

The Germans were reported to have retired on Ebolowa, so Colonel Haywood received orders to follow them up with his 2nd Nigerians, two companies Gold Coast Battalion, one section 1 A.N.R. and field section 36th Company Royal Engineers.

8th January 1916

Colonel Haywood's columns, unopposed, reached Widemenge and pushed forward the same day to the Nyong River crossing at Kolmaka. Here were handed over to him 34 Europeans, of which 24 were British, and of these seven were combatants, one a lieutenant Royal Artillery captured at Nsanakang.

9th January

Major Coles left Yaunde down the Kribi road. He had with him the 1st Nigerians, one gun Nigerian Battery and the Gambia Company.

Colonel Haywood arrived at Ebolowa on 22nd January and found that the enemy were making for Ngoa. In spite of very scanty rations, supplemented by bananas picked from the farms at places, he pushed on from Ebolowa next day for Ngoa, where the German Governor Ebermayer was reported to be on his way to Spanish Muni.

Mafub, 24th January

An enemy force under Buhler held up Colonel Haywood most of this day. There were no paths to outflank the position, but the Nigerian troops crept down through the bush on either side of the road to try and turn the flanks of the German position, which was on the far bank of a small stream in thick cover. The Germans counter-attacked, killing Lieutenants Anthony and McIver and almost capturing Captain Waller's telephone party which that officer was attempting to get to a position on the right flank of the German position from which to observe the battery fire. Captain Waller extricated the party, and returning to his gun position at the top of the hill about 500 yards to the rear, fired several rounds at where he judged the main German position to be. The casualties amounted to 22 British and one French, also one of the telephone-carriers, a civilian. It may be mentioned here that these telephone-carriers, all of whom were civilian, had on many occasions behaved with great coolness under fire. The enemy eventually retired and Colonel Haywood, continuing his advance on the 25th January, occupied Abang in face of slight opposition. Immediately south of that position, however, he encountered stubborn resistance from the hostile rearguard posted in two successive positions behind streams from which they were only driven at dusk. According to the official report 'this success was largely due to Captain Waller's guns whose effect was so demoralizing that in spite of the expenditure of a very large amount of ammunition by the enemy only four of the British were wounded'.

This fight concluded the participation of the British Contingent, and it is satisfactory to have to report that 1 A.N.R., who were almost the first to fire at the enemy in the Cameroons, also had the honour to fire the last rounds at the enemy as far as British troops were concerned.

The conduct of the gunners and gun-carriers of this Hausa battery was at all times admirable and their conduct, even under the most trying circumstances, a pattern of steadiness and loyalty to their officers.

LIST OF OFFICERS W.A.F.F., ROYAL ARTILLERY

Northern Nigeria Regiment:	*Date of appointment to W.A.F.F.*
Robinson, Captain W. A.	1 Dec. 1897
Cubitt, Lieutenant T. A.	14 Feb. 1898
Robertson, Lieutenant G. C.	15 Feb. 1898
Macnaghten, Lieutenant E. B.	16 Feb. 1898
Russel, Lieutenant A. C.	3 Mar. 1898
MacDougall, Lieutenant J. P.	14 Jan. 1899
Sheppard, Captain H. C. R.	11 Feb. 1899
Scott, Lieutenant C. W.	11 Mar. 1899
Edwards, Brevet-Major W. E.	8 Apr. 1899
Phillips, Second Lieutenant E. H.	22 Apr. 1899
West, Lieutenant G. E. J. A.	2 Aug. 1899
Kemball, Major G. V. (Later Inspector-General W.A.F.F.)	9 Sept. 1899
O'Neill, Major W. H.	9 Sept. 1899
Merrick, Captain G. C.	27 June 1900
Stewart, Second Lieutenant D. R.	28 Nov. 1900
Stevens, Second Lieutenant A. C. C.	9 Jan. 1901
Wilson, Second Lieutenant P. H.	17 Jan. 1901
Browne, Lieutenant E. W.	15 May 1901
Farquhar, Captain J.	5 July 1901
Grayson, Captain A. Q. H. A.	30 Oct. 1901
Griffin, Lieutenant J. Mc. C.	16 Nov. 1901
Kinsman, Captain G. V. R.	7 Dec. 1901
Tompson, Lieutenant R. H. D.	14 Dec. 1901
Cock, Captain H. C. L.	17 Jan. 1902
Elliott, Captain E. H. H.	24 Jan. 1902
Henvey, Captain R.	9 Feb. 1902

Northern Nigeria Regiment:	*Date of appointment to W.A.F.F.*
Lowther, Lieutenant E. St. G.	2 Mar. 1902
Goodwin, Captain R. H.	12 Apr. 1902
Graham, Lieutenant E. S.	12 Apr. 1902
Heelas, Lieutenant P. J. B.	22 Aug. 1902
Spinks, Lieutenant C. W.	1 Sept. 1902
Woods, Lieutenant A. N.	1 Sept. 1902
Lyon, Captain F.	(?) Oct. 1902
Lee, Lieutenant W. H.	12 Dec. 1902
Maturin, Lieutenant R. C.	20 Dec. 1902
Galloway, Lieutenant L.	14 Mar. 1903
McLay, Lieutenant W. J.	16 May 1903
Phillips, Captain E. H.	24 Jan. 1904
Mackworth, Lieutenant F. J. A.	2 Apr. 1904
Roberts, Lieutenant L. D. E.	2 Apr. 1904
Maclaverty, Lieutenant C. F. S.	28 May 1904
Dunbar, Lieutenant J. C.	25 June 1904
Lamb, Lieutenant R. W.	25 Mar. 1905
Eden, Lieutenant A. G.	31 Mar. 1905
Mann, Lieutenant G. D.	17 June 1905
Clayton, Lieutenant W. A.	19 Aug. 1905
Kincaid-Smith, Captain K. J.	28 Oct. 1905
Buckill, Lieutenant L. M.	20 Apr. 1907
McGrath, Captain A. T.	8 June 1907
Massy, Lieutenant, H. R. S.	6 July 1907
Guthrie, Lieutenant J. C.	26 Oct. 1907
Robertson, Lieutenant N. B.	26 Oct. 1907
Cogan, Lieutenant F. J. L.	7 Nov. 1908
Baxter, Lieutenant H. H.	6 July 1910
Howell, Captain H. G.	14 Sept. 1910
Willoughby-Osborne, Lieutenant D'Arcy	25 Jan. 1911
Cummins, Lieutenant A. A.	10 May 1911
Waller, Lieutenant R. J. R.	2 Nov. 1912
Fairbank, Lieutenant H. N.	29 Jan. 1913
Haygate, Lieutenant G.	26 Feb. 1913
Edwards, Lieutenant B.	16 Apr. 1913
Frith, Lieutenant G. T.	6 Aug. 1913
Weatherbe, Lieutenant W.	8 July 1914
Peele, Temp. Lieutenant H. J. J.	27 July 1915
McCorkindale, Second Lieutenant	20 Oct. 1915
Shaw, Second Lieutenant M.	3 Nov. 1915
Robinson, Second Lieutenant E. W. J.	7 Jan. 1916
Southern Nigeria Regiment:	
Turner, Lieutenant A. J.	20 May 1900
Moorhouse, Captain H. C. (Later Commandant)	1 Aug. 1900

Southern Nigeria Regiment:	*Date of appointment to W.A.F.F.*
Mair, Captain G. T. (Later Commandant Nigeria Regiment)	15 Aug. 1900
Mackenzie, Brevet-Major A. M. N.	22 Dec. 1900
Montanaro, Brevet-Lieut-Colonel (The First Commandant)	12 Feb. 1901
Jones, Lieutenant R. P.	24 July 1901
Boddam-Whetham, Lieutenant C.	4 Sept. 1902
Vickery, Lieutenant C.	4 July 1903
Burton, Lieutenant F. C. D.	9 Apr. 1904
Smith, Captain E. de H.	2 July 1904
Hamilton, Lieutenant H. H.	26 Aug. 1904
Gibbon, Lieutenant J. H.	24 Sept. 1904
Steel, Lieutenant E. A.	8 Oct. 1904
Hulton, Lieutenant H. H.	26 Aug. 1905
Rudkin, Captain W. C. E.	27 Jan. 1906
Williams, Lieutenant R. C.	24 Feb. 1906
Marshal, Lieutenant E. T.	29 Sept. 1906
Vaughan, Lieutenant H. H. S.	27 Oct. 1906
Rowe, Lieutenant R. H.	1 June 1907
Rose, Lieutenant D. D.	22 June 1907
Griffith, Lieutenant G. M. R.	3 Oct. 1907
Leech, Lieutenant C. J. F.	12 Oct. 1907
Sterling, Lieutenant W. A.	12 Oct. 1907
Hickes, Lieutenant L. D.	29 Feb. 1908
Forbes, Lieutenant J. L.	10 Oct. 1908
Cogan, Lieutenant F. J. L.	7 Nov. 1908
Sturges, Lieutenant C. H. M.	3 June 1909
Benham, Lieutenant F. B.	13 Sept. 1911
Rees, Lieutenant L. W. B.	21 May 1913
Dobbin, Lieutenant A. W.	18 June 1913
Body, Second Lieutenant C. G.	17 Sept. 1913
Nigeria Regiment:	
Hill, Lieutenant J. N.	1 July 1917
Gold Coast Regiment:	
Smith-Rewse, Captain H. B. W.	5 June 1901
Mathews, Lieutenant H. de C.	5 June 1901
O'Kinealy, Captain J.	12 June 1901
Allen, Captain W. J. B.	16 Nov. 1901
Greenway, Lieutenant J. J. K.	30 Nov. 1901
Sedwick, Captain F. R.	7 Dec. 1901
Collins, Lieutenant G. M.	14 Dec. 1901
Griffith, Lieutenant G. M.	15 Jan. 1902
Macleay, Lieutenant D.	24 Jan. 1902

Gold Coast Regiment:	*Date of appointment to W.A.F.F.*
Ford, Lieutenant J. E. H.	10 Apr. 1902
Murray, Lieutenant F. M.	9 May 1902
Scrottky, Lieutenant C. E. C.	7 Feb. 1903
Beor, Lieutenant B. R. W.	26 Sept. 1903
Jackson, Lieutenant F. W. F.	30 July 1904
Clarke, Captain H. C. S.	18 Feb. 1905
Simpson, Lieutenant R. C.	26 Aug. 1905
Rich, Lieutenant C. S.	21 Oct. 1905
Barne, Lieutenant W. B. G.	25 Nov. 1905
Oliver, Lieutenant G. B.	30 Dec. 1905
Cockcraft, Lieutenant L. W. La T.	10 Feb. 1906
Anstey, Lieutenant E. C.	13 Apr. 1907
Harris, Captain O. M.	11 Apr. 1908
Pask, Lieutenant I. A. J.	24 Aug. 1908
Scovil, Lieutenant F. H.	27 Nov. 1909
Smeed, Lieutenant C. W.	9 Mar. 1910
Bryant, Captain F. C.	14 Sept. 1910
Saunders, Lieutenant J. D. G.	28 June 1911
Ralton, Lieutenant H. J.	1 Sept. 1911
Custance, Lieutenant S. N.	26 Mar. 1913
St. Clair, Lieutenant W. L.	10 Sept. 1913
Simpson, Lieutenant W. A. J.	27 May 1914
Foley, Lieutenant J. G.	16 June 1916
Parker, Second Lieutenant G. H.	29 Dec. 1916
Lagos Battalion:	
Haywood, Captain A. H. W. (Later Inspector General W.A.F.F.)	5 Sept. 1903
Sierra Leone Battalion:	
Palmer, Captain C. E. (Later commanded the Battalion)	23 Nov. 1901
Bond, Captain H. H.	9 July 1904
Ayton, Lieutenant H. R.	23 Oct. 1905
Patterson, Lieutenant J.	11 Aug. 1906
Gilbert, Lieutenant D. P.	1 Dec. 1909
Gambia Company:	
Hill, Lieutenant O. C. R.	18 Jan. 1913

APPENDIX I

Battle Honours of the Royal West African Frontier Force

The Nigeria Regiment[1]

'ASHANTEE, 1873–4'
'ASHANTI, 1900'
'DUALA'
'GARUA'
'BANYO'
'CAMEROONS, 1914–1916'
'BEHOBEHO'
'NYANGAO'
'EAST AFRICA, 1916–1918'
'Juba'
'Goluin'
'MARDA PASS'
'BABILE GAP'
'Bisidimo'
'COLITO'
'OMO'
'Lechemti'
'ABYSSINIA, 1940-41'
'North Arakan'
'KALADAN'
'Mayu Valley'
'MYOHAUNG'
'Arakan Beaches'
'Kangaw'
'Dalet'
'TAMANDU'
'CHINDITS, 1944'
'BURMA, 1943–45'

The Gold Coast Regiment[2]

'ASHANTEE, 1873–4'
'ASHANTI, 1900'
'KAMINA'
'DUALA'
'CAMEROONS, 1914–1916'
'NARUNGOMBE'
'EAST AFRICA, 1916–1918'
'Wal Garis'
'EL WAK'
'JUBA'
'BULO ERILLO'
'Gelib'
'Alessandra'
'WADARA'
'ABYSSINIA, 1940–41'
'NORTH ARAKAN'
'KALADAN'
'Tinma'
'Mayu Valley'
'MYOHAUNG'
'Arakan Beaches'
'Kangaw'
'TAUNGUP'
'BURMA, 1943–45'

The Gambia Regiment

'CAMEROONS, 1914–16'
'NYANGAO'
'EAST AFRICA, 1916–18'
'NORTH ARAKAN'
'KALADAN'
'MOWDOK'
'NYOHAUNG'
'BURMA, 1943–45'

The Sierra Leone Regiment

'DUALA'
'CAMEROONS, 1914–16'
'NORTH ARAKAN'
'KALADAN'
'MYOHAUNG'
'BURMA, 1943–45'

Honours shown in capitals are borne on the Colours.

[1] Now the Queen's Own Nigeria Regiment.
[2] Now the Ghana Regiment.

APPENDIX II

Inspectors-General W.A.F.F.: Commanders of Formations: W.A.F.F. Battalion Commanders W.A.F.F.

Inspector-General (Local or Temp. Rank of appointment)	*Date of appointment*
Brigadier-General and Major G. V. Kemball, D.S.O., Royal Artillery	23 July 1901
Brevet-Colonel T. L. N. Morland, C.B., D.S.O., King's Royal Rifle Corps	1 Sept. 1905
Brevet Lieutenant-Colonel P. S. Wilkinson, Northumberland Fusiliers	1 Sept. 1909
Brevet-Colonel C. M. Dobell, D.S.O., Royal Welch Fusiliers	1 Sept. 1913

Note. Till the end of the 1914–18 War the appointment was vacant and was not again filled until 1st January 1920, from which date Brigadier-Generals were abolished. Subsequent appointments were held first as Colonel-on-the-Staff and later as Brigadier.

Commandant W.A.F.F., or Northern Nigeria Regiment (Local or Temp. Rank of Colonel)	*Date of appointment*
Captain and Brevet-Major F. D. Lugard, C.B., D.S.O., Norfolk Regiment	26 Aug. 1897
Lieutenant-Colonel James Willcocks, Leinster Regiment	9 Sept. 1899
Brevet-Colonel F. L. N. Morland, C.B., D.S.O., King's Royal Rifle Corps	23 July 1901
Brevet Lieutenant-Colonel A. W. G. Lowry-Cole, D.S.O., Royal Welch Fusiliers	24 Sept. 1904
Brevet Lieutenant-Colonel J. Hasler, East Kent Regiment	25 Sept. 1907
Major E. F. Strickland, D.S.O., Norfolk Regiment	8 Feb. 1909

Commandant Oil Rivers, Constabulary, or Southern Nigeria Regiment (Local or Temp. Rank of Lieutenant-Colonel)	
Captain C. H. P. Carter, Royal Scots Regiment	21 Sept. 1896
Captain (Brevet-Major) C. H. P. Carter, C.M.G., Royal Scots Regiment	1 Jan. 1900
Major and Brevet Lieutenant-Colonel A. F. Montanaro, Royal Artillery	12 Feb. 1901
Captain and Brevet-Major H. C. Moorhouse, D.S.O., Royal Artillery	3 Aug. 1905
Captain and Brevet-Major H. M. Trenchard, D.S.O., Royal Scots Fusiliers	1 June 1908
Major F. H. Cunliffe, Middlesex Regiment	25 Sept. 1911

Commandant Nigeria Regiment (Temp. Rank of Colonel)	*Date of appointment*
Brevet-Colonel C. H. P. Carter, C.B., C.M.G., Royal Scots Regiment	24 Oct. 1913
Major F. H. Cunliffe, Middlesex Regiment	6 Sept. 1914

Note. During the 1914–18 War 'Acting' Commandants for the Nigeria Regiment were appointed as required. The appointment of Commandant Nigeria Regiment was not filled again until early 1920 (10 March).

Commandant, Gold Coast Regiment (Local, or Temp. Lieutenant-Colonel)	*Date of appointment*
Major P. S. Wilkinson, Northumberland Fusiliers	17 May 1900
Captain C. E. Rew, West India Regiment	24 Dec. 1904
Major E. C. Tidswell, D.S.O., Lancashire Fusiliers	11 Mar. 1905
Brevet-Colonel C. H. P. Carter, C.B., C.M.G., Royal Scots Regiment	4 June 1906
Major W. T. M. Reeve, Leinster Regiment	27 Feb. 1909
Captain and Brevet-Major E. M. Panter-Downes, Royal Irish Regiment	5 Sept. 1911
Captain R. A. de B. Rose, Worcestershire Regiment	6 Aug. 1914

1st Special Service Battalion W.A.F.F., or 1st Battalion Northern Nigeria Regiment (later 1st Battalion Nigeria Regiment, (Local, or Temp. Lieutenant-Colonel)	
Major T. D. Pilcher, Northumberland Fusiliers	18 Oct. 1897
Captain T. L. N. Morland, King's Royal Rifle Regiment	20 June 1899
Brevet-Major A. H. Festing, D.S.O., Royal Irish Regiment	9 Jan. 1901
Captain A. McClintock, D.S.O., Seaforth Highlanders	1 Oct. 1902
Major C. M. Dobell, D.S.O., Royal Welch Fusiliers	29 July 1905
Major E. P. Strickland, D.S.O., Norfolk Regiment	5 Oct. 1906
Major E. L. Mackenzie, D.S.O., Royal Sussex Regiment	8 Apr. 1909
Major R. L. McDougall, D.S.O., East Kent Regiment	16 Mar. 1912
Major J. B. Cockburn, Royal Welch Fusiliers	16 Mar. 1913

2nd Battalion Northern Nigeria Regiment (later 2nd Battalion Nigeria Regiment) (Local, or Temp. Lieutenant-Colonel)	
Major H. S. Fitzgerald, Durham Light Infantry	5 Feb. 1898
Captain A. W. G. Lowry-Cole, Royal Welch Fusiliers	12 Dec. 1898
Captain H. R. Beddoes, Royal Dublin Fusiliers	23 July 1901
Brevet-Major J. Hasler, East Kent Regiment	29 Apr. 1904
Captain F. H. G. Cunliffe, Middlesex Regiment	31 July 1905
Brevet-Major A. M. N. Mackenzie, Royal Artillery	25 July 1907
Major E. E. Williams, D.S.O., Northumberland Fusiliers	18 Feb. 1910
Captain T. A. Rose, D.S.O., Royal Scots Fusiliers	4 Oct. 1911
Captain J. B. Cockburn, Royal Welch Fusiliers	16 Aug. 1913
Major P. Maclear, Royal Dublin Fusiliers (Killed in action at Garua, 30/8/14)	15 Apr. 1914

3rd Battalion Nigeria Regiment (Temp. rank of Lieutenant-Colonel)	*Date of appointment*
Major G. T. Mair, D.S.O., Royal Artillery	30 Oct. 1913
4th Battalion Nigeria Regiment (Temp. rank of Lieutenant-Colonel)	
Captain A. H. W. Haywood, Royal Artillery	8 Oct. 1913
3rd (Mounted Infantry) Battalion Northern Nigeria Regiment (Temp. Lieutenant-Colonel, or Temp. Major)	
Brevet-Major E. C. Crawley, 12th Lancers	10 Dec. 1902
Brevet-Major J. Hasler, East Kent Regiment	28 July 1903
Brevet-Major T. A. Cubitt, D.S.O., Royal Artillery	29 Apr. 1904
Brevet-Major C. W. Barlow, Essex Regiment	10 Dec. 1904
Captain A. D. Green, D.S.O., Worcester Regiment	28 July 1905
Captain H. F. Searight, 1st Dragoon Guards	15 Nov. 1906
Captain Lord J. S. Cavendish, D.S.O., 1st Life Guards	1 Sept. 1909
Major J. B. Orr, Norfolk Regiment	12 Jan. 1913
Major S. J. B. Barnardiston, Suffolk Regiment	2 Mar. 1914
Captain Lord Henry Seymour, Grenadier Guards	10 June 1914
Captain J. T. Gibbs, 3rd Dragoon Guards	13 Nov. 1914
Major J. P. D. Underwood, D.S.O., North Lancs Regiment	8 Aug. 1916
Captain C. H. M. Venour, O.B.E., Hants Regiment	1 Jan. 1919

Note for the Nigeria Regiment. On the conclusion of the Cameroons Campaign, until the Armistice, that is, from early 1916 until November 1918, there were a succession of Battalion or Acting Battalion Commanders, whom it has not been possible to identify by dates. Some of their names are as follows:

1st Battalion. E. C. Feneran, The Queens Regiment; C. E. Roberts, Northants Regiment; R. G. Coles, Suffolk Regiment; M. H. Willis, Suffolk Regiment.

2nd Battalion. W. I. Webb-Bowen, Middlesex Regiment; R. H. West, Royal Highlanders; G. L. Uniacke; C. Gibb, Royal Scots Fusiliers.

3rd Battalion, J. Crookenden, East Kent Regiment; J. F. E. Archer; J. F. Badham, Worcester Regiment; J. P. D. Underwood, D.S.O., North Lancs Regiment.

4th Battalion. J. Sargent, Lancashire Fusiliers; S. N. Webb, South Wales Borderers; J. P. D. Underwood, D.S.O., North Lancs Regiment.

From November 1918, when the partially or organized 1st West African (Palestine) Service Brigade was demobilized, until the end of 1919, when the Nigeria Regiment was restored to peace establishments, there was no permanency in the command of battalions.

Sierra Leone Battalion (Temp. Major or Temp. Lieutenant-Colonel)	*Date of appointment*
Major E. C. Blakeney, 4 Essex Regiment	15 June 1901
Captain C. E. Palmer, Royal Artillery	30 Apr. 1904
Captain F. N. Le Mesurier, Royal Dublin Fusiliers	20 Feb. 1907
Captain G. P. Newstead,[1] Suffolk Regiment	1 Apr. 1913
Major W. C. Hastings, D.S.O., Manchester Regiment	5 Mar. 1915
Major A. N. Ogilvie, North Staffordshire Regiment	22 Oct. 1919

[1] Killed in action at Harmann's Farm, 4/3/15.

Gambia Company	*Date of appointment*
Captain F. O. Graham, Royal Marines	30 Nov. 1901
Captain W. C. N. Hastings, D.S.O., Manchester Regiment	12 Sept. 1906
Captain R. D. F. Oldman, D.S.O., Norfolk Regiment	Mar. 1909
Captain I. G. Sewell, Royal Fusiliers	3 Sept. 1910
Captain H. T. Dobbin, Duke of Cornwall's Light Infantry	7 Jan. 1911
Captain V. B. Thurston, Dorset Regiment	11 Jan. 1913
Captain R. Law, Royal Dublin Fusiliers	20 Oct. 1916
Captain H. T. Stronge, M.C., East Kent Regiment	1 June 1919

APPENDIX III

Pamphlet—Africa (West): C.O. No. 588—June 1899

SELBORNE COMMITTEE

Interdepartmental Committee on Amalgamation of Military Forces in West Africa

Proposed designation	*Units*	*Original composition (at present)*
N.N. Regt.	1st Bn. (8 coys.) 2nd Bn. (8 coys.) 1 and 2 Btys (guns) 1 coy. Engineers	Original W.A.F.F. and Coys. of R.N.C. in N.N.
S.N. Regt.	Inf. Bn. (8 coys.) 2 btys. (guns)	N. Coast Protectorate, Force and coys. R.N.C. in S.N.
G.C. Regt.	G. C. Bn. N. T. Bn. } (12 coys.) 2 btys.	G. C. Constab. of 2 bns. and 2 btys.
Lagos Bn.	1 Bn. (3 coys.)	Lagos Constab.
S/L Bn.	1 Bn. (4 coys.)	S/L Frontier Police

When the difficulties with the French in the hinterland of Lagos and on the Niger in the years 1897–8 brought to the front the question of the responsibility of the Imperial Government in connection with Niger Territory and the necessity for the relinquishment by the Royal Niger Company of the administration of those territories became apparent it became necessary to form the nucleus of a new military force for Imperial purposes on the Niger. This force was called 'The West African Frontier Force' and with the transfer of the Royal Niger Company's territories and of the Niger Coast Protectorate from the Foreign Office to the Colonial Office was chosen as a convenient moment to consider as a whole the position of military forces of the Crown under control of the Colonial Office throughout West Africa to make their forces mutually self-supporting, and to obviate as far as possible bringing reserves to Imperial troops for purposes of small West African Expeditions it was considered necessary the various constabularies and newly raised West African Frontier Force should be amalgamated into one organization and bear a military name.

APPENDIX IV

Extracts from Dress Regulations: W.A.F.F. 1903

OFFICERS

Levee dress or review order	*Field dress*	*Mess dress*
Khaki serge jacket; red piping	Khaki drill jacket Khaki drill breeches or	White jacket; rolled collar
Khaki serge jacket; overalls strapped	Khaki drill overalls Wolseley helmet	White trousers Black tie
Wolseley helmet; regimental puggaree	Sam Browne belt Brown shooting boots	Wellington boots
Sam Browne belt	Khaki puttees or	Silk kamerband
Black Wellington boots; spurs	Stohwasser gaiters Tie of battalion colours	

Special distinctions

Colours of puggarees and kamarbands:

Artillery
Khaki puggaree topped with ¼ in. red and blue (red above blue); royal blue kamarband.

Infantry
1 Nigeria Battalion: Khaki puggaree and red flash; red kamarband.
2 Nigeria Battalion: Khaki puggaree and green flash; green kamarband.
Southern Nigeria: Red puggaree; long red kamarband with fringed ends.
Lagos: Khaki and red puggaree; red kamarband.
Gold Coast: Khaki puggaree and old gold flash; red kamarband.
Sierra Leone: Khaki puggaree and blue flash; blue kamarband.
Gambia: Khaki and brown puggaree; brown kamarband.

LIST OF UNIFORM AND EQUIPMENT FOR NATIVE SOLDIERS OF THE WEST AFRICAN FRONTIER FORCE

Article	*Scale of issue*
Zouave jacket (red with yellow braiding, for infantry and mounted infantry; blue, with yellow braiding for artillery)	1 every 2 years
Khaki blouse; khaki knickerbockers (drill, or serge, according to local option)	3 first year, 2 second year; then 3 and 2 in alternate years; 3 a year
Bedford-cord pantaloons (mounted infantry only)	1 a year
Shirt, drab union mixture	1 a year
Brown jersey	1 a year
Kamarband of regimental colour	2 a year
Fez	1 a year
Tassel of regimental colour	1 a year
Kilmarnock cap	1 a year
Khaki puttees	2 pairs a year
Chupplies	1 pair a year, but a reserve of 1 pair a man to be kept in Quartermaster's stores in West Africa

APPENDIX V

(1) *London Gazette: 15th January 1901*

VICTORIA CROSS

Captain (Temp. Major) C. J. Mellis: Indian Staff Corps and West African Frontier Force

On 30th September 1900, at Obassa, 12 miles north-west of Kumassi, seeing the enemy very numerous and intended to make a firm stand, hastily collected all stray men and any he could get together, and charged at their head into dense bush were the enemy were thick. His action carried all along with him, but the enemy were determined to have a hand-to-hand fight. One fired at Major Mellis, who put his sword through the man and they rolled over together. Another Ashanti shot him through the foot, the wound paralysing the limb. His wild rush had, however, caused a regular panic among the enemy, who were at the same time charged by the Sikhs and killed in numbers.

Major Mellis also behaved with great gallantry on three previous occasions.

Sergeant J. Mackenzie: Seaforth Highlanders (Rosshire Buffs, The Duke of Albany's; employed with the West African Frontier Force)

On 6th June 1900, at Dompaassi, in Ashanti, Sergeant Mackenzie, after working two maxim guns under a hot fire and being wounded while doing so, volunteered to clear the stockades of the enemy, which he did in the most gallant manner, leading the charge himself and driving the enemy into the bush.

(2) *London Gazette: 11th September 1903*

VICTORIA CROSS

Lieutenant (now Captain) W. D. Wright: Royal West Surrey Regiment and Northern Nigeria Regiment

On 24th March 1903 Lieutenant Wright, with only one officer and 44 men, took up a position in the path of the advancing enemy, and sustained the determined charge of 1,000 horse and 2,000 foot for two hours, and when the enemy, after heavy losses, fell back in good order, Lieutenant Wright continued to follow them up till they were in full retreat.

The personal example of this officer, as well as his skilful leadership, contributed largely to the success of this brilliant affair. He in no way infringed his orders by his daring initiative, as though warned of the possibility of meeting large bodies of the enemy he had been given a free hand.

(3) *London Gazette: 23rd August 1915*

VICTORIA CROSS

Captain John Fitzhardinge Paul Butler: King's Royal Rifle Corps and West African Frontier Force

For most conspicuous bravery in the Cameroons. On 17th November 1914 with a party of 13 men went into thick bush and at once attacked the enemy about 100 strong, including several Europeans. He defeated them, capturing machine guns and ammunition.

On 27th December 1914 with a few men he swam the River Ekam, held by the enemy. Alone and in face of brisk fire he completed his reconnaissance on the farther bank and returned in safety. Two men were wounded while he was in the water.

APPENDIX VI

Medals

1. *The East and West Africa Medal*

Authorized 1892 (A.O. 212). This medal, in silver and bronze, was the same as that issued for the Ashanti Campaign of 1873–4; obverse the head of Queen Victoria, reverse British troops fighting Africans in the bush; ribbon yellow with black borders and two narrow stripes.

2. *The Ashanti Star 1896*

3. *The Ashanti Medal 1900*

Authorized 1901 (A.O. 249). This medal was issued to all who served with the Ashanti Field Force between 31st March and 25th December 1900. It bore on the obverse a bust of King Edward VII in Field-Marshal's uniform, and on the reverse the British lion standing on a rock, looking towards the rising sun. Below was a shield with two spears and in the exergue the word 'Ashanti' on a scroll. The ribbon was black with two dark green stripes.

4. *The African General Service Medal*

Authorized 1902 (A.O. 132). A silver medal that for some campaigns was also cast in bronze for issue to carriers. The obverse of the original bore a bust of King Edward VII in Field-Marshal's uniform; the reverse was the same as that of the East and Central Africa Medal, except that the word 'Africa' appeared in the exergue. The ribbon was yellow, with black borders and two narrow green stripes.

The African General Service Medal replaced the East and West Africa Medal for the commemoration of campaigns in East, Central and West Africa, and was never issued without the appropriate clasp.

5. *The Medal for Distinguished Conduct in the Field*

This medal is commonly known as the African D.C.M. It was first approved for the Royal West African Frontier Force, and its adoption for the W.A.F.F. was suggested by the Interdepartmental Rewards Council in 1903. Prior to this the Imperial D.C.M. had sometimes been awarded to African askaris. Mention of this medal was included in the provisional W.A.F.F. Regulations of 1905, though the Army Council did not agree to its issue until the following year. The obverse shows a military trophy with the royal arms in the centre; the reverse the words 'For Distinguished Conduct in the Field' and W.A.F.F. The ribbon is red, with two blue stripes and one green.

6. *The Long Service and Good Conduct Medal*

A special medal for the W.A.F.F., approved at the same time as the African D.C.M. The obverse bears an effigy of the King in Field-Marshal's uniform, the reverse the words 'For Long Service and Good Conduct' and W.A.F.F. The ribbon is crimson with a green stripe.

The period of service originally required to qualify for this medal was 18 years. This meant that it was issued on the day of discharge, when the recipient had no opportunity to wear it. In 1932, in reply to a representation from the Colonial Office, the War Office refused to modify the period on the ground that 'any alteration may affect conditions of service of other native corps and possibly British personnel', but in March of the following year, after a renewed approach by the Colonial Office, sanction was given for the reduction of the qualifying period to 16 years.

APPENDIX VII

Awards to the Nigerian Brigade for Service in German East Africa

In the following list of awards the narratives concerning each award have been taken from the records of the Nigeria Regiment. They will, therefore, not agree word for word with the narratives published in the *London Gazette*. In most cases individuals have been recommended by their Commanding Officers for an award on more than one occasion. It is quite impossible to state for which recommendation an award was granted. In several actions out of which these recommendations arose individuals have earned an award apparently for no particular action, but seem to have been given the award for the sum total of these recommendations. Therefore, all recommendations before an award was actually granted are given in the following list:

Name	*Rank*	*Unit*	*Date of award*	*Remarks*
Badham, J. F.	Maj. T/Lt.-Col.	3 N.R.	New Year Honours List, 1918	To be Bt. Lt.-Col. for continual good service in the field when commanding a battalion.
Mann, G. C., D.S.O.	Maj. T/Lt.-Col.	Brig. H.Q.	27/7/18	To be Bt. Lt.-Col. for valuable services rendered when acting as Brig.-Gen. of the Nigerian Brigade.
Sargent, J., D.S.O.	Maj. T/Lt.-Col.	4 N.R.	27/7/18	To be Bt. Lt.-Col. for good services rendered when acting as G.S.O.1 of the Lindi Force.
		ORDER OF ST. MAURICE AND ST. LAZARUS		
Cunliffe, F. H. G., C.B., C.M.G.	Br.-Gen.		26/5/17	Award of the above order, Officers' Class, for distinguished service during the campaign.
		CROIX de GUERRE		
Feneran, E. C.	Maj. T/Lt.-Col.	1 N.R.	26/5/17	Good services as a Battalion Commander.
Crichton, Hon. J. A., D.S.O.	Capt.	Brig. H.Q.	26/5/17	Good work on the staff of the Brigade.
Leonard, T. M. R.	T/Lt.-Col.	W.A.M.S.	26/5/17	Good work as P.M.O. to the Brigade.
		D.S.O.		
Sargent, J.	Maj. T/Lt.-Col.	4 N.R.	4/6/17	Skilfully handled two companies of the 4 N.R. at Ngwembe, on 24 Jan. 1917 when in support of the 3 N.R. so as to cover the retirement of that Battalion, which was being closely pressed by the enemy. He personally took over the command of the rearguard and by bold and skilful handling of his troops saved a very critical situation and enabled the retirement to be carried out in safety.

Name	*Rank*	*Unit*	*Date of award*	*Remarks*
		D.S.O.—*cont.*		
Uniacke, G. L.	Bt.-Maj. T/Lt.-Col.	2 N.R.	29/10/18	Continuous good work throughout the Campaign and skilful leadership since being promoted to the command of a battalion.
Badham, J. F.	Bt. Lt.-Col.	3 N.R.	27/7/18	Continuous good work throughout the campaign and skilful leadership in the field whilst serving in Brig.-Gen. O'Grady's column in the Lindi area.
Leonard, T. M. R.	P.M.O., T/Lt.-Col.	W.A.M.S.	27/7/18	Continuous good work as P.M.O. throughout the campaign.
Crichton, Hon. J. A.	Capt.	Brig. H.Q.	27/7/18	Continuous good work on the staff. Most marked when on the Rufiji when that river was in flood. At Mahiwa from 15 to the 18 Oct. 1917, he displayed marked coolness in action and devotion to duty, personally superintending the distribution of ammunition under very heavy fire. in spite of ill health he has at all times shown the greatest devotion to duty.
		BAR TO D.S.O.		
Uniacke, G. L., D.S.O.	Bt. Maj. T/Lt.-Col.	2 N.R.	New Year Honours List, 1918	Conspicuous gallantry at Bweho-Chini on 22 Sept. 1917, when in command of his battalion.
		BAR TO THE MILITARY CROSS		
Pring, F. J. H., M.C.	Capt.	1 N.R.	Jan. 1917	Displayed great initiative and judgment under heavy fire at Mkindu on 18 Jan. 1917. Owing to his correct appreciation of the situation the position was taken with only slight loss to the attackers.
Gardner, A., M.C.	Capt.	2 N.R.	Jan. 1917	Displayed the greatest gallantry at Bweho-Chini on 22 Sept. 1917. This officer, with Capt. Fowle, M.C., held the left flank during repeated and most determined attacks. His company charged the enemy during the most critical time, and inflicted heavy loss on them with the bayonet.

Name	*Rank*	*Unit*	*Date of award*	*Remarks*
		BAR TO THE MILITARY CROSS—*cont.*		
Hawkins, A. S. G., M.C.	Lieut.	3 N.R.	24/12/17	Displayed the greatest gallantry and devotion to duty at Mkwera on 8 Nov. 1917.
Collins, J. G., M.C.	Capt.	3 N.R.	15/1/18	Conspicuous gallantry at Nyengede on 30 Sept. 1917, where he was wounded.
Waters, C. L., M.C.	Capt.	1 N.R.	15/1/18	Conspicuous gallantry and devotion to duty at Mahiwa, 15 to 18 Oct. 1917.
Fowle, C. H., M.C.	Capt.	2 N.R.	27/7/18	Has at all times displayed marked coolness and gallantry in action, and has been a most reliable officer throughout the campaign. At Bweho-Chini, on 22 Sept. 1917, he commanded his company with the greatest ability, helping to repulse several most determined attacks. Owing to his fine personal leadership his men have the greatest confidence in him.
Gardner, A.	Capt.	2 N.R.	4/1/17	Displayed fine initiative Jan. 1917 at Tachimbe, when he led a charge resulting in the capture of an enemy's howitzer and several prisoners.
Armstrong, H. W. R.	Capt.	3 N.R.	10/6/17	When under heavy fire assisted No. 5701 Pte. Olubi Ijero (since died of wounds) to carry Sgt. Dixon, who had been wounded, out of action at Ngwembe on 24 Jan. 1917. He subsequently held on with a section under very heavy fire so as to allow the wounded to be brought in.
Robinson, A. C.	Capt.	3 N.R.	10/6/17	Handled his company with the greatest judgment and coolness at Ngwembe on 24 Jan. 1917. His action kept the enemy in check at a most critical period until reinforced, thus enabling the main body and guns to get clear.
Burney, C. T.	Capt.	1 N.R.	29/10/18	Continual good work as Adjutant of his battalion and great devotion to his work, also conspicuous gallantry in the action at Bweho-Chini on 22 Sept. 1917.

Name	*Rank*	*Unit*	*Date of award*	*Remarks*
		BAR TO THE MILITARY CROSS—*cont.*		
Winter, N.	Lieut.	4. N.R.	10/6/17	Skilfully handled his men under heavy fire at Ngwembe on 24 Jan. 1917, where by his personal example and skilful fire control, caused the enemy to withdraw their attack against the Nigerian right.
Waters, C. L.	Capt.	1 N.R.	29/10/18	With the greatest skill frequently commanded patrols. Also at the capture of Mkindu on 18 Jan. 1917 was in command of the supporting company, where his skilful leadership and fire control greatly aided in the capture of the position. Gallantry at Bweho-Chini on 22 Sept. 1917.
		M.C.		
Studley, G.	Lieut.	2 N.R.	29/10/18	Bweno-Chini, 22/9/17
Collins, J. G.	Capt.	3 N.R.	5/11/17	Ngwembe
Southby, R.	Lieut.	3 N.R.	5/11/17	Nyengedi, 30/9/17
Hetley, C. R.	Capt.	4 N.R.	26/11/17	Mahiwa, 15/11/17
Hart, J. J.	Lieut.	1 N.R.	26/11/17	Bweho-Chini, 22/9/17
Hawkins, A. S. C.	Lieut.	3 N.R.	26/11/17	Mahiwa, 18/10/17
Fell, M. E.	Capt.	2 N.R.	27/12/18	Beho-Beho, 3/1/17 Bweho-Chini, 22/9/17 Mahiwa, 16/10/17
Finch, H. S.	Capt.	3 N.R.	27/12/18	Mahiwa, 18/10/17
Fox, D. B.	Lieut.	4 N.R.	27/12/18	Mahiwa, 7/6/17; 15/10/17
MacLean, G. D. M.	Lieut.	Gambia Coy.	27/12/18	Mahiwa, 16–18/10/17
Maxwell, J. E. H.	Capt.	4 N.R.	27/12/18	Mahiwa, 15/10/17
Vise, T. A.	Capt.	A/N.R.	1/1/18	Mkindu, 14/3/17
Webb, S. N. C.	Capt. (Ag. Maj.)	4 N.R.	1/1/18	Sibiti R., 8/6/17
Barber, L.	Lieut.	2 N.R.	27/12/18	Mahiwa, 17/10/17
Blackmore, C. W. P.	Lieut.	A/N.R.	27/12/18	Mahiwa, 16/10/17
Budgen, T. A.	Capt.	1 N.R.	27/12/18	Bweho-Chini, 22/9/17
Crowe, D. M.	Lieut.	4 N.R.	27/12/18	Mahiwa, 16/10/17
Beck, D. M. H.	Lieut.	1 N.R.	24/12/17	Mahiwa, 16/10/17
Catt, A. W.	Lieut.	3 N.R.	24/12/17	Mahiwa, 8/11/17
Ambrose, W. G.	Capt.	3 N.R.	1/1/18	Itete R., 26/7/17
Buchanan-Smith, W.	Lieut.	3 N.R.	1/1/18	Mkindu, 14/3/17
Downes, W. D	Capt.	4 N.R.	1/1/18	Mahiwa, 16/10/17
Roberts, C. E.	Maj.	4 N.R.	1/1/18	Ngwembe, 24/1/17
Stronge, H. C.	Capt.	2 N.R.	1/1/18	Mahiwa, 16/10/17
Milne-Home, A. C.	Capt.	3 N.R.	27/12/18	Ngwembe, 24/1/17
O'Connell, H. G.	Capt.	3 N.R.	27/12/18	Mahiwa, 18/10/17
Raby, H. S. V.	Lieut.	1 N.R.	27/12/18	Bweho-Chini, 22/9/17 (Mahiwa, 16/10/17)
Rumbold, W. R.	Lieut.	Pioneer Sect. and 3 N.R.	27/12/18	Devotion to duty 1917

Name	*Rank*	*Unit*	*Date of award*	*Remarks*
		M.C.—*cont.*		
Shaw, M.	Lieut.	Stokes Bty. and 4 N.R.	27/12/18	Mahiwa 15–18/10/17; Luchimi Val, 16–17/11/17
Steed, R.	Lieut.	2 N.R.	27/12/18	Bweho-Chini, 22/9/17; Mahiwa, 18/10/17
Wood, L. C.	Lieut.	2 N.R.	27/12/18	Devotion to duty
Gibson, E.	Capt.	W.A.M.S.	27/12/18	Good service
Morehead, H. R.	Capt.	W.A.M.S.	27/12/18	Nyongedi, 30/9/17
Sandeman, T. R.	Capt.	W.A.M.S.	27/12/18	Devotion to duty

OFFICERS MENTIONED IN DESPATCHES

Armstrong, H. W. R.
Badham, J. F.
Barber, L.
Barclay, C. E.
Buchanan-Smith, W.
Budgen, T. A. G.
Burney, G. T.
Burr, W. E.
Catt, A. W.
Cavanagh, B. G.
Collins, J. G.
Crichton, The Hon. J. A.
Cunliffe, F. H. G.
Elliott, D.
Fell, M. E.
Fox, D. B.
Gardner, A.
Gibb, C.
Green, C. H.
Hetley, C. R.
Kilby, R. N.
Leonard, T. M. R.
Mann, G. D.
Migeod, G. E. A.
Maxwell, J. E. H.
Milne-Home, A. C.
Murray, G. G.
Parr, B. C.
Pring, J. H.
Robinson, A. C.
Sandeman, T. R.
Sargent, J.
Stobart, A. M. St. C.
Stretton, A. L. de C.
Stronge, C. T.
Taylor, R. R.
Uniacke, G. L.
Vice, T. A.
Vicars, W. G.
Waters, G. L.
Webb, S. N. C.
Whetton, F. H.
Winter, N.

Name	*Rank*	*Unit*	*Date of award*	*Remarks*
		BAR TO D.C.M. (EUROPEAN)		
Element, R.	Sgt.	4 N.R.	3/10/18	Mahiwa, 15/10/17; Ngwembe, 23/1/17
		D.C.M. (EUROPEAN)		
Tanti, J.	T/Sgt.	2 N.R.	29/10/18	Bweho-Chini, 22/9/17
Badger, C.	Sgt.	2 N.R.	29/10/18	Bweho-Chini, 22/9/17
Fraser, J. H.	O.R.S.	2 N.R.	1/1/18	Devotion to duty
Hunsworth, W.	C/Sgt.	2 N.R.	1/1/18	Bweho-Chini, 22/9/17
Russell, C.	Sgt.	3 N.R.	1/1/18	Kibengo, 21/1/17
Darke, B. J.	Sgt.	3 N.R.	3/10/18	Nyangedi, 28–30/9/17
Empringham, H.	Sgt.	4 N.R.	3/10/18	Mahiwa, 16/10/17
Hawes, A. R.	Sgt.	2 N.R.	3/10/18	Bweho-Chini, 22/9/17
Sanders, W. T.	Sgt.	2 N.R.	3/10/18	Bweho-Chini, 22/9/17
Tasker, P. T.	Sgt.	1 N.R.	3/10/18	Mahiwa, 16/10/17
Watkins, J. H.	Sgt.	1 N.R.	3/10/18	Bweho-Chini 22/10/17
Gillan, A.	Bat.S.M.	A/N.R.	9/10/18	Mahiwa 15–17/10/17
Payne, C. W.	Sapper	Wireless/ N.Bde.	29/10/17	Bweho-Chini, 22/9/17
Botha, J. H.	Sgt.	S.A. Inf./ N.Bde.	24/12/17	Mahiwa, 16/10/17
Boyd, W. J.	Sgt.	S.A.Inf./ N.Bde.	24/12/17	Mahiwa, 16/10/17

Name	*Rank*	*Unit*	*Date of award*	*Remarks*
		MILITARY MEDAL (EUROPEAN)		
Dixon, F. J.	Sgt.	3 N.R.	30/3/17	Ngwembe, 24/1/17
Hunt, A.	Sgt.	4 N.R.	26/11/17	Mahiwa, 16/10/17
MacEwan, W. P.	Sgt.	S.A.Inf./ N.Bde.	24/12/17	Mahiwa, 8/11/17
		ITALIAN BRONZE MEDAL		
Newbrook, H.	C/Sgt.	1 N.R.	15/5/17	Mkindu, 18/1/17
Badger, C. W.	Sgt.	2 N.R.	15/5/17	1/1/17
Woolley, G.	Sgt.	3 N.R.	15/5/17	Ngwembe, 24/1/17
Tanner, W.	Sgt.	4 N.R.	15/5/17	24/1/17

MENTIONS IN DESPATCHES

Baigent, S/Sgt. H.	Badger, Sgt. C. W.
Carfree, C.S.M. W.	Blair, Sgt. H.
Catt, Q.M.S. A. W.	Dixon, Sgt. F. J.
Kelliher, Sgt. J. C.	Newbrook, Sgt. H.
Lamb, Sgt. F. E.	Ruffell, Sgt. F.
O'Bergin, Sgt. C. M. D.	Tanner, Sgt. W.
Russell, Sgt. G.	Woolley, Sgt. C.
Scott, Sgt. J.	Hunt, Sgt. A.
Wilton, C.S.M. E.	Kerry, Sgt. A.
Vicars, S.S.M. W. G.	Walter, Sgt. F. B.

AWARDS TO AFRICAN RANK AND FILE

No.	*Rank*	*Name*	*Unit*	*Date of award*	*Remarks*
			2ND BAR TO D.C.M.		
3087	C.S.M.	Sumanu	3 N.R.	10/10/18	Nyengedi, 30/11/17
			1ST BAR TO AFRICAN D.C.M.		
6410	C.S.M.	Momadu Kukawa	2 N.R.	15/1/18	Beho-Beho, 3/1/17
4245	C.S.M.	Momadu Bauchi	4 N.R.	10/10/18	Continuous devotion to duty and gallantry
3780	Sgt.	Andu Katsena	4 N.R.	10/10/18	Mkwera, 8/11/17
			Total 3		

	AFRICAN D.C.M.	MILITARY MEDAL	MERITORIOUS MEDAL	MENTION
Company Sergeant-Majors	8	6		10
Sergeants	7	8		10
Corporals	6	—		3
Bombardiers	1	—		2
Lance-Corporals	9	3		7
Gunners	1	—		2
Privates	15	12	1	7
Gun-Carriers	1	—		—
Machine-gun Carriers	2	1		1
Trumpeters	1	—		
Stretcher-bearers	1	—		—
Dressers	—	—		1
Carriers	—	—		2
Totals	52	30	1	45

LIST OF HONOURS AND DECORATIONS AWARDED TO EUROPEAN STAFF AND NATIVE RANK AND FILE OF THE GOLD COAST REGIMENT DURING THE EAST AFRICAN CAMPAIGN

Award	*Name*	*Date*
	(1) OFFICERS	
Bt. Lt.-Col.	Temp. Lt.-Col. R. A. de B. Rose, D.S.O.	7/10/17
	Maj. G. Shaw, M.C.	5/8/18
Bt.-Maj. on promotion to Capt.	Temp. Capt. T. B. C. Piggott, M.C.	5/8/18
D.S.O.	Maj. H. Goodwin	10/6/17
	Capt. H. A. Harman	10/6/17
Bar to D.S.O.	Temp. Lt.-Col. R. A. de B. Rose, D.S.O.	5/8/18
M.C.	Capt. G. Shaw	24/11/16
	Capt. A. J. R. O'Brien	24/11/16
	Capt. R. H. Poyntz	24/1/17
	Captain J. Leslie-Smith	13/8/18
	Capt. J. G. Foley	29/10/17
	Capt. H. B. Dawes	5/8/18
	Capt. T. B. C. Piggott	10/6/17
	Capt. G. H. Parker	11/3/18
	Capt. R. F. Beech	11/5/18
	Capt. G. B. Kinley	30/4/18
	Capt. L. B. Cumming	27/7/10
Bar to M.C.	Capt. G. Shaw, M.C.	13/8/17
	Capt. A. J. R. O'Brien, M.C.	13/8/17
	Capt. E. B. Methven, M.C.	5/11/17
	Capt. J. G. Foley	17/10/18
O.B.E.	Maj. H. Read	9/9/18
	(2) BRITISH N.C.O.S	
D.C.M.	7024 Cpl. J. Campbell	24/1/17
	9532 R.S.M. F. C. Medlock	10/6/17
	28399 Sgt. E. Thornton	19/7/17
	69845 Pte. S. G. Radford, R.A.M.C.	19/7/17
	1847 Sgt. C. A. Thornett	17/6/18
	7024 Cpl. J. Campbell	19/7/17
	(3) NATIVE RANK AND FILE	
D.C.M.	3948 Cpl. Akanno Ibadan	19/7/17
	113 M. G. C. John Lagos	19/7/17
	3844 C.S.M. Mumuni Moshi	19/7/17
	6727 Cpl. Jessufu Kotokoli	19/7/17
	5827 Sgt. Morismbah Moshi	19/7/17
	5737 Cpl. Musa Fulani	6/7/17
	6557 Temp. Cpl. Seti Frafra	24/11/16
	8427 Pte. Yaw Kums	19/7/17
	5493 Temp. Sgt. Chililah Grunshi	No date
	8581 L/Cpl. Granda Dikale	19/7/17

Award	*Name*	*Date*
	(3) NATIVE RANK AND FILE—*cont.*	
D.C.M.	7339 Tptr. Huaga Kusase	18/4/17
	5048 Cpl. Sandogo Moshi	No date
	5397 Dr. Musa Karaki	No date
	5655 Sgt. Alhaji Grunshi	19/7/17
	7817 Pte. Seidu Chokesi	20/9/17
	5860 L/Cpl. Issaka Dagarti	18/10/17
	4188 Sgt. Jessufu Mamprusi	18/10/17
	7426 Bglr. Nufu Moshi	1/10/17
	4157 C.S.M. Musa Womgara	11/4/17
	5225 Sgt. Mandu Moshi	25/5/17
Bar to D.C.M.	4961 Sgt. Bukara Kukawa	24/11/16
	6557 Temp. Cpl. Seti Frafra	15/8/17
M.M.	4188 Sgt. Yessufu Memprusi	19/7/17
	6689 Pte. Akuluga Moshi	19/7/17
	6414 Sgt. Palpuku Grumab	19/7/17
	182 M. G. C. Kwejeh Moshi	19/7/17
	109 M. G. C. Degali	19/7/17
	7842 Pte. Adama Bazaberimi	19/7/17
	7248 Pte. Allassan Grumah	15/12/16
	4765 Sgt. Braima Dagarti	15/12/16
	6690 L/Cpl. Kuka Moshi	15/12/16
	6756 Cpl. Timbala Busanga	15/12/16
	6675 Cpl. Yero Fulani	15/12/16
	13 H. G. C. Imoru Dodo	6/2/17
	5593 Cpl. Nuaga Moshi	11/4/17
	6688 Pte. Sebidu Moshi	11/4/17
	4388 B. S. M. Bukare Moshi	23/5/17
	137 Hdmn. G. C. Kwesi John	23/5/17
	94 G. C. Lawain Ibadan	23/5/17
	959 Sgt. Member	23/5/17
	8481 L/Cp. Ntonge Etun	24/11/16
	3851 Sgt. Ali Wongara	24/11/16
	200 S. B. Musa Kano	24/11/16
	170 S. B. Bawa Hausa	24/11/16
	5658 L/Cpl. Sulley Ibadan	24/1/17
M.S.M.	V.103 Cpl. J. W. H. Amartey	17/6/18
	O.R. Sgt. G. M. Fraser	17/6/18
	31 Q.M.Sgt. S. Amonoo Aidoo	17/6/18

APPENDIX VIII

Casualties (East African Campaign)

Below is given the Roll of Honour of the Nigerian Overseas Contingent for the whole period that they were in East Africa.

Officers Killed in Action or Died of Wounds

Maj. Green
Capt. Barclay
Capt. Cook
Capt. Dudley
Capt. Higgins
Capt. Stretton, M.C.
Capt. Norton Harper
Capt. Waters, M.C.
Lieut. Strong
Lieut. Ewen
Lieut. W. H. Harrison
Lieut. F. Oliver
Lieut. Joseland
Lieut. Stevenson
Lieut. F. H. Robinson
Lieut. H. W. Robinson
Lieut. Miller-Stirling
Lieut. Ryan
Lieut. Sutherland-Brown

British Non-commissioned Officers Killed in Action or Died of Wounds

C.Q.M.S. Lamb, D.C.M.
Sgt. Spratt
Sgt. Evans, D.C.M.
Sgt. Booth
Sgt. Tomlin
Sgt. Packe
Sgt. Riley

Officers Died of Diseases

Capt. the Hon. R. E. Noel
Lieut. Huddart
Lieut. Baker
Lieut. Catt, M.C.

British Non-commissioned Officers Died of Disease

Sgt. Powter
Sgt. S. Walker
Sgt. North
Sgt. Kelly
Sgt. Whitaker
Col.-Sgt. Duggan
Sgt-Maj. Dwyer

Officers and British Non-commissioned Officers Wounded and Prisoners of War (subsequently released unconditionally)

Maj. Gard'ner
Lieut. Jeffries
Col.-Sgt. Speak
Col.-Sgt. Wroe
Sgt. Woolley

Officers Severely Wounded

Maj. Waller, D.S.O.
Capt. and Adj. Collins, M.C.
Capt. A. C. Robinson, M.C.
Capt. Carson
Capt. O'Connell
Capt. Budgen
Capt. Allen (twice)
Capt. Armstrong, M.C.
Capt. Rickards
Capt. Pring, M.C.
Capt. Gardner, M.C.
Capt. Finch
Lieut. Newton
Lieut. Young
Lieut. Thompson
Lieut. Winter, M.C.
Lieut. Mytton
Lieut. Southby, M.C.
Lieut. Buchanan-Smith, M.C.
Lieut. Spaxman
Lieut. Graydon
Lieut. Fox
Lieut. Kellock
Lieut. Mulholland
Lieut. Bovill
Lieut. Cunningham
Lieut. Hawkins

Officers Slightly Wounded

Lieut.-Col. Feneran
Lieut.-Col. T. M. R. Leonard
Maj. Gibb
Capt. O'Connell
Lieut. Studley, M.C.
Lieut. and Adj. Winter, M.C.
Lieut. Steed
Lieut. Grandfield
Lieut. Hillman
Lieut. Edwards
Lieut. Snape
Lieut. Jerrim
Lieut. Dyer
Lieut. Pomeroy

British Non-commissioned Officers Severely Wounded

Sgt. Reilly
Sgt. Dixon
Sgt. Trandark
Col-Sgt. Kerry
Col.-Sgt. Watkins
Sgt. M'Knight
Sgt. Ward
Sgt. Darke
Sgt. Manad

British Non-commissioned Officers Slightly Wounded

Col.-Sgt. Hunsworth
Sgt. Fraser
Sgt. Booth
Sgt. O'Bergin
Sgt. Hunt, M.M.
Sgt. Tanner
Sgt. Empringham

Accidentally Wounded

Capt. Drake

Officers Invalided out of German East Africa from Diseases Contracted on Active Service

Lieut. and Act. Adj. Travers
Lieut. H. de B. Bewley
Capt. R. R. Taylor
Lieut. R. H. Wortham
Capt. H. C. Faussett
Capt. E. T. P. Ford
Lieut. Harris, M.M.
Lieut. B. G. Cavanagh
Lieut. Harrison
Lieut. R. F. Forrest
Lieut. Rutland
Lieut. W. E. Burr
Lieut. W. B. Preston
Lieut. Avary
Lieut. Marlow
Lieut. Hobson
Lieut. Wood

British Non-commissioned Officers Permanently Invalided out of German East Africa from Diseases Contracted on Active Service

B.S.M. Thorogood
Arm. Sgt. Collins
Sgt. Pearce
Sgt. Grinyer
Sgt. Taylor

The following table gives the numbers of native ranks and file killed or died of wounds, or died from the result of accidents incurred by Active Service conditions, died of disease, and wounded, during the whole campaign. In addition many deaths occurred during the return voyage to Nigeria, which are not included in this table. This list does not include deaths of men repatriated on account of wounds or disease, who died after leaving East Africa.

Company	*Killed*	*Died*	*Wounded*
No. 1	38	10	52
No. 2	17	8	38
No. 3	15	16	63
No. 4	7	8	11
No. 5	7	12	47
No. 6	11	11	33
No. 7	13	14	24
No. 8	9	7	26
No. 9	35	5	76
No. 10	41	16	75
No. 11	16	10	24
No. 12	32	7	86
No. 13	22	15	38
No. 14	14	11	19
No. 15	13	18	26
No. 16	22	19	49
Battery	23	17	22
Pioneer Section	3	3	6
Drafts	12	56	31

CASUALTIES (EAST AFRICAN CAMPAIGN)

GOLD COAST REGIMENT

	Killed	*Wounded*	*Missing*	*Died of disease*	*Invalided*
Officers	9	21	—	3	30
B.N.C.O.s	6	9	—	4	15
Rank and file	181	603	13	206	469
Gun-carriers	9	56	—	16	28
Stretcher-bearers	—	3	—	—	—
Clerks	—	—	—	1	1
Carriers	10	33	—	40	24
Total	215	725	13	270	567

APPENDIX IX

W.A.F.F. Honours

CAMEROONS

Officers

		Date
K.C.B.	Maj.-Gen. C. M. Dobell, C.M.G., D.S.O.	29/4/16
C.B.	Brig.-Gen. F. H. G. Cuncliffe, C.M.G.	3/6/16
	Brig.-Gen. C. M. Dobell, D.S.O.	1/1/15
C.M.G.	Major W. D. Wright, V.C., D.S.O.	3/6/16
	Brig.-Gen. F. H. G. Cunliffe	23/6/15
	Major J. Brough, M.V.O.	23/6/15
D.S.O.	Maj. (Temp. Lt.-Col.) A. H. W. Haywood	23/6/15
	Capt. J. Crookenden	3/6/16
	Capt. J. F. P. Butler, V.C.	3/6/16
	Capt. J. P. D. Underwood	3/6/16
	Capt. R. J. R. Waller	3/6/16
	Maj. C. F. S. McClaverty	23/6/15
	Maj. G. Howell	23/6/15
	Capt. M. H. S. Willis	3/6/16
	Maj. R. A. de B. Rose	14/1/16
	Maj. D. G. Mann, R.A.	14/1/16
	Maj. C. R. U. Savile	14/1/16
M.C.	Capt. A. E. Beattie	23/6/15
	Capt. H. D. S. O'Brien	23/6/15
	Capt. C. H. Fowle	3/6/16
	Capt. F. J. H. Pring	3/6/16
	Capt. R. H. Rowe	23/6/15
	Capt. E. L. Salier	14/1/16
Bt. Lt.-Col.	Maj. J. B. Cockburn, R. Welch Fus.	23/6/15
	Maj. J. Brough, C.M.G., M.V.O., R. Marines	3/6/16
Bt.-Maj	Capt. C. Gibb, R. Scots Fus.	3/6/16
	Capt. R. H. Rowe, R.A.	3/6/16
	Capt. A. E. Beattie, R.W. Surrey Regt.	3/6/16
Victoria Cross	Capt. J. F. P. Butler, K.R.R.C.	23/8/15
Promotion to Maj.-Gen.	Brig.-Gen. C. M. Dobell, C.M.G., D.S.O.	23/6/15

TOGOLAND

C.M.G.	Capt. (Temp. Lt.-Col.) F. E. Bryant, R.A.	28/10/14
D.S.O.	Capt. H. B. Potter, E. Kent Regt.	28/10/14
M.C.	Capt. C. G. Hornby, E. Lancs Regt.	28/10/14

FOREIGN DECORATIONS (FRENCH)

Legion of Honour

(Commandeur)	Maj.-Gen. Sir Charles Dobell	22/10/17
(Officier)	Lt.-Cols. Cockburn, Haywood, Rose	22/10/17
(Chevalier)	Majors Coles, Crookenden, Mair	22/10/17

Croix de Guerre, with Palm

Major (Temp. Lt-Col.) A. H. W. Haywood 9/2/16

Rank and File

	Artillery	*Infantry*
Nigeria Regiment	10	119
Gold Coast Regiment	2	16
Sierra Leone Battalion		4
Gambia Company		3
Total	12	142
Grand Total	154	

Note. Owing to the difficulty of tracing names and confirming records, it has not been found possible to give names.

APPENDIX X

Order of Battle

CAMEROONS ANGLO-FRENCH EXPEDITIONARY FORCE

23rd September 1914

G.H.Q.

G.O.C.	Brig.-Gen. C. M. Dobell, D.S.O., A.D.C. (I.G. W.A.F.F.)
A.D.C.	Lieut. G. E. R. de Miremont, R. Welch Fus. (S/L Bn. W.A.F.F.)
Senior G.S.O.	Lt.-Col. A. J. Turner, R.A. } (Staff Officers to I.G. W.A.F.F.)
G.S.O.	Maj. J. Brough, M.V.O., R.M.A. } (Staff Officers to I.G. W.A.F.F.)
French G.S.O. attached	Capt. A. Charvet
D.A.A. and Q.M.G.	Capt. R. H. Rowe, R.A.
D. of Signals	Capt. F. L. N. Giles, R.E.
D. of Medical Services	Maj. J. C. B. Statham, R.A.M.C.
D.of S. and T.	Capt. S. A. Wallbach
Financial Officer	Mr. H. St. J. Sheppard
Political Officer	Mr. K. V. Elphinstone
Intelligence Officer	Lieut. D. McCallum

G.H.Q. Troops

Camp Comdt. — Lieut. A. McC. Inglis, Gloucester Regt. (Gambia Coy., W.A.F.F.)

H.Q. Escort
Signal Coy.
(Railway Sec., Lieut. H. E. Kentish, R.E.)
Capt. P. J. Mackesy, R.E.
(Telegraph Sec., Lieut. H. M. Woolley)
(Field Sec., Lieut. C. V. S. Jackson, R.E.)

BRITISH CONTINGENT

B.H.Q.

O.C.	Col. E. H. Gorges, D.S.O.
2 I.C.	Lt.-Col. F. H. Cunliffe (Nigeria Regt., W.A.F.F.)
G.S.O.	Maj. W. D. Wright, V.C., Queens' Royal Regt. (Nigeria Regt., W.A.F.F.)
Attached G.S.	Capt. H. G. Howell, R.A. (Nigeria Regt., W.A.F.F.)
Staff Capt.	Capt. C. R. U. Savile, R. Fusiliers (Nigeria Regt., W.A.F.F.)
Staff Capt. attached	Capt. C. H. Dinnen, King's Liverpool Regt.
Sen. Medical Officer	Maj. W. G. H. Best, R.A.M.C. Spec. Res.
Ordnance Officer	Maj. H. W. G. Meyer-Griffith

H.Q. Troops

Pioneer Coy., G.C. Regt. — Capt. H. Goodwin, Middlesex Regt. (G.C. Regt., W.A.F.F.)

Artillery

S/Leone Coy. R.G.A.	Capt. N. d'A. Fitzgerald, R.A. Four 2·95 in. guns
No. 1 Bty. Nigeria Regt.	Capt. C. F. S. Maclaverty, R.A. Four 2·95 in. guns (W.A.F.F.)
Sec. Gold Coast Regt. Bty.	Lieut. W. L. St Clair, R.A. Two 2·95 in. guns (W.A.F.F.)

Infantry

West African Regt. (W.A.R.)	Lt.-Col. E. Vaughan, Manchester Regt. H.Q. and 6 coys.
No. 1 Bn. Nigeria Regt. (1 N.R.)	Lt.-Col. J. B. Cockburn, R. Welch Fus. (W.A.F.F.) H.Q. and 4 coys.
No. 2 Bn. Nigeria Regt. (2 N.R.)	Lt.-Col. A. H. W. Haywood, R.A. (W.A.F.F.) H.Q. and 4 coys.
Composite Bn.	Lt.-Col. R. A. de B. Rose, Worcester Regt., (W.A.F.F.) H.Q. and 2 coys. G.C.R. and 2 coys. S/L Bn. (W.A.F.F.)

Medical

S. and T.

Total: 154 officers; 81 B.N.C.O.s; 2,460 native ranks; 3,563 carriers; 10 guns (2·95 in.).

FRENCH CONTINGENT

O.C. Col. Meyer

Four Staff Officers and Capt. H. T. Horsford, Gloucester Regt., attached for liaison.

Artillery

One Mtn. Bty. (Capt. Gerrard) (six guns)

Infantry

One Coy. European Colonial Inf. Capt. Salvetat

No. 1 Senegalese Bn. (Commandant Mechet)

No. 2 Senegalese Bn. (Commandant Mathieu)

Engineers

One sec. (Capt. Chardy)

Medical, Ammunition and Transport details

Total: 54 officers; 354 Europeans; 1,859 native ranks; 1,000 carriers; 200 animals (Bty. mules and horses).

APPENDIX XI

Dispositions of W.A.F.F., 1919

NIGERIA REGIMENT

1st Battalion	H.Q. and 2 companies	Kaduna
	1 company	Sokoto
	1 company	Kano
	1 company	Keffi
	1 company	Bauchi
	1 company	Katagum, Zungeru
2nd Battalion	H.Q. and 3 companies	Lokoja
	1 company	Nafada
	1 company	Abinsi, Womba
	1 company	Yola, Ankpa
3rd Battalion	H.Q. and 2 companies	Calabar
	1 company	Bamenda
	1 company	Obudu, Okigwi
	1 company	Owerri, Abakaliki
	1 company	Ossidinge
4th Battalion	H.Q. and 1 company	Lagos
	1 company	Okwoga
	1 company	Onitsha
	1 company	Soppo
	1 company	Agbor
	1 company	Udi
5th Battalion	H.Q. and 1 company	Kano
	1 company	Sokoto
	1 company	Geidam (or Maiduguri)
Artillery	1st Battery	Zaria
	2nd Battery	Calabar

GOLD COAST REGIMENT

Infantry	H.Q. and 5 companies (1 Pioneer)	Kumasi
	1 company	Accra
	1 company	Lome
	1 company	Tamale
Artillery	1 battery (4 guns)	Kumasi

SIERRA LEONE BATTALION

H.Q. and 3 companies	Daru
1 company	Makene
1 company	Bandajuma
1 company	Kanrelahun (or, Kailahun)

GAMBIA COMPANY

H.Q. and 1 company	Bathurst

APPENDIX XII

Bibliography

Histories of campaigns	*Title*	*Author*
Ashanti, 1900	*Kabul to Kumasi*	Willcocks
	Official History	Beddoes
	History of Gold Coast and Ashanti	Claridge
	Official Despatches, W. Africa	*London Gazettes*
Cameroons and Togoland, 1914–16	*Official History*	Moberly
	The Great War in W. Africa	Gorges
	War Diaries and Despatches	War Office Records
	The Empire at War, Vols. I–IV	Lucas
	Der Grosse Krieg, Vol. IV	Schwartze
East African Campaign, 1914–18	*Official History*, Vol. I, 1914–16	Hordern
	With the Nigerians in E. Africa	Downes
	The Gold Coast Regiment in the E. African Campaign	Clifford
	General Smuts's Campaign in East Africa	Crowe
	E. African Force 1915–19	Fendall
	War Diaries and Despatches	War Office Records
	My Reminiscences of E. Africa	Von Lettow-Vorbeck
Minor Tribal Campaigns and Operations, 1892–99	Parliamentary Papers for the relevant years	Foreign or Colonial Office
Minor Tribal Campaigns and Operations, 1900–9	Annual Reports for Nigeria. (Northern and Southern Nigeria are shown separately.)	Colonial Office
North Sudan Campaign,	*Campaigning on the Upper Niger and Nile*	Vandeleur
Sierra Leone Rising, 1898	*The Advance of our West African Empire*	C. B. Wallis

Note. The two last are not official, but give a very good account of these important 'Small Wars'.

Histories of Countries of Origin	*Author*
Gambia	Lady Southern
Ghana, History of	W. E. F. Ward
Gold Coast and Ashanti, History of	Claridge
Making of Northern Nigeria	Orr
Nigeria, History of	Alan Burns
Native Problems in Africa	R. L. Buell
Natives of the Northern Territories	A. W. Cardinall
Lugard, Vols. I and II	Margery Perham
Ibo and Ibibio Speaking People	D. Forde and G. I. Jones
Short History of Sierra Leone	J. J. Crowe
Tropical Dependency, A	Lady Lugard (Flora Shaw)
Transformed Colony (Sierra Leone), A	T. J. Aldridge
Yorubas, A history of the	Johnson

W.A.F.F. Records and Narratives

Colonial Office files in P.R.O.
Serial Nos. 642(7) and (8)
Serial Nos. 445 (10 to (28)

Barracks and Bush in Northern Nigeria	H. C. Hall
Bush Warfare	Heneker
Short History of the Nigeria Regiment	Lt.-Col. G. S. Taylor
Short History of the Sierra Leone Battalion	Lieut. R. P. M. Davis
Five Years Hard Northern Nigeria	Crozier
With the W.A.F.F. in Northern Nigeria	Lord Esme Gordon-Lennox

Various articles in the *R.U.S.I. Journal* and other magazines

The History of the Ghana Regiment	H.Q. Ghana Army
Nigerian Regimental Museum	Pamphlet by Capt. H. A. J. W. Stacpoole

APPENDIX XIII

Glossary

askari	African soldier trained by Europeans.
C.A.R.	Central African Rifles.
doki	Hausa name for horse.
G.C.R.	Gold Coast Regiment.
I.G.	Inspector-General W.A.F.F.
jehad	holy war.
K.A.R.	King's African Rifles
K.	abbreviation for German company.
mallam	term for Mussulman holy man, or learned man.
matchet	a heavy knife, or cutlass, part of W.A.F.F. rank and file equipment.
N.N.R.	Northern Nigeria Regiment.
N.R.	Nigeria Regiment.
N.T.	Northern Territories of the Gold Coast (now Ghana).
patrol	often used to denote a small military operation.
S/L	Sierra Leone
S.N.R.	Southern Nigeria Regiment.
W.A.R.	West African Regiment.
W.A.M.S.	West African Medical Service.
W.I.R.	West India Regiment.

PART II, 1920–1961

By

BRIGADIER F. A. S. CLARKE

D.S.O., p.s.c†.

PREFACE TO PART II

THIS Part of the History of the R.W.A.F.F. is based on official documents, supplemented by reminiscences and narratives by officers who served with the Force in peace and war. The object has been to present the facts as correctly as possible with but few comments, the author believing with Francis Bacon that the reader should exercise his own judgment.

During the Second World War the R.W.A.F.F. served in the East African campaign and on the Arakan front in Burma. Both are of considerable interest as examples of major operations in different types of undeveloped country against dissimilar adversaries. It is thought that descriptions of the operations in some detail will be of value to officers as the Official History of the campaigns deals with them on a very high level with practically no tactical narratives. Therefore, every effort has been made to produce a detailed narrative of the part played by the R.W.A.F.F. in these campaigns, and also to provide the strategic background.

There has been considerable difficulty in furnishing this Part with suitable maps and sketch-maps. The Burmese place names are often long and full of apparently useless consonants; the spelling on the East African maps was found to be much varied. However, with the aid of the Ordnance Survey, an attempt has been made to produce maps and sketch-maps which will enable the narratives to be followed intelligently.

I feel that this History will bring back happy memories to old 'Waffs' and will enhance their admiration and affection for their African comrades. Furthermore, I trust that this History will provide inspiration for those whose honour it is to carry on the traditions of the three Regiments now and in the future. I also venture to hope that this History will be read by many who have not served in the R.W.A.F.F. From it they will learn something of the sterling qualities of the West African soldier and of his splendid achievements under British officers about which so little is generally known.

ACKNOWLEDGMENTS

My thanks are due to those who have given me assistance either by providing material and/or reading the chapters covering events in which they were particularly concerned. These include, among several others General Sir George Giffard, G.C.B., D.S.O.; General Sir Hugh Stockwell, K.C.B., K.B.E., D.S.O.; Major-General C. G. Woolner, C.B., M.C.; Major-General J. Y. Whitfield, C.B., D.S.O., O.B.E.; Major-General C. R. A. Swynnerton, C.B., D.S.O.; Major-General A. H. G. Ricketts, C.B.E., D.S.O.; Major-General A. V. Paley, C.B., C.B.E., D.S.O.; Major-General C. B. Fairbanks, C.B., C.B.E.; Major-General J. H. Inglis, C.B., C.B.E.; Brigadier G. B. S. Hindley, O.B.E.; Brigadier E. H. G. Grant,

C.B.E., D.S.O., M.C.; Brigadier P. G. F. Young, C.B.E.; Lieutenant-Colonel P. F. Pritchard, O.B.E., M.C., late 4th Battalion the Nigeria Regiment; Lieutenant-Colonel C. G. Bowen, late 5th Battalion the Gold Coast Regiment; Major S. G. B. Francis, Depot The Queen's Own Nigeria Regiment; Captain F. K. Butler, late 3rd Battalion the Nigeria Regiment.

I owe much to my wife for her cheerful assumption of responsibility for the discharge of the various tiresome jobs that accumulate during the preparation of a history of this nature. Of course, parts of the story awakened pleasant memories of the days of long ago.

I am also indebted to the Editor of *The Army Quarterly and Defence Journal* for permission to reproduce in Chapter 3 extracts from an article of mine which appeared in the October 1947 number of that publication. My thanks are also due to Miss P. C. McGlinchy (of Camberley), who speedily accomplished the monumental task of typing the fair copies of the History for the printer and others.

Finally, I must acknowledge the many kind offers received from 'Old Coasters' to provide photographs, but at the same time to signify my regret that so few can be accepted owing to the expense involved in reproduction.

F.A.S.C.

June 1961

CHAPTER 7

The Years Between the Wars

(i) *Conditions in West Africa*

WEST AFRICA was still a land where the improbable is normal and the impossible occurred often enough to make life interesting. Plenty of uncanny things did happen but, what was worse, some people tried to explain them. However, the 'Coast' by the twenties had ceased to warrant the title of the 'White Man's Grave',[1] and those who contemplated serving in Nigeria, or even other parts of West Africa, had no longer need of the warning contained in the old jingle:

'Beware and take heed of the Bight of Benin,
Where few come out though many go in.'

Government House, Lagos, too, had long since ceased to be 'a corrugated iron coffin that contained a dead Governor once every year'.

Most of the improvement was due to increased medical knowledge, improving sanitary conditions and the adoption of simple precautions such as the daily dose of quinine. Nevertheless, a tour of 18 months was considered long enough. However, even in the late twenties there were still large numbers of 'bush houses' which harbour all kinds of pests. These, like their counterparts in North-Western India, were cool enough by day but infernally hot by night.

Juju was, and probably still is, a power in the land. As late as 1937 the following warning was given to troops competing in the Annual Regimental Sports in Nigeria, and confirmed in print on the programmes: 'Any team or individual displaying a juju, or anything purporting to be a juju or charm, or claiming to possess a juju, will be disqualified.'

The following contribution by an officer who served in West Africa from 1927 to 1933 gives a good picture of service in Southern Nigeria during that period:[2]

'I arrived in Nigeria in February 1927 and was to enjoy the happiest time of my life there until I returned to my British Regiment. I found I had been posted to the 4th Battalion of the Nigeria Regiment which was stationed at Ibadan. . . . At Ibadan we lived in "bush houses", that is houses built of mud, with grass roofs and matting "doors" and "window" coverings. Since we received five pounds a month Bush Allowance for this we were contented enough. The visit of the then Prince of Wales in 1925 had led to the construction of a very roomy and airy officer's mess and a squash court. The mess was not elaborate, but it was well laid out and

[1] In Lagos in 1896, 28 out of 150 Europeans died within a few months. In 1926, out of an estimated European population for the whole of Nigeria of just under 5,000, there were only 42 deaths.

[2] Lieutenant-Colonel P. F. Pritchard.

comfortable. A long *punkah*, hand—or usually foot-operated—from behind a screen by a *punkah* boy, kept the dining-room coolish and the table reasonably clear of flies, flying ants and all the other winged insects which abounded. In those days no wives were permitted to join their husbands in the Nigeria Regiment and so consequently every officer lived in the mess. This led to a real regimental life and the building of houses for married officers and the arrival a few years later of their wives in the country detracted, in my humble opinion, from the pleasant mess life which had previously existed.[1]

'The troops were first-class. I have served with and in the company of many troops—British, Indian, African, Burmese, Egyptian and Gurkha to name most of those with whom I am familiar, but for my money and for enjoyable soldiering give me the Hausa soldier of the 1920s. He was as keen as mustard, as clean as a new pin, as hard as nails and as brave as a lion. Superimposed on all this was his delightful childish nature. His infectious smile and cheerful laugh were a great inspiration to those of us who had the privilege of training and leading him.

'The officer strength of the Battalion would be composed of a dozen or more British Regiments. A number of the officers had 15 to 18 years' service, were much decorated, but due to the system of promotion then obtaining in the British Army were still subalterns. Service in the W.A.F.F. gave them the chance to escape from the deadly boredom of home service—with its too frequent tours of duty as orderly officer. It also provided opportunities for sport—including polo, racing, shooting and fishing. These activities, and many more, could all be done on one's pay. Furthermore, it also afforded prospects of promotion to local rank in the W.A.F.F. For the British non-commissioned officer who was seconded to the W.A.F.F. there was also the valuable factor that his service counted as double.

'Transport, as known in the British Army, did not exist. All loads were carried on the heads of porters (or carriers as they were called). In each company the Lewis-gun team was accompanied by their "gun-carriers". All weapons, other than personal weapons, ammunition and equipment were similarly carried on men's heads. This even extended to the Mortar Battery and the "Mountain Gun" Battery. I forget how long it took this very efficient Gunner unit to assemble their guns and fire the first round, but it was an amazingly short time. No tentage existed, so none was carried. On manoeuvres we lived in huts made by the troops from grass and branches.'

Domestic arrangements in barracks were equally simple. The troops fed themselves, receiving 'chop money' each week in addition to their pay, which was issued monthly. All African troops, except recruits, had 'wives' in barracks who cooked for their lords and kept the huts and lines clean. Each company had a head-woman, the *magajia*, who was responsible for the cleanliness of the lines as well as the dress, deportment and general behaviour of the 'wives'. These head-women attended on 'company request day', usually a Thursday, which was a similar institution to that which existed in the old Indian Army. One of their duties was to accom-

[1] Some notes on regimental customs will be found in Appendix I.

pany any inspecting officer or other personage round their lines. They wore a sergeant's red sash and in the South wore a khaki drill jacket with sergeant's stripes as well. In the North they curtsied, Hausa fashion, in the South they saluted—and very well they did it.

After his first leave Pritchard was sent to one of the small out-stations which existed in those days. The detachment consisted of a platoon, commanded by a subaltern, who had a British N.C.O. to assist him. Pritchard's destination, Agbor, was a small village to the east of Benin City. It was the headquarters of an Assistant District Officer and a doctor, both of whom spent most of their time on tour. A prison completed the Government establishments at the place.

'The country', he writes, 'was very enclosed and it was necessary to turn the troops to grass cutting practically every day, after the conclusion of morning parades. Armed with their formidable matchets they would form long lines and commence to move steadily forward, cutting down the grass as they went. I always thought this showed the happy-go-lucky African soldier at his best. As they worked, snatches of song and topical quips and jokes broke out up and down the line. Every man was happy and smiling and if one listened carefully one could pick up many interesting asides on matters of the moment. In the wet season it rained almost continuously and the downpour had to be experienced to be believed and appreciated. My bush house had a tin roof and the noise of the rain beating down on that was only countered by my playing the most tumultuous passages from Wagner's Ring, using the loudest needles I possessed.

'During the eleven months of my stay in Agbor I lived on tinned food almost exclusively. There were practically no fresh vegetables, no bread or fish, and meat was a great rarity.

'On taking over the outstation I saw that the map pinned to my office wall had the surrounding country marked as "Impenetrable Bush". Being young, keen and a "new broom", I soon decided to burst this fallacy wide open, and one bright morning sallied forth with my command to carry out a march through this unconquerable terrain. After a very few hours I was forced to the conclusion that my predecessors had been correct in the nomenclature they had applied. We were almost torn to shreds by the creepers and other tropical growths, had made progress which a snail would have rejected and were all physically exhausted from our efforts. I had set out to hack our way through the bush on a compass bearing, but I had reluctantly to admit that if any progress was to be made, we should have to keep to the bush-paths. In the event of operations, these paths were invariably death traps to the unlucky men detailed as point of the advanced guard to a force using them. An enemy had only to poke his weapons through the dense bush, let fly at the oncoming troops and then melt away into the obscurity of the undergrowth. The weapons took the form of "dane guns"—long-handled, muzzle-loading guns—which were filled with old bits of iron, nails, etc., rather unpleasant objects which invariably caused shocking wounds. It was a country which was ideal for ambushes and progress had necessarily to be slow. Added to any expedition's worries was always the long "tail" of unarmed porters who had to be sandwiched in among the fighting men and in addition to being protected had also to be watched in case they should suddenly take fright at any enemy offensive action, down loads and take to the bush.' (See Appendix II.)

By 1935 'bush houses' had disappeared from all but the small stations and Zaria. There also, the old bush mess, an affectionately regarded 'Heath Robinson' building, was still going strong. It continues to do so and, in fact, seems likely to be scheduled as an 'ancient monument'.

Kaduna had the appearance of an Indian cantonment, especially in its layout, but the bungalows were better and instead of a 'cantonment magistrate' the civil authority was represented by a 'local authority' who was also lord of the mango trees. The station was the Headquarters of the Northern Provinces and as such boasted an imposing Secretariat office where, no doubt, files passed from one official to another in slow decorum. At intervals a red-painted basket mounted on three wheels, surely a relic of Victorian London's parcel post, emerged from the Secretariat and was pedalled in leisurely fashion to Government House, some distance away. Those in the know whispered that this exotic vehicle carried files—weighty in both senses of the word. Kaduna also possessed a discreet building where the Freemasons conducted their ceremonies and had their feasts. This was called by local African the *gidan juju*. Such establishments in India were known as the *jadu Ghar*, which being interpreted means 'the house of magic'. Curious uninamity between Africa and Asia.

Some stations were, of course, more popular than others. In Nigeria, Kaduna, Zaria and Kano were preferred by most people. The new station at Enugu and that at Ibadan were rather 'steamy', while Lagos and Calabar suffered from excessive humidity. At Calabar, too, no ponies could be kept, and the old hands were said to grow web feet. To be sent there was regarded by some, not without reason, to be a form of banishment.

In Gold Coast, Kumasi and Accra seemed to be most favoured, though Tamale had a better climate—hot and dry. Kintampo, a very bush place with a similar climate, had been a large and important station of the old Gold Coast Constabulary up to the turn of the century. It was closed down in 1933, reopened in 1940 and abandoned at the end of the war. It seems to have had a bad name, possibly due to the 'Juju Rock', a large block of granite some 20 ft. high facing the old civil station. Though not so imposing as the 'Juju Rock' in the Niger at Jebba, there are almost as many stories about its power: the local population believed it had an especially malign influence over white men. Be this as it may, Kintampo was disliked and during the last war was regarded, perhaps unjustly, as a penal station.

It is said that in Sierra Leone, the up-country stations of Mekene and Daru were preferred to Freetown, possibly on account of the humid climate of the latter. In Gambia, the 'Coast of Dreams', there was, of course, no choice of stations.

It was often necessary to warn new arrivals, especially those who had served east of Suez, not to use the word 'jungle' when referring to the bush or even to the tropical forest, such a term being anathema to all good old 'Coasters'. However, various descriptions were applied by British N.C.O.s to the bush in general. A polite version, overheard from the upper veranda of Headquarters at Kaduna, was: 'Miles and miles of sweet Fanny Adams', applied to the impressive view of miles and miles of orchard bush extending to the far horizon and shimmering in the midday sun.

New-comers were often struck by the jovial, well-fed appearance of the convicts and were usually told they regarded their detention as a good Government job. There were many stories extant about these prisoners of which the following is an instance.

The warder with a gang out grass-cutting near the Kaduna Racecourse suddenly decided to desert. Putting down his carbine, he started to take off his uniform. The prisoners gathered round, surprised and annoyed. The warder said 'I'm off', or words to that effect.

'Oh, no, you not go,' replied the senior prisoner, picking up the carbine and assuming command. 'We catch plenty trouble too much if you done run away.'

Forming up the gang, with the warder in their midst, and carrying the carbine correctly at the slope, the senior prisoner marched the party back to the prison. One would like to add that he afterwards became a warder, but that would not be true.

There is also a much older story of a convict who stepped out of the ranks when a work party was being marched back to the prison and assaulted a passer-by. When the affair was enquired into the man was asked why he had beaten a peaceful citizen. His reply was: 'He no salute the King's Prisoners!'

It is necessary, perhaps, to establish clearly that many queer tales are told in Africa. Lots of them are hardly believable even when they are true.

Few will disagree with the statement that West Africa, though a hard taskmaster, has a peculiar attraction. Further, that many, not least those who served in the R.W.A.F.F., fell under its spell. What is more likely to linger in his memory than the 'Hausa Farewell' sounded for an officer when he leaves Nigeria for the last time?[1]

After the lapse of quite a short period at home recollections of the trials and discomforts of service in Africa are apt to become overshadowed and thoughts to dwell on the pleasant things, and on memories of the Regiment and its African soldiers. All of which leads to a type of nostalgia, not the true kind perhaps, but a longing for the haunts of yesteryear tinged with regrets for the days that are no more. Who has not on a cold, raw winter's day at home thought kindly of the orchard bush shimmering in the sun, or even of the sticky heat of Lagos or Accra?

(II) *Peacetime Soldiering*

During the early twenties the W.A.F.F. settled down to peacetime soldiering once more, but suffered the usual post-war economies. In Nigeria, during 1922, the 5th (Mounted Infantry) Battalion and one of the batteries were disbanded. Out of the ashes of the latter unit arose a short-lived mortar battery which was stationed at Ibadan. A Regimental

[1] See Appendix I (5).

Depot was formed at Zaria in 1924 and a signal unit was established there during the same year. Regimental Headquarters had moved to Kaduna and from 1924 the troops' records were kept there instead of by units. There were at this time a number of small detachments, but the headquarters of battalions were stationed as follows:

1st	Kaduna	3rd	Calabar
2nd	Kano[1]	4th	Ibadan

Each now consisted of four rifle companies and a machine-gun section.

After the reductions at the end of the war the Gold Coast Regiment consisted of a Headquarters, one infantry battalion and a battery. The battalion was organized in four companies, each of three platoons. There was also a machine-gun platoon and a pioneer company. The stations of the Regiment at this period were Tamale, Kumasi, Accra and Kintampo. During 1923 one rifle company and the pioneers were disbanded. However, in 1926, the fourth rifle company was restored, a Regimental Depot was formed and four years later the machine-gun platoon was expanded into a company of eight guns.

The Sierra Leone Battalion consisted of Headquarters, a signal section and two companies which alternated between Daru and Mekene. Gambia retained its single company.

In 1922 Colours were presented to battalions of the W.A.F.F. in recognition of their services in the War of 1914–18. Six years later the W.A.F.F. had the honour of becoming a Royal Corps with H.M. King George V as the first Colonel-in-Chief. In the same year an Imperial unit, the West African Regiment, stationed at Freetown, was disbanded, and thus the R.W.A.F.F. became responsible for safeguarding the Colony and Protectorate of Sierra Leone instead of only the latter.

There is an old story about the receipt of the news by the Sierra Leone Battalion that H.M. King George V would become the first Colonel-in-Chief of the R.W.A.F.F. It appears that the Commanding Officer tried to translate the notification to the assembled Battalion into pidgin English and to explain what the honour meant. When he had finished the men broke into three lusty cheers and he then ordered that 'the rest of the day would be observed as a holiday'. That night he asked his orderly why the troops had suddenly cheered and was somewhat nonplussed at the reply: 'Sah. Dey t'ink we get new C.O.'

Since the war a number of minor patrols had been carried out. In 1929, however, the R.W.A.F.F. in Nigeria was called upon for 'Duty in Aid of the Civil Power' on a larger scale. At this time the detailed distribution of the Nigeria Regiment was as follows:

1st Battalion		*3rd Battalion*	
Headquarters	Kaduna	Headquarters	Calabar
Three companies less two platoons	Kaduna	One company	Calabar
One company	Zaria	One company	Abakaliki
Two platoons	Zuru	One company	Okigwi
		One company	Ankpa

[1] Moved from Lokoja to Kano in 1925.

African N.C.O.'s in full dress

Guard of Honour, Kaduna, 1936

Hausa Soldier of the Nigeria Regiment in full marching order, 1937

Face page 321

2nd Battalion		*4th Battalion*	
Headquarters	Kano	Headquarters	Ibadan
One company	Kano	Three companies less one platoon	Ibadan
One company	Maiduguri		
One company	Sokoto	One company	Lagos
One company	Yola	One platoon	Agbor

Light Battery	Zaria
Signal Company	Zaria
Regimental Depot	Zaria
Mortar Battery	Ibadan

In early December 1929 widespread disturbances began in the Calabar and Owerri Provinces of Southern Nigeria which developed into what afterwards became known as the 'Aba Riots' or *Yakin Mata.* The cause of the trouble appears to have been primarily a prevalent rumour that the Government, having taken a census, intended to impose a tax on all women; secondly, that the prices of local produce had fallen very low. There are indications, however, that there was a guiding hand at work behind the scenes.

During the second week in December riotous crowds of women broke into the 'factories' at Aba and Imo River. Meeting with no serious resistance, they looted the stores and were successful in getting away with their booty by land and water. The sight of canoes loaded with loot going down-river past Opobo led to the belief that women could sack the factories with impunity. Furthermore, the women had become convinced that the authorities would not allow the troops or police to fire on them. The disturbances spread rapidly throughout the two Provinces and lasted until the middle of January 1930.

The 3rd Battalion was the first to become involved and on 15th December one platoon, sent to Opobo, was forced to open fire on a large mob of women; on the same day another platoon had to open fire on a similar gathering at Abak and at Uti-Etim-Ekpo. A description of the former episode will be found in Appendix III.

Reinforcements were soon despatched to Aba, the centre of the disturbed area. Two companies of the 1st Battalion left Kaduna on 14th December by rail and arrived on the 16th. Two companies of the 4th Battalion arrived, one on the 18th and the other on the 20th. They were employed in patrolling, 'showing the flag' and dispersing mobs of women. It is interesting to note that on one occasion a platoon formed square with bayonets fixed at a place called Okpala.

An officer of the 4th Battalion, hastily summoned from his detachment at Agbor, spent six weeks trekking from place to place in the district north of Calabar and living on the country. He was successful in dispersing small mobs without firing, though sometimes by the use of rifle butts. At one place, N'de Okporo on the Cross River above Calabar, he was thrown into the river by a woman ringleader! He later voiced the opinion, agreed with by others who took part in the 'operations', that the women of this part of Nigeria were a far more potent force for trouble than the men. In fact, he likened them to the famous Amazons of Dahomey, who had formed a third of the force that attacked Abeokuta 70 years before, and who had since given the French troops, including the Foreign Legion, some exciting moments during the last decade of the nineteenth century.

In January the disturbances began to abate, and in the middle of the month the troops returned to their normal stations. As usual, an enquiry was eventually held, the findings of which affecting the Nigeria Regiment are stated in Appendix III.

During 1933 there was a reorganization of the R.W.A.F.F. In Nigeria the four battalions were transformed into six battalions, each of headquarters, two companies and a machine-gun section. These were commanded by majors. The country was divided into two areas, North and South, each under a lieutenant-colonel with a small headquarters. The 1st, 2nd and 5th Battalions were stationed in the Northern Area and the 3rd, 4th and 6th in the Southern; the latter in a new station—Enugu. In the Gold Coast, too, similar changes were made. The infantry was re-organized into two battalions each of two rifle companies and a support company, but until 1936 the companies consisted of only three platoons.

The record of the R.W.A.F.F. would be incomplete without reference to the European Reserve Force, formed in 1933, which consisted of potential officers and N.C.O.s who would be called up for service on the outbreak of war and did a certain amount of training in peace. To this also belonged the Engineer Cadres in Nigeria and the Gold Coast, whose function it was to provide the European personnel of the field companies necessary in war. They also helped to form the survey sections required in East Africa in 1940. Just before the Munich crisis another unit—the Lagos Defence Force—was formed to man Vickers machine guns for the defence of the beaches and the entrance to the lagoon.

The Signal Company in Nigeria and the Section in the Gold Coast had by now reached a considerable degree of efficiency. In addition to the old means of transmitting messages they possessed portable long-range wireless sets improvised by the British officers and N.C.O.s seconded from the Royal Corps of Signals. Each set, however, required seven carriers to be mobile. In Nigeria the main stations each had one of these sets and communication was kept up between them and between Zaria and Kumasi. When the telegraph lines between Kaduna, Kano, Sokoto and Maiduguri were down, a not unusual event in certain seasons, the regimental signallers transmitted all civil telegrams between these places.

About this time some European civilians stationed in the Southern Province of Nigeria openly stated that another war was 'unthinkable'. 'Why, therefore,' they argued, 'retain an expensive force of soldiers when the police were capable of dealing with all matters of internal security?' They appear to have forgotten the *Yakin Mata*, and unfortunately for them some trouble broke out in Lagos and an urgent call had to be sent to the R.W.A.F.F. for assistance which, it was specified, must come from the North. The 1st Battalion left Kaduna by train at four hours' notice and on their arrival at Lagos the trouble and local panic subsided.

At Lagos the Battalion was billeted in the Customs Shed alongside which the mail ship happened to be tied up. None of the troops, probably, had ever seen the sea and were vastly intrigued by the ship towering above the wharf. One hopeful private was heard to ask his platoon sergeant how the white men found their way across the sea. The answer was: 'Oh, bush ape, this canoe runs on iron things under the water just like the *girigin kassa*.'

Some time previous to the events recorded above H.M.S. *Ramillies* had visited Lagos, anchoring, of course, outside the bar. A party from the 4th Battalion was taken over the ship and all were duly impressed; in fact, everything was 'fine past all'. On their departure, loaded with presents from the matelots and marines, an African sergeant approached the officer superintending the disembarkation. Pointing to the huge guns protruding from one of the turrets he asked: 'Sah, if a man gets seven days for having a dirty rifle, how much would he get for having one of these dirty?'

The standard of drill and turn-out was excellent and such difficult ceremonies as Trooping the Colour were carried out with precision. The troops liked drill, particularly big ceremonial parades, and *esprit-de-corps* was very strong. Weapon training and gunnery reached a very high standard in the thirties, and in 1937 the combined figure of merit for all the Nigerian battalions was as good, if not better than that of the Army at home. During the years 1923–37 the R.W.A.F.F. won the African Cup twelve times; they also won the African Machine Gun Match four times. (See Appendix IV.)

The following anecdote gives some idea of the keenness with which the African soldier was imbued. A senior officer strolling through the Depot lines at Zaria just before dark one afternoon saw a squad of recruits drilling. To his astonishment he noticed they were being drilled by an old man in a stained and ragged *rega* squatting under a big tree. Finding the Depot Commander he asked why if it were necessary for recruits to do extra parades they should be drilled by an adjectival sitting scarecrow. The Commanding Officer hastily assured the visitor that all parades had finished an hour ago. Subsequent enquiries produced the explanation that the squad of recruits had hired an old retired N.C.O. to drill them for one shilling an hour.

During 1936 it was decided that, owing to the improved internal situation and the increasing efficiency of the Nigerian Police, a number of detachments could be dispensed with, a course which would facilitate collective training. Consequently, Calabar, Okigwi and Yola were closed down. The cycle of training was similar to that at home, but modified to suit the climate. Thus, individual and weapon training were carried out during the rainy season; platoon, company and higher training took place during the dry weather. When funds permitted Nigerian units were concentrated for formation training often at Kachia, where the battery also went for 'practice camp'. In collective training more time was now devoted to methods applicable to warfare in open country.

When the Italians used mustard gas with devastating effect against the totally unprepared Abyssinians in 1935 they presented the R.W.A.F.F. with a difficult problem. Mustard gas sprayed from the air seemed to be the most dangerous, particularly at that time, when the only means of transport was expected to be carriers or animals. It was thought, however, that in the hot dry weather the liquid would vaporize before reaching the ground unless sprayed from a very low altitude. It would be possible to provide respirators and protective clothing for the troops and to train them in anti-gas measures, but this could not be done for large numbers of hastily raised and undisciplined carriers. The main problem so far as the troops were concerned was to instruct them so that their morale could not be affected by what they might regard as a strong *juju*.

As equipment arrived progress in training units was made. But, as usual in West Africa, funny incidents took place. For instance, at Kano one morning when some troops were practising movement wearing respirators they suddenly came upon a party of country folk on their way to market. These unfortunates promptly cast their loads and 'went for bush', thoroughly scared at the sight of men with devil's faces. It was thought that the soldiery might exploit their power to terrorize simple folk as a joke or worse, so preventive measures had to be taken.

The R.W.A.F.F. sent detachments to London for the Jubilee of H.M. King George V in 1935 and the Coronation of H.M. King George VI in 1937. The members of these detachments enjoyed themselves enormously and said they had seen many and strange things. The escalators on the London Underground appear to have been one of the major attractions. One N.C.O., however, expressed surprise that there was nobody to be seen asleep outside the big 'canteens'.

It is said that officers listening in Kaduna to the broadcast about the Coronation procession in 1937 were surprised and pained to hear the commentator say: 'Ah! Here come the King's African Rifles in their scarlet zouave jackets. A fine body of men.' That evening, however, having heard the same commentator announce the glad tidings: 'The Fleet's lit up', they decided not to cable to the B.B.C. pointing out that the King's African Rifles do not wear scarlet zouave jackets, these being the preserve of the Royal West African Frontier Force!

Included in the detachments sent to London for both functions was an African sergeant-major of many years' service.[1] One morning the Coronation party was being shown a Guards battalion on parade at Wellington Barracks. After some evolutions had been performed, the Guards sergeant-major conducting the party turned to our African sergeant-major and asked: 'Well, what do you think of that?'

'O'right, sah,' was the answer.

'All right,' spluttered the Guardsman. 'Why, there are no smarter troops in the world.'

Our sergeant-major grinned and replied: 'You no see my battalion, sah!'

(iii) *Preparations for War*

Some time before the Coronation, however, the threat of war became more apparent. In 1935, when Mussolini attacked Abyssinia, Nigeria was warned to hold a battalion and the Battery in readiness to proceed to East Africa. Then, in October 1936, Major-General G. J. Giffard was appointed Inspector-General R.W.A.F.F. and King's African Rifles, and

[1] Sergeant-Major Chari Maigumuri. See Appendix V.

Brigadier D. P. Dickinson became Commandant of the Nigeria Regiment.

A thorough reorganization was now to be undertaken with a view to the formation of an Expeditionary Force to be sent to East Africa, if required, and as a preparation for expansion on the outbreak of war. But this had to be done without greatly increasing the cost of the forces paid for by each Colony. After Munich, however, the Inspector-General obtained a grant from the home Government of £1,000,000 for the provision of new weapons and equipment for the East and West African forces.

The defence schemes of the West African territories had also to be revised in the light of the changed international situation. It must be emphasized that all plans were to be based on two suppositions laid down by the Overseas Defence Committee; first, that we should retain command of the sea; secondly, that *France would be an Ally.*

Both Nigeria and Gold Coast were required to provide a brigade group for the Expeditionary Force, each consisting of headquarters and signal section, three battalions, light battery, field company and field ambulance. The Sierra Leone Battalion and Gambia Company were to be retained for local defence. The Vickers machine guns were withdrawn from battalions and replaced by four 3 in. mortars. The reorganization was carried out as detailed in the following paragraphs.

In Nigeria the 1st, 2nd and 3rd Battalions were brought up to war establishment in Africans; the 4th and 5th to approximately 50 per cent of it.[1] The area headquarters were abolished and the 6th Battalion disbanded, its personnel being distributed among the other units. On mobilization the two battalions at half-strength were to absorb the reservists, of whom there were 900 on the books, though it was thought that most of them would be a long time in joining, while many would, it was expected, be found unfit for active service on arrival. On completion of the reorganization the battalions were distributed as follows:

1st	Kaduna	4th	Ibadan (with one company at Lagos)
2nd	Kano	5th	Zaria (with detachments at Maiduguri and Sokoto)
3rd	Enugu		

The situation in the Gold Coast was more difficult, as a much smaller establishment existed; there were only two of the small '1933' battalions. These were reorganized into the 1st Battalion at full strength and a 2nd (Cadre) Battalion at about half war strength. On the outbreak of war the 2nd Battalion would have to expand into two battalions, using recruits and reservists. The Gold Coast Brigade would therefore take much longer to mobilize than the Nigerian. It was proposed, however, to attach the 1st Battalion to the latter formation until its own Brigade arrived in the field.[2]

In both Brigade Groups the field company and field ambulance would have to be formed on the outbreak of war. The former units would be raised by the Engineer Cadres; the latter were to be composed of volunteers from the West African Medical Service. Some of the extra Europeans

[1] See Appendix VI.

[2] In the event, the Expeditionary Force was not required to go overseas until nine months after the outbreak of war, by which time the Gold Coast Brigade Group was complete.

required on mobilization for the infantry and artillery would be drawn from the European Reserve Force and the remainder would be provided by Rhodesia.

The reorganization, revision of defence schemes, preparation of war establishments, mobilization schemes, as well as load and movement tables involved a considerable amount of staff work. All these were completed in good time. It was clear that expansion would be necessary, as after the departure of the Expeditionary Force, very few organized units would be left in West Africa. In Nigeria, which had the largest resources in manpower, definite plans were worked out for expansion in stages commencing on the outbreak of war, the first of which would be the formation of two new battalions and a battery. At the same time the Gold Coast would mobilize its Territorial Battalion and commence the formation of a fourth battalion as soon as possible. The Sierra Leone Battalion was to increase from three to four companies. Gambia would raise a reserve company and hold the original company to increase the garrison of Sierra Leone.

It was during this period that steps were taken to introduce the now familiar slouch hats. The Kilmarnock cap, tortured into the shape of a pill-box and kept in place on the top of the head with a chin strap, even when covered with khaki cloth and a neck flap, was not really suitable for active service. Europeans were too conspicuous in their pith helmets, so something had to be found which would be suitable for all ranks. The choice fell on the type of hat worn for many years by the Gurkha regiments. It was sad to part with the old headgear, which to some extent had become traditional, coupled as it was with memories of the War of 1914–18 in East Africa, when the 'Green Caps' as they called them, had won the admiration of the other units engaged. It was also decided to substitute a specially designed boot for the *chaplis* hitherto worn in the field. These *chaplis*, of a pattern common on the North-West Frontier of India, were made of soft leather with stout soles; they were eminently suitable for the African soldier, but were expensive and had to be specially made, a difficulty which would be intensified in another major war.[1]

A notable event in December 1938 was a conference held at Nairobi under the Inspector-General, and attended by representatives of the R.W.A.F.F. and King's African Rifles, to discuss the reinforcement of East Africa by West African troops. An important item was the coordination of war establishments and equipment tables. It was also decided that 300 trained mechanical transport drivers should be added to the West African Contingent, 200 being provided by Nigeria and 100 by Gold Coast.

On the surface life went on very much as usual after the Munich affair, but there was a bad earthquake at Accra in the following year. The behaviour of the African telephone girls at the telephone exchange who stuck to their posts throughout, may be described as a 'good show'. A few miles away in the cantonment there was an African company sergeant-major who did not believe in earthquakes. It so happened on this particular afternoon that all the British officers and N.C.O.s were away from

[1] See Appendix XVI for scale of clothing, etc.

barracks either playing games or preparing to do so. When the shock came they hurried to the lines, the first to arrive being the company commander. He found the company parading in full marching order under the African company sergeant-major, who ran up to him and asked for the keys of the magazine. When asked why, etc., he replied:

'Sah! I t'ink dem Germani come.'

The first task undertaken by the R.W.A.F.F. in connection with the war fell to the lot of 'B' Company 3rd Battalion the Nigeria Regiment under Captain G. Laing. The Company, with a mortar detachment, left Enugu at very short notice on 26th August 1939 and travelled by sea from Port Harcourt to Victoria, Cameroons. Their orders were to prevent a hostile landing there and to support the police in controlling the Germans who were working the banana plantations at Tiko. One platoon was sent to the latter place, but there were no untoward events, and after some three months the Company was relieved by one from the 5th Battalion.

The months of the *sitzkrieg* provided a welcome chance to continue preparations and training and for the units formed on the outbreak of war to settle down. On 4th June 1940 the Nigerian Brigade embarked in H.M.T.s *Lancashire*, *Devonshire* and *Dilwara* and met the Gold Coast Brigade at sea in the *Orion* and *Reina del Pacifico*. So, once more, the R.W.A.F.F. went overseas in the King's service.

During the voyage news of the evacuation of Dunkirk, the Italian entry into the war and the fall of France came through, the second item being received with acclamation by the officers. The effect of the third event on the situation in West Africa and the action taken will be described in a subsequent chapter, after following the fortunes of the R.W.A.F.F. in East Africa.

CHAPTER 8

The Campaign in East Africa

(Maps Nos. 29 and 33)

(i) *The Situation in the Middle East*

THE fall of France in June 1940 caused a dangerous situation in the Middle East. When the Italians declared war on 11th June, Lieutenant-General Sir Archibald Wavell, Commander-in-Chief Middle East Command, had at his disposal only some 65,000 British troops, not all organized in normal formations or fully equipped. In Cyrenaica, facing the western frontier of Egypt, the enemy had an army of over 215,000 men under the infamous Marshal Graziani. On the south-east another army of some 225,000 was located in Eritrea, Abyssinia and Italian Somaliland. In the air, the R.A.F. was greatly inferior in everything except skill and morale.

Holding the western frontier of Egypt were 7 Armd. and 4 (Indian) Divs. and two British brigades.[1] Facing the Italians on the frontier of the Sudan were three British battalions and the Sudan Defence Force with the combined total of some 7,000 all ranks. In British Somaliland, which could only be reached by sea, was one battalion of K.A.R. and the Somaliland Camel Corps. On the frontier of British East Africa were five battalions and two light batteries. Such being the case, offensive action was apparently out of the question, and the intention was to carry out a fighting withdrawal on all fronts if attacked and, in any case, to harry the enemy with light forces. A major factor was that any enemy advance would have to be made through vast desert areas, short of water, which we could afford to give up. On the other hand, though the Italians were now cut off from all supplies by sea, the vital importance of the Red Sea as a link in our communications with Egypt made it necessary to gain control of the western shores as soon as possible.

In the middle of August, British Somaliland was invaded and taken by an enemy force of some 25,000. The small garrison, which had received some reinforcements since June, was, however, safely evacuated to Aden after a gallant resistance which cost the enemy 1,800 casualties.

Towards the end of August the flow of reinforcements and stores from the United Kingdom and Commonwealth was under way, though 1 (S.A.) Bde. Gp. and two brigade groups of the R.W.A.F.F. from Nigeria and the Gold Coast had already arrived in Kenya. The decision to reinforce the Middle East, in spite of the situation in Europe, was one of the most momentous acts in the realm of grand strategy during the war.

It has been said that General Wavell always thought that, with his inferior numbers, it could be less risky to take the offensive than to await

[1] In the narratives of operations the titles of units and formations will be given in abbreviated form. (See Glossary, Appendix XX.)

attack. Late in August, when he became aware that 5 (Indian) Div. would soon arrive, he called on Major-General Platt, commanding the British Forces in the Sudan, for an appreciation of the ways and means of invading Italian East Africa. At the same time he made arrangements to incite the Abyssinians to revolt by various methods, including the use of irregulars, later known as 'patriots'. On 1st December, just before the start of his offensive in Libya, General Wavell made the startling statement at a conference of higher commanders that it was essential to clear the Italians out of Eritrea, Abyssinia and Italian Somaliland by the autumn of 1941. Further, that 4 (Indian) Div. would be switched from the Western Desert to the Sudan as soon as the first phase of the coming operations had been carried out, and would be replaced by other troops. The offensive against the Italians in the south-east would take the form of a pincer movement from the Sudan in the north and from Kenya in the south. It was timed to start in early February, 1941.

(ii) *Events in Kenya up to January 1941*

In June 1940 there were in Kenya very few troops for the defence of such an enormous territory. An important factor, however, was the distance between the frontier and the vital areas, namely, the port of Mombasa and those served by the Mombasa–Uganda Railway.

The frontier district consists of what is practically a sunbaked desert lying between the highlands of Kenya on the one hand and the foothills of Abyssinia on the other. Though much of this vast space is almost treeless, the coastal districts are covered with dense bush which also extends to large areas round Bura, El Wak, Wajir, Buna and Garissa, as well as north-east to the hills of British Somaliland. In this bush, though easily passable by men on foot and sometimes by armoured cars and other vehicles, visibility is never more than 100 yards, and often less. The river banks are lined with tall trees and thicker bush; malaria is rife in their vicinity. The few tracks across this inhospitable country become impassable to vehicles for days at a time during the rains which occur in this part of East Africa from April to June and from mid-October to mid-December.

On the outbreak of war with Italy, Lieutenant-General D. P. Dickinson, who had succeeded General Giffard as Inspector-General of the R.W.A.F.F. and K.A.R., was appointed to command the East Africa Force. His instructions from General Wavell were 'to defend Kenya, and without compromising that defence to contain as many Italians as possible on his front'. The force then at his disposal consisted of six African battalions, African light battery, a mountain battery from India and the East African Reconnaissance Regiment. To carry out the first part of his task General Dickinson decided to deny the enemy access to the River Tana and to the water at Wajir, to post detachments at Marsabit, at Moyale on the frontier, and in the vicinity of Lake Rudolf, thus covering the most likely lines of approach. This involved the dispersion of his force on a front of over 800 miles facing an enemy force of some five colonial, brigades, and numerous *banda*, whose main centres were Yaveilo, Dolo, Mogadishu, Kismayu and Moyale.

29. The campaign in East Africa

The *banda* mentioned above were irregular troops recruited from local natives, organized in 'groups' and officered by Italians who 'lived native'. They were often used as a screen on the front or flanks of the regular troops. They had a considerable nuisance value and also provided the enemy with information about our movements and dispositions. We also used irregular companies to co-operate usually on the flanks of the regular troops and occasionally in raids behind the enemy's positions. They were recruited at first from local Somalis and later from Abyssinian 'patriots'.

Soon after Italy came into the war there were a few patrol clashes at points on the frontier with Italian Somaliland and about Moyale. It was at the latter, on the edge of the Abyssinian escarpment and covering the junction of the tracks from Marsabit and Wajir, that the Italians were most active. The garrison consisting of one company of 1 K.A.R. was unsuccessfully attacked on 1st July and, as a precautionary measure, reinforcements were moved up to the vicinity. On 10th July the defences were heavily shelled and an attack by some four battalions developed. The attack was repelled and intermittent fighting went on for three days. It was then decided that to hold Moyale would be too much of a strain on our scanty forces and the garrison was successfully withdrawn. After an interval the enemy advanced as far as the water holes at Buna on the track to Wajir and then stopped. The evacuation of Moyale, followed by the loss of British Somaliland, had a depressing effect in Kenya and plans were discussed at Nairobi for the evacuation of the British women and children.

On the arrival of the two West African brigade groups at the end of June, two weak divisions, 11th and 12th African, were formed. 11 (A.) Div., consisting of 23 (N.) Bde, and 21 (E.A.) Bde., took over the River Tana and coastal sector of the defences. 12 (A.) Div. with 22 (E.A.) Bde. and 24 (G.C.) Bde., became responsible for the northern sector.

The men of the R.W.A.F.F., most of whom had never seen the sea or anything larger than a canoe, found much to interest them on the voyage. Many were firmly convinced that the sea was running away from the ships, which they thought were stationary. They were all very impressed with Durban and Mombasa, but disliked the Kenya frontier district, where, strangely enough, they felt the heat. The district had, as one Hausa put it, 'no women, no houses, no water, nothing'. But they were always very interested in any form of local 'beef', and the sight of any animal would always cause a stir, or if possible, a wild chase. They were much intrigued by the giraffes, which they named 'dem bush camel' or 'long, damfool bushmeat'. They were soon on good terms with the K.A.R., but, as in 1916–18, referred to them as 'Jumbo-jumbos'.

At the end of June, 1 (S.A.) Bde. Gp. arrived and continued its training near Nairobi. It was followed at intervals by the remainder of 1 (S.A.) Div., and by non-divisional troops, technicians, transport and equipment. By the end of the year some 9,000 vehicles had arrived and the long drive from the railhead in Northern Rhodisia had provided training for the drivers which was to prove invaluable later. New East African units had been raised and were in training and, at the beginning of December, the total strength in British East Africa had risen to some 70,000 Europeans and

Africans. It must be remembered, however, that a large proportion of these comprised the big 'tail' essential in such circumstances.

In the meantime, there was more patrol activity in which the R.W.A.F.F. began to play an increasing part. There was, however, one unfortunate incident. On 30th July, 1 N.R. was ordered to capture an Italian fort at Korondil near Wajir. The attack, which was badly managed, failed and the Battalion withdrew thoroughly disheartened.

Early in November Lieutenant-General Alan Cunningham relieved General Dickinson, whose health had broken down. The latter had well and truly laid the foundations on which the force was based and had overcome many difficulties.

General Cunningham gave orders for a forward movement of part of his forces to the frontier in January; meanwhile, action was to be taken to secure moral scendancy over the enemy troops. The first, and most important, enterprise was carried out by 12 (A.) Div. (Major-General Godwin-Austen) against the frontier post of El Wak, which consisted of five localities defended by a colonial battalion and *banda*, a total of some 2,000 men with 16 light guns and a few light armoured fighting vehicles.

In the neighbourhood of El Wak the boundary between Kenya and Italian Somaliland, marked by a rough road, ran north and south. The Italian position ran approximately east and west across the border. On the eastern flank was a group of defended camps astride the road to Bardera; to the west of this stood the Somali village of El Buro Hachi, also defended. Just inside the Italian frontier was the fort of El Wak and a huddle of native huts behind strong barbed wire entanglements. Across the frontier there existed a water hole and a junction of camel tracks known as El Ghala. Farther west stood the abandoned British post of El Wak.

As it was important to gain success, General Godwin-Austen decided to employ a large force consisting of 1 (S.A.) Bde. Gp.[1] 24 (G.C.) Bde. Gp.,[2] and a company of South African light tanks. On 16th December, after a long night march in vehicles through difficult, boulder-strewn bush, the force arrived at its assembly positions. The timing, co-operation and work of the ancillary units proved to be excellent.

The attack was to be made in three columns whose objectives were as follows:

Right: 1 (S.A.) Bde., less one battalion, the defended camps on the Bardera road and the village of El Buro Hachi.

Centre: 1 G.C.R., 51 (G.C.) Lt. Bty., and the tanks, the El Wak fort locality.

Left: 1 D.E.O.R., with armoured cars, British El Wak. 3 G.C.R. in reserve.

It was intended that the three attacks should be synchronized as far as possible in order to prevent the enemy moving troops from one locality to another. The attacking troops were to leave their assembly positions at first light.

In the centre 1 G.C.R. attacked with great dash. Having blown gaps in

[1] 1 (S.A.) Bde. consisted of 1 Royal Natal Carabineers, 1 Duke of Edinburgh's Own Rifles and 1 Transvaal Scottish.

[2] Composed off 1, 2 and 3 G.C.R., etc.

the wire with Bangalore torpedoes, they followed the tanks through them, spread out and attacked with the bayonet. The objective was captured by 0930 hours. The left column reached British El Wak at 1355 hours and the armoured cars then turned eastward. The right column, which had had to follow behind the centre column for some distance and was also delayed by bad going, was astride the Bardera road by 1000 hours. The action finished with a gallant bayonet charge by 1 R.N.C. into the village of El Buro Hachi at 1500 hours. The force began to withdraw on the evening of 17th December, having burnt or otherwise destroyed the enemy's localities. They brought away 13 guns and a few prisoners, most of the Italian troops and *banda* having 'gone for bush'. This proved an excellent rehearsal for future operations and the Gold Coast troops had lived up to their reputation. On 20th December, the C.I.G.S. sent the following message to General Wavell:

> 'Please convey my congratulations to G.O.C. East Africa and South African and Gold Coast troops for their most daring and successful raid on El Wak. In every way a brilliant action.'

In mid-January, 1 (S.A.) Div., less 1 (S.A.) Bde. Gp., crossed the Abyssinian frontier between Moyale and Lake Rudolf with the object of encouraging a rising against the Italians. This failed to materialize and, after enduring considerable hardship, the force turned south-east, captured Mega on 16th February and found Moyale abandoned on the 22nd.

It had become evident to General Cunningham during January that, judging from events on other fronts, especially the Western Desert, great risks could be taken with the enemy. Moreover, since the raid on El Wak it had become apparent that the Italians were withdrawing behind the Juba, leaving on the western bank a few detachments, including a single battalion at the landing ground and wells at Afmadu and a garrison at Kismayu. General Cunningham decided, therefore, that four brigade groups would suffice for the opening stage of the offensive instead of the six originally thought necessary. There was now sufficient transport to move and maintain such a force.

During January preparations to meet the administrative requirements of an offensive continued. Distance, lack of water, shortage of equipment and poor routes leading forward were the main difficulties. The Juba is 250 miles from the Tana, which itself is some 250 miles from railhead at Nairobi. The routes eastward from Garissa and Bura were bush-tracks unfit to stand the passage of many vehicles; this factor and the expected onset of the spring rains made the early capture of a port essential.

Stocks of supplies, ammunition and stores had been built up at Garissa and Bura, while advanced depots were being established as far forward as the frontier. The South African engineers located and developed supplies of water on the main routes forward, which they also strove to improve.

During the later stages of the preparations a comet appeared in the sky which, by a strange coincidence, had previously been known as 'Cunningham's Comet'. It was thought that this manifestation would be taken by the superstitious troops on both sides as an omen foreshadowing a British victory. Probably they were encouraged in this belief by various methods.

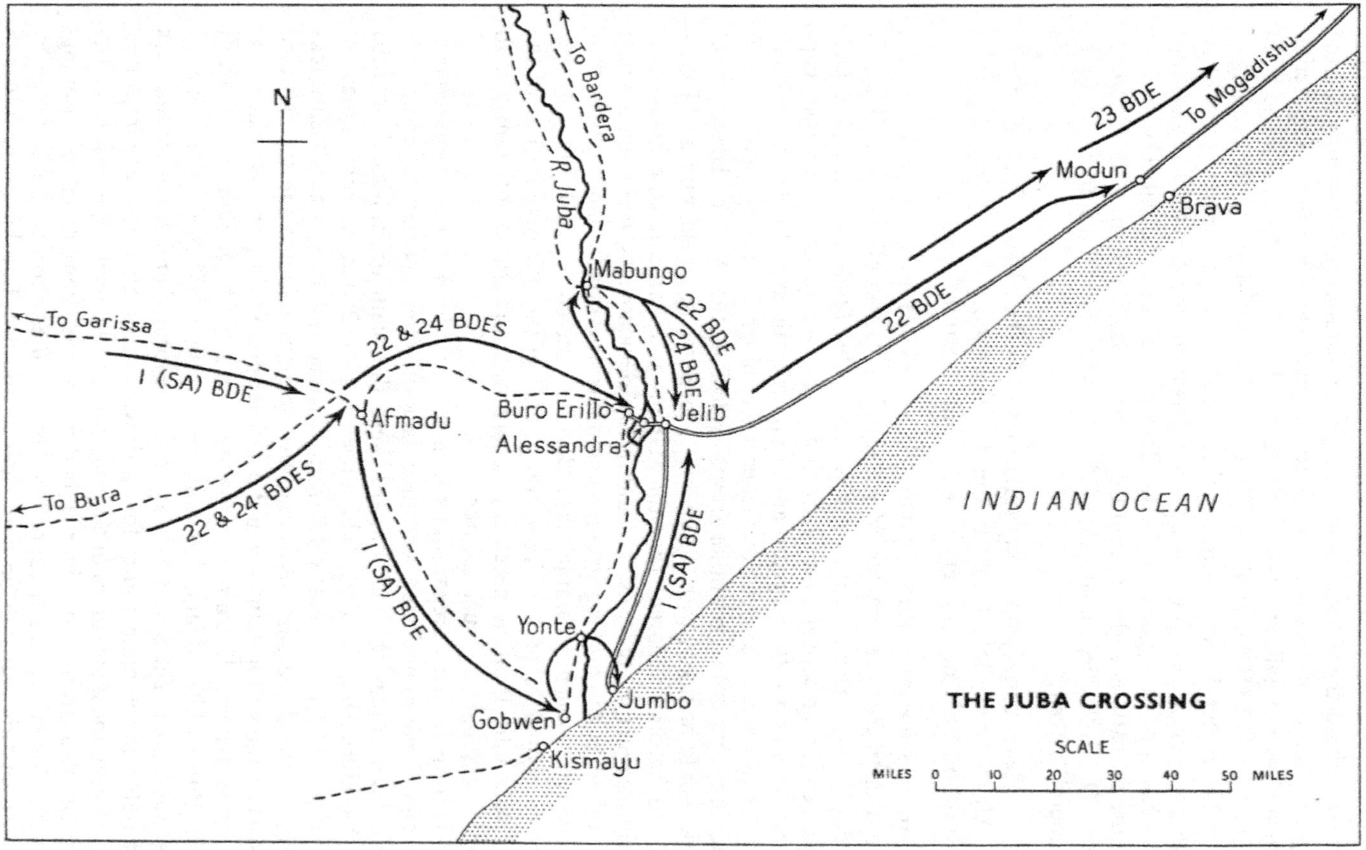

30. The Juba crossing

(iii) *Across the Juba to Mogadishu*

(See Map No. 30)

On either side of the Juba there extended a belt of tropical forest and thick bush anything from a few hundred yards to a few miles in breadth. South of Jelib[1] this belt of forest and bush was broken by patches of cultivation. A good fast road ran from Jelib to Mogadishu and there were roads on either side of the river to Bardera and Dolo at the foot of the Abyssinian highlands. The river offered the best natural position for the defence of Italian Somaliland; on the other hand, the vegetation on both banks favoured mobile, bushworthy troops.

The enemy forces holding the lower Juba, south of and inclusive of Jelib, were estimated to be about 14,000 strong, consisting of 102 Col. Div. of four brigades, divisional troops, three groups of *banda* and the garrison of Kismayu, which comprised three battalions, two groups of field artillery and some coast defence guns. Farther north, from exclusive Jelib, was 101 Col. Div. of two brigades, divisional troops and three groups of *banda*, with a total strength of 8,000.

The plan for the opening of the offensive envisaged the employment of both African divisions to clear the west bank of the river. The main effort to be made by 12 (A.) Div., consisting of 1 (S.A.), 22 (E.A.) and 24 (G.C.) Bde. Gps. After taking the well-wired position at Afmadu on 11th February, 1 (S.A.) Bde. was then to move south, capture the airfield at Gobwen and secure a bridgehead at Jumbo. In the meantime, 24 (G.C.) Bde. Gp. would move east on Buro Erillo and secure another bridgehead. Farther south, 23 (N.) Bde. Gp.[2] of 11 (A.) Div. was to advance on Kismayu when the enemy's attention should be distracted by the action of 12 (A.) Div. The Royal Navy would co-operate in the early stages by bombarding Brava, the coastal route and, if necessary, Kismayu. Precautions were to be taken to preserve secrecy and no written orders were issued. One of the means adopted to mislead the enemy was the phantom '4th Australian Division' at Wajir, represented by a few officers and a number of wireless operators who kept up a constant traffic in realistic messages.

From 2nd February onwards the South African Air Force attacked the enemy airfields at Gobwen, Afmadu and Dif. After a particularly heavy attack on the defences of Afmadu on 10th February the garrison disintegrated and 22 (E.A.) Bde. moved in unopposed next morning. This formation was followed by 24 (G.C.) Bde. (Brigadier C. E. M. Richards), which still had 60 miles to cover before reaching its objective—Buro Erillo.

On 10th February the following signal was sent to 11 and 12 (A.) Divs.:

> 'The following message from the Force Commander will be made known to all troops under your command. Force Commander also directs that the operation and its scope should also now be explained to troops. Begins. The victories of Imperial troops farther north have

[1] Sometimes spelt 'Gelib'.

[2] Consisting of 1, 2 and 3 N.R., etc.

filled us in East Africa with pride and excitement though no doubt the ensuring period has been touched with envy and strong desire to emulate achievements. Chance is now before you to prove what I well know that E.A. Force is no whit behind in dash courage and endurance. In this connection I send to South African East African West African and Indian troops taking part in operation message of good luck. Hit them hard and hit them again. Cunningham.'

The River Juba splits into two channels about Buro Erillo; that on the west was at that time empty and was known as the 'dry Juba'. Buro Erillo lies west of the dry Juba, and the town of Jelib is 10 miles to the east just beyond the eastern branch of the river. These two places are joined by the road which runs eventually to Mogadishu, and on the island between the two channels is the village of Alessandra. The Italian position at Buro Erillo was situated in thick bush and consisted of an area 1,400 yards long and 600 yards wide enclosed by thick barbed wire. It contained tank traps, rifle and machine-gun pits as well as a battery of field guns. The garrison was estimated at one colonial battalion with a few armoured cars.

24 (G.C.) Bde. Gp. moved up during the night 12th–13th February and debussed behind a covering force which had been in position since 1930 hours. This force consisted of one company 3 G.C.R., one machine-gun company of 1/3 K.A.R. and armoured cars. The intention was to make the main effort against the enemy position from the south with a holding attack from the west. Debussing one mile west of the covering force, 1 G.C.R. (Lieutenant-Colonel I. R. Bruce) and 2 G.C.R. (Lieutenant-Colonel J. W. Hayes) moved to their assembly positions as follows:

1 G.C.R., with a detachment of sappers, to strike the road Buro Erillo–Kismayu two miles south of Buro Erillo and then to take up a position facing east astride the road Buro Erillo–Alessandra–Jelib.

2 G.C.R., with a detachment of sappers, to follow 1 G.C.R. and assemble east of the road Buro Erillo–Kismayu facing north-north-west.

At 0830 hours 2 G.C.R. started their attack. Gaps were blown in the wire by Bangalore torpedoes through which the companies passed and swept right across the area from south to north. Meanwhile, 1 G.C.R. had been attacked by armoured cars coming down lanes cut in the bush. The anti-tank rifles proved most effective and even bullets from Bren guns were found to have penetrated the vehicles. During the action the light batteries fired with great precision and the sappers showed themselves skilful in detecting and destroying mines.

The casualties incurred by 2 G.C.R. were three officers and one British N.C.O. killed, three officers and one British N.C.O. wounded, nine Africans killed and 18 wounded. Many of the Italian troops dispersed into the bush, but 141 prisoners, all their artillery and most of their machine guns were taken. As one excited African private remarked to an officer: 'Fine fight, sah! We done beaten 'em.'

On the evening of 13th February information reaching General Cunningham suggested that the enemy were withdrawing from the west bank of the river. So 22 (E.A.) Bde. Gp. was ordered to move at once on Kismayu, as 23 (N.) Bde. was still too far back. Kismayu was occupied late in 14th February. In the meantime, 1 (S.A.) Bde. had moved southward and secured Gobwen early on 14th February, but too late to intercept the garrison of Kismayu. One small port had been secured and General Cunningham was now determined to force the Jaba with all speed.

At Gobwen the pontoon bridge over the 200-yard wide river had been destroyed; at Buro Erillo the crossing were also found to be strongly held. In either case an attempt to force a crossing would have been very costly. However, a suitable place was found by the South Africans at Yonte, 10 miles up-stream, and a company crossed in assault boats on 17th February. Next day a strong counter-attack was beaten off with heavy loss. On the 19th a pontoon bridge was completed and 1 (S.A.) Bde. crossed and turned south to capture Jumbo.

In the meantime, patrols from 24 (G.C.) Bde. had discovered a suitable place to cross at Mabungo, 30 miles to the north. Leaving 2 G.C.R. and a light battery at Buro Erillo to threaten a frontal attack, the rest of the Brigade started north at 1800 hours on 18th February and by 0100 hours on the 19th had reached assembly areas near Mabungo. At 0300 hours 1 and 3 G.C.R. moved down to the river and all were across by 0530 hours, quite unopposed. By 0900 hours a bridgehead was established and bridging began. At 1600 hours on 21st February the Brigade moved south down the east bank of the river. In the meantime, 2 G.C.R., still on the west bank, had captured Alessandra.

Jelib was taken on 22nd February by a converging attack from the north by 24 (G.C.) Bde., and by 1 (S.A.) Bde. from the south. Crossing at Mabungo after 24 (G.C.) Bde., 22 (E.A.) Bde. moved in a south-easterly direction by camel tracks and through virgin bush to cut the Jelib–Mogadishu road, which they reached 18 miles east of Jelib. Then, turning east along the road, they reached Modun, 150 miles on the way to Mogadishu.

When 24 (G.C.) Bde. had left Mabungo to drive southwards to Jelib the defence of the bridgehead at Mabungo was taken over by 2 N.R. with a machine-gun platoon of 1/3 K.A.R. attached. The Battalion took up a position with one company astride each of the roads approaching the crossing and on the newly made track of 22 (E.A.) Bde. On the morning of 22nd February the Italians attacked the position three times. At 0930 hours a preliminary attack was made by *banda*, presumably to ascertain the positions of the defenders. At 1040 hours the main attack by Colonial infantry and artillery began, apparently with the object of working round the defenders' left flank and of cutting it off from the bridge. Owing to the staunchness of the defence and the thick bush—visibility not exceeding 10 yards—the enemy failed to achieve his object. Another attack was put in at 1210 hours, probably to cover the retreat of the Italian main body, and a small counter-attack at 1400 hours found that the enemy had withdrawn. In spite of quite heavy artillery and mortar fire 2 N.R.'s casualties were very slight.

A large number of prisoners had been captured, many Colonial units had vanished into the bush and the Italian command was evidently in great confusion. It seemed to General Cunningham that there was nothing to stop him reaching Mogadishu or even Harar. He could move and maintain three brigade groups for that distance and had been able to remove restrictions on the movement of convoys by daylight owing to the enemy having been driven from the air. On 22nd February he suggested to General Wavell that, if his proposal to move on Harar were approved, the port of Berbera should be captured so as to shorten his land communications. He was informed in reply that the advance on Harar was sanctioned and that a force from Aden would land at Berbera. This was a momentous decision and the long, rapid pursuit commenced next day.

The task was given to 23 (N.) Bde. Gp. (Brigadier G. R. Smallwood, M.C.) was the pursuit of the enemy to Mogadishu. While waiting west of the Juba, news of the capture of Jelib was received at 1615 hours on 22nd February. During the evening the whole Brigade Group passed the Mabungo bridgehead and spent the night on the Jelib road some 15 miles to the south. Next morning they advanced through Jelib, turned on to the road to Mogadishu, leap-frogged the main body of 22 (E.A.) Bde., and by nightfall had covered about 100 miles. During the night it was heard that the Navy had bombarded Brava. (See Map. No. 31.)

On 24th February, the leading elements of 23 (N.) Bde. Gp.[1] consisting of 'C' Sqn. (E.A.) Armd. C. Regt., 52 (N) Lt. Bty., 1 (S.A.) Anti-Tk. Bty., 1 N.R. (Lieutenant-Colonel B. J. D. Gerrard) and one machine-gun platoon 1/3 K.A.R., started at 0345 hours. No opposition was encountered at Modun and a detachment of 22 (E.A.) Bde., moving farther south-east, occupied Brava without incident.

The advance towards Mogadishu continued in country more open than the thick bush recently met. About 1120 hours an Italian rearguard was located by the armoured cars of 23 (N.) Bde. Gp. in a cultivated area seamed with irrigation channels and one car was put out of action by a minefield. 'A' Coy. 1 N.R. debussed and deployed south of the road, and after moving over a mile gained touch with the enemy. After a short fire fight they attacked with the bayonet—the Italians retired. At the same time 'B' Coy. 1 N.R. had debussed and moved north of the road to the edge of the minefield. At 1300 hours detachments from 16 (S.A.) Fd. Coy. and 51 (N.) Fd. Coy. arrived to clear the minefield, and by 1430 hours the column had embussed and was again moving forward. At 1545 hours the enemy was bumped again. 1 N.R. debussed on the north side of the road, and after a brisk action, in which 52 (N.) Lt. Bty. scored a least one direct hit on a machine-gun post, the enemy withdrew, leaving behind five guns and eight machine guns. This action took 2 hours 15 minutes to complete, after which 'A' Coy. 1 N.R., following up, reported the road clear.[2] A light force was then sent forward to search for the Vittorio D'Africa landing ground, but failed to find it in the dark.

The landing ground was located early on 25th February and occupied by a company of 3 N.R. During the morning there was some delay in finding the way and the main column was embarrassed by enemy troops

[1] Each Brigade group had a brigade-group company (A.S.C.) which provided second-line transport.

[2] These attacks on the Italian rearguards took place about Goluin, which lies inland from Mercia and 50 miles south-west of Mogadishu.

surrendering in large numbers, but Afgoi, 15 miles north-west of Mogadishu, was occupied by 1600 hours. A squadron of armoured cars and two companies 2 N.R., moved on into the town and found it unoccupied by the enemy. Next morning representatives of all units of 23 (N.) Bde. Gp. entered the town without incident. The formation had moved 235 miles in three days.

Though there had been a number of sharp engagements since the offensive started, the enemy had nowhere offered systematic resistance nor mounted a counter-offensive, and it seemed that their higher command was bewildered by the speed of the advance and the tactics employed. The British troops had proved superior in morale and training; they had shown endurance and determination, having moved fast and far in extreme heat, with little water, over difficult country.

There had to be a short halt at Mogadishu to allow of supplies, etc., being accumulated and to get the port into working order. The town, which was completely undamaged, contained great quantities of stores, most valuable of which were 350,000 gallons of motor fuel and 80,000 gallons of aviation spirit.

The intention was to push on to Harar as quickly as possible, little opposition being expected. At the same time, it was considered desirable to give the impression that our main advance would be through Neghelli. This task was given to 12 (A.) Div.; 24 (G.C.) Bde. Gp. moved up the Juba and 3 G.C.R. occupied Bardera on 27th February. Iscia Bardoa was cleared two days later, followed by Lugh Ferrandi on 3rd March and Dolo on the 5th. On 17th March a small column of 3 G.C.R. left for Neghelli, an important airfield, which was reached on the 21st. Nothing on a larger scale was then possible owing to supply and transport difficulties and the need to clear the area of disbanded soldiers and dissident tribesmen.

(iv) *On to Addis Ababa*

(See Maps Nos. 31, 32 and 33)

Before describing the next stage of the advance it is necessary to give some idea of the roads used and of the surrounding country. From Mogadishu to Belet Uen, 209 miles, the Strada Imperiale with tarmac surface, good culverts and grading is a memorial to the excellence of Italian road-making. For the next 205 miles to Gabredarre the road was rougher, though all-weather, and followed the slopes of the hills. From Gabredarre to Daghabur, 165 miles, the road rises considerably and there was more vegetation, but for some 20 miles the road virtually ceased and each vehicle had to make its own course. From a few miles north of Daghabur to 30 miles south of Jijiga the road did not exist and vehicles had to find their way amongst trees and grass. From that point, however, to Jijiga, Harar and eastwards towards Hargeisa there was an excellent metalled all-weather road. The town of Jijiga lies in an open plain some 5,000 ft. above sea-level; to the east are bare rolling downs, while to the west, rising almost sheer out of the plains, is an escarpment which marks the eastern edge of the Abyssinian mountains, through the gorges and valleys of which the road to Harar had been built. Water was so scarce that

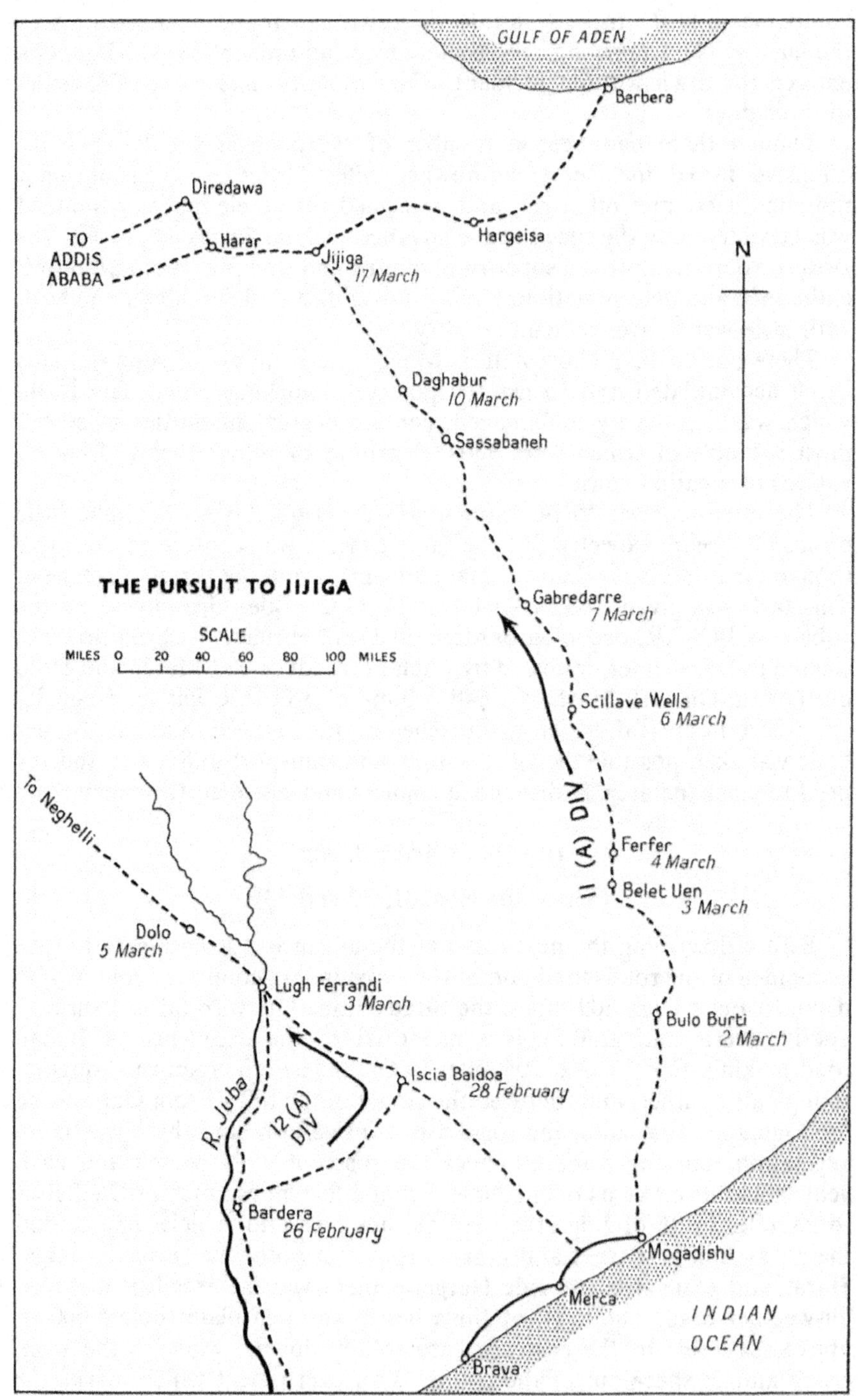

31. The pursuit to Jijiga

supplies for three days had to be carried by all troops moving between Belet Uen and Daghabur. (See Map No. 31.)

The advanced guard of 23 (N.) Bde. left Mogadishu on 1st March and reached Bulo Berti next day. Belet Uen, an oasis 209 miles from Mogadishu, was occupied on the 3rd. It was now necessary to call a halt to allow of supplies catching up, but a small column was to be pushed forward boldly to secure landing grounds and to report on water supplies. It was not to move beyond Sassabaneh before 9th March, as the main body of the Brigade would not be able to leave Belet Uen before then. This column, under the command of Lieutenant-Colonel J. A. S. Hopkins, consisted of 2 N.R. 'C' Coy. 1/3 K.A.R., 'C' Sqn. (E.A.) Armd. C. Regt., and detachments of 51 (N.) Fd. Coy. and 3 (N.) Fd. Amb., and moved rapidly towards Daghabur. This place was reached on the tail of the enemy on 10th March by the advanced guard of the column, the rest of which was 100 miles behind. The main body of the Brigade caught up on 13th March. On the 17th the advance continued and Jijiga, 744 miles from Mogadishu, was reached the same evening. To facilitate the movement on Jijiga and the landing at Berbera, the Diredawa airfields were attacked on two successive nights by the R.A.F. from Aden and by South African fighters by day.

During the advance from Mogadishu 11 (A.) Div., now composed of 1 (S.A.), 22 (E.A.) and 23 (N.) Bde. Gps., had been strung out along a single road with its groups moving at about 48-hour intervals to permit the passage of the necessary supply convoys. It was expected, however, that by 23rd March Divisional Headquarters and 1 (S.A.) Bde. Gp. would arrive in the Jijiga area.

On 16th March the landing at Berbera commenced and 3 N.R. with some armoured cars had been sent to cut off the Italian garrison of British Somaliland, which, however, melted away. A number of difficulties had to be overcome in getting this primitive port into working order, yet within a week 11 (A.) Div. was being partly maintained through it.

The Division was now about to leave the flat bush country and to move into the Abyssinian highlands, its first objective being the important town of Harar. The road from Jijiga winds steeply out of the plains and is the only practicable route for vehicles. It was found to be blocked at the Marda Pass, where the enemy held a position astride the road on a line of hilltops which completely overlooked the plain across which any attack would have to be made. The hilltops were wired and tunnelled and a system of minefields and tank traps had been found in the few areas over which armoured cars could move. The enemy strength was estimated to be three or four battalions, pack artillery and two groups of *banda*. There appeared to be no chance of making a quick frontal thrust, together with a flanking movement, such as had always caused Italian resistance to collapse. Looking towards the Italian position, the main features were named as follows: On the right Camel Saddle Hill, then came the Right and Left Breasts of Marda. On the left of the road were Observation Hill, the Ledge and Saddle Hill. (See Maps 32 and 33.)

Active patrolling had been carried out from 18th March onwards as a result of which General Wetherall decided to await the arrival of 1 (S.A.)

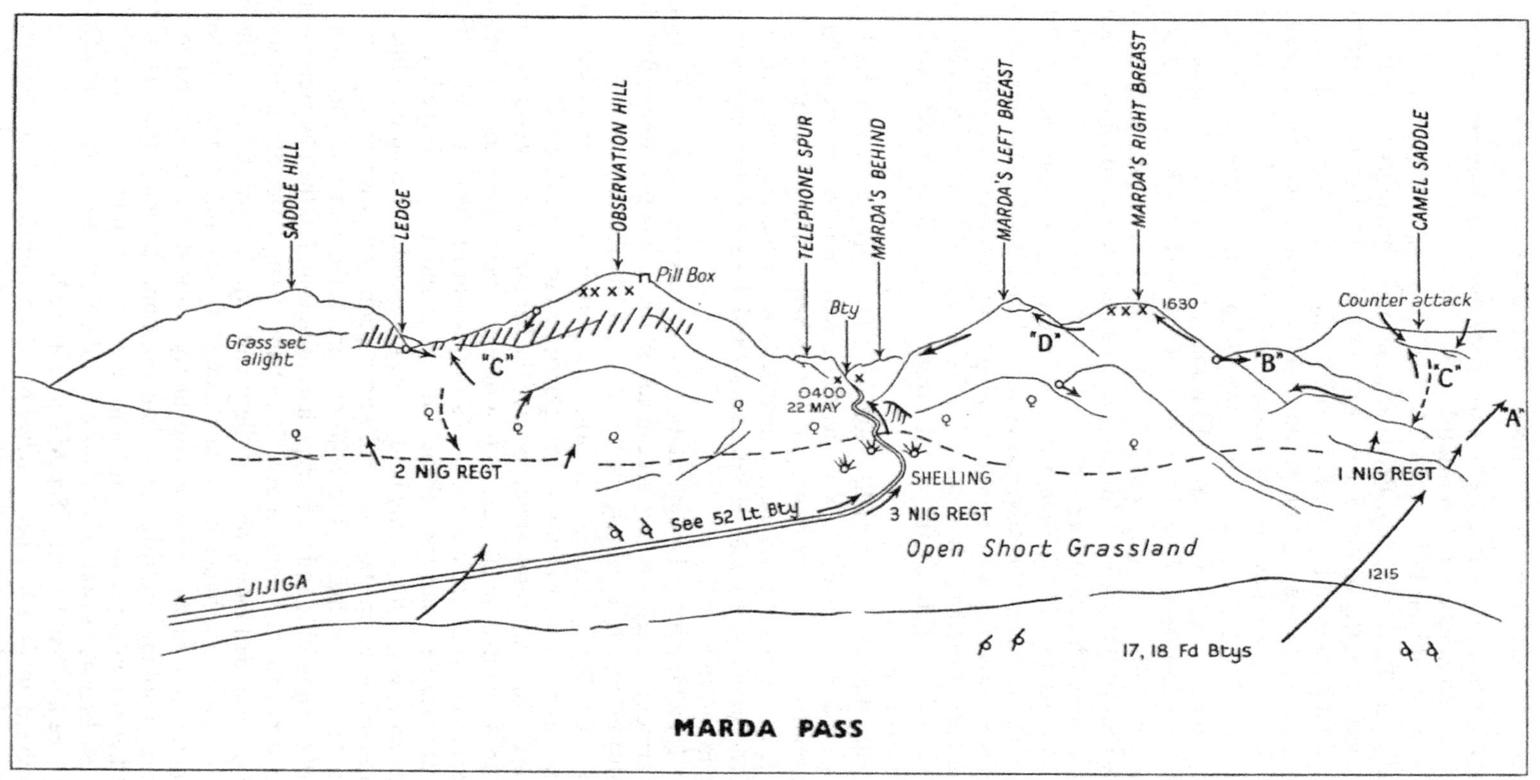

32. Marda Pass

Bde. and more artillery. This would mean postponing the attack until the 23rd. Meanwhile, the position was being attacked from the air, as were troop movements on the road in rear and the railway between Diredawa and Awash. On the morning of the 21st, however, information from patrols and deserters indicated that the enemy intended to withdraw. It was then decided that 23 (N.) Bde., supported by all the available artillery, which amounted to three South African field batteries and one light battery, should attack as soon as possible. This, in spite of the fact that 3 N.R. (Lieutenant-Colonel H. Marshall) had not yet returned from Hargeisa.[1]

The plan was for 1 N.R., supported by two field batteries, to take Camel Saddle Hill, which was believed to be unoccupied, and then to capture Marda's Right Breast. On the left, 2 N.R. was to make a holding attack against Observation Hill and the Ledge between that feature and Saddle Hill, supported by 52 (N.) Lt. Bty. One additional field battery, 5 (S.A.) was to be sited to fire on both objectives. The following description of the action is given by a liaison officer of H.Q. 23 (N.) Bde.[2]

'Soon after midday 1 N.R. started their attack on Camel Saddle Hill, the supporting artillery having already gone into action, and a troop of armoured cars having cleared one of the villages in the foothills. The leading troops were held up in the foothills by machine gun, mortar and light-artillery fire, but the machine-gun posts in the villages were silenced by artillery as soon as a message was received from the foremost troops. As the troops were approaching the south end of Camel Saddle Hill they were driven back temporarily by a well-timed counter-attack. This, in its turn, was driven back with loss by a furious burst of fire from the supporting batteries. The left company then pushed on and by 1630 hours, after having been under fire continuously for four hours and after silencing several machine guns, two platoons succeeded in establishing themselves on Marda's Right Breast. Here they were joined by the rest of the company, another company and one platoon of machine guns (1/3 K.A.R.). Another company, with its objective the north end of Camel Saddle Hill, met unexpected opposition from the whole ridge; however, they were able to give the guns targets and so effective was the shelling that only darkness prevented the objective being gained.

'Meanwhile, 2 N.R. had begun their attack on Observation Hill, but were held up by extremely heavy machine-gun and rifle fire from wired posts dotted all over the hill. 52 (N.) Lt. Bty. early knocked out the observation post on top of the hill and by means of some artistic shooting succeeded in setting fire to the grass near to the top, which burned for the rest of the day. The accuracy of their shelling was confirmed next day when it was seen that the enemy had suffered heavily in casualties and damage to positions.

'On several occasions during the day armoured cars had made their way nearly to the wire guarding the pass, but had always come under shell-fire. When the sun went down behind the pass, however, the flashes

[1] This Battalion arrived during the afternoon and was placed in reserve on the right.

[2] Captain F. K. Butler, late 3 N.R.

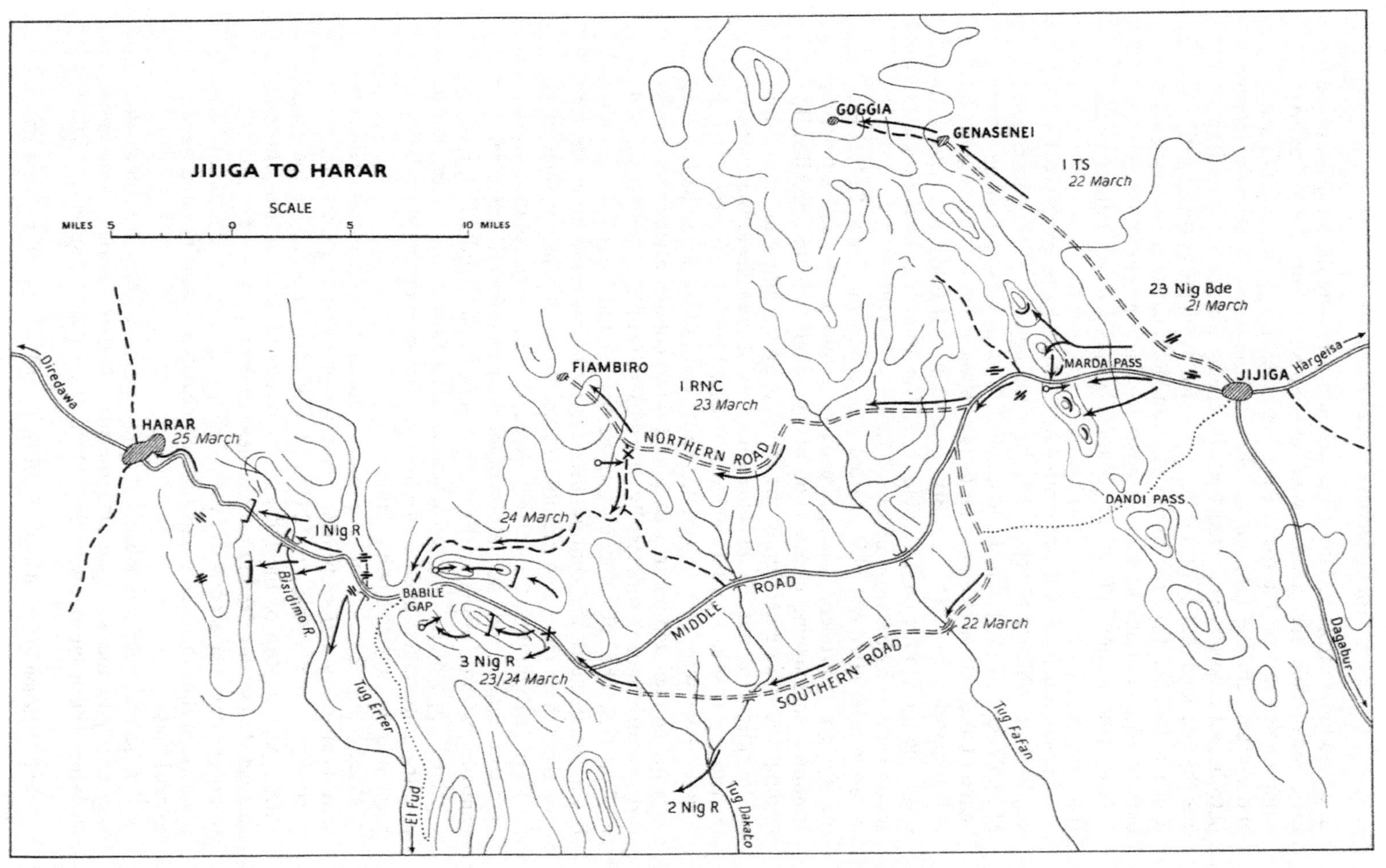

33. Jijiga to Harar

of a gun in the middle of the pass could be seen in the shadows by members of Brigade and Divisional staffs who, throughout the day, had been able to see clearly the general course of the battle from a ridge between the batteries. 5 (S.A.) Fd. Bty promptly opened fire, though it appeared on inspection next day that nothing short of a direct hit would have had any effect on the tunnel in which the gun was situated. (This tunnel also held a casualty clearing station.)

'During the afternoon "C" Coy. 2 N.R. had obtained a footing on the Ledge. Later, orders were issued for a night attack by two companies on Wart Hill[1] and by one company on Saddle Hill. "C" Company was to patrol and occupy the Ledge.

'During a bitterly cold night, after the Battalion Quartermaster and mechanical transport drivers had carried a hot meal to the troops on top of the mountain, 1 N.R. patrolled towards Marda's Left Breast, which was found to be still occupied. A patrol of 3 N.R. went straight up to the pass towards the blue searchlight which shone down the road, and the pass was also found to be occupied. Lights were seen flickering on Camel Saddle Hill—probably Italians collecting their dead and wounded—and lorry lights were seen first approaching and then leaving the pass. It was uncertain at the time whether these lorries were bringing reinforcements or preparing for a withdrawal. 1 N.R. decided to attack the Left Breast by moonlight, with support from 5 (S.A.) Fd. Bty., which had registered during daylight, but at 0315 hours the searchlight went out and at 0400 hours a patrol from 3 N.R. found the pass unoccupied. At about the same time a patrol from 1 N.R. found that the enemy had withdrawn from the Left Breast.

'It was discovered later that the Italian casualties were heavy, whereas ours, considering the amount of fire of all sorts for several hours on end, were also unbelievably light—two officers killed and three wounded, five Africans killed and 34 wounded. The field batteries—themselves under fire from long-range guns—and the light battery were responsible for extremely accurate shooting throughout the day, observation being good and new targets being shelled quickly and effectively.

'The morning of 22nd March was spent by 51 (N.) Fd. Coy. making a bridge across the tank trap, removing and marking mines and making a deviation round a huge hole blown in the road to the west of the pass. The slight delay gave time for inspecting the enemy positions; these were so strong and so carefully prepared that an enemy with any determination at all should have held us up for a considerable time.' This was the second important victory gained during the campaign.

There were three roads from the Marda Pass leading to Harar. Both the south and central were good metalled roads which join at the Babile Pass, 30 miles to the west. Farther to the north ran an old Abyssinian road which linked up with the other two west of the Babile Pass. The plan was for 23 (N.) Bde. to advance by the southern road, while a small column of South Africans moved by the northern route with the object of reaching Harar behind the flank of the enemy's main position outside the town. The centre road was not used, as it was believed to be heavily mined and

[1] Wart Hill, not shown on the panorama, is to the left of Saddle Hill.

blocked. On the afternoon of 22nd March, 23 (N.) Bde started and continued to advance until nightfall, when the head bivouacked 15 miles west of the Marda Pass.

The next obstacle, the Babile Pass, consisted of a narrow defile with high rocky features on either side. Early on the morning of 23rd March the leading armoured cars met a road block in the defile and came under machine-gun fire from the heights on either side. The enemy was quickly driven from his positions by 3 N.R., who captured nine machine guns. By 1430 hours, following good work by the engineers, the road block was cleared and the column moved on. About two miles farther along the road the leading troops came under severe and accurate shell-fire. As only two hours of daylight remained it was decided to halt for the night. (See Map No. 33.)

Next morning strong patrols were sent out by 3 N.R. on either flank to discover a route leading to the rear of the enemy's position. This does not appear to have been achieved, though their presence probably worried the enemy, as 3 N.R., supported by 52 (N.) Lt. Bty., attacking down the middle of the defile about midday, made steady progress and reported at 1720 hours that they hoped to reach the end of the pass by nightfall. The leading troops hacked their way through wire obstacles with their matchets under machine-gun fire and succeeded in breaking into the enemy's position. But once more darkness intervened and a perimeter camp was formed back along the road. Next morning patrols reported that the enemy had gone. The column on the northern road did not achieve its object, though it is probable that its approach caused the enemy to retire.

On 25th March the advance continued with 1 N.R. in the lead. By evening a pass above the River Bisidimo was reached and it was decided to attack at first light next morning. By daylight the forward companies of 1 N.R., supported by 52 (N.) Lt. Bty., were approaching the foothills near the river when they came under heavy artillery fire. It was decided to call up three South African field and two medium batteries and for 2 N.R. to get into position for an attack on the enemy's right flank. After a fire fight lasting two hours the enemy's artillery was silenced and fire was directed on to his machine-gun positions. At 1400 hours 1 N.R. moved forward and half an hour later had crossed the river and were advancing through the hills where the enemy artillery had been sited. About the same time 2 N.R. developed their attack on the enemy's right flank, only to find him in the process of withdrawing. In this action over 500 prisoners were taken and a number of machine guns and 13 guns captured. At 1800 hours 1 N.R. and the armoured cars entered Harar, which was unconditionally surrendered.[1]

The fall of Harar marked the end of a period during which the Nigerians had led the pursuit and invasion. General Cunningham paid them the following tribute:

'In 30 days they had covered 1,054 miles, an average of 35 miles a day. The final 65 miles into Harar entailed an advance through the most difficult country in face of opposition from three strong positions, yet the

[1] The Italian flag on the barracks was hauled down by 1 N.R. and is now in the Regimental Museum.

distance was covered in three and a half days. The Nigerian soldier, unaccustomed to cold and damp, fought his way from the hot and dusty bush to the wet and cold highlands of Abyssinia, where he maintained his cheerfulness and courage in spite of strange conditions and strenuous climbing operations made necessary by the terrain.'[1]

The lead was now taken over by 1 (S.A.) Bde., which passed through Harar on 27th March, the day when the victory of Keren was won in the north. Their objectives were, first, Diredawa, and then Miesso on the road to Addis Ababa. Whilst the main body of 23 (N.) Bde. remained in the vicinity of Harar, 2 N.R. helped the South Africans in clearing demolitions and later, after the capture of Diredawa, garrisoned the town. However, as 1 (S.A.) Bde. approached Miesso it ran out of petrol owing to the unexpectedly heavy expenditure due to the roads, and 22 (E.A.) Bde.[2] was ordered to take the lead. During the night 1st–2nd April the Brigade poured through, drove in an enemy rearguard on 2nd April and made for the River Awash, the last obstacle before Addis Ababa. As this Brigade was short of one battalion, left on the lines of communication, 2 N.R. was attached and the remainder of 23 (N.) Bde. moved up to Diredawa.

The aerodrome at Addis Ababa was heavily bombed on 4th, 5th and 6th April. In the meantime, on the 4th, a crossing over the Awash was forced, the village of that name captured and a bridgehead formed under cover of which a road bridge was built. Early on 5th April, 22 (E.A.) Bde. crossed and moved on towards the outskirts of Addis Ababa, but also sent two columns to the south-west of the main road, in which direction some enemy troops were retiring. One of these columns, commanded by Lieutenant-Colonel J. A. S. Hopkins, contained among other troops 2 N.R. and 52 (N.) Lt. Bty. This force secured a bridgehead at Ponte Malcasa on 7th April, a day after representative detachments of South African, West African and East African troops had marched into Addis Ababa.

On 5th May the Emperor Haile Selassie, who had entered his country from the Sudan a few months previously, arrived at his capital. He was received by a guard of honour found by 1 N.R.

In eight weeks the British forces had advanced from the River Tana to the enemy's capital, a distance of some 1,700 miles. There were occasions when the ground favoured the defence, but the general lack of will to fight prevented the imposition of delay to the advance—and delay, because of the approaching rains, was what General Cunningham had to fear most. The plan was carried through with energy, determination and brilliant administration. Great credit is due to the South African Engineers, whose work made the rapid advance possible. Nevertheless, it had been no picnic for the troops; there had been great hardship, cheerfully borne. Among other trials, the Europeans of the force had lived for weeks on end on bully and biscuit. Mails were slow and uncertain and there was generally a shortage of cigarettes.

'The total casualties of the British forces during the period 11th February to 5th April were:

[1] In his Report to the C. in C. Middle East.

[2] This Brigade normally consisted of 1/1, 5 and 1/6 K.A.R.

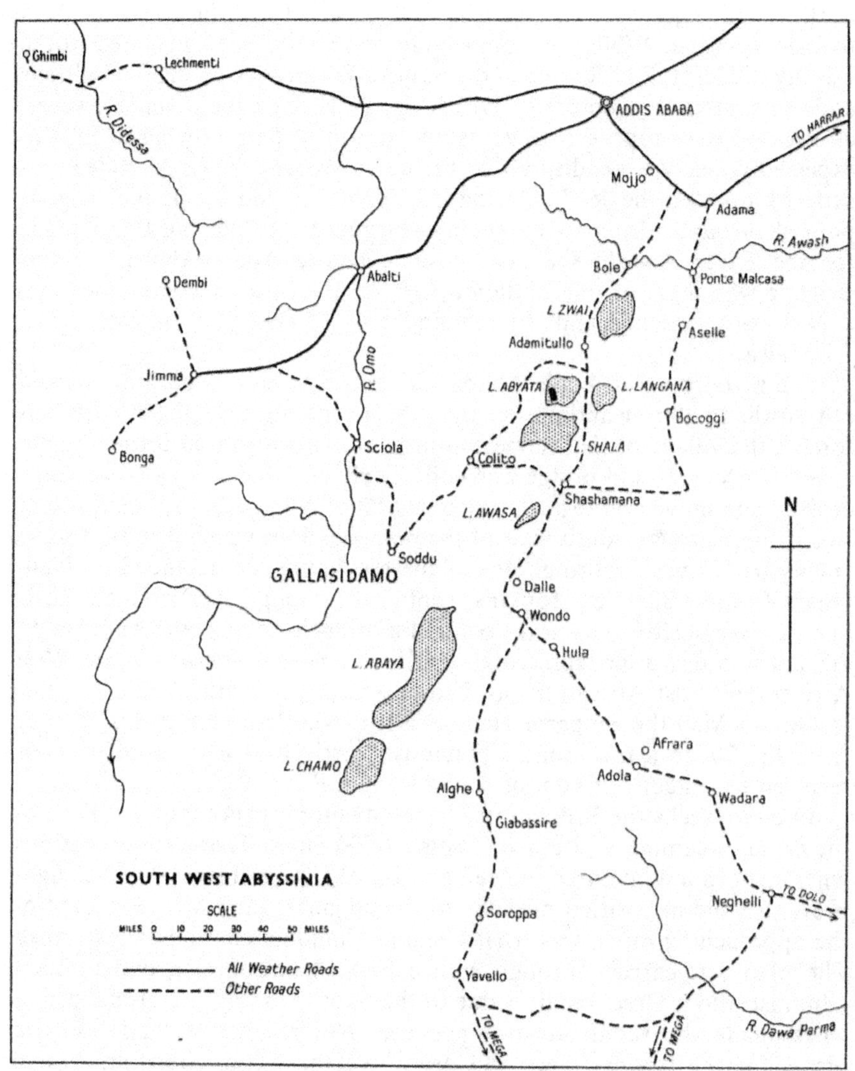

34. South-West Abyssinia

Killed	135
Wounded	310
Prisoners	4
Missing	52
	501

'It might appear from this figure that there was very little serious fighting. This is by no means the case. Nearly always when our troops met the enemy they were heavily fired on, and the number of automatics and heavy machine guns captured testified to the firepower the enemy could develop. I attribute the low number of casualties firstly to the superior mobility of our forces which enabled them quickly to find the "soft spot", secondly to the cover provided by the bush, and thirdly to the lack of marksmanship of the Italian Colonial infantryman who, when pressed, was inclined to shoot high.'[1]

(v) *Destruction of the Italian Forces in the South-West*

Just prior to the capture of Addis Ababa a number of Italian formations had been forced to retire south-westwards into the Provinces of Galla-Sidamo. By mid-April the enemy's dispositions were as follows:

Group 1		
Wadara	24 Col. Div.	25 and 85 Bdes. and attached troops
Alghe	21 Col. Div.	9 and 18 Bdes. and attached troops
Shashamana	25 Col. Div.	Militia, remnants of Eastern Command and attached troops
Soddu	101 Col. Div.	Lakes Bde. and attached troops
Group 2		
Jimma	22 Col. Div.	1 Bde. and attached troops
Lechmenti	26 Col. Div.	7 and 23 Bdes. and attached troops
Ghimbi	23 Col. Div.	10 and 86 Bdes. and attached troops

with detachments on lines of approach. All were very weak in numbers and morale, but still possessed some 30 light tanks and 200 field guns. Their orders were to detain as many British troops as possible in Abyssinia. (See Map. No. 34.)

Early in April the South African Division was already on the move to Egypt, though most of the artillery remained, and two battalions were to be attached to 22 (E.A.) Bde. until the end of May, owing to shortage of shipping. The British forces available for operations now consisted of 11 (A.) Div., of which 22 (E.A.) Bde. was south of Adama and 23 (N.) Bde. about Addis Ababa, less 3 N.R. who had relieved a South African battalion

[1] General Cunningham's Report to the C.-in-C. Middle East.

where the main Addis Ababa–Jimma road crosses the River Omo. South of the lakes, in 12 (A.) Div. area, were 24 (G.C.) Bde. concentrating at Neghelli and 21 (E.A.) Bde. about Yavello. A third Brigade, 25 (E.A.), was north of Lake Rudolf, struggling to gain touch with forces coming from the Sudan.

General Cunningham's object was to destroy the enemy forces in Galla-Sidamo, which he proposed to do in two stages. First, by a converging attack by 11 (A.) Div. from the north with Soddu as its objective, and by 12 (A.) Div., less 25 (E.A.) Bde., moving from the south in two columns. The next step was to be the occupation of Jimma, administrative capital of the province, followed by an advance along the Addis Ababa-Ghimbi road.

It has been seen that 22 (E.A.) Bde. had secured a bridgehead at Ponte Malcasa on 7th April and it was decided to continue the advance east of the lakes. On 9th April Aselle was entered and Bocoggi was reached on 13th April. Rain was falling in torrents and the unmetalled road climbing into the mountains became a sea of mud. By the 24th the Brigade had retraced its steps with the intention of moving by the road running south from Bole. After some fighting on both sides of the lakes, Shashamana was occupied on 14th May and a small column was, sent farther south to Dalle, which was reached on 17th May.

In the meantime, 12 (A.) Div. had met strong opposition on the Neghelli–Dalle road and both its columns were delayed by heavy rains and the state of the roads. By 17th May it had become apparent that the Division would not arrive in time to co-operate immediately in the advance on Soddu and Jimma. The plan was therefore modified and 11 (A.) Div. was ordered to press on to Soddu, and after its capture to move on alone to Jimma, while 12 (A.) Div. was to be responsible for the security of the rear areas during the movement. For the advance on Jimma 23 (N.) Bde., which had been retained about Addis Ababa, would be made available. To replace 2 N.R., serving with 22 (E.A.) Bde., 1/1 K.A.R. had been brought up from the lines of communication and attached to 23 (N.) Bde.

At 0900 hours on 18th May, 2 N.R. joined 1/6 K.A.R. about Colito, where they were in touch with an enemy position on the far bank of the River Bilatte. 1/6 K.A.R. attacked the position frontally on the 18th, while 2 N.R. made a long march on the night 18th–19th to turn the enemy's right flank. At 0600 hours on the 19th, however, they found the enemy had gone. 2 N.R., with some attached troops, followed the retreating Italians, entered Soddu on 23rd May, and took a large number of prisoners.

At this stage a digression is necessary to follow the fortunes of the two Brigades advancing from Neghelli and Yavello respectively. Their lines of communication were long and difficult: 24 (G.C.) Bde. was supplied from Mogadishu via Dolo, and 21 (E.A.) Bde. from Kenya via Marsabit and Mega; and transport was limited. The only lateral road—a very bad one—for connection between the two columns ran from Neghelli to Yavello.

For a good many miles north of Neghelli the road along which 24 (G.C.) Bde. was advancing passes through bush country. It then begins to rise towards the Wadara highlands. Some five miles from Wadara, after crossing a comparatively open tableland, the forest becomes noticeably thicker and there is a succession of ridges each higher than its predecessor and offering almost complete concealment from the air, but sufficiently open to give a good field of fire. It was here that the Abyssinians held out for eleven months when the Italians conquered the country some years before the war, and it was here that the enemy decided to oppose our advance. (See Map No. 35.)

There was sufficient depth in the position to give three distinct defensive lines. The flanks rested on almost impenetrable forest and in front of what became the second or main position ran a steep ravine which could only be reached by crossing a forward slope in full view. In rear of the third line there was room for reserves and headquarters completely concealed from the air. The main position was distinguished by having two high hills to the right centre which came to be known as the 'Twin Pimples'. The enemy's front extended for approximately 2,000 yards to the north-east of the Pimples and 1,000 yards to the south of them. Through the left sector ran the main road, passing near a white house, the area around which had been strongly fortified. The enemy's left proved most difficult to locate, as it was situated in a very thick forest, but was eventually found to be echeloned back and to terminate in an open glade some 2,000 yards from the Pimples. The enemy's right extended to a high feature to the south of the Pimples. The ground to the west of this feature fell away to a precipice; to the east it sloped gradually down to the ravine previously mentioned, which crossed the road forward of the 'White House' and then swung north approximately parallel to the road. To the east of the ravine was an old Abyssinian track which took off from the main road south of the enemy position and offered a possible line of approach for armoured cars or a turning movement. On the main road south of the ravine was a formidable road block covered by machine guns and, forward again, was a sucession of ridges, two of which comprised the enemy's forward position. The ground throughout was steep and extremely difficult to move over.

The enemy force holding the position was estimated to be two brigades of 24 Col. Div., with 10 field guns and one medium gun, as well as some 200 'Blackshirts'. Most of the N.C.O.s and machine gunners were Eritreans, noted for their hatred of the English, and who were able to keep some semblance of discipline. The units, however, varied in value; they were known to be affected by our propaganda and to be short of food.

Patrols from 24 (G.C.) Bde. had been in touch with the Italian position since 8th April and on the 19th several forward localities had been taken, one of which, a feature east of the main road, was named 'French's Hill'. On the 21st 3 G.C.R. had made a gallant attempt to break into the main enemy position which failed. The situation that evening was that 3 G.C.R. was astride the main road just short of the ravine, with 1 G.C.R. behind them. It was now decided that a full-dress attack would have to be staged, but which could not take place until 4th May, by which time the Bde. Gp. could be concentrated. From 25th April onwards there was continual patrolling to locate the enemy's dispositions—which were difficult to find—and to gain information about the terrain. All this was done in torrential rain by troops on short rations.

The troops under the command of Brigadier Richards were as follows:

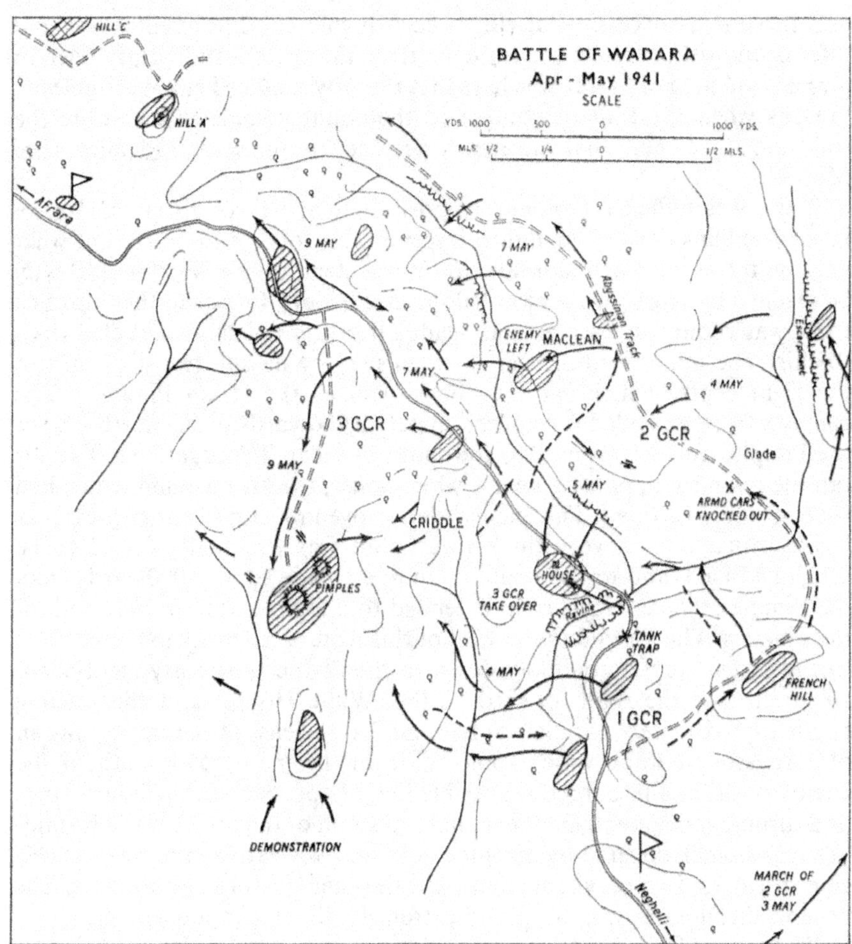

35. Battle of Wadara, April–May 1941

1, 2 and 3 G.C.R.; 'A' Coy. 1/3 K.A.R.; 51 (G.C.) Lt. Bty; 52 (G.C.) Fd. Coy.; 'A' Sqn. (E.A.) Armd. C. Regt.; 7 (S.A.) Fd. Bty.; Fd. Pk. Coy.; 2 (E.A.) Pioneers; three pls. of irregulars.

It was considered that by rolling up the enemy's left flank it would force his withdrawal from the strong position on the right. The plan for the opening of the attack was as follows:

2 G.C.R., starting on 3rd May, to make a long, and it was hoped secret, approach march, climb the escarpment and attack the enemy's left flank. The objective given to the Battalion was the main road from the White House to a point on the road 600 yards to the north-west. The advance would be preceded by two platoons of irregulars. One Tp. Armd. C.s to move up the Abyssinian track and to support the Battalion when their attack began to develop.

1 G.C.R. to hold the captured enemy positions astride the main road with two companies and to develop a holding attack on the Pimples,

[*Photo: Imperial War Museum*

Gold Coast Troops marching into a town in Italian Somaliland

Guard of Honour for the Emperor Haile Selassie, Addis Ababa, 5th May 1941

[Photo: Imperial War Museum

A British Officer studying Italian positions across the River Omo

but not to become heavily engaged. A platoon of irregulars would make a demonstration against the feature forming the enemy's right flank.

3 G.C.R. in reserve, prepared to advance should the enemy collapse.

An elaborate artillery programme was to be fired from 0545 hours, 4th May.

On 1st May, leaflets were to be dropped on the position, followed by a day in which there was to be no air activity to give deserters a chance to come in. On 3rd May bombing was to go on all day while the troops got into position. During the night 3rd–4th May there was to be occasional bombing, followed by air action as required during the attack.

At 0700 hours 3rd May, 2 G.C.R. began their wide flank movement, often having to cut their way through the gloomy, dripping forest with their matchets. It was not until late afternoon that they reached their assembly position with one company on the escarpment. During the night 3rd–4th two companies of 1 G.C.R. crossed the ravine and about 0730 hours next morning began to move on the Pimples. They encountered heavy artillery and machine-gun fire and after a short time the advance ceased. On the right 2 G.C.R. started to move forward to the Glade area on the enemy left. Heavy firing was heard in that direction about 0745 hours, but nothing could be seen from the rear, owing to the forest. The armoured cars had gone forward along the Abyssinian track and inflicted casualties on the enemy. Later, as heavy fighting seemed to be going on in the forest, one company of 1 G.C.R. was ordered from French's Hill to work round and come in on the left of 2 G.C.R.

By midday, however, it appeared that no progress was being made. The two companies of 1 G.C.R. were pinned down in front of the Pimples; 2 G.C.R. was held up in the forest and artillery support for them was impossible; and the armoured cars had withdrawn, having come under heavy artillery fire and lost some vehicles. But at 1430 hours a message from 2 G.C.R. reached Brigade Headquarters to the effect that 'A' Company (Captain Maclean) had worked through the forest from the Abyssinian track, had come in on the rear of the enemy's position and had driven them out. They captured six machine guns and put a field gun and mortar out of action. This success enabled the remaining companies of the Battalion and the company of 1 G.C.R. to push on until darkness and exhaustion put an end to the advance. Patrol encounters continued during the night.

Early on 5th May three companies of 2 G.C.R. and the attached company of 1 G.C.R. reached their objectives on the road, including the White House area, which was consolidated. The remaining company of 2 G.C.R. (Captain Criddle) pushed across the road and made a gallant effort to take the Pimples. After some progress, the company was counter-attacked and forced to withdraw. That evening 1 G.C.R. moved back into reserve, 3 G.C.R. took over the White House area and 2 G.C.R. concentrated on the Abyssinian track with one company in the Glade.

At midday on the 6th 2 G.C.R. reached a point on the Abyssinian track 2,000 yards to the north-east of the White House, with one company forward about 200 yards at an anti-tank ditch. At the same time 3 G.C.R. had two companies 1,000 yards north-west of the White House and two companies a further 1,000 yards to the north-west. 1 G.C.R. was again moving up to the White House area. It was uncertain where the enemy's left now rested, but it was thought to be just east of the road. There were also, it was considered, prepared positions on the high ground. The plan for the following day was for 3 G.C.R. to attack the position to the east of and across the road with two companies moving on a compass bearing through the forest and to come out on the rear of the enemy locality. At the same time 2 G.C.R. were to move along the Abyssinian track and to attack any position contacted.

Early on 7th May the two Battalions moved forward as arranged. But, owing to the Abyssinian track petering out, the leading company of 2 G.C.R. found itself in contact with 3 G.C.R. and the two Battalions advanced more or less on the same alignment. The country was too thick for the artillery to take part. After confused fighting in the bush, 3 G.C.R.'s effort to dislodge the enemy from two small hills failed, but a counter-attack on one of their companies was defeated. Meanwhile, 2 G.C.R., trying to cut their way through the bush, were held up at a steep ravine near the track.

There was heavy rain next day, but patrols were active. They found the forest in places to be practically impassable and visibility limited to a few yards. Orders were issued for the resumption of the advance next day, in which 3 G.C.R. were to turn south-west to the track leading on to the rear of the Pimples locality.

The troops were still in good heart, although all ranks were feeling the strain, when 2 and 3 G.C.R. advanced on the morning of 9th May. On the right, 2 G.C.R. moved along the Abyssinian track and made contact with the enemy. On the left, two companies of 3 G.C.R. moved on the rear of the Pimples, which the enemy hurriedly evacuated. The position was occupied by 1015 hours. Later, the rest of the Battalion took the position attacked on 7th May, the enemy slipping away to the north-east at dusk in torrential rain. By the morning of 10th May the enemy had withdrawn from all his remaining positions.

At 0600 hours on 10th May, 1 G.C.R. passed through 3 G.C.R. and began to advance on the main road towards Afrara, which was found to be obstructed by tree trunks, minefields and demolitions. At 1415 hours the Battalion had only covered five miles and between 1630 and 1830 hours were heavily engaged with an enemy rearguard. Fighting was continued during the night, and when the position was captured it was found that the enemy had suffered heavy casualties.

Wadara was one of the stiffest and longest fights in East Africa, second only to Keren and the crossing of the Juba. General Godwin-Austen afterwards paid the following tribute to the Gold Coast troops: 'In every situation,' he said, 'they have distinguished themselves. Their spirit, their efficiency, their burning patriotism, and their high courage are admired and envied by all.'

The British casualties in this action amounted to 22 Europeans and 96 Africans killed, wounded and missing. The Italian casualties are known to have been 20 Europeans and 150 Africans killed and four times that number wounded. In addition, according to deserters, there had been heavy casualties in the early stages from artillery and air bombardments. They lost three guns, nine heavy machine guns and quantities of small arms and equipment.

The Italians had used the ground well. Machine guns dug in and difficult to locate were sited to fire down and across the occasional glades in the forest; rifle trenches were equally well positioned; the artillery was sited to cover all forward slopes and mortars to fire into the ravine. It was considered to be an area which could be held almost indefinitely by determined men.

On 11th May the pursuit continued in heavy rain. A convoy with supplies, ammunition and medical assistance was sent forward to 1 G.C.R. on captured pack animals.

The Battalion reached Adola on 14th May, but was stopped short of Afrara by a deep ravine covered by machine guns. The next day was spent climbing the escarpment to make a flank attack, but, on the 16th, the enemy was found to have gone. The Battalion followed up, halting 11 miles north of Adola, and moving on again next morning at first light towards Hula, which lies some 15 miles south of Wondo. The roads, owing to rain and demolitions, were in a shocking state. In the meantime, the remainder of the Brigade concentrated below Afrara late on the 18th.

The Divisional Commander constantly urged Brigadier Richards to push on more quickly because of the urgency of making contact with 11 (A.) Div. But it must be remembered that 24 (G.C.) Bde. was not only on half-rations and short of petrol, but on a road which had disappeared in slush. Movement by vehicles in such conditions is bound to be slow and uncertain. The Divisional Commander was apparently not fully aware of the state of the roads or of the difficult mountain country through which the advance was being made.

On 19th May 1 G.C.R. moved on again with one company in lorries and a section of armoured cars. The motorized company and armoured cars sent on ahead, under Captain McGavin, made contact with the Italians next day, hit them hard and took a number of prisoners. Soon afterwards another action took place with an enemy battalion. The total number of prisoners captured in these two actions amounted to 91 Europeans, 1,300 Africans and 300 horses and mules. Leaving a platoon to guard the prisoners, McGavin pushed on to Hula, where he captured 36 Europeans and approximately 1,000 Africans. Wondo was reached on 22nd May, where 600 Europeans and 1,000 Africans were taken. Patrols moved forward to Dalle and made contact with 11 (A.) Div. the same day.

Orders were now given for 24 (G.C.) Bde. to concentrate in the Dalle–Soddu area. On 25th May 3 G.C.R. less one company, 51 (G.C.) Lt. Bty. and some armoured cars started for Soddu to take over from 22 (E.A.) Bde. to allow the latter to move on towards Jimma. They arrived on 27th May.

In the meantime, 21 (E.A.) Bde. on the left had struggled on under appalling conditions: at one period they only advanced 47 miles in 10 days, pushing their lorries up hills and hampered by surrendering Italians at every village. They had fought a very successful action at Soroppa on

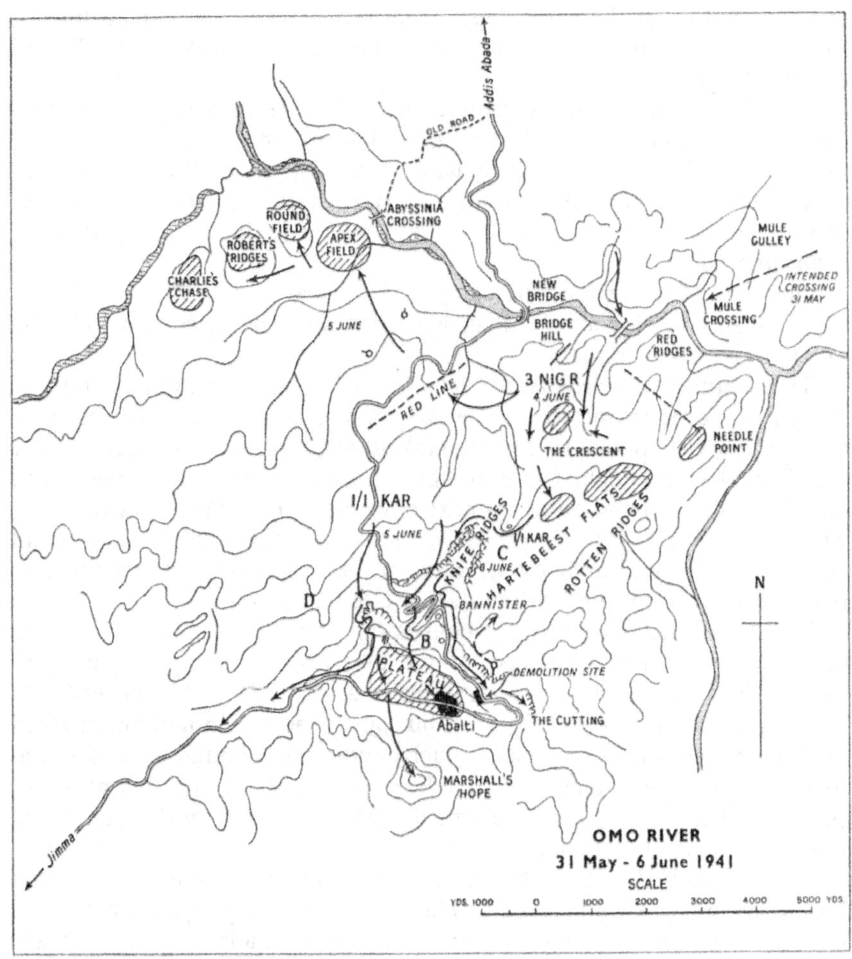

36. Omo River, 31st May–6th June 1941

31st March; and on 11th May, after some minor actions, had reached the strong enemy position of Giabassire, which was surrendered without a fight. Now, owing to the state of the roads, it became impossible to continue the advance in vehicles. One battalion, however, placed on an improvised pack basis, continued to move forward.

To return to 11 (A.) Div., which was about to move on Jimma by two routes, 23 (N.) Bde. by an all-weather road from Addis Ababa which crossed the River Omo at Albalti and 22 (E.A.) Bde., on the south, by a road from Soddu crossing the Omo at Sciola.

The Omo is one of the three largest rivers in Abyssinia, which, rising in the northern highlands of the country, flows in a southernly direction until it loses itself in the waters of Lake Rudolf. Though only some 50 ft. wide in the dry season, the Omo in May and June is liable to come down in spate and expand to a width of 100 yards and to become a formidable obstacle 15 ft. deep. In the area to be crossed the river flowed through a gorge with a steep sides 1,500 ft. below the ground-level of the plateau, which was some 5,000 ft. above sea-level. The bottom of the gorge on either side of the river was covered with dense bush. The Divisional plan provided for a simultaneous crossing by both Brigades.

The Northern Crossing

The position occupied by the Italians was naturally very strong. This was due partly to the rugged terrain and partly to a bend in the river on which the right flank of the position rested, and to the presence of the Little Ghibi, a tributary of the Omo, on the enemy left or western flank. There had been two crossing places over the Omo. One, known as the Abyssinian crossing, on the left of the position was on the course of an old track. The other, about a mile down-stream, known as the New Bridge, carried the main Addis Ababa–Jimma road. Both bridges had been destroyed. (See Map. No. 36.)

The strength of the enemy troops holding this position was estimated as 2,200 with a numerous artillery whose sites were not known at the outset. A group of localities covering the Abyssinian crossing was strongly held, as it was here the enemy apparently expected the main attack. Opposite the New Bridge they were thin on the ground, in fact, it was afterwards ascertained that only a weak company was posted in this area. There were other infantry and machine-gun positions in rear on the forward slopes overlooking the Omo, and the plateau was considered certain to be held.

The troops under command of 23 (N.) Bde. consisted of the following: 1 N.R.; 3 N.R.; 1/1 K.A.R.; one pl. 1/3 K.A.R.; 52 (N.) Lt. Bty.; 51 (N.) Fd. Coy.; 'C' Sqn. 1 (E.A.) Armd. C. Regt., less one tp.; 1 (S.A.) Med. Bde., less two guns; 7 (S.A.) Fd. Bde. and A/Tk. Bty.; 7 (S.A.) Fd. Pk. Coy.

Since 10th April 3 N.R. had been on the hills above the left bank of the river opposite Abalti; they had seen it change from a fordable stream 18 in. deep to a rushing torrent and vice versa. After careful patrolling a crossing place was selected some distance from the demolished New Bridge. On the night 30th–31st May all preparations for the attack had been made, but the river came down in spate, rose 4 ft. and expanded 25 yards. The attack had to be cancelled.

Next day a more suitable site one mile down-stream of the New Bridge was found. But the accumulation of stores and ammunition had to be moved to it, partly by head loads and through difficult country. Eventually the night 4th–5th June was selected for the assault; fortunately the two previous nights passed without rain. In the meantime, the artillery and South African Air Force concentrated on the hostile guns.

Owing to the change of site for the crossing the original plan for the attack had to be altered. The modified plan was as follows:

> 3 N.R. and one company of 1/1 K.A.R. to assault Bridge Hill-Crescent-Hartebeest Flats, with 7 (S.A.) Fd. Bde. in support.
>
> Then 3 N.R. to wheel to their right and secure Red Lines, while the company of 1/1 K.A.R. was to push on towards the escarpment cutting.
>
> The remainder of 1/1 K.A.R. to be held for the assault on the plateau.

1 N.R. in reserve.

During 4th June the river began to fall and Lieutenant J. D. Heath, 51 (N.) Fd. Coy., was able to swim across carrying a rope for the assault boats. 3 N.R. crossed during the early hours of the night and advanced on their first objectives, which were very soon taken. The company of 1/1 K.A.R. (Captain Bannister) crossed behind 3 N.R. and reached Hartebeest Flats at 0200 hours.

After advancing some 2,000 yards, 3 N.R. swung to their right and by midday, in spite of a counter-attack on their left flank, had consolidated on Red Lines and sent patrols towards Apex Fields. The engineers now commenced the construction of a footbridge and a pontoon ferry. At 1700 hours 3 N.R. attacked Apex Field, supported by artillery concentrations. The objective was occupied and next morning a patrol took Round Field after some opposition and captured 100 prisoners. They then moved on to Charlie's Chase.

In the meantime, Captain Bannister's company of 1/1 K.A.R., moving towards Knife Ridges, covered 10 miles of difficult country without being observed and reached a spot where the road climbed the escarpment. There they laid concealed until dusk. At nightfall the company was disposed astride the road, and soon after found and destroyed the wires of a demolition prepared to cut the road. The main body of 1/1 K.A.R. and a company of 1 N.R. began to cross the river at 1830 hours. All were over by 2330 hours and 1/1 K.A.R. marched up the road and joined the company on the escarpment. The advance continued and by first light on 6th June they were on the north-west and north-east ends of the escarpment. By 1045 hours the whole plateau was in our hands and Abalti had been occupied.

Organized resistance now ceased and 1 N.R. relieved 3 N.R. in the task of clearing pockets of the enemy. Italian casualties had been heavy, particularly in killed, and 2,800 prisoners were taken. The enemy's artillery support had been scanty during the action, which was undoubtedly due to the work of own gunners and air force previous to the attack.

The Southern Crossing

Here, 60 miles to the south of the crossing at Abalti, the chief antagonists of 22 (E.A.) Bde. were cliffs, floods and bush. The enemy's main position was on the high ground west of the river astride the Soddu–Jimma road. The west bank of the river was also held and there was a small bridgehead on the east bank covering an undamaged footbridge.

On 25th May the advance of 22 (E.A.) Bde. started from Soddu. A small mixed force consisting of two companies 2 N.R., light tanks and light artillery reached Sciola on the 29th and reported three large demolitions on the road leading down to the river. During the following day the main body of the Brigade arrived at Sciola. On 31st May 'D' Coy. 2 N.R. was in position 500 yards east of the river and an attempt was made to rush the enemy covering the bridgehead. This gallant attempt failed. Late that night 'B' and 'D' Coy. 2 N.R. were in position overlooking the river, with the rest of the force some three miles behind. During the night the enemy withdrew across the river and the bridge was blown. That night, too, the river came down in spate.

During 1st June all attempts to cross failed owing to the strong current. Next day an easier site was found three miles south of the destroyed foot-bridge. A few platoons of 2 N.R. and 5 K.A.R. were got across during the day, but damage to assault boats slowed down the movement. During the night one more platoon of 5 K.A.R. was put across, but the assault boats by this time were nearly all out of action or destroyed. Those remaining were used to maintain the troops who were across the river. In spite of considerable shelling this force of less than two companies hung on to their little bridgehead for nearly three days. During this period 1/3 K.A.R. managed to work their way forward and to bring some of the enemy guns under machine-gun fire.

On the night of 4th–5th June two more companies of 2 N.R. and three of 5 K.A.R. were ferried across and by first light in the morning were ready to attack. The plan decided on was for 2 N.R. to advance up-stream along the river bank while 5 K.A.R. made an encircling movement northward through the foothills at the base of the western wall of the gorge.

At 0745 hours 2 N.R. moved off through the thick bush along the river bank and at 0900 hours made contact with a small enemy force which was driven off. By midday they were a mile beyond the ruins of the foot-bridge and about an hour later 'C' Coy. had established a bridgehead astride the Jimma road about a mile from the demolished road bridge. 5 K.A.R. had started their outflanking movement at 0530 hours and for hours struggled through the gullies below the main escarpment, out of range of artillery, support and counter-attacked more than once. Nevertheless, they captured an enemy battery and arrived in rear of the enemy's right flank with one hour of daylight remaining. Although almost exhausted, they attacked and were doing well when darkness fell. The enemy withdrew during the night, leaving 1,100 Italians and 100 Africans in the hands of 5 K.A.R., who also captured or destroyed nine 105 mm. and eight 65/77 mm. guns and 150 lorries.

The Italians, who had the advantage in numbers and equipment, had displayed unbelievable lack of tactical skill and energy. The position had little depth and there appeared to have been no general reserve for use in emergency.

After the northern crossing, Brigadier Smallwood sent a signal to Brigadier Fowkes, commanding 22 (E.A.) Bde., praising the Nyasas of 1/1 K.A.R. He received the following reply: 'Glad my Nyasas did you well, as Hoppy's Nigerians have done fine work for me.'

Some days later 22 (E.A.) Bde. advanced to within a few miles of Jimma, which, for political reasons, was not occupied until 21st June. The total number of prisoners taken in this town was 12,000 Italians and 3,000 Africans, including four generals and eight brigade commanders. On 27th June 1/1 K.A.R., who had rejoined the Brigade, captured a rearguard at Dimbi, north-west of Jimma.

In the meantime, and after gaining touch with 22 (E.A.) Bde. west of the Omo, 23 (N.) Bde. had been transferred to the Addis Ababa–Lechmenti road, where they fought a minor action 15 miles west of the latter place on 15th June. The scene was a feature appropriately known, perhaps, as 'Massacre Hill'. The enemy were a rearguard about 400 strong covering the demolition of the bridge over the River Didessa. The attack was carried out by two companies of 1 N.R., one platoon of 1/3 K.A.R., 52 (N.) Lt. Bty., and some gangs of 'patriots'. The action was short and sharp; the enemy lost more than 200 killed and 150 prisoners, four guns and 11 heavy machine guns. By 24th June 1 N.R. and 3 N.R. had crossed the River Didessa, while the relics of the Italian 23 and 26 Divs. retired westward, only to be captured by a force advancing from the Sudan.

This practically completed the operations in Galla–Sidamo. So far as the R.W.A.F.F. were concerned, except for two units, this was also the end of the campaign in East Africa, though fighting went on about Gondar until November. The only West African units taking part in these final operations were 51 (G.C.) Lt. Bty. and 53 (G.C.) Fd. Coy., both serving in 25 (E.A.) Bde. The British Chiefs of Staff, anxious for the security of the vital convoy port of Freetown from Vichy French interference, had ordered the return of all West African units as soon as possible. In August the Nigerian Brigade left East Africa, but the Gold Coast Brigade did not sail until October.

'It seems worth mentioning, in view of the many enemy claims that they were overwhelmed by superior numbers, that at no time were more than three brigade groups, plus two battalions, engaged in operations against the 40,000 enemy infantry and militia in Galla–Sidamo, where at the commencement of operations the enemy had five times as many guns as we had. After the fall of Shashamana only two brigade groups were used.'[1]

As to the risks taken during the campaign from February to June, they were more apparent than real. Our African troops were better led, more tactically mobile, much more efficient, especially in bush, and of incomparably higher morale than their opponents. This, however, does not detract from the reputation of the commanders who took these risks.

In all respects the old R.W.A.F.F. units had added to the reputation they had gained in the War of 1914–18 in spite of the heat of Somaliland and the cold and wet of the highlands of Abyssinia. The field companies had done splendid work throughout and the brigade group companies had proved most efficient. Finally, a tribute must be paid to the African drivers of all the ancillary units. Continuous driving, first over tracks in the high temperatures of Somaliland and later over shocking mountain roads in the cold and rain of Abyssinia, was a considerable strain. In spite of the hard work and hardships incurred they displayed a most praiseworthy willing and cheerful devotion to duty.

As the Official Historian remarks, this campaign 'marked a memorable stage in the development of the African soldier and their success was the fruit of skill and determination'.[2]

[1] General Cunningham's Report to the C.-in-C. Middle East.

[2] Official History of the War, Mediterranean and Middle East, Volume II.

(vi) *Chronological Table of Main Events in the Middle East and East Africa: June 1940 to November 1941*

Date	*Middle East*	*East Africa*	
1940 June	11: Italy declares war Frontier operations	Frontier operations	
July	Frontier operations	4: *Sudan:* Loss of Kassala and Gallabat 15: *Kenya:* Loss of Moyale	
Aug.	Frontier operations	12: *Sudan:* Sandford's Mission enters Abyssinia 19: Loss of British Somaliland	
Sept.	13: Italians advance into Egypt	Indian 5th Division arrived in Sudan	
Nov.		6–9: *Sudan:* Action at Gallabat	
Dec.	9: British offensive commences	16: *Kenya:* Raid on El Wak	
1941 Jan.	4: Bardia captured 22: Tobruk captured	OFFENSIVE FROM NORTH 19: Kassala taken	OFFENSIVE FROM SOUTH
Feb.	6: Benghazi captured 5–7: Battle of Beda Fomm. Italian10th Army surrenders	3: Battle for Keren commences 23: Emperor enters Abyssinia from the Sudan	14: Kismayu taken 16: Mega taken 19: R. Juba crossed 22: Moyale reoccupied 25: Mogadishu taken
Mar.	30: Axis offensive under Rommel commences	27: Battle of Keren won	16: Berbera recaptured 17: Jijiga taken 27: Harar taken
Apr.	6–28: Invasion of Greece 10: Tobruk cut off by Rommel	8: Massawa taken Patriot operatons in Gondar	5: Addis Ababa taken 10: Campaign in Galla Sidamo starts
May	4: Rommel's attack on Tobruk fails Fighting at Sollum and Halfaya	Patriot operations continued 16: Italian Viceroy surrenders at Amba Alagi	5: Emperor enters Addis Ababa 3–10: Battle of Wadara 23: Soddu taken
June	1: Crete evacuated 8: British invade Syria 15–17: British attack on Halfaya–Sollum fails	Patriot operations continued	4–5: River Omo crossed 21: Jimma taken

Date	*Middle East*	*East Africa*	
July		Patriot operations continued	6: Italians in Galla–Sidamo surrender
Aug.		Patriot operations continued	NIGERIAN BRIGADE LEAVES FOR WEST AFRICA
Sept.		25: Italians at Wolchefit surrender	
Oct.		Preparations for attack on Gondar fortress	GOLD COAST BRIGADE LEAVES FOR WEST AFRICA
Nov.	18: British offensive in Libya commences	27: Italians surrender Gondar END OF CAMPAIGN IN EAST AFRICA	

CHAPTER 9

The Fall of France and the Expansion of the R.W.A.F.F.

(i) *The Situation in West Africa*

WITH the fall of France, and the assumption of power by a hostile government at Vichy, the potential danger of our West African territories caused considerable anxiety. As has already been mentioned, very few organized troops were left after the departure of the Expeditionary Force to East Africa. There were no aircraft other than a few antiquated machines belonging to the Navy at Freetown. To make matters worse the pre-war plans for expansion in Nigeria had not been completely implemented. The geographical situation was also unfavourable. Thus Gambia, surrounded by French territory, could be invaded overland or down the Gambia River. Though the approaches to Sierra Leone from the west and north were through difficult country with poor communications, and Freetown could only be approached overland down a narrow peninsula, the harbour was only two days' steaming from Dakar by fast ships and within range of French aerodromes. Both Gold Coast and Nigeria could be attacked from three sides by land, while Lagos, the capital of the latter, and the main railway to the north, are only a few miles from the Dahomey frontier.

Although the West African ports were important for the export of much-needed raw materials, Freetown and Takoradi had special significance. The magnificent harbour of Freetown, capable of holding large numbers of ships, was a vital convoy centre, particularly since the virtual closure of the Mediterranean route; the second was the port where crated aircraft were unloaded, assembled and flown to the Middle East via Nigeria and the Sudan. There was a small coastal battery at Freetown, while Takoradi possessed an old 4 in. gun taken from a sunken merchantman. Lagos harbour had no guns, its only protection being a volunteer machine-gun unit.

The French had a strong force of native units, with a number of armoured fighting vehicles, which could be reinforced from North Africa. They also had aircraft, including American Glen Martin bombers, together with adquate airfields within range of our ports. Dakar was a well-protected Naval base where, besides small craft, there was a damaged battleship and, in early September, three heavy cruisers and several destroyers arrived from Toulon. On the other hand, it was believed that French morale was very low, except at Dakar, which seemed to be a nest of virulent Vichyites strongly supported by the French Navy.

As regards enemy operations by sea, raids by heavy ships or seaborne aircraft were considered to be possible; also that blockships might be used at Takoradi or Lagos. The coastline of the British territories was very long: Sierra Leone 200 miles, Gold Coast 330 miles, and Nigeria about

600 miles. Owing to heavy surf or mangrove swamps, however, there were few beaches suitable for landings, though, unfortunately, some of these were near Freetown and Takoradi. A small force could also have been landed inside the mole at Lagos at the entrance to the harbour. Generally speaking, however, nothing more than raids appeared possible unless we lost command of the sea for an appreciable period. The main threats were considered to be an invasion overland and/or sporadic but not sustained bombing.

It had been agreed that the War Office should assume responsibility for the defence of West Africa on the outbreak of war. In the event they did not do so, and it was not until after much discussion with the Colonial Office that they decided to appoint a general officer commanding and to take over from the date of his appointment. This was one of the causes of the delay in providing for the defence of the West African territories before the Expeditionary Force left for East Africa.

On 7th July 1940 Lieutenant-General G. J. Giffard arrived at Freetown with one Staff Officer to take up his appointment as General Officer Commanding West Africa, and his Headquarters was finally established at Achimota College near Accra on 15th July. His task was the defence and co-ordination of effort of all the West African territories. The remainder of the staff, a large proportion of whom had previous service in the R.W.A.F.F., began to arrive in early August, but the heads of services and their staffs and the bulk of the Headquarters clerks did not arrive until some weeks later.

It was clear that the situation called for expansion on a large scale and two major problems required immediate attention. First, the defence of Freetown was of vital importance; and secondly, the provision of reinforcements for Gambia if any attempt was to be made to hold it.

(ii) *Preparation for Defence and Expansion*

As a first step in organization each territory was placed under an Area Commander who was to be responsible for its defence and for raising and training the units to be formed therein, including those of the medical, ordnance and supply and transport services. In the meantime, General Giffard had informed the War Office of his immediate requirements. He also told them 'there was nothing we could not teach the African provided we had the necessary instructors'. In response, one British battalion had been placed under orders for Freetown: it was to be followed by two more as well as coast-defence and anti-aircraft units. In addition, he had asked for the personnel and equipment for the casualty clearing stations and general hospitals required in West Africa; the latter to be held in readiness for despatch as soon as accommodation would be available. The authorities at home stated that the artillery and medical units would be sent out with only 80 per cent of their establishment, the remainder to be provided by West Africa, and the proportion of Africans to be increased by stages as quickly as possible. It was also specified that the British battalions were to be relieved by units of the R.W.A.F.F. as soon as available.

The expansion envisaged at this stage was intended only to provide for the defence of West Africa. The new formations and units it was proposed to raise consisted of the following: Nigeria, three brigade groups; Gold Coast, one brigade group; Sierra Leone, one battalion; Gambia, one battalion. Each brigade group was to have an army service corps unit capable of carrying one day's supplies and second-line ammunition. In addition, general transport companies and other ancillary units such as supply and ordnance depots were to be formed.

On 26th September 4 G.C.R. embarked for the Gambia. This was the last unit of the immediate post-war expansion and with its departure the Gold Coast was left almost defenceless. A welcome event was the arrival of the first British battalion, 1/4 Essex, at Freetown early in September.

The Dakar operation, about which General Giffard had not been consulted, commenced on 23rd September and proved a complete fiasco. Fortunately there were no repercussions elsewhere in West Africa. However, the British Headquarters of the expedition and a battalion of Royal Marines appeared at Freetown without warning. The latter had to be accommodated in a new camp earmarked for one of the British battalions expected to arrive for the defence of the port.

(iii) *Expansion: First Stage*

It is proposed in this section to deal mainly with manpower. One of the main problems at the outset was the provision of European cadres and African N.C.O.s. No European could be obtained locally at this time and reliance had to be placed on drafts from the United Kingdom. The first party arrived early in August, including, as General Giffard had requested, a large proportion of regular officers and N.C.O.s who had had previous experience in the R.W.A.F.F. A few of the field officers took command of new units at once, which enabled a good start to be made. After European cadres, the next requisite was experienced African N.C.O.s, and application was made to East Africa for as many as could be spared from the two brigades there. The numbers available, however, did not suffice. Fortunately a number of ex-N.C.O.s and old soldiers re-enlisted who were fit for training recruits and garrison duties even if too old for active service. Units ran cadre courses and, as soon as possible, schools were formed. The regimental depots were expanded into infantry-training centres, though at one time the intake was so large that battalions had to train some of their own recruits, a course which had its disadvantages.

Training was as intensive as possible, though hampered in some respects by the language difficulty and the shortage of arms and ammunition in the early stages. Steps were taken to overcome the language difficulty by engaging African schoolmasters, on a scale of eight per battalion and *pro rata* in the other arms, to teach English to the troops. Considerable progress was made, which was particularly noticeable when the units went to Burma.

The aim of infantry training was the same as in peace, namely, first to make the recruits into disciplined soldiers with a thorough grounding in their weapons and infantry subjects, then to pass on to collective training under normal as well as bush warfare conditions. Company marches in bush and long-distance patrols were a feature of the training. Recruits of the engineer and signal units did their primary training at infantry-training centres, as did some of the recruits for the services. The latter units were, however, mainly dependent on their British cadres, who, new to the country and mostly non-regular, had a difficult task which they carried out very well.

As Headquarters, West Africa, had no signal unit for many months, dispersion and space were troublesome factors. All communications with the United Kingdom had to be by cable or a slow and most erratic postal service; the same applied to communications with Nigeria, Sierra Leone and Gambia. Visits by officers from Headquarters to units, except in the Gold Coast, had to be made by sea: opportunities were rare and there was always the difficulty of getting back. Officers could occasionally travel by Imperial Airways to Nigeria and, eventually, the G.O.C. was allowed a personal aircraft.

By the time Headquarters, West Africa, had been in existence for six months the R.W.A.F.F. had approximately twenty-three battalions in being, including the six in East Africa who, of course, had to be provided with drafts. The ancillary units were taking shape, particularly the West African Army Service Corps. A good start had been made in building new hospitals and barracks. Freetown had two British battalions and the Sierra Leone Battalion, as well as British anti-aircraft and coast-defence batteries. But most of the other units were incomplete in equipment and not past the elementary stages of their training. The French in the surdounding territories were still hostile, though quiescent. Their morale was low; they were getting short of European food and clothing, and were feeling the effects of delayed leave to Europe.

A good deal had been achieved, but much remained to be done. There had been considerable enthusiasm among all ranks who had worked hard, and the African recruits were shaping well. But the progress made can also be attributed to quick, firm decisions, decentralization and a mimimum of correspondence and talk. It now remained to complete the training and equipment of the field units, to raise garrison units, to relieve the British battalions, and to Africanize the coast and anti-aircraft artillery as well as the medical units up to 80 per cent of their establishment.

In the following sections an outline is given of some of the main problems which had to be solved in the early days by the Administrative Staff at Headquarters, West Africa, as well as some of those which confronted the General Staff. The administrative side is considered first, as so much depended on quick action to meet the needs of the rapidly expanding forces in West Africa.

(iv) *Administrative Problems*

It must be remembered that no services existed in peacetime; each had to be formed from scratch. There was a shortage of everything for the new units except potential manpower. Hospital and barrack accommodation was insufficient and sites for new buildings had to be selected, though, in some cases, old stations were reopened.

'Early in August it was decided that a start must be made to provide hospitals and barracks. But the Chief Engineer had not arrived and, in any case, he would not have the staff to cope with the work to be done; moreover, there were no engineer stores. The medical staff were also not available, though said to have embarked.

'There was a small British military hospital at Freetown and the Navy had a hospital ship anchored there. There were, in addition, some old hospital buildings near the town which could be renovated and have more space added. Otherwise the steadily mounting numbers of European and African troops were entirely dependent on the West African Medical Service hospitals in the various territories. The estimated number of hospital beds and the locations of the units, assuming we should have to fight in West Africa, were worked out with the Director of Medical Services, Gold Coast, whilst the co-operation of the West African Medical Service and the Public Works Departments in all the territories was enlisted. The former undertook to design the hospitals and to advise as to the exact sites. In the meantime, they would endeavour to expand their European and African hospitals to take the additional patients. The Public Works Departments undertook the building and the requisition of the necessary material from the United Kingdom. In spite of many difficulties the work was finished in good time. Those who served in West Africa during that period, and later on too, owe a great debt of gratitude to these two Departments.

'More barracks were required in each Area. Though the Africans could, at a pinch, have built their own, this could not be allowed, for obvious reasons; and, moreover, a great deal of new accommodation was required for British troops. Once more the Public Works Department helped until the Sappers were in a position to deal with contractors or employ direct labour, but even then the Departments often acted as agents for "works" of various kinds. Tented camps are not suitable in West Africa, and, anyway, there were no tents.

'The most urgent problem during the early part of August 1940 was the provision of accommodation for the British battalions coming to Freetown, one of which was expected within a few weeks, and two more later. Accommodation for the first battalion was secured by taking over the R.W.A.F.F. barracks at Wilberforce, near Freetown, by enlarging them and by adding various amenities. The local authorities made a very good job of this indeed and managed to have the place very nearly ready when the unit disembarked. It was, however, a nightmare to "Q" and the Chief Engineer. The other two battalions had to be located within the Freetown peninsula for tactical reasons, and this made the choice of sites very limited. In the event, the third battalion did not arrive, but the accommodation prepared for them was useful for other purposes. One of the trials of the Staff was the repeated threat to dump British troops on the Coast at short notice. Sierra Leone always seemed to be the first favourite, though quite the worst from the point of view of space and accommodation.

'The roads in the Freetown peninsula required immediate attention or they would not stand up to the anticipated traffic. At a later stage there was considerable road development in Nigeria, particularly as regards the completion of two north and south routes.

'Existing aerodromes were enlarged and a number of landing grounds were hacked out of the bush in various parts of the territories. These landing grounds were always a source of anxiety to Area Commanders, first because the bush came back with surprising rapidity; secondly, because it was essential to deny their use to hostile aircraft, but the means of prevention, mostly oil drums filled with earth, had to be removed before our aircraft could use them; and thirdly, because many of them were far from any military station.

'There were many other requirements, all urgent. Command posts, gun emplacements, magazines, etc., for the new coast defences at Freetown, Takoradi and Lagos had to be designed and constructed, also magazines and covered accommodation in each Area for reserves of ammunition and all kinds of stores.

'As already pointed out, no supply and transport organization existed in peace. Various local arrangements were made at the outset for feeding the units, but rations were to be issued in the normal manner as soon as possible. So the new Supply and Transport Service was faced with starting the whole organization from zero and without delay. African rations could be obtained from local contractors, but British rations in the main would have to be imported. But it was known that West Africa was required to be self-supporting as soon as possible, except for groceries, so every endeavour had to be made to use local resources. Nigeria could produce meat and butter, but Gold Coast could not supply enough for its own rations and Sierra Leone practically none. This gave rise to the problem of shipping animals along the coast from Nigeria. But Sierra Leone was always a difficulty, and more than once the Navy came to our help from their own ample stocks or by lending refrigerated space afloat for meat from overseas. Vegetables were grown in all the territories and attempts were made to produce bacon and jams; the latter was more successful than the former! Yams were sometimes issued instead of potatoes, but were hardly popular with English personnel. Yeast was always a difficulty, and so palm wine was substituted for bread-making. Cooking was done by wood, so S. & T. were not bothered about coal, though Nigeria could have produced ample supplies.

'In addition to setting up an organization for the purchase, storage and issue of local supplies, S. & T. had to prepare for the receipt of vehicles and stores from overseas and for building up reserves of all commodities in the right places. They also had to find and train their African personnel. They had to deal with the hire of transport and for requisitioning it in an emergency. They were, of course, also deeply concerned with the formation and training of the field units of the West African Army Service Corps.

'In peace the R.W.A.F.F. had no regimental cooks, as the West African soldier was accustomed to having his food prepared by his women. So with the issue of rations came the necessity for training unit cooks. But a British Catering Corps instructor would not know the language or the type of cooking required. The problem was solved in the Gold Coast by

General Sir George Gifford, G.C.B., D.S.O.

Face page 368

The Kaladan Valley

Face page 369

getting the African lady contractor who dealt in jam and marmalade for the S. & T. to provide teachers and run a school for a specified fee. She produced a collection of *mammies* and the local School of Cookery became a great success. On state occasions Madam always appeared in a *Paris* creation from Dakar, ready to receive distinguished visitors.

'There was no Ordnance service at the outset, so the Staff used the rough and ready method of indenting by cable for the complete war outfits of the units to be raised in each Area, plus reserves. A pitiful trickle arrived at first, which is not surprising in view of the situation at home. So far as weapons and ammunition were concerned, releases were made to West Africa in bulk, and sub-allotted to Areas in proportion to their requirements, the War Office being notified to which ports the articles were to be consigned. Great care was taken about this, because the home authorities' knowledge of the geography of West Africa seemed to begin and end at Freetown. After a month or so the flow started to increase, and the mass of vehicles which began to arrive from Canada and the U.S.A. early in 1941 was astonishing.

'In the meantime, resort had to be made to local resources once more. For instance, all stocks of khaki drill in the territories were bought up—strangely enough the quantities were quite large, though it was very poor stuff. The cloth was made into uniforms by local tailors. Rifles were borrowed from the Police! Other articles such as blankets were procured somehow; boots did not matter so much at the moment, at least for the bush recruits.

'West Africa started with one representative of Transportation and Movement, but a suitable organization and the necessary units were slowly built up. As the Areas were separated from each other by sea or by the Vichy French, the only means of moving stores and troops between them was by ship. So, very early in the proceedings, a request was made for a suitable coaster. This met with a blank refusal. But the bombardment was continued until finally, probably through the good offices of "Admiral, Freetown", a somewhat cranky craft of uncertain origin was produced on "temporary loan". This was, at least, a minor triumph.

'The Record Offices remained under the Areas; they were mainly an expansion of the peacetime Regimental Record Offices. The "Records" in Africa were not the virtual dictators they always appear to be to units on the normal British establishment. Generally speaking the infantry and light batteries were recruited from the bush and there was little difficulty in getting the numbers required, though the physical condition of recruits in some places was disappointing to those who knew the pre-war soldiers. Usually, however, suitable men suffering from tropical ailments which would yield rapidly to modern medical treatment were accepted. The Sappers made efforts to recruit village craftsmen with some success in certain areas. The recruitment of suitable types for signals and the services, as well as clerks, presented more difficulty, as the semi-educated were not so keen to join as the bushmen.

'The Pay Branch had to start from nothing and was partly Africanized: in spite of early troubles due to inexperience it functioned. The Paymaster and Financial Adviser, who was a tower of strength, was strangely enough the first head of a service to arrive, which was just as well, as the forces in West Africa were not considered to be "on active service" from the financial point of view.

'The first British battalion arrived at Freetown with no mosquito nets. Thanks to the Royal Navy it was kept on board ship until the nets could be traced. They turned up in a convoy a fortnight later. It was not good for the unit to be kept on board so long in the anchorage and it was shocking waste of ship's time. But there can be no doubt as to the wisdom of the decision. To have landed a raw battalion at Freetown in September without protection would have been to court disaster.

'As always in malarial areas, it was found that the incidence of malaria with British personnel in general and British units in particular was in direct relation to their observance of local orders, which were the result of considerable experience in West Africa. The well-disciplined units were always outstanding in this respect. It is curious that the same lesson had to be learned in the following years in Malaya, North Africa and Burma.'[1]

(v) *Some Defence Problems*

The problems facing the General Staff were, as usual, more intangible than the administrative ones. Defence schemes, operation instructions and demolition plans had to be thought out and prepared. All this brought home to the planners how exiguous our forces were in the first few months. For instance, in the Gold Coast it was found necessary to rely on the Escort Police—armed constabulary—to provide 500 men in an emergency. There were new establishments to be worked out and there were always 'courses open to the enemy' to be studied as circumstances altered which might lead to repercussions in West Africa. A perennial question was whether the Germans would succeed in goading the Vichy French into taking action against Freetown, or one of the other territories. It was fortunate, perhaps, that the Trans-Sahara railway had remained merely a project.

'For instance, there was speculation as to the possibility of an Italo/German force, based on Tripolitania, carrying out a *blitz* with a mechanized column on one of the territories. Such an attack would be made down one of the main north and south routes in Nigeria or Gold Coast, and co-ordinated with French action to keep us occupied elsewhere. The thin orchard bush of the northern provinces would be little or no obstacle to tracked vehicles, and we had neither aircraft not anti-tank guns. The tropical forest might constitute an obstacle if properly utilized, but it was far south of the northern frontiers. It looked as if we should have to go back to an obstacle, either one of the big rivers or the forest, but this would entail giving up country which produced ground nuts for export and native corn for home consumption, as well as being the main recruiting area for the infantry. It was clear that an attack of this nature would require a good deal of preparation and a backing of French African troops to operate on the flanks of the route used. Some considered the project unlikely, if not

[1] Excerpts from 'The Development of the West African Forces in the Second World War', *Army Quarterly*, October 1947.

impossible, but if the Germans had thought it worth while and given their attention to it, they could have reached our frontiers. The feasibility of a column crossing the Sahara was afterwards proved when General Le Clerc took a force from Lake Chad area to join the Eighth Army in Tripolitania.'[1]

There is no *juju* in connection with bush warfare and no new principles are involved. It is simply war in a peculiar type of country which demands the common-sense application of suitable tactical methods to give circumstances and conditions, but untrained troops are simply useless off the roads. The R.W.A.F.F. had had plenty of experience of fighting in bush against good native troops trained and led by Europeans in the War of 1914–18. Doctrine on the matter was clear and the brigades in East Africa were gaining further experience. But now the effect of aircraft and armoured fighting vehicles in the possession of the enemy had to be considered in relation to the defence of West Africa, bearing in mind that we had neither of these weapons, no anti-tank guns or mines and only a small amount of static anti-aircraft artillery.

On 7th June 1941 a cryptic message was received from the War Office indicating the possibility of hostile French action, especially by air, any time after first light next day. All concerned were warned to take every precaution possible, but in the event the local French did nothing. The reason for this little flutter was soon apparent—we had invaded Syria on the morning of 8th June. In the meantime, the declaration of the Governor of Chad for de Gaulle and the occupation of the French Cameroons and Equatorial Africa by the Free French Forces had closed Nigeria's back door and now the attack on Syria made the Vichy French in West Africa extremely nervous.

(vi) *Completion of Expansion and Events: 1941–42*

Early in 1941 it was decided that the R.W.A.F.F. should consist only of the infantry. All other units, raised or being raised, including the light batteries, would form part of the African Colonial Forces with the prefix 'West African' before their titles, thus: 'West African Engineers, A.C.F.'

By July 1941 we had a force in being in West Africa,[2] equipped, not yet fully trained, but steadily improving. The British Battalions in Freetown had been relieved by Nigerians and the coast and anti-aircraft artillery as well as the medical units were progressing with their Africanization. The signal units and the services, particularly the West African Army Service Corps, had made remarkable progress and the African recruits, including those from the bush, had shown considerable mechanical aptitude. The G.O.C. had become the G.O.C.-in-C., but the four Governors still retained their titles of 'Commander-in-Chief'. So there were five commanders-in-chief—a curious anachronism, though four of them could exercise no command. This was laid down in King's Regulations.

Much hard work had been done and devoted service given since Headquarters, West Africa, had been formed a year before. Many difficulties

[1] Ibid.

[2] The distribution of units and formations is shown in Appendix VII.

had been overcome and awkward situations resolved without fuss. Though a few small units had still to be raised, the main task was now to complete the training of the existing units and formations.

Transport had been mechanized, but this did not solve the problem of movement off the roads nor give the necessary flexibility and mobility. The only solution in the absence of animal transport was to use carriers, but these must be enlisted and disciplined men. Early in 1941, therefore, an Auxiliary Group was added to each brigade group. These units consisted of a headquarters and three companies each of 500 carriers with a small European cadre.[1] Each group could carry about 36 tons of supplies and ammunition up to 15 miles a day. When not required for mobile operations these units would be used to provide labour. Though originally designed for service in West Africa, these groups were found to be extremely useful in Burma.

Just before the outbreak of war the Governor of the Gold Coast had suggested that the time had come to grant commissions in the R.W.A.F.F. to Africans. A scheme was worked out that educated Africans, recommended by carefully stipulated persons, should be enlisted in the Gold Coast Territorial Battalion as cadets. They were to serve for two years, at the end of which they would have to pass the examination laid down for candidates for commissions in the Territorial Army at home. Twelve cadets enlisted, only two stayed the course and, in 1941, one of these was rejected, leaving only Sergeant Seth Antony, an Old Achimotan. He was sent to England to attend an O.C.T.U. and after three months was reported to be doing well. Having passed out, he was awarded an emergency commission in the Gold Coast Regiment and, after doing well in Burma, returned as a temporary major. It is understood that he afterwards became a Civil Servant.

By the middle of 1941 the new hospitals had been built and were functioning. The personnel were very keen. One Quartermaster in checking his stores discovered an item missing. He wrote in to Area Headquarters on behalf of his commanding officer as follows:

> 'As this hospital is now open to receive patients we shall require twelve coffins.'

An Allied Conference was held at Accra on 5th–6th August to consider plans for the defence of West Africa. This was attended by the Belgians and Free French and arrangements were made for mutual assistance. Among other things, it was agreed that a Belgian Brigade Group from the Congo would, if necessary, move to Nigeria and come under British command.

The expansion had by now nearly reached the ceiling finally laid down by the War Office. A reconnaissance squadron was added to each brigade group in August 1941. The formation of the much needed anti-tank batteries had been delayed owing to lack of weapons, which in the circumstances is understandable. However, in November, seven 12-gun batteries were authorized and a training unit was formed in Nigeria. About this time there was a shortage of officers in the Army and the War Office

[1] The strength of these units was afterwards increased.

was unable to provide any more officers for West Africa. The deficit was made up by posting some 200 Polish officers.

On 1st September the Nigerian Brigade Group arrived at Lagos from East Africa and was stationed in the Ilorin–Ibadan Area until leaving for Sierra Leone at the end of the year. The Gold Coast Brigade Group arrived at Takoradi early in December and was stationed temporarily in the Gold Coast. These formations now became the 1st and 2nd (West African) Brigade Groups respectively. The return of these two experienced formations made all the difference to our defensive potential and enabled us to reinforce the garrisons of Sierra Leone and Gambia in 1942.

During the early months of 1942 there was a series of disasters in the Middle and Far East, but the tide slowly began to turn. Madagascar was taken from the Vichy French by a British Expeditionary Force, the victory of El Alamein was won and an Allied Army landed in North-West Africa. At least two of these events could have caused repercussions in West Africa.

There was, however, a flutter in April when it was thought the battleship *Richelieu* was about to attempt to break out of Dakar. If so, she would be intercepted by the Royal Navy and probably sunk. Warnings were issued to all concerned to be particularly alert, especially against air attack.

As in the case of the attack on Syria in the previous year, there was the possibility that the operation against Madagascar would lead to reprisals on West Africa. Warnings were sent out, but again no hostile action took place.

The state of special alertness was hardly ended when another crisis arose. It was learnt on 10th October that there was a state of intense nervous tension in Vichy circles caused by the impression that an Allied attack on Dakar was imminent. It also appears that the Germans thought the offensive being mounted in the United Kingdom and United States was to be against Dakar. This was probably due to the cover plan for the landings in Morocco and Algeria and, to some extent, to the arrival of American troops in Liberia. In the meantime, the leading elements of a Belgian Brigade Group had arrived in Nigeria. The dispositions in West Africa at this time are shown in Appendix VIII.

Once more there was no hostile action against British territory and eventually the whole of French West Africa opted for General de Gaulle. Thus the main threat to the security of British West Africa ceased to exist and it became possible to employ the African forces elsewhere.

(vii) *Formation of the 81st and 82nd Divisions*

In December 1942, whilst on a visit to the War Office, General Giffard had suggested that the West African formations and units could be usefully employed in Burma. On 1st January 1943 the War Office notified Headquarters, West Africa, that a division and a large number of non-divisional ancillary units would be required for service in Burma. A fortnight later orders arrived for the preparation of a second division for despatch to the same destination. Steps were taken at once for the necessary internal movement of units and formations and the concentration of the first division in Nigeria. It was also agreed that the Belgian Brigade Group should leave Nigeria for service elsewhere. Later in the month General Giffard flew to India to make arrangements for the reception of the West African troops.

The 81st (West African) Division came into being on 1st March. A few days later preliminary orders were issued for the formation of the 82nd (West African) Division which involved taking the last three of the six trained brigade groups. This was possible since a radical alteration in the general situation had occurred, so much so that on 14th March the Chiefs of Staff issued the following appreciation in regard to West Africa:

> 'No attack by land forces, surface craft or air forces is considered possible in the foreseeable future.'

It was then decided to reduce the coast-defence and anti-aircraft artillery in West Africa, some of the latter units being made available for service overseas. Furthermore, it was settled that 10 battalions of the R.W.A.F.F., in addition to training units, would suffice for general defence and internal security. The order of battle of the two West African Divisions and a list of the battalions remaining in West Africa are given in Appendix IX.

On 25th March 1943 General Giffard relinquished command of West Africa on appointment as G.O.C.-in-C., Eastern Army, India. It was due to the firm foundations he laid as Inspector-General before the war that the East and West African troops were able to play so great a part in the campaign in East Africa and Abyssinia. Furthermore, the rapid expansion of the R.W.A.F.F. during 1940–2 depended not only on this foundation but above all on his organizing ability, determination, mental and physical energy.[1] He was so fully trusted by the Colonial Office and the Governors in Africa that he was able to settle difficult problems which might otherwise have proved insurmountable. Moreover, his knowledge of Colonial systems of government was also of great value to the War Office.

The 81st Division was concentrated in Nigeria in April, began to move overseas in July and was in action in Burma by February 1944. The 82nd Division, after concentrating in Nigeria, began to embark in November and commenced to assemble at Ranchi in Western India during January 1944.

A monumental task had been completed. The main object in West Africa was now to provide the necessary drafts to keep the formations up to strength. In July 1944 preparations were made to reduce staffs and services as well as coast defences. Disbandment commenced in October.[2]

[1] In the immediate post-war years he was justly regarded as the 'Father' of the R.W.A.F.F.

[2] The Lagos Defence Force had been disbanded in July 1943.

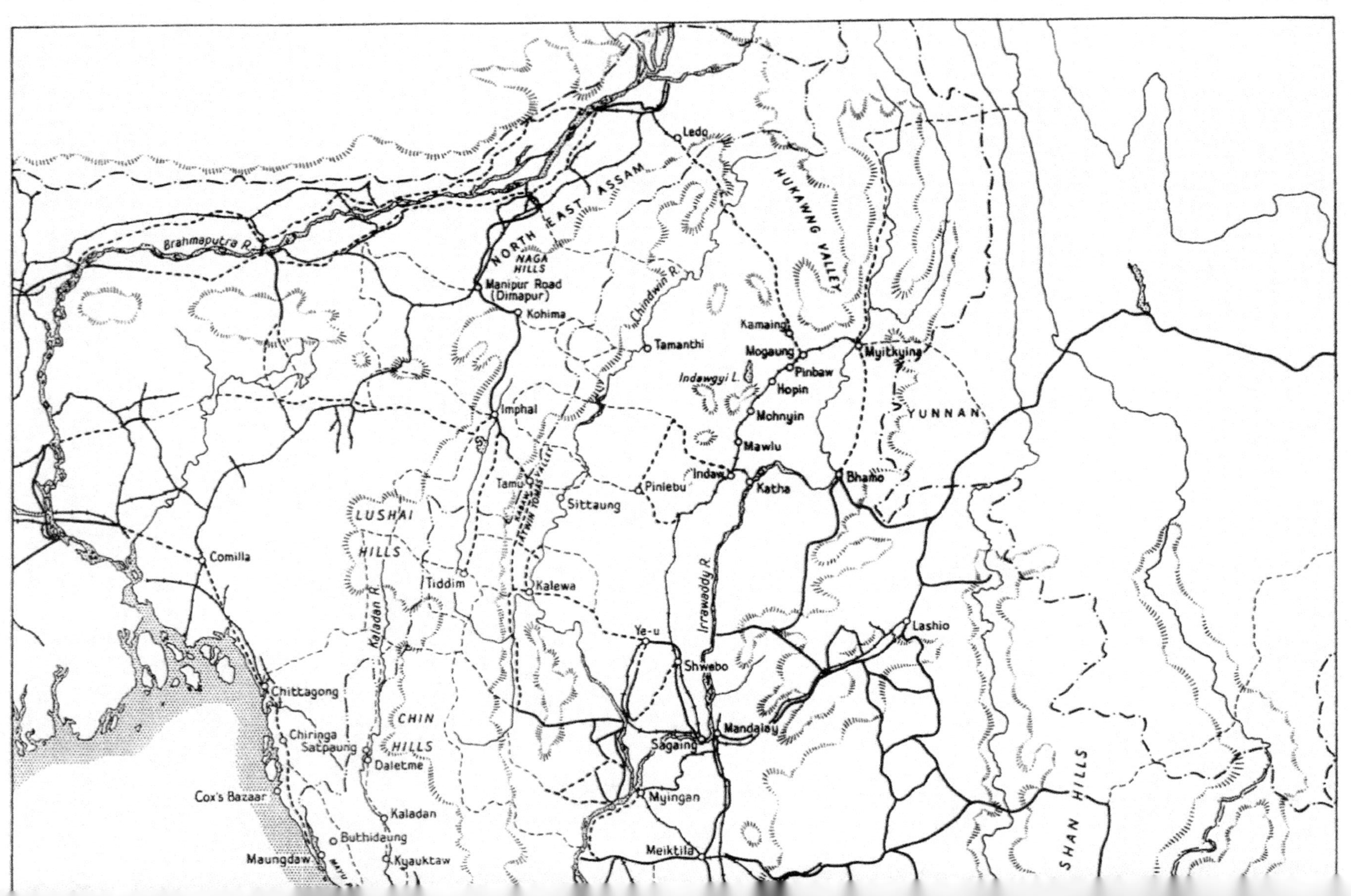

Ledo
NORTH EAST ASSAM
HUKAWNG VALLEY
NAGA HILLS
Brahmaputra R.
Manipur Road
(Dimapur)
Kohima
Chindwin R.
Tamanthi
Kamaing
Mogaung
Myitkyina
Pinbaw
Indawgyi L.
Hopin
Mohnyin
YUNNAN
Imphal
Mawlu
Indaw
Bhamo
Katha
Tamu
Pinlebu
Sittaung
LUSHAI HILLS
Comilla
Tiddim
Kalewa
Kaladan R.
Irrawaddy R.
Lashio
Ye-u
Shwebo
Chittagong
CHIN HILLS
Chiringa
Satpaung
Daletme
Mandalay
Sagaing
Cox's Bazaar
Myingan
Kaladan
Buthidaung
Maungdaw
Kyauktaw
Meiktila
SHAN HILLS

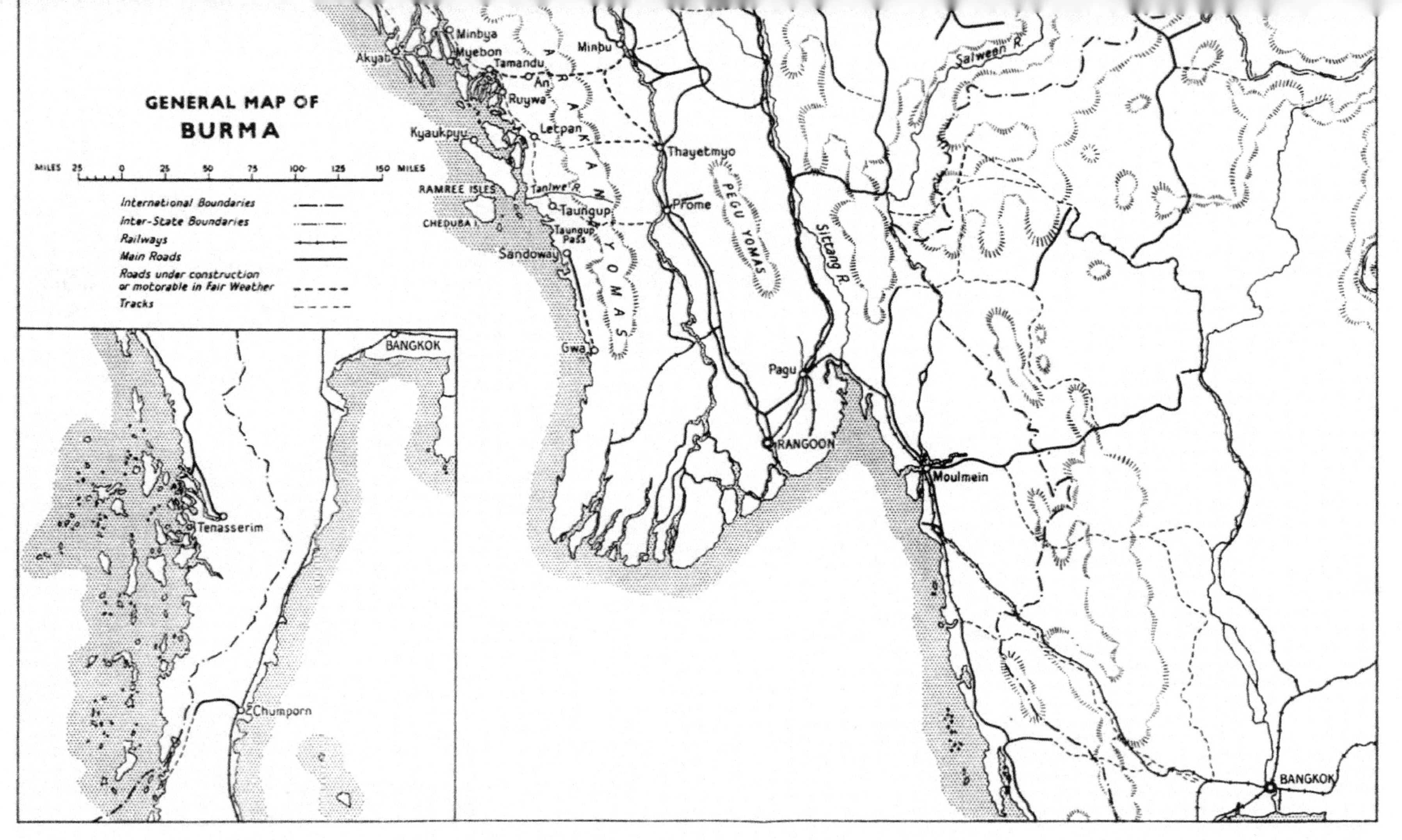

37. General map of Burma

Face page 375

81st (WEST AFRICAN) DIVISION: DIVISIONAL SIGN

GIZZO (Anase) the spider is a traditional hero of West African folk-lore. His outstanding quality is subtlety; and by using his wits he repeatedly discomforts those who would harm him. He achieves many 'impossible' feats such as the capture alive of a hive of bees, a leopard and a snake.

CHAPTER 10

The Campaign in Burma: 1943–4

(Maps Nos. 37, 38 and 39)

(i) *The Situation in November 1943*

LATE in May 1942 the 900-mile retreat of the Burma Corps from Rangoon came to an end on the Indo-Burma frontier. It had been a fighting withdrawal, conducted with spirit and courage under conditions of great hardship. Gaunt, ragged as scarecrows, but still a disciplined force, they found on arrival that their hopes of retiring behind other troops were in vain. Reinforced by no more than a half-trained brigade, they had to hold the Assam frontier. Fortunately, the enemy were in no state to press their advantage; the wet season commenced in earnest and there was a lull in operations.

We had lost Hong Kong, Malaya and Burma, and had now arrived at the last ditch in the Far East, a state of affairs which also came to pass about six weeks later in the Middle East. Nevertheless, as has so often happened before in our long history, we held the last ditch until emerging from it to win the final victory. But the time had not yet come for our emergence from this ditch in Burma. Early in 1943 an attempt had been made to drive the enemy from the Arakan to remove the air threat to Calcutta. It was a near disaster and resulted in lowered morale. The first 'Chindit' expedition had been an expensive failure which achieved practically nothing, though it had some psychological effect.[1]

The series of disasters and setbacks in the Far East was mainly due to lack of preparedness. So far as operations in Burma were concerned, a major factor was that India's resources and communications had for many years been organized to deal with an invasion of the North-West Frontier. There was neither a rail nor a road link between the Indian Province of Assam and the Burma systems.

As recorded in the previous chapter, General Giffard left West Africa in March 1943 to command the Eastern Army. On arrival in India he took steps to counter the deterioration in morale and to improve administration. He also instituted hard, intensive training during the monsoon period of 1943. In these measures he was ably seconded by Lieutenant-General W. J. Slim, who succeeded in raising the morale of all ranks under his command. The result was that more and better bush-trained formations became available towards the end of the year.

It had been decided at the Ottowa Conference in August 1943 to set up an Allied Headquarters with Admiral Lord Mountbatten as Supreme Commander. This Headquarters, termed South-East Asia Command,

[1] See also Chapter 11 (i).

became operational in mid-November. General Sir George Giffard was appointed to command the newly formed 11th Army Group, and General Slim to command the Fourteenth Army. Thus, the forces in Assam and Burma passed from the command of the Commander-in-Chief, India, but that country remained the main base and General Auchinleck rendered most valuable services in training and maintenance.

The land forces allotted to S.E.A.C. consisted of the under-mentioned, deployed in three distinct groups each separated from the next by mountainous, roadless country:

11th Army Group

Fourteenth Army

XV Corps (Lieutenant-General Sir Philip Christison): Four divisions, including 81 (W.A.) Div., less 3 (W.A.) Bde., in the Arakan based on Chittagong and in process of gaining contact with the enemy.

IV Corps (Lieutenant-General Sir G. Scoones): Three divisions deployed on the Central Front and based on Imphal.

Army Reserve: one division.

Assigned to S.E.A.C.; to be allotted later

XXXIII Corps of three divisions:

Commando Brigade.

50th (Indian) Tank Brigade.

3 (Indian) Division (Chindits).

Northern Area Combat Command (Lieutenant-General Stilwell, U.S.A.)

The troops under command consisted of three Chinese Divisions each 10,000 strong, trained and equipped by the Americans. Also a combat group of U.S. troops trained for long-range penetration, known as 'Merril's Marauders'. These forces were starting to move southwards from their base at Ledo in north-east Assam.

There was also the Chinese Yunnan Force consisting of 12 divisions—each equivalent to a British brigade group—on the upper Salween in Eastern Burma. This force was not under command of S.E.A.C., but directly under the Chinese 'Generalissimo', Chiang Kai-shek, and was simply watched by small Japanese detachments.

In mid-November the Japanese had some five divisions in the forward area in addition to army, garrison and lines of communication troops. Their 55 Div. was in the Arakan, 31 and 33 Divs. on the Central Front and 18 and 56 Divs. on the Northern Front. Their 54 Div. was assembling at Prome, other reinforcements were known to be moving in, and there was a steady flow of drafts to replace casualties. It was believed that the Japanese air force amounted to 370 fighters and bombers. The fighters were superior to our Hurricanes, and it was not until January 1944 that the R.A.F. began to achieve local superiority and finally to achieve command of the air.

(ii) *The Two Enemies*

The Army in Burma had to face two enemies—the Japanese and the combined effect of the geography, topography and climate of the country. This second enemy was the cause of the greatest problem at this stage of the war in Burma, namely, that of moving and maintaining sufficient forces in the forward area to beat the Japanese.

By the end of 1943 we were beginning to understand the Japanese characteristics sufficiently well to take advantage of their weak points. Though fanatically brave when ordered 'to succeed or die', the Japanese soldier was liable to panic when surprised or in doubt; and, though skilful at infiltrating and rushing a position from an unexpected direction, he became, at times, upset by determined resistance. Their plans were generally bold, but their junior officers and N.C.O.s, lacking in initiative and self-reliance, were at a loss when faced by the unexpected or when events did not go according to plan.

The Japanese were skilful at digging in and camouflaging their positions, yet nullified the result by chattering at night like a lot of monkeys. Although good at the use of ground and at moving silently, patrolling was often badly done and the men were not good shots. Officers and other ranks had the habit of carrying diaries, military papers or even orders into battle.

Apart from their ability to march and fight on very scanty rations, the outstanding characteristic of officers and men was that, due to their upbringing and outlook, they regarded capture as the worst disgrace and any individual when cornered would sell his life dearly or commit suicide. Mopping up after a successful attack was, therefore, apt to be a slow process, as every Japanese officer or other rank had to be 'winkled out' and killed.

Before narrating the operations which took place it is essential to appreciate the topographical and climatic conditions of the theatre of war—the second enemy. It will be apparent that the Japanese had, up to the early months of 1944, the advantage of fairly good communications by road, water and rail, and that the Allies were badly handicapped in this respect.

The Indo-Burmese frontier, from where it leaves the sea in Arakan, near Maungdaw, until it joins the Sino-Thibetan frontier on the Salween River north of Myitkyina, follows a series of mountain ranges, the general axes of which run from north to south. The main features of these mountain ranges are their precipitous sides and the fast-flowing rivers in the deep valleys. These mountains are at their maximum heights at the north-east end of the frontier, where they rise to 10,000 to 12,000 ft. and more. Their height gradually declines as the ranges run southwards, though in the Naga and Chin Hills there are many peaks of 9,000 ft. until they reach the lesser ranges of the Arakan, where the maximum heights are seldom over 2,000 ft. The main spine of these ranges, however, continues southwards, parallel to the coast, towards the mouth of the River Irrawaddy and finally disappears just north of the town of Bassein. Throughout these ranges the hillsides are for the most part covered with forest and jungle in which the undergrowth is dense evergreen interspersed with large areas of bamboo or tiger grass where, unless moving by tracks, paths have to be cut. Except in the Arakan the foothills are covered with teak forests which have little undergrowth and through which infantry can move easily.

In the whole length of this mountain system there were only three roads, none of them of good quality, over which wheels could pass. These are the Ledo–Myitkyina road, the Dimapur–Imphal–Tamu road and the Taungup–Prome road, none of which had been completed to a standard which would carry heavy traffic all the year round.

East and south of this great mountain system lies the main river basin of the Irrawaddy and its principal tributary the Chindwin on the west which flows almost parallel to it until it joins the Irrawaddy at Myingyan. The Irrawaddy is navigable by various craft, according to the time of year, as far north as Myitkyina, and the Chindwin can be navigated up to Tamanthi. These two rivers provide, therefore, first-class lines of communication throughout the year. The valley of the Irrawaddy and other tributary valleys provide access for a system of railways which, starting from Rangoon, pass through Mandalay to Myitkyina. There are various branches such as that from Rangoon to Prome and from Saigaing to Ye-U. The road system of central Burma was reasonably good, especially from Ye-U southwards.

There is a dry belt in central Burma from Swebo in the north between the Irrawaddy, Chindwin and the Shan Hills. This is open cultivated country over which tracked vehicles can move with ease, where wheeled vehicles can use the tracks, and where the annual rainfall is 20–40 in. as opposed to 200 in the Arakan. From November to April this area is hot and dry.

In Arakan the 'chaungs' or waterways with which the coastal strip is intersected are almost as great an obstacle as the hills and the jungle. In dry weather they can be forded by infantry at low water, but at other times a 6-ft. tide makes them difficult to cross. In the rains of the south-west monsoon they are swollen by flood water which makes them greater obstacles. The banks are usually muddy and crumbling. Bridging presents considerable difficulties and special arrangements have to be made at each for the passage of tanks and mechanical transport.

There are two ranges of hills in the Mayu Peninsula and another between the Rivers Kalapanzin and Kaladan. These hills rise up sheer on one side to a knife-edged ridge and drop down equally steeply on the other. The lower slopes are covered with ordinary jungle that soon gives way to bamboo which is extremely hard to penetrate and which has to be cut with matchets with consequent noise and movement. This area has been described as the worst fighting country in the world, and one in which large-scale operations are impossible during the monsoon.

There were other disadvantages for our forces operating southwards in Arakan. The two main rivers, Kalapanzin and Kaladan, with their tributaries, converge on Akyab, which was the main Japanese base. By this command of the entrance to these two waterways, the enemy was able to make use of excellent water communications which were denied to us.

The climate of Burma is affected by two monsoons, the north-east in the winter and the south-west in the summer. The influence of the former produces fine dry weather with little cloud and conditions are good for operations both on land and in the air. The south-west monsoon, on the other hand, blowing across the Bay of Bengal, discharges torrential rain over Burma and Eastern Bengal during the months May to October. Precipitation of rain, especially in the Arakan, is extremely high, reaching in places as much as 200 in. a year. The climate varies, too, according to the altitude, the temperature above 3,000 ft. being reasonably low and above 5,000 ft. cool and invigorating. In the lowlands along the coast the temperatures are high, with great humidity, which makes campaigning in these areas exhausting.

While the south-west monsoon has a bad effect on the health of the troops and causes them acute discomfort from wet, its really worst effect is on the communications in the country. The heavy rain turns Arakan, a rice-growing area, to a muddy swamp quite impassable to wheeled vehicles unless the roads have proper foundations and surfaces capable of withstanding heavy rain.

In Assam and Burma there is very little stone, most of the hills being composed of soft shale quite useless for road-making. The construction of roads, therefore, is very difficult, as they have to be built to a very high standard in order to stand up to the weather in spite of a shortage of proper material. The heavy rains also make the ordinary native tracks very nearly impassable, as they get so slippery on the steep slopes that neither man nor beast can stand up on them. Finally, rivers and streams become very formidable obstacles, all of which have to be bridged to allow the passage of troops and transport. Indeed, campaigning in Burma during the monsoon may be said to be one of the most arduous operations anywhere in the world today.

Malaria is endemic throughout Burma below 3,000 ft., but was worse in some areas than in others. The rate of infection was highest at the beginning of May and at the end of the monsoon in October. By the beginning of 1944 much had been done to reduce the incidence of malaria and other tropical diseases such as dysentery. There was also a little-known disease, 'scrub typhus', which caused a good deal of worry. Various skin complaints occurred in the rainy season and at the same time the large numbers of leeches in the jungle were very troublesome.

(iii) *Plans and Preparations for the Dry Season: 1943–4*

In November 1943 we were in contact with enemy troops in the Arakan and there was intensive patrolling on the Central Front. The plans for the coming dry season were briefly as follows:

(*a*) In the Arakan, XV Corps, already advancing, was to secure positions from which it would eventually be possible to capture Akyab. The immediate objective given was the mouth of the River Naf-Maungdaw-Buthidaung. It was originally intended that there should be a landing by 2 (British) Div. behind the enemy opposing XV Corps. This had to be cancelled, as the necessary landing craft were not available.

38. Burma—Araka

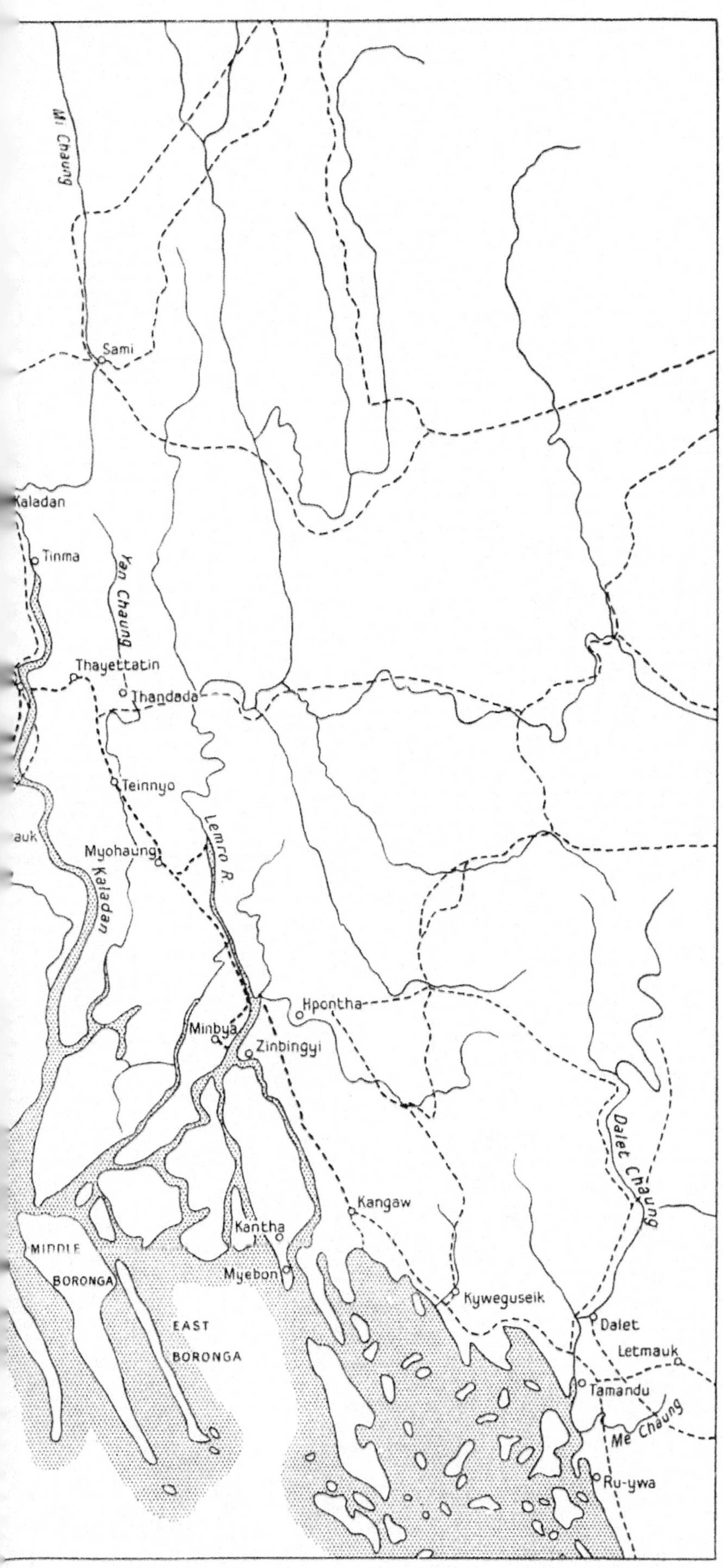

nd Akyab Area

Face page 381

(*b*) On the Central Front, IV Corps were to clear the Chin Hills as far as the foothills south-east of Tiddim and dominate the area between the Yu and Chindwin Rivers south of the Tamu–Sittaung road. Also 'to contain and kill Japanese' in the Kebaw Valley and the Atwin Yomas.

(*c*) The N.A.C.C. to advance through Kamaing to the general line Mogaung–Myitkyina, helped by 'Chindits', who were to draw off and disorganize the enemy opposing them.

During the Arakan campaign of the previous year the enemy had moved up the Kaladan Valley and had threatened the British communications. It was considered that the obvious Japanese reaction to a threat to Maungdaw-Buthidaung would be a counter-advance up this same valley. General Slim therefore proposed that XV Corps, in addition to moving on both sides of the Mayu Hills, should throw out 81 (W.A.) Div. as a flank guard to move down the distant Kaladan Valley. It was also hoped that this detachment would, in addition to protecting the left flank of XV Corps, menace the Japanese flank and threaten their east-to-west communications.

The feasibility of such an operation, however, depended on a solution of the supply problem. In the circumstances there were only three ways of maintaining troops in the Kaladan Valley. These were:

(*a*) A mixture of pack, porter and sampan transport.
(*b*) By air.
(*c*) By a combination of (*a*) and (*b*).

But to move even a brigade group maintained by (*a*) would be a most precarious operation needing large, and probably unprocurable, quantities of these types of transport. Moreover, even if this transport could be obtained, movement would be slow and vulnerable. Furthermore, it would limit the size of the force, so that it would be inadequate for its task. It was worked out that the total maintenance for the Division, less 3 (W.A.) Bde., would amount to 51,000 lb. per day, including ammunition. This lift would require 22 aircraft with 12 in reserve, a number that could be made available. It was decided therefore, to use this method of supply, and so 81 (W.A.) Div. became the first normal formation to be entirely maintained by air. Its ground transport consisted of a 'jeep train', mostly for the artillery, and the Auxiliary Groups, consisting of head-load carriers.

Though the Division was to be supplied by air, the Valley had to be reached overland. It was therefore necessary to construct a jeep track, 75 miles long, from Chiringa to Daletme in the Kaladan Valley and, moreover, to continue making tracks as the advance proceeded. The track to Daletme became known as the 'West African Way'. It crossed four ranges of high, steep hills, was begun on 18th November and finished on 17th January. When it is considered that the only tools were picks, shovels, matchets and sticks of gelignite, that no road-making machinery whatever was available and that the work was done at the tail end of the monsoon, it is evident that it was not only a feat of engineering skill, but also a remarkable performance on the part of the troops.

6 Bde. (Brigadier J. W. A. Hayes) left Chiringa on 7th December and 4 N.R., the leading battalion, reached Mowdok on 18th December and sent forward detachments to Satpaung and Daletme on the Kaladan River, where a base of operations was to be prepared. 5 Bde. (Brigadier E. H. Collins) had been delayed owing to a fire on the ship which was to have brought them to Chittagong, and rear elements of the Division had not yet reached the concentration area at Chiringa. In addition, a period of heavy rain also caused the move forward from Chiringa to be bogged down for a week. For the next three weeks the main effort had to be directed to work on the West African Way.

(iv) *Outline of Operations in Arakan, 1944*

After moving down towards the Mayu Peninsula, 5 and 7 (Indian) Divs. of XV Corps had by mid-January driven in the enemy outposts prior to attacking the main positions on the line Maungdaw-Buthidaung. During this period 81 Recce R. had carried out several successful amphibious raids behind the enemy's lines. As already mentioned, 81 (W.A.) Div. had been concentrating in the Satpaung–Daletme area in the Kaladan Valley east of Cox's Bazar. Their task was to advance down the valley to capture Kyautaw with the ultimate object of cutting the Htizwe–Kanzauk road—the enemy's main communication between the Kalapanzin and Kaladan Valleys.

The attack on the Japanese main position, which was naturally strong and had been well prepared for defence, commenced on 19th January, by which date 81 (W.A.) Div. was also on the move. The operation was going well when, on 4th February, the enemy, who had been reinforced, launched a counter-offensive which was the first phase of an attempted invasion of India.

Their plan, a bold one, involved the movement of several columns up the eastern side of the Kalapanzin Valley before wheeling to the west. One force was to surround and destroy 7 (Indian) Div. on our left and another was to cross the Mayu Hills, disrupt the communications behind 5 (Indian) Div. on our right, and then to surround and destroy this formation. In addition, holding attacks were to be made on the troops deployed opposite the Japanese defensive position.

Although they succeeded in surrounding 7 (Indian) Div., no part of it surrendered. Holding a number of 'boxes' and supplied by air, this fine formation fought its opponents to a standstill. Meanwhile, the reserve division of XV Corps—26 (Indian)—moving down from the north and parts of 5 (Indian) Div. moving from the south, dealt with the enemy columns attempting to disrupt the communications of the latter formation. By the end of February the enemy had been driven back, their known casualties in killed and wounded being 4,500 out of a total of some 7,000 engaged. This action marked the turning-point in the Arakan campaigns and the myth of the 'invincible Jap' had been exploded.

By 5th March XV Corps, now reinforced by 36 (British) Div., was ready to resume the offensive, and by 3rd May the enemy's strongholds had all been taken. Whilst this fighting was going on in the Arakan the enemy, reinforced by two more divisions, had opened the second phase of his invasion of India by an attack on the Central Front.[1] In this offensive the Japanese Army suffered a greater defeat than ever before in its history. Their 31 Div. had practically lost all fighting value and their 15 and 33 Divs. had been greatly reduced by losses. Between March and mid-June their battle casualties on the Central Front alone had amounted to not less than 30,000, of whom 13,500 were killed. They also lost 100 guns.

In the meantime XV Corps had secured all their objectives in the Arakan in spite of the transfer of 5 and 7 (Indian) Divs. to the Central Front and of 36 (British) Div. to prepare for an operation elsewhere. By 22nd June the Corps had taken up its monsoon dispositions as follows:

25 (Indian) Div.: In the Tunnels area, covering the Maungdaw–Buthidaung road up to and including the east tunnel.

26 (Indian) Div.: One brigade in the Bawli–Goppe–Taung Bazars area; one brigade at Taungbro–Tumbru; and the third at Cox's Bazar.

81 (W.A.) Div.: Headquarters and one brigade at Chiringa. One brigade taking up new positions to protect the eastern approaches to the Chiringa–Singpa track, with detachments on the Sangu River to block enemy attempts to infiltrate into that area.

It must be remarked that the term 'monsoon dispositions' does not imply passive defence or that opportunities for local offensive action were not taken. The object was to get the troops away from the worst of the low-lying country.

It is now necessary to go back in time to January 1944 and to describe the part played by 81 (W.A.) Div. in these operations.

(v) *81 (W.A.) Div. in the Kaladan Valley*

(See Maps Nos. 39, 40 and 41)

The Division had arrived at Bombay during the previous August and September and was encamped in the Deolali area. It had been hoped that a good deal of training in jungle warfare would have been possible before moving to Burma. Unfortunately the country near Deolali was unsuitable for the type of training necessary. However, an area of jungle-covered hills 50 miles away was discovered and a certain amount of company and battalion training was done. Except for one exercise for each brigade no formation training was possible in the time available. The move to Calcutta, by sea to Chittagong and thence to Chiringa commenced early in November and, as already mentioned, work soon started on the West African Way.

On 4th January, XV Corps issued instructions to 81 (W.A.) Div. that their advance from the Daletme area was to start not later than the 21st, and detailed the objectives referred to in the previous section. The instruction mentioned that attacks on Japanese in prepared positions were not to be made without previous softening by concentrated air strikes for which the aircraft would be made available.

[1] The Japanese now had at least nine divisions and one or possibly two independent brigades in Burma as well as garrison and lines of communication troops.

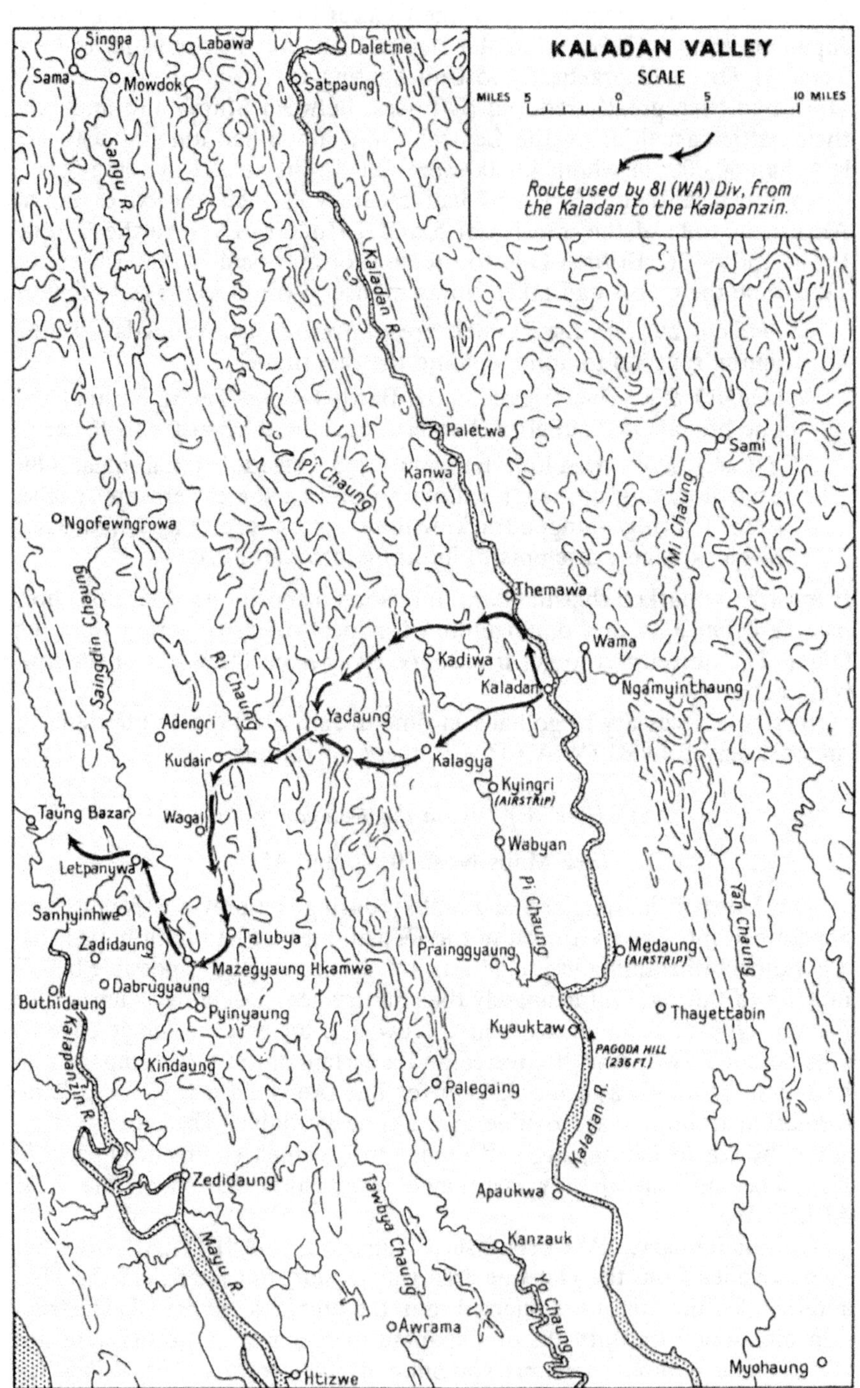

39. Kaladan Valley

It must be remarked at the outset that the Division was without its third infantry brigade[1] and that the artillery consisted of one light regiment armed with 3·7 in. howitzers and moved by jeeps and 15 cwt. trucks.[2] In addition there was a 3 in. mortar battery of three troops.[3] This being the case, Major-General C. G. Woolner, the Divisional Commander, had issued an instruction on the policy to be adopted if organized positions were encountered. Briefly, this policy was to make use of the mobility conferred by air supply to surround the position and force the Japanese to make attempts to break out.

The Division was also without 81 Recce R., whose vehicles were considered unsuitable for employment in the Kaladan Valley. In place of this unit 11 (E.A.) Scout Bn. was attached to the Division. No tanks were allotted as they could not be got into the valley.

The main body of the Division, less the artillery which had not arrived, commenced to move forward on 19th January, although 6 Bde., in the lead, started a day earlier. The first bound to be made by the latter formation was to Kanwa, just south of Paletwa, beyond which there was to be no movement until 5 Bde. had closed up. It was expected that the Scout Bn. would also arrive in time to take part in the advance from Kanwa.

The Japanese troops in the Kaladan at that time consisted of one battalion 213/R. based on Kyauktaw. A detachment was reported at Paletwa and small parties at Pansanwa and Mangkhol the former just west and the latter just south of Murgai. Burma Traitor Army forces, in unknown strength, were said to be at Murgai and Tringhat, both places about 12 miles south of Daletme.

6 Bde. advanced on a broad front. On the right 4 N.R. moved down the Kaladan; on the left, 1 G.R.[4] moved up the Daletme Chaung and across the watershed into the Mila and Palet Chaungs. Brigade Headquarters, with 1 S.I.R. followed 1 G.R., on the axis of whose route was on a track reported 'jeepable', or easily made so, all the way to Paletwa. The objective given was the general line Milawa–Sepalaung. The former lies in the bend of the Kaladan River opposite Paletwa, the latter two miles east on the Palet Chaung. The following intermediate bounds were specified on which the leading battalions were to make contact:

(*a*) Murgai, between 1750 and 1830 hours, 19th January.

(*b*) Milawa, between 1700 and 1900 hours, 20th January.

The timing was, however, too optimistic. Although no enemy were met the first bound was not reached until the 20th. Both forward battalions met opposition on this day, 4 N.R. at Pansanwa on the Kaladan and 1 G.R. at Murgai. Both units attacked with dash and the results of this first clash were quite satisfactory. Identification of 1/213 R. was obtained and two live Japanese were acquired who gave much accurate information, some of which confirmed what had hitherto been mere conjecture.

[1] See Chapter 5.

[2] A very accurate weapon, but with a maximum range of only 6,000 yards.

[3] When it was decided that head-loads could not be used for the 3·7 in. howitzers in the Arakan, the gun-carriers were formed into three troops of mortars.

[4] 1 G.R. is an abbreviation of 1st Battalion the Gambia Regiment. (See Glossary.)

It appears that the Japanese soldier was not told what to do if captured, presumably it was considered 'unthinkable' for anyone to be taken alive. The two prisoners referred to surrendered, an almost unprecedented occurrence at this time, the reason being, they said, that they believed African troops ate the killed in battle, but not prisoners. They feared that, if eaten by Africans, they would not be acceptable to their ancestors in the hereafter.

The final bound to Milawa–Sepalaung was reached on 22nd January by 1 G.R. and later by 4 N.R. There was no opposition to the advance, patrols found Paletwa clear of enemy and reports indicated that no Japanese intervention on the right flank was likely.

Paletwa was occupied on the 24th as the first phase of an attack on Kanwa, where the enemy was found to be well dug in on two small hills south-west and south of the place. The Japanese works were, as usual, mutually supporting. The plan was for 4 N.R. to surround the position, attack from the north-west with one company, while the main effort was to be made from the south. The artillery had not yet arrived, but support was to be given by the mortars of 3 Lt. Bty. and the brigaded mortars of 1 S.L.R. and 1 G.R. under the command of a gunner officer. Positions were found on the east bank of the river which afforded good observation over Kanwa. The east or left flank was to be watched by 1 S.L.R., who took up a position a mile east of Kanwa. 1 G.R. were in brigade reserve.

4 N.R., less 'A' Coy., moved on 24th January, and after a long flank march over difficult hill country reached an assembly area south of Kanwa. The attack was to be carried out as follows:

> 'A' Coy. to advance down the west bank of the river from Paletwa and attack enemy positions in Kanwa from the north.
>
> 'B' Coy. to advance from the south along the west bank of the river to attack the enemy position south of the village and the village itself.
>
> 'D' Coy. to move to a flank and attack the positions west of the village.
>
> 'B' Coy. in reserve and to stop Japanese reinforcements coming up the river.

The attack ran into trouble from the outset. The troops could not keep touch and direction in the dense jungle, communications broke down, the wireless sets being unsatisfactory in such terrain, and it was found extremely difficult to judge the distance and direction of firing. 'A' Coy. failed to make any headway. 'C' Coy. captured the village after fierce fighting. 'D' Coy. took one position in the hills, but failed to take the other. By 1600 hours so little progress had been made that the Brigade Commander called off the attack. An air strike was requested for the following day, but could not be made available. However, next morning patrols found that the enemy had hurriedly evacuated their positions. On 28th January the advance was resumed, and patrols of 1 S.L.R. encountered enemy at Naiwa, eight miles south of Paletwa on the east bank of the river.

While 6 Bde. was clearing up the neighbourhood of Paletwa the rest of the Division was closing up. Reports had been received that enemy troops were moving towards Paletwa from the east through the mountains.

5 G.C.R. was therefore sent forward from 5 Bde. to protect the left flank of the Division. The Battalion arrived on 25th January and patrolled to Sami, but found no sign of the enemy.

In the meantime, the jeeps had been having a difficult time on the hills between Chiringa and Daletme. There were a number of accidents resulting in casualties to both men and vehicles, but the personnel, with the greatest skill and determination, pressed on. Eventually only two jeeps had to be 'written off'. Whenever possible work was continued on the jeep track and the construction of small airstrips as the Division advanced.

On 30th January the Scout Bn. arrived to join the Division. This was not a regular battalion. It was lightly armed and had only been trained for reconnaissance and tip-and-run guerilla tactics.

Reports received about this time indicated that the enemy were in strength on the line Kreinggyaung–Bidonegyaungwa–Kaladan. 5 Bde., which had now closed up, was ordered to carry out a deception plan to simulate an advance in strength down the Pi Chaung. The main thrust, however, was to be through the hills between Bidonegyaungwa and Kaladan Village directed on Palegaing seven miles south-west of Kyauktaw. The task given to 6 Bde. was to secure the site for a Dakota strip at Medaung by moving astride the Kaladan as quickly as possible. Opposition encountered at Kaladan Village was not to be allowed to delay the advance east of the river. After taking Medaung the Brigade was to establish itself at Thayettabin.

On 4th February, the day on which the Japanese launched their counter-offensive against the main body of XV Corps, the situation of 81 (W.A.) Div. was as follows:

> *5 Bde.* 7 G.C.R. on the Pi Chaung with two companies forward at Kadiwa and the rest of the Battalion expected there next day. The remainded of the Brigade was moving via Themawa on the west bank of the river in four columns; 8 G.C.R., Bde. H.Q., Admin. Gp., 5 G.C.R.
>
> *One Coy. Scout Bn.* covering the gap between 5 and 6 Bdes.
>
> *6 Bde.* Astride the river with 1 G.R. three miles north of Kaladan Village on the west bank of the river. 1 S.L.R. on the east bank moving towards the Mi Chaung. Scout Bn. operating on the left of 1 S.L.R.

Two days later 1 G.R., following the west bank of the river and closing in on the enemy in Kaladan from the north and west, found them strongly entrenched on a commanding position. An attack was launched on the 7th, but the dense jungle and deep chaungs rendered co-operation difficult and no progress was made. By 10th February all three light batteries had arrived and were in action. Supported by their fire and very accurate dive bombing of a fortified pimple south of the village, another attack was launched which resulted in a small advance. Next day another attempt was made supported by artillery and mortar fire, but this also failed. The Battalion was by this time thoroughly discouraged, and no further progress was made until 15th February, when patrols discovered that the enemy had vacated his positions. It was afterwards ascertained that the Japanese had left in boats during the night 14th–15th taking their dead and wounded

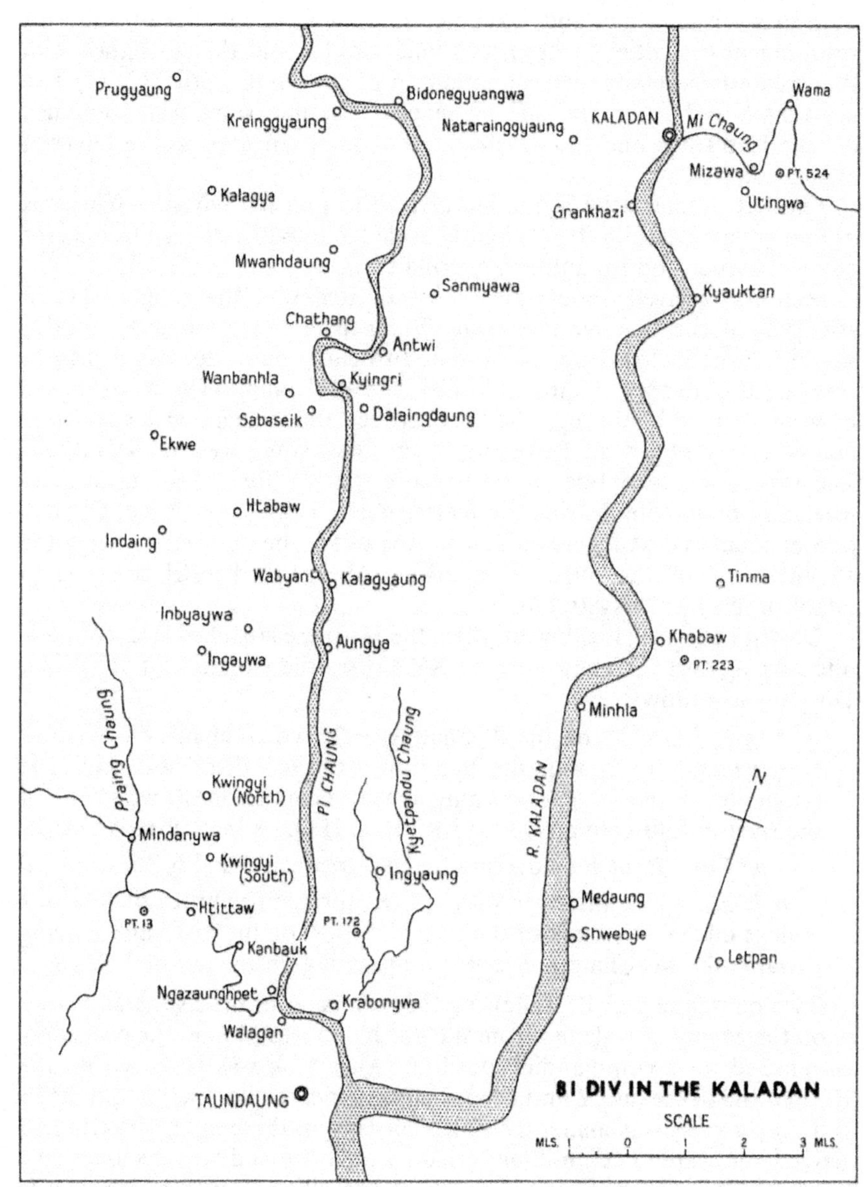

40. 81 Division in the Kaladan

with them. An identification of 55 Div. Cav. was obtained during this action.[1]

On the east bank of the river the advance of the rest of 6 Bde. had gone well. By 1st February patrols of 1 S.L.R. were already as far south as the Mi Chaung and the Battalion reached Wama three days later. Crossing the chaung in boats and dugouts, 1 S.L.R. continued southward, preceded by patrols well ahead. The enemy was met at Khabaw on 12th February and driven through Minhla, but south of the village they were found in prepared positions. After two attacks from the east had failed, the enemy was driven out by a night bayonet charge from the south and retired in disorder, leaving arms and equipment. Shwebye was then occupied to enable work to be commenced on airstrips. By the 15th a strip was ready to receive Moths and by the 21st the Dakota strip had been completed. In the meantime, the Scout Bn. was patrolling towards Kyauktaw and 4 N.R. at Letpan had found no enemy north of Mahamuni.

South of Kaladan Village the valley begins to broaden out and at Kyauktaw is some 15 miles wide, consisting of open paddy with numbers of scattered villages. Between the Pi Chaung and the river, however, there is a strip of bush-covered hills running down to the bend in the river where it is joined by the Pi Chaung. South of this bend and opposite Kyauktaw, rising abruptly straight from the east bank, is Pagoda Hill, an isolated cone-shaped feature 236 ft. high and crowned by a pagoda. Its sides are steep and covered with light bush. This was a most important feature, as it afforded observation over a wide area round Kyauktaw.

Information was received from XV Corps on 15th February that the advance towards Myohaung was not to take place. Instead the Division was to concentrate in the area Kanzauk–Apaukwa so as to form a serious threat to the Mayu river area.

The advance of 5 Bde. had continued with 7 G.C.R. on the right in the Pi Chaung and 8 G.C.R. on the left along the west bank of the river. 7 G.C.R. overcame a small ambush on 5th February and fought a sharp action on the following day near Prugyaung. On 7th February 8 G.C.R., having overcome some slight opposition, reached Sanmyawa on the 9th. 5 G.C.R., after working on the jeep track, crossed the river and joined the Brigade on 7th February. By this time 7 G.C.R. had found the enemy's positions about Kreingyyaung abandoned and the country clear as far south as Mwanhdaung. A company of 7 G.C.R. despatched to Prugyaung on 10th February encountered strong opposition and a second company failed in an attack on Kalagya. These companies remained in contact for several days, but could make no headway. The enemy apparently attached great importance to the entrance of a route to the Kalapanzin at the Romadaung Pass about a mile south-west of Yadaung (Map 39).

There was some delay to 5 Bde. while the Pi Chaung was crossed, supplies were accumulated and distributed for what was hoped to be a rapid movement on Palegaing. However, by 17th February the Brigade was on the move again. 8 G.C.R. were then approaching Indaing and Headquarters and 5 G.C.R. were at Ekwe, but 7 G.C.R. were still at Prugyaung and Kalagya. On 19th February 8 G.C.R. and 5 G.C.R.

[1] This unit, less its light tank squadron, had been converted into an infantry battalion.

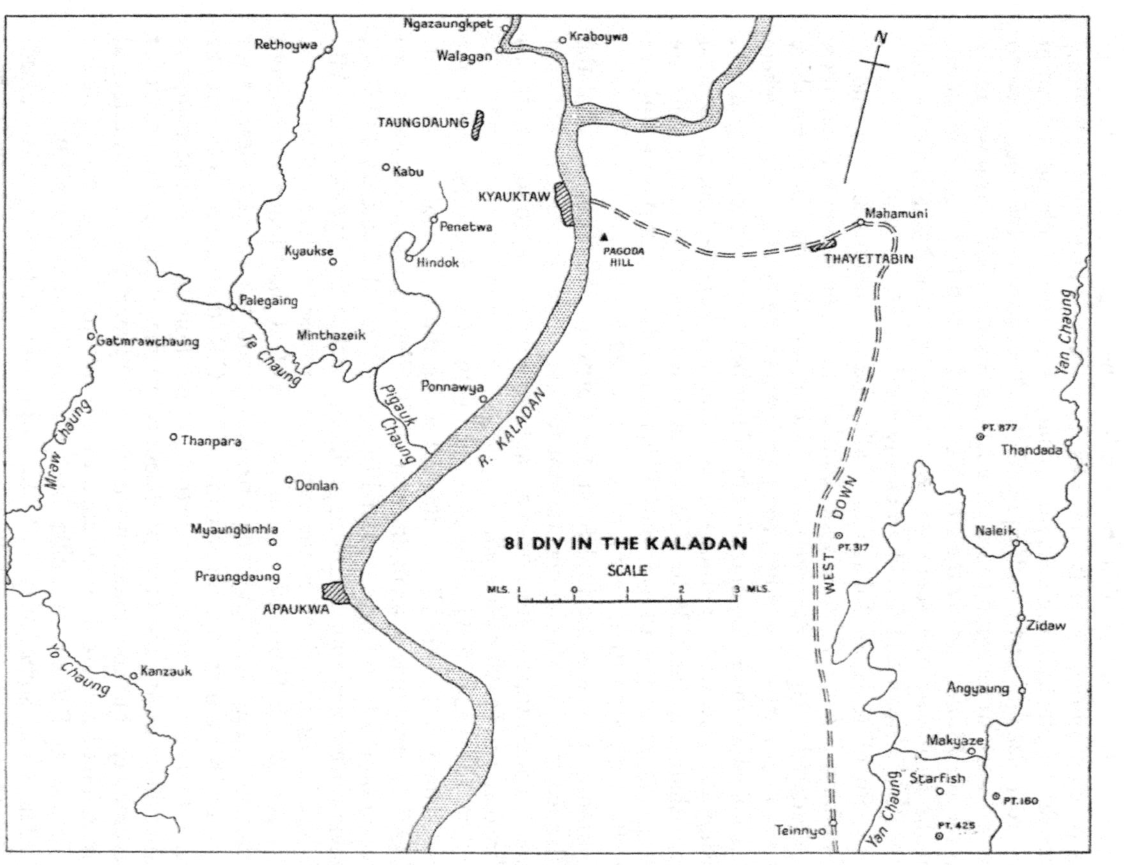

41. 81 Division in the Kaladan

forced the line of the Praing Chaung on both sides of Mindanywa after a stiff fight, but the advance was held up by strong positions at Pt. 13, one mile down-stream, and at Htittaw. Our casualties at Mindanywa amounted to seven British and 48 Africans. (Map 40.)

In 6 Bde. area the Scout Bn. gained no contact with the enemy and on 17th February occupied Pagoda Hill. Next day 4 N.R. found no signs of the enemy on the road running south from Thayettabin. On the 19th 4 N.R. took over Pagoda Hill and the Scouts moved to the left flank at Mahamuni to continue patrolling deeply to the south and south-east. 1 S.L.R. were protecting the airstrips and 1 G.R. were trying against stiff opposition to establish a bridgehead across the Pi Chaung near its confluence with the Kaladan. The object of this move was to come in on the rear of the Japanese holding up 5 Bde. They succeeded in crossing the Pi Chaung on 23rd February at Walagan and by the evening of the 24th the whole of Taungdaung and Kyauktaw were in our hands. (Map 41.)

Thus, the first objective had been reached a month after the advance began. A welcome message of congratulations from the Corps Commander was communicated to all ranks.

It is necessary to digress from the actions now in progress to give some account of the plans for the future role of the Division.

On learning of the occupation of Pagoda Hill, XV Corps emphasized the importance of holding it firmly. The Divisional Commander then applied for a battalion with a machine-gun company to be flown in to garrison it. This request was not granted on the grounds that air supply resources available were not sufficient. On the 24th the Corps Commander flew in to Medaung and discussed the situation with General Woolner, to whom he outlined the plans for the future. The latter asked if a detachment of 81 Recce R. could be sent now that the West African Way was capable of taking 15 cwt. trucks. This, he was told, would be considered.

After the Corps Commander had left, orders were issued for 6 Bde. to cross the river at Kyauktaw, leaving the Scout Bn. on the east bank to cover the flank and hold Pagoda Hill. Preparations for the crossing had already been made.

Three days later XV Corps Instruction dated 26th February defined the tasks of the Division as the following extracts show:

'I am taking the offensive on the main front and I appreciate I shall be delayed by rearguards while the Jap will try and direct his main effort against you, as you have now become a serious threat.'

'After 15th March he will be prepared to denude Akyab of the bulk of its garrison now believed to be 111 R. of 54 Div. He may therefore be able to make available a maximum force of five battalions to oppose you and I appreciate he will hold you on the Kanzauk Pass and strike by the east of Kyauktaw.

'2. Your object is to protect the left flank of the Corps and contain and destroy as many Japs as possible.'

'3. The enemy will be prevented from obtaining control of the Kaladan Valley north of a general line Kanzauk–Teinnyo and must not be allowed to establish himself at Kyauktaw under any circumstances.' (Map 41.)

'4. Subject to para 3 you will keep the Jap guessing as regards your three main potential threats:

(*a*) To Minbya,
(*b*) To Akyab,
(*c*) To Rathedaung.

Your main effort will be west of the Mayu River to cut his line of communications Akyab–Buthidaung.'

On receipt of these instructions the Divisional Commander sent an appreciation to XV Corps. At the same time he repeated his request for a squadron of 81 Recce R. and also asked for a third brigade. Corps replied that a squadron of the Recce R. could not be spared and that a third brigade could not be sent owing to the limitations of air supply. The Corps Commander agreed with the appreciation, the plan stated in which was as follows:

(*a*) 11 Scout Bn. to watch enemy on road Mahamuni–Myohaung in order to give the earliest warning of any advance. To work forward as far as possible through the hills east of the road and the tidal chaungs west of it.
(*b*) Whole Division to make a rapid thrust via Kanzauk towards Htizwe.
(*c*) Plans to be worked out in detail for moving the whole Division back again to the area Kyauktaw–Mahamuni with a view to surrounding and destroying any Jap force which attempts to thrust northwards.
(*d*) Operations to be confined as far as possible to the hills west of Kanzauk and those east of road Mahamuni–Myohaung.
(*e*) Continuous and deep patrolling in all directions to give early warning of enemy intentions and to deceive him as to ours.

It is apparent that this plan is based on the assumption that no counter-offensive would take place until the middle of March and that there would, therefore, be time for effective action about Htizwe. It is to be remarked that the routes chosen in paragraph (*d*) were based partly on the fact that the troops, having been trained for and having shown considerable aptitude for fighting in jungle, did not feel so confident of themselves in the open plain around Kyauktaw.

Meanwhile 5 Bde. had been fighting hard at Pt. 13 and Htittaw. Repeated attacks and local outflanking movements failed to dislodge the enemy. In the end, 8 G.C.R., making a wide turning movement, reached a point on the track north of Rethoywa and by 24th February opposition collapsed. On the following day the advance commenced and by 27th February the Brigade was in contact with the enemy about Palegaing.

On 25th February the Scout Bn. patrols towards Myohaung gained information of a 'large Japanese Headquarters' there.[1] On the same day the crossing of the Kaladan by 6 Bde. at Kyauktaw commenced and was

[1] Colonel Koba, commanding 111 R., had, in fact, established his Headquarters there.

completed on the morning of 28th February. This was a considerable feat, since the river was 750 yards wide with a strong tide. Anti-aircraft protection was provided by a troop of 1 L.A.A./A. Tk. Bty. which had arrived by air. 1 S.L.R. crossed the Pigauk Chaung during the night 26th–27th February and patrolled towards Apaukwa, and 4 N.R. followed next day.

In 5 Bde. area on 29th February 7 G.C.R. were preparing to move into the Mraw Chaung leading to Kanzauk and 5 G.C.R., after beating off three Japanese attacks, had established themselves on the high ground east of Praungdaung. By this time 4 N.R. were moving on Praungdaung with the object of attacking Apaukwa from the west. 1 S.L.R. had previously located the enemy in the town, but had been unable to cross the open ground north of it.

On 1st March 5 Bde. was ordered to bypass the Japanese position about Palegaing and to continue the advance on Kanzauk. During the day 4 N.R. having bypassed Donlan, also held by the enemy, moved forward towards Apaukwa. The assault went in at dawn under cover of an artillery bombardment on 2nd March. Half the town was captured at once and the remainder during the day. By nightfall on the same day patrols from 5 Bde. were on the line Gatmrawchaung–Thanpara–Myaungbinhla, with no sign of the enemy between them and Kanzauk. The whole of 6 Bde., with the exception of 1 G.R., which was in reserve at Ponnaywa, were south of the Pigauk Chaung. Divisional Headquarters was just south of Ponnaywa. In the north, 7/16 Punjabis, now under command 81 (W.A.) Div., had one company at Mowdok, headquarters and two companies at Paletwa and one company at Mizawa.

The first clear indication of a Japanese counter-offensive was on the night 1st–2nd March, when the Scout Bn. was surprised in the Thayettabin area. After some resistance the defenders were driven back on Pagoda Hill. A company of 1 G.R. was sent across the river to clear up the situation and next morning the rest of the Battalion was moved over to secure Pagoda Hill. During the afternoon 29 (W.A.) C.C.S., floating down the river on rafts, was fired on south of Minthla. At 1800 hours a message was received from XV Corps stating that the western move of the Division towards Kanzauk was to be cancelled and that the denial of Kyauktaw to the enemy would be its main task. Consequently orders were sent to 5 Bde. at 2000 hours to stop their advance and to 6 Bde. to cross the Kaladan and restore the situation on the east bank: 1 G.R. to hold Pagoda Hill at all costs.

1 G.R. had got into position during 2nd March, but their dispositions were faulty, the companies being so widely dispersed that the enemy were able to infiltrate during the night. The Japanese attacked at dawn on 3rd March, control broke down and the unit, unable to take effective action, lost the hill. A gallant defence was made by individuals of both units, but they were overwhelmed by the fanatical determination of the Japanese. News of the disaster reached Divisional Headquarters at 1100 hours.

The Divisional Commander now had to consider whether to attempt the recapture of Pagoda Hill. In the event of failure the result would be that the Division, split by the Kaladan half a mile wide, and situated in an area completely overlooked from Pagoda Hill, with no cover whatsoever on the banks for the boats, could be defeated in detail. 1 S.L.R., by a magnificent effort, had crossed the river by dawn and were moving up the east bank to the assistance of 1 G.R. and the Scouts who were beginning to rally south of Pagoda Hill, but 4 N.R. from Apaukwa could not follow until after dark. An immediate counter-attack by 1 S.L.R. alone might lead to a major reverse; 4 N.R. could not be available until the 4th, or possibly even the 5th, by which time the enemy would have had time to consolidate and build up their forces, the strength of which was not precisely known. Moreover, the Commander 6 Bde. had informed him that with 1 G.R. temporarily out of action he did not feel confident of success. After taking all these factors into consideration, General Woolner reluctantly decided to abandon the attempt to counter-attack with 6 Bde. He intended instead to transfer the Division into the hilly area north of the confluence of the Pi Chaung and Kaladan, then to endeavour to cross the river higher up and turn south again. This would allow of movement through the forest-covered hills for an operation against Thayettabin.

Orders were issued to 5 Bde. to act offensively during the rest of the day west of Apaukwa and to withdraw during the night 3rd–4th March to an area about Kyaukse–Minthaziek and to send two companies to Walagan to secure bridgeheads across the Pi and Priang Chaungs. All troops east of the Kaladan were to be transferred to the west bank and the rest of 6 Bde. were to move north of the Pigauk Chaung. Divisional Headquarters and administrative units were to move to Hindok. All moves were satisfactorily carried out by dawn on 4th March, when 1 S.L.R. proceeded to secure the west bank of the river at the mouth of the Pi Chaung.

(vi) *The Withdrawal from Kyauktaw*

(See Maps Nos. 40 and 41)

During the night 4th–5th March 5 G.C.R. crossed at Walagan into the area between the Pi Chaung and Kaladan and moved off before dawn, preceded by one company 8 G.C.R. Strong opposition was met three-quarters of a mile east of the Kyetpaung Chaung and the movement came to a standstill with the left flank on Pt. 172. Bitter fighting continued all day with attack and counter-attack, while the enemy began to appear in some strength south and south-west of Ingyaung. In the meantime, 8 G.C.R. had established a bridgehead across the Praing Chaung at Ngazaungphet. The Brigade was well supported during the day by 5 and 6 (W.A.) Lt. Btys. That night Divisional Headquarters moved from Hindok into Taungdaung and 6 Bde., with 7 G.C.R. and 3 (W.A.) Lt. Bty. under command, withdrew to the line Kabu–Penetywa–Kyauktaw. The African drivers and men of the Aux. Gps. displayed great devotion to duty during these moves.

It was now apparent that no useful purpose would be served by persisting with the plan to recross the river and turn back southwards towards Thayettabin. It had become necessary to switch the axis of the withdrawal west of the Pi Chaung and to go into close harbour in the friendly jungle for a period. Aircraft photographs revealed a suitable site between Kwingwe North and Kwingwe South. Orders were issued for the move there after dark.

Throughout 6th March 5 G.C.R. continued to beat off the enemy's attacks and the light batteries had some good targets—once they fired salvoes into Japanese charging in close order. Nevertheless, they attacked again on the right and left flanks, but the companies at Kranonywa and Pt. 172 stood firm and beat them off. Finally, at 0200 hours on the 7th, a fresh attack penetrated to Battalion Headquarters, but it was foiled by a bayonet charge. The Battalion was then able to withdraw across the Pi Chaung according to timetable. 5 G.C.R. had stood its ground with great gallantry, had inflicted some 150 casualties on the enemy, and had prevented enemy interference with the movement of the main body, which had gone well. A bridge had been constructed across the Praing Chaung just south of Kanbauk which was ready by 2200 hours on 6th March. From that time there was a continuous stream across the bridge until 1200 hours next day, when it was dismantled and taken up to the harbour. The full moon was of great assistance.

The movement had also been covered by 8 G.C.R. on the north and east by 6 Bde., with 7 G.C.R., on the south; anti-aircraft protection of the bridge was provided by the troop of Bofors guns. All units, complete with every vehicle and all their equipment, were under cover in the new harbour by 1500 hours, 7th March. On the previous day enemy patrols had been in contact with 7/16 Punjabis in the Mizawa area. Direct wireless communication between this unit and the Division had broken down.

The Division had been successfully withdrawn, though the enemy's plan, which will now be discussed, was calculated to prevent it. The Japanese Commander, Colonel Koba, had approximately five and a half battalions, with artillery including one 150 mm. howitzer. The units were as follows: Headquarters 111R.; 55 Div. Cav.; 3/111 R.; Composite Bn. H.Q. and one company 143 R. and one company 144 R.; a temporary unit 1,000 strong under Captain Honjo formed from reinforcements for 144 R.; one Bn. I.N.A. He considered this force ample for his purpose and by not waiting for more troops he gained surprise. 55 Div. Cav., far from being demoralized, was in good heart and proud of its success in delaying a much larger force for so long in the Kaladan Valley.

Koba's object was to destroy 81 (W.A.) Div. on the Kyauktaw plain. His plan was to cross the Kaladan from east to west with his main body one and a half miles north of Pagoda Hill on 5th March, cut the Division's communications about Walagan and then attack towards the south. At the same time 55 Div. Cav. and Honjo's unit were to move northwards from Apaukwa. In the event, 5 Bde. and Koba's main body were converging on Walagan on 5th March, but the Japanese had crossed the Kaladan too late to achieve effective interception. Their plan was bold and typical, but they failed to take advantage of their early successes, particularly the capture of Pagoda Hill, and do not appear to have grasped the effect of air supply on the flexibility of their opponents. Nevertheless, they had removed the threat to their right flank in the main battle and Koba was rewarded by promotion to Major-General.

The troops were relieved to be in the jungle again, but the Division could not remain where it was for the following reasons:

(*a*) The enemy was in all probability advancing up the Kaladan.

(*b*) Water supply in the area was precarious.

(*c*) Casualties with which the Division was encumbered were a drag on mobility, though 42 had been evacuated from a Moth strip constructed on arrival.[1]

An immediate move was therefore necessary in spite of the exhaustion of the troops, who had been marching, fighting and working on jeep tracks for ten weeks almost without ceasing.

The first move was to be to the area Htabaw–Inbyaywa–Ingaywa, which was to be held by a ring of battalion localities, 5 Bde. occupying the northern half and 6 Bde. the southern. A site for a Dakota strip was found just south of Htabaw. The move commenced on 8th March and was completed during the following night. A Moth strip was finished on 10th March, so that the evacuation of casualties could begin while the Dakota strip was under construction.

There now occurred an event which did much to raise the spirits of all ranks. In the early morning of 11th March 7 G.C.R. ambushed a column of Japanese near Htabaw. After some confused fighting, the enemy withdrew, leaving 38 unburied dead, a quantity of arms, ammunition, equipment, three officer's swords, as well as documents, including the Battalion war diary and Koba's orders for the offensive. Later, the Battalion Commander's grave was found among a number of others. It was afterwards ascertained that this force had consisted of Battalion Headquarters, 10, 11 and machine-gun companies of 3/111 R., with two infantry guns. These troops after fighting near Kyauktaw had headed north, crossed the Pi Chaung about Kreinggyaung and had then turned south to attack the Division. Believing that this formation was still just north of the Praing Chaung, they were moving carelessly and were completely surprised. It was stated by a prisoner that most of the officers had been killed or wounded and that only about 200 survivors remained. Some of these were seen by a patrol crossing the Pi Chaung, carrying wounded with them. A much-needed identification had been obtained and 55 Div. Cav. were again identified, at this time by 6 Bde. south of their positions.

The enemy's discomforture provided a good opportunity for continuing the move unmolested towards Kyingri, where the Pi Chaung, broad, deep and tidal, forms a loop suitable for all-round defence. On 12th March 5 Bde. sent a company from each battalion to seize the high ground round the loop; 5 G.C.R. east of Sabaseik, 7 G.C.R. west of Wanbanhla and 8 G.C.R. north of Chathang. This was accomplished without trouble. The rest of the Brigade and Divisional Headquarters followed the next day, leaving 6 Bde. to cover the evacuation of the casualties from the Dakota airstrip which had opened on 12th March. After 5 Bde. had left, 6 Bde. withdrew to positions on the high ground round the airstrip from which they succeeded in keeping it open in spite of two determined attacks on 4 N.R.

The strip was kept open until 15th March and during the three days 34 Dakotas landed. They took out 212 casualties and some salvage, mostly

[1] Battle casualties up to date had been 120 killed, 300 wounded and 180 missing. The sick had amounted to 280. It was estimated that the casualties inflicted on the enemy amounted to about 1,000.

parachutes. They also evacuated the water-borne ambulance column and the Indian Inland Water Transport personnel, both of which had displayed gallantry and devotion to duty in the operations about Kyauktaw, during which the latter put no less than 11,000 troops across the river. Finally, the R.A.F. flew in 72 British and 674 African reinforcements and some engineer stores.

On 14th March, one company 5 G.C.R. and 5 and 6 Fd. Coys. crossed the Pi Chaung into the loop and took up positions across the neck. When they were in position the batteries and administrative units crossed into the loop. A company column from each of 7 and 8 G.C.R. left to establish bases at Kalagya and Kreinggyaung from which to harass any Japanese who could be found and to obtain identifications. Next day 5 Bde. sent their advanced companies to occupy their final positions 5 G.C.R. south of Dalaingdaung, 8 G.C.R. at Antwi and 7 G.C.R. half-way between them. That night 6 Bde. took over from 5 Bde. west of the Pi Chaung.

On the 17th parties of Japanese were seen moving north towards 4 N.R. positions west of Wanbanhla, and about a dozen casualties were inflicted on them. This position was rather too far out; it was also overlooked from a ridge towards the west and had the Pi and another chaung behind it. In the meantime, it had been decided to withdraw the Battalion into the loop on 18th March to take over the positions held by the field companies. This would leave 1 S.L.R. on the high hill on the bend of the chaung east of Sabaseik, from which the whole harbour was commanded, and 1 G.R. on the ridge half a mile north of Wanbanhla. At the same time all the combatant technical units were allotted defensive positions along the banks inside the loop. Thus, the whole of 5 Bde. would be relieved of defensive commitments and become available for offensive operations.

At dawn on 18th March a company of 4 N.R. was heavily attacked and, after beating off two assaults, lost some ground during a third, but with the assistance of 3 (W.A.) Bty. succeeded in stopping the enemy. Casualties on both sides were about 40. The Battalion then withdrew to its new position in the neck of the loop. It was in this action that Sergeant Hama Kim (now R.S.M. at the Regimental Depot, Zaria) greatly distinguished himself.

A Moth strip had been made on arrival and another was put in hand in the valley east of the neck in case the first became unusable. Work on the Dakota strip had started—there was just enough room for this across the widest part of the loop.

On 18th March the enemy started to shell the harbour with a 75 mm. gun, a nuisance which continued intermittently so long as the place was occupied, in spite of air strikes and counter-battery fire by the light batteries. On 20th March, and again on the 21st, the Dakota airstrip was shelled by two high-velocity 37 mm. guns from a position north-east of Minthaye. This could not be tolerated, so a company of 1 S.L.R. with a demolition party was sent out to destroy them. Covered by an airstrike and by 3 and 5 Lt. Btys., the attackers went in with great dash and drove off the gunners. After blowing up the guns they returned with a quantity of booty, including three officer's swords and documents which identified the anti-tank platoon of 55 Div. Cav. This thoroughly well-conducted operation still further encouraged the troops, whose spirits were already rising.

While this was going on two companies of 5 G.C.R. had made a raid to the south and found no Japanese except at Aungya, where they killed 35. Extensive patrolling in all directions revealed few traces of the enemy. West of the Pi Chaung 55 Div. Cav. appeared to have 'had enough' for the time being and to have withdrawn to a small area round Kalagyaung where they were completely static.

On the night 6th–7th March a company of 7/16 Punjabis at Mizawa had been attacked and for some time there was no news of it. The Battalion, out of touch by wireless with both XV Corps and 81 (W.A.) Div., short of supplies, with one company apparently destroyed and another still held back at Mowdok, withdrew from the Kaladan Valley. The missing company eventually rejoined, and the Battalion, once again in touch with XV Corps and at full strength, began to advance again, reaching Paletwa on 23rd March.

The Divisional Commander flew to XV Corps on 23rd March, where he learnt of the impending move of the Division to the Kalapanzin Valley. On his return he was met by Brigadier R. N. Cartwright, who had been appointed to command 6 Bde. in place of Brigadier Hayes, evacuated sick. Brigadier Cartwright had distinguished himself in command of 81 Recce R. on the main front. Inspired by him they had quickly established complete ascendancy over the enemy and their many exploits had shown once again what could be done by well-led African troops. (See also Appendix XIV.)

(vii) *81 (W.A.) Div. Ordered to the Kalapanzin Valley*

(See Maps No. 39 and 40.)

It had been decided early in March to evacuate the positions east of the Kalapanzin River south of Taung. But it was considered that when 7 (Indian) Div. left for the Central Front the Japanese would certainly infiltrate up the east bank. Once the retreat of 81 (W.A.) Div. became general the possibility of turning this adverse situation to our advantage was mooted. It was thought that this could be achieved by bringing the Division across to the Kalapanzin to strike in flank any large scale move by the enemy towards or beyond Taung. The Corps Commander thought that this course would at least impose caution on the enemy and possibly afford an opportunity to inflict heavy loss if they advanced too boldly. Even a moderate success, which would be certain if the move could be kept secret, would help to raise the morale of 81 (W.A.) Div. and offset the effect of the retreat.

An instruction was issued on 25th March ordering the move to take place as soon as possible. After stating that the force opposed to 81 (W.A.) Div. was estimated to be: 55 Div. Cav., less one sqn.; 3/111 R., less one company; a weak composite bn., with a total strength of 1,200, the instruction went on as follows:

2. Your first task is to destroy this force.

3. (*a*) Your second task, which will be carried out irrespective of the degree of success of the first, is to move your Div. (less one bn.) and all wheeled transport, into the Kalapanzin Valley, debouching between 20th April and 17th May.

(*b*) Your object will be to bring your main body out at the Saingdin Chaung, but you will avoid a major battle on the way and the actual points at which you emerge will be governed by this.

4. It is most important to deceive the Jap higher command as to your intention and to create the impression that you are moving southwards down the Kaladan.

5. The move westwards will be on a porter basis, wheels and baggage will be evacuated, or as a last resort destroyed, before leaving the Kaladan.

The Battalion remaining in the Kaladan—1 G.R.—was to come under the command of the officer commanding 7/16 Punjabis. The two units would be known as 'Hubforce'.

On 24th March preparations to evacuate the personnel, baggage and stores not to be taken to the Kalapanzin began. The column formed was to cross to the east bank of the Kaladan at Themawa, where it would come on to the main jeep track to the north. The Japanese were known to have occupied Kaladan Village, so it would be necessary to destroy, or at least pin down this detachment while the column moved to Themawa. So 5 Bde. left Kyingri on the 26th and advanced on Kaladan Village. In the meantime, 7/16 Punjabis would begin to move south from Paletwa.

By 27th March the Dakota strip at Kyingri had been completed and on that day 25 sorties were flown to evacuate 212 casualties and stores. The column of administrative personnel moved off the same day. On 28th March 6 Bde. left the defended area and moved east to the Kaladan at Tinma, where, led by 4 N.R., they crossed the river unopposed, although 1 Bn. I.N.A. was only three miles to the south. The Brigade then moved north towards Mizawa on the Mi Chaung. In the meantime, 5 Bde. had closed in on Kaladan Village and Grankhazi from the north-west and south-west through wild country, with the Scout Bn. forming a screen astride the river to the south.

7 G.C.R. captured Grankhazi on 2nd April by a well-organized attack under cover of an artillery 'barrage'. Next day 8 G.C.R., having driven the enemy off another position, found Kaladan empty, the enemy having escaped across the river.

Identifications of 2/143 R. were obtained. That evening the enemy, probably 55 Div. Cav., started probing from the south.

By 31st March 6 Bde. had 1 S.L.R. on Pt. 524, 4 N.R. at Utingwa and 1 G.R. with Brigade Headquarters south of Kyauktan who closed up next day to Utingwa. On 3rd April elements of 1 S.L.R. had a hand-to-hand fight with two platoons of Japanese south of Pt. 524. Next morning the Battalion's positions were shelled and on the night 4th–5th April they were vigorously and repeatedly attacked by a mixed force of Japanese and I.N.A. The enemy gained a footing on the north of Pt. 524 feature, but were driven off by a counter-attack. They then established themselves on the jeep track south of Mizawa, where they were unsuccessfully attacked by 1 G.R. on 6th April. Next day, another attack by two companies of 1 S.L.R. and one of 1 G.R. supported by 3 (W.A.) Lt. Bty. was successful; 38 graves were found after the action, together with evidence of more casualties. The Japanese, attempting to withdraw during the night 7th–8th April, were cut off by a platoon of 1 G.R., who fought them for four hours in the dark. The enemy in these actions were identified as 3/111 R., who had already suffered heavily at Pagoda Hill and on two other occasions, the last of which was at Htabaw on the 11th March, and of its original strength of 500–600 it was estimated that only some 140 remained.

Meanwhile, the first transport column to leave had crossed the river at Themawa and withdrawn behind 7/16 Punjabis on 3rd April. By the 7th the Punjabis had cleared the country north of the Mi Chaung and had occupied Wama on the jeep track.

While 6 Bde. was fighting around Mizawa the rest of the Division had concentrated at Kaladan, 5 Bde. being responsible for keeping the routes to the west open. It remained to get 212 casualties as well as the guns and trucks away. A column was formed which left on 9th April—the guns firing until the last minute—and with the safe move of the last column assured, 6 Bde. crossed the river and joined the rest of the Division. 55 Div. Cav. had ceased probing from the south and had disappeared into the hills. Their strength was now estimated to be down to about 130.

The difficult trek to the Kalapanzin started on 10th April. The enemy attacked 1 S.L.R., acting as rearguard, in a position south-west of Kaladan. They set fire to the undergrowth, but the wind changed and blew the smoke and flames back on them. A second attack was made later, but finding the position still firmly held the Japanese gave up. The Battalion retired unmolested before dawn on the 11th in accordance with their timetable. The Japanese now lost contact with the Division altogether.

The enemy pursuit had been carried out by small widely dispersed parties. They never seem to have concentrated even a battalion strength against any one objective after the capture of Pagoda Hill. The ease with which the Division broke contact is astonishing. So far as the enemy were concerned they appear to have been under the impression that Hubforce, whom they pursued, was the tail of the Division.

'The Division had had a most difficult month. It had been through the unpleasant period of initiation to danger which every new unit and formation has to experience before it finds itself, and it had done this in a very lonely part of the world where no one else, except the R.A.F., could possibly come to its assistance if it got into trouble. There had been some hard fighting which made the evacuation of casualties a constant problem. In all 536 casualties were flown out during the month from seven different airstrips.

'The evacuation of the guns, mechanical transport and baggage had given cause for anxiety up till the last moment, but it had been successfully accomplished and nothing was abandoned.

'All this was due to good staff work, and to the unfailing willingness and cheerful obedience of all ranks. The guns had been an outstanding success; the Sappers and Auxiliary Groups had made the track so quickly that we were never delayed by it; the F.B.E.[1] and assault boats had been transported overland from river to river, thus enabling the many crossings to be carried out without a hitch and at great speed; and signal communication had continued with its usual efficiency in spite of frequent moves and the difficult nature of the country.'

In conclusion, it may be stated as a fair claim that the Division's quick advance down the Kaladan to Apaukwa had contributed to the success of the operations of XV Corps on their main front.

(viii) *The Move to the Kalapanzin and Subsequent Events*

(See Map No. 39)

The march started in two columns, 5 Bde. via Kalagya–Yadaung–Kudair–Wagai, 6 Bde. and divisional troops moved north to just south of Themawa, then westward to the Pi Chaung, and then south-west to Yadaung, where they joined 5 Bde. The route is shown on Map No. 39.

5 Bde. moved out from Kaladan during the night 10th–11th April. The march went smoothly except for the difficulties caused by the path, especially at a narrow gorge south-east of Yadaung which caused considerable delay. However, a company of 8 G.C.R. sent on ahead to secure the Romadaung Pass, about a mile south-west of Yadaung, succeeded in getting to Yadaung only 40 minutes after their opposite number, 4 N.R., from the northern column.

On the northern route the march had begun on the afternoon of 10th April. 6 Bde. had sent 6 (W.A.) Fd. Coy. on a day ahead to improve the path for headloads, which they succeeded in doing so well that the column moved steadily forward behind them, encountering no obstacles except the steepness of the hills. The head of the column reached Yadaung on 13th April and 1 S.L.R. at the tail closed up next day. They had laid a false trail to Themawa and had obliterated their own tracks for half a mile. After leaving the Pi Chaung not a single inhabitant was seen by the column, though there were many signs of wild elephants.

By the evening of 13th April 8 G.C.R. were on top of the Romadaung Pass, which, with its towering cliffs on either side, bore some resemblance to the Pass of Thermopyle. As 5 Bde. had been delayed at the first gorge, units were passed over as they arrived. It so happened therefore, that the first unit to get to Wagai was 4 N.R., who reached there on 14th April and immediately made a dropping zone.

There are several points of interest which must be mentioned here. Since wireless silence was in force, control of a column had to be by cable, laid by Signals at the head and reeled up after the column had passed. This was a notable feat of endurance, as all the cable had to be carried as head loads. Not only was wireless silence maintained, but the columns marched in silence—no voices were raised, a test of discipline for the Africans! On the march all side tracks were blocked by sentries and the column did not close up at night. Each unit went into a close harbour allotted to it by a 'harbour party' sent on with the leading troops. All-round protection was organized by sub-units.

[1] Folding boats, engineers.

The whole Division was concentrated about Wagai by 16th April, where the troops were given a short rest and a large air drop was received. On this day contact was made with the outside world in the form of a Gurkha patrol from 7 (Indian) Div. at Taung. This was closely followed by one from 81 Recce R. During this period patrols were sent out in all directions, including one to the Yo and Tawbya Chaungs, west of Kyauktaw. Either none or only small parties of enemy were encountered by these patrols. Contact was also made with 'V' Force in the vicinity, who had only heard of the Division 48 hours after its arrival.[1]

The Divisional Commander had been ordered to keep the Division concentrated in the hills in the neighbourhood of Kindaung and, while avoiding a major battle, to operate against the Japanese communications east of the Kalapanzin River. On 18th April the Division began to move south on Talubya. During the move 6 Bde. found the north bank of the Saingdin Chaung impassable; moreover, the chaung itself was 200 yards wide, unfordable and flowing through a deep gorge. It was also discovered that the water was too salt to be drinkable. In addition, about this time it was learnt that the enemy had a company in Pyinyaung and at Kindaung there was a battalion. It was then decided not to push on towards Kindaung until Pyinyaung had been cleared. This was done on 24th April by 5 G.C.R., after some difficulty caused by the nature of the ground.

With the approach of the monsoon XV Corps plan was to withdraw from Buthidaung in stages commencing on 5th May whilst continuing to hold the Maungdaw–Buthidaung road up to and including the Tunnels. 81 (W.A.) Div. was ordered to protect the movement by continuing to harass the Japanese lines of communication between Kindaung and Buthidaung until 9th May. The Division was then to slip away through the hills, reappear for a few days at Oktaung, three miles north of Sanhyinhwe, and, finally, to establish itself east of Taung. The Division was to remain about Taung until the rain made the country impassable and the garrison would no longer be liable to attack.

It would have been impossible to find a suitable base in the hills north of Kindaung and there were strong objections against the other sides. The Divisional harbour was therefore located just east of Mazegyaung Hkamwe, from which raiding parties would be sent out. The site was a beautiful one with plenty of good water and fish in the chaung. 4 N.R. and 8 G.C.R. formed the first raiding columns and were later joined by 81 Recce R. This left 5 Bde., less 8 G.C.R., on the north and 1 S.L.R. on the south to hold the harbour. A good deal of work was done on defences, including the construction of wide belts of *panjis*.

During the night 25th–26th April a party of some 30 Japanese bypassed a forward company of 1 S.L.R. and penetrated the harbour. They ran into a platoon of 5 G.C.R. who happened to be on the dropping zone. A bayonet fight ensued in the darkness and in their flight the enemy were caught by the Sierra Leone company and suffered further losses. On 29th April a similar party infiltrated into one of 1 S.L.R.'s positions, from which they were ejected leaving a number of bodies transfixed on the *panjis*,

[1] 'V' Force was an intelligence organization which maintained posts in various places for the collection of information.

after hand-to-hand fighting. The survivors were located and dive-bombed next day, which cost them another 12 casualties. Identifications in both cases were of 111 R.

On 27th April 81 Recce R. arrived after a quick march from Taung. Three days later, 'C' Sqn. on their way to establish a patrol base encountered some 100 enemy. The Squadron charged at once and killed about 20 at close quarters. There were also some minor clashes, including one between 5 G.C.R. and a mixed party of 30 Japanese and I.N.A. north-west of the harbour, after which it was not disturbed again.

While the enemy were probing the harbour the two battalions columns were forcing the defiles to the west. 8 G.C.R. got through first, and on 28th April reached Sanhyinhwe and established a base just north of it from which patrols searched the hills to the north and west. No enemy were encountered. On 29th April 'A' Sq. of the Recce R. joined the base and passed their patrols through into the paddy. Their orders were to dominate the whole country as far west as the Kalapanzin River, to destroy supply installations and any enemy found. In the event of large numbers being located they were to call on 4 N.R. or 8 G.C.R.

Meanwhile, 4 N.R., after cutting paths and surmounting various obstacles, reached the vicinity of Dabrugyaung on 29th April. From this time until 9th May the Recce R. and the two battalions infested the whole countryside east of the Kalapanzin within range of their bases. Whenever Japanese were reported they were hunted relentlessly, occupied villages were raided by night and dive-bombed by day. Three supply and two ammunition dumps were destroyed. A mule column was 'shot up' near Dabrugyaung; 4 N.R. captured 250 mules north of Kindaung, and a bridge just west of the former place was demolished. 4 N.R. were unable to occupy Kindaung itself, but they succeeded in raiding the northern part of it before the time came to withdraw and rejoin the Division.

Reconnaissance had shown that the paths running north-west from the harbour were unsuitable and two new ones were cut which joined some four miles to the north where an existing track was found to be passable. As the diversion to Oktaung had been cancelled, an advanced party left on the night 5th–6th May for Letpanywa. On 8th May 6 Bde., less 4 N.R., moved out by the western path and divisional troops by the eastern one. 5 Bde., less 8 G.C.R., took over the defence of the harbour. 4 N.R. withdrew from their position north of Kindaung during the night 8th–9th May and joined their own brigade column on the 10th. 5 Bde. withdrew by the eastern route and 8 G.C.R. acted as rearguard. By 11th May the whole Division, less the Recce R., which was to follow later, had assembled about Letpanywa and after a halt of two days moved on to the hills east of Taung.

In the meantime, 1 S.L.R. had pushed on to the Taung area to relieve 4/14 Punjabis of 7 (Indian) Div. They covered the whole distance of 30 miles from Mazegyaung Hkamwe in two days and, on arrival, in spite of a gruelling march, they made an impression on the Indian troops well worthy of the R.W.A.F.F.

The positions now held by the Division formed a horse-shoe of battalion-defended localities with the open end covered by the Taung Keep, which was being prepared for monsoon defence and accommodation. The paddy land to the south was dominated by the Recce R., a task at which they were expert. Throughout the period these positions were held there was no major action.

On 18th May 6 Bde., less 4 N.R., started to move to Chiringa for operations in the Mowdok area which will be described in the next section. They were followed later by the divisional troops, and Headquarters opened at Chiringa on 2nd June. 5 Bde., plus 4 N.R., remained in their positions patrolling and inflicting casualties in ambushes until 8th June, when they left for Chiringa, arriving there on 11th June.

If the operations of the Division be considered as a whole, there is no doubt that the outstanding characteristics were mobility and flexibility. For instance, Divisional Headquarters covered at least 325 miles and moved no less than 36 times between its departure from Chiringa and its arrival at Taung. It is difficult to estimate how far the average infantryman marched, but it must have been 1,500 miles or more. The mobility of the Division may be attributed to forethought, including reconnaissance well ahead, to rapid and orderly harbouring and to march discipline. This was particularly apparent during the march from the Kaladan to the Kalapanzin. But all this would have been in vain but for the endurance of the troops and the work of the engineers in track- and path-making and ferrying. Experience showed the usual halts of ten minutes each hour to be unsuited to the conditions, so halts of half an hour every two hours were substituted, which gave the carriers time to relax.

Patrolling was maintained at a high standard throughout the campaign. The average depth to which infantry patrols penetrated was eight miles and long-distance patrols went very much farther. The result was that Divisional Headquarters always had a good idea of the enemy's movements, etc., in the vicinity. The exception was at Thayettabin during the first days of March, when this was not the case and a disaster occurred. Experience gained during the campaign points to the necessity in jungle warfare of gaining the ascendancy over the enemy in a given area, much as a fleet controls an ocean. In either case it is impossible to prevent a small enemy unit penetrating the area, but it does so at its peril. This ascendancy is to be obtained by continuous aggressive action by patrols from platoon to company strength.

In African bush warfare it was usually possible for one side to attack the other either by existing paths or by cutting. In the Arakan jungle/hill warfare this was not the case. There, the extremely steep slopes, deep chaungs and razor-backed ridges usually confined movement to a few narrow routes. These could easily be blocked by a small party well sited and dug in. In these conditions the Japanese were often most difficult to dislodge, especially when their exact position could not be located.

The presence of large numbers of unarmed carriers was, as it always had been in bush warfare, a source of continual anxiety to a commander, owing to their tendency to panic and drop loads. During this campaign it became apparent that the carriers would be less liable to panic if provided with weapons, and the Divisional Commander recommended that at least a proportion should be armed with a light carbine.[1] Nevertheless, the men of the Auxiliary Groups displayed the same qualities of devotion and endurance that West African carriers had always shown in the past. During this campaign these characteristics earned them the respect and admiration of the whole Division, which resulted in their enhanced morale and *esprit de corps*. This was strengthened by allotting Auxiliary Group personnel permanently to one unit.

It might have been better if the Division, inexperienced, not fully trained and composed mainly of young soldiers, could have been introduced into battle *en cadre* with other formations. But it was not to be, and the Division had to overcome its teething troubles by itself. In doing so the troops displayed the characteristics of their forebears and showed once more how difficulties can be surmounted and setbacks overcome by fit, determined troops such as the R.W.A.F.F. had always been.

The battle casualties were:

	British	*African*	*Total*
Killed	25	162	187
Wounded	101	726	827
Missing	7	150	157
			1,171

In many ways the Division's operations in the Kaladan and Kalapanzin resembled those of the Chindits in central Burma, though they attracted very much less public attention. This had a discouraging effect on the British ranks, who, knowing their Division had been first in the field with large-scale air supply, the construction of airfields in enemy territory, the flying in of guns and other heavy equipment, and the flying out of casualties, could not understand why it was not given credit for these achievements. Some reasonable publicity could surely have been given without compromising security.

General Woolner, in his report to the G.O.C.-in-C. West Africa, paid the following tribute to the R.A.F.:

'No words of mine can do justice to the achievements of the R.A.F. in support of the Division. Their faultless supply dropping, the skill with which they landed their Dakotas on our airstrips in rapid succession, the devotion of the Moth pilots in evacuating casualties, the promptitude and accuracy of their airstrikes, the plentiful supply of air photographs which they provided, together with the air-letter service and the daily message dropping, taken together, constituted an outstanding effort of co-operation. Above all, there was the most heartening feeling of comradeship between the two Services.'

The report referred to above ends as follows: 'It must be many years since a Divisional Commander has lived for so long in such close contact with his men and we got to know each other intimately. It is impossible to express in words my gratitude to them for their irrepressible cheerfulness

[1] Many carriers acquired Japanese rifles during the campaign. Later 25 per cent were officially armed.

under all circumstances, or for their unfailing and enthusiastic support whatever I asked of them. By sharing triumph and disaster together the various arms of the Service have acquired a remarkable respect and affection for each other. The "Spider" has become the symbol of a very strong Divisional *esprit de corps*. I am proud of having had a share in bringing it about.'

Before many months were to pass the 'Spider' was carried once more down the Kaladan Valley to the victory of Myohaung.

(ix) *The Withdrawal of Hubforce from the Kaladan*

(See Map No. 44)

For two days after the Division had left, Hubforce maintained its position near Kaladan Village. But, finding that the enemy were working round their flanks, a withdrawal was commenced on the 13th April and 7/16 Punjabis fell back to Naiwa, eight miles north of Kaladan. The enemy advanced with caution, apparently unaware that the Division had left the valley. Thus, the transport columns with their large walking element, including 212 wounded, sick and unfit, were able to get a good start. All arrived safely, the last reaching the main road to Chiringa on 27th April. One vehicle was lost on the way.

On 17th April, however, the enemy attacked the Punjabis at Naiwa and the Battalion fell back through Paletwa, held by 1 G.R., to Dokhan, 12 miles farther north. Enemy pressure now increased and on the 23rd, 1 G.R. withdrew through Dokhan to a position covering Daletme. But as it became obvious that the enemy intended to thrust up the Pi Chaung on Labawa and Mowdok it was decided not to attempt to hold the Satpaung–Daletme area. Consequently, 1 G.R. took up a position on a ridge four miles east of Labawa and about half-way between that place and Satpaung on 1st May. Two days later the Pinjabis fell back through 1 G.R. to Labawa and the latter withdrew on 7th May to the frontier where the track crosses a ridge some 3,000 yards north-east of Mowdok, afterwards known as 'Frontier Hill'. Meanwhile, 1 Tripura Rifles,[1] who had been watching the Pi Chaung, withdrew towards Labawa closely followed by the enemy.

The enemy, now reinforced by a fresh battalion, 1/29 R., attacked the Labawa position. As it now appeared that there was a danger of the enemy penetrating between 1 G.R. and 7/16 Punjabis, the latter withdrew to a position in the Mowdok area in touch with 1 G.R. On 16th May, when the Punjabis had hardly settled in their new positions, 1 G.R. was attacked. The enemy pressed vigorously throughout the 17th and thereafter by continually harassing attacks. On 20th May 1 G.R. was relieved by the Punjabis and moved back to a position covering Mowdok.[2]

As early as 18th May the situation was causing some anxiety to XV Corps, who ordered 6 Bde., less 4 N.R. left with 5 Bde. and 1 G.R. to move from Taung to Chiringa with the object of taking control of the Mowdok area. Heavy rain had made the West African Way impassable,

[1] This was a local State unit very lightly armed.

[2] The Gambia Regiment was awarded the battle honour 'MOWDOK' for its services in these actions.

so the move had to be via Dohazari, but rapid movement was not possible, as only 200 men could be sent along this route each day.

The Commander, 6 Bde., had been warned by a Corps Instruction that he would either find the way to Mowdok open, or he would have to fight his way into the place. He was given the following tasks:

(*a*) At minimum to ensure that dumps and installations at Mowdok are in our hands with a secure land line of communications to the Sangu River when the rains break on 5th to 19th June.

(*b*) If at all possible to drive the Japanese back to Labawa and even to the Kaladan Valley.

He was also told that once the monsoon had broken he was to withdraw the force, less the Tripura Rifles, via the Sangu River. But no more was to take place until he was satisfied that 'the rains have conferred immunity from serious threat to 1 Tripura Rifles'.

While 6 Bde. was struggling to reach Mowdok the enemy launched their most determined attack on 7/16 Punjabis holding the frontier position north-east of Mowdok. A counter-attack by 1 G.R. made little progress, and on the following day the enemy offensive was renewed. On the 25th the Commander Hubforce decided to concentrate round Mowdok and next day the force was disposed as follows: 1 G.R. on the north; 1 Tripura Rifles on the south and west; 7/16 Punjabis on the east.

Headquarters 6 Bde. reached Tranchi from Bandarban by boats on 1st June, but then three days' heavy rain practically stopped all movement.[1] The Brigade Commander with one Staff Officer managed to get through and assume command, while two companies of 1 S.L.R. arrived on 5th June. Next day it was considered safe to withdraw all the troops except 1 Tripura Rifles, and on 7th June 7/16 Punjabis moved back to Tranchi, followed during the next two days by 1 G.R. and 1 S.L.R. By 11th June all but one company of 1 S.L.R. were beyond immediate recall. On that day the enemy attacked and captured Mowdok, though 1 Tripura Rifles managed to set fire to the store bashas before leaving. The unit then fell back to Kumai.

The move of 6 Bde. was stopped at once and 1 G.R. was ordered to turn back and establish a firm base at the junction of the Sangu River and the Remanki Chaung seven miles north of Singpa. 1 Tripura Rifles were ordered to patrol to Singpa and to keep a close watch on Mowdok. The Brigade now began to take up preliminary monsoon positions as follows: Bandarban, one battalion; Ruma, one company; Tranchi, one battalion, less one company; Alikadam, one company from a battalion at Chiringa forming a patrol base; Chiringa, one battalion, less one company ready to move at short notice.

It is considered probable that the aim of the Japanese attack on Mowdok was to disguise the withdrawal of 1/29 R. Prior to this, and possibly on arrival of 1/29 R., 3/111 R. had moved back to join its division, as had the detachment of 144/R. The Japanese monsoon position, which was astride the Labawa–Mowdok track where it crosses the Mowdok Taung, was held by 55 Div. Cav.

[1] The difficulties of moving in this area during the monsoon were stated in Section (ii) of this chapter.

The monsoon positions of 81 (W.A.) Div. were:

H.Q. 5 Bde.	Chiringa.	H.Q. 6 Bde.	Bandarban.
5 G.C.R.	Chiringa.	4 N.R.	Sangu River. H.Q., Tranchi.
7 G.C.R.	West African Way. H.Q. at Alikadam.	1 S.L.R.	Singpa.
		1 G.R.	Sangu River, H.Q., Bandarban.
8 G.C.R.	Chiringa.		

(X) *Chronological Table of Events in Burma: November 1943 to October 1944*

Date	*Arakan*	CENTRAL AND NORTHERN FRONTS
1943 Nov.	16: *Headquarters, South-East Asia Command becomes operational* XV Corps pushing back enemy outposts north of the Mayu	N.A.C.C. begins to move south from Ledo.
Dec.	7: 81 (W.A.) Div. begins to move from Chiringa to the Kaladan Valley	
1944 Jan.	19: XV Corps begins attack on Mayu fortress 19: 81 (W.A.) Div. starts to move down Kaladan Valley 24: Paletwa occupied	Positive signs of enemy build-up on the Chindwin River to launch offensive on Central Front
Feb.	4: Enemy counter-offensive on XV Corps starts 14: 81 (W.A.) Div. occupied Kaladan Village 24: 81 (W.A.) Div. occupies Kyauktaw 28: Japanese offensive against XV Corps collapses	5: 16 Bde. (Chindits) marches south from Ledo
Mar.	2: 81 Div. takes Apaukwa Japanese counter-attack starts 4: 81 Div. begins to withdraw from Kyauktaw 5: XV Corps ready to resume offensive 12: XV Corps captures part of Mayu fortress 16–29: 81 Div. at Kyingri 30: XV Corps capture more positions	5: Fly in of Chindits starts 8: Japanese offensive on Central Front commences
Apr.	3: 81 Div. retakes Kaladan 6: Eastern Tunnel (Mayu) captured by XV Corps 10: 81 Div. begins to move from Kaladan Valley to Kalapanzin Valley	5: Kohima invested by enemy 12: Fly in of all Chindits completed 20: Kohima relieved
May	3: Pt. 551 taken. Capture of Mayu fortress completed 13: 81 Div. arrives at Taung XV Corps begins to take up monsoon positions	17: Outskirts of Myitkynia reached and airfield taken by Sino-American force

Date	*Arakan*	CENTRAL AND NORTHERN FRONTS
1944 June	11: Japanese capture Mowdok 13: 81 Div. begins to take up monsoon positions	22: Kohima–Imphal road opened 26: Mogaung taken by Chindits and Chinese 30: Japanese offensive finally defeated FOURTEENTH ARMY CONTINUES PURSUIT THROUGHOUT THE MONSOON PERIOD
Aug.		3: Myitkyina captured by a Sino-American force
Oct.	1: 81 Div. concentrated in Mowdok area 29: 81 Div. ready to advance down Kaladan Valley	18: Tiddim occupied by Fourteenth Army

THE SPECIAL FORCE SIGN

This sign depicts the 'Chinthe'—Guardian of Burmese temples. The word 'Chindits' appears to be a corruption of this term.

CHAPTER 11

'Chindits' (Wingate's W.A.F.F.)

(Map No 37)

(i) *Plans and Preparations for the Second Chindit Operation*

(See Map No. 42)

As already mentioned, the first Chindit operation resulted in nothing but propaganda value. This, skilfully handled, not only distracted attention from the first Arakan campaign, but had some effect on the troops in Burma and on the general public of the Allies.

General Slim, for one, considered that the raid had been an expensive failure from which about a third of the total force of 3,000 failed to return. There was little tangible or no return for the losses suffered and the resources squandered. Such damage as was done to enemy communications was repaired in a few days; it had inflicted few casualties; and it had not affected enemy dispositions or plans. Nevertheless, it was decided at the highest level, namely the Combined Chiefs of Staff, to mount a second and larger operation.

The characteristics of Major-General Orde Wingate are by now well known, as is his flair for getting support for his theories from the highest authority. His original notion was to penetrate behind the enemy's lines with small, lightly equipped columns whose task would be to harry their communications and installations while the main army fought the decisive battle. Later it appears that, carried away by his theories, he began to think in terms of long-range penetration groups playing a major part whilst the rest of the forces would remain comparatively static.

By late 1943 the troops under Wingate consisted of five brigades of British and Gurkha troops as well as 3 (W.A.) Bde. To provide these troops 70 (British) Div., a well-knit formation with considerable battle experience in the Middle East, and the only British Division trained in jungle warfare, was disbanded. This was done in spite of the fact that orthodox military opinion believed it would be more effective against the enemy if employed as a normal division. Subsequent experience confirmed this view. In addition, 81 (W.A.) Div. was much weakened by the loss of a third of its infantry; moreover, a division composed of only two brigades is an unsound organization. Not yet satisfied, Wingate demanded that 26 (Indian) Div. should be handed over to him. General Slim refused point-blank, in spite of Wingate's threat to complain to the Prime Minister direct.

Meanwhile, the scope and role of the Chindits had been decided by 11 Army Group, who placed them under the direct command of Fourteenth Army. On 4th February 1944 an order was issued by General Slim

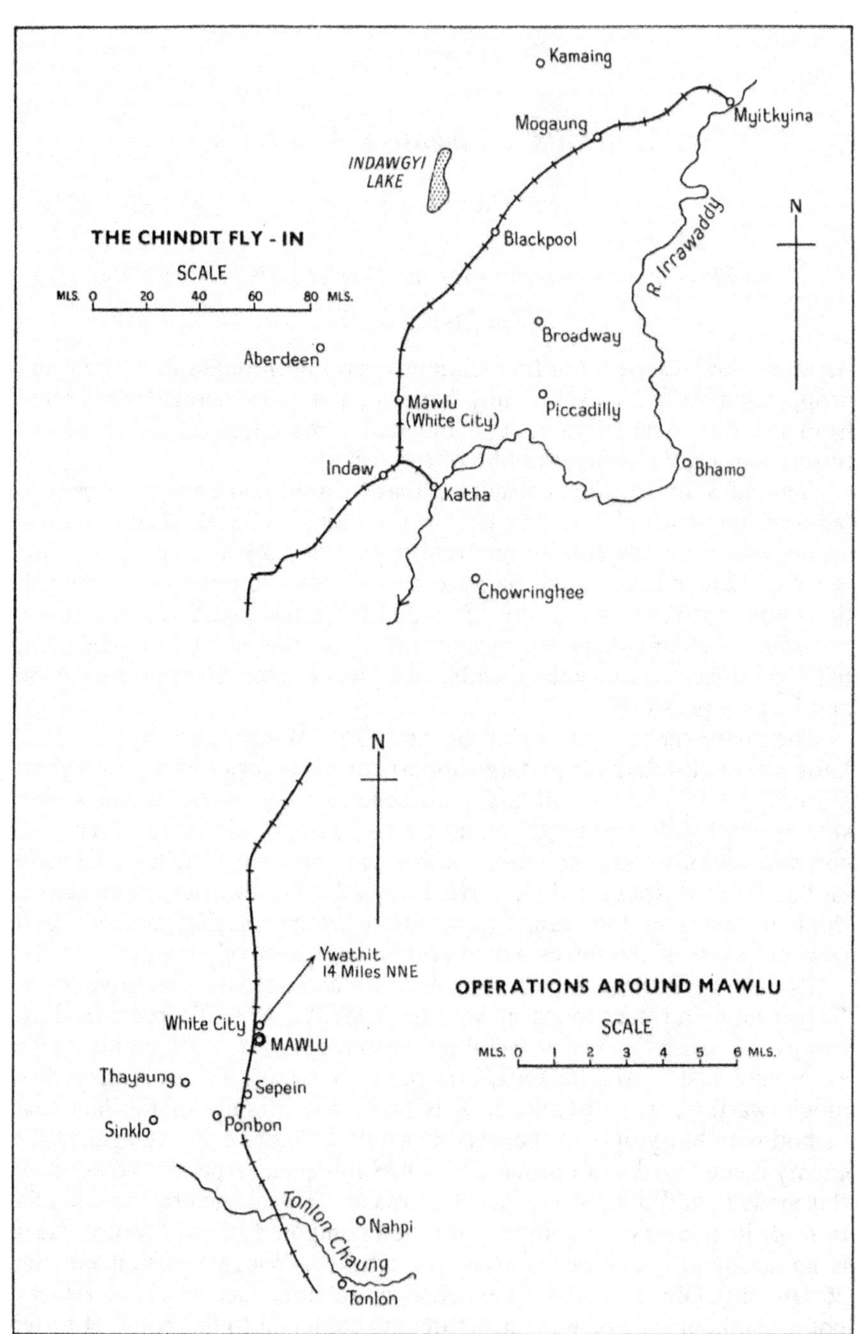

42. The Chindit fly-in

that the force would march and fly into the Indaw area[1] and operate there under the direct command of Fourteenth Army with the objects of:

(*a*) Helping the advance of N.A.G.C. on Myitkyina by cutting the communications of the Japanese 18 Div., harassing its rear and preventing its reinforcement.

(*b*) Creating a favourable situation for the Yunnan Chinese to cross the River Salween and enter Burma.

(*c*) Inflicting the greatest possible damage on the enemy in Northern Burma.

It was also hoped, in some quarters, that their operations might interfere with the imminent Japanese offensive on the Central Front.

Wingate's conception was to concentrate the first three brigades in the Indaw–Katha area and to capture and dominate it to the line Tamu–Pinlebu–Katha–Bhano. From here it would be possible to cut the road, rail and river communications of the enemy opposing the Sino-American forces advancing down the Hukawng Valley. He seems to have clung to the delusion that a division would eventually be flown into this 'liberated' area to relieve his brigades and garrison it.

The tactical plan for getting the forces into position was based on four assembly areas given fictitious names on the map. The sites selected were in uninhabited country, away from roads, with water in the vicinity and enough flat ground to admit of the rapid construction of airstrips. They were as follows: Aberdeen, Piccadilly, Broadway, Chowringhee—all within a radius of 50 miles from Indaw. The intention was to fly in 77 Bde. in two halves to Piccadilly and Broadway, and 111 Bde. to land at Chowringhee. But a last-minute reconnaissance showed that Piccadilly was obstructed, so the landings on the first night were confined to Broadway. 16 Bde. was to march from Ledo to Indaw.

The other Brigades, 14, 23 and 3 (W.A.) were to be kept back as a second wave to relieve the first in two or three months. In the event, 23 Bde. was sent to take part in the main battle and rendered excellent service on the left flank of Fourteenth Army. 3 (W.A.) Bde. was to have had the same role as the other brigades, but, before operations started, it was decided to split up the Brigade and to attach one battalion to each of 14, 77 and 111 Bdes. Their new task was to garrison the 'strongholds' which were to be the bases of these three brigades. It was also decided to fly in both 14 and 3 (W.A.) Bdes. as soon as possible.

The 'strongholds' referred to above were one of Wingate's later ideas which appears to be in direct opposition to the original plan 'to penetrate behind the enemy lines with small, lightly equipped columns to harry his communications and installations'. Being static, they offered the Japanese a chance to concentrate against one or more of them. It will be seen later that this is exactly what they did.

The instructions for the formation of these strongholds issued by Wingate's Headquarters included the following: 'A stronghold must be sited far enough from any form of road to prevent its attack by other than pack-supported enemy. It must have a suitable space to allow of the

[1] This refers to the Indaw on the Rangoon–Mandalay–Myitkyina railway.

construction of a fair-weather airstrip for transport aircraft. There must be an inner defence area—with adequate water supply—which is capable of being fortified and from which the garrison can repel attacks. Floater columns, which are essential to all strongholds, operate outside the perimeter, attack all attackers and prevent them from having any firm base. Surprise is essential in the early stages of the occupation in order to allow of the landing of fortress stores and the preparation of fortifications.'

Soon after arrival in India in mid-November 1943, 3 (W.A.) Bde. was selected to join the Special Force, or 3 (Indian) Div., as it was called for security reasons. The Brigade was soon moved to Orccha in the Central Provinces for special training in 'Long Range Penetration' operations. This included air support with live bombs, air supply, jungle shooting, digging, column marches and bivouacs, patrols, watermanship, animal transport and a good deal of ordinary marching.

The units had also to be reorganized to the Chindit pattern, that is to say, each battalion was split into two 'columns' each composed of a headquarters; one rifle company of four platoons each of four sections; a reconnaissance platoon, consisting of two sections of Burma Rifles and two sections of men from the unit all under a Burma Rifles officer; a commando platoon, with R.E. officer and N.C.O.s, the rest being men from the unit trained in demolitions; a support platoon with two medium machine guns and two 3 in. mortars; and an animal transport platoon.

The officer who commanded 3 (W.A.) Bde. during the latter part of the Chindit operations comments on the 4 × 4 company organization as follows: 'In the campaign where full all-round defence, not merely lip-service to it, was wanted every halted moment, this organization gave a three-point defensive perimeter with one sub-unit either (A) in reserve in the centre and able to really rest and be at a lower degree of readiness or (B) be away at some distance on patrol or detachment. Secondly, all offensive operations at column level such as blowing an ammunition dump, railway calvert, etc., involved establishing a carefully concealed assembly area as near to the objective as possible:

(*a*) Whence reconnaissance could be made.
(*b*) Where supplies of explosives, if needed, could be dropped by night and made up into the correct charges.
(*c*) Where unwanted elements of the column which have no role in the particular operation could remain or mules and spare ammunition could be left.
(*d*) Where an aid post could be formed and a light airstrip constructed for flying out casualties directly after the operation.
(*e*) From where communications could be opened.

Whether the operation was at platoon level or column level, one might say diagrammatically, that sub-unit "A" actually did the job; sub-unit "B" was to a flank on a protection task; sub-unit "C" was covering the immediate get-away and in immediate reserve to be thrown in if "A" were failing; sub-unit "D" protected the assembly area described above. Finally, it ensured that one could remain at any rate 75 per cent effective after several engagements and considerable losses from casualties, sickness, etc., by dropping to a 4 × 3 organization as numbers dwindled, which actually happened.'

The units and brigades were neither organized nor equipped for the attack of Japanese in position. Yet this is what they were called upon to do.

(ii) *Outline of Events*

(See Maps Nos. 42 and 43)

Since 3 (W.A.) Bde. did not fight as a formation until the middle of May the activities of each battalion will be described separately up to that time, completed as far as it is possible to do so with the data available. Further, an outline of operations in general will be given as a background, with emphasis on those of 77 and 111 Bdes., with whom 7 and 12 N.R. served until May.

The fly-in of 77 and 111 Bdes. commenced on the night 5th–6th March and by the night of the 10th–11th, 9,500 troops and 1,100 animals had been landed. No opposition on the ground was met until 11th March. The fly-in of 14 and 3 (W.A.) Bdes. started on 22nd March, but was not completed until 10th April, owing to bad weather and shortage of aircraft due to the enemy offensive on the Central Front. During the last phase 6,000 troops and 850 animals were landed at Aberdeen and a new airstrip at a bloc, known as 'White City',[1] located 16 miles north of Indaw. In the meantime, 16 Bde., which had left Ledo on 15th February, reached Aberdeen during the third week in March after a march of 450 miles through difficult, mountainous country. They met only slight opposition from the enemy.

The tasks of the four brigades were as follows:

14 Bde. to establish permanent interruption of enemy communications in the Pinlebu area.

16 Bde. to capture Indaw and its airfield.

77 Bde. to take Mawlu and cut communications of enemy 18 Div. south of Myitkyina.

111 Bde. to establish permanent interruption of enemy communications in the Pinlebu area.

On 16th March 77 Bde. attacked Japanese positions near Mawlu and established the White City block and airstrip which severed the rail and road communications of 18 Japanese Div. During the nights 18th–19th, 19th–20th and 20th–21st and in daylight on 21st March the Japanese made probing attacks on the block which were easily dealt with. The garrison of White City at this time consisted of 1 S. Staffords, 3/6 Gurkhas and the Brigade defence company with commando and reconnaissance platoons in reserve. 1 L.F., from bases in the hills overlooking the valley, harassed enemy communications from 10 to 20 miles north and south of the block.

The Japanese attacked White City on the night 21st–22nd March and gained some small footholds, but were driven out in the morning. The next four days were spent in improving the defences, thickening the wire and laying minefields, as well as probing towards Mawlu and dominating

[1] Although a 'block', White City had most of the characteristics of a 'stronghold'.

the surrounding paddy. On 27th March the enemy was driven from Mawlu.

On 1st April the situation was as follows: 14 Bde. and 3 (W.A.) Bde. were still being flown in; and 16 Bde., having failed to take Indaw, had concentrated at Aberdeen. 77 Bde. was firmly established at Broadway, which had been subjected to air and some slight ground attacks, and at White City, where a strong block had been established across the enemy rail and road communications to Myitkyina. A detachment known as 'Morris Force' had cut the Bhamo–Lashio road south of Bhamo. 111 Bde. had landed partly at Chowringhee and partly at Broadway. Brigade Headquarters and one column had crossed the Irrawaddy to the west and were moving towards Pinlebu. Another column which had failed to cross the Irrawaddy was sent to join Morris Force to the east. The remainder of the Brigade from Broadway was moving south-west to join their Headquarters at Pinlebu.

On 4th April a striking force of 77 Bde. was sent north to attack Mohnyin. At White City there remained a detachment of Brigade Headquarters, 1 S. Staffords, a column of 1 L.F. and some extra support weapons.

The Japanese had by this time organized a detachment to deal with the Chindits, but they did not divert any formation from their main front in Assam. The anti-Chindit force, based on 24 Independent Brigade, consisted of six battalions, a battery of 77 mm. and one of 105 mm. guns, a number of 6 in. mortars and ancillary troops. They also had a few light tanks which were used against White City on two or three occasions without any result.

As White City seems to have been the principal objective of this force and as 12 N.R. took part in its defence, a description of the place is apposite. The perimeter was 1,000 × 800 yards and situated round a series of 'mole hills' rising to a height of about 30–50 ft. above the plain, with numerous little valleys in between and water at both the northern and southern extremities. The village of Henu was included in the defended area and also a slightly higher hill known as 'O.P. Hill', from which a good view over the surrounding countryside could be obtained. Since there was cover from both view and fire within the perimeter, the Commander 77 Bde. (Brigadier J. M. Calvert) decided to bring Brigade Headquarters and all the mules into the block. By the time the siege began the wire on the perimeter consisted of two rows of double apron fence with at least a triple concertina fence as well. Company and platoon posts were also wired in, telephone lines had been laid and buried, and water had been stored. Defensive fire from medium machine guns and mortars had been co-ordinated and checked. The narrative of the siege of White City will appear in Section (iv) of this chapter, which is devoted to 12 N.R.

About the time of the death of Wingate late in March there seems to have been a good deal of 'order and counter-order' which resulted in unnecessary moves. Early in May, however, Major-General W. D. A. Lentaigne, who had succeeded to the command of Special Force, was ordered to move north in close support of the Sino/Americans, who were progressing slowly towards Mogaung and Myitkyina. 16 Bde., exhausted after their long march and abortive attack on Indaw, were flown back to India.

Owing to the move north, Aberdeen, Broadway and White City were to be evacuated. The plan was briefly as follows:

77 Bde. to advance along the hills east of the railway corridor on Mogaung and support the Chinese in the capture of the place.

111 Bde., with 6 N.R. under command, to open a new block at Hopin on the railway. This block was afterwards known as 'Blackpool'.

14 Bde. and 3 (W.A.) Bde., less 6 N.R., were to move through the hills west of the road and rail corridor to the vicinity of Blackpool and provide floater columns in support of 111 Bde. in the block.

Blackpool was never properly established and, in any case, did not conform to the requirements laid down for a stronghold. It was attacked almost from the time the first troops arrived on 7th May, when the floater brigades earmarked to co-operate were still involved at White City, which was not evacuated until the 11th. It appears that Headquarters Special Force did not appreciate that Japanese reactions were likely to be much quicker at a point so close to their forward area, especially after their experience at White City.

The Japanese soon concentrated both field and medium artillery against the place and brought anti-aircraft guns to within range of the airstrip. When, after a few days, the weather broke and rendered close air support by dive-bombing and 'strafing' quite unreliable, the garrison was deprived of a weapon which had been invaluable at White City. Moreover, the combination of bad weather and hostile anti-aircraft guns prevented the evacuation of casualties and reduced supply by air, as everything had to be dropped by parachute.

There were particularly heavy attacks on 23rd and 25th May by strong enemy forces, including a regiment of 53 Div.—a fresh formation. After the latter attack the block could no longer be held. The Brigade broke out and, retiring through the Nigerians, concentrated at Mokso on the shores of Lake Indawgyi.

On 17th May the Sino/Americans captured Myitkyina airstrip[1] and, on the same day Special Force came under the command of the American General (Vinegar Joe) Stilwell. It was not until 16th June that a Chinese Division took Kamaing but four days later 77 Bde. stormed Mogaung with the help of a Chinese unit. Soon after the taking of Mogaung both 77 and 111 Bdes., much under strength and completely exhausted, were flown out. This left 14 Bde., 3 (W.A.) Bde. and Morris Force to co-operate with the Sino/Americans until the arrival of 36 (British) Div.

(iii) *6th Battalion the Nigeria Regiment*

The Battalion landed at Broadway in March and was ordered to march to Aberdeen; why they were not landed at the latter place is not apparent.

As 77 Bde. was at this time fanning out to establish a block on the railway north of Mawlu, it was decided to route the unit to the advantage of

[1] The town of Myitkyina was not taken until 3rd August, after an untidy and uninspired siege.

that operation. 6 N.R. was therefore ordered to move round north of Mohnyin in the hope that their presence might delay the enemy garrison there from advancing on Mawlu. The Brigade Commander afterwards admitted not having taken fully into account the difficult open valley containing the railway which the Battalion would have to cross.

In the event, the Battalion moving in two parties, having advanced well and without opposition as far as the railway, were surprised in column of route when about to cross it. A confused engagement ensued in which a number of casualties were suffered and many mules were lost. No explanation is available as to how or why the unit was surprised, but it must be assumed that elementary protective measures were not taken.

Brigadier Calvert afterwards wrote: 'It says much for the leadership of the officers and the common sense and loyalty of the men and the standard of training that, in spite of this incident, they soon re-formed at their rendezvous and were a fighting unit again.' After this unfortunate occurrence, the Battalion moved south-west and reached Aberdeen on 31st March. Here they remained for weeks waiting for a Japanese attack which never came.

The Battalion left Aberdeen on 9th May with 111 Bde. and moved north, but was left in the hills west of Blackpool. Throughout the siege of the block they waited on the hills within hearing of the firing, but were never ordered to assist by direct action. It was not until July, when the 3 (W.A.) Bde. had been re-formed some time, that the unit had a chance of fighting the Japanese.

(iv) *12th Battalion the Nigeria Regiment and the Defence of White City*

The Battalion landed at Aberdeen and marched to White City, the first half arriving on 7th April, and the second on the 9th. Their arrival coincided with a heavy attack, the forerunner of what was to become more or less a siege of over a fortnight's duration. Fortunately, the garrison had been reinforced a few days before by the arrival of six Bofors anti-aircraft guns and four 25-pounders with adequate crews.

The attack on 9th April started with a number of air-burst ranging shots and soon settled down into a heavy bombardment of the 'box'. This was thickened up by a few bombs from aircraft and some 6 in. mortars. The troops on the forward slopes and on O.P. Hill took a heavy pounding. Most of these positions were held by 12 N.R. But, owing to the Commanding Officer's and other officers' example of visiting each post during the shelling, the troops remained unshaken and gave a very good account of themselves during the fighting in the night. This was a very severe test for a raw unit.

The shelling continued from 1700 hours to 1800 hours; the enemy then gave the garrison an hour at dusk to repair the wire and generally to prepare for the expected attack. The assault commenced soon after dark. It came in from the east on the sector held by 1 L.F., on 1 S. Staffords at the northern end and also against 12 N.R. holding O.P. Hill. The Japanese, after passing through the defensive fire put down by the garrison's mortars, during which they must have suffered heavy casualties, reached the wire, where they were lit up by star shells and literally mown down by machine-gun and rifle-fire as well as being 'strafed' with grenades. Many dead and wounded were found on the wire next morning.

On 9th April, Headquarters 3 (W.A.) Bde. (Brigadier A. H. Gillmore) had arrived to take over the garrison. Next day—10th April—the bombardment started about 1730 hours and continued until dusk, when the Japanese put in an identical attack on O.P. Hill and the eastern sector. Later in the night they attacked the northern sector, and this continued until first light in the morning. The floater company outside the perimeter had been ordered to put in a counter-attack on the enemy's rear, but soon became heavily involved and was only extricated by a strong counter-attack from the perimeter on which 12 N.R. were prominent.

Headquarters 77 Bde. left on 11th April to organize a counter-offensive against the besieging force. As 7 N.R. took part in this offensive and subsequent operations north of White City, their actions will be described in the following section of this chapter.

There was a further attack on the evening of 11th April, and for several days after, which always followed the same sequence though varying in intensity. During the day the enemy was invariably quiescent and the garrison could wander about the perimeter at will. But lack of sleep and the stink of putrefying Japanese corpses on and near the wire were beginning to affect the garrison. So much so that Brigadier Gillmore sent a message to Calvert on 13th April to the effect that he was doubtful of being able to hold out much longer.

On 16th April, O.P. Hill was lost by the S. Staffords, but was recaptured by a platoon of that Regiment and two platoons of 12 N.R. There was fierce hand-to-hand fighting on the hill and its forward slopes before the Japanese were driven off. The platoons of 12 N.R. on their return startled the British troops by displaying 32 Japanese heads which they had removed with their matchets. An eyewitness is reported as saying after this action: 'I never saw men fight with more dash or ferocity. They came back and just dumped the heads. We were amazed.'

The defenders of White City had done well and on 17th April Brigadier Gillmore issued the following order of the day:

> 'I wish to express my deepest appreciation and admiration for the cool and determined way in which all ranks in the block have met repeated enemy attacks. For six nights they have tried and failed and this last effort has cost them dear. Much equipment and many valuable documents have been captured and we have inflicted heavy casualties. We will stand fast tonight while Brigadier Calvert is moving upon the enemy's flank. Rest assured that the deeds and determination of all ranks will not go unrecognized. All casualties have been evacuated.'

The final Japanese attack had been a very heavy one and continued in broad daylight on the 17th. Next day 500 Japanese bodies were counted on or about O.P. Hill and there were more in and in front of the perimeter wire.

The Colonel commanding 24 Independent Brigade, after furious exhortations from his Army Commander to 'do or die', had led the final assault and was afterwards found among the dead. After this last failure, coupled with news of Calvert's operations to the south, Japanese morale broke and they began to straggle away. They never attacked the place again.

(v) *7th Battalion the Nigeria Regiment*

(See Map No. 42)

This was the last battalion of 3 (W.A.) Bde. to arrive. Soon after flying to Aberdeen the Battalion was placed under command of 77 Bde. and ordered to rendezvous at a point west of Mawlu and marched off short of officers and without its support weapons.

It will be remembered that Brigadier Calvert had left White City on 11th April to organize a counter-attack on the Japanese attacking the box. The force collected for the relief of White City consisted of: Headquarters, 77 Bde., and defence company; 16 Bde. Recce R.; a column of 1 L.F.; 3/6 Gurkhas; 7 N.R. A total of about 2,400 men. This left a column of 1 L.F., 1 S. Staffords and 12 N.R. to hold White City.

The village of Sepein was a nodal point in the Japanese organization for the siege; in fact, the whole Indaw–Katha–Sepein area was an important centre on the enemy's line of communications. Brigadier Calvert's intention was to use Sepein as a base for attack on the enemy concentration against the box. Sepein was visible from O.P. Hill, so that observed fire from the 25 pounders in the perimeter could be brought down on it. After practically no reconnaissance, it was decided to attack Sepein from the west, using an assembly position about Thayaung where there was good cover and a possible site for an airstrip. The place was taken by 1 L.F. on the evening of 11th April and the rest of the Brigade moved into the villages of Sinklo and Ponbon the same night.

The objectives for the attack were as follows. 3/6 Gurkhas were to take the village and 1 L.F. a lorry park on the road. The Recce R. was to advance in between these two units and 7 N.R. was to be in reserve. The Gurkha's attack started well and Sepein was reported to have been taken; 1 L.F. reached their objective. But the main position was found to be in thick scrub beyond Sepein, and in spite of support by the 25-pounders the Gurkhas could make no progress. In the meantime, and on the assumption that Sepein had fallen, 7 N.R. were ordered to take Mawlu. This they did with *élan* and reached and held the railway station. It was afterwards established that the enemy troops in Sepein amounted to three battalions.

The counter-offensive by 77 Bde. had failed and the Brigade Commander had to decide on a new plan. This was to block all enemy communications until he was weakened sufficiently to be beaten or until he turned away from White City and attacked the Brigade. The force moved south in the direction of the Tonlon Chaung, leaving 7 N.R. to maintain a road block about Nahpi, while the remainder of the Brigade took up a blocking position on the Tonlon Chaung.

The Japanese, however, continued to attack White City, and when Gillmore's message to the effect that he could not guarantee to hold out much longer arrived, Calvert changed his mind. The new plan was to move north again and to attack the enemy outside White City from the rear. This counter-attack failed and the force retired southward and concentrated in the Nahpi re-entrant.

During this operation 7 N.R. had been retained on the road at the Tonlon Chaung, where they succeeded in ambushing and destroying a convoy of six lorries and killing 39 Japanese. They also reported encounters with enemy trying to infiltrate past their block on the Tonlon Chaung. One rifle patrol encountered a party of Japanese stragglers some 400 strong, presumably from the force which had been attacking White City. They appeared to be quite demoralized and when fired on most of them fled, dropping kits and even arms as they ran away.

The fact was that not only 77 Bde. 'shot its bolt' for the time being, but the Japanese, too, were severely shaken and withdrawing southward. On 25th April, after blocking the railway and harassing enemy road communications for six weeks, 77 Bde. withdrew to the cool safety of the hills east of the railway, which were occupied by loyal Kachins.

At the end of the month Japanese were found dug in at a village called Ywathit and Lieutenant-Colonel P. Vaughan, 7 N.R. asked permission to attack them, using a combination of medium machine guns and mortars in support. The attack was to take place on 1st May and on the previous night the commanding officer reconnoitred to within 50 yards of the enemy position. The Battalion was guided by Kachins to an assembly position for the attack at dawn. The mortar and machine-gun combination proved effective, but the action lasted three hours before the village was finally taken for the loss of one African killed and 11 wounded. When the action was over the Battalion marched south-west towards White City, whilst 77 Bde. moved over the hills to Broadway. Brigadier Calvert was sorry to say 'good-bye' to 7 N.R., who 'came when we were feeling exhausted and battle-worn and their enthusiasm for action had been a great help to us'.

(vi) *3 (W.A.) Bde. in the Final Phase*

(See Map No. 43)

Early in May, Colonel A. H. G. Ricketts[1] arrived to take command of 3 (W.A.) Bde. and the garrison of White City, which also now included two R. Leicester columns with 7 N.R. acting as a floater unit on the north. The new Commander was faced with a difficult problem on his arrival; the evacuation was to be carried out within a few days and there was no plan in existence. He had been informed, however, that 14 Bde. was moving up from the south into the area round the White City with the object of creating some distraction and thus of providing indirect protection for the garrison during the evacuation. An important factor was that there were only two gates in the wire through which the troops, with 250 miles, would have to pass in single file. It was apparent, therefore, that even after the guns and stores had been flown out the withdrawal of the garrison would be slow.

The enemy had pulled back, especially on the western side, but Mawlu,

[1] Colonel Ricketts afterwards commanded 4 (W.A.) Bde. in the third Arakan Campaign, 1944–5.

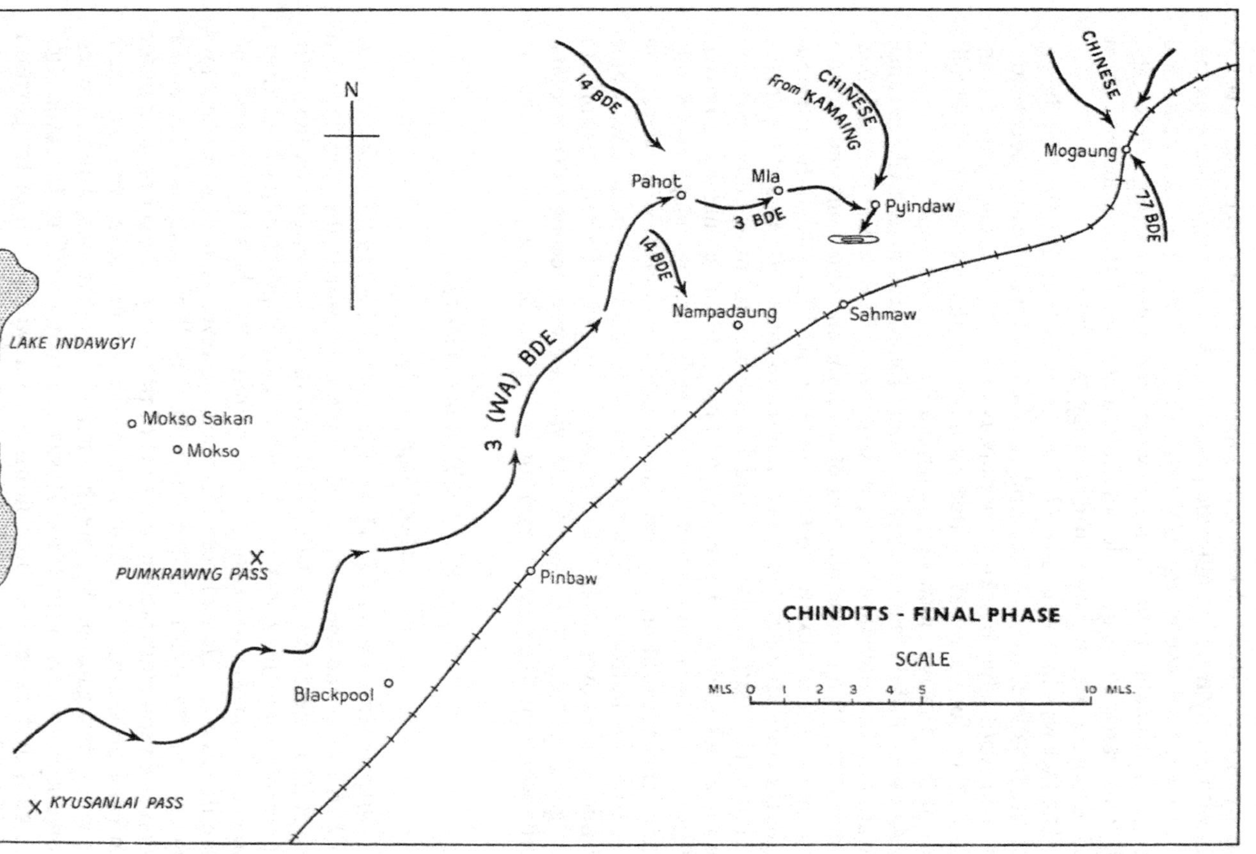

43. Chindits—final phase

only some 1,100 yards to the south of the perimeter, was strongly held. It was therefore considered essential to keep the enemy in their positions in Mawlu by alarms and feints during the evacuation. But White City was not in communication with Headquarters 14 Bde., still less with its columns, which it was vital to locate in places where they fitted in with the withdrawal cover plan.[1] However, Commander 3 (W.A.) Bde. rode out alone on a pony and made contact with two Column Commanders in the vicinity and by this somewhat old-fashioned method secured their co-operation in covering the evacuation.[2] The plan evolved was for a company of 12 N.R. to operate against Mawlu from the east, whilst one column of 14 Bde. made a feint attack from the west. In addition, another column of 14 Bde. would provide protection for the airstrip.

Soon after dark on 10th May the first aircraft landed and about the same time the detachments investing Mawlu began to put up a noisy fight. By 0300 hours 11th May, 30 Dakota flights had been completed and all the guns and stores had been lifted. Before first light the rearguard, consisting of one column of 12 N.R., had manned the perimeter, the rest of the garrison had marched out in a westerly direction, and the columns around Mawlu had disengaged. The rearguard remained in the perimeter until the night 11th–12th May and then slipped away without interference.

Both 3 (W.A.) and 14 Bdes. moved northwards through the hills to the west of the railway, at first by separate routes. However, after minor interference by Japanese patrols against them, 14 Bde. followed the same route as 3 (W.A.) Bde., which caused some delay in reaching their destination on the shores of Lake Indawgyi.

After a difficult march of over 50 miles the Brigade, less 6 N.R. still with 111 Bde., started to arrive in the vicinity of Lake Indawgyi on 21st May. By the 23rd Brigade Headquarters, with 7 N.R., were in and about the Kyusanlai Pass, with 12 N.R. on the point of rejoining after their spell as rearguard from White City.

A column of 1 R. Leicester had been the first to reach the top of the Pass from the Lake Indawgyi side on the morning of the 21st. Within two hours of their arrival a Japanese force about a company strong marched up in fours from the railway valley—singing. Surprised by the Leicesters, they suffered heavily. Lieutenant-Colonel Vaughan with a column of 7 N.R. arrived at the foot of the Pass about 1400 hours on the same day, after marching since 0530 hours that morning, and settled into an empty camp of *bashas* belonging to the Japanese. Firing could be heard from the Pass above and word of the action soon reached Colonel Vaughan, who sent two platoons with two mortars, tired though they were, up the Pass to the Leicesters.

There was further fighting on the slopes of the Pass on the railway side of the crest during the next few days, whilst successive columns of 3 (W.A.) and 14 Bdes. arrived. A column of 7 N.R. and one of the Leicesters took part in this fighting, the whole under the command of Lieutenant-Colonel Vaughan. It soon became apparent that the Japanese, having failed to

[1] Some notes on Chindit intercommunication are given in Appendix XV which show why formations and columns were sometimes out of step.

[2] He kept to the line of open paddy and was prepared to gallop for it if the Mawlu machine guns had opened on him. This, it turned out, they were too surprised to do.

forestall the Chindits by a matter of hours and having failed to turn them out, where determined to deny the exit of the Pass down into the railway valley. This prevented aid reaching Blackpool, where, unknown to the two Brigade Commanders, the sands were fast running out.

As soon as Headquarters 14 Bde. arrived the two Brigadiers agreed to a course of action whereby 3 (W.A.) Bde. would hand over the Pass and work their way over or along the crest northwards and debouch on the railway side wherever a track could be found. The move was under way and the leading column had got half-way down to the railway when the news of the fall of Blackpool came in. The Brigade accordingly pulled back the column now needlessly exposed on the railway side of the ridge, picquetted the crest with one column and awaited orders by the side of Lake Indawgyi. There was much despondency at having expended so much exertion in vain, the leading troops having literally only a few more miles to go before they must have made contact with the fringe of the force invested in Blackpool.

The exhausted men of 111 Bde. from Blackpool owed much to the troops of 6 N.R., who, besides providing a screen to cover their withdrawal, cut steps in the hillsides, built staging camps along the route, took over their loads, carried the sick and wounded, gave them cigarettes and made them laugh. It is said that some of the men in the last stages of exhaustion found new heart and are alive today because of the ministrations of the Nigerians.

As so often occurs when a period of strenuous exertion for men under great strain ends in failure, the rate of sickness increased rapidly. Many Europeans, particularly those under 25 years of age, seemed suddenly to crumple. It was essential to commence the evacuation of the rapidly growing number of casualties at all costs. No airstrip was available for transport aircraft and no light plane could land, as the country was awash. Eventually an arrangement was made which must have no equal in the history of casualty evacuation. A Sunderland flying boat, from anti-submarine tasks based on Colombo, was flown to the upper reaches of the River Bramaputra in Assam. Here it alighted for refuelling and briefing, but with great difficulty owing to the raging monsoon currents. It was then escorted by fighters over the Naga Hills to alight on Lake Indawgyi, where the combined commando platoons of 3 (W.A.) and 14 Bdes. had erected a bamboo jetty and made a buoy. The first flight took the most desperately sick and wounded, including many of the survivors of Blackpool. Several more such trips were made without incident and 500 casualties were evacuated.

During the lull after the failure to reach Blackpool the Brigade Special Intelligence Officer who, by a strange coincidence, had once lived in the Indawgyi Lake area cutting teak for his firm, set off to gain touch with the Company's old elephant *mahauts.* They were known to be in hiding from the Japanese, but the elephants had been let loose; however, two were caught and brought in to help their old master. They afforded much assistance for several days and no little light relief, too. Rations went up and casualties came down from the picquets on the ridge which enabled men and mules to obtain rest and to build up. Until the supply ran out opium was the payment preferred by the *mahauts.* Incidentally, the steps an elephant made up a near hillside simply with his feet were a great help to columns climbing the ridge later.

To resume the narrative. On 12th June the Brigade started forward again with 6 N.R. under command once more. The Brigade task was part of a plan to hasten the fall of Mogaung and to cut off the Japanese retiring from Kamaing. The rendezvous was Pahot, 15 miles west of Mogaung, and here the Brigade concentrated in the first week of July for the first time since entering Burma. Morale went up accordingly.

The monsoon was now at its height and movement through the hills became a nightmare. The tired, sodden columns in single file climbing the narrow tracks up the hills, pushing and pulling their mules, and occasionally rescuing those that slithered down the hillside, moved slowly. The descent eastward into the main valley was, if possible, worse. Between 2nd and 8th July patrols encountered Japanese blocks astride the tracks and 7 N.R. fought several platoon actions before an unguarded one was found.

The tactical situation which had arisen at the Kyusanlai Pass now repeated itself. Although Mogaung had by now fallen it was still possible to aid the Chinese by debouching on to the Kamaing road behind the enemy. But the presence of British troops in the hills was known to the Japanese, who had detachments on all the tracks down their side of the watershed. So, whilst the columns of 3 (W.A.) Bde. slowly and painfully crawled into Pahok, the earliest arrivals were trying to find ways down the other side.

Scrub typhus had now broken out and many Europeans and Africans alike had only arrived at Pahok on stretchers thanks to the really extraordinary strength and stamina of their African comrades. Pahok had a bamboo hut and here the very sick were concentrated. In the words of Lieutenant-Colonel Vaughan: 'The scene, particularly at night with the big *basha* illuminated only by the flickering light of one hurricane lantern and one of three doctors continually on duty among so many delirious and groaning men, was not a pleasant one.'

Lieutenant-Colonel Vaughan himself had been badly wounded in the arm on the way to Pahok during a reconnaissance. Sergeant Alhassan Geiri in charge of the escort had immediately made a 'right flanking' movement which restored the initiative to the party and enabled the commanding officer to be extricated. Sergeant Geiri was awarded the D.C.M. for this and other kindred acts of courage and leadership.

Once clear of the hills the Brigade moved towards Pyindaw with 6 N.R. leading, over flat country covered with secondary jungle. So close was it that accurate map reading became most difficult, if not impossible. Some opposition was encountered and quickly overcome at Mla and, on the 11th, near Pyindaw there was a brush with troops who afterwards turned out to be Chinese. In fact, the point of intersection on the road which the Brigade had aimed for had been reached by the leading Chinese troops a few hours before. A serious inter-allied battle was only averted by the remarkable energy and boldness of an American artillery colonel who had walked right round our flank, being guided by a light plane netted on to a 'walkie talkie' radio set slung on his shoulder. He, himself could see nothing and went simply where he was told. It was still raining heavily.

The Brigade was now ordered to turn and move southwards on Nampadaung. About three miles south of Pyindaw the Japanese were found in position astride the road from Kamaing on an elongated bush-covered feature known as 'Hill 60'. This position was unsuccessfully attacked by 6 and 12 N.R. on 14th July and again on the 16th. At this time 7 N.R. were still in the foothills. As the Brigade Commander has pointed out, this stage involved conventional operations in flat or slightly undulating country for which the units were ill equipped. There were neither telephones nor wireless with platoons and companies. The Brigade could only muster two or three mortars owing to casualties and the only other support available was a few Chinese guns. Moreover, the hillside was covered with secondary jungle in lush monsoon growth like acres of nettles about six feet high.

The following account by an eye-witness of the final attack by 12 N.R. on Hill 10 is of considerable interest. 'The attack of 12 N.R. was cruelly unfortunate. By the evening the last sub-unit had been thrown in as each one, casting wider than its forerunner, tried to get on to the hilltop somewhere. Lieutenant-Colonel Hughes (the Commanding Officer) could see nothing and touch was really lost through continual outflanking. A company of 6 N.R., going wider still in an effort to get right round the hill, was out of touch, too. Colonel Hughes therefore asked the Brigade Commander for permission to pull back before nightfall. The latter, well knowing how hard it is to ask troops to advance again on the morrow over ground gained the day before but given up, went forward with Colonel Hughes to see whether 12 N.R. could sit out the night on the hillside somewhere. Together with one or two orderlies, and picking up one or two from companies *en route*, this party emerged on the top of the hill as the sun was setting to find it unoccupied at that point. While efforts were being made to get the nearest elements on the move once more, the Japanese took courage again and their patrols emerged at the top, seeing off the party and landing a bomb splinter in the Brigade Commander's shoulder.'

It was not until three weeks later that Hill 60 was attacked and captured by a battalion of 36 (British) Div., who were advancing southward on the left flank of Fourteenth Army. These fresh troops, belonging to a normal formation, were properly equipped and had adequate artillery support. Moreover, as the weather improved and this Japanese rearguard position remained the sole obstacle to further advance, the power of the air forces became available and the enemy's cover was destroyed by their action. The attacking battalion was provided with guides by 12 N.R., who by then knew each game track thoroughly.

To quote the eyewitness again. 'From the 18th to the end of July about 16 U.S.A. "Mustangs" were daily talked down by the Staff of (3 Bde.) Headquarters from an O.P. on a lone tree. During the last few days before 36 Div's attack 18 bombers in addition were talked down by Brigade Headquarters and it was an impressive sight to see 1,000 lb. bombs raking the hill less than half a mile ahead. Incidentally, the lone tree was hit by a Japanese shell one day during this period with about the fifth or sixth shot. Luckily it was realized that a single gun was making a deliberate shoot at this target and the O.P. aloft was called down just in time. But a splinter from the air burst which ensued when the tree was hit killed the Brigade Intelligence Officer in a small, shallow water-logged trench near-by.

'12 N.R. followed the 36 Div. attack up and took over the hill to enable them to continue the advance. R.S.M. Bolland stood triumphantly on the tattered summit whence the further advance of 36 Div. could be seen continuing below with concentrations of artillery fire preceding them in the dawn sunlight. He was feeling the elation of all the Brigade as it was known that this was their final performance before going back to India. A last "Parthian" Japanese bullet passed harmlessly through his thigh as a reward for his premature indiscretion.

'That night there was laughter and song around the open camp fires for the first time in months instead of vigilance, silence, darkness and strain.'

The Brigade was flown out from the Myitkyina all-weather airstrip during the 21st–25th August and rejoined their Division early in 1945.

Where the results achieved by the Special Force worth the cost in lives, effort and material? The answer is given by the G.O.C.-in-C. 11th Army Group, General Sir George Giffard, as follows: 'I have nothing but praise for the organization of the initial landings, and the gallantry and endurance displayed by all ranks in the operations which followed. Events have shown, however, that these operations had less effect upon the enemy than I had hoped for. The enemy did not divert troops from his forward areas, nor did he alter his main strategical plan. In fact, the results achieved did not prove to be commensurate with the expenditure in manpower and material which had been employed.'[1] This view has since been supported by the Official History.[2]

[1] In his despatch to the Secretary of State for War, 'Operations in Burma and North-East India from 16th November 1943 to 22nd June 1944'.

[2] *The War Against Japan*, Vol. III, in which this question is discussed in some detail.

82ND (WEST AFRICAN) DIVISION: DIVISIONAL SIGN

The two crossed spears passing through an African's head-pad symbolize: 'Through our carriers we fight.' It recognizes the vital part played by the Auxiliary Groups of the Division who carried heavy loads by head in the traditional African style, enabling the Division to move across country a non-African division could not contemplate.

CHAPTER 12

The Campaign in Burma: 1944–5

(Maps Nos. 37, 38 and 39)

(i) *Plans for Dry Weather Operations, 1944–5*

THROUGHOUT the monsoon of 1944 the Fourteenth Army on the Central Front had steadily driven back the Japanese, who suffered heavy casualties both in action and from starvation and disease. British formations crossed the Chindwin early in December, while the enemy retired to the Irrawaddy. In the meantime, preparations for the British offensive to clear central Burma and recapture Rangoon had been made. During this period the Japanese were receiving drafts to replace casualties at the rate of 6,000 a month.

In the Arakan, XV Corps remained in its monsoon positions patrolling actively and conducting minor offensive operations, though 81 (W.A.) Div. began to move towards the Kaladan Valley in September. The original instructions issued to XV Corps on 29th July for the coming dry season contemplated an offensive-defensive to:

(*a*) Secure with the minimum forces the present forward positions in the Maungdaw–Tunnels area.

(*b*) Prevent enemy penetration of the Kaladan Valley which might endanger the operations of our air forces and the lines of communication west of the Mayu Range.

As the monsoon drew to a close it became apparent that the enemy in Arakan were in no position to launch a serious attack. The bulk of 55 Div. had been transferred to the lower Irrawaddy Valley leaving approximately four battalions in the forward area. Three more battalions belonging to 54 Div. were in the coastal area between the Borongas and Cheduba Island. There were also detachments in the Kaladan Valley about Paletwa.

At the end of September additional tasks were given to XV Corps as follows:

(*a*) To secure the Chittagong–Cox's Bazar area.

(*b*) To secure the estuary of the Naf as a base for light coastal forces and landing craft.

(*c*) To carry out reconnaissance bombardments and raids from the sea along the whole Arakan coast to force the enemy to lock up troops in this area.

(*d*) To exploit any withdrawal or thinning out of the Japanese in Arakan.[1]

[1] As will be seen later in this chapter, this operation was afterwards extended.

From midnight 15th–16th November, XV Corps was removed from Fourteenth Army and came directly under 11 Army Gp., which later became Headquarters, Allied Land Forces South-East Asia. The order of battle of the Corps was now as follows: 25 and 26 (Indian) Divs.; 81 (W.A.) Div., less 3 (W.A.) Bde.; 82 (W.A.) Div., on arrival in Arakan; 3 Commando Bde.; 22 (E.A.) Bde., on arrival from Ceylon; 50 (Indian) Tk. Bde.; Corps Tps.

The aim of operations now to be undertaken was to tie down and destroy Japanese forces in Arakan which might otherwise be used against Fourteenth Army on the Central Front. It would then be possible to release formations for further amphibious operations. An Instruction to XV Corps, dated 9th November, again stressed the necessity of securing the area Chittagong–Cox's Bazar and gave the following specific tasks:

(*a*) A land advance in Arakan down the Mayu Peninsula, the Kalapanzin and Kaladan Valleys to destroy or expel the Japanese within the area north of a general line Foul Point–Kudaung Island–Minbya. The advance to start as soon as possible.

(*b*) An amphibious assault on Akyab Island about 15th January supported by maximum sea and air bombardment.

(*c*) Consolidation to secure firmly the area north of a general line Akyab–Minbya.

While XV Corps could make use of the sea not only for landings but for supply, and combined headquarters had already been established for these purposes, their land communications were very restricted. The only roads along which they could move military traffic were:

(*a*) Chittagong–Taungbro–Bawli Bazar–Maundaw–Buthidaung–Myinbu–Foul Point.

(*b*) A track from Maungdaw along the coastal strip to Foul Point.

(*c*) The jeep track linking Chiringa with Paletwa in the Kaladan.

On the other hand, the Japanese had the advantage of very much better land communications in Arakan:

(*a*) From the Irrawaddy Valley: Prome–Taungup and a new road Minbu–An.

(*b*) From Taungup southward to Gwa, and northward to Ru–Ywa–Kangaw–Hpontha.

(*c*) Two routes into the Kalapanzin Valley. One from Akyab via Kudaung Island to Htizwe; the other from the Kaladan Valley at Kyauktaw via Kanzauk to Htizwe.

(*d*) An indifferent road running north from Myebon–Minbya–Myohaung–Kyauktaw.

The above had ferries over the many chaungs and there was an anchorage at Myebon through which he could pass supplies inland.

(ii) *Outline of Operations in Arakan: November 1944–May 1945*

After an uneventful voyage via the Suez Canal, 82 (W.A.) Div. (Major-General McI. Bruce) concentrated about Ranchi early in 1944.[1] Some time was spent in re-equipment, but very little training was possible, as the surrounding country was unsuitable. In September the Division began to move to Chiringa and at the end of October relieved 26 (Indian) Div. in the upper Kalapanzin Valley at Goppe and Taung Bazars, as the latter formation was now being withdrawn to rest and train for amphibious operations. During November 25 (Indian) Div. continued active patrolling and other minor operations while 81 (W.A.) Div. was advancing down the Kaladan Valley in the neighbourhood of Paletwa.

D-Day for the main Arakan offensive was to be 14th December, though preliminary operations started on the 12th. The offensive proceeded well and on 15th December 82 (W.A.) Div. occupied the town of Buthidaung. They established a bridgehead on the east bank of the Kalapanzin on the same day and so secured control of the Maungdaw–Buthidaung road. This enabled 650 river craft, required for the maintenance of 25 (Indian) Div. in operations they were about to commence on the Mayu Peninsula, to be transported through the Tunnels to Buthidaung and launched on the Kalapanzin River. This was completed by 21st December.

Supplied entirely by water, 25 (Indian) Div. advanced rapidly down the Mayu Peninsula and reached Foul Point on 26th December. By the 29th, Rathedaung and Kudaung Island had been occupied. These successes were only possible because of the tactical mobility afforded by supply from the sea. In the meantime 81 (W.A.) Div. had advanced steadily down the Kaladan and had reached Thandada 10 miles east of Kyauktaw, whilst 82 (W.A.) Div., having cleared the east bank of the Kalapanzin River, were concentrating about Htizwe at the entrance to the Kanzauk Pass.

On 3rd January 3 Commando Bde. and a brigade of 25 (Indian) Div. landed and occupied Akyab Island unopposed. 'But in a sense the battle for Akyab had been won in the Kaladan Valley; for it was later learnt that two of the three battalions defending Akyab had been thrown into the battle there, and when these had failed to stem our advance the third battalion, which would not be able to hold Akyab on its own, had been withdrawn 48 hours before we arrived.'[2]

Nine days later 3 Commando Bde. assaulted Myebon, and on the following day 25 (Indian) Div. began to land. After a week of hard fighting Kantha was captured and the Myebon Peninsula secured against counter-attack. The next step was to capture Ramree Island, especially the airstrip and anchorage at Kyaukpyu on its north-western tip. Both these were important as future bases from which Fourteenth Army could be supplied by air. On 21st January 26 (Indian) Div. successfully assaulted Kyaukpyu under cover of a sea and air bombardment. By nightfall the place had been captured and steps were immediately taken to begin the development of

[1] Composed of 1 Bde., Brigadier C. R. A. Swynnerton, 1, 2 and 3 N.R.; 2 Bde., Brigadier E. W. D. Western, 1, 2 and 3 G.C.R.; 4 Bde., Brigadier A. H. G. Ricketts, 5, 9 and 10 N.R.

[2] Report to the Combined Chiefs of Staff by the Supreme Allied Commander, South-East Asia.' (H.M.S.O., 1951).

the airfield, while the Division moved southward to clear the rest of the island. But it was not until 22nd February that all formed bodies of enemy troops were disposed of with the assistance of the Navy.

On the mainland it was essential to prevent the escape of the Japanese troops retreating down the Kaladan Valley in front of 81 (W.A.) Div. The place on the escape route where interception would be possible was Kangaw on the road leading southward. It was therefore decided to undertake an amphibious assault on Kangaw on or about 22nd January with 3 Commando Bde. and one from 25 (Indian) Div. At the same time the other two brigades of that Division would advance northward from Myebon and take Minbya. It was also decided to attack Myohaung, the ancient capital of Arakan, with the object of forcing the Japanese commander to order a general retreat from that area. The attack was to be carried out from the north by 81 (W.A.) Div. and from the west by 82 (W.A.) Div. This, however, was not to take place until after the landing at Kangaw had been made good.

The landing in the neighbourhood of Kangaw was carried out on 22nd January and surprise was gained, but the enemy reacted quickly and heavy fighting ensued in desperate Japanese counter-attacks. On the 30th our troops took the offensive, captured the village of Kangaw and established a road block on the escape route. Next day the enemy made a savage counter-attack which failed and turned out to be his last. In the meantime, the two West African Divisions had entered Myohaung on 25th January and 82 (W.A.) Div. was advancing south on Kangaw.

By early February 81 (W.A.) Div. was being withdrawn from Arakan to ease the strain on maintenance. The Division, with 3 Bde. restored to it, was to rest and train in India for another operation.[1] The remains of the enemy 54 Div. were now in two main groups, one covering the An–Minbu road, and the other in the neighbourhood of Taungup covering the road to Prome. Most of their 55 Div. was by this time in southern Burma.

Instructions issued to XV Corps by S.E.A.C. at this time ordered the extension of operations to the clearance of the whole coastal strip as far south as Sandoway and Gwa and the destruction of the Japanese remaining in Arakan. It seemed likely that the enemy would make a stand on the two passes leading to the Irrawaddy Valley, the northern from An to Minbu being defended by 54 Div., less 121 R., and the southern Taungup–Prome by 121 R. Farther south there were elements of 55 Div. The terrain was highly suitable for protracted defence and it was anticipated that the maintenance of our forces would present a formidable problem.

The first object was to destroy the Japanese detachments on the An–Minbu road; the second, to hold or destroy the remainder of 54 Div.about Taungup. The plan was to encircle the An detachment by 82 (W.A.) Div. moving from the north supported by 25 (Indian) Div. landing at Ru-Ywa. This assault took place on 16th February and Ru-Ywa village was reached on the next day. A heavy counter-attack came in on the 19th which was beaten off, and during the following week the rest of the Division was put ashore and 74 (Indian) Bde. began to advance on Tamandu, an enemy supply base and rallying place, though it was not taken until 11th March

[1] A landing on the Isthmus of Kra.

as will be described later. But at the end of February the whole plan had to be curtailed as the Fourteenth Army required more and more air supply to maintain their advance. XV Corps quota was reduced from 130 to 30 tons a day, so the encirclement of the An area had to be given up. This was because 82 (W.A.) Div. would have had to be entirely supplied by air in the roadless area through which the advance was to be made.

On 13th March another amphibious operation was carried out by 26 (Indian) Div. against Letpan with the object of cutting the road to Taungup. The Division was soon afterwards moved back to Akyab to further ease the strain on maintenance.

At the end of March 82 (W.A.) Div., which had concentrated on the Tamandu–An–Minbu road, was ordered to send a brigade up the road to hold the Japanese in this area. Another moved south and occupied Taungup on 29th April and afterwards moved up the Prome road to hold the Japanese in this area also. The third brigade pushed on southwards from Taungup, entered Sandoway on 9th May and Gwa on the 13th.

The third and last campaign in the Arakan was over. In the meantime, 26 (Indian) Div., after an assault landing on 2nd May, entered Rangoon on the 4th.

Having given an outline of events in this campaign as a background, the operations of the two West African Divisions will now be narrated in detail.

(iii) *81 (W.A.) Div. Advances Down the Kaladan Valley*

(See Maps 41 and 44)

The Division, now under the command of Major-General F. J. Loftus-Tottenham, concentrated just west of Mowdok, was to make the first move in XV Corps drive through the Arakan. This involved a march of over 60 miles through difficult, mountainous country to their first objective Bidonegyaungwa–Kaladan Village, which they were due to reach by 1st December. The Division was to be supplied by air and carriers were to be used as before, but, this time, these means were to be supplemented by pack mules and more river transport. 81 Recce R. would be available on this occasion as well as an Indian Mountain Artillery Regiment. The Division's own batteries on a head-load basis had been found unsuitable in the Arakan.

There were a number of courses open to the Divisional Commander. One of these was to advance on a broad front with one brigade in the Pi Chaung and another in the Kaladan Valley. But, with only two brigades, there would be a lack of depth and danger of defeat in detail. Another course was to advance with the whole Division down one valley—but which? If the Pi Chaung were used a strong flank guard would be needed in the Kaladan Valley. On the other hand, should the Kaladan be used a smaller detachment would suffice on the west. In the event the Division used both routes at first, probably owing to the necessity of taking Kyingri for the airstrip. In the later stages the Division moved on the east bank of the Kaladan River with the Recce R. as flank-guard on the west.

On 9th October Mowdok was occupied by 6 Bde. (Brigadier A. A.

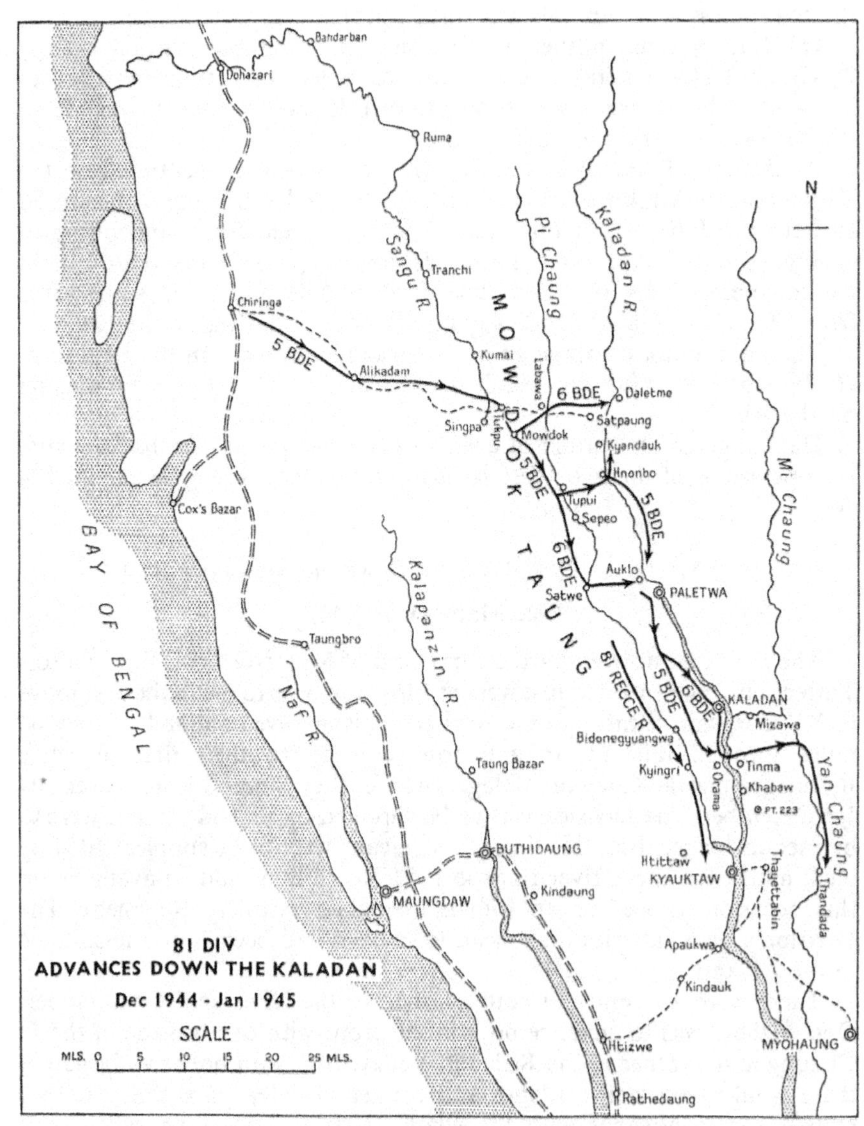

44. 81 Division advances down the Kaladan, December 1944–January 1945

Crook).[1] The next step was to capture the enemy's position north of Mowdok on the Mowdok Taung, known as 'Frontier Hill'. In the meantime, 5 Bde. (Brigadier P. J. Jeffreys) was to cross Frontier Hill farther south and concentrate at Tupui on the Pi Chaung before crossing the next range of hills into the Kaladan Valley, with the object of cutting off the enemy's escape from Daletme and Satpaung.

The position of Frontier Hill, which was thought to be held by one company, was actually held by two, plus a machine-gun troop who put up a stubborn resistance. On 11th October, after an air strike, 4 N.R. attacked and was held up in most difficult country by light automatic and medium machine-gun fire. On the 14th, after another air strike, 4 N.R. captured the feature and exploited towards the north-east. Next day the enemy made an unsuccessful counter-attack. By the 17th 1 S.L.R. was also firmly established on Frontier Hill and went on to take Labawa. Patrols soon reached Satpaung and enemy resistance appeared to have collapsed, the defenders on Frontier Hill probably having escaped in small parties.

5 Bde., who were at Tukpu, had great difficulty in finding a suitable track over the Mowdok Taung, south of Frontier Hill. After persistent reconnaissance, however, a game track was found through the very thick bush. On 9th October 7 G.C.R. reached Topui and by 18th October the Brigade was concentrated on a general line from Sepco on the Pi Chaung, two miles south of Tupui, to Hnonbo on the west bank of the Kaladan River. The Brigade was now ordered to turn north as a force of Japanese, estimated to be 200 strong, was thought to be trapped between the two Brigades at Kyandauk. The place was found to be deserted on 21st October, but mopping-up operations were continued for the rest of the month and a few Japanese were killed, but most of them had made a hurried retreat down the east bank of the Kaladan.

While 5 G.C.R. were at Sepeo the crew of a crashed American aircraft were rescued unhurt but shaken. They were made as comfortable as possible, but the aftermath of the incident is described by an officer of the Battalion as follows: 'At that time we were under the impression that our rations were pretty good, but we could not help noticing that the Americans thought they were very, very bad. It was not rudeness; they just felt that we deserved something better, and promptly sent off a long message for specialities and beer. Unfortunately, practically nothing turned up, and they ate very little for the first few days. Porridge was quite beyond them, and tea was no substitute for their beloved coffee. We were not hurt about it. In fact, we felt with some satisfaction that we must be pretty tough if it were possible to enjoy something which others viewed with such obvious distaste. It delighted us when one of them asked us how far it was to the nearest town.

'After about a week a signal came through for them to go back and we sent them off with an African escort to a half-way point on their journey. Three days later the Corporal confirmed our worst fears about their reactions to our hills.

' "Sah," he said with a mixture of indignation and amazement. "Dem men no fit march at all." '

[1] Brigadier R. N. Cartwright had died of typhus in July.

' "Why, Corporal?" we asked. What had happened?

' "Uh! Sah," the Corporal grinned. "Dat big man, sah, he march ten minutes: den he halt for one hour. When I try help him, he lie for ground. He say, 'Go, go! Leff me, Corporal, I go die.' " The Corporal chuckled. "Dey no savvy dis march palaver at all." It was no more than we had feared.'

To revert to the narrative. The Division commenced its advance southward on 2nd November. The second bound was to be to the area Kyautaw–Myohaung–Kanzauk. The enemy opposing the Division was thought to consist of 55 Div. Cav., one battalion 111 R., 1 Bn. I.N.A., one company 143 R. and possibly 1/29 R.

5 Bde., advancing down the Kaladan River, concentrated at Auklo on 14th November. 6 Bde., leaving 4 N.R. on Frontier Hill, moved unopposed down the Pi Chaung to Satwe, where some resistance was encountered. On 13th November, having been ordered to concentrate at Auklo, they crossed the dividing range of hills and arrived on the 18th. The enemy who had faced them at Satwe were discovered dug in on a knife-edged ridge between Auklo and Paletwa and driven east on 23rd November. In the meantime, Division had ordered the advance to be resumed, 5 Bde. by the track Auklo–Khawei–Mizawa.[1] The Brigade moved off to secure a base at Mizawa, but, as the enemy were known to be in Bidonegyaungwa, 8 G.C.R. were detached to Htangshan, four miles south of Mizawa, to harass and contain them as a deceptive measure, while the rest of the Brigade moved on Kyingri.

In the meantime, 6 Bde., with 4 N.R. rejoined, and moving quickly, reached Natarainggyaung, two miles west of Kaladan Village, on 28th November without meeting much opposition. The enemy had at last evacuated Paletwa and were moving south on the east bank of the river. Patrol contacts with enemy from Themawa identified 55 Div. Cav. Meanwhile 81 Recce R., who had been west of the Pi Chaung, by-passed Bidonegyaungwa and occupied the loop of the Pi Chaung at Kyingri on 30th November.

6 Bde. continued to advance and gained contact with enemy near Sigyaung, three miles south-west of Kaladan Village. Identification of 3/111 R. was obtained. The Japanese had failed to close the gap between Bidonegyaungwa and Kaladan owing to their having held on too long to Paletwa and so the Division had gained its first objective up to time and in doing so had outmanoeuvred the enemy.

In mid-October the Japanese in fact, had built up a 'Kaladan Defence Force' under Major-General Koba, whose task it was to cover the withdrawal of the Japanese forces on the Mayu front and to hold the general line Akyab–Kaladan. His troops consisted of 55 Div. Cav., 111 R., 4 Coy. 143 R., 1 Bn. I.N.A. and about 3,000 divisional and army troops. 3/111 R., taken from Akyab, had been moved up in support of the troops in the north, 2/111 R. was in reserve, leaving only 1/111 R. to hold Akyab.

The Divisional Commander now decided to concentrate east of the

[1] Khawei is on the Pi Chaung some five miles south-west of Auklo, and Mizawa is some six miles farther down the chaung. The latter place must not be confused with the village of the same name two miles east of Kaladan Village.

Kaladan River about Tinma, prior to moving through the hills round the Japanese right flank. The immediate object was to occupy a firm base in the hills dominating the road Thayettabin–Myohaung. Patrols were to be sent out to reconnoitre the routes and fighting patrols were to go towards Kyauktaw and Thayettabin to indicate impeding attacks in that direction.

On 4th December 6 Bde. occupied Orama and sent a detachment across the river to Tinma where contact was made with enemy troops withdrawing southward. The bridgehead was rapidly enlarged and the ferrying of troops continued for several days. 6 Bde. made a firm base two miles east of the river. 5 Bde., who had joined 81 Recce R. at Kyingri, now moved across to Orama and crossed to the east bank, where they formed a separate 'box' on the river bank near Tinma. A small force was left at Kyingri consisting of 81 Recce R., less one sqn., and 21 (W.A.) A/Tk. R., acting as infantry, with a troop of mortars. This detachment known as 'Holdforce', besides being responsible for patrolling to the south, was also detailed to clear the Soutcol route to the Kalapanzin and for maintaining contact with patrols from Taung.[1]

By 11th December the Division, less Holdforce, had been concentrated on the east bank of the river about Tinma. A new airstrip was opened, re-equipment proceeded, and the patrols mentioned above were sent out. The patrol to Thayettabin, known as 'Coaster', consisted of one company from 5 Bde. and a troop of artillery its task being to give the impression that a divisional advance was about to start on the plain. To add to the deception Holdforce patrolled vigorously southwards as if to tie down the enemy in preparation for an advance down the west bank of the river. Three old jeeps, brought in by air, were driven about ostentatiously by day and with blazing headlights after dark around Kyingri to give the impression that heavy equipment had been received. It appears that these actions to mystify and mislead the enemy were quite successful and that he never was certain on which bank the main thrust would come. According to the information available at this time the Japanese were thought to be on a wide front from Htittaw to Kyauktaw and Thayettabin. This was afterwards found to be correct.

The bridgehead had been shelled on 9th December by four 77 mm., four 105 mm. and 150 mm. guns firing about 100 rounds, but our casualties were only three killed and nine wounded. On 15th December, Coaster had secured a base at Pt. 223 near Khabaw and on patrolling forward had immediately made contact. Japanese reaction was swift. On the night 15th–16th December at least one battalion, supported by a number of 77 mm. and 105 mm. guns, attacked Coaster and 5 Bde's position at Tinma for six hours without success. 'A' Coy. 5 G.C.R. bore the brunt of the attack on 5 Bde. which was made against the ridge south of Tinma. All localities were firmly held. Coaster force became heavily engaged and one platoon and two guns were overrun, but the position was restored by a counter-attack and the guns recaptured. 6 Bde. was not involved, except 1 G.R., whose forward elements were engaged near Sanon two and three-quarters

[1] The Soutcol route ran from Kaladan via Kalagya–Yadaung–Wagai–Letpanywa to Taung. It was used by the Japanese in their counter-offensive in the first Arakan campaign. Parts of it were also used by 81 (W.A) Div. in the move from the Kaladan to Kalapanzin Valley in April–May 1944 (See Map 39.)

miles south-east of Tinma. Next morning 46 Japanese bodies were found; our losses amounted to nine killed and 36 wounded.

Of 'A' Coy.'s fight on this night, an officer of the Battalion writes as follows: 'On this narrow ridge the battle swayed backwards and forwards for nearly seven hours in the darkness, amidst "Banzais" from the Japanese and counter yells from the Africans, who were in their element. At one stage Jap and African were actually firing at each other at less than five yards' range, and one African, worried by the fire of a wounded Jap near-by, crawled out of his foxhole and finished him with his matchet. . . . The troops had excelled themselves. As the ground lay they could be given none of that flanking fire which normally is the real strength of a defensive position, but with rifle, grenade and automatic they had fought the battle out themselves at a few yards' range. It was estimated afterwards that the enemy had used the greater part of two companies in their efforts to wipe out our forward platoon. Individual acts of bravery that night earned the Company no less than one D.C.M. and five M.M.s. The case of a Bren gunner from the standing patrol was particularly pleasing. When his section came back, this man stayed behind, and during the earlier stages of the battle dodged about, firing his gun into the assaulting Japanese from varying positions on the flank. Next morning he was found by his gun, alive but unconscious from loss of blood, with all his ammunition expended.'[1]

The plan for the next advance was to move the Division into the hills east of Tinma, then to turn southward down the Yan Chaung and establish a firm base astride the chaung where it turns west below Thandada. Deception parties were to be left about Tinma to give the impression of strength remaining in that area. Wireless silence was to be maintained during the move.

On the 18th December, 6 Bde., with 1 G.R. leading, moved through the hills to the Yan Chaung, brushing aside slight opposition. Thandada was reached on the 23rd and 1 S.L.R. occupied Pt. 877 two miles to the west and ambushed a Japanese patrol, killing 13 and taking one prisoner. The remainder of the Division followed with no trouble other than occasional shelling of the chaung route. Divisional Headquarters reached Thandada on the 24th, where a message conveying the Supreme Commander's congratulations was received. The movement had been carried out very quickly; the enemy had been deceived and were still in their positions across the valley on either side of Kyauktaw, waiting for an attack from the north. Koba had been outmanoeuvred for the second time in a month.

5 Bde., passing through 6 Bde., met some opposition at villages where the Yan Chaung turns westward, but for the time being the Division remained in its firm base. Their immediate task was to dominate the surrounding country, particularly the Japanese communications to Thayettabin by air strikes, artillery and mortar fire and fighting patrols.

There was an important feature west of the area occupied by the Division, situated close to the Thayettabin–Myohaung road. It is an isolated hill, the highest point of which is 317 ft., three and a half miles

[1] Private Kweku Pong, 5 G.C.R., who afterwards received the M.M.

long from north to south and rather less than a mile across at its widest part. The hill was thickly wooded, had many gullies on its sides, and so made an admirable forming-up position for an attack on the Divisional area from the west. This feature, which came to be known as 'Westdown', was too far out to be held by less than a battalion, but the intention was to use it as a company base for patrols. (See Map No. 41.)

The Division now completely overlooked the Japanese on the paddy, who replied by shelling the base area, by an abortive attack on 1 S.L.R., holding Pt. 877, and by continual probing from the west. On the east our patrols went as far as the River Lemro without encountering any great Japanese strength. 5 Bde. cleared the enemy from the northern end of Naleik Chaung and reached Zidaw, thus enabling a Dakota strip to be made in the vicinity which the Brigade became responsible for guarding.

After some days it became evident that the Japanese were intending to mount an attack using the western slopes of Westdown as a forming-up place. It was accordingly decided by XV Corps that all available air support should be allotted to 81 (W.A.) Div. for a period of three days. The intention was to put down saturation bombing on Westdown to knock out the enemy's guns and to smash the impending attack in its assembly areas. This action would, it was hoped, compensate for the shortage of artillery with the Division. The air attack was made on 29th, 30th and 31st December, when waves of bombers were continually over the target all through the hours of daylight. Each night during this '*blitz*' patrols went across to the feature to report on its effect and to give clearer pin-points for targets the following day. Preparations for an attack were undoubtedly being made on the slopes of Westdown and, just as certainly, they were abandoned in face of the terrific onslaught from the air. In any case, probing from the west ceased. The Divisional Commander sent a signal to XV Corps on conclusion of the operation: 'Any Jap intention of attacking Pt. 317 shattered. Am resuming advance.'

On 4th January 81 Recce R. left Holdforce at Kyingri and began to move south on the west bank of the Kaladan River towards Apaukwa and Kanzauk, where they were to meet 82 (W.A.) Div. coming from Htizwe. The Soutcol track was now clear of Japanese and 'C' Sqn., which had been with 82 (W.A.) Div., had rejoined.

The narrative of 81 (W.A.) Div. must now be left for the time being.

(iv) *82 (W.A.) Div. in the Mayu Offensive*

(See Map No. 45)

The first task allotted to the Division was to act as left or eastern flank guard to 25 (Indian) Div. during their move south down the Mayu Peninsula. The Division had also to protect the eastern flank of XV Corps from Goppe Bazar to Htizwe on the line of the Kalapanzin River.[1] Having achieved these two tasks the third would be to move by the Htizwe–Kanzauk Pass road into the Kaladan Valley to relieve 81 (W.A.) Div. prior to an advance on Myohaung.

[1] It should be noted that south of Kwason the Kalapanzin is known as the Mayu River.

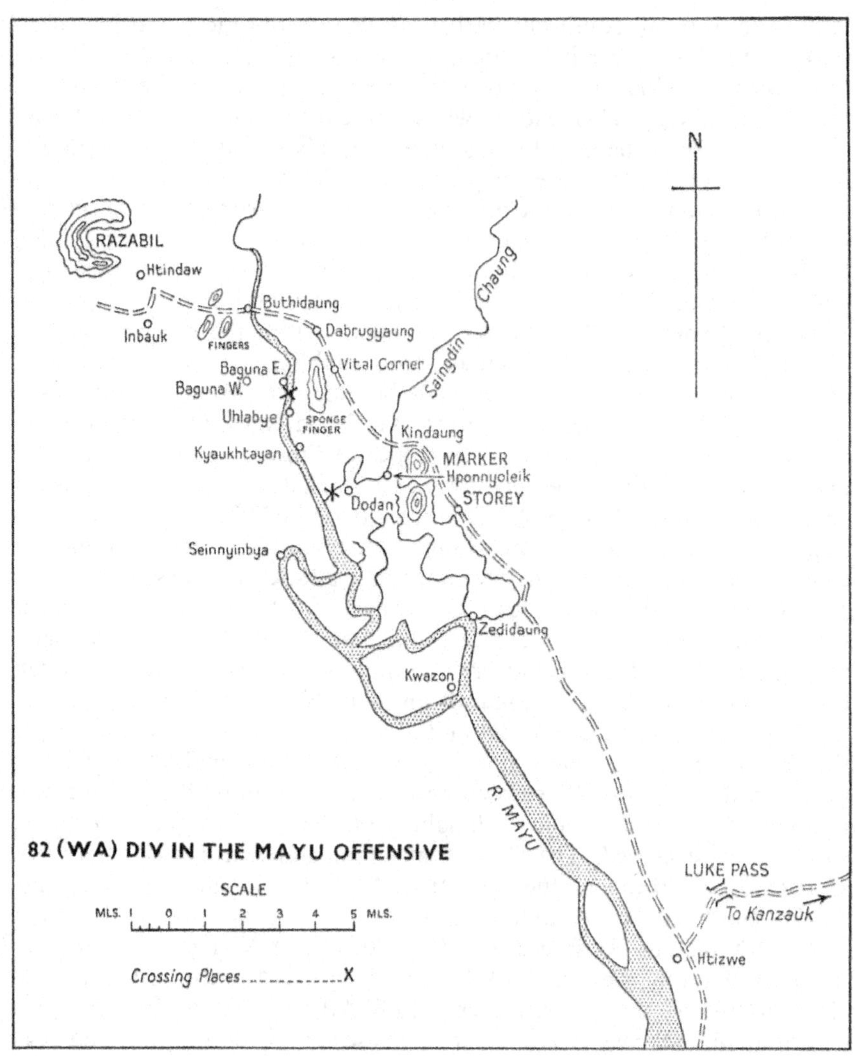

45. 82 (W.A.) Division in the Mayu Offensive

On 11th November 2 Bde. assumed responsibility for the Kalapanzin area. This Brigade was relieved by 4 Bde. on 29th November and moved to Razabil, where 1 Bde. also arrived on 8th December.

By 12th December the Division, less 4 Bde., had concentrated in the Htindaw 'bowl', a stretch of paddy between Razabil and Buthidaung. The first steps on 14th December were to be an advance by 1 Bde. on Baguna and on Buthidaung by 2 Bde. The former were to move during the previous night to the neighbourhood of Inbauk. 4 Bde., in the north, were to exert pressure on the Japanese still in the upper Kalapanzin.

South of Taung Bazar the Kalapanzin/Mayu River runs through a broad, flat valley which widens rapidly as it gets farther south. The entire floor of the valley was paddy, interrupted by isolated hill features rising abruptly from the level plain. The valley is also broken by a mass of chaungs feeding the river, which broadens out to a width of nearly two miles south of Kwazon. East of the valley high hills separate it from the Kaladan Valley. From the southern outskirts of Buthidaung a line of small hills stretches southward for 1 and a quarter miles; 1 and a half miles farther west a somewhat similar line of hills stretches southward from the main road for about the same distance. From their appearance on the map these two lines of hills were known respectively as 'East' and 'West Finger'. A block of hills north of West Finger, and separated from it by the road, was known as the 'Massif'. Between this and West Finger was known as the 'Gate', which had been secured on 13th December by 25 (Indian) Div.

During the morning of 14th December 2 Bde., supported by artillery and tanks, took over the Gate from 51 (Indian) Bde. and passed through with 1 G.C.R. directed on East Finger and 3 G.C.R. directed on Buthidaung. By the morning of 15th December the Brigade had cleared East Finger and Buthidaung, while 3 G.C.R. had one company across the Kalapanzin in a tight bridgehead. Next day 2 Bde's bridgehead was 1,000 yards east of the river but still under machine-gun and mortar fire. By 18th December the forward troops were exploiting east of Dubrugyaung. The Brigade was now made responsible for the defence of XV Corps maintenance area near Buthidaung.

As soon as 2 Bde. had reached West Finger, 1 Bde. started with 1 N.R., whose objective was Baguna East, leading. This Battalion detached a company and a section of mortars north of a chaung skirting the southern edge of the two Fingers. A fighting patrol was also sent towards some high ground south of the line of advance in order to discover if any Japanese were located in the foothills in that direction. The main body advanced without incident, but the left company was held up for a short time by opposition from the southern end of East Finger. This was disposed of by the company in conjunction with 1 G.C.R.; and by afternoon the Battalion was concentrated at Baguna East. In the meantime, the patrol to the hills had located enemy in position and an attempt to outflank them only succeeded in drawing fire from positions sited to cover the first post encountered. However, the Patrol Commander succeeded in inflicting 12–15 casualties on the enemy by skilful manoeuvre before he was recalled. The remainder of the Brigade moved to Baguna West, less 2 N.R. in divisional reserve.

During the early hours of 16th December 3 N.R. crossed the river unopposed and by nightfall had established themselves on 'Sponge Finger'. 1 N.R. formed a close bridgehead round the point of disembarkation. Next day, 3 N.R. moved northwards, occupied 'Vital Corner' and gained touch with 2 Bde.'s bridgehead east of Buthidaung. The next object of 1 Bde. was to cross the Saingdin Chaung near its junction with the river. As a first step 1 N.R. were to move to Uhlabye, leaving one company to cover the crossing of the remainder of the Brigade.

2 N.R., now released from divisional reserve, were given the task of forming the bridgehead over the Saingdin Chaung just west of Dodan. Moving partly by water, one company and another platoon established

themselves on the south bank of the chaung by the evening of 17th December. Next day the troops in the bridgehead were increased to three companies and a troop of 104 Mortar Bty. The enemy commenced to shell both banks of the chaung and a patrol found that they were in occupation of Dodan village, which commanded the exits of the bridgehead. An attack on the village supported by artillery and mortar failed to drive the enemy out, though the leading troops entered the place. As dusk was now falling, the enemy's strength was unknown and the surroundings were unfamiliar to the troops, it was decided to withdraw into the bridgehead That night fire from field and medium artillery was put down on the village. Next morning—the 19th—another company attacked. This, too, was unsuccessful, the enemy gunners bringing down heavy and accurate defensive fire upon the troops advancing over the open paddy around the village. After a pause an air strike and a concentration of all the artillery and mortars was put down on the objective. Under cover of this bombardment a company tried once more. Again the attack failed to dislodge the enemy from the deep dugouts and heavily constructed bunkers.

While these frontal attacks were going on other elements of 2 N.R. had been moved, partly by water and partly on foot hugging the bank, to Seinnyinbya to get behind the enemy and cut them off. A minor skirmish took place at Seinnyinbya in which an enemy patrol was driven out. During this little action an African soldier calmly walked up to a tree and shot out of it a Japanese sniper who had been causing casualties to his comrades in the open paddy.

The flanking force was gradually built up from the bridgehead, which was still being shelled and sniped. The detachment found the country extremely difficult, as it consisted of a succession of deep tidal chaungs with muddy banks. However, both these obstacles and enemy resistance were overcome and by 22nd December both Dodan and Hponnyoleik had been cleared and the feature known as 'Storey' occupied. This was an action calling for considerable gallantry and determination on the part of all concerned.

Meanwhile, 1 N.R. had taken the southernmost tip of the high ground north of Kindaung and the village itself on 18th December, where some slight resistance was eliminated. Next day a company crossed the Saingdin Chaung and established themselves on the high ground north of the road by nightfall. That night they were subjected to their first Japanese 'jitter party', but only one shot was fired and that by an African soldier who suddenly found a foreign body within a yard of the muzzle of his rifle. Thus, one round, one dead Jap and one captured automatic. On 20th December the company consolidated while another company passed through and worked their way southwards through thick jungle. This company was also visited by 'jitter parties' during the night, but, like the other company, remained 'calm, cool and collected'. Next day, the whole of this big feature, known as 'Marker', was cleared.

The southward advance was now taken over by 4 Bde., who had cleared small parties of enemy from the Kalapanzin Valley from Taung to Buthidaung and had then moved up behind 1 Bde. to Kindaung. The latter Brigade was now disposed as follows: Headquarters and 3 N.R., Kyaukhtayan; 1 N.R., Marker and 2 N.R., Storey. The casualties incurred exceeded 100, over 80 of these being suffered by 2 N.R. in their operations around Dodan. It is interesting to note that the casualties of these few days fighting were about the same as those sustained by the Brigade in the whole of the East African Campaign of 1940–1.

To facilitate the advance of 4 Bde., 3 N.R., less two companies, were sent by water to Zedidaung to threaten the enemy's lines of communication and also to secure the left flank of 53 (Indian) Bde., who were operating on the west bank of the river. Zedidaung was occupied on 25th December after some fighting; 3 N.R. then exploited eastward and made contact with 4 Bde.

At the beginning of January 4 Bde. was concentrated about Htizwe, preparing to advance via Kanzauk to the Kaladan Valley, where they would come under command of 81 (W.A.) Div. On 2nd January 1 N.R. took over the western end of the pass, known as 'Luke', sent patrols as far as Rathedaung and established two forward companies along the road to Kanzauk. The remainder of the Brigade concentrated in the western end of Luke awaiting orders to follow 4 Bde. into the Kaladan Valley. 2 Bde. remained responsible for the security of the Corps maintenance area around Bathidaung.

(v) *Myohaung: January 1945*

(See Maps Nos. 41, 46 and 47)

After the bombardment of Westdown the Japanese retired towards Myohaung, leaving behind large dumps of stores and ammunition. The force opposing 81 (W.A.) Div. on 1st January was estimated to be four battalions, a battery and some army troops. One of the battalions was thought to be south and south-east of the Division's concentration area, guarding the approaches to Myohaung, the rest of the force being in the Teinnyo–Myohaung area. In addition to the above, 55 Div. Cav. were on the west bank of the Kaladan, withdrawing southwards.

The city of Myohaung lies in a pass running east and west through the narrow southern neck of foothills which border the eastern side of the Kaladan Valley. Farther north in the same latitude as Thayettabin, the foothills are divided into several close parallel ranges, giving a considerable width of difficult mountain country from the general line of the Thayettabin–Myohaung road east to the Lemro River. As they flow south the Kaladan and the Lemro draw closer together, thus squeezing out the hill ranges, which cease one by one until only the western range remains. Myohaung lies on this ridge six miles north of the point where it ends in the junction of the Paungdok and Naragauk Chaungs. The hills bordering the town are generally about 300–400 ft. above the paddy fields, while the width of the range is little more than two miles.

On the west side the city is separated from the Kaladan River by six or seven miles of flat paddy land which is considerably intersected by chaungs and minor waterways. To the east the Lemro River is only four or five miles distant and the intervening terrain is also flat and cultivated. Although it is almost free of water obstacles, several prominent and isolated hill features stand up from the valley's bed and dominate the country between the river and the city.

The intention had been to relieve 81 (W.A.) Div. by 82 (W.A.) Div. when the former had completed its task of securing the area Kyauktaw–Thayettabin–Teinnyo–Apaukwa by 14th January. But, owing to the speed with which the Division had advanced and the Mayu operations had progressed, it was decided to commence the relief earlier. The first phase was to be the relief of one brigade by 4 Bde., with 82 Recce R. and 40 Mortar R. attached. On 4th January, however, after the occupation of Akyab, this was modified and 4 Bde. was to come under command of 81 (W.A.) Div. as its third brigade. Headquarters 82 (W.A.) Div. with 1 and 2 Bdes. were to follow, the latter formation being relieved at Buthidaung by a battalion of 22 (E.A.) Bde. 81 Recce. R. was placed under command of 82 (W.A.) Div. On completion of the relief, 82 (W.A.) Div. was to move southwards and cut the Japanese lines of communication east of Myebon.

In the meantime, General Loftus-Tottenham was planning to continue his advance with the troops at his disposal, though he expected 4 Bde. to arrive in time for the final phase commencing on 10th January. His object was to capture Myohaung and establish a bridgehead over the River Lemro to the south-east of the city.

On 1st January 6 Bde. started to regain contact with the enemy by moving south from Zidaw by a track through the hills. The enemy was encountered at Makyaze and Pt. 160, a mile south-east of it. On 3rd January 4 N.R. took Pt. 160 and the rest of the Brigade closed up to a point half a mile south of Angyaung. After bridging the chaung through Makyaze, the next objective was to be Pt. 555 on the ridge running southward to Myohaung. Then 5 Bde. was to advance along the western slopes of the ridge and occupy Thingyittaw Pagoda. The Commander 6 Bde. decided to build up on the north feature of the ridge immediately south of Makyaze which, from its appearance on the map was named 'Starfish'. The first attempt to cross the chaung at Makyaze by 1 G.R. on 5th January was stopped by shell-fire; on the same day the enemy made an unsuccessful counter-attack on Pt. 160. The advance was postponed to await an air strike.

On 9th January the old base was evacuated; 5 Bde. concentrated north of Teinnyo and Divisional Headquarters opened at Westdown. Bombing of Starfish by four squadrons failed to enable 6 Bde. to cross the chaung at Makyaze on 8th January, but next day 1 S.L.R. crossed and occupied Starfish by the 11th. The Japanese were, however, still holding out on Pt. 425 farther along the ridge to the south.

Leaving Kanzauk on 7th January, 4 Bde. arrived on the 13th and concentrated near Westdown. For the reasons given in Section (ii) of this chapter it was essential not to spring the trap too soon. The Divisional Commander, therefore, under orders from XV Corps, postponed the projected advance of 5 Bde. until 15th January and modified his plan. The revised plan was as follows:

6 Bde., before 15th January, was to limit its efforts to patrol activity if the enemy still found in position south of Starfish, but to maintain vigorous deception patrols on the left flank. On 15th January the Brigade with 41 Mortar R. under command was to mount an attack along the ridge, the objectives to be Pt. 555 and three pimples, just south of it. Additional support would be provided in the form of a 20-minute air strike on the ridge north of Pt. 425, followed by a 20-minute air strike to the south of it.

5 Bde., with 50 Mtn. R. under command, in the paddy on the right, were to advance on 15th January under cover of the diversion by 6 Bde. Objective Thingyittaw Pagoda.[1] Additional support would be provided by a force of Hurricanes at call.

4 Bde., whose artillery had not yet arrived, in reserve at Teinnyo Ferry.

On 15th January 6 Bde. attacked from Starfish, but, in spite of repeated air strikes, 4 N.R. were unable to dislodge the enemy from a strong position north of Pt. 425. An officer of the Battalion writes as follows: 'Almost immediately the Battalion met very determined resistance. As usual, the enemy position was very cunningly sited on a knife-edged ridge which made it impossible to attack on more than a platoon front, and any attempt to outflank ran into strong covering positions. During the following three days each company in turn assaulted the position after an air strike had been made.' But a wide turning movement was in progress and on 18th January Pt. 425 was taken after 1 G.R. with air support exerted pressure on the Japanese right flank.

In 5 Bde., 5 G.C.R., after hard fighting on 15th January, secured a footing on the edge of the ridge west of Pt. 425. One company of 8 G.C.R., operating from Mudein, five miles north-west of Myohaung, to harass the main road north of the city, was joined by another company and directed on Thingyittaw Pagoda. They captured the feature after a short resistance on 18th January and were joined there by the rest of the Battalion, while 7 G.C.R., moving on the paddy, reached Thangyaung Ywathit. On the same day 4 Bde., less 10 N.R., began to move south from Teinnyo, making a detour through the paddy to by-pass an enemy position on the main road. By 21st January the Brigade had concentrated in the foothills below Thingyittaw Pagoda with 9 N.R. in contact with the enemy on the main road.

There were unconfirmed reports about this time that the enemy had an escape route northward from the Lemro or along its east bank and thence eastwards from Pyelongi[2] by a rocky jungle path unfit for wheels or even mules. 10 N.R. were sent with some sappers to Pyelongi to cross the river and cut the route. They found no Japanese using the route, but did not rejoin the Brigade until the end of the month.

It was also considered important to cut any escape route farther south. As it had now been decided not to relieve 81 (W.A.) Div. by 82 (W.A.) Div., the latter Division was to be brought forward to take part in the capture of Myohaung. Consequently, 82 (W.A.) Div. (Major-General

[1] This Pagoda was situated on the crest of the western ridge running down to Myohaung, about 1,500 yards from the road. Some 500 ft. above the level of the paddy, it afforded an extensive view.

[2] On the River Lemro, six miles east of Thandada.

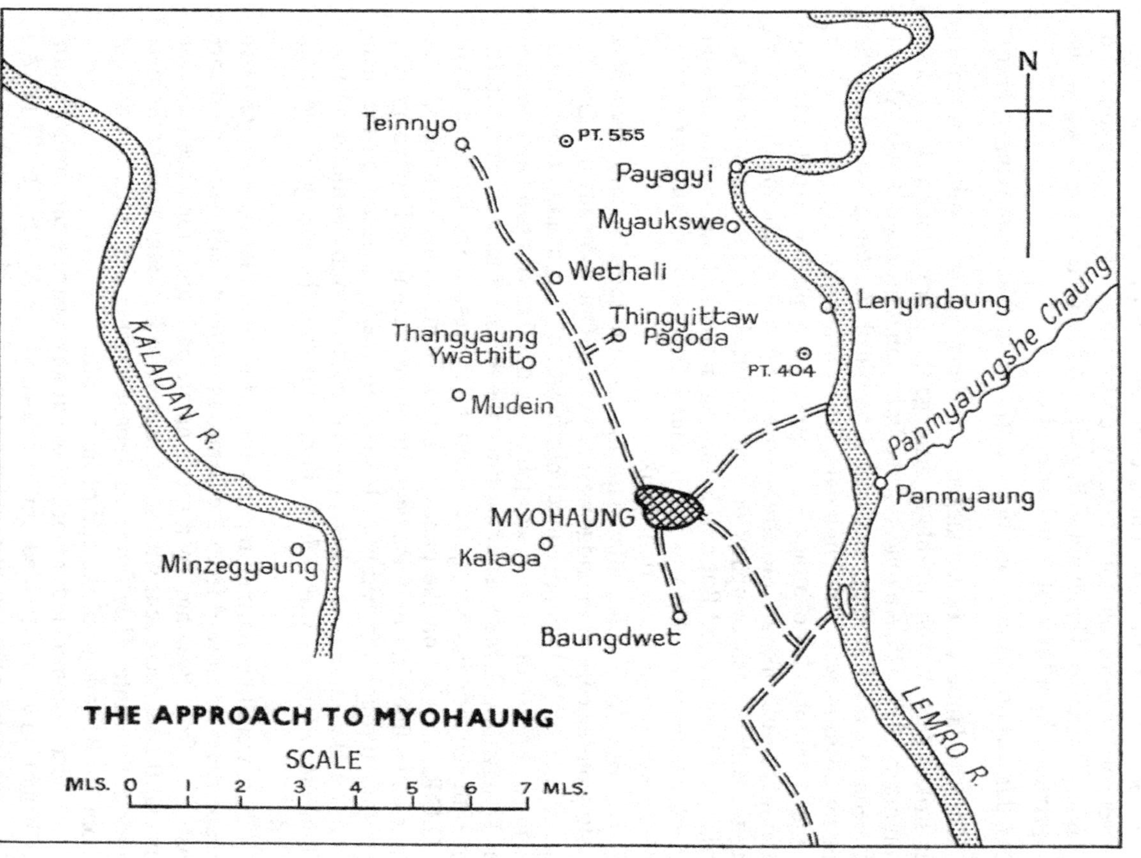

46. The Approach to Myohaung

H. C. Stockwell)[1] was ordered to move from the Mayu via Kanzauk, directed on Baungdwet, two miles south of Myohaung, to cut across the Lemro River. 1 Bde., which had moved in accordance with the original relief plan, was already through the Kanzauk Pass and 2 Bde. was moving from Buthidaung to follow them. Both Brigades marched with commendable speed. 81 Recce R. was attached to 82 (W.A.) Div. and 82 Recce R. to 81 (W.A.) Div. as a matter of convenience.

After the capture of Pt. 425, 6 Bde. were not only to exploit forward to Pt. 555, but were to secure control of the Lemro River at Payagyi Ferry: 5 Bde. were to move north-east from Thingyittaw Pagoda, with the same task two miles south of Payagyi. 4 Bde. was to attack Pt. 403 from the west. This feature is situated on the ridge two miles north of Myohaung and overlooks the place. 10 N.R. from Pyelongi to stop all traffic on the Lemro and would be reinforced by 82 Recce R., who would cross the river and move down the east bank to meet its own Division when it crossed the river south of Myohaung.

6 Bde. found Pt. 555 unoccupied and moved southwards. By 22nd January Brigade Headquarters were at Myaukswe, with forward battalions at Wethali and Lenyindaung on the Lemro, where the only contact was made. 5 Bde. was concentrated at Thingyittaw Pagoda, in the vicinity of which there were still pockets of enemy in the hills and chaungs to the north-east. On this day, also, 5 N.R. of 4 Bde. captured Pt. 403 and 1 Bde. crossed the Kaladan River due west of Myohaung with 81 Recce R. on their right flank.

On 22nd January fresh instructions were issued for the final elimination of the Japanese from the Myohaung area. The operation was to commence on 24th January, but, as a preliminary, 5 Bde. were now to capture the two ridges between Myohaung and Panmyaung Ferry. 1 and 4 Bdes. were to be under command of 81 (W.A.) Div., but the former were relieved of their task of cutting the Lemro River which had been the original intention.

The plan was as follows: On 23rd January 5 Bde. was to concentrate north of its objectives while 4 Bde. simulated an attack north of Myohaung. On the night 23rd–24th January 5 Bde., supported by 81 (W.A.) Div. artillery, was to attack its objectives. At the same time 4 Bde., supported by 82 (W.A.) Div. artillery, was to send forward fighting patrols and, if possible, secure the enemy's main positions north of Myohaung. 1 Bde.'s objective was the ridge to the south of Myohaung between Pt. 268 and Pt. 326. After 0800 hours, this Brigade would send patrols to the high ground surrounding the lakes south of the city. 10 N.R. was to move south on the east bank of the river on Panmyaung Ferry, while 82 Recce R. crossed the river at Payagyi to cut an enemy escape route via the Panmyaungshe Chaung, which leads north-east from Panmyaung. 6 Bde. was to concentrate on the west bank of the river south of Payagyi.

By 23rd January the Japanese had disappeared from the Thingittaw Pagoda area. 4 N.R., of 6 Bde., moved from Wethali to the west bank of the river. 5 Bde. completed its concentration.

4 Bde., after capturing Pt. 403, had found a determined body of enemy

[1] Major-General Stockwell had assumed command of the Division, *vice* Major-General Bruce, evacuated sick. General Stockwell was an old W.A.F.F. officer.

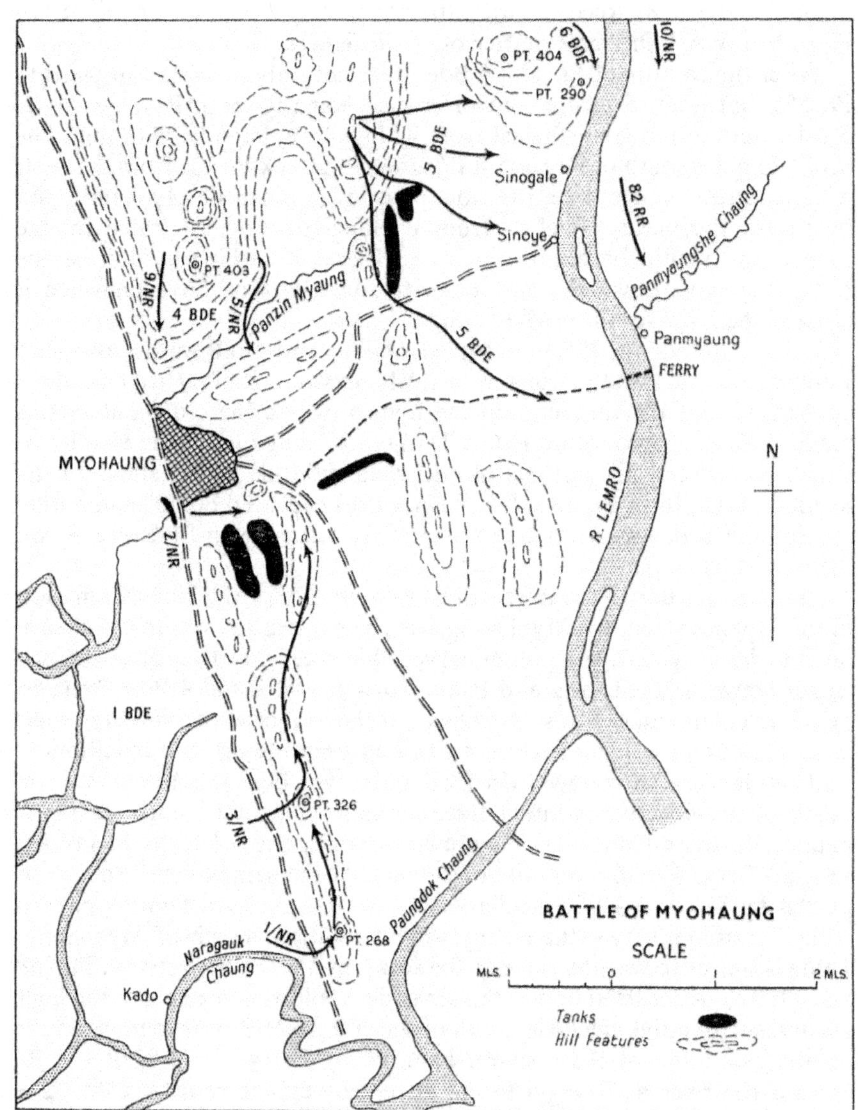

47. Battle of Myohaung

Carriers on the march in bush

Carriers on the march in paddy country

Face page 448

[Photo: Imperial War Museum

Hurri-Bombers attack Japanese position at Paletwa

[Photo: Imperial War Museum

Supply Drop

between them and Myohaung on the line of the Panzin Myaung and on a number of pagoda-topped pimples bordering the road. On 23rd January, in spite of air strikes, several attacks by 9 N.R. failed to capture the hill feature bordering the road, but in the evening 5 N.R., after fighting all day, forced the crossing of the Panzin Myaung. 5 Bde. occupied its objectives on the ridges east of Myohaung, but the enemy maintained a firm hold on Pt. 404 and the river bank to the south of it. East of the Lemro 82 Recce R. was within four miles of the Panmyaungshe Chaung. It is now necessary to leave the formations closing in on Myohaung to narrate the movements of 1 Bde. and its action on 24th January.

1 Bde., after a hard march and overcoming by improvised means a number of obstacles, mostly chaungs, and having its axis switched south-eastwards, began to arrive at Minzegyaung on the west bank of the Kaladan River on 19th January, three days after leaving Htizwe. 1 N.R. was the first unit to reach Minzegyaung, but, by the following morning, Brigade Headquarters, 3 N.R. and attached troops came in with 2 N.R. following closely behind, spurred on by the sounds of battle going on to the east. The arrival of 1 Bde. in time had, in fact, been considered improbable if not impossible, and the corresponding surprise of the enemy at its sudden appearance must have been greater still. It may be remarked here that this Brigade had adopted the form of march discipline recommended by 81 (W.A.) Div. and described in Chapter 10, Section (viii) of this volume.

On 20th January 1 Bde. started to cross the Kaladan. Before final orders had been received 3 N.R. had been ordered to occupy Kalaga, where they had established a bridgehead over a chaung. It was therefore necessary to side-step the Battalion for the coming attack on the high ground south of the city. This was carried out with the assistance of landing craft, enemy opposition being limited to snipers and small patrols.

2 N.R. took over Kalaga and pushed a platoon up to the outskirts of Myohaung, where they encountered a party of enemy attempting to destroy an important bridge. The enemy, taken by surprise, were driven off, but in the ensuing fighting, which lasted two days, the enemy were eventually cleared from the area around the bridge. A very gallant African N.C.O., Sergeant Ibrahim Wadai, 2 N.R., who personally accounted for seven Japanese and cleared the bridge virtually single-handed, was awarded the D.C.M. for his exceptionally fine conduct.

Meanwhile, 1 N.R. had been taken by landing craft to Kado, a village about a mile west of their objective—Pt. 268—and were concentrated by 23rd January. The enemy on the ridge reacted strongly to patrols and it appeared they had no intention of being hustled out of the position.

Next day—24th January—was to see the finale of the operations around Myohaung. It was to be an historic day in the annals of the R.W.A.F.F., when twelve of their battalions, representing all four of the West African Territories, took part in the same battle. This was the greatest concentration of force ever achieved by the R.W.A.F.F.

While 1 Bde. was to attack from the west, 4 Bde., supported by an air strike, was to assault from the north. To eliminate chances of a mishap, no patrols were to be sent into the area south of Myohaung city before 0800 hours, and the area was not to be bombarded by artillery or mortars during the same period. Unfortunately, the objective of 3 N.R., the ridge Pt. 328, was in this area. In the event the Battalion was lucky; they took their objective without any trouble.

Farther south, 1 N.R. attacked Pt. 268, supported by 30 Mtn. R. The fire plan involved an air strike by eight Thunderbolts as well as support by guns and mortars. The leading company moved up as close to the objective as possible during the bombardment, followed by another company in support. At the end of the air strike the leading company assaulted with great dash and secured their objective, while the following company exploited northwards and linked up with 3 N.R. The artillery with the Brigade was then switched to support 4 Bde., who were still engaged just north of the city. Later, patrols entered Myohaung, where no Japanese were seen. During the following night fighting patrols of 1 and 2 N.R. engaged withdrawing parties of enemy from the Paungdok Chaung to the south-east of the city and inflicted more casualties.

The Japanese stated after the war that they were surprised by the direction and strength of the attack by 1 Bde. When they first became aware of the threat to their flank and rear they thought the troops concerned were their old enemy—a detachment from 81 (W.A.) Div.

On 25th January 4 Bde. occupied Myohaung. 5 Bde. found Pt. 404 and the bank of the Lemro to the south clear of enemy and occupied Sinogyi and Sinogale. It appears that this area had been held to the last to preserve an escape route for the last of the garrison of Myohaung. 2 Bde., to their great disappointment, arrived too late to take part in the battle.

81 (W.A.) Div., having completed their task, received the congratulations of the Supreme Commander and the Corps Commander.[1] Success with the minimum of light artillery support had been attained by the selection of ground suited to the African soldier for skilful manoeuvre. For more than four months they had marched south through most difficult country, ceaselessly in contact with the enemy, to whom they had given no rest.[2] With no lines of communication and little contact with the outside world, but well supported by the air forces, they had fought and defeated parts of the enemy 54 and 55 Divs., with such success that the enemy had been forced to thin out and weaken the garrisons of Akyab and Mayu to try to prevent the Division's advance and the threat to their communications. The easy occupation of Akyab was due to the Division's successful advance, during the latter part of which they had acted as the 'Hammer' to the 'Anvil' of Kangaw. All this had been achieved at a cost of 438 battle casualties. (See Appendix XI.)

The experience gained in the first Kaladan operations had served them well in the second. An officer of 5 G.C.R. writes: 'In the second campaign we experienced the advantage of all the little things which one learns and goes on learning, so long as fighting continues. To travel light was both necessary *and* comfortable, once you learnt how. . . . That morale was

[1] See Appendix X (1) and (2).
[2] In addition, 6 Bde. had been holding the Sangu Valley throughout the previous monsoon. *Vide* Chapter 10 Section (ix).

higher in our second attempt was only to be expected. Nobody any longer overestimated the Jap as they had before all the well-meaning propaganda had been debunked in action: and the Africans and Europeans had developed a greater trust and confidence in each other. Both had learnt their limitations. The African relied on his officers for imagination and foresight, for quick apprisal of a situation and clear orders; the European, to rely far more on the African's instinct for danger, and to trust much more to his amazing powers of hearing and observation. We had all learnt that speed in a jungle battle is purely relative and that, if anything, it was to be regarded as a tactical danger. There were other much more important requirements: to acquire a complete knowledge of the ground before you struck; to maintain control if possible, but to leave room for initiative where the unexpected is so commonplace; to allow time, and more time, in which to ensure that nothing can go wrong.'[1]

The Division, after mopping up around Myohaung, began to march via Kanzauk to Buthidaung and moved thence to Chiringa on the way back to India.

[1] *West African Way, The Story of the Burma Campaign, 1943–1945*, by Lieutenant-Colonel C. G. Bowen, late 5 G.C.R.

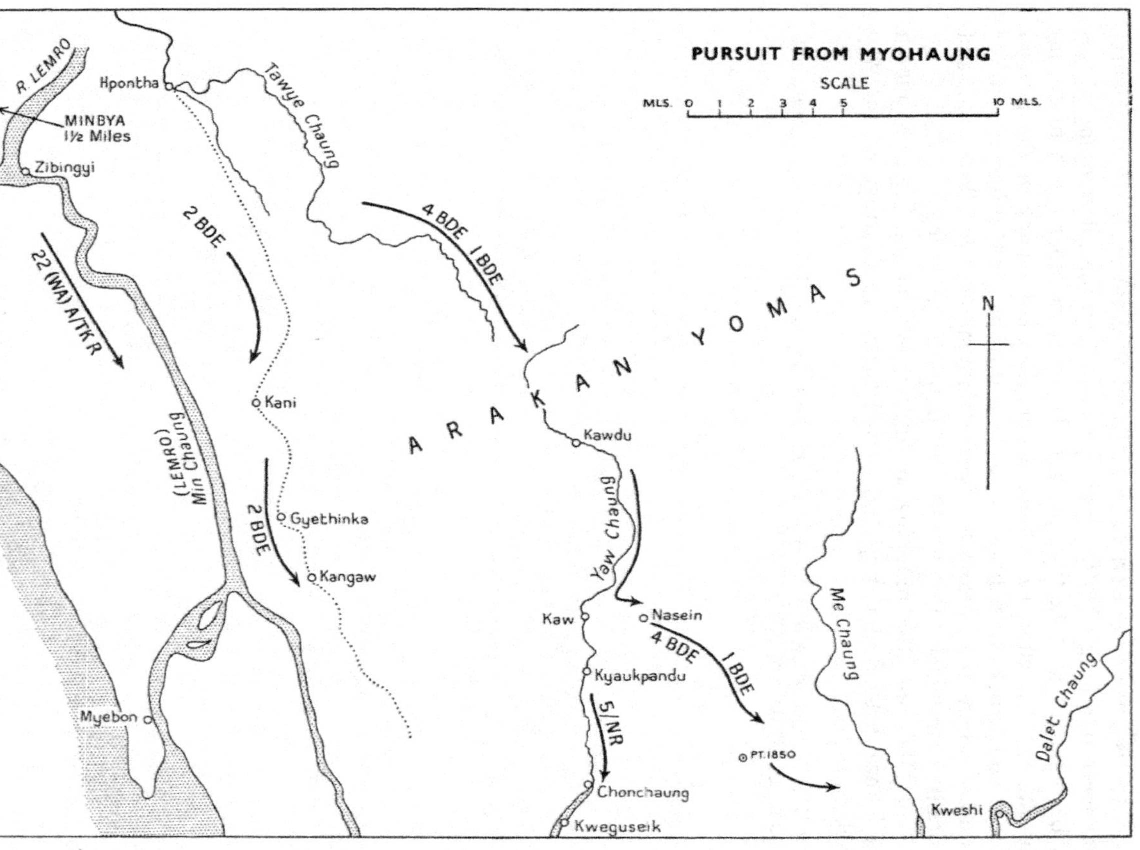

48. Pursuit from Myohaung

CHAPTER 13

Operations in South Arakan: 1945

(Maps Nos. 37 and 38)

(i) *82 (W.A.) Div. in the Pursuit from Myohaung*

(See Map No. 48)

AFTER the battle of Myohaung the role allotted to the Division was to cross the River Lemro between Myohaung and Minbya and carry out a parallel pursuit:

(*a*) Down the axis Hpontha–Kangaw.

(*b*) Down the axis Hpontha–Kyweguseik.

The main effort to be on (*a*) and touch to be gained with 25 (Indian) Div. south of Minbya. The Division, now forming the 'Hammer', commenced to advance on 27th January.

There had been heavy fighting since the landing at Kangaw on 22nd January and by the end of the month the battle was reaching a climax. By this time, however, the Division, supplied by air and advancing southward, was beginning to influence the situation.

The Division moved in several columns. On the right, 22 (W.A.) A./Tk. R.[1] and 81 Recce R. were moving down the west bank of the River Lemro directed on Minbya. 4 Bde., with Hpontha as the objective, was going down the Lemro in river craft. On the left, east of the Lemro, was 1 Bde., also moving on Hpontha. 2 Bde., after a pause at Myohaung, was on its way to join the Division.

Hpontha was reached by 1 Bde. on 29th January after a few brushes with retreating Japanese in which all three battalions took part. 22 (W.A.) A./Tk. R. and 81 Recce R. encountered some delaying forces before making contact with units of 25 (Indian) Div. at Minbya. The town was entered on 1st February and the surrounding area cleared on the following day. The Division, with its forward elements on the line Zinbingyi–Hpontha, was now concentrating for a further advance, while 81 Recce R. moved north to rejoin its own Division.

The advance from Hpontha started on 3rd February. 2 Bde., moving in three columns east of the River Lemro with 22 A./Tk. R. on the west bank, were to act as the final stroke of the 'Hammer' by driving the enemy on the 'Anvil' at Kangaw. 4 Bde., farther to the east, moved along the Taywe Chaung with the intention of by-passing the Kangaw block and cutting the main road south of it at Kyweguseik with one battalion. This was an attempt to cut off the enemy opposing the block from the south side. The rest of the Brigade with 82 Recce R. was to move towards Dalet.

[1] This unit was acting as infantry.

The plan for the extension of operations, referred to in Section (ii) of Chapter, 12 now began to affect the formations engaged in the Kangaw battle. 82 (W.A.) Div. was ordered to destroy the Japanese northern group in the vicinity of An. For this reason 1 Bde. was ordered to join 4 Bde. at Kaw and left Hpontha on 7th February. As already mentioned, it was intended that the Division should be entirely supplied by air, should avoid making a frontal attack on An from the west and should move round by the north. By this approach the strong positions the enemy was known to have constructed to guard the end of the pass east of the town could be outflanked.

At the outset the Division, less 2 Bde., and leaving one battalion to continue to advance in the Kyweguseik operation, was to move south-east from Kaw towards Dalet, whilst 25 (Indian) Div. was to land a brigade at Ru-Ywa and obtain a bridgehead due west of An. On the conclusion of the Kangaw action, 2 Bde. was to be brought round by sea, pass through Ru-Ywa and rejoin the Division. In the meantime, 25 (Indian) Div., less one brigade but plus 2 (W.A.) Bde., was to complete the destruction of the Japanese at Kangaw, followed by pursuit by a small force to Kyweguseik and the release of 2 Bde.

Good progress was made by 2 Bde. in spite of efforts by small parties of enemy to impose delay. On 8th February the Brigade was as far south as Kani, where they drove a party of Japanese off a hill feature immediately north-east of the village. Next day, now only nine miles north of Kangaw, the Brigade came under command of 25 (Indian) Div. Opposition began to strengthen and on the 14th Gyethinka, about four miles north of Kangaw, was cleared by 1 G.C.R. who killed 14 Japanese for the loss of one African wounded. On the following day 3 G.C.R. secured the crossing of the Gyethinka Chaung and the Brigade pressed on southwards.

After some confused fighting in the tangled area around Kangaw, resistance ceased on the 18th and next day the first flight of the Brigade embarked for Ru–Ywa. A few days later 7/16 Punjabis were sent by 25 (Indian) Div. to follow up the success at Kangaw by moving southward on Kyweguseik and thence to Tamandu, while troops already landed at Ru-Ywa approached the latter place from the south.

The Japanese had been surprised at the landing at Kangaw and, attacked in such a vital spot, were forced to stay and fight. They suffered casualties estimated at 2,500 and lost 26 guns there. The retreat from Myohaung had been a hasty one and 2 Bde. were cheered by the sight of guns and lorries sticking out of the mud in the chaungs at low tide.

The advance of 4 Bde., and later of 1 Bde., by the same route, was through some of the thickest, most mountainous and difficult country—the Arakan Yomas. Throughout the whole length of the route 4 Bde. was constantly in contact with assorted parties of Japanese endeavouring to escape through the hills and prepared to fight hard for a chance of survival. Nevertheless, Kawdu on the Yaw Chaung was reached on 8th February with the forward battalion at Kaw.

On 10th February 10 N.R., who had been detailed for the advance on Kyweguseik, moving down the Yaw Chaung past Kaw, came into contact with the enemy near Kyaukpandu, where they were halted by sustained rifle and machine-gun fire from positions covering the chaung. The two leading companies climbed on to a ridge, later known as 'Banana Ridge', and began to dig in. In the midst of this the leading company was attacked and forced back through the rear company. By dusk, however, the rear company had finished digging in, which was fortunate, as they were attacked eight times during the night with great ferocity. Early next morning the remainder of 10 N.R. arrived and a platoon was sent off on a wide flanking movement while a company was ordered to assault the enemy on Banana Ridge. The attack was made with great vigour, but was unsuccessful against a well dug in enemy. For over an hour charge and counter-charge took place and the company, when withdrawn, was found to have suffered heavy casualties. For their distinguished conduct on these two days Major C. R. Kalshoven, Sergeant Yaro Zuru and Lance-Corporal Bagadu Lamurdi were awarded decorations.

During the night 11th–12th February the Japanese withdrew about 500 yards along the top of the ridge and one company 10 N.R. moved forward and occupied the vacated position which was on higher ground. About 21 Japanese dead were found in the position and in some cases both African and Japanese dead lay in the same trenches. Nothing had been heard of 10 N.R. flanking platoon since its departure. 9 N.R. were moved up round the right of 10 N.R. with one company on Banana Ridge farther south and the remainder tried to encircle the enemy by deploying through the hills to the west. But the enemy held up all attempts to move round him. 5 N.R. now occupied the position vacated by 9 N.R. and sent a company out to the left to establish itself on a feature Pt. 1021 (not marked on map) preparatory to a battalion concentration in that area with the object of cutting the enemy's communications in the Yaw Chaung.

The Brigade had now reached the tidal section of the chaung, which was only fordable at special places at low tide. Moreover, the banks were quite precipitous in most places from Kyaukpandu southwards. This made communication with 9 N.R. and the evacuation of casualties from that side most difficult and slow. Meanwhile, the remainder of the Brigade had concentrated south of Kaw and 30 Mtn. R. arrived in support. A Moth strip was built and casualties evacuated. During the night 13th–14th February Japanese jitter parties were active and drew more response than should have been the case.

On 14th February Brigade Headquarters was at Kyaukpandu, 10 N.R. concentrated on Banana Ridge and 5 N.R., after a terrific climb, had assembled on Pt. 1021 without being interfered with. The missing platoon of 10 N.R. returned and reported having sat astride the Japanese communications and killed five of them. The platoon had had hardly any food for two days; however, the acting Platoon Commander, Company Sergeant-Major Hawes, remarked, 'It was so exciting I barely noticed I was hungry.'

During 15th February 30 Mtn. R. harassed the enemy while 5 N.R. moved into position overlooking the enemy's Yaw Chaung communications. This manoeuvre, which entailed great exertion, was entirely unseen by the enemy. Before the Battalion could pounce, however, the Brigade was ordered to return to Kaw, owing to a change in the Divisional plan which called for 4 Bde. to follow 1 Bde. over the hills south-eastward towards Dalet. An officer who was present writes: 'This was particularly aggravating at the time, for the enemy were still in position and had brought up a heavy mortar. The Bde. had worked hard for the kill, had some old scores to pay off and a miniature "Sedan" was at least in prospect. By way of consolation 10 N.R. staged two jitter parties on a scale far more elaborate than the Jap model. That the demonstration was not appreciated could be deduced from nervous Jap reaction. The fireworks were followed by heavy rain and 4 Bde., sipping their rum issue, hoped that the not-so-lucky Jap would catch pneumonia.'

On 18th February, the day on which the battle of Kangaw ended, 4 Bde. began to withdraw on Kaw. On the next day, before following, 9 N.R. reported that the enemy had withdrawn. 5 N.R., now detailed to take over the task of reaching Kyweguseik, started to move southwards. The advance was along the east bank of the chaung as far as Chongchaung. At this point a patrol reached Kyweguseik and, though fired on, sustained no casualties. The place was found unoccupied on 22nd February and the Battalion took up a position to the south overlooking the coastal road. There were signs of occupation by a considerable force and large dumps of various natures of artillery ammunition were found. On the 23rd contact was made with 7/16 Punjabis coming from Kangaw and with 102 Lt. R.

Next day 5 N.R. with 1 Lt. Bty. moved off along the coast road towards the Dalet Chaung and Tamandu. After overcoming slight opposition, Satya, six miles north-west of Tamandu was occupied on 27th February. The Dalet Chaung was reached without interference on 4th March and the Battalion and Battery were ordered to cross as soon as landing craft became available. The Battalion would then come under command of 74 (Indian) Bde.

This may be said to have been the end of the pursuit. Before proceeding any further with a description of the operations to capture Tamandu, it is necessary to commence the story of the difficult and complicated operations of the Division on the road Tamandu–An.

(ii) *Operations by 82 (W.A.) Div. on the Tamandu–An Road*

(See Maps Nos. 48 and 49)

It will be remembered that early in February the Division had been ordered to destroy the Japanese Northern Group in the vicinity of An. The first phase of General Stockwell's plan to carry out his task was the concentration of 1 and 4 Bdes. in firm bases east of the Dalet Chaung and ready to advance on An by 24th February. It was hoped that by this time 2 Bde. from Kangaw would also be available.

On 15th February, 82 Recce R. led the advance from Kaw, followed by 1 Bde. on the 17th, who were under orders to establish a firm base at Kunywa on the road Dalet–An by 22nd February. The route was to be south-east from Nasein to Pt. 1850, thence due east to the Me Chaung, which was to be crossed about two miles above its confluence with the Dalet Chaung. Finally, the Dalet Chaung was to be crossed about two

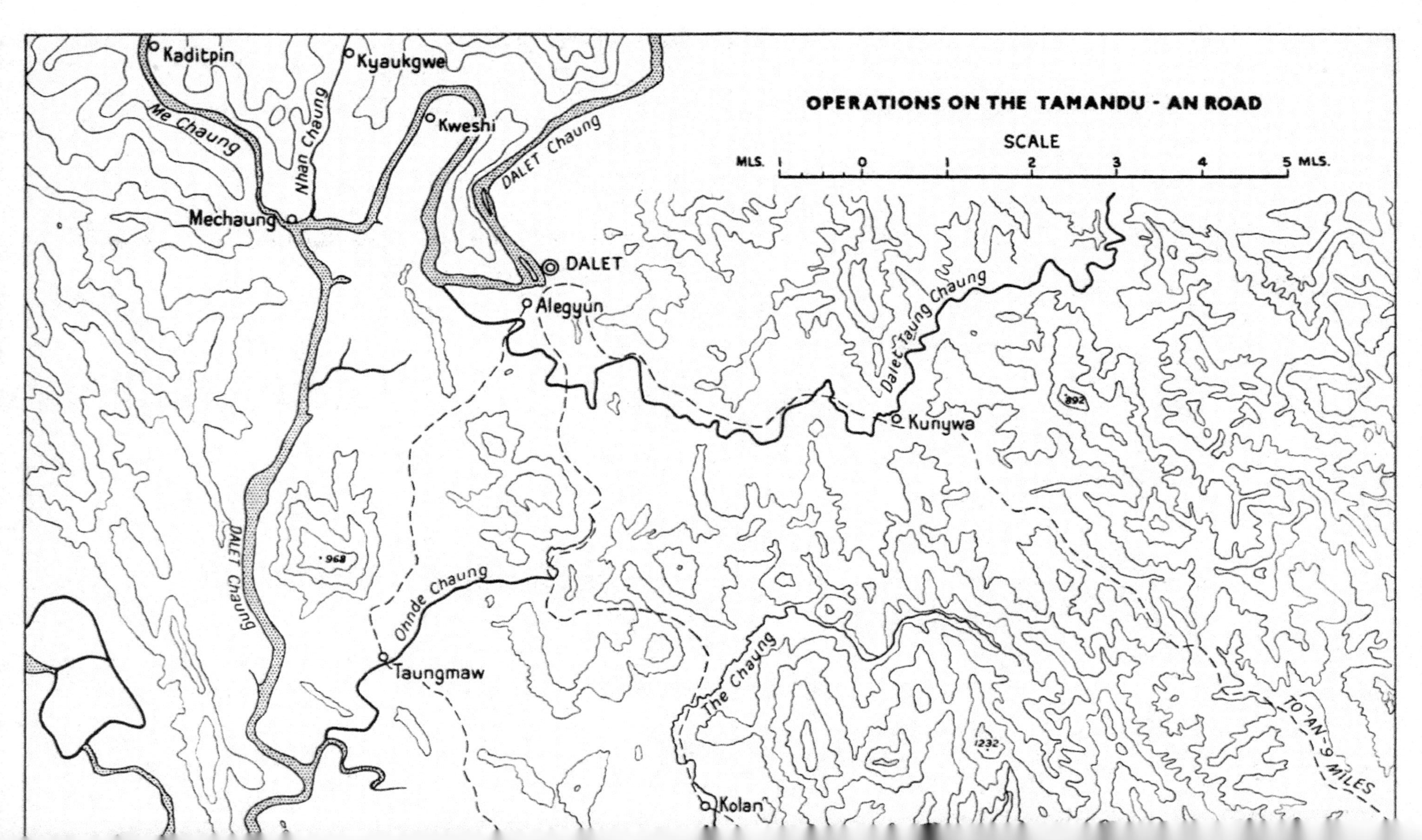
OPERATIONS ON THE TAMANDU - AN ROAD
SCALE
MLS. 1 0 1 2 3 4 5 MLS.
Kaditpin
Kyaukgwe
Me Chaung
Nhan Chaung
Kweshi
DALET Chaung
Mechaung
DALET
Alegyun
Dalet Taung Chaung
Kunywa
892
968
DALET Chaung
Onnde Chaung
Taungmaw
The Chaung
1232
Kolan
TO AN - 9 MILES

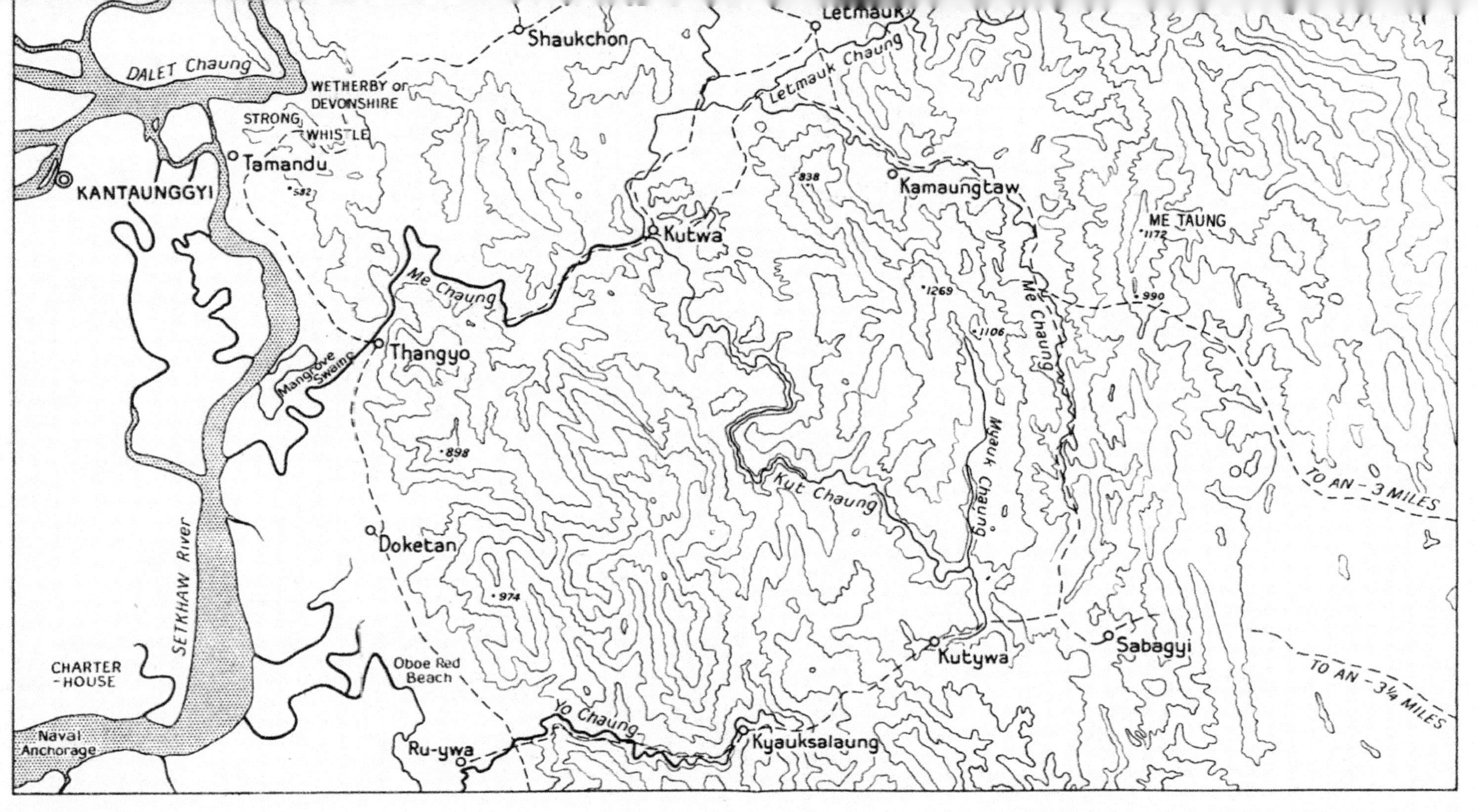

49. Operations on the Tamandu-An Road

miles north of Dalet Village. 4 Bde. followed from Kaw on the 18th with orders to establish a firm base on the road Dalet–Letmauk. The intention was to advance from these bases in conjunction with 2 Bde. coming up from the south, the object being to approach An from three directions.

82 Recce R. found the country south-east of Nasein increasingly difficult as the advance progressed; in fact, game tracks were the only passable routes and the descent from the main ridge entailed the cutting of tracks through dense bamboo. Only slight resistance was met and 1 Bde. crossed the Me Chaung on 18th February after considerable difficulty in finding a track out. 82 Recce R. moving down the west bank of the Me Chaung, whilst 1 Bde. crossed it at Kaditpin, moved over a ridge of hills and concentrated on the 22nd at Kyaukgwe, three miles north-west of Dalet. 4 Bde., less 5 N.R., arrived at Kaditpin on the same day. During the next two days 82 Recce R. was fighting north-west of Mechaung Village, while 1 Bde. drove in an enemy post south of Kyaukgwe and reached the Dalet Chaung opposite Kweshi.

An incident showing the inherent persistence of the Japanese occurred at this time at Kaditpin, while part of 82 Recce R. was there and 1 Bde. was moving into the area. Some 40 or 50 Japanese appeared from the hills to the west and were surprised by the Regiment. They suffered some casualties and retreated leaving no less than 40 packs behind, which proved to be a mine of information to the Intelligence Staff. That night the remnants of the force tried to attack down the same axis, but were driven off after achieving an initial and local success. But they dug in on the high ground during the night and were ejected next day by a company of 1 N.R. Nevertheless, they stayed in the vicinity and proved a nuisance when, a few days later, units of 4 Bde. occupied the same area.

It was intended to cross the Dalet Chaung at Kweshi, but before this could be done some hills west of the loop had to be cleared of enemy parties. 3 N.R. mounted a company attack which gained its objectives, but the country was so dense that it was impossible to keep a determined enemy at a distance. That night the company was unsuccessfully counter-attacked. Meanwhile, 1 N.R. were improving and making a track to the northern tip of the westerly loop of the Dalet Chaung.

The chaung was tidal and the current in both directions very strong. Only a few rubber boats were available and these, with parachute cord strung across the water, had to suffice. Nevertheless, 1 N.R., with some mortars, crossed during the night 24th–25th February just below Kweshi. There was no opposition and the Battalion reached some high ground about a mile to the south. On the following night 3 N.R. crossed by a ford which had been discovered a little farther down the chaung, passed through 1 N.R. and began to advance on Dalet. By the evening of the 26th their patrols had reached Alegyun. However, before Brigade Headquarters and 2 N.R. could cross, Japanese advanced in strength from Mechaung Village up the right bank of the Dalet Chaung, seized the high ground west of Kweshi and blocked the crossing places. 82 Recce R. at the junction of the Me and Dalet Chaungs had reported considerable enemy movement northwards up the Dalet Chaung, presumably from Tamandu. It was now apparent that quite a substantial body of Japanese had succeeded in infiltrating into positions from which they could cover the ford.

2 N.R. were ordered to drive the enemy away from the area of the ford, but, after initial progress, failed to clear it. A company of 1 N.R., left in Kweshi, however, threw out a screen of snipers to cover the ford. Bitter fighting continued during the night 26th–27th February, and next day, but 2 N.R. could make no progress. The Battalion was by then exhausted and had suffered heavy casualties. It was now decided to mount a deliberate attack by 4 Bde. and, as a preliminary, 10 N.R. took over from 2 N.R. the hill feature originally captured by 3 N.R. and 2 N.R. held the approaches thereto from the west.

The attack was to be made by 9 N.R. supported by the mountain artillery and an air strike. The time chosen was 1100 hours, 1st March, as it was proposed to use a proportion of inflammable oil bombs and it was hoped by that hour the dew would have evaporated. The bombs burst with enormous flames and threw up columns of dense black smoke, but the jungle did not catch fire. 9 N.R. followed up the air strike, but they, too, failed to dislodge the enemy. In the afternoon, also, 500 3·7 in. howitzer shells were fired at the tip of the hill where the Japanese had another position and an attack was put in by 10 N.R. But the approach lay along the top of the usual razor-backed spur and the attack was unsuccessful. Meanwhile, 3 N.R. had crossed the Dalet Chaung, using two or three three-man canoes, and had occupied Alegyun after a short skirmish. In the evening the Japanese counter-attacked, but were driven back. Next morning 3 N.R. occupied Dalet and detached one company to a high feature, known as 'Big Contour', to the south of what afterwards became the airstrip.

Unfortunately, the time had now arrived when the Division's operations would be affected by the reduction in air supply. The encirclement of An was no longer possible, as, in future, the Division would have to be supplied from a field maintenance area to be established at Tamandu. though to allow for readjustment an air lift would be available until 7th March. In the meantime, XV Corps had decided to concentrate the Division on the Tamandu–An road and to make a frontal attack on the enemy positions about An. General Stockwell, therefore issued the following orders on 1st March:

2 Bde. from Ru-Ywa, to form a firm base on the road Letmauk–An at the track junction four miles south-east of Letmauk.

1 Bde. to move on Letmauk and strike the road Tamandu–An and to open the road between Letmauk and the firm base of 2 Bde. by 7th March. During this period the Brigade would be supplied by air.

4 Bde. to break off the engagement on the right bank of Dalet Chaung, march to Tamandu and clear the Tamandu–Letmauk road for the maintenance of the Division. 30 Mtn. R. and 82 Recce R. placed under command.

Divisional Headquarters to move with 4 Bde.

It was decided on the afternoon of 1st March that the balance of 1 Bde. should attempt to cross the Dalet Chaung that night. Further, that 4 Bde.

should leave a detachment to contain the enemy near the ford until the main portions of both brigades were clear. As soon as darkness fell, 1 Bde. started to move and the crossing continued all that night and part of next day without any enemy interference. By 3rd March the Brigade was concentrated in a defended area around Dalet village with one company of 3 N.R. on Big Contour. An airstrip was put in hand and preparations made for the move on Letmauk.

The next obstacle was the Dalet Taung Chaung, which was fordable on the track one mile south of Dalet. The enemy not only opposed the crossing of the ford, but also retained firm possession of the block of hills immediately east of the track between Dalet and the ford. On 4th March an attack on these positions by 3 N.R., supported only by the mortar battery, failed after lasting all day. As it was evident that no more progress would be possible in this particular area without heavy casualties, an attempt was made farther west and a crossing was effected. On the morning of the 5th a company of 1 N.R. passed through the bridgehead and occupied a large feature some 1,000 yards south of the chaung. But the enemy reacted quickly and, after repeated attacks during the day, which were repulsed, succeeded in penetrating the company's area as darkness fell. The company with all its British officers and N.C.O.s wounded withdrew to the area of the bridgehead. A detached platoon, however, maintained its position all through that day and part of the next. When running short of ammunition, and finding by means of a patrol that the company had gone, they were skilfully withdrawn and rejoined the Battalion on the afternoon of 7th March.[1]

The Divisional Commander now decided to postpone the advance of 1 Bde. until a new plan could be devised. The Brigade had suffered a considerable number of casualties, though claiming to have killed at least 80 Japanese. However, the Brigade was restricted to patrol activities for two or three days. It is now necessary to describe the operations of the other brigades.

It had originally been intended that 2 Bde. would move direct on An by a narrow jungle track from Ru-Ywa but this route turned out to be impassable. The Brigade, now with the objective on the Letmauk-An road referred to above, moved down the head-waters of the Me Chaung. The enemy, fully aware of the threat to their lines of retreat from Tamandu, sent two companies and some artillery to slow down the advance. Nevertheless, the Brigade advanced with determination in spite of continual harassment and infiltration, and by various means kept the enemy guessing. 22 A./Tk. R. held the lines of communication open for as long as possible and ultimately moved to Letmauk.

On 6th March two companies of 1 G.C.R. and two of 2 G.C.R. blocked the road Tamandu-An at a junction some nine miles west of An. There was hand-to-hand fighting round the block, but the engineers managed to mine the road, on which a Japanese light tank was destroyed. Three 105 mm. guns were rushed and spiked by two platoons of 3 G.C.R. But the road block, which was in the valley and under attack from both east and west, could not be maintained, so the withdrawal of the enemy from

[1] The Platoon Commander, Sergeant Hedley, was awarded the D.C.M.

Tamandu and elsewhere was not permanently arrested. By 9th March the forward troops on the road had disengaged with considerable skill after fierce hand-to-hand fighting. In all 60 Japanese were known to have been killed. The Brigade then concentrated west of the road in the hills surrounding Pts. 1106 and 1269.

After the cessation of hostilities the Japanese admitted that the road block set up by 2 Bde. south-east of Letmauk had caused them considerable anxiety. A counter-attack was ordered by 54 Div. to be carried out by two battalions of 111 R., supported by all available artillery and a company of tanks. They stated that about 30 vehicles were using the road at the time of the block and that the harassing fire of our artillery and snipers had been very effective. It was also learnt at the same time that Headquarters 54 Div. were at Kolan until 11th March.

Thus, on 9th March, 1 Bde. was still at Dalet and 2 Bde. was some three and a half miles south of Letmauk. 4 Bde. was still fighting round Tamandu, the future supply base of the Division, whose flexibility had decreased owing to the stoppage of air supply. It is now necessary to revert to the operations of the latter Brigade until they rejoined the Division at Letmauk.

As already mentioned, 4 Bde. had commenced to withdraw from the Dalet area during the night 1st–2nd March. The Brigade was concentrated just south of Kaditpin on 4th March. In the meantime, patrols of 82 Recce R. had been sent to discover the best route across the hills west of the Dalet Chaung. The track selected had to be cut and graded in places to allow of the passage of 30 Mtn. R. with their mules. The move in three groups at intervals of 24 hours began on 5th March, and by the 7th Headquarters and 9 N.R. had reached Tamandu, after crossing the Dalet Chaung. Next day 5 N.R. reverted to command of 4 Bde.

Tamandu village had been occupied a few days earlier by 74 (Indian) Bde., who had landed at Ru–Ywa, but fighting had been going on for some days to the north, where the enemy held a series of hill features astride the road to An. On 3rd March 74 Bde. held Pt. 582 on the right of the road and a feature known as 'Pig' on the left of it. 3/2 Gurkhas, who had taken Pt. 582, were heavily counter-attacked and fought all through 4th March to regain the half of the feature which had been lost. After a hard fight, in which they suffered heavy casualties, the whole feature was regained. The plan for 5th March was for 7/16 Punjabis to attack from Pt. 582 and capture 'Whistle' and thence across the road to take 'Strong'. The role of 5 N.R. was to pass through on the capture of these hills and take 'Dog', a feature overlooking the road about a mile farther on.

Whistle was captured early on 5th March, but Strong held out; another battalion was brought up to continue the attack and 5 N.R. moved out to undertake an outflanking movement on Dog. After clearing some features, part of Dog was captured, but attempts to push on northward were held up on a steep, razor-backed ridge. After beating off a counter-attack, some progress was made during the 6th and 7th. But a further attack on the northern end of Dog, supported by the light battery, timed for 8th March did not go in, as orders had been received from 4 Bde. to stand fast.

On 8th March, 9 N.R. assembled behind 74 Bde., prepared to pass through on the capture of Strong, which was still being attacked. As the position was not captured the Battalion had to follow the tortuous route taken by 5 N.R. along the ridge right-handed. In addition, 10 N.R. were to make an assault landing up the Dalet Chaung to link up with 5 N.R. via the left flank. Considering the unit had had no training in amphibious operations this was asking a good deal of the Royal Navy and the African troops.

4 Bde. was now committed to a right and left hook, the former which only African troops and their carriers could attempt. To add to their difficulties there was a great shortage of water. But the relief of 2 Bde. was now becoming so urgent that the risks involved in a complicated and hazardous operation had to be accepted. The following written by officers who took part gives some idea of the difficulties faced and overcome: 'Changing climatic conditions were now affecting our tactics. The useful and comforting early morning mists of the winter no longer existed to cover awkward attacks or the risky passage of chaungs, defiles or open ground. . . . 5 N.R. could only be maintained by exertions which only troops of the R.W.A.F.F. are capable of; their food and water was passed from hand to hand, or rather head to head, and initially took 36 hours to reach the forward troops. Casualties, trying to come back by the same route, in some cases took just as long. Many parties of carriers and runners were left marooned here and there during the night. 9 N.R. now struck off along this same via Dolorosa. The early part of the line of communication was through the forward defended localities of 74 Bde., and their carrying parties and ours frequently clashed at the steepest places with both parties unable to move up or down.'

10 N.R. were ferried up the Dalet Chaung after dark on 8th March, passing within 50 yards of the Japanese positions on Strong. The actual landing, which took place on a mangrove swamp slightly away from the place intended, was unopposed. As usual the Royal Navy was 'magnificent'. That night 10 N.R. failed to reach their objective, a hill known as 'Cat' and towering above the chaung. Next day two unsuccessful attempts were made to take the feature. On the right flank, 9 N.R. were following 5 N.R. round the Strong position and whilst on the move both battalions were shelled by observed fire. On this day, too, Japanese artillery caused the suspension of movement on the chaung until nightfall, when the crossing of ancillary units, supplies and water was resumed.

The enemy on Strong continued to hold further attacks by 74 Bde. throughout 10th March and a plan for a deliberate attack with the maximum air support was planned to take place next day. The Japanese still clung on to their positions on Cat and Dog, but 9 N.R. managed to establish a block astride the An road on the exit from the bowl behind Strong. The jaws of the pincers had nearly closed; realizing this, the enemy vacated Strong during the night 10th–11th March through a very narrow gap. Early next morning fighting patrols from 9 and 10 N.R. reported that final resistance on Cat and Dog had ceased. On the 12th 9 N.R. moved off along the An road towards Shaukchon and Letmauk.

The Brigade had suffered a considerable number of African casualties at Kayaukpandu, Dalet and Tamandu. Two Commanding Officers had been killed on 1st March and a large proportion of British officers and N.C.O.s had become casualties.[1] On the other hand, since the landing at Ru-Ywa and up to the end of the battle for Tamandu, 243 dead Japanese had been counted. On this basis it was estimated that their total casualties had amounted to over 600.

4 Bde. with one troop 19 L. (Sherman tanks), 8 Fd. R., 102 Lt. R., and a troop of 5·5 in. medium guns, leaving 74 (Indian) Bde. to guard temporarily the influx of supplies and transport at Tamandu, advanced on Letmauk. On 13th March, whilst the Brigade was marching along the road, 9 N.R., moving rapidly out of the hills on to the road, quickly located enemy positions; the remainder of the Brigade concentrated about a mile from Shaukchon. During the afternoon 9 N.R., with the troop of 19 L. in support, attacked two thickly wooded features, known as 'Lion' and 'Tiger' which lay astride the road. The attack was successful and the features were both cleared by the following morning. 10 N.R. now took the lead and overcame a number of cleverely sited ambushes. On 15th March, 5 N.R. came forward and passed through 10 N.R. then driving the enemy back they eventually gained some high ground above Kolan. Exploiting this success at first light next morning they paved the way for 9 N.R. to take Kolan after encountering small parties of the enemy who quickly retired. 9 N.R. pressing forward to Letmauk were halted by the enemy just short of the village but, supported by the tanks, drove them off a small feature to the left of the road.

On 17th March 10 N.R. entered Letmauk and seized the bluff on the farther side of the Letmauk Chaung which dominated the plain around the village. The direct route to the chaung was through lentana scrub on the left of the road. The chaung itself and many gaps in the bush were overlooked from the bluff. The enemy had small parties on the fringe of the lentana and movement in the gaps drew fire from the bluff. The leading company had a very 'sticky' time beating through the bush, despite covering fire from the tanks. Late in the afternoon Captain Tolmie's company was sent round to make a left hook on the bluff in the hope that an assault at twilight would surprise the enemy. Nothing was seen or heard of this company while the original leading company kept creeping forward to the edge of the chaung. Suddenly in the gathering darkness they heard distant cheers and a few scattered shots. In the last rays of the setting sun the company had rushed the bluff from the flank and surprised the Japanese many of whom were shot in flight. The enemy made no counter-attack and the risks taken were justified by a quick success.

During the previous day a company of 9 N.R. and another of 10 N.R. had been sent round on a right hook to cut the road on the An side of the Letmauk plain. This was the first time the country had allowed of a rapid and easy hook. The operation was entirely successful, the road was cut in several places; and the Japanese pulled out during the night leaving a 47 mm. anti-tank gun and some dead.

Operations to make contact with 2 Bde. continued although the troops

[1] Lieutenant-Colonel L. J. Oliver, 5 N.R. and Lieutenant-Colonel C. A. Wade, 10 N.R.

were very tired and enemy opposition hardened. Every yard of ground was now contested by gun, mortar and machine-gun fire. 5 and 9 N.R. followed up the axis of the two companies who had blocked the road. But where the road crosses the Letmauk Chaung it becomes hemmed in by high bamboo-covered hills and on either side the enemy was found holding all the key positions. The road then ran through a gorge closely flanked by the Me Chaung with steep winding banks and thick undergrowth in the sides of which the enemy was strongly established. Attempts to make progress were made daily in one of which 9 N.R. lost their Second-in-Command, Adjutant and Signal Officer from one burst of machine-gun fire. The last attack in this area by 5 N.R. was led by Captain Ross Tod and Sergeant Kent—the only remaining Europeans in the company. The former was severely wounded in this action.

It must have been a sad blow to 4 Bde. when it became apparent that, although 2 Bde. was only two miles away, they were unable to break through. However 1 Bde. had arrived and on 20th March were ordered to link up with 2 Bde. During this operation 4 Bde. continued to 'hold the ring', making small gains and inflicting casualties.

In the meantime, 1 Bde. at Dalet had not been idle; efforts were still being made to find a way across the Dalet Taung Chaung, but the Japanese had gained a foothold on Big Contour. However, on 9th March, a patrol from 2 N.R., composed entirely of swimmers, moved through Alegyun and discovered a rough track which led from near the junction of the chaungs over the hills into the paddy, where air photographs revealed that the approach to Shaukchon was relatively easy. In spite of a failure to clear Big Contour it was decided to use this route. A track, screened from observation by the enemy on Big Contour, was cut to the crossing place whilst normal movement and activities were carried out until after dark on 10th March.

The breakout began at 0430 hours on 11th March, when 2 N.R., accompanied by 1 (W.A.) Fd. Coy. carrying a floating bridge, which had been made at Dalet, set off to secure a bridgehead. Two companies of 1 N.R. held a position at Alegyun and except for 3 N.R. on Big Contour these were the last to withdraw. The breakout was accomplished without any interference from the enemy, and by nightfall the Brigade was located in a ravine between the Dalet Taung Chaung and the paddy. The Japanese afterwards admitted that they had not observed this move, but asserted that their own troops were at that time preparing to withdraw to Kunywa.

On 12th March the move began to the wide belt of paddy running south to the Ohnde Chaung. No enemy were seen. Next day 1 N.R. took the lead and came up against opposition in a small pass. This was cleared on the 14th; 2 N.R. exploited towards Taungmaw, and it was decided to advance on Shaukchon through this place. 1 N.R., however, moved by a route farther east and reached Shaukchon on 16th March; the rest of the Brigade arrived next day and the whole formation was concentrated at Letmauk by the 20th.

In the meantime, the Japanese between 2 Bde. and Letmauk had been reinforced. The Brigade was still in possession of its firm base, hampered by many casualties who could not be evacuated, and faced by a shortage of supplies, especially forage for the transport animals. The situation was not eased by a lucky hit on Brigade Headquarters by a mortar shell which wounded the Commander, Brigadier E. W. D. Western, and his brigade major and killed the G.S.O.3. However, the Gold Coast Battalions not only repulsed all attacks on their positions but continued to take such offensive action as was possible.

On arrival at Letmauk, 1 Bde. was ordered to break the block and relieve 2 Bde. The first efforts were directed to capturing the commanding hills to the east; so little progress was made, however, that by the 22nd it was clear that advance on this axis offered no prospect of an early junction. Brigadier Swynnerton then switched operations to the south of the road, and 22 A./Tk. R. was placed under his command.

1 N.R. captured Pt. 838 on 23rd March, but attempts to continue down the ridge to Pt. 1269 met with strenuous opposition. The ridge was of the usual variety—about 12 ft. wide at the top, which was fairly clear, but the sides were covered by a very thick growth of bamboo. By the skilful use of mortar smoke bombs, which set fire to the dry bamboo leaves, the enemy positions were burnt out one by one. In the meantime, 3 N.R. had moved north-east from Pt. 838 and occupied a prominent hill known as 'Camel'. From there a company was pushed forward into a depression where, in very thick country, a good deal of fighting of a hide-and-seek nature took place. 1 N.R., now reinforced by a company of 2 N.R. and 22 A./Tk. R., continued to press along the ridge to Pt. 1269, cutting, grading and picquetting a path wide enough for the mules of 2 Bde. to pass along. The break through to Pt. 1269 was made late on 24th March and next day 2 Bde. began to withdraw. By the evening of 26th March the Brigade had concentrated in an area around the airstrip south of Letmauk, and two days later, having evacuated the casualties, left Letmauk to rest and refit at Tamandu.

A party of Japanese coming in from the north staged a demonstration on the night of 26th–27th March with automatics, tracer, light mortars and grenades on the part of the perimeter held by 2 Aux. Gp. There was no penetration, but the firing was so heavy that parts of all three brigades joined in. It should be remembered, however, that this took place at a time when a night attack was expected. It appears that a Japanese runner, who had been killed a day or two previously, was found to be carrying an operation order for the assembly of a mixed force which was to 'destroy the enemy in the Letmauk area at one stroke'. This operation was to be completed by the 26th. However, beyond some patrol clashes with 5 N.R., there was no enemy activity on the 27th.

During these operations 4 Bde. had been engaged with the enemy east and north of Letmauk. But now, however, the enemy were beginning to thin out north and north-east of the place and by the end of March withdrawal towards An was evident. At this time 82 (W.A.) Div. was ordered to move south along the coast to the area Tanlwe–Taungup,[1] leaving one brigade to harass and contain as many Japanese as possible. 22 (E.A.)

[1] 4 (Indian) Bde. of 26 (Indian) Div. had landed at Letpan, 35 miles north of Taungup, on 13th March.

[Photo: Imperial War Museum

The Taungup–Prome Road

Bde., who had landed at Ru-Ywa, would come under command of the Division. On 1st April, General Stockwell issued orders as follows:

1 Bde., with 82 Recce R., 1 Lt. Bty., 105 and 106 Mortar Btys. and 22 A./Tk. R. under command, to exploit forward from Letmauk to occupy An and contain the enemy on the high ground east of the An Chaung. After 4th April the Brigade would be responsible for their own maintenance from Tamandu.

2 Bde. from Tamandu and *22 (E.A.) Bde* from Ru-Ywa, to move south by road.

4 Bde. to begin withdrawal from Letmauk to Shaukchon prior to embarking as soon as the area northward to Kunywa was reported clear.

In the event, as the Kunywa area had been reported clear, 4 Bde. moved back to Shaukchon–Tamandu between 1st and 4th April. 10 N.R. was left temporarily under command of 1 Bde. owing to shortage of shipping.

Leaving 10 N.R. to hold the airstrip and 82 Recce R. and 22 A./Tk. R. to patrol in all directions, 1 Bde. left Letmauk on 1st April to carry out their task. Moving south-east, they soon came into contact with enemy holding the road and the Me Taung east of it. On 5th April 3 N.R. captured and held Pt. 990. During the next two days the hills on the right and left of the road were cleared, but elsewhere little progress was made owing to stubborn resistance and thick bamboo.[1]

Soon enemy patrols appeared again on the Me Taung ridge and reports were received of large numbers of Japanese on the parallel track from An to Kunywa. The Brigade was ordered to withdraw to Letmauk and concentrated there on 10th April. The first sign of enemy reaction was on 11th April, when a large party of Japanese appeared on the road from the east. Marching in threes, apparently quite unaware that Letmauk was still held, they were ambushed by 2 N.R. and disappeared after suffering heavy casualties. But about the same time a number of enemy attacks, mostly from the north, began to develop. The latter were thought to be made by a force from Kunywa with the object of cutting off the Brigade's communications with Tamandu. All these attacks were repulsed with heavy loss, but, in the meantime, the enemy had blocked the road south-west of Shaukchon and occupied the high ground on either side. 10 N.R. were sent off to Shaukchon at once.

The situation at Tamandu on 12th April was that 4 Bde., less 10 N.R. and 2 Aux. Gp. had already embarked. 2 Bde. was already well on the way towards Taungup by road. An enemy detachment, working their way round from the west, had blocked the road about 'Lion' and 'Tiger'. The first intimation that the road was blocked was when a lorry convoy was ambushed. Next day the Officer Commanding 7 Aux. Gp. was flown in to take command. He immediately raised a force, afterwards known as the 'Canteen Commandos', from 2 and 7 Aux. Gps., various R.A.S.C. N.C.O.s and volunteers from various detachments, including 4 (W.A.) Fd. Coy. Aided by an air strike, this scratch force so successfully occupied

[1] In this area a patrol of 22 A/Tk. R. took eight hours to cover 500 yards without any opposition.

the enemy that 10 N.R., coming from the north by a track through the bush, arrived in time to embark early on 14th April.

Letmauk was considered untenable and the large supply dumps at Wetherby, now seriously threatened, had no infantry for their protection and on 12th April XV Corps ordered the withdrawal of the Brigade. During the night 12th–13th April, after 82 Recce R. and a company of 3 N.R. had foiled an enemy attempt to block the road to the west, the main body disengaged and reached Shaukchon next day. The Japanese, however, were still holding positions south-west of the village. These were cleared by 1 N.R. and the Recce R. on the 14th, then, having picquetted the road on either side and covered by 3 N.R., the Brigade moved down to Tamandu and Wetherby which were reached on the 15th. The enemy did not follow up: he was already many days overdue in crossing the Yomas to Minbu.

The next few days were spent in putting the place into a state of defence. All ranks were badly in need of a rest, especially the overworked British element, who had been much reduced by casualties.[1] During this period the following message was received from XV Corps:

> 'Well done 1st Brigade but essential you continue maintain patrol contact with enemy.'

Details for the establishment of patrol bases forward were already being worked out and they were soon in being. Some long-distance patrols were carried out to the vicinity of Letmauk and An, but, acting on instructions, no attempt at any extended operation was made. However, on 13th May, the Brigade Commander, with the headquarters platoon and another from 1 N.R., entered An. This was the end of the campaign for 1 Bde., and a few days later all the units had left for Kindaunggyi.

It has since been ascertained that the Headquarters of the Japanese 54 Div. did not leave An until 24th April and that the troops in the vicinity consisted of 111 R., 154 R., and 54 Recce R., with artillery and probably some army and lines of communications troops. At the same time 121 R., less one battalion, was at Taungup. Three or four battalions, including 54 Recce R. were used in the attack on Letmauk and Shaukchon on 12th April. It appears that the operations of 82 (W.A.) Div., and the later advance south-east from Letmauk by 1 Bde., had not only forced the Japanese to keep troops west of the Yomas, but in April had also compelled them to move some units about 20 miles to the west to remove the threat to their own withdrawal.[2]

After the cessation of hostilities the Commander of 54 Div. was asked why he had held the extreme western ends of the An and Taungup passes for so long instead of contesting the more favourable defensible ground actually within the Yomas. His reply was: '54 Div's role was to annihilate the British forces on the waterline and not let them into the hinterland at all.'[3] In this connection General Stockwell afterwards stressed the following points.

[1] Since 14th December 1944, 1 Bde. had lost from battle casualties alone 39 officers and 25 B.N.C.O.s and had received practically no replacements. 4 Bde. had suffered in the same way and at the end of March 9 N.R. had been organized on a three-company basis owing to shortage of Europeans.

[2] See also Appendix X (3).

[3] 82 (W.A.) Div. Intelligence Report No. 16 of 10th April 1946.

'In this campaign the Japanese Commander almost invariably disposed his forces with the object of defeating the British landings on the water-line. In his own words he "kept close to the coast". This tendency was common to most Japanese coastal defence practice. While it fulfilled the principle of offensive action, it partially sacrificed those of mobility and security. As a consequence the overland hooks of 82 (W.A.) Div. went far to disorganize his defence on at least three occasions.

'The first occasion was at Myohaung, when the possibility of a coastal attack in the rear had been foreseen by the construction of strong defences at Kangaw. The landward flank had, however, been left open by the failure to hold the Kanzauk Pass.

'The second occasion was the arrival of 1 and 4 Bdes. at Dalet. At this time the main Japanese force was stubbornly resisting the landings both at Myebon and Kangaw, and so little provision had been made for flank protection that the Dalet thrust was met, not by a mobile reserve, but by pulling out 154 R. from the Kangaw battle.

'The third occasion was the establishment of 2 Bde.'s road block on the An road. At this time the Japanese Commander had once again disposed the bulk of his striking force at strategic points on the coast from Dalet to the mouth of the An Chaung, a total of some 70 miles, and against a superior force. One would have considered that under such circumstances it would have been imperative to hold a reserve in the area of An. However, there does not appear to have been any such reserve, and the force which was used to attack 2 Bde. was 111 R., which was withdrawn from its position on the coast.'[1]

It remains to describe the final operations of the Division and to make a few general comments.

(iii) *The Last Phase: 82 (W.A.) Div. clears South Arakan*

(See Map No. 50)

As previously mentioned, 26 (Indian) Div. had landed a brigade at Letpan on 13th March to form a bridgehead from which to attack the Southern Group of the Japanese 54 Div. holding the Taungup Pass on the road to Prome. Considerable resistance had been met but, by the end of the month, 82 (W.A.) Div., with 22 (E.A.) Bde. under command, was moving south from Tamandu and Ru-Ywa. On 5th April Divisional Headquarters opened at Kindaunggyi taking over all troops of 26 (Indian) Div. until their relief by a West African Brigade. General Stockwell's object was to destroy or contain the enemy about the Taungup area and to clear the coastal belt of Southern Arakan. This he proposed to do by seizing the general line of the Prome road at Yebawgyi and then to exploit towards Prome, Sandoway and Gwa.

On 3rd April 2 Green Howards of 4 (Indian) Bde. captured Hill 370, three miles north of Taungup, and on the following day 22 (E.A.) Bde. began to move east along the Tanlwe Chaung. The enemy, however, launched a counter-attack on Hill 370 which was successful, but later in

[1] Ibid.

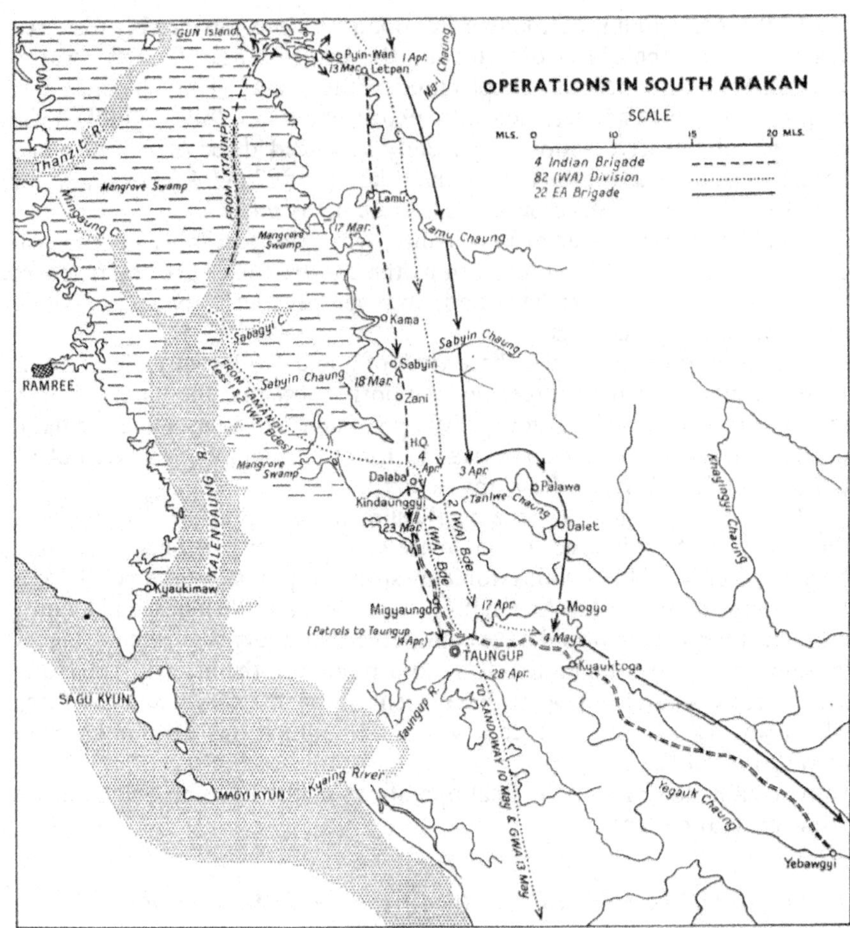

50. Operations in South Arakan

the day—5th April—two counter-attacks were put in, the second of which regained the feature.

The relief of 4 (Indian) Bde. commenced on 11th April and 22 (E.A.) Bde. had now reached the Tanlwe Chaung nine miles north of Taungup. On the same day the leading units of 2 Bde. reached the Chaung after dislodging tenacious parties of enemy. 22 (E.A.) Bde. captured Dalet, some nine miles north-east of Taungup, and a week later were in touch with the enemy one and a half miles north of Mogyo.

By 20th April 4 Bde. had concentrated at Kindaunggyi and units on arrival were detailed to protect the field maintenance area. Active patrolling took place and numerous stragglers were hunted down.

At this time there was a spirited little action by a patrol of four Africans commanded by Corporal Musa Doki Augungu, 9 N.R. Returning from a routine patrol in which he had found no enemy on his objective, he suddenly bumped into a Japanese patrol of the same strength but commanded by an officer. He at once shot the officer and two other ranks with his rifle, and then charged the other two, setting them on fire with 77 grenades. He returned with the officer's sword and a marked map which proved of considerable value.[1]

The two West African Brigades were now detailed to take Taungup. The town lies on the south bank of a chaung with the same name on a plain of paddy land completely dominated on the east by a large, jungle-covered hill around which passes the road to Prome. The Divisional Commander's intention was to by-pass this hill—still held by the Japanese —by moving 4 Bde. to the south of it whilst 2 Bde. attacked it from the north.

During the night 26th–27th April, 4 Bde., less 9 N.R. covering Divisional Headquarters at Kindaunggyi but with 2 Green Howards attached, crossed the Taungup Chaung against slight opposition while 2 Bde. cleared the enemy from their bunker positions on the dominating hill. On the 29th, Taungup was occupied by 4 Bde., who joined hands with 2 Bde. on the hill referred to above. Next day patrols cleared the main road for seven miles east of Taungup.

2 Bde. now joined 22 (E.A.) Bde. in moving along the road to Prome. After a joint attack on a road block at Milestone 99, 11 miles from Taungup, 22 (E.A.) Bde. took up the advance alone and entered Yebawgyi on 15th May. Next day Milestone 60 from Prome was reached without further contact with the enemy. Vast stores of ammunition, supplies and equipment were found abandoned on either side of the road.

Meanwhile, 4 Bde. had pushed on southwards along the coastal road and had occupied Sandoway on 10th May. Gwa was reached by a motor patrol three days later. The Arakan was now clear of formed bodies of Japanese and most of those who escaped were either destroyed by Fourteenth Army or perished from starvation and disease in the Pegu Yomas. A few belated stragglers, mostly from Ramree Island, were found and dealt with during the next two or three months.

By the end of May the Division had settled in monsoon quarters as follows: Divisional Headquarters and 1 Bde. in the Kindaunggyi area, 2 Bde. at Taungup and 4 Bde. at Sandoway.

Between 14th December 1944 and the end of operations in May 1945 the Division had marched a long way: 1 Bde. 285 miles, 2 Bde. 274 miles and 4 Bde. 428 miles. No unit marched less than 190 miles out of the total distance covered by its formation. Casualties in the Division had been the heaviest in XV Corps. The casualties in both West African Divisions are given in Appendix XI, which also shows the total casualties in XV Corps as well as those of the enemy.

A notable feature of both campaigns was the ease with which units and formations disengaged, and even disappeared so far as the Japanese were concerned, by making use of the cover provided by the jungle and a few minor deceptions. Outstanding examples are 81 Div.'s withdrawal to the Kalapanzin Valley from Kaladan in 1944 and their advance to Thandada in 1945, 1 Bde.'s withdrawal from Dalet in March 1945 and from Letmauk in the following month.

[1] Corporal Musa Doki was awarded the M.M. The sword was afterwards presented to the Sarikin Augungu.

The term 'jungle warfare' is, today, a common expression, but the fact that there are varieties of jungle was and is often overlooked. For instance, the orchard bush is very different to the tropical forest of Ashanti, which again differs very much from the hill jungle of the Arakan. The African soldier brought up in the orchard bush of Northern Nigeria or the northern provinces of the other territories has to become accustomed to the African tropical forest or Burmese hill jungle. But he is used to moving in 'bush', is not frightened of it and, in fact, regards it as a friend. Moreover, the African soldier's instinct for approaching danger and powers of hearing and observation are very great assets in close country. Nevertheless, some difficulties arose with illiterate troops in patrolling and in action when they could not see their objective. They were at their best when they could see both the objective they were attacking and their leaders, as was shown in some instances in East Africa and Burma. In the latter country, it must be remembered, they were fighting against a fanatically brave and resourceful enemy, though they were quick to spot his weak points and benefit by them.

A Japanese view of the African soldier is given in an unexpected and and unsolicited testimonial found in a captured diary which is worth recording though it ends with a blatant understatement. It reads as follows:

> 'The enemy soldiers are not from Britain but from Africa. Because of their belief they are not afraid to die, so even if their comrades have fallen they keep on advancing as if nothing had happened. They have an excellent physique and are very brave, so fighting against these soldiers is somewhat troublesome.'

In Burma the R.W.A.F.F. had faced the greatest test in their half-century of existence, where their qualities of gallantry, loyalty and cheerful endurance had been tried as never before. They emerged from this test with great credit and enhanced traditions. That they were able to undertake operations of a kind no other formation could attempt was due not only to the qualities of the troops in general but to the magnificent work of the Auxiliary Groups who carried their head loads for long distances in most appalling country.

A few remarks on the subject of carriers, additional to those in Chapter 10, Section (viii), will not be out of place. It must be remembered that many of them were recruited from primitive tribes and required handling with perception and patience. This is illustrated by an anecdote given in Appendix XIV.

The carriage of loads on the head was in accordance with West African tradition and skill. The use of carriers by West African formations in the hill jungles of Burma made them far more mobile than those relying on mules or other transport and, when supplied by air, remarkably flexible. The disadvantages, well known from the experience of previous wars in Africa, were the large numbers required, the consequent length of columns and their vulnerability on the march; finally, normal movement in single file along a jungle track made concentration at the end of a move somewhat lengthy. In the first campaign the carriers of 81 Div. were unarmed, though in the later stages many of them acquired weapons, Japanese or otherwise. In the second campaign a proportion were officially armed and sometimes took part in the defence of perimeters.

In this connection, too, tribute must be paid to the units of the African Colonial Forces, the reconnaissance regiments, gunners, sappers, signals and the ancillary units who fought with or otherwise supported the R.W.A.F.F. Battalions of the two West African Divisions. The A.C.F. ceased to exist after the war and the gunners reverted to the R.W.A.F.F. However, in order that the units of the A.C.F. who took part in the operations in Burma shall not be forgotten, the order of battle of the two Divisions, as organized in 1943–5, is set out in Appendix XII.

Referring to his period in command of 82 (W.A.) Div., General Sir Hugh Stockwell writes: 'To me it was an experience never to be forgotten. The staunch determination of the African soldier in face of not only a fanatical and determined enemy, but also terrain in which no self-respecting soldier would ever seek battle, carried us through. Added to which the careful and thoughtful leadership of the Brigadiers, Commanding Officers and, indeed, of all officers and B.N.C.O.s, eventually bore us into the calm waters of Sandoway, Gwa, Prome and Rangoon.

'They fought splendidly and stood up to much privation and hardship. They never turned their heads at any task I asked of them—cheerful—resolute—and truly men, their shining bodies and enduring friendship remain with me always.

'They certainly played a most valuable part in the Burma Campaign and History will, I am sure, show how these difficult days have led to a close and understanding relationship between this Country and West Africa.

'I am so glad it is all being recorded and it will serve as a valuable reminder of the confidence of Europeans and Africans in each other.'

Early in 1946, while the rest of the Division remained in their monsoon quarters, 1 Bde. marched across the Arakan Yomas to Prome, where they remained for a few weeks policing the area. Meanwhile, two companies of 1 N.R. were sent farther north to the area of Thayetmyo to patrol against the local *dacoits* in conjunction with the Burma Police. Shortly afterwards the Brigade moved to Rangoon to await embarkation.

(iv) *Chronological Table of Events in Burma: November 1944 to September 1945*

Date	*Arakan*	*Central and Northern Fronts*
1944 Nov.	2: 81 (W.A.) Div. starts to move down Kaladan Valley 82 (W.A.) Div. begins to move towards Maungdaw	
Dec.	3: 81 (W.A.) Div. reaches Kaladan 14: Arakan offensive starts 15: Buthidaung taken by 82 (W.A.) Div. 24: 81 (W.A.) Div. reaches Thandada 26: 25 (I.) Div. reaches Foul Point	3: Fourteenth Army begins to cross the Chindwin 10: 36 (B.) Div. captures Indaw 11: 36 (B.) Div. captures Katha

Date	*Arakan*	*Central and Northern Fronts*
1945 Jan.	3: 82 (W.A.) Div. at Htizwe preparing to advance on Kanzauk 3: Akyab occupied by Commandos and 25 (I.) Div. 12: Landing at Myebon 21: Kyaukpyu captured by 26 (I.) Div. 22: Landing near Kangaw 24: 81 and 82 (W.A.) Divs. drive Japanese from Myohaung 27: 82 (W.A.) Div. in pursuit of Japanese 29: 82 (W.A.) Div. reaches Hpontha 30: Japanese escape route to the south blocked near Kangaw	9: 19 (I.) Div. seizes two bridgeheads over Irrawaddy east of Swebo
Feb.	14: 2 (W.A.) Bde. arrives north of Kangaw 15: 82 (W.A.) Div. less 2 Bde. begins to move towards An 16: 25 (I.) Div. lands at Ru-Ywa 18: Kangaw battle ends 24: 1 and 4 Bdes. engaged around Dalet until 1 Mar.	12–13: 20 (I.) Div. crosses Irrawaddy 13–14: 7 (I.) Div. crosses Irrawaddy 21: 19 (I.) Div. passes through 7 Div. bridgehead 26: 19 (I.) Div. begins to advance on Mandalay 26: 2 (B.) Div. moves towards south of Mandalay
Mar.	2: 4 Bde. leaves Dalet for Tamandu 6: 2 (W.A.) Bde. from Ru-Ywa blocks Letmauk–An road and is eventually surrounded 11: 1 Bde. leaves Delat for Letmauk 12: Battle for Tamandu ends. 4 Bde. leaves for Letmauk 13: 26 (I.) Div. lands at Letpan 17: 4 Bde. reaches Letmauk 18: 1 Bde. reaches Letmauk 20: 1 Bde. begins relief of 2 Bde. 26: 2 Bde. relieved by 1 Bde. reaches Letmauk and moves to Tamandu on 28th	4: 17 (I.) Div. takes Meiktila 20: Mandalay surrenders to Fourteenth Army 30: Sino-American forces take no further part in the campaign
Apr.	1: 1 Bde. moves towards An 2: 4 Bde. leaves Letmauk for Tamandu 10: 1 Bde. back at Letmauk 11: Enemy counter-attack on Letmauk defeated 13: 1 Bde. leaves Letmauk for Tamandu 29: Taungup occupied by 4 Bde.	29–30: 17 (I.) Div. takes Pegu
May	10:–13: Sandoway Gwa occupied by 82 (W.A.) Div.	2: 26 (I.) Div. lands south of Rangoon and enters the city on the 4th 2: Prome occupied
Aug.		4: Last Japanese fugitives cross the Salween (6,000 escaped out of 18,000)
Sept.	2: Formal surrender of all Japanese forces in South-East Asia	

CHAPTER 14

The Post-War Years

(i) *Return to Peacetime Soldiering*

THE first to embark for West Africa was naturally 81 (W.A.) Div. from India, but, in April 1946, units of 82 (W.A.) Div. began to take ship at Rangoon. The Division, however, did not complete embarkation until early in September. On the 2nd of that month the following message was sent to King George VI:

> '82 (West African) Division now beginning final phase of embarkation at Rangoon for repatriation and demobilization offer His Majesty their humble duty and affirm their resolution to continue to serve him with all loyalty and devotion as soldiers or civilians whatever may be their individual futures.'

The following reply was received from the Secretary of State:

> 'Your telegram of 2 Sep has been laid before the King. His Majesty has commanded me to thank you for your message of loyalty a loyalty which has already been actively expressed by your service in Burma. He wishes you God Speed on your journey home and hopes that you will further efforts of peace with same resolute courage as you fought the terrors of war.'

The long time awaiting shipping was very trying to the Division, but there was not so much as the breath of an incident in lapse of discipline. During this period, whilst all leaders did their duty, Regimental Sergeant-Major Chair Maigumeri was a tower of strength, as was also the senior Mallam. Both of them were of the greatest help in keeping the troops in good spirits.

With the same object in view, some units, notably those of 1 (W.A.) Bde., reconstituted a corps of drums on the nucleus of the survivors of their original corps. They had brought their instruments and full dress for the men from West Africa and stored them in India. As soon as the new entry were trained and the old hands were in practice again, units 'beat retreat' every evening. The troops, African and British, as well as local Burmese, crowded in to see and hear this ceremony, which was invariably well performed and seems to have had the desired moral effect.

1 N.R. inserted 'John Peel' at the end of their last ceremony before handing over Prome to a battalion of the Border Regiment. This totally unexpected performance of their regimental march brought the watching Borders to their feet, and they cheered so heartily and long that 'Old Calabar', played as customary when marching off, was almost completely drowned.

Another who played a great part in dealing with problems affecting the troops both during and after the end of the war must be mentioned here. This was Tim Foley, who arrived in Nigeria from Australia in the early days and later became one of the world authorities on tin and one of the magnates of the Plateau. The following appreciation is given by Major-General Swynnerton, who was in command of the Division during the waiting period after having commanded 1 (W.A.) Bde. throughout the campaign. He writes of Foley as follows: 'In the early part of the war he spent a lot of his private fortune in financing B.N.C.O.'s messes in Nigeria, thus enabling them to obtain decent chairs and other equipment. He was appointed Welfare Officer to the R.W.A.F.F. by General Giffard in 1941. During the campaign in Burma he made his headquarters in Calcutta—all at his own expense—and busied himself with all sorts of problems affecting the troops. Although by no means young (over 60 years of age) he flew into Burma as soon as the campaign was over and went round the jungle camps talking to everybody and telling the most ribald stories in Hausa, which never failed to put the troops into paroxysms of laughter. He was immensely popular not only with the troops and their officers and B.N.C.O.s, but also with all the mining community around Jos. He died shortly after returning to Nigeria.'

The R.W.A.F.F. sent a detachment to take part in the Victory Parade in June 1946. Whilst in London the African troops were entertained by Headquarters Eastern Command at the official residence of the G.O.C.-in-C. (General Sir Oliver Leese). As many officers as possible who had served with the R.W.A.F.F. or K.A.R. were especially invited to attend and to help entertain the guests. There was a circus, several bands played during the afternoon and 'plenty fine chop' was provided.

A small party, including Regimental Sergeant-Major Chari Maigumeri represented the R.W.A.F.F. at the funeral of H.M. King George VI. A contingent of all ranks went to London in 1953 for the coronation of H.M. Queen Elizabeth II. They made a great impression on the spectators during the march of the coronation procession through London. In February 1958 the R.W.A.F.F. was represented at the unveiling of the Rangoon War Memorial, where the names of 1,608 West African soldiers who have no known graves are recorded.

Reduction of the West African Forces began in 1946. The disbandment of a unit is always a sad event, but particularly so at the end of a war. A living entity, welded together by training, discipline, experience and comradeship, is destroyed and its human elements are dispersed. It is, however, an event which usually cannot be avoided, but we can, at least, record the deeds of those wartime units who fought with and contributed to the history and traditions of the R.W.A.F.F.[1]

The R.W.A.F.F. in Nigeria was reduced to four battalions but, after a few months, the 5th Battalion was re-formed. In Gold Coast all the war-time battalions disappeared, but the 3rd Battalion was re-formed again after the disturbances in 1948. In Sierra Leone only the 1st Battalion remained; the two Gambia Battalions were reduced to one company which formed part of the Sierra Leone Battalion. However, the wartime R.W.A.F.F. training school at Teshi, near Accra, was retained to ensure

[1] See also Appendix XII.

common doctrine and methods of training in the units of the four contingents.

Nigeria and Gold Coast re-formed both engineer and signal units as well as the ancillary services sufficient for the peacetime establishment. These units, descendants of the wartime A.C.F., did not form part of the R.W.A.F.F., and they now bear the name of the territory in which they are raised, such as 'Nigerian Military Engineers'.

Arrangements had been made before the end of the war to further the resettlement of discharged soldiers, and pamphlets on the subject had been circulated to units overseas and in West Africa. The difficulties which eventually arose were mainly due to the fact that so many, having been looked after by the Army on active service better than they had ever been, found the return to civil life irksome. A factor which aggravated the situation was the rising cost of living. In Nigeria most of the dissatisfaction was in the South, particularly among the literate and semi-literate classes in the ancillary units, who seem to have expected preferential treatment in the form of soft, well-paid Government jobs.

Apart from resettlement problems there was an incident at Lagos in 1948 when the men of the R.E.M.E. Workshop staged a 'mutiny'. This was quite orderly: the troops simply fell in and marched on Government House. They were intercepted by the G.O.C., who had no difficulty in getting them back to barracks. This trouble was mainly due to bad administration, including indifferent relations between the officers, B.N.C.O.s and the African personnel. There was some unrest about the same time in the Ordnance Depot and in a W.A.A.S.C. company, both at Lagos. The units of the R.W.A.F.F., however, remained contented and loyal in spite of the fact that Headquarters West Africa Command had blundered by insisting on the W.A.A.S.C. providing standard rations irrespective of the fact that Northerners could not stomach Southern forms of food and vice versa.

The disturbances in the Gold Coast during February and March 1948 were by no means due entirely to the grievances, real or illusory, of the ex-servicemen, though these were exploited by the dissidents. The short supplies of necessaries from overseas and their high cost was a very real cause of popular discontent and was also made use of by the organizers of the disturbances. Rioting, looting and arson broke out in Accra on 28th February and continued next day.[1] On 1st March the disturbances spread to Kumasi, Korforidua, Nsawam and other towns. There was a further outbreak in Kumasi on 15th and 16th March. The existing two battalions of the Gold Coast Regiment were fully employed in aid of the Civil Power during these months: 'a duty which they carried out exceptionally well'.[2] The many calls on their services, however, were more than their resources could cope with. Help was therefore sent from Nigeria. Three companies of the 1st Battalion and one of the 3rd moved by air early in March. The remainder of the 1st and 3rd Battalions and one company of the 2nd went by sea. It appears that there was only one

[1] See Appendix XVII.

[2] Major-General C. R. A. Swynnerton, acting G.O.C.-in-C. West Africa at the time.

incident in which the Nigerians had to use their weapons; most of the time they were engaged in patrolling and in finding town picquets. Their presence undoubtedly had a steadying effect and enabled the local troops to get some rest. All the Nigerian troops were back in their own stations by 19th June.

Late in 1949 the aircraft normally used for passenger and freight services by the West African Airways Corporation were made available for military use in emergency under the control of Headquarters West Africa Command. They were placed at immediate call for use when required to transport military or police reinforcements to any area within the Command. During the coal strike at Enugu at the end of 1949 these aircraft were used to transport several hundred reserve police to Enugu. At the same time the Battery, organized as infantry, was sent to Lagos, whilst the R.W.A.F.F. battalion at Enugu stood by to help the police.

Since the war R.W.A.F.F. barracks have been named after the actions and campaigns in which the Force has gained distinction during the past 60 years. For instance, the infantry barracks at Kaduna are named 'Mogadishu' and 'Dalet', those at Abeokuta bear the name 'Nyangao', whilst those at Enugu commemorate the capture of Apaukwa in March 1944. There are also 'Ashanti', 'Ethiopia' and 'Chindit' barracks. A new station has been opened at Abeokuta; Kano has been abandoned—why is not clear—and Kaduna has become a two-battalion station, with the new Reconnaissance Squadron and the Military Training College also located there. The Depot remains at Zaria with a new School of Physical Training, a Military School and a Boy's Company. Battalions no longer have permanent stations as in the old days, but move at intervals. Nigeria has once more been divided into two districts, Northern and Southern, with Headquarters at Kaduna and Lagos respectively.

The three battalions of the old Gold Coast Regiment are stationed at 'Giffard Camp', Accra; 'Kaladan' Barracks, Tamale; and 'Ranchi' Barracks, Takoradi, with the Depot and a Boy's Company, formed in 1953, at 'Wadara' Barracks, Kumasi. There is also a Reconnaissance Squadron, formed from the Gold Coast Battery, located at 'Gondar' Barracks, Accra.

The Sierra Leone Battalion was stationed at Freetown with the Depot at Daru. In the Gambia the quarters at Cape St. Mary were known as 'Frontier Hill' barracks to commemorate the defence of this feature during the fighting around Mowdok in May 1944.

The African Cup of the Army Rifle Association was won in 1948 and 1950 by the 3rd and 5th Battalions the Nigeria Regiment respectively. The cup was also won by the 2nd Battalion Gold Coast Regiment in 1952.

During the war, when the R.W.A.F.F. was otherwise engaged, polo in Nigeria suffered a decline. In fact, it was only kept alive by the Emir of Katsina and a small number of keen and usually overworked civilians. In the war years it was frequently necessary for some of these few remaining enthusiasts to make their own sticks and balls. The revival started in 1946, and though due to a great extent to the R.W.A.F.F., some energetic district officers and members of the Veterinary Department played their part in it, too.

In the North, polo began again at Kaduna, Zaria, Kano, Daura, Kazure, Jos and Sokoto and, of course, continued to flourish at Katsina. In the South, Ibadan and Lagos have enthusiastic clubs but Enugu has dropped out, perhaps for ever. Regular annual tournaments were re-started in 1947 at Kaduna, Kano, Katsina and Zaria, during which all the pre-war competitions, except the Enugu Captain's Cup, take place.

The Empire Day Cup between the Army and Civilians in Nigeria is still a hard, well-fought match and shows some of the best polo in the country. Lieutenant Hassan Katsina played very successfully for the Army in this match in 1960. A number of other Nigerian officers are also playing, some only as beginners, but polo is becoming very much a matter of national interest. In the Inter-Regimental Commandant's Cup, 1959–60, the Depot fielded a private soldier, one Gindma Ngala, a hardworking and useful member of the team.

The Nigeria and Gold Coast Regiments both started museums after the war. The former is housed in the Depot at Zaria, the latter in the old fort at Kumasi. Both are doing well.

During 1948 it was decided to have an annual day of remembrance for the whole of the R.W.A.F.F. to be held on the anniversary of the battle of Myohaung. This was well chosen, as the action was fought by the largest concentration of R.W.A.F.F. units ever assembled and consisted of battalions from all four Territories—namely seven from Nigeria, three from Gold Coast, and one each from Sierra Leone and Gambia. The other troops taking part belonged to the A.C.F., except two Indian Mountain Artillery Regiments.

(ii) *Events in the Fifties*

This decade saw the introduction of a number of constitutional changes leading up to the independence of the four Territories. The military forces, except for some terminal grants, ceased to be a charge on the Government of the United Kingdom and Headquarters West African Command was closed down. Furthermore, new conditions and terms of service had to be introduced for all personnel seconded from the British Army which would be on a voluntary basis.

In the following paragraphs an outline will be found of events during this decade as far as possible in chronological order. This outline will, of course, be confined to those events which affected the units of the R.W.A.F.F.

During the fifties considerable advances were made in the selection and training of potential officers by the development of the following method. The soldier or civilian applicant for a commission has first to satisfy a board of carefully chosen examiners as to his character and standard of education before appearing before a selection board. If he passes, the candidate has to go through a special course of training lasting six months before appearing before a final board.[1] If selected by this board, candidates for regular commissions are sent to the R.M.A. Sandhurst; those for short-service commissions go to the O.C.T.U. at Aldershot. In Nigeria, by

[1] This course was originally run by the R.W.A.F.F. School at Teshi, but is now done locally, as the R.W.A.F.F. Training School has ceased to exist.

1958, there were approximately 50 African commissioned officers the majority of whom had passed through Sandhurst and several have passed through the Staff College. During the same period most of the British warrant and non-commissioned officers were replaced by Africans. In fact, by the end of the decade, those remaining were all technicians.

On 10th February 1950 the Gambia Regiment was reconstituted as a separate entity to be maintained in peacetime at the strength of one company. In the following April Colours were presented to the 'Regiment'.

In 1951 there was some minor trouble with the Engineer Squadron, stationed at Kaduna, who marched in from their camp with the object of demanding an interview with the Area Commander. They were easily stopped by one of the R.W.A.F.F. battalions at Kaduna. A more serious incident, involving a mutiny and injuries to British officers, B.N.C.O.s and senior African N.C.O.s, took place at the R.E.M.E. Workshop at Lagos. The G.O.C. arrived very soon after the mischief started, and with the aid of the R.W.A.F.F. Company stationed at Lagos the disturbance was quickly under control. A number of ringleaders, etc., were awarded sentences of several years' imprisonment by courts martial.

The same year there were widespread disturbances in the Cameroons. The one road, from Mamfe into the Cameroons, was blocked in many places and the police were having difficulty in their efforts to restore order and re-open communications. In order to support the police the District Commander established an advanced air head at Mamfe and flew in a detachment from the R.W.A.F.F. Battalion at Enugu. This air head provided administrative support for the police operating in the Cameroons and any further armed reinforcements which might be required.

Robert Ben-Smith served in the Gold Coast Regiment for at least 30 years and retired as African Chief-Clerk. About 1950 he was brought back to deal with welfare problems at District Headquarters, where he had direct access to the Commander. Ben-Smith was a man of outstanding loyalty and integrity who knew the G.C.R. 'backwards' as well as its regimental 'characters'. He was an expert on tribal customs and could advise on the basic causes of any probable trouble. In 1952 he was commissioned as an Honorary Lieutenant and awarded the M.B.E. The Gold Coast Legion raised a subscription to give him a sword which was presented on Myohaung Day 1954 by the District Commander.

Contrary to expectations the Gold Coast elections for the first all West African Legislative Council in June 1954 passed off quietly. By October, however, Ashanti nationalism became a threat to security which increased during the winter. The only unit in Ashanti was the Regimental Training Centre at Kumasi, which could only produce a few trained soldiers for security duties. Tamale was the most convenient station from which to reinforce Kumasi, but was 237 miles away and, although the road was good, the ferry across the River Volta at Yegi could only be operated in daylight. Early in 1955 the Government of the United Kingdom sent out a flight of transport aircraft, However, by autumn the situation had improved sufficiently to allow of the aircraft being withdrawn. But there were numerous occasions during the following years when a company from

Tamale, if not sent into Kumasi, was moved to the south bank of the Volta.

Rioting and looting broke out at Freetown in February 1955 and the Sierra Leone Battalion was called upon to aid the Civil Power. Their intervention, which included the firing of a few rounds, quickly brought the disturbances to an end.

An outstanding event was the visit of H.M. The Queen and H.R.H. Prince Philip to Nigeria early in 1956.

The itinerary of the Queen, moving from Region to Region with an entourage, baggage and a large Press party and carrying out visits to many places in each Region presented a difficult movement control problem. At the request of the G.O.C.-in-C. West Africa, the War Office sent out an experienced movement-control officer—Lieutenant-Colonel S. J. Cornfoot—who worked out a complete, detailed progamme for all Her Majesty's moves. In the event, everything went according to plan and Her Majesty's party was always punctual. The R.W.A.F.F. were also faced with a crowded programme of conflicting requirements, for, in addition to ceremonial parades, guards of honour on arrival and departure at various stations, guards wherever Her Majesty was accommodated during the tour had to be provided.

The Queen arrived at Lagos airport at 1000 hours on 28th January where a Royal Salute was fired by the Nigerian Battery and a Guard of Honour was found by the 2nd Battalion, who also mounted a Sovereign's Guard at Government House. Next morning Her Majesty attended the Myohaung Commemoration Service in the Cathedral. The service was most impressive. H.R.H. Prince Philip read the Lesson and an address was given by the Bishop of Lagos.

On the morning of 30th January Her Majesty presented new Colours to the 2nd Battalion to replace the Old Colours, which had been carried since 1933. The ceremony took place without a hitch and the Queen was most impressed by the parade and standard of drill. In the evening Her Majesty was photographed at Government House with the officers of the 2nd Battalion and also with the Warrant and Non-Commissioned officers of the Battalion.

The Queen left Lagos on 1st February and arrived at Kaduna at 1220 hours, where a Royal Salute was fired by the Battery and a Guard of Honour was found by the 1st Battalion, who also found the Sovereign's Guard at Government House. Next day Her Majesty attended a 'Durbar' in which the Emirs of the Northern Region took part, together with their picturesque retinues. The 1st Battalion 'kept the ground'. On 3rd February Her Majesty visited the Officer's Mess at Mogadishu Barracks, the home of the officers of the 1st Battalion for many years. Here, the famous 'Dan Fodio Flag', which had been in the possession of the Battalion for over fifty years, and other trophies were on view.[1]

Next morning Her Majesty left Kaduna for Jos, where she was accommodated at Tundun Wada. The Sovereign's Guard at the residence was found by the 1st Battalion.

[1] After Nigeria had attained independence, the Flag was handed back to the Sarik-Musalmi with due ceremony. (See also Appendix XVIII.)

On Monday, 5th February, Her Majesty left Jos for Makurdi and Enugu. At the latter place the Guard of Honour was found by the 3rd Battalion, who also provided the Sovereign's Guard at Government House. On the following evening there was a display at the Enugu Stadium, during which the 3rd Battalion staged a ceremonial parade.

After visiting Port Harcourt and Calabar, the Queen returned to Lagos, where she arrived at 1900 hours on 9th February. On the 11th Her Majesty left Lagos by train for Abeokuta and Ibadan. The 5th Battalion found the Guard of Honour at the latter place also the Sovereign's Guard at Govern-House, Ibadan. On the 15th Her Majesty opened the Parliament Building of the Western Region at Ibadan, the Guard of Honour being provided by the 5th Battalion, who also found three or four extra guards on this day. Her Majesty left Ibadan that evening for Lagos.

The Queen arrived at Lagos airport at 1120 hours on 16th February to depart for Kano on her way back to England. The Battery fired a Royal Salute and the 2nd Battalion found the Guard of Honour. Mention must be made here of the Regimental Band which had performed in front of Her Majesty over a dozen times during the visit.

It is understood that the Queen said she wished to make an announcement before leaving Nigeria which would leave a lasting memory of her visit. Among the suggestions considered was the the Nigeria Regiment should receive some special distinction. Probably as a result of Her Majesty seeing so much of the Regiment during her tour and realizing how much they had done so well, she decided that the Regiment should be 'The Queen's Own'.

So, at the end of a message broadcast to the people of Nigeria, Her Majesty announced the granting of a great honour to their Regiment. Her actual words were as follows:

> 'On the eve of our departure I would like to leave all Nigerians a reminder of this visit, which has been a great experience to us and I believe also to you. I have therefore decided that from now on the Nigeria Regiment is to be called the Queen's Own Nigeria Regiment. In this way I can also pay my tribute to the gallantry and loyalty of the people of the whole Federation who have served the Crown and their country so faithfully in peace and war.'

On 10th December of the same year the 5th Battalion the Queen's Own Nigeria Regiment was presented with new Colours by H.E. the Governor-General. These Colours were the first to bear the new title of the Regiment.

During the years 1952 to 1956 the only major incident affecting internal security in Nigeria was at Kano where fighting broke out between Ibos and local Hausas. Several people were killed and it appeared that serious communal rioting might ensue. The 1st Battalion was flown up to Kano from Kaduna and the police with such backing soon got the situation under control. The troops were not called upon to take action.

In January 1957 H.R.H. the Duke of Edinburgh visited Ghana and Gambia. In the latter Territory the R.W.A.F.F., in spite of their limited resources, carried out the necessary ceremonial and hospitality with commendable skill. Some months later H.R.H. the Princess Royal, during a

[*Photo: Topical Press*

H.M. Queen Elizabeth II, Colonel-in-Chief Royal West African Frontier Force, inspecting a Guard of Honour formed by the 3rd Battalion The Nigeria Regiment on 5th February 1956, during the Royal Tour in Nigeria

General Sir Lashmer Whistler, G.C.B., K.B.E., D.S.O., D.L.

Born 1893; Royal Sussex Regiment 1917; G.O.C. 3rd Infantry Division 1944–47; G.O.C. British Troops in India 1947–48; Kaid, Soudan Defence Force 1948–50; G.O.C. 50th (Northumbrian) Division (T.A.) 1950–51; G.O.C.-in-C. West Africa Command 1951–53; G.O.C.-in-C. Western Command 1953–57; Colonel Commandant R.W.A.F.F. 1958; Hon. Colonel Royal Nigerian Military Forces 1959; Hon. Colonel Royal Sierra Leone Military Forces 1959; died 1963.

visit to Nigeria, spent a morning with the units in Lagos. She also inspected the Nigerian Signal Squadron and lunched in the Mess at Apapa.

About this time Gambia decided to convert her small force into an armed constabulary and it seems that Sierra Leone had been contemplating a similar move. But during August 1957 the Sierra Leone Battalion was again called out in aid of the Civil Power, this time in connection with the disturbances arising out of the outbreak of illicit diamond mining. The fact that the police had failed to restore order in the Freetown riots of 1955 and in the diamond disturbances of 1957 has so far acted as a deterrent to any attempt to follow the example set by Gambia.

The Gold Coast became independent on 6th March 1957, and the troops were styled the Ghana Military Forces. Owing to the trouble taken personally by the G.O.C.-in-C., Lieutenant-General Sir Otway Hubert, the new Forces started with a sound organization.

For two and a half years Ashanti had been the focus of unrest, but now a new threat arose in mandated Togoland. Most of the inhabitants of this Territory were agreeable to incorporation with the new state of Ghana; there was, however, a minority who wanted the whole of this former German Colony to be formed into an independent state together with that part of south-eastern Ghana in which the Ewe tribe lived. It was shortly before the independence ceremonies were to take place that reports were received to the effect that training camps had been established in the bush north-east of Ho. There is little doubt that the dissidents not only hoped to disrupt the celebrations, but to focus world attention to the supposed plight of an unwilling Togoland being forced to join the new state of Ghana.

In spite of other heavy commitments at this time, two platoons of armed police were sent into Togoland and were soon followed by four more. So far as the R.W.A.F.F. were concerned, Accra had already been reinforced from Takoradi owing to the number of ceremonial guards, etc., to be found. On 7th March a company at full strength from Takoradi and the Battery, less guns and such personnel as were required for firing salutes, were sent by road to Togoland. About the same time a skeleton brigade headquarters started for Ho, where the Battery joined them. On 7th March also, Headquarters 1st Battalion with two companies left Tamale for Togoland. Numerous sweeps and searches were carried out and an important camp was discovered in the Kpandu district. However, the troops were not called upon to use their weapons and after a few weeks returned to their normal stations.

During the celebrations in Accra the R.W.A.F.F. was involved in finding guards of honour, etc., for Her Majesty's personal representative H.R.H. the Duchess of Kent and the new Governor-General. There was also a big ceremony of welcome in the Accra stadium, in which six companies of the R.W.A.F.F. took part as well as two companies of the other arms and a saluting battery. Her Royal Highness was pleased to express her admiration at the smartness of the troops.

In Southern Nigeria during 1957 there was considerable unrest followed by disturbances in the area Enugu–Onitsha–Port Harcourt—practically the same area in which the *Yakin Mata* took place. The causes were also similar, namely, the imposition of various financial measures and new taxation by the Regional Government. Also, as in 1929, the Ibo women played a leading part in the disturbances which lasted for several weeks. Large forces of police eventually restored order, but not without some difficulty. Though the R.W.A.F.F. were not actually engaged, transport, wireless communications and administrative backing were given to the police by the military authorities.

Serious trouble broke out in the French Cameroons during the same year. Bands of armed bandits caused serious incidents and it was found that many of the gangs were lying up in the British Cameroons in between forays across the border. After a visit by the G.O.C. to the French authorities at Duala, security along the border was strengthened and police operations, supported by military forces, were conducted against the bandits. This incident led to plans being made for the despatch of strong military forces to the Cameroons should the necessity arise. Eventually units of the R.W.A.F.F. were stationed in British Cameroons until just before Nigerian independence, when they were relieved by a British battalion. (See also Appendix XIX.)

The Governor-General of Nigeria established a Federal Defence Council under his own chairmanship in 1958. The members consisted of the Federal Prime Minister, the Regional Prime Ministers, the G.O.C. and the Director of the Nigerian Naval Service. One of the activities of the Council was the preparation of plans for the establishment of a Defence Ministry when Nigeria became independent. A programme for making the battalions of the Queen's Own Nigeria Regiment more mobile, hard-hitting and capable of sustained independent operations was approved by the Council in 1958. Sanction was also given for the raising of another battalion—the 6th. Approval was also given for the establishment of an Infantry Training School, at Kaduna as the R.W.A.F.F. School at Teshi was closing down. The old pre-war Engineer Cadre at Jos was reconstituted on a voluntary part-time basis as a reserve squadron for the Nigerian Engineers.

After 60 years of distinguished service at home and abroad, the Nigerian Battery was converted into a reconnaissance squadron. On 14th April 1958 H.E. the Governor-General paid a farewell visit to the unit and made a valedictory speech to the troops. The act of conversion was marked by a special ceremonial on the occasion of the Queen's Birthday Parade at Kaduna on 22nd April, during which the salute was taken by H.E. the Governor of the Northern Region. What must have been an impressive ceremony began with the firing of a 21-gun salute and a *feu de joie*, following which the guns of the Battery were trooped for the last time, after which the unit was played off the parade ground to 'Auld Lang Syne' by the Regimental Band. Then, with the Band playing 'Old Calabar', the 1st Reconnaissance Squadron of the Queen's Own Nigeria Regiment drove on to parade in their patrol vehicles. The first commanding officer of the Squadron was Major R. E. G. Scott, M.C., Durham Light Infantry.

Though all ranks, past and present, of the Nigerian Forces regret the passing of the Battery, one of the original units of the W.A.F.F., they will look to the Reconnaissance Squadron to maintain its fine traditions, combining them with those of the two West African Reconnaissance Regiments, A.C.F., disbanded in 1946 after a distinguished record in the war. A brief account of their services including the remarkable amphibious operations carried out by 81 (W.A.) Div. Recce R., will be found in Appendix XIV.

H.R.H. the Duke of Gloucester visited Nigeria in May 1959. On the 19th he inspected the Boys' Company at Zaria and on the 28th took the salute at a Combined Services parade at Lagos. Before his departure the Duke laid a wreath on the War Memorial at Lagos and met many ex-servicemen.

The Boys' Company which the Duke inspected had been formed in 1953, recently expanded to a strength of 250 and housed in excellent and well-equipped barracks at Zaria. The Company has a fine reputation throughout Nigeria for its high standard of turn-out, discipline and physical efficiency. Like a similar unit in Ghana, the Company is intended mainly for soldiers' sons, although others may be taken if vacancies exist. These units are a potential source of officers, N.C.O.s and technicians for the years ahead.

During the fifties considerable progress was made in the building of new barracks and married quarters. Pay codes were overhauled and simplified, rates of pay were increased and pensions for long service were instituted.

On 1st October 1960 Nigeria became independent. During the ceremonies and celebrations the Queen's Own Nigeria Regiment displayed their traditional smartness on parade.

In the meantime, the G.O.C. Nigeria had been made responsible for certain supervisory duties in Sierra Leone which were carried out by visits during 1958 and 1959. At this time the Sierra Leone Battalion was stationed as follows:

Battalion Headquarters	Freetown
The Headquarters and three rifle companies	Freetown
One rifle company	Daru
Training Company	Juba

During 1960 the Battalion, in addition to normal training, carried out a number of company marches 'showing the flag'. Thus, practically every district in the Protectorate, including the frontier areas, was visited. The troops were well received everywhere.

The Battalion was faced with heavy ceremonial duties in connection with the Independence Celebrations in 1961, which had to be carried out without the company at Daru, which was required to remain there for security reasons. The programme included Trooping the Queen's Colour, three guards of honour for the Duke of Kent and a searchlight tattoo preceding the flag-raising ceremony on 27th April—Independence Day. The Battalion was heartily congratulated on its performance.

There was an added complication. A self-styled opposition to the new Government had caused sufficient trouble and unrest for a state of emergency to be declared. This involved the provision of patrols, picquets and extra guards, so that every officer and other rank was fully employed.

Officers and B.N.C.O.s provided guards on bridges along the Royal route, as no troops were available. In spite of this the celebrations were completed with no sign of trouble and were an outstanding success.

The Government of Sierra Leone has decided that the *Kwakwa* shall remain the principal symbol in the new badge of the Regiment. So some touch with the R.W.A.F.F. will remain.

(iii) *Epilogue*

With the granting of self-government it followed that each Territory would bear the cost of its own defence commitments, as, indeed, they had done before 1940. It had been agreed by the four Territories in 1956, though reluctantly by Gold Coast, that a Lieutenant-General should be appointed to 'assist their governments in the co-ordination of defence'. But as time went on it became apparent that neither was willing to commit its forces to a common pool. In the end the appointment of a co-ordinating officer was abandoned, the holder having the power to advise without being able to implement his advice.

Headquarters West Africa Command had closed down in June 1956. The R.W.A.F.F. Training School at Teshi, however, continued to function until the end of 1959. Ghana severed its connection with the R.W.A.F.F. on 6th March 1959 and the units became the Ghana Army.

By March 1960 the units previously belonging to the R.W.A.F.F. were absorbed into the Royal Nigerian Military Forces, the Royal Sierra Leone Military Forces, and the Ghana Army. The R.W.A.F.F. had ceased to be an entity. It was eventually agreed that the formal date for the end of the R.W.A.F.F. would be on 1st August 1960, and in the *London Gazette* of 2nd August it was announced that General Sir Lashmer Whistler, Colonel Commandant of the R.W.A.F.F., had 'relinquished his appointment'. In the meantime, H.M. The Queen had accepted appointments as Colonel-in-Chief of the Royal Nigerian Military Forces, the Royal Sierra Leone Forces and the Ghana Regiment of Infantry. In addition, General Whistler had been appointed Honorary Colonel of the Nigerian and Sierra Leone Military Forces.

So the R.W.A.F.F. has 'faded away' almost unnoticed. It is a pity, perhaps, that the descendants of the original W.A.F.F.[1] units have not had the words 'Frontier Force' added to their titles.

The contingents which composed the R.W.A.F.F. have a fine history of achievement, as is shown by the 66 battle honours awarded for their services in two continents.[2] It must also be remembered that, particularly in their early days, units took part in many minor expeditions, sometimes involving heavy fighting, and always considerable hardship, for which medals but no battle honours were given. They have, too, a record of duties in aid of the Civil Power carried out with commendable restraint and efficiency.

During the Ashanti campaign of 1900, the first occasion when a purely African force defeated the redoubtable Ashantis, the original W.A.F.F.

[1] Now the 1st and 2nd Battalions and 1st Reconnaissance Squadron, the Queen's Own Nigeria Regiment.

[2] Nigeria 28, Gold Coast 24, Gambia 8, and Sierra Leone 6. (See Appendix I Part I)

units quickly proved their superiority over the local Constabularies. The upshot was that all the West African forces were reorganized and re-formed on the W.A.F.F. model.

The first major test, however, came in the War of 1914–18, when the W.A.F.F. was called upon to fight highly trained African regular troops armed with modern weapons and led by German officers. Both in the arduous Cameroon and East African campaigns they won the approbation of their commanders for gallantry, endurance and cheerful obedience. General Dobell remarked of them: 'No day appears too long, no task too difficult.'

Once more in East Africa, during 1940–1, fighting against Italians and Italian-trained, well-armed African troops, the Nigerian and Gold Coast Brigades displayed the same sterling qualities as their forebears. The battle honours 'Juba', 'Marda Pass', 'Wadara' and 'Omo' were earned by skill, bravery and endurance against an enemy who, on these occasions, put up a much stronger resistance than usual. In fact, 'Wadara' may be classed with 'Keren' as one of the two hardest-fought and arduous battles of the campaign.

The year 1940 saw the safety of the British West African Territories threatened by a hostile French Government. After tremendous efforts the R.W.A.F.F. was increased to a strength of 28 battalions. Many units of other arms and services were also raised, often on R.W.A.F.F. cadres, as part of the African Colonial Forces. When the danger had passed West Africa was able to send two divisions to Burma, which included 18 R.W.A.F.F. infantry battalions. In Burma the R.W.A.F.F. met a tough, skilful and fanatically brave enemy in very difficult country, but in spite of setbacks, mostly minor ones, accomplished the arduous tasks allotted to them.

81 (W.A.) Div., composed of units from all four territories, and the first normal formation ever to be entirely supplied by air, displayed great mobility and flexibility in the roadless Kaladan Valley and contributed to the success of XV Corps on the main Arakan front. In the third Arakan campaign this Division, moving quickly down the Kaladan, out-manoeuvred the enemy and by a skilful use of ground outmanoeuvred them a second time. As a result of this operation the Japanese were forced to evacuate their important base on Akyab Island. Then, by a series of laborious actions the Division, reinforced by 4 Bde., paved the way for the victory of Myohaung in which 1 Bde. of 82 (W.A.) Div., moving up rapidly from the west, surprised the Japanese and struck the final blow.

Previous to Myohaung, 82 (W.A.) Div. had taken part in the Mayu offensive on the main Arakan front, and afterwards, supplied entirely by air, carried out the pursuit over some of the most difficult country in Burma. At the end of the pursuit 2 Bde. arrived behind the defenders of Kangaw in time to hasten their decisive defeat, whilst the remainder of the Division moved towards An with the object of destroying or holding the Japanese forces west of the Arakan Yomas. In their later operations on the Tamandu–An road the Division was unfortunate in having to change the plan for surrounding An from the north and west owing to the necessity for switching more aircraft to maintain the main offensive on the Central

Front. Nevertheless, though mobility and flexibility were much reduced by having to rely on supply by land transport, the Division, after taking a leading part in the final capture of Tamandu, succeeded by hard fighting in the neighbourhood of An in holding large numbers of the Japanese 54 Div. west of the Yomas and in inflicting heavy casualties on them. The last operation carried out by the Division was the clearance of the enemy from southern Arakan and the occupation of Sandoway, Gwa and later of Prome.

The 13 battle honours awarded to the units of the R.W.A.F.F. for their services in Burma were well earned. Their skill in jungle, their mobility, endurance, fortitude, and gallantry are deserving of the highest praise. These qualities, coupled with good leadership and staff work, made the two divisions most formidable opponents.

The units which composed the R.W.A.F.F. have splendid traditions to sustain them in whatever the future may hold. The many British officers and N.C.O.s who have served with them in the past, and who have happy memories of the gallant and cheerful West African soldier, will watch their progress with interest and pride.

And so we say 'Hail and Farewell' to the Royal West African Frontier Force, and '*Allah shi dede rainka*' to all ranks, past, present and future.

Annexures to Part II

ANNEXURE I

(i) *Commandants Nigeria and Gold Coast Regiments*

Nigeria

Colonel G. T. Mair, C.M.G., D.S.O.	1920–1924
Colonel J. F. Badham, D.S.O.	1924–1926
Colonel W. B. Greenwell, C.M.G., D.S.O.	1926–1929
Colonel C. C. Norman, C.M.G., D.S.O.	1929–1931
Colonel W. R. Meredith, C.B.E., D.S.O.	1931–1936
Brigadier D. P. Dickinson, D.S.O., O.B.E., M.C.	1936–1939
Brigadier W. R. Smallwood, D.S.O., M.C.	1939–1940
Major-General C. R. A. Swynnerton, C.B., D.S.O.	1946–1949*
Major-General C. B. Fairbanks, C.B., C.B.E.	1949–1952*
Major-General J. H. Inglis, C.B., C.B.E.	1952–1956*
Major-General K. G. Exham, C.B., D.S.O.	1956–1960*

Gold Coast

Lieutenant-Colonel J. R. Meiklejohn, D.S.O.	1922–1924
Lieutenant-Colonel I. H. MacDonnel, D.S.O.	1924–1928
Lieutenant-Colonel W. C. Wilson, D.S.O., O.B.E., M.C.	1928–1930
Colonel G. V. Breffit, M.C.	1930–1933
Colonel H. H. Beattie	1933–1936
Lieutenant-Colonel D. S. Marchant, M.C.	1936–1937
Colonel M. A. Green, O.B.E., M.C.	1937–1939
Brigadier C. E. M. Richards, C.B.E., D.S.O., M.C.	1939–1940
Brigadier J. A. Daniel, C.I.E., D.S.O., M.C.	1945–1946
Brigadier P. J. Jeffreys, D.S.O., O.B.E.	1946–1947
Brigadier G. B. S. Hindley, O.B.E.	1944–1949†
Brigadier E. H. G. Grant, C.B.E., D.S.O., M.C.	1949–1952†
Brigadier W. S. Ritchie, O.B.E.	1952–1954†
Major-General A. G. V. Paley, C.B., C.B.E., D.S.O.	1954–1960†

(ii) *Inspectors-General R.W.A.F.F.*

Colonel A. H. W. Haywood, C.M.G., C.B.E., D.S.O.	1921–1924‡
Colonel R. D. F. Oldman, C.M.G., D.S.O.	1924–1926‡
Colonel S. S. Butler, C.M.G., D.S.O.	1926–1930‡
Brigadier C. C. Norman, C.M.G., C.B.E., D.S.O.	1932–1936
Major-General G. Giffard, C.B., D.S.O.	1936–1939

* Also Commander Nigeria District.
† Also Commander Gold Coast District.
‡ Colonel on the Staff equivalent to the modern appointment of Brigadier.

ANNEXURE II

Honours and Awards Granted to the R.W.A.F.F. During the Second World War

(See note after Gambia Regiment)

THE CAMPAIGN IN EAST AFRICA

The Nigeria Regiment

D.S.O.

Brig. G. R. Smallwood
Lt.-Col. B. J. D. Gerrard
Lt.-Col. J. A. S. Hopkins

M.C.

Capt. C. A. Wade
Capt. C. A. V. Brownlie
Capt. K. B. M. Carter
Capt. J. R. Filmer-Bennett
Capt. J. H. Patterson
Capt. J. E. L. Corbyn
Capt. A. J. Stewart
Lieut. J. MacBean
Lieut. E. M. Kidner
2/Lieut. J. McNeil
2/Lieut. J. E. L. Willis

M.M.

R.S.M. Chari Maigumeri
C.S.M. Mursal Doba
C.S.M. Alam Bari
Sgt. R. H. C. Strong
Sgt. G. P. Roberts
Sgt. Abdul Bagarimi
Sgt. Musa Abinsi
M/S/Sgt. E. D. Childes
Cpl. Momadu Mubi
Cpl. Musa Dikwa
Pte. Momadu Wase

O.B.E.

Maj. I. L. Wight
Maj. A. E. Hillier

M.B.E.

Capt. R. W. Dodds
Capt. J. T. Ennals
Capt. H. M. Greenspan

Mention in Despatches

Lt.-Col. B. J. D. Gerrard
Lt.-Col. J. A. S. Hopkins
Lt.-Col. H. Marshal
Maj. R. Carr
Maj. W. T. B. Webb
Maj. T. L. Fasson
Capt. T. W. S. Moss
Capt. C. O. O. O'Flynn
Capt. W. P. B. Arkwright
Capt. F. K. Butler
Capt. A. A. Couzens
Capt. G. F. Upjohn
Lieut. A. Burtles
Lieut. R. T. Kerslake
Lieut. G. T. McChlery
Lieut. B. O. O'Shea
Lieut. O. S. Swainson
Lieut. S. J. Watt
Lieut. W. G. H. Race
Lieut. C. J. V. Fisher-Hoch
2/Lieut. R. G. Hunter
2/Lieut. A. G. Spicer
2/Lieut. G. G. Lytle
R.S.M. G. E. W. Harvey
M/S/Sgt. E. D. Childes
M/S/Sgt. G. H. Gull
Sgt. A. R. Hayter
Sgt. G. B. Hendrie
Sgt. L. R. Hendry
Sgt. C. Matitos
Sgt. L. Ralston
Sgt. O. H. Templar
Sgt. D. G. Trow
Sgt. J. G. Wade
Sgt. N. L. Lally
L/Cpl. Amadu Sanin

(ii) *The Gold Coast Regiment*

D.S.O.

Lt.-Col. J. W. A. Hayes
Lt.-Col. E. W. Western
Maj. J. A. French

M.C.

Capt. A. J. Ainley
Capt. E. H. Muldoon
Capt. B. E. Hazelton

M.C.—cont

Lieut. S. E. Ellis
Lieut. V. Porter
Lieut. E. Morris
Lieut. E. Zacks
2/Lieut. D. M. M. Kellas
2/Lieut. G. Brydon
2/Lieut. G. L. Levett
2/Lieut. C. H. Allen

Bar to M.C.

2/Lieut. C. W. Ballenden, M.C.

D.C.M.

C.S.M. H. C. Russell
C.S.M. W. H. Twyman
L/Cpl. Zakare Busanga
Pte. Bukare Frafra
Pte. Kwaku Mensah

M.M.

C.S.M. Bawa Bazabarimi
C.S.M. Issa Bazabarimi
Sgt. Mamudu Kanjarga
Sgt. Mumuni Dagarti
Sgt. Musa Grumah
Sgt. Tallata Kanjarga
Pte. Amadu Frafra
Pte. J. Q. Lamptey
Pte. Seidu Isalla

M.B.E.

Capt. P. M. Hughes
Lieut. A. G. Johnson
Lieut. C. J. Taylor
R.S.M. Lanyian Dagarti

B.E.M.

C.Q.M.S. R. Martin
Sgt. Aniah Frafra

Mention in Despatches

Lt.-Col. E. W. D. Western
Lt.-Col. J. W. A. Hayes
Maj. H. P. Fowler
Maj. J. A. French
Maj. W. S. Reid
Maj. J. C. Liesching

Mention in Despatches—cont.

Maj. P. Van Straubenzee
Maj. N. G. McLean
Maj. C. H. Allen
Maj. D. W. Ponting
Capt. E. A. T. Boggis
Capt. J. C. Hooten
Capt. R. P. M. T. Barrett
Capt. A. D. Campbell
Capt. R. B. Ross
Capt. B. B. Waddy
Capt. G. J. Williams
Capt. A. G. Ames
Lieut. A. J. Ainley
Lieut. A. Ellman Brown
Lieut. J. McGavin
Lieut. M. Maude
Lieut. P. J. Wauchope
Lieut. D. W. Breakspear
Lieut. K. A. Sinclair
Lieut. T. L. Bowden
Lieut. D. M. Dyer-Ball
2/Lieut. H. Willis
2/Lieut. G. L. Levett
2/Lieut. T. E. Norbury
2/Lieut. D. Bookless
2/Lieut. D. A. Lane
2/Lieut. E. C. Lanning
2/Lieut. A. G. Thorburn
2/Lieut. O. Holmes
C.S.M. N. A. Abbey
C.S.M. Awuni Nangodi
C.S.M. W. W. Cluff
C.S.M. H. C. Russell
C.S.M. E. E. Engman
Sgt. B. K. Abbey
Sgt. I. Buliga
Sgt. J. V. Burgess
Sgt. L. J. Church
Sgt. Kusasi Aduku
Cpl. A. G. Sampong
Cpl. Chokosi
Cpl. J. K. Jumoh
Col. Kobina Buama
L/Cpl. Abudu Bazabarimi
L/Cpl. A. Kanjara
L/Cpl. Braima Moshi
L/Cpl. Busanga Businga
L/Cpl. V. C. Dei
Pte. Ali Dagarti
Pte. Mama Fulani
Pte. Grunchi Jatto
Pte. Wongara Deriman

THE CAMPAIGN IN BURMA, 1943–1945

(i) *The Nigeria Regiment*

D.S.O.

Lt.-Col. R. M. V. Ponsonby
Lt.-Col. Paltridge

M.C.

Maj. C. C. A. Carfree
Maj. C. R. Kalshaven
Capt. C. E. Coaton
Capt. H. C. Fisher
Lieut. D. K. Lamb
Lieut. J. F. Ross
Lieut. K. G. Moore

D.C.M.

Sgt. F. E. Hedley
C.S.M. Momadu Krawa
Sgt. Ibrahim Wadai
Sgt. Osuman Sumari
Sgt. Yaya Chikena
Sgt. Dogo Yerwa (attached G.C.R.)
Sgt. Al Hassan Geiri

M.M.

C.S.M. H. P. A. Staunton
C.S.M. A. Kitt
C.S.M. Issa Sokoto (attached G.C.R.)
C.S.M. Shellem Suli
Sgt. W. J. Best
Sgt. C. Lynch
Sgt. Aba Dikwa
Sgt. Abdullai Banana
Sgt. Audu Yola
Sgt. Hamakim
Sgt. Hassan Biliri
Sgt. Moma Fort Lamy
Sgt. Osuman Doba
Sgt. Umoru Numan
Sgt. Yaro Zuru
Cpl. Adamu Bauchi
Cpl. Adamu Gafasa
Cpl. Amadu Doso
Cpl. Amadu Katsina
Cpl. Audu Tuberi
Cpl. Dogo Manga
Cpl. Garaba Sokoto
Cpl. Issa Yola (attached G.C.R.)
Cpl. Garaba Sokoto
Cpl. Abrahim Mansu
Cpl. Musa Banana
Cpl. Musu Dokin Argungu

M.M.—cont.

Cpl. Osuman Banana
L/Cpl. Baguda Lamurde
L/Cpl. Eke Akaji
L/Cpl. Issa Zuru (attached G.C.R.)
L/Cpl. Ibrahim Hadeija
L/Cpl. Sherifi Fort Lamy
L/Cpl. Ibrahim Tilla
Pte. Adamu Gala
Pte. Agara Mbaya
Pte. Abdulai Di (attached G.C.R.)
Pte. Alleiji Gasson
Pte. Banjeram Hassan (attached G.C.R.)
Pte. Mailafia Shangev
Pte. Saidu Sokoto
Pte. Umoru Malanawa
Pte. Idrisa Malabu

M.B.E.

Capt. R. L. Williams
Lieut. J. G. Crowne

B.E.M.

R.S.M. Chari Maigumeri, M.M.
R.S.M. Sule Yola
C.S.M. Hassan Lai (attached G.C.R.)
Sgt. Musa Yola
Cpl. Bassey Okon

Mention in Despatches

Lt.-Col. G. F. Upjohn
Lt.-Col. P. M. Hughes
Maj. A. D. Mackenzie
Maj. L. W. S. Tayler
Maj. K. F. Fullager
Maj. J. T. Alexander
Capt. J. B. Bell
Capt. M. B. Cooke
Capt. C. Tighe
Capt. J. S. Binns
Lieut. C. P. Banfield
Lieut. J. K. T. Earle
Lieut. C. H. Mercer
Lieut. (Q.M.) Parkinson
Lieut. N. S. McNeil
R.S.M. Chari Maigumeri, M.M.
R.S.M. Abdullai Bagarami
C.S.M. R. A. Keevil
C.S.M. H. Hill
C.S.M. Garaba Kano

Mention in Despatches—cont.

C.S.M. Issa Sokoto
C.S.M. Jallo Mundi
C.S.M. Mamman Zuru
C.S.M. Mati Marwa
Sgt. Abasin Numan
Sgt. Adamu Fort Lamy
Sgt. Adamu Katsina
Sgt. Akanbi Salami
Sgt. Audu Yola
Sgt. Ali Gutiba
Sgt. Busaini Gwaronye
Sgt. Benjamin Blackie
Sgt. Diga Kaltungo
Sgt. Hama Kim
Sgt. Hassan Maiduguri
Sgt. Isufi Janingo
Sgt. Jatto Kano
Sgt. Johnson Igbe
Sgt. J. F. S. Kent
Sgt. Momo Dogo
Sgt. Moman Tangada
Sgt. Thomas Olu
Sgt. Sanda Peni
Sgt. Dogo Yerwa (attached G.C.R.)
Sgt. Shaibu Godabwa
Sgt. Tugui Banana
Cpl. Adamu Doso
Cpl. Ameka Ogoja
Cpl. Anara-Wa-Biliri
Cpl. Audu Sara
Cpl. Bubu Biu
Cpl. Bukar Bedde

Mention in Despatches—cont.

Cpl. Jemo Maidoba
Cpl. Kachella Banana
Cpl. Madaki Numan
Cpl. Maman Kazel
Cpl. Mijin Waya Womba
Cpl. Usuman Ankwa
Cpl. Yaro Peni
Cpl. Emegu Enugu (attached G.C.R.)
L/Cpl. Bukar Marwa
L/Cpl. Hassan Dee
L/Cpl. Phineas Lamurde
L/Cpl. Musa Pella
L/Cpl. Musa Gurin (attached G.C.R.)
Pte. Abdulai Di (attached G.C.R.)
Pte. Abdullai Mundu
Pte. Afi Abaji
Pte. Ajayi Kano
Pte. P. Atia
Pte. Cheku Egu (attached G.C.R.)
Pte. Jedda Manga
Pte. Paterick Lamurde
Pte. Mbuka Ribah
Pte. Moman Bashir
Pte. Nagima Bagundi
Pte. Nufu Demsa
Pte. Sackio Lamba
Pte. Sule Hadeija
Pte. Umumi Zuru
Pte. Umuru Habu
Pte. Usuman Yola
Pte. Yilcam Kabir
Pte. Audu Gando

(ii) *The Gold Coast Regiment*

D.S.O.

Lt.-Col. M. J. A. Paterson
Lt.-Col. F. J. Goulson

M.C.

Maj. F. Myatt
Maj. H. C. Russell, D.C.M.
Lieut. P. S. Evans

Bar to M.C.

Maj. D. G. Dickson

D.C.M.

Sgt. L. J. Rawlins
Sgt. Hassan Bazabarimi
Sgt. Sidi Hausa
Sgt. Sidiki Moshi

M.M.

C.S.M. Ali Moshi
Sgt. T. Monteith
Sgt. Yamba Grunshi
Sgt. Amadu Bazabarimi
Sgt. Potopoa Dagarti
Sgt. Diewoo Kwesi
Sgt. Kado Seidu
Sgt. Issaka Moshi
Sgt. Sigiya Moshi
Cpl. Amadu Bazabarimi
Cpl. Anipuma Kassena
Cpl. Buri Moshi
Cpl. Alakum Dagarti
Cpl. Niama Dagomba
Cpl. Idrissa Kanate
Cpl. Musa Frafra
Cpl. Maina Beriberi

M.M.—cont.

Cpl. Norga Busanga
Cpl. Issaka Moshi
Cpl. Musa Grunshi
L/Cpl. Bedoli Bazabarimi
L/Cpl. Issa Dagomba
Pte. Salitu Kanjarga
Pte. Kweku Pong
Pte. Yiowa Moshi

M.B.E.

Capt. S. K. Anthony

B.E.M.

R.S.M. Issa Bazabarimi, M.M.
R.S.M. Musa Kanjarga
C.S.M. Banjogo Wangara
C.S.M. Musa Moshi
C.S.M. Salifu Moshi
C.S.M. Musa Moshi
Sgt. Moses Masoperh
Sgt. T. O. D. Bempong

Mention in Despatches

Lt.-Col. C. G. Bowen
Maj. F. T. Jeffries
Maj. F. J. Moore
Maj. R. A. James
Maj. R. W. McFayden
Capt. V. L. Watts
Lieut. L. G. M. Tanfield
Lieut. A. Q. Mesure
Lieut. T. Strachan
R.S.M. G. Moshi
R.S.M. Bachana Grunshi
C.S.M. Sam Dagarti
C.S.M. Tallata Kanjarga
C.S.M. O. Wangara
C.S.M. M. McFarland
C.S.M. Ali Moshi
C.S.M. Ali Frafra
C.S.M. Ali Grunshi
C.S.M. H. G. Hammond
C.S.M. Salifu Kanjarga (twice)
R.Q.M.S. R. N. Lowell
C.Q.M.S. W. H. Hilton
Sgt. J. Jamieson
Sgt. Abdulai Kanjarga
Sgt. Abudumia Kanjarga

Mention in Despatches—cont.

Sgt. Amadu Moshi
Sgt. Bukari Kanjarga
Sgt. E. T. T. Maxwell
Sgt. Iyeni Omege
Sgt. A. Moshi
Sgt. I. Moshi
Sgt. Omoru Bima
Sgt. Sibiri Grumah
Sgt. Tumani Sisshoer
Sgt. Yamba Grunshi
Cpl. Anipuna Kassena
Cpl. Akumboa Frafra
Cpl. Alhandu Grunshi
Cpl. Bawa Grunshi
Cpl. Eno Boat
Cpl. Bosofo Dagarti
Cpl. A. Builsa
Cpl. B. Dagarti
Cpl. Jabina Issalla
Cpl. Jumsia Moshi
Cpl. Kasuwin
Cpl. L. A. Laryea
Cpl. Mahamadu Zambrama (twice)
Cpl. Mama Fulani
Cpl. Seidu Moshi
Cpl. Tuonare Dagarti
Cpl. N. Yallense
Cpl. Taro Yaga Dagarti
L/Cpl. J. Arthur
L/Cpl. A. Prang
L/Cpl. J. K. Paterson
L/Cpl. Kwami Lassor
Pte. A. B. Macninday
Pte. Adonga Frafra
Pte. Ali Fulani
Pte. Allandu Sissella
Pte. Allason Zabarama
Pte. K. Anani
Pte. Attah Basare
Pte. Baroa Shadai
Pte. Bawa Chokosi
Pte. F. Bazabarimi
Pte. B. Dagarti
Pte. Iddrissu Moshi
Pte. Effah Kanina
Pte. Kofi Mensah
Pte. Kofi Tann
Pte. Koto Abochi
Pte. Peter Kwami
Pte. Donkor Kwami
Pte. Kwami Lassor
Pte. Saler Bazabarimi

(iii) *The Sierra Leone Regiment*

D.S.O.

Maj. P. T. van Straubenzee

M.C.

Maj. P. L. McArthur
Maj. P. M. Pitt
Capt. C. W. M. White

D.C.M.

Sgt. Beya Asana

M.M.

Sgt. J. Goude
Cpl. Karonka Samuna
L/Cpl. Bobo Jumbo
Pte. Ansumana Turay
Pte. Bumpe Kontieh
Pte. Thomasi Bwaindu

B.E.M.

R.S.M. Tamba Bayma
R.S.M. Bokari Farandugu

Mention in Despatches

Lt.-Col. K. P. M. Carter, M.C.
Maj. H. L. George
Maj. T. Forrester
Maj. A. F. Dawkins (twice)
Maj. P. M. Pitt, M.C.
Capt. E. Sayers (twice)
Capt. S. E. Drake
Capt. M. G. Megginson
Lieut. D. A. Anderson
Lieut. G. W. N. Greenhouse
Lieut. R. F. Grocott

Mention in Despatches—cont.

R.S.M. F. A. Aldous
C.S.M. Abdulla Serabu
C.S.M. Bennett
C.S.M. Bandi Kove
C.S.M. J. Harding
C.S.M. Brima Kaikai
C.S.M. Kalli Koinadugu
C.S.M. Francis Va Va
C.S.M. Momadu Kamara
Sgt. J. Kershaw
Sgt. Kalfalla Kamara
Sgt. Salamu Turay
Sgt. Thomas Ajax
Sgt. Kargbo Frankie
Sgt. Legawo Tiama
Sgt. J. Limba
Sgt. M. Mamie
Sgt. Morlar Kamara
Sgt. Surie Gberia
Sgt. Santiggi Tibilla
Cpl. Dambarra Faiera
Cpl. Mambain Mara
Cpl. Samba Kargbo
Cpl. W. G. Senesse
Cpl. Dansa Turay (twice)
Pte. Ansumana Sillah
Pte. Bokart Piama
Pte. Josiah Dumbarra
Pte. Jusu Baio
Pte. Kontehmatuh
Pte. Mohammed Marrah
Pte. Seffa Segbwema
Pte. Thomasi Braindu
Pte. Bokari Blana
Pte. Konte Matru

(iv) *The Gambia Regiment*

D.S.O.

Lt.-Col. J. A. J. Read, M.C.

M.C.

Capt. Jan Zieleznik

M.M.

Cpl. Bubu Kaita
L/Cpl. Jallow Samba
L/Cpl. Jallow Yaryah
Pte. Bojan Bokari
Pte. Kamara Kinti

M.M.—cont.

Pte. N'Dowe Dudu
Pte. N'Jie Musa

B.E.M.

C.S.M. Samba Sillah

Mention in Despatches

Capt. D. G. N. Wetmore
Lieut. W. R. Golder
C.S.M. Samba Sillah
C.Q.M.S. T. Farrell

Mention in Despatches—cont.

Sgt. Bokari Kanara
Sgt. Demba Jalloh
Sgt. Momodu Barrie
Cpl. Ansumana Chatti (twice)
L/Cpl. Peirre Tamba
L/Cpl. Lawarie Braimah

Mention in Despatches—cont.

L/Cpl. Ansumana Chatti
Pte. Bokari Kamara
Pte. Massere Turay
Pte. Tala Barrier
Pte. Tumble Sekane
Pte. Yusufu Fatti

NOTE. There has been considerable difficulty in obtaining the material to compile these lists in spite of help by the Military Secretary's Branch at the War Office. It is feared that some names may still be missing, particularly British officers and N.C.O.s whose names may have appeared in official notifications under their own Regiments and without reference to the R.W.A.F.F. Nevertheless, the author expresses his regret that this should be the case and offers his apologies to anyone concerned.

Appendices to Part II

APPENDIX I

Notes on Regimental Customs, etc.

NIGERIA

1. *Dress:* Officers of the Headquarters Staff wore the crest of the crown bird (West African Crowned Crane) on the front of their helmets instead of the hackle worn by others on the left side. A black tie was worn by all officers on ceremonial parades.

2. *Crests and Marches:* Some battalions adopted distinctive crests for use on their notepaper, mess appointments and unit flags. These same units played a battalion march past in addition to 'Old Calabar'. Thus:

	Crest	*Battalion March*
1st Battalion	A burutu bird	'The Lincolnshire Poacher'
2nd Battalion	A crown bird	'Father O'Flynn'
5th Battalion	An antelope (*Ferrin Gindi*)	'The British Grenadiers'
6th Battalion	A wart hog	The March from 'The Vagabond King'

The first three kept living specimens of their crest. That of the 1st Battalion was hardly a pet, being a large, hideous bird possessing enormous, prominent eyes which swivelled round about 150 degrees on either side. It also had a tendency to eat knives and forks as well as cycle tyres. The 3rd and 4th Battalions kept to the *Kwakwa* for all purposes; the 3rd Battalion played only 'Old Calabar', but the 4th Battalion used, in addition, an Irish tune, 'The Orangeman', as a unit march. The Battery marched past to the 'Mountain Artillery'.

3. *Ordeals:* Some Officer's Messes had customary ordeals for those dining in Mess for the first time on a guest night. One—in the 4th Battalion—was to climb to the top of the Mess flagstaff and, at the top, drink a bottle of beer hoisted up by the halyards. This fell into disuse during the thirties owing to the action of white ants on the flagstaff.

The 1st Battalion prized their ceremony of the 'DRUM'. This was not really a drum but a large, circular, copper cooking pot captured from the Germans in the Cameroons. Soon after dinner the 'Defaulters Call' would sound and the victim was ceremoniously approached by two officers bearing lances who advised him to 'Come quickly or . . .' He was then arranged in the drum, like a winkle in its shell, by the Adjutant. The contraption was then up-ended and rolled by willing hands across the room to a flight of steps where, gathering its own momentum, it clattered down and raced across the veranda until brought up to a shattering stop by the concrete balustrade. But that was not all. The dazed passenger was then invited to drink a brandy and soda in one gulp and then to sign his name in a special book kept for the purpose. By this signature the individual could claim exemption if challenged at any future date.

The 2nd Battalion invited its victim to stand on a box and conduct the Band playing his own regimental march. When well under way the dupe was upset backwards on to a carpet and tossed. An officer who passed this ordeal twice writes as follows: 'When this happened to me the four subalterns holding the carpet were not strong enough to toss my thirteen stone very high. But I had to face this ordeal again when I was dined out by the Battalion at the end of my time. Having been carried round the dining-room pick-a-back by the Drum-Major to the wailing of fifes and deafening throbbing of the drums hammering out "Father O'Flynn", I was deposited on a box in the ante-room. After protesting that I had already done this once, I proceeded to conduct the Band. When I fell on to the carpet I saw to my horror that it was held by six large gun-carriers. They were quite expert and when I was allowed to stagger away I had gained a considerable knowledge of the taste and smell of Kano dust and, moreover, had a thirst as good as any ever acquired east of Suez.'

4. *The Regimental Week:* This yearly 'festival', which was held at Kaduna and which lasted a fortnight, attracted every British officer and N.C.O. who could be spared from his unit. It was a tumultuous mixture of work and very strenuous play. Not only did the Annual Sports Meeting take place, but polo tournaments were played off and a rifle meeting was held. So, with all these activities, plus the running of conferences and several T.E.W.T.s, the Headquarters Staff and the officers of the 1st Battalion had a hectic time and not overmuch sleep. It was customary for the Staff to entertain officers from outstations at the Staff Officer's bungalow, followed by a fancy dress ball at the Club, which usually led to one or two amusing incidents.

5. *The Hausa Farewell:* This was a long medley of bugle calls believed to be based on Hausa tunes played when men went to war. In the Regiment it was played when a unit went on active service or as a farewell to an officer leaving for the last time. It was played at his station or on the mole at Lagos; sometimes in both places. In most cases there was a feeling of regret at leaving the country and the African soldiers. The following, contributed by an officer, gives some impression of this: 'The last evening. A look round the garden of which I had been so proud; farewell to dear old Musa my head garden boy, followed by the final misery of the bath and change in the now desolate bungalow. Dinner out—with whom I do not remember. The last drive through the *Sabon Gari* and over the long, rattling bridge to the station with its smell of hot dust and the bustle and excitement always caused by the departure of the "Ocean Mail". And this was to be one of the nights when eight or nine buglers in full dress were lined up at the far end of the platform. Final drinks with the party who had come to see me off and futile attempts at conversation: more farewells to my orderly and a row of dejected servants as the whistle blew. Then, as the long, dusty train began to move very slowly, the bugles sounded. I stood at the window while all the figures on the platform became blurred in the dim light and, as the last sad notes of the Hausa Farewell rang out my compartment passed the buglers. Almost mesmerized, I remained staring out of the window long after the station lights had disappeared and the train, gathering speed, had plunged into the dark bush. There are some memories, grave or gay, which remain for ever fresh. To me, after a quarter of a century, this is one.'

GOLD COAST

6. *An Unusual Club:* An officer joining the Gold Coast Regiment in 1935 noticed that some of the old hands wore an attractive blue tie on which a red raspberry was embroidered. He was informed that the tie, specially made to order by a London firm, showed the wearer to be a member of an exclusive fraternity known as the 'Raspberry Club'. To qualify for membership a candidate had to produce a letter of censure from Regimental Headquarters.

7. *Regimental March:* 'I'm 95'.

8. *Farewell:* Officers leaving were given the Hausa Farewell.

9. *Ordeal:* Newly joined officers were required to conduct the Band playing their own regimental march on their first guest night.

SIERRA LEONE

10. *March Past:* The Battalion March during the twenties was 'South Carolina's a Sultry Clime'. At this period there was no band only a small corps of drums and fifes.

11. *Piety and Patriotism:* Practically all the training of recruits was in the hands of the African R.S.M., who was also responsible for teaching them the Lord's Prayer and the National Anthem. An officer who served in the Battalion during the twenties writes: 'On Tattoo Staff Parade all the troops assembled on the square and after the roll was called would recite the Lord's Prayer and sing 'God Save the King'. As the R.S.M. was a Moslem and the instructors Moslem or pagan (as probably were most of the troops) the resulting gabble and cacophony may be imagined. I don't know when this custom started nor when it was stopped.'

12. *Living in the Bush:* Living in the bush stations, before the move to Freetown on the disbandment of the West African Regiment, appears to have been very rough. Snakes occasionally intruded on the meditations of the occupant of a hard seat in the totally inadequate convenience outside each quarter. We are assured, however, that 'life was extremely enjoyable nevertheless'.

Fresh food was scarce. This was remedied to some extent as explained by the abovementioned officer. 'In the dry season a "fishing man" (a soldier with a rifle) would be sent daily to the river to shoot fish. He used old Mark VI S.A.A. of which we had a lot to spare. He would stun the fish by shooting into a shoal of Nile perch in the river, upon which his small son would jump in and sling the concussed fish ashore before they could recover. In the wet season the river was too dirty and the fish too muddy to eat. There was also a "hunting man" who would go out and shoot guinea fowl and bush fowl when they settled down to roost for the night. This "*shikari*" used a 12-bore gun.'

APPENDIX II

Method used for Advancing through Thick Tropical Forest

A NEW development took place in the dense tropical forests of Southern Nigeria during the 'twenties. The tribesmen began to cut a path or paths by which they could escape quickly after firing at an advanced guard. (See also Part 1, Chapter 3, (C).) The method employed was for a section of men to move on each flank and roughly in line with the point of the advanced guard moving along a bush path. These flankers had to cut their way through the virgin bush and each rifleman was partnered by a comrade who, with his matchet, hacked a way through the dense vegetation. So thick was the bush that, even at a range of a few feet or yards, the pairs could not see each other. Contact was maintained by short quiet signals—made by the mouth—from pair to pair. In this way they gauged the proximity and position of the next pair and remained in touch with the point of the advanced guard.

The formation was something like the head of a cow. The flanking pairs constituted the 'horns' and were calculated to cut off the retreat of any enemy who tried to get away down his escape path after firing into the head of the column. A rough sketch illustrates the layout:

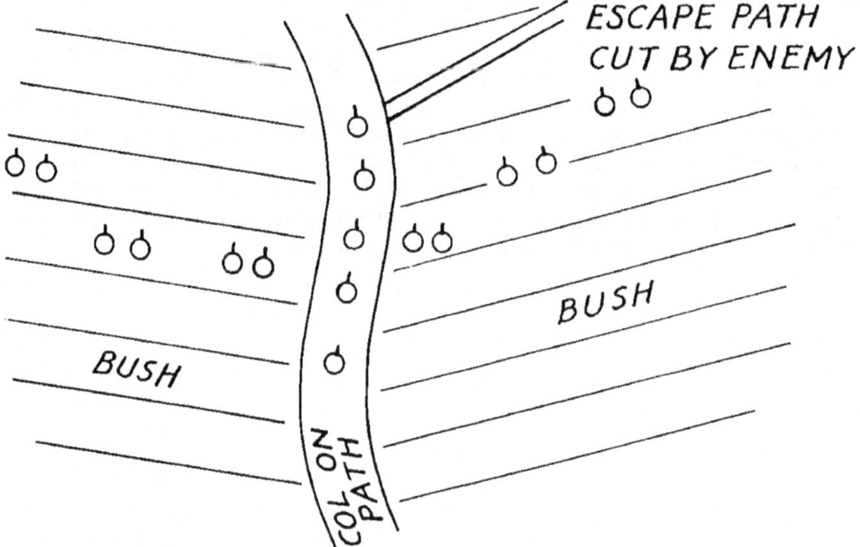

In the main body of the column the carriers were interspersed with the troops. On being fired on from a flank the 'drill' was still to turn outwards towards the bush and blaze off into it with every available weapon. This was known as 'burning powder' and there was very little else one could do to counter a hidden enemy in such conditions.

Notes. (i) This method of browning the bush was frowned on in some quarters as being a waste of ammunition and detrimental to fire discipline. But it is difficult to suggest a workable alternative.

(ii) Modifications of this method were used in more open country. In the northern orchard bush the elastic square was the usual formation employed.

APPENDIX III

The Aba Riots or the Woman's War, 1929

(i) *The Incident at Opobo*

ON the morning of 15th December the District Officer at Opobo held a *palaver* with the leaders of a large crowd of women outside his office. He endeavoured to explain to them that the Government had no intention of levying a tax on women. The leaders asked for this statement to be put in writing, which he did. They then asked for five typed copies, and so on, making frivolous demands apparently to gain time for more contingents to arrive.

As time went on the mob increased, grew more excited and pressed slowly forward. The women, of all ages, were wearing fronds of palm leaves—emblem of solidarity and warlike intent—were stripped to the waist and wearing only old loincloths. Many had their faces daubed with red or white clay, also a sign of war. They were armed with stout sticks, heavy pestles used for pounding corn and, in some cases, with matchets. At times they chanted an Ibo war song: 'What is the smell? Death is the smell!' They also danced and waved their weapons. All this took place while the *palaver* dragged on. At last, becoming more and more excited, the mob reached a state of frenzy; its numbers continued to increase, and canoe-loads of women were awaiting events on the river behind the D.O.'s office and Government buildings.

Lieutenant Hill with a platoon of the 3rd Battalion had arrived early that morning after an all-night journey. During the *palaver* the troops were drawn up in front of the D.O.'s office, facing the mob. The officer was with the right half platoon; an African N.C.O. was in charge of the left half.

Finally, the mob began to surge forward. So great was the noise that Hill had to signal with his revolver to the D.O. for permission to open fire. He then ordered the right half to fire a volley. The mob still moved on and some men and women armed with matchets tried to rush the post office. A second volley was fired. In the meantime, the left half fired two volleys, the second when the mob was only six or seven yards from them. Fire discipline was good—there was no more firing.

After the second volleys the mob broke and scattered, leaving 21 dead and 19 wounded. The fleet of canoes lying out in the river opposite the factories began to disperse and about another hundred coming down the river turned back and paddled hastily away.

(ii) *Report of a Commission of Inquiry appointed to inquire into certain incidents at Opobo, Abak and Utu-Etim-Ekpo*

As regards the incident at Opobo, the Commission reported as follows:

(*a*) That the firing at the time it took place was absolutely necessary in order to protect life and property.

(*b*) That it was done with all reasonable caution.

(*c*) That it produced no further injury than was absolutely necessary for the prevention of felonous outrage.

We have no doubt that had the troops been overpowered, the Government offices would have been destroyed and the factories looted. The latter held large stocks of gin and other intoxicants and had the savage passions of the mob become further inflamed by alcohol, it need hardly be said that the lives of the Europeans on the station, which included three ladies, would have been in the greatest danger. Indeed it is difficult to see how they could have escaped destruction.

The Commission reported in similar terms on the firing carried out by another platoon of the 3rd Battalion in practically the same circumstances at Abak and Utu-Etim-Expo on the same day.

APPENDIX IV

Army Rifle Association Decentralized Matches won by the R.W.A.F.F. between the Wars

THE AFRICAN CUP

Year	*Winners*
1923	1st Bn. the Nigeria Regiment
1924	2nd Bn. the Nigeria Regiment
1926	1st Bn. the Nigeria Regiment
1927	4th Bn. the Nigeria Regiment
1930	2nd Bn. the Nigeria Regiment
1931	3rd Bn. the Nigeria Regiment
1932	2nd Bn. the Nigeria Regiment
1933	2nd Bn. the Nigeria Regiment
1934	3rd Bn. the Nigeria Regiment
1935	4th Bn. the Nigeria Regiment
1936	4th Bn. the Nigeria Regiment
1937	The Gambia Company

(Match suspended until after the war)

THE AFRICAN MACHINE-GUN MATCH

1931	2nd Bn. the Nigeria Regiment
1935	Sierra Leone Battalion
1936	4th Bn. the Nigeria Regiment
1937	1st Bn. the Gold Coast Regiment

(This match no longer in existence)

APPENDIX V

Hon. Captain Chari Maigumeri, M.M.

A BERI-BERI from the Maiduguri District, Chari Maigumeri joined the *Kaiserlichen Shutztruppe fur Kamerun* in 1913. He fought against us in the Cameroons Campaign, where he won the Iron Cross for gallantry. Captured by us at the battle of Garua in 1915, he enlisted in the W.A.F.F. early in 1917 and served in East Africa during the latter part of the campaign. He was promoted sergeant in 1920, Company Sergeant-Major in 1924, and Regimental Sergeant-Major in 1928. All his service was spent in the 3rd Battalion the Nigeria Regiment.

He was one of a representative detachment sent to London for the Jubilee of H.M. King George V and for the Coronation of H.M. King George VI in 1937. He served throughout the campaign in East Africa, 1940–1, being awarded the Military Medal for conspicuous gallantry, particularly at the crossing of the River Omo. He accompanied the 3rd Battalion to Burma and was mentioned in despatches for his action during a night attack by the Japanese. In the Birthday Honours of 1944, Chari was awarded the British Empire Medal for his long, loyal service to the Crown.

After the war he came to London for the Victory Parade and again in 1952 when he represented the Regiment at the funeral of H.M. King George VI. In 1953 he came to London once more as one of a detachment sent home for the Queen's Coronation. The same year he retired after 36 years' service in the Regiment, 24 of which were spent as Regimental Sergeant-Major of the 3rd Battalion. By the order of H.M. the Queen he was made an honorary captain to mark the conclusion of his long and distinguished military career. The officers of the Regiment presented him with a sword.

He was a first-class drill instructor and would, on suitable occasions, give a demonstration of German arms drill with the appropriate words of command. He was a great trainer of tug-of-war teams, and the final of this event at the annual Regimental Sports during the thirties was usually between the 3rd Battalion and the mighty men of the Light Battery—who were, more often than not, the losers. In spite of the fact that the Battalion's successes were due to long and arduous training for each event, it was firmly believed in certain quarters that they possessed a very strong *juju*.

Captain Chari has settled down near Kaduna and, as was to be expected, has not entirely severed his connection with the Regiment. He has on several occasions rendered assistance in recruiting drives. In 1958, he was selected to represent the Regiment at the unveiling of the Rangoon War Memorial, which commemorates all those men of the land forces who fell in Burma and have no known grave. He laid wreaths not only for Nigeria but also on behalf of Sierra Leone and Gambia. He was, indeed, a worthy representative of them all.

APPENDIX VI

Organization and Establishment of a Battalion and Battery, R.W.A.F.F., 1938

BATTALION

Headquarters.
Headquarter Company:
Intercommunication Pl. (Runners)
Mortar Pl. four 3 in. Mortars*
A.A. Pl. four L.M.G.s
Administrative Pl.

Four rifle companies each:
Headquarters,
Four pls. each of three sections.
(each pl. had two L.M.G.s)
Each rifle company had two A./Tk. rifles, 16 discharger cups and 96 grenades.

Total Strength: 80 Europeans, 591 African troops and 219 gun-carriers.†

LIGHT BATTERY

Headquarters. Two A.A. L.M.G.s and two A./Tk. rifles.
Two sections, each two 3.7 in. howitzers, carried as head loads.

Total Strength: four officers, five B.N.C.O.s, 81 gunners, 251 gun carriers.†

NOTES:

* Later increased to six mortars.

† These gun-carriers were trained men and formed an integral part of units and teams of the various weapons.

APPENDIX VII

Distribution of Troops in West Africa: July 1941
(With details of R.W.A.F.F. Units)

NIGERIA

3 (W.A.) Bde.	*4 (W.A.) Bde.*	
7 N.R.	5 N.R.	8 N.R. (Training Bn.)
9 N.R.	6 N.R.	13 N.R. (Coast Defence Bn. for Lagos forming)
12 N.R.	10 N.R.	

Coast Defences, Lagos: Two 6 in. and other smaller guns.

GOLD COAST

5 (W.A.) Bde.		
5 G.C.R.[1]	6 G.C.R.	(Training Bn.)
7 G.C.R.	9 G.C.R.	(Coast Defence Bn. for Takoradi forming)
8 G.C.R.		

Takoradi Fortress: One C.D. and A.A. Bty.; one Tp. Lt. A.A.

SIERRA LEONE

6 (W.A.) Bde.		
4 N.R.		
1 S.L.R.	3 S.L.R.	(Coast Defence Bn. for Freetown forming)
2 S.L.R.		

Freetown Fortress: Two C.D. Btys.; three Heavy A.A. Btys.; Lt. A.A. Bty, less one tp. 11 N.R. (Coast Defence Bn.)

GAMBIA

4 G.C.R.	3 G.R.	(Coast Defence Bn. forming)
1 G.R.		

Coast Defences: One C.D. Bty.

NOTES: Each brigade had one Lt. Bty., a Fd. Coy., a Gp., W.A.A.S.C., a Fd. Amb., one Res. M.T. Coy. earmarked for each. An Auxiliary Gp. (carriers) was forming for each Bde. Gp.

[1] This was originally the Gold Coast Territorial Battalion

APPENDIX VIII

Dispositions in West Africa, October–November 1942

(Showing R.W.A.F.F. Units in Detail)

NIGERIA

3 (W.A.) Bde.	*4 (W.A.) Bde.*	*Area Units*
7 N.R.	5 N.R.	8 N.R.
9 N.R.	6 N.R.	13 N.R.
12 N.R.	10 N.R.	

One Belgian Bde. Gp.

GOLD COAST

5 (W.A.) Bde.	*Area Units*
5 G.C.R.	14 N.R.
7 G.C.R.	6 G.C.R.
8 G.C.R.	9 G.C.R.

SIERRA LEONE

1 (W.A.) Bde.	*6 (W.A.) Bde.*	*Area Units*
1 N.R.	4 N.R.	11 N.R.
2 N.R.	1 S.L.R.	3 S.L.R.
3 N.R.	2 S.L.R.	

GAMBIA

2 (W.A.) Bde.	*7 (W.A.) Bde.*
1 G.C.R.	4 G.C.R.
2 G.C.R.	1 G.R.
3 G.C.R.	2 G.R.

APPENDIX IX

Order of Battle of 81 and 82 (W.A.) Divs. 1943 and List of R.W.A.F.F. Units remaining in West Africa, 1943–5

81 (W.A.) Div.

3 (W.A.) Bde.	*5 (W.A.) Bde.*	*6 (W.A.) Bde.*
H.Q. and Def. Pl.	H.Q. and Def. Pl.	H.Q. and Def. Pl.
6 N.R.	5 G.C.R.	4 N.R.
7 N.R.	7 G.C.R.	1 S.L.R.
12 N.R.	8 G.C.R.	1 G.R.

82 (W.A.) Div.

1 (W.A.) Bde.	*2 (W.A.) Bde.*	*4 (W.A.) Bde.*
H.Q. and Def. Pl.	H.Q. and Def. Pl.	H.Q. and Def. Pl.
1 N.R.	1 G.C.R.	5 N.R.
2 N.R.	2 G.C.R.	9 N.R.
3 N.R.	3 G.C.R.	10 N.R.

Divisional Troops, each Division

H.Q. and Div. Sigs.
H.Q. Lt. Arty. R.
One L.A.A./A. Tk. R.
Recce R.
Provost Coy.
Ancillary units

Each Bde. Gp. had:

Sigs. and Survey Secs.
One Lt. Bty.
One Fd. Coy.
One Bde. Gp. Coy. W.A.A.S.C.
One Auxiliary Gp. (carriers)
One Fd. Amb. and Fd. Hyg. Sec.
One Inf. Bde. Workshop and an L.A.D.
One Pro. Sec.

R.W.A.F.F. UNITS REMAINING IN WEST AFRICA

Nigeria	*Gold Coast*	*Sierra Leone*	*Gambia*
8 N.R.	4 G.C.R.	2 S.L.R.	2 G.R.
11 N.R.	6 G.C.R.	3 S.L.R.	
13 N.R.	9 G.C.R.		
14 N.R.			

There was also a number of Garrison Companies.

APPENDIX X

Congratulatory Orders and Message to 81 and 82 (W.A.) Divs.

(i) *Message from Supreme Commander S.E.A.C. to 81 (W.A.) Div. dated 26th July 1945*

'Now that the operations in which you have been engaged in Burma have been so successfully completed and your return to your home country is imminent, I wish to acquaint all officers, N.C.O.s and men of 81st West African Division of my sincere appreciation and gratitude for their outstanding services in fighting for the liberation of Burma. From the commencement of your active operations in the Arakan in December 1943, you have shown magnificent fighting qualities, both in your advance down the Kaladan Valley and in your determined battle through the jungles of the Kaladan in October 1944. You have withstood and overcome the rigours of the 1944 monsoon in the upper Sangu Valley day by day and established a reputation for your division which will always be remembered in the annals of the Burma campaign. I wish you all the best of luck.'

(ii) *XV (Indian) Corps Special Order of the Day to 81 (W.A.) Div., 14th February 1945*

'You have just completed an arduous campaign in some of the most difficult mountain jungle and chaung intersected country in the whole S.E.A.C. theatre.

'You have built up a fine reputation as a Division since your entry into the theatre of operations, which began in December 1943 and ended with the capture of Myohaung, the ancient capital of Arakan, in January 1945.

'You have fought and defeated parts of 54 and 55 Japanese Divs. from Kaladan to the Kalapanzin. You have shown a fine fighting spirit. Aggressive and relentless in attack, you have learned to defend skilfully, to hold your fire and your ground when yourselves attacked. I am very proud of you all and have specially asked that you may be retained under my command.

'You had the unenviable role of drawing off from the main front the maximum possible of enemy forces in order to so weaken his Mayu and Akyab garrisons that the latter place could be assaulted from the sea.

'So successful were you that the Jap Command had to thin out his Akyab garrison piecemeal to stop your advance down the Kaladan, an advance which threatened his main lines of communication via Mynba for all his forces in Arakan.

'He found himself finally with only one battalion to defend Akyab, and concluding that this had little chance of achieving its object he pulled it out as we landed, again in order to try to stem your advance. The fate of Akyab was sealed when you won the battle of Tinma and outflanked his Kyauktaw positions. I thank you for this fine contribution to the overall plan and congratulate you on your fine spirit and your successes.

'You will, I hope, have a considerable period of rest and refitting ahead of you. I know I can rely on you to get the best out of this period and that you will maintain that high standard of discipline and correct relationship to the civil population for which you have also won a name. I hope most of you will get and enjoy some leave, and I wish you a pleasant time and all good luck for the future.

(*Signed*) A. F. P. Christison,
Leutenant-General Commanding'.

(iii) *XV (Indian) Corps Special Order of the Day to 82 (W.A.) Div., 26th April 1945*

'On your passing from my command I wish to congratulate all ranks on the splendid performance they have put up since they came into the Arakan in November.

'The part played by the 82nd (W.A.) Division in the Arakan Campaign as a whole has been not only a major one but a decisive one. You have advanced over 300 miles, and marched every mile of it, through what is probably the most difficult country in the whole of Burma. You have fought and defeated parts of two Japanese divisions and your part in the decisive battle of Kangaw, directly and indirectly, was a major factor in it being won.

'One of the hardest tasks that can be given a formation is to contain the enemy forces and prevent them disengaging and fighting elsewhere. This task you have performed so satisfactorily that out of the whole of 54 Division only one battalion was able to be withdrawn to oppose Fourteenth Army during the vital time that you were ordered to contain these forces, and that battalion had been reduced to only 150 strong.

'I congratulate you all on this splendid achievement which has not been won without hard fighting and considerable sacrifice. I want all ranks to know that it has had a decisive effect not only on the Arakan Campaign but on the Battle of Burma as a whole. You have, to your credit, the infliction of over 4,000 casualties on the Japanese, you have captured 30 prisoners, a number of guns and a large quantity of enemy stores, ammunition and equipment.

'I deplore the loss of your comrades in attaining your object, but they have not made their sacrifice in vain.

'I have watched you under your gallant and experienced Commander, Major-General H. Stockwell, D.S.O., becoming steadily more and more skilled and battle worthy. You have gained great experience and all this will stand you in good stead in any future operations you may be called upon to undertake.

'I do not know what the future holds, but if there is any chance of having your Division under my command again I shall be very proud, and all ranks of 15 Indian Corps join me in wishing you the very best of luck and will give you a rousing welcome should you return to us again.

(*Signed*) A. F. P. Christison,
Lieutenant-General Commanding.'

APPENDIX XI

Casualties in XV Corps during the Campaign of 1944–5

81 (W.A.) Bde.	*Killed*	*Wounded*	*Missing*	*Totals*
Officers	3	9	1	13
British O.R.s	5	20	—	25
African O.R.s	66	314	20	400
				438

82 (W.A.) Div.	*Killed*	*Wounded*	*Missing*	*Totals*
Officers	29	94	2	125
British O.R.s	19	61	1	81
African O.R.s	428	1,417	34	1,879
				2,085

Total Casualties other Formations XV Corps

25 (Indian) Div.	1,374
26 (Indian) Div.	606

Grand Total in XV Corps (including Corps Troops and 22 (E.A.) Bde.)=5,093

Japanese Casualties

Killed	3,950
Wounded	5,274
P.O.W.	129
Total	9,353

NOTE: Enemy killed are actual counted bodies. Wounded assessed at one and a half times number of counted dead. But it must be assumed that there were many dead neither seen nor counted.

APPENDIX XII

Order of Battle of the West African Divisions as Organized in Burma 1943–5

(Full titles of A.C.F. Units given)

81st Division

5th (W.A.) Infantry Brigade
  5, 7, 8 G.C.R.
  3 Auxiliary Group

6th (W.A.) Infantry Brigade
  4 N.R., 1 S.L.R., 1 G.R.
  4 Auxiliary Group

Divisional Troops

81 Reconnaissance Regt.
101 Light Regt. 41 Mortar Regt.
21 Anti-Tank Regt.
3, 5, 6 Field Companies
8 Field Park Company
10 Divisional Survey Section
81 Divisional Signals
Ordnance Field Park
5, 6 Field Ambulances
83 Field Hygiene Section
1001, 1002, 1006 Mobile Workshops
1010, 1011, 1012, 1013, 1014, 1015 Light Aid Detachments
816, 817 Divisional Transport Companies, 1780, 1781, 1782 Composite Platoons
1, 4, 8 Field Butchery Sections
Divisional Pack Bullock Company
1 Auxiliary Group
Divisional Postal Unit
Divisional Salvage Unit
108 Field Cash Office
6 Field Security Section
275 Divisional Provost Company
Divisional Base Forwarding Party

82nd Division

1st (W.A.) Infantry Brigade
  1, 2, 3 N.R.
  5 Auxiliary Group

2nd (W.A.) Infantry Brigade
  1, 2, 3 G.C.R.
  6 Auxiliary Group

4th (W.A.) Infantry Brigade
  5, 9, 10 N.R.
  2 Auxiliary Group

Divisional Troops

82 Reconnaissance Regt.
102 Light Regt. 42 Mortar Regt.
22 Anti-Tank Regt.
1, 2, 4 Field Companies
9 Field Park Company
11 Divisional Survey Section
82 Divisional Signals
Ordnance Field Park
1, 2, 4 Field Ambulance
82 Field Hygiene Section
1003, 1004, 1005 Mobile Workshops
1016, 1017, 1018, 1091, 1020, 1021, 1022 Light Aid Detachments
825, 836 Divisional Transport Companies, 1784, 1785, 1786, 1787, Composite Platoons
26, 29 Field Butchery Sections
7 Auxiliary Group
Divisional Postal Unit
119 Field Cash Office
81 Field Security Section
276 Divisional Provost Company

NOTE: 3rd (W.A.) Infantry Brigade, 6, 7, 12 N.R., detached to Special Force.

APPENDIX XIII

Primitive Soldiers of the Auxiliary Groups: An Anecdote

It must be remembered that Brigade Auxiliary Groups had to be in front and in isolated positions in jungle where there is no 'line'. Their platoons carried forward and got shot up from time to time. They 'went for bush' quite shamelessly and indeed at times cheerfully.

'The Munshis in 2 Aux. Gp. in support of my Brigade spoke no English and none of us in the Brigade spoke Munshi even haltingly. Communication was by (*a*) the odd Munshi who spoke a little Hausa; (*b*) one or two normal African other ranks who spoke a little Munshi. So they were quite clueless as to what was going on!

'On one occasion Commander 4 Bde. was sitting on his pack at the end of a day's march whilst all around him, in the last rays of the sun, harbour drill was being carried out. Bde. H.Q. office area, admin. area, signals area and perimeter defence positions had just been marked out and each man was clearing the necessary minimum growth and now digging his slit or cover for his wireless set as the case might be. Parties were drawing water, cooking the evening meal, cleaning weapons and so forth. Long experience had taught the Brigadier that this was just the moment when it was most tactful for him to do simply NOTHING and this was best done in a congested area by just sitting down and relaxing.

'Suddenly, an agitated African rushed up to him wearing only his cotton pants which he whipped down as he faced about on arrival. So the Brigadier found himself looking up at an African posterior at a few inches range above his face whilst its owner poured a torrent of tears and words over his shoulder and pointed to two weals which at that range could all too clearly be seen. As the Brigadier scrambled to his feet an Aux. Gp. officer arrived, almost equally agitated, and it transpired that this Munshi had just been sentenced, and received, two strokes for consuming a whole 7 lb. tin of bully beef entirely by himself, contrary to orders and thereby causing various comrades to go without their share of it for their evening meal.

'A supply drop had been taken that morning before the day's march, to the annoyance of all; a veritable last straw on our backs, moreover an indivisible one and one which it was almost impossible to isolate without rendering our huge loads lopsided. This man had been detailed to carry this tin for the day on behalf of his section, but now at sunset when the tins were being called in for hotting up and distribution he had eaten it.

'The Brigade Commander sent for the African sergeant-major, who, with many gestures and repetition of words of one syllable, finally made clear to the Munshi what it was all about. So smiles succeeded tears and the party broke up with the Brigadier patting the man's wooly head in gestures of eternal friendship. It was indeed a case of all's well that ends well.

'A few explosive sentences over the admin. signals net that night ensured that no more of these 7 lb. tins were ever dropped on the Brigade. The Munshi, for the rest of the campaign, let out a yell of friendship whenever his Brigadier passed within miles of him on the march. A chastened Aux. Gp. officer learned to develop his powers of explanation and curb the strong arm of the punishment traditional in the R.W.A.F.F., but officially frowned upon during the war.'

APPENDIX XIV

The 81st (W.A.) Reconnaissance Regiment on the Main Arakan Front, 1944

(See Map. No. 38)

THE two West African Reconnaissance Regiments, formed from R.W.A.F.F. cadres mainly in Nigeria and the Gold Coast, both served in Burma, the 81st from the end of 1943 until January 1945, and the 82nd in the campaign of 1944–5 The 81st, detached from the Division, was on the Arakan main front until the opening of the third campaign in December 1944, for which they rejoined their own formation. During January, February and March 1944 the Regiment was engaged in a series of amphibious raids along the coast in addition to normal patrolling. In April and May 1944 part of the Regiment joined their Division temporarily in the hills east of the Kalapanzin as related in Chapter 10, Section (viii). The 82nd served throughout almost entirely with their own Division as described in Chapter 6. Both Regiments earned an enviable reputation for efficiency and fighting qualities.

The 81st arrived at Chiringa from India on 26th December 1943 and came under command of XV Corps. On 9th January 'B' Sqn. took over the mobile defence of the Teknaf Peninsula. Next day 'A' Sqn. came under command of an Indian Division to cover their move forward from Ramu to Bawli Bazar, and later, was attached to 9 (Indian) Bde. of 5 (Indian) Div. in the Razabil area to provide foot and mounted patrols in front of the infantry.

On 19th January the Regiment, now under command of 5 (Indian) Div., began to concentrate at Maungdaw. 'A' and 'B' Sqns. rejoined on 22nd January, but 'C' Sqn. from XV Corps reserve did not arrive until the 31st. The role allotted to the Regiment was the domination of the paddy on the south or coastal flank of the Division, which was to attack in the Tunnels area. The Commanding Officer (Lieutenant-Colonel R. N. Cartwright) decided that the area could only be dominated by active offensive patrols from bases forward of Maungdaw and by carrying out raids on enemy-occupied localities down the coast. Troop bases were established in two villages about seven miles south of Maungdaw. Patrols operating from these bases went as far south as Lambaguna and also penetrated into the Mayu Hills south and east of Maungdaw. A variety of information was obtained as to Japanese movements, air-strike and artillery targets were pin-pointed, and casualties were inflicted on the enemy.

Towards the end of the month the Regiment was warned that they must be prepared to prevent the Japanese moving guns to the area near the entrance to the Naf River to harass naval patrols or shipping moving up to Maungdaw. This led to a number of raids on the Alethangyaw area from a temporary base at Nahkaungdo, an island off the coast west of Hinthaya. The first raid failed, as half the boats carrying the raiding party were sunk in the surf. A second raid was carried out on 30th January at Alethangyaw and Dodan. At the first-named place 'A' Sqn. routed the garrison and secured a quantity of booty which, among other things, led to the first identification of 144 R. in Arakan. Dodan was successfully attacked by 'B' Sqn., who then occupied Nahkaungdo. About this time documents were captured which foretold the impending enemy counter-offensive on XV Corps.

XV Corps offensive was halted by the enemy counter-offensive and on 4th February 'C' Sqn., was ordered to the Kalapanzin Valley to locate Japanese infiltration north of Taung Bazar. Next day 'A' Sqn. was sent north to assist in the defence of Headquarters, 5 (Indian) Div. on whose area the enemy were advancing. 'B' Sqn. had to be withdrawn from Nahkaungdo to form with the 'H.Q.' Sqn. the only combatant force for the defence of Maungdaw.

However, by 10th February 'A' and 'B' Sqns. had rejoined and the original patrol bases had been re-established. 'A' Sqn. reported 30 enemy with a battalion gun five miles to the south of one of the bases. This party was attacked by 'B' Sqn. coming in from the sea through Nahkaungdo. One Japanese officer and six other ranks were killed and a further number wounded. The remnants, withdrawing eastward into the hills, were located by 'A' Sqn. and successfully dive-bombed. On the 16th 'A' Sqn. made a raid on a small post at Kanyindan, near Nahkaungdo, accounting for six Japanese and taking two prisoners. Three days later a small patrol from the same squadron raided Indin, killing six Japanese and obtaining some identifications. On 29th February, 'B' Sqn. reoccupied Nahkaungdo and patrolled extensively east and south. In the meantime, 'C' Sqn. had rejoined after valuable patrolling in the Goppe–Taung area.

The Japanese counter-offensive having failed, XV Corps attacks on the Mayu fortress recommenced early in March, and the Regiment's activities were intensified south of Maungdaw. On 4th March a Japanese patrol was annihilated a few miles south of one of the patrol bases. On the following night a troop of 'C' Sqn., *en route* to occupy Ywathitke, two miles north of Hinthaya, to control the entrance to the Naf River, successfully ambushed an enemy force, killing 12 and wounding others. These operations were the beginning of the gradual occupation of the whole paddy strip between the sea and the hills for a distance of 20 miles south of Maungdaw which was designed to prevent Japanese infiltration from the south. This was not accomplished without some minor actions. For instance on 11th–13th March 'A' and 'B' Sqns. attacked Dodan and a garrison just to the east of it. The latter, consisting of over 30 Japanese, resisted until all were killed with the exception of two or three who escaped and two taken prisoner; a 75 mm. gun was also captured. On 18th March a Commando Brigade took over from the Regiment, which was withdrawn to Maungdaw. During the period under command of 5 (Indian) Div. the regiment had carried out upwards of 150 patrols and amphibious raids in addition to routine mounted patrols between Maungdaw and Razabil.

The Regiment came under command of 26 (Indian) Div. on 28th March and moved to Taung Bazar, where their task was to watch the left flank of the Division. During the period with this formation the Regiment carried out over 100 separate patrols, many of these being of a week's duration or more. In addition a number of mounted patrols were made. On 23rd April two assault troops from each squadron, three composite troops and a small regimental headquarters assembled at Taung Bazar preparatory to moving down the Saingdim Chaung to join 81 (W.A.) Div. as mentioned above.

APPENDIX XV

Chindits: Problems of Intercommunication

CO-ORDINATION in the field and with base was naturally supremely important. The real difficulty lay in there being no means of communication when on the move and no means whereby one column could know when another was moving or going to stop. Even pre-arranged times of stopping to open up sets were often upset by any one of many unforeseen circumstances, of which enemy action was only one. To mitigate this every column tried at all costs to halt and open up at midday, even if it had nothing to say and was trying hard to get on, because someone else might have something important for it.

The set for intercommunication between the columns was the current No. 22 Army Set, capable of much rough handling and quite handy. However, it lacked power to overcome bad siting and a column, unavoidably in a narrow valley bed, might well be out of contact with some one the other side of the ridge. In the twilight hour all columns tried their utmost and the result was often congestion in the air. After dark, especially in the monsoon, atmospheric conditions grew rapidly worse.

For use at base was a large R.A.F. set believed to have originally been devised for use between armoured cars and aircraft in Iraq. It had power to overcome most siting problems, but not the conditions imposed by nightfall. It required four very big mules to carry it and its batteries. At base there were 'guard sets' which swept the air for messages from any columns or brigade headquarters wishing to get rid of a message and move on, having failed to make contact with the intended recipient. The guard set then watched for the intended recipient coming on the air later on and relayed the originator's message. Messages from a headquarters to more than one recipient might well take two days before the last recipient's answer came in.

A column commander would stand over a wireless set, gnawing a strand of his beard in an agony of indecision, whilst an operator tried to get a message through. To delay his march another few minutes might endanger plans, on the other hand to fail to pass information was often equally hazardous to the column or to others.

APPENDIX XVI

Scale of Clothing and Necessaries for Rank and File (1920–39)

	Troops	*Gun Carriers*
Badges, W.A.F.F., Fez	1	—
Blankets, G.S.	2	2
Blouses, K.D.	3	2
Brasses, button	1	—
Brushes, brass	1	—
Brushes, scrubbing	1	1
Brushes, polishing	1	—
Buttons, W.A.F.F., sets of six	2	—
Capes, Zouave	1	1
Caps, Kilmarnock	1	2
Chaplis	1	1
Cover, cap Kilmarnock	2	2
Fez, red	1	—
Jackets, Zouave	1	—
Jerseys, brown	1	1
Kamarband	1	—
Putties	2	2
Shirts, drab	2	1
Socks, pairs (held in Mob. stores)	1	1
Soap, Properts	1	1
Tassels, black	1	—
Titles, shoulder, pairs	2	2
Knickers, K.D.	3	3
Number plate and chain	1	1

NOTE. In 1939 Caps Kilmarnock and chaplis were being withdrawn and slouch hats and boots were in process of issue.

APPENDIX XVII

Disturbances in the Gold Coast, 1948

THERE was an ex-serviceman's rally on 20th February at Accra arranged by the Ex-Servicemen's Union[1] who were closely linked with the organizers of the boycott of imported goods. This boycott was started at the end of January, but, after negotiations between the Government and other bodies, was to cease on 28th February.

By an apparent coincidence a march had been arranged by the Ex-Servicemen's Union on the afternoon of the same day. The route was agreed with the police, who appear to have assumed it would cause no trouble. In the event the marchers soon turned away from the agreed route and headed for Christiansborg Castle, the residence and office of the Governor. The march was led by a few ex-servicemen, but was composed mostly of riff-raff from Accra. The unarmed police were unable to stop or divert the procession, which was some 2,000 strong. In the meantime, a party of armed police had arrived by another route and were disposed to bar the way at the cross-roads some 900 yards from the Castle. The crowd refused to stop and continued to surge forward. The police were forced to fire. Five or six rounds were fired at about 1500 hours and soon afterwards the mob began to disperse mainly towards Accra.

Trouble in the shops and stores started well before midday and minor acts of violence took place. By 1500 hours real looting and violence was well under way and liquor stocks in the stores were broached. The police by this time were unable to exercise any real control and no troops had yet arrived.

According to the internal security scheme the 1st Battalion the Battery and the Engineeer Field Squadron were to be used in a mobile role, whilst the other units stationed at Accra were to be available for static tasks. On this occasion, however, the Governor had ordered the raising of the boycott and the march of the ex-servicemen to be regarded as normal occurrences and did not wish any military or police preparations to be visible. The District Commander, however, ordered one company of 1 G.C.R. to be at half an hour's notice from midday on the 28th February and placed the town out of bounds to British troops and families from 1300 hours. It was not until 1545 that he was asked on the telephone 'to turn out troops to help the police'.

The first platoon moved off at 1614 hours and the second at 1650 but were despatched to the Castle instead of the town. The District Commander who arrived at 1800 hours found the situation around the Castle had cleared and was then told there was 'serious trouble in the town'. He ordered 1 G.C.R. to move into the town to secure the General Post Office, bank and cable office and 'to send patrols to disperse the crowds and stop rioting and looting in close co-operation with the police'. A troop of the Battery was ordered to garrison the Castle and dispositions were made for the protection of the European residential area and to collect them from hotels in the town. By 1830–1900 all the available troops were in the town at the principal vital points and attempting to restore order. By 1930 there were still a number of 'vital points' to be secured and it was apparent that matters had got far beyond the powers of the police. In fact, the police barracks were seriously threatened by a large crowd until dispersed by a troop of the Battery.

About this time the District Commander[2] came to the conclusion that the use

[1] This body, with a reputed membership of 6,650, had no connection with the Gold Coast Legion, with a membership of 30,246 and in receipt of financial assistance from the Government.

[2] Brigadier G. B. S. Hindley, O.B.E.

of troops would not be confined to a short period. The troops would require rest and relief and he regarded it as certain that the disturbances would spread to other towns. The 2nd Battalion at Tamale was therefore ordered to move as quickly as possible to Accra dropping a company at Kumasi. Starting soon after first light on the 29th the leading company, closely followed by the rest, reached Accra on Sunday night. The distance is over 400 miles and the River Volta had to be crossed by a ferry; the vehicles were impressed, but the drivers were Northern Territories ex-soldiers.

Throughout the night 28th–29th February and the following day there were almost continuous clashes between troops and looters. It appeared that the whole population, including old men, mammies and pickins, was engaged in looting and burning. The local people were abetted by crowds from suburbs and villages outside.

During the night 28th–29th February the acting G.O.C.-in-Chief[1] decided that the Gold Coast forces were not strong enough to cope with the disturbances existing and likely to spread. He therefore ordered Nigeria to be prepared to send troops to the Gold Coast by sea and air. By 0400 on the 29th one Nigerian battalion was ready to move.

While the situation in Accra was being got under control disturbances broke out on 1st and 2nd March at Kumasi and again on 15th–16th March. On 1st March there were outbreaks at Nsawam, Korforidua, Akuse and elsewhere. There were signs of trouble at Takoradi and Secondee, but the timely arrival of Nigerian troops had a steadying effect.

Conditions did not return to anything like normal for another three weeks; and it was not thought desirable to reduce the number of static guards and patrols as well as the concentration of troops around Accra for some months.

[1] Major-General C. R. A. Swynnerton.

APPENDIX XVIII

The Return of the Flag of Sultan Attahiru Ahamadu to Sokoto

IN 1903 Sir Frederick Luguard launched a military expedition against Kano and Sokoto. Sultan Attahiru Ahamadu, the great-grandson of Shedu Dan Fodio who founded the Fulani Empire, collected a large army and opposed the British Forces outside the gates of Sokoto. He was defeated, but with a few faithful followers he made his way eastwards to Burmi in Bornu. Here he was attacked by another British Force and after a fierce and gallant resistance was killed.

Sultan Attahiru's Standard was found lying near his body. Later it came into the hands of the 1st Battalion the Queen's Own Nigeria Regiment, who have for nearly 60 years held it in safe custody and treated it with the respect it deserved both as the Standard of a valiant and worthy foe and, as it was thought, of the great Shehu Dan Fodio himself. Indeed, it was always known as 'Dan Fodio's Flag', though latterly there has been some doubt cast on this. However, it is significant that the present Sultan of Sokoto referred to it as such when it was returned to him.

In 1959, when Northern Nigeria was given Regional Self-Government and the Independence of Nigeria in October 1960 was fast approaching, it was suggested by Mr. H. A. S. Johnston, then Secretary to the Premier and later Deputy Governor of the Northern Region, that the return of this Standard to Sokoto would be a much appreciated and timely gesture and one symbolic of the new relationship between Britain and Nigeria. The then G.O.C., of the Nigerian Military Forces, Major-General K. G. Exham, readily agreed, and the return of the Standard to Sokoto in 1960 was set in train.

The day selected was the 6th November 1960, just over a month after Nigeria's Independence. The scene was the Durbar Ground at Sokoto, which is also the site where the battle was fought in 1903. Among those present to take part in or witness the ceremony were the Sultan of Sokoto; Sir Ahmadu Bello, Sardauna of Sokoto and Premier of the Northern Region; Major-General N. M. Foster, G.O.C. Royal Nigerian Army; and, Mr. Johnston, the Deputy Governor, whose last public appearance it was. On parade there was on one flank a Guard of the 1st Battalion the Queen's Own Nigeria Rebiment and on the other flank the Sultan's Bodyguard in their traditional dress. In the centre was the Standard framed and suitably inscribed.

After the Sultan had arrived and been appropriately received and saluted by each Guard, he advanced to the middle of the ground and was there presented with the Standard by Lieutenant-Colonel A. Dunlop, Commanding Officer of the 1st Battalion the Queen's Own Nigeria Regiment. In a short speech Colonel Dunlop traced the history of the Standard and concluded by saying:

'It is most appropriate that in this year of Independence, the Standard should now be returned to you, sir, in recognition of the very great friendship which, for many years now, has existed between Great Britain and Nigeria. Many of your peoples died as soldiers alongside ours in mutual defence of freedom from oppression in the World Wars. The days of strife which existed at the turn of the century are long forgotten and it is with the greatest respect and affection for your peoples, whom I personally have known in East Africa, Burma, and now in your own country, that I return to you, sir, the Standard of Sultan Attahiru Ahamadu. I am sure that you will honour it and treasure it as we have done, as a symbol of the great fighting qualities of your people.

The Sultan, in his speech thanking Colonel Dunlop, said: 'On behalf of all the Muslim Community in the Sudan, I hereby take over the Standard with respect and gratitude to Her Majesty's Government for this kind gesture.' He then presented to the 1st Battalion a sword and two spears from himself and the Council of Sokoto. Mr. Johnston then presented to Colonel Dunlop for the 1st Battalion a silver statuette of a Nigerian soldier of the period when the Standard was captured, to replace the Standard and in memory of the occasion and the generous spirit which has led to the return of the Standard to its original home. This statuette was generously subscribed to by the 'Friends of Sokoto', who were all British Administrative Officers who had at some time served in the Province.

Alhaji Sir Ahmadu Bello, Premier of the Northern Region, concluded the speeches by thanking the 'Friends of Sokoto' for their generosity. In the course of his speech he said: 'The exchange of this Standard and this statuette symbolizes all that has been achieved in half a century which began with war and has now ended in co-operation and friendship between ourselves and the United Kingdom.' And again: 'It is also a symbol of that characteristic British trait to turn enemy into friend.'

The ceremony ended with a march past by the Guard of the 1st Battalion followed by the Sultan's Bodyguard and contingents of horsemen from Sokoto. The rest of the day was spent in feasting and rejoicing.

In the many speeches made at this parade there were repeated references to this 'symbolic gesture'. To many of those present, and particularly the Army officers, the real significance of the event was that it marked, more than anything in the Independence Celebrations, the changed nature of the Nigerian Army. This ceremony was symbolic of the fact that the Army was no longer the agent of the United Kingdom and the Colonial Government. Henceforth it was Nigeria's own Army.

APPENDIX XIX

Operations in the Southern Cameroons, 1959–60

For many months terrorists, mainly of the Bamileke tribe from the French Cameroons, had been raiding villages in the British Trustee Territory of the Southern Cameroons. The problem facing the Government of this Territory was to prevent terrorists from crossing the border and lying up in the frontier area in between raids. Operations by the police eventually became inadequate and the situation had so deteriorated by October, 1959 that the Government of the Territory called for military aid from Nigeria.

Two companies of 1 Q.O.N.R. from Enugu were sent into the Territory ostensibly to carry out military training. One company was based on Bamenda in the north and the other at Kumba in the south of the Territory. The presence of these troops overawed the terrorists and both companies were withdrawn to Enugu during November. But the situation soon began to deteriorate again, added to which the French Cameroons were due to become independent on 1st January, when it was anticipated the Bamileke would cause trouble. The police therefore asked for the troops to be returned and so, during December, 1959, 1 Q.O.N.R. moved in and were based on Bamenda.

As a result of 1 Q.O.N.R. operating entirely in the north, the terrorists increased their activities in the south. To counter this 4 Q.O.N.R. was moved from Ibadan to Kumba in February, 1960. The move was carried out by sea from Lagos to Victoria, the troops being carried in ships of the Royal Nigerian Navy and their transport by coaster. During the following month 1 Q.O.N.R. was relieved in the Bamenda area by 5 Q.O.N.R. from Kaduna; the move was made by road and rail, Enugu being used as a staging post.

In these operations battalions were deployed in company groups, the main task of each company being to cover a large frontier area by active patrolling. In one instance a patrol of 5 Q.O.N.R. surprised a terrorist camp, capturing 30 terrorists and a strong box containing £10,000. It was subsequently ascertained that this camp was almost certainly the main headquarters of Singap Martin, who was one of the most important terrorists leaders.

During May, 4 Q.O.N.R. was relieved in the Kumba area by 3 Q.O.N.R. from Abeokuta, and in the following month 2 Q.O.N.R. took over from 5 Q.O.N.R. at Bamenda.

It had been decided that once Nigeria became independent military operations in Southern Cameroons would be a United Kingdom commitment. In August an advanced party of the 1st Battalion, The King's Own Border Regiment arrived by air. Their transport came by L.S.T. which was used to move the vehicles of 3 Q.O.N.R. back to Lagos.

The process of thinning out now commenced and 3 Q.O.N.R. returned to Abeokuta, their area in the south being taken over by one company of 2 Q.O.N.R. from Bamenda. On 22nd September, 1960 2 Q.O.N.R. was relieved by the 1st Battalion, The King's Own Border Regiment and so ended Nigeria's responsibility in the Southern Cameroons. The whole operation had lasted eleven months and five battalions of the R.W.A.F.F. had taken part.

APPENDIX XX

GLOSSARY

Allah shi dede rainka	May Allah prolong your life (Hausa)
banda	irregular troops employed by the Italians in East Africa
basha	a hut made of bamboo (Burma)
chaplis	a kind of sandal worn in Pakistan
chaung	a river or stream, tidal for some distance from the sea; often navigable by small craft for a considerable distance inland (Burma)
dacoits	armed bandits, India and Burma (Urdu)
ferrin gindi	a small antelope with white buttocks (Hausa)
gidan juju	house of magic (Hausa)
girigin kassa	land canoe=railway (Hausa)
jadu ghar	magic house (Urdu)
kwakwa	the West African oil palm, badge of R.W.A.F.F. (Hausa)
magajia	queen=the headwoman of a company (Hausa)
mahaut	elephant driver (Urdu)
paddy	flat rice fields (Burma)
panjis	obstacles made of bamboo stakes sharpened at one end, firmly fixed in the ground with points towards the enemy at an angle of 45 degrees (Burma)
punkah	a large swinging cloth on a frame hung from the ceiling and pulled by a rope (Urdu)
rega	a long robe worn by Hausas and other northern tribes in West Africa (Hausa)
sabon gari	new town built on outskirts of an old one (Hausa)
sitzkrieg	sit-down war—the phoney war (German)
taung	a hill feature (Burma)
yakin mata	women's war (Hausa)

ABBREVIATIONS

Div.	Division
Bde.	Brigade
Bde. Gp.	Brigade Group
Bn.	Battalion
Coy.	Company
Pl.	Platoon
Sqn.	Squadron
Tp.	Troop
Armd. Cs.	Armoured Cars
Med. Bty.	Medium Battery
C.D. Bty.	Coast Defence Battery
Fd. R.	Field Regiment
Fd. Bty.	Field Battery
Lt. R.	Light Regiment
Lt. Bty.	Light Battery
Mtn. R.	Mountain Regiment
Mtn. Bty.	Mountain Battery

A./Tk. R.	Anti-Tank Regiment
L.A.A.	Light Anti-aircraft
Fd. Bde.	Field Brigade } now obsolete
Med. Bde.	Medium Brigade } now obsolete
Fd. Pk. Coy.	Field Park Company
Fd. Coy.	Field Company
Aux. Gp.	Auxiliary Group (Carriers)

EXAMPLES—FORMATIONS

S.E.A.C.	South East Asia Command
N.A.C.C.	Northern Area Combat Command (U.S.)
I.N.A.	Indian National Army (Traitors)
A.C.F.	African Colonial Forces
23 (N.) Bde.	23 (Nigerian) Infantry Brigade
22 (E.A.) Bde. Gp.	22nd (East African) Brigade Group
1 (S.A.) Bde.	1st South African Infantry Brigade
7 Armd. Div.	7th Armoured Division
4 (Indian) Div.	4th (Indian) Division
81 (W.A.) Div.	81st (West African) Division
2 (W.A.) Bde.	2nd (West African) Infantry Brigade

EXAMPLES—UNITS

4 N.R.	4th Battalion the Nigeria Regiment
2 G.C.R.	2nd Battalion the Gold Coast Regiment
1 S.L.R.	1st Battalion the Sierra Leone Regiment
1 G.R.	1st Battalion the Gambia Regiment
K.A.R.	The King's African Rifles
1/3 K.A.R.	1st Battalion 3rd King's African Rifles
19 L.	19th Lancers (Indian Army)
2 Green Howards	2nd Battalion the Green Howards
1 L.F.	1st Battalion the Lancashire Fusiliers
1/4 Essex	1st/4th Battalion the Essex Regiment
1 S. Stafford	1st Battalion the South Staffordshire Regiment
7/16 Punjabis	7th Battalion 16th Punjab Regiment
3/2 Gurkhas	3rd Battalion 2nd Gurkha Rifles

Japanese

2/111 R.	2nd Battalion 111th Infantry Regiment
54 Div. Cav.	54th Divisional Cavalry Regiment

LIST OF SUBSCRIBERS

We gratefully acknowledge the financial help which we have received from the following governments, organisations and individuals and without whose help it would not have been possible to produce this work.

The Governments of:
- The Federation of Nigeria
- The Republic of Ghana
- Sierra Leone
- The Gambia

Military Establishments:
- Royal Military Academy, Sandhurst
- 5th (West African) Infantry Brigade Club

Firms and Companies:
- Ashanti Goldfields Corporation Limited
- Bank of West Africa Limited
- Barclays Bank D.C.O.
- British & French Bank Limited
- Elder Dempster Lines Limited
- John Holt & Company (Liverpool) Limited
- A. G. Leventis & Company Limited
- Lever Bros (Nigeria) Limited
- G. B. Ollivant Limited
- Sierra Leone Development Company Limited
- Sierra Leone Selection Trust
- United Africa Company Limited

Individual subscribers:
- Adye, Colonel J. E. (D.S.O.)
- Allt, G.
- Armstrong, Colonel J. F. (M.B.E.)
- Aston, T. B.
- Baker, Lieut.-Colonel E. T. L.
- Baker, G. L.
- Barlow, H. E.
- Barlow, Brigadier V. W. (D.S.O., O.B.E.)
- Barrow, R.
- Blackmore, Lieut.-Colonel C. W. P. (M.C.)
- Blake, Captain T. N. S.
- Boulton, Lieut.-Colonel C. H. (M.B.E., T.D.)
- Bowler, E. J. H.
- Brett, Sir Lionel (Kt.)
- Brown, Brigadier J. Gilbert (C.M.G., C.B.E., D.S.O.)
- Cairns, Lieut.-Colonel D. (M.B.E.)
- Campbell-Baldwin, Major A. N.
- Chater, Captain J. K.
- Cheal, A. S.
- Chrystal, Major A. J.
- Clarke, Brigadier F. A. S. (D.S.O.)
- Cocksedge, Lieut.-Colonel A. E. (D.S.O.)
- Collins, Captain D. E.
- Cromartie, Major the Earl of (M.C., J.P.)
- Crowe, Major D. M.
- Davis, Simon
- Dean, Major K. J. (T.D.)
- Exham, Major-General K. G. (C.B., D.S.O.)
- Field, Major C. S. (O.B.E.)
- Fitzgerald, B. E. Major (T.D.)
- Gardner, Major A. (O.B.E., M.C.)
- Gaskell, W. P.
- Gedge, J. B.
- Gibb, Lieut.-Colonel C.
- Giffard, General Sir George (G.C.B., D.S.O.)
- Grant, Brigadier E. H. G. (C.B.E., D.S.O.)
- Green, Lieut.-Colonel R. G. M. (M.C.)
- Greenwell, Colonel J. B. (C.B.E., D.S.O., D.L.)
- Hardman, Major F.
- Harrison, Lieut.-Colonel B. E.
- Haywood, Colonel A. (C.M.G., C.B.E., D.S.O.)
- Hazleton, Lieut.-Colonel B. E. (D.S.O., M.C.)
- Heards, Major J. R.
- Herbert, Lieut.-General Sir Otway (K.B.E., C.B., D.S.O.)
- Hillyard, Lieut.-Colonel H. L. S.
- Hooper, Major G. W.
- Hudson, Major E. C. R.
- Huffam, Major J. P. (V.C.)
- Inglis, Major-General G. H. (C.B., C.B.E., D.L., J.P.)
- Jeffrey, Major D. G. V.
- Johnson, Brigadier A. C. C.
- Keene, Lieut.-Colonel P. F.

Keylock, Major J. E. H. (O.B.E., T.D.)
Knocker, Lieut.Colonel H. S.
Knott, Lieut.-Colonel Sir Harold (K.C.B., O.B.E., Q.H.P.)
Knowles, Major J. M.
Laing, Brigadier G. (C.B.E.)
Lawrence, H. I. C.
Leniewski, J.
Linder, Brigadier J. F. (O.B.E., M.C.)
Loftus-Tottenham, Major-General F. J. (C.B.E., D.S.O.)
MacDermott, O. A.
Macpherson, Sir John (G.C.M.G.)
McNie, T. M.
Mitchell, Lieut.Colonel D. B.
Monckton, Major D. P.
Napier, Lieut.-Colonel G. H. C.
Nash, Captain K. H.
Nicholas, W. B.
Nichols, G. F.
O'Brien, Lieut.-Colonel D. D.
Paley, Major-General Sir Victor (K.B.E., C.B., D.S.O.)
Parkes, Major D. A.
Parry, Brigadier F. W. B. (C.B.E.)
Patrick, Major P.
Patten-Thomas, W. F. (M.C.)
Pickford, Major G. R. A. (T.D.)
Proudlock, Brigadier A. G. (D.S.O., O.B.E.)
Quinn, Colonel N. O.
Read, Major-General J. A. J. (C.B.E., D.S.O., M.C.)
Renwick, Major E. W.
Richards, Brigadier H. U. (C.B.E., D.S.O.)
Ritchie, Brigadier W. S. (O.B.E.)
Robertson, Sir James (G.C.M.G., G.C.V.O., K.B.E.)
Robson, T.
Rumball, F. G. L.
Scott, Captain C. H. N.
Sinclair, Major Sir George (C.M.G., O.B.E.)
Somerville, Lieut.-Colonel B. A.
Speer, Lieut.-Colonel M. C.
Stewart, Lieut.-Colonel A. D. J.
Stockwell, General Sir Hugh (G.C.B., K.B.E., D.S.O.)
Stroud, Capt. G. M. I.
Swynnerton, Major-General C.R.A. (C.B., D.S.O.)
Thackrey, Major B. E. (T.D.)
Theobald, Major W. A.
Thomas, D. K. N. L.–Capt.
Thomlin, B.
Vesey, D. M. E.
Wadell, Captain R. B.
Waller, Major R. J. R. (D.S.O.)
Ward, Brigadier P. S. (O.B.E.)
Webster, Major H. R. J. (T.D.)
Wenham, Lieut.-Colonel A. H.
Wheatley, Lieut.-Colonel H. C. (O.B.E., T.D.)
Whistler, General Sir Lashmer (G.C.B., K.B.E., D.S.O.)
Whitaker, J.
Whitfield, Major-General J. Y. (C.B., D.S.O., O.B.E.)
Willett, G. J.
Williams, Captain P. M.
Winward, F. G.
Woolner, Major-General C. G. (C.B., M.C.)
Young, Major-General P. C. F. (C.B.E.)

Our grateful thanks are also due to Messrs. Gale & Polden, and in particular to Mr. A. L. Kipling for the great interest they have taken in the preparation of the History and for their kind help and advice on the many problems of production.

INDEX

PERSONAL NAMES

Abdurahman, Sultan, 45, 46, 47
Abu Bekr, 13
Abubeker Gombai, Sheikh, 42
Abudu Dinga, Gun Carrier, 223
Abudulai, Cpl., 226
Adametz, Capt. (G), 112
Adams, Lt. F. D., 48
Adams, Capt. G. S. C., 110–11
Afolabi Ibadan, Pte., 223
Alafin, The, of Oyo, 26
Alhaji Diko, 48
Alhaji Grunshi, R.S.M., 99
Aliyu, Emir of Kano, 45–46
Amanda Fulani, Cpl., 204
Ambrose, Capt., 222
Anderson, Maj. F., 167, 174
Anderson, Capt., 53
Andrews, 2/Lt. F. E., 141
Anthony, Lt. G., 171
Aplin, Capt., 41, 51, 53
Archer, Lt.-Col., 189, 195
Armitage, Capt. C., 52–53, 258
Armstrong, Capt., 197, 222
Arnold, Capt. (Niger Coy.), 28–29
Arnold, Lt. (Gold Coast Regt.), 181
Askia the Great, 13
Aubin, Capt. A. C., 111
Awudu Argungu, L/Cpl., 207
Awudu Bakano, Sgt., 211
Awudu Kaduna, L/Cpl., 198
Awudu Katsena, Sgt., 227
Awudu Katsena, Gun Carrier, 196, 229
Awudu Sakadade, Pte., 109
Awufu Eloof, Pte., 193
Aymerich, Gen. (F), 120, 137, 147, 149, 151, 155, 160, 161, 164, 168

Baden-Powell, Maj., 26
Badger, Sgt., 219
Badham, Capt. G., 193, 196, 234, 239
Baikie, Capt., 5, 8, 19
Bail, Lt., 213
Baillie, Lt., 236–8
Baker, Capt. A. W., 33
Balders, Capt. A. W., 165
Bari-Bureh, Chief, 21, 23
Barker, Capt., 98–99
Barlow, Maj., 45
Beattie, Lt. A. E., 118, 148, 253
Beattie, Col.-Sgt., 179
Beaty-Ponall, Capt., R.N., 129
Beauclerck, Lt., 32
Beddoes, Maj., 37, 56–59
Bedford, Adml., 27
Beech, Lt., 205
Beecroft, Consul, 19
Beeves, Maj.-Gen., 207–13, 225–6
Belo Akure, Sgt.-Maj., 127–8, 198–9
Ben-Smith, R., 478
Biddulph, Capt. L. S., 165, 184–5
Bila Busanga, Cpl., 220
Biltcliffe, Lt., 206
Blackburn, Capt. C. J., 254
Blakeney, Capt., 22–23, 40, 43, 258
Blakiston, Mr., 3
Body, Lt. O. G., 115
Boileau, Lt., 22
Boisragon, Capt., 27
Bond, Capt. H. H., 105, 123, 135
Booth, Capt. A. H., 31–32
Booth, Col.-Sgt., 217
Bostock, Lt., 118
Bower, Capt., 27
Bowyer-Smijth, Lt., 110, 154, 159, 174
Brady, Capt., 213
Brake, Lt.-Col. C. J., 53, 55, 60
Bray, Lt., 179, 181, 206
Briscoe, Capt., 213
Brough, Lt.-Col. J., 174
Brown, Lt. H. L., 111
Browne, Brig. J. G., 3
Brownlie, Lt., 56
Bryan, Capt. H., 38, 40, 57, 60
Bryant, Capt. F. C., 97, 99, 100, 105
Bryne, Col.-Sgt., 116–18
Buchanan-Smith, Capt., 198, 222
Budgen, Lt., 217
Burgess, Lt. H. A., 43
Burney, Capt. G. T., 219
Burns, Sir Alan, 3
Burroughs, Maj., 53, 56–57
Butler, Capt. J. F. P., 130, 134, 166, 179

Calvert, Brig. J. M., 416, 418–21
Cardew, Sir Frederick, 28
Carré, Capt., 45
Carroll, Lt. J. W. V., 32
Carter, Capt. C. H. P., 28, 34, 53, 55–57, 81, 88, 106–7
Carter, Sir Gilbert, 17
Cartwright, Brig. R. N., 398, 435 *n.*
Cary, Lt. A. J. L., 155
Castaign, Capt. (F), 100–3
Cathie, Lt. H. W., 163
Chadwick, Sgt. W., 165
Chamberlain, Joseph, 31
Chamley, Capt. J. W., 132
Chapman, Capt. P., 83
Charles, Lt. J. R. E., 32
Chartres, Lt. J., 159
Cheesman, Mr. B., 3
Clapperton, Capt., 10
Clausnitzer, Mr., 99
Clifford, Sir Hugh, 121, 176
Cobbe, Maj., 58
Cockburn, Capt. J. B., 35, 88, 121, 139, 140, 150, 165, 168–9
Cockcraft, Capt. L. de la T., 84

Coles, Maj. R. G., 155, 171
Collins, Brig. E. H., 382
Collins, Lt. H. S., 101
Collins, Capt. J. G., 223
Cooke, Capt., 195
Coombs, Lt. A. E., 166
Corner, Lt. H. E., 167
Cotton, Lt.-Col., 159
Crailsheim, Capt. von (G), 136, 146, 153
Crane, Capt. J. H. C., 81
Craven, Capt. Hon. R., 165
Crawley, Capt. Eustace, 32, 45, 51
Crewe-Read, Capt., 44
Crook, Brig. A. A., 435
Crooke, Lt., 80
Crookenden, Capt. J., 112–15, 137, 157
Crowe, Lt. D. M., 166
Crozier, Brig., 47
Crutchley, Capt., 35
Cubitt, Capt. T. A., 51
Cuneen, Col.-Sgt., 236–7
Cunliffe, Capt. F., 111, 121, 137, 146, 153, 154–61, 164, 172–3, 188, 193, 217, 220, 224, 238, 255
Cunningham, Lt.-Gen. Alan, 332–3, 336, 338, 350
Cunningham, Col., 24

D'Amico, Dr., 130
Dawes, Lt. G. (Sierra Leone Bn.), 140, 174
Dawes, Capt. H. B. (Gold Coast Regt.), 240
Decoeur, Capt. (F), 20
de Miremont, Lt., 142
Dennis, Sgt. J., 115, 118
Denton, Sir George, 40, 87
Dickinson, Lt.-Gen. D. P., 325, 329, 332
Dinnen, Capt. C. H., 143
Dobbin, Capt. H. J., 87
Dobell, Capt. C. M., 48, 82, 83, 88, 97, 99, 106, 119, 121–2, 131, 145, 147, 149–58, 160–66, 168, 172, 174
Doering, Maj. von (G), 98–99
Dokes, Sgt. R., 147
Dorchester, Lord, 3
Downer, Lt., 185
Downes, Capt., 201, 217
Dudley, Capt., 195
Duncan, Lt., 184
Dykes, Col., 200

Eames, Capt., 24
Earle, Lt., 150
Easton, Capt. P. T., 253
Ebermaier, Governor (G), 168–9, 175
Eden, Capt., 56–57
Edwards, Brig.-Gen., 177, 200, 241
Edwards, Lt., 53, 57
Eglon, Lt., 207, 211
Element, Sgt., 227
Eley, Sgt., 229
Elgee, Capt. A., 53, 55
Elgee, Capt. P. E. L., 100, 112
Elizabeth II, H.M. Queen, visit to Nigeria, 479–80
Elliott, Sgt., 166
Ellis, Col., 22
Englebrechten, Lt. von (G), 133
Evans, Capt. J. S. P., 255
Evans, Sgt., 229
Ewart, Capt. F. R. C., 81

Fairtlough, Capt., 23–25
Fane, Maj. J., 135
Faucon, Lt.-Col. (F), 166–8, 171
Fell, Capt. M. E., 155, 165, 174
Feneran, Lt.-Col., 159, 217
Fergusson, Capt., 25
Ferrandi, Capt. (F), 107, 121, 153
Festing, Maj. A. H., 34, 106, 258
Finch, Lt. H. S., 142
FitzGerald, Lt.-Col., 29, 31, 33
Fitzpatrick, Lt. J., 146
Flanagan, Sgt., 166
Fodi Kabba, Chief, 59, 60
Fodi Silah, Chief, 22
Foley, Tim, 474
Foley, Capt., 25–26
Foster, Lt., R.A., 231, 238
Foulkes, Maj.-Gen. C. H., 46
Fowle, Capt. C. H., 154, 174, 217
Fox, Capt. H. C., 84
Fox, Capt. R. W., 106–8, 136
Francis, Maj. S. F. B., 3
Fraser, Dr., 108
Fraser, Sgt., 146
Freeman, Lt., 87
Fuller, Capt. C., R.N., 106, 126

Gallagher, Lt. C. E., 48
Gallwey, Sir Henry, 87
Gardner, Capt. A., 155, 195, 217, 219
Gethin, Col.-Sgt., 101
Gibb, Capt. C., 131, 133, 147–8, 174, 212
Gibbs, Capt. J. T., 109, 110
Giffard, Lt.-Col., 234; Gen. Sir George, 3, 324, 329, 364, 373, 376, 377, 427, 474
Giles, Capt. A. H., 131, 174
Gill, Capt. C., 131, 133
Gillmore, Brig. A. H., 419, 420
Glover, Capt., R.N., 5, 17
Godwin-Austin, Maj.-Gen., 332
Goering, Capt. Von (G), 230
Goldie, Sir George, 8, 19, 28–31
Goodwin, Capt. H., 181, 184, 206, 221, 237
Goodwin, Capt. R. H., 83
Gordon, Capt. H. P., 44
Gorges, Col. E. H., 119, 130, 133, 140–5. 161–9
Graham, Capt. F. O., 40, 42, 81
Grant, Capt. A., 7
Green, Capt., 195, 239
Greene, Capt. H. R., 181
Grieve, Dr. K. K., 163
Grove, Lt. K. S., 124
Guillemart, Lt. (F), 103
Gush, Capt., 231

Haedike, Maj. (G), 148, 166, 167
Hagen, Lt.-Col. (G), 169
Hall, Capt. W. M., 53, 55, 57

Hamilton, Lt.-Col. Bruce, 27
Hamilton, Lt., R.N., 137
Hannan, Mr. H., 3
Hanyngton, Brig.-Gen., 177, 182, 212-13
Harman, Capt., 184
Harrison, Lt., 195
Hartland, Capt., 213
Haskett-Smith, Lt., 85
Hasler, Capt. J., 51, 82
Hastings, Capt. W. C. N., 81, 85
Hawker, Lt., 33
Hawley, Maj. F. H., 255
Hawthorn, Col., 217
Hayes, Brig. J. W. A., 382, 394, 398
Haywood, Col. A., 118, 121–30, 134–7, 145–9, 161, 163–9, 171–2, 253–4
Headlam, Lt. T. E., 32
Heathcote, Capt. G. N., 87, 157
Heelas, Lt., 81
Henderson, Lt., R.N., 18, 26
Heneker, Capt. W. G., 41
Henry of Portugal, Prince, 17
Herodotus, 11
Hervey, Sgt., 227
Hetley, Capt. C. R., 226–7, 239
Higgins, Capt. P. C., 217
Hill, Lt. O. C. R., 88
Hills, Lt. E. R., 165
Hilton, Lt., 196
Hince, Lt. A. H., 43
Hobson, Lt., 216
Hodgson, Sir Frederick, 52
Holford, Maj., 58
Hollis, Capt., 185
Holme, Lt. A. C., 115–16
Hooker, Col.-Sgt. H. R. G., 139
Hopkinson, Capt. C. R. T., 112–16
Hopkinson, Capt. E. H., 40
Hornby, Capt. C. G., 174, 213
Hoskins, Maj.-Gen., 177, 197, 200, 204
Hoskyns, Lt., 40, 42
Humphries, Sgt., 56
Hutchinson, Sgt. J., 161
Hutin, Lt.-Col. (F), 138, 161, 171

Inglis, Lt. A. McC., 88
Isaacs, Lt., 181

Jeffries, Sgt., 196
Jenkins, Maj. F., 88, 253
Joseland, Lt., 217

Kano, Emir of, 45
Keating, Lt. H. C., 30, 32
Kellock, Lt., 227
Kelton, Lt., 185
Kemball, Maj. G. V., 34–40, 45–57, 96
Kennedy, Sgt., 166
Keyes, Capt. C. V., 36
King, Sgt. W., 159
Kinley, Lt., 205–6
Koba, Maj.-Gen., 395, 436, 438
Kofi Kofia, Chief, 59
Kyngdon, Lt., 102

Lalor, Capt., 27
Lamb, Col.-Sgt., 196
Lander, R., 10
Largeau, Col., 107, 120
Latham, Brig. H., 3
Law, Capt., 212
Le Meillour, Lt.-Col. (F), 138, 171–2
Le Mesurier, Capt. F. E., 83
Leggett, Lt. P. H. A., 53
Lettow, Col. von (G), 181, 183, 187, 204, 207, 213, 225–7, 230, 233, 235, 241
Lindsay, Dr. J., 111
Loch, Lt. E. E., 111
Locke, Capt., 27
Loftus-Tottenham, Maj.-Gen. F. J., 433
Looff, Capt. (G), 213
Lowry-Cole, 33, 35, 83
Lugard, Sir F. D., 15, 19, 29, 30–31, 33–34, 36–37, 42, 45–48, 111, 121, 131, 158, 172
Lugard, Lady, 14
Lyon, Maj. F., 38–39, 51

McCallum, Lt.-Col. H. C., 32
MacCarthy, Sir Charles, 6, 7
McClintock, Capt. A., 33, 37, 258
Macdonnell, Capt. D. H., 109
McElligot, Capt., 213–15
MacGregor, Laird, 7, 8
MacIver, Lt. K., 171
Mackenzie, Capt. A. J. L., 45
Mackenzie, Capt. A. M. N., 44, 63
Mackenzie, Col.-Sgt. J., 33, 58
Mackesy, Capt., 102
Mackinnon, Capt. L. W. A., 159
McLachlan, Lt., 42
Maclaverty, Capt. C. F. S., 142–3
Maclear, Capt. P., 44, 50, 88, 106, 108–11
Macleod, Sgt. R., 166
MacNaghten, Lt. E. B., 32, 35
Macpherson, Capt., 206
Magaji of Keffi, 45
Maifundi Shua, Sgt., 218
Mair, Capt. G. T., 50, 88, 106, 112–13, 115–16, 121, 131, 133, 135, 137
Manger, Lt. F. V., 87
Mann, Capt. G. D., 135, 157–8, 224–6, 230–1
Mannion, Sgt. J., 115
Marchand, Capt. (F), in Togoland, 99
Maritz, Lt. (F), 22
Markham-Rose, Lt. K., 148
Maroix, Maj. (F), 99, 100, 102–3
Marsh, Maj., 145
Marshall, Capt. G., 53
Marshall, Lt.-Col. (W.I.R.), 23, 95
Martin, Lt. L. H. T., 50
Mathieu, Cmdt. (F), 126, 147
Maud, Capt. W. H., 39, 49
Mawa Juma, Sgt.-Maj., 237
Maxwell, Capt. J. E. H. (Nigeria), 195, 226, 254
Maxwell, Lt. (Gold Coast), 213
May, Col.-Sgt., 181
Mayer, Col. (F), 125–6, 136–7, 143, 145, 147, 149, 164
Mechet, Cmdt. (F), 148–9, 163
Mellis, Maj. C. J., 37, 55, 57–59
Merrick, Capt. G. C., 42, 48

Mésségué, Capt. (F), 171
Milne-Home, Lt. A. C., 113–18, 195, 198, 238, 253
Miquelard, Maj. (F), 138
Mizon, Lt. (F), 19
Mohammed Belo, Sultan, 15
Molesworth, Lt. A. B., 34
Moloney, Capt., 45
Monde, Pte., 140
Montanaro, Maj. A. F., 34–35, 41, 44, 58, 84, 96
Montgomerie, Capt. H. G., 200
Moore, Maj., 21
Moorhouse, Capt. H. C., 44, 84, 258
Morakinyo Ibadan, C.S.M., 196
Morisson, Lt.-Col. (F), 120, 138, 154, 161, 168–72
Morland, Maj. T. L. N., 30–36, 42, 45, 51, 53, 58, 83, 85
Morley, Lt., 40, 81
Morris, Maj. A. H., 40, 43, 50–52
Mountbatten, Adml. Lord, 376
Mulholland, Lt., 227
Mundy, Capt. G. C. R., 47
Mungo Park, 10, 17
Muri, Emir of, 19

Nachtigall, Dr. (G), 20, 97, 105
Nana, Chief, 27
Naumann, Capt. (G), 200–3
Nelson, Sgt., 187–8, 203
Newlands, Mr., 99
Newstead, Lt.-Col. G. P., 139, 141–2
Nicholl, Capt. Rev., 203
Noble, Sgt., 39
Northey, Brig.-Gen., 182–3, 200, 204

O'Brien, Lt. D. H. W., 134
O'Brien, Capt. (R.A.M.C.), 185
O'Grady, Brig.-Gen. D. de C., 184, 187, 204, 213, 222, 224, 233
Oldman, R. D. F., 85, 187
Oliver, Lt., 217
Ollivant, Capt. A. H., 87
Ologboshiri, Chief, 95
O'Neill, Maj. W. H., 34–35
Ord, Capt. J. C., 43
Orr, Col., 220, 241
Othman dan Dodio, 14, 46–47
Overami, Chief, 27

Palmer, Capt. C. E., 43, 50, 83
Parker, Lt. G. H., 246–7
Parker, Lt. M. J., 140
Parr, Capt. B. C., 157
Partridge, Lt. P. J., 84
Pawle, Lt. D. W., 146
Percy, Lt., 216
Phillips, Capt., 27
Piggott, Capt., 184–5
Pilcher, Lt.-Col., 29, 32, 34
Poole, Capt. G. A. E., 164
Pomeroy, Lt., 196
Popp, Capt. (F), 155
Porter, Lt. H. A., 32
Potter, Capt., 100–1
Power, Maj. R. E., 84
Poyntz, Lt. R. H., 131, 179–80, 184
Pretorius, Maj., 224–5
Pring, Capt., 157, 201, 216–17
Puckle, Maj. T. N., 110–11
Pye, Capt., 184

Rabeh, 42
Raben, Capt. Von (G), 107
Rattray, R. S., 100
Rawson, Adml., 27
Read, Maj., 182
Redfern, Capt. A. F., 102
Remond, Capt. (F), 155
Rich, Lt., 184
Ricketts, Brig. A. H. G., 421
Roberts, Maj., 195–6, 229–33
Robertson, Mr. (Acting Governor), 97, 100
Robinson, Capt., W. A., 31, 34, 82–83
Rose, Lt.-Col. R. A. de B., 3, 119, 123, 124, 127–9, 143, 150, 161, 164–5, 167–8, 176, 184, 204, 213, 241–6
Rudkin, Capt. W. C. E., 82
Ryan, Lt., 234

Salami Yola, Sgt., 111
Sali Bagirmi, Cpl., 227
Salier, Lt. G., 118
Sambur, L/Cpl., 32
Sanderson, Lt., 237
Sanni Zozo, L/Cpl., 109
Sargent, Capt. J., 122, 174, 189, 195–6, 203, 255
Savage, Lt. J. A., 85, 87
Schneider, Lt. H. H., 132
Schmoll, Capt. (F), 169
Scott, Sir F., 26
Scott, Lt., 207
Scott-Moncrieff, Lt. R., 111
Seccombe, Capt. G., 159
Seymour, Maj. Lord Henry, 88, 108–9
Sharpe, Capt., 23, 25
Shaw, Capt. G., 179, 185, 206, 209, 211, 214–15, 220, 241
Shearing, Sgt.-Maj., 139
Sheffield, Capt. G. N., 159
Shehu of Burnu, 20
Sheppard, Maj.-Gen., 177
Sherlock, Lt. L. S., 109
Sherston, Lt. A., 84
Shields, Lt. G. H., 180, 187–8, 203
Silva (Trade Commissioner), 59
Sitwell, T. C. S., 59
Skeffington-Smyth, Capt., 82
Slater, Sir Ransford, 254
Slater, Lt., 54
Slim, Gen. W. J., 376–7, 411
Smallwood, Brig. G. R., 338, 359
Smith, Capt. E. de H., 82
Smith, Lt. S. B., 213–15, 236–7
Smuts, Lt.-Gen., 177–8, 181, 204
Sneyd, Lt.-Cmdr. R.N., 129
Somerset, Capt. Honble. F., 32–33
Sommerfeld, Capt. (G), 114
Southby, Capt., 222
Speak, Sgt., 196
Spratt, Sgt., 226

Stacpoole, Capt. H. A., 46
Stanley-Clarke, Capt., 84
Statham, Lt.-Col., 147
Steed, Sgt.-Maj., 110
Stein, Capt. (G), 169
Steptoe, Lt. H. N., 163
Stevenson, Lt., 217
Stewart, Lt. A. H., 111
Stewart, Sir Donald, 52
Stirling-Miller, Lt., 231
Stockwell, Maj.-Gen. H. C., 447, 456, 458, 465–7
Stretton, Lt. A. L. de C., 115–16, 216, 230–1
Strickland, Capt. E. P., 82
Studley, Capt., 217–19
Sully-Ibadan, L/Cpl., 187
Sumanu, Sgt.-Maj., 223
Swynnerton, Maj.-Gen. C. R. A., 431, 464, 474–5 *n.*

Tafel, Capt. von (G), 213, 221, 240–1
Tanti, Sgt., 219
Tarbett, Capt., 22–23, 25
Tasker, Sgt., 233
Taylor, Lt. R. R., 115, 118
Taylor, Cpl. W., 32
Taylor, Col., 207, 222
Taylor, Sub-Inspector, 22
Taylor, Lt., 185
Thompson, Lt. (Gold Coast Regt.), 103
Thompson, Lt. (Nigeria Regt.), 196
Thomson, Lt. (R. Niger Coy.), 29
Thurston, Capt. V. B., 87
Tidswell, Maj. E. C., 41, 44, 50
Timbela Busanga, Cpl., 204
Tombeur, Gen. (B), 182
Tomlin, Sgt., 234
Travers, Lt., 198
Trenchard, Capt. H., 50, 77, 84
Trengrouse, Lt. R. V., 163
Trollop, Sgt., 227
Trumper, Dr. W. A., 111
Tukuru Bouchi, Sgt.-Maj., 227
Turner, Lt.-Col. A. J., 143–74
Turner, Sgt., 108
Tyler, Col., 234

Underwood, Capt. J. P. D., 122, 174
Uniacke, Maj. G., 193

Van Deventer, Lt.-Gen., 177, 205, 212, 240
Vandeleur, Lt., 28–29
Vassall, Capt. G., 50
Vaughan, Lt.-Col., 141
Vise, Lt., 198

Wahle, Maj. (G), 182–3, 200, 221, 225–6, 233
Walker, Lt. G., 165
Wallace, Sir William, 29, 42
Wallace Wright, Capt., 45, 57, 88, 153, 174
Waller, Capt. R. J. R., 3, 166, 171, 174, 189, 198
Wallis, Capt. C. B., 24
Wanke, Capt. (G), 153
Waters, Capt. C. L., 219, 235
Waters, Lt. R. E. M., R.N., 112
Watherston, Maj. C. C., 43, 50
Wavell, Gen. Sir Archibald, 328–9, 338
Webb, Maj. S. N. C., 201
Webb-Bowen, Maj. W. I., 111, 136, 146, 154, 156, 158, 169
Webster, Assistant Resident, 45
Wesché, Lt. E. B., 113
West, Lt.-Col. C. C., 189, 193
Western, Brig. E. W. D., 431 *n.*, 464
Wetherall, Maj.-Gen. H. E. de R., 341
Wheatcroft, Col.-Sgt., 40
Wheeler, Capt., 179, 184
Whistler, Gen. Sir Lashmer, 484
Wickham, Capt. T. S., 109
Wilford, Lt. K., 44
Willcocks, Lt.-Col. J., 29, 31, 34, 36, 52–53, 55, 57–59, 95
Willis, Capt. M. H. S., 174
Wilkinson, Capt. C. A., 48
Wilkinson, Capt. P. S., 31, 35, 40, 53, 55
Wingate, Maj.-Gen. Orde, 411, 413, 416
Winter, Col.-Sgt. J. J., 134
Winter, Capt. N., 197
Wintgens, Capt. (G), 100
Wood, Lt., 215, 236–7
Woodgate, Col. E. R. P., 24
Woodley, Sgt., 196
Woolner, Maj.-Gen. C. G., 385, 391, 394, 405
Wray, Capt., 185
Wray, Lt., 215–16

Yates, Lt. W. G., 115

Zimmermann, Col. (G), 175

GENERAL

Aba, 321
Abakaliki, 50, 51
Abeokuta, 17, 27, 322, 476
Abyssinia, 324, 329, 341, 347, 349, 360
Accra, 9, 17, 81, 84, 318–19, 326, 372, 474–5, 481
Ada, 98
Adamawa, 14, 42
Adansis, 53, 55, 57–58
Addis Ababa, 347, 349, 365
Adegkape, 101
Agbanake, 99
Agbeluvoe, 101–2
Agbor, 51
Agreements: Anglo-French (1896), 18; (1898), 33; Anglo-German (1899), 20; Franco-British (1898), 18
Ain Walata, 13
Air supply, 381, 385, 405, 431, 433, 458, 485–6
Air support, 335, 341, 347, 353, 383, 387, 400, 405, 424, 426, 439, 442, 444–5, 449, 458, 465, 476
Akyab, 379, 380, 392, 431, 433, 444, 485
Aku (minor operation), 21
Akuse, 98
Alegyun, 457–8, 463
Alessandra, 336–7
Almoravides, 13
Ambam, 171
An, 432–3, 454, 456, 458–9, 461, 465–7, 485–6
An Chaung, 465, 467
Anecho, 98, 102
Apaukwa, 389, 393–5, 401, 439, 444
Appam, s.s., 119
Arabia, 16
Arakan, 377, 379–80, 383, 429–33, 467, 486
Arakan Yomas, 454, 466, 471, 485–6
Archibong, 118
Argungu, 30, 34
Aro Expedition, 41–43
Asaba, 44
Ashanti, 478, 481, 484; recruiting, 84; Wars (1802–43), 6; (1873), 7, 25, 49; (1895–6), 26; (1900–1), 35, 51
Assam, 376, 380, 424
Astraca, H.M.S., 146
Atabubu, 26
Atahiru, 48
Audoghast, 13
Auklo, 436

Babile Pass, 345–6
Badagry, 10
Bafing, 12
Bagwema, 22
Bamako, 18
Bamenda, 135
Bandajuma, 23–25, 43
Banjol, 7, 17
Banyo, 156, 158
Bare, 133, 135, 139–41
Barewa, 19
Baro, 11, 157
Bassa Province, 48
Bathurst, 7, 8, 42, 83
Bauchi, 9, 14, 15, 33, 42, 45, 48
Bawli Bazar, 383
Beaufort Island, Expedition, 28
Beho-Beho, Battle of, 193
Bekwai, 25, 55–57
Bende, 50
Bende-Onitsha-Hinterland Expedition, 50
Benin, 9, 27
Benin City: Operations, 95; Territories Expedition, 95
Benue River, 8, 19, 35–36, 48
Bepele Bridge affair, 122
Berber, 13, 15
Berbera, 338, 341
Bida, 28–30
Bidonegyaungwa, 387, 433, 436
Bilonde, 146–53
Bissidemo River, 346
Bita (Gambia), 40
Blackwater fever, 43, 48
Blockade, Cameroons, 151, 174
Bole, 50
Bonaberi, 105, 123, 135
Bonthe, 24
Borgu, 19, 29–33
Bornu, 14–16, 20, 42
Boundary Commission, Anglo-French, 46
Brazzaville, 145–9
British N.C.O.s, 38
Brohimie, 27
Buea, 127, 130–1, 140
Bulingo, 109
Bum, River, 24
Bum-Kittan, 21
Burma: situation, November 1943, 376–7; topography and climate, 378–93; health in, 380; communications, 379
Burmi, 45, 47–48
Buro Erillo, 335–7
Bussa, 10, 19, 32–33
Bush warfare, 317, 371, 404, 470, 485; experience in Burma, 450–1; mobility and flexibility, 360, 404, 449, 469; march discipline, 401, 404, 449; patrols in, 404; carriers, 404, 470–1
Buthidaung, 380, 382–3, 392, 431, 440–1, 443–4
Bweho-Chini, Battle of, 216–19

Cadamosto, 17

Calabar, 8, 106, 318, 323, 480
Cameroons, 327; Allied Expeditionary Force, 150; Allied dispositions in September 1914, 119–21;—in October 1915, 158–61; disturbances in 1951, 478;—in 1957, 482; German forces in 1914, 105; plan for invasion, 106; history and topography, 9, 20, 105
Campaigns. *See under* Tribal
Campo, 146, 155, 174
Cap, Kilmarnock, issue of, 49
Cape Coast Castle, 10, 53, 55
Cape St. Mary, 22, 43
Carrier Corps (Porters), 188, 206
Chad, Lake, 9, 16, 19, 20, 42, 105
Challenger, H.M.S., 106, 119, 146
Chang, 134–6
Chang-Mangas, 165–7
Charter, Royal, 5
Cheti, 102
Chibuk, 83
Chindwin River, 379, 381
Chiringa, 381, 383, 387, 404, 406, 431, 451
Chittagong, 383
Chop boxes, 38
Chupplies, issue of, 49
Colito, 350
Combo, district, 22
Commandants: Gold Coast Regt., 81, 88; Northern Nigeria Regt., 36, 37, 53, 85, 88; Nigeria Regt., 88, 106, 111; Southern Nigeria Regt., 84; West Africa Regt., 84
Companies: African Merchants, 6; National Africa, 8; Royal Adventurers, 6; Royal Africa, 6; Royal Niger, 19, 37
Congo, 105
Constabulary. *See* Units and Formations Index
Convention. *See under* Agreement
Cox's Bazar, 383
Creoles, 7
Cross River, 321
Cumberland, H.M.S., 106

Dabaskum, 107, 155
Dagh, Battle of, 15, 46
Dagomba, 14, 97
Dahomey, 17, 19, 29, 97, 99
Dakakeri, 48
Dakar, 19
Dalet, 453–4, 457–9, 461, 463, 469; Dalet Chaung, 456–7, 460–1
Dalet Taung Chaung, 459, 463
Daletme, 381, 385, 387, 406, 435
Dalle, 350, 355
Dar-es-Salaam, 177, 182
Daru, 43, 84, 88, 318, 320, 483
Dehane, 155
Dibombe, 145
Dikwa, 42
Dinassi, 58
Dixcove, 17
Dodan, 441–2
Dodoma, Battle of, 6
Dodowa, Battle of, 6
Dompoassi, 54
Duala, 97, 105, 111; surrender of, 121, 150, 167
Dumie, 143
Dutch Settlements, Gold Coast, 6
Dutumi, River, 180, 193, 195

East Africa, 1940–1: situation, June 1940, 328–9
Ebolowa, 166–9
Edea, 125–7, 136, 150, 164
Egba, Rising and Operations, 253–5
Egbaland, 16, 26–27
Ejisu, 58
Eket, 44
Ekom, 139, 141, 143
Ekumuku Society, 82
Ekwanta, 56
El Wak, 332–3
Elmina, 17
Enugu, 318, 322, 327, 476, 478, 480–1
Epe, 32
Eritrea, 329
Eseka, 105, 147–9, 163–7
Esumeja, 55, 57
Euphrates, River, 13
Expeditionary Force, Cameroons. *See under* Cameroons

Fad-el-Allah, 42
Falaba, 23
Fantis, 6
Fashoda, 29
Fernando Po, 8, 19
Fezzan, 161
Flogging, abolition of, 85
Fra Fra. *See* Mamprussi
Freetown, 8, 9, 11, 43, 318, 360, 363, 479, 483
'Frontiers' (e.g. Sierra Leone Police), 7, 20–25, 40, 43, 53, 56, 59
Fula (Fulani), 11–16, 28, 29, 96
Fumsu, 55–56
Futa Jallon, 9, 12, 18

Gabon, 105
Galla-Sidamo, 350, 360
Gallinas, 12, 21
Gambaga, 50, 51, 98
Gambia, 318, 320, 326, 474, 478, 481; Colony and River, 7, 10, 12, 17, 39, 50, 87; Expedition, 59
Gando, 14
Garua, 106–11, 137, 146, 153–4
Gashiga, 154
Gazawa, 14
Geidam, 107
Ghana, 11, 13, 481
Gober, 14, 46
Gogobiris, 16
Gold Coast, disturbances in 1948, 475–6
Gold Coast Hill, 184
Goldie, Fort, 33
Gonja, 14
Goppe Bazar, 383, 431, 439
'Grosse Krieg, 1914–18, Der', 105, 167, 172

Gujba, 42, 45
Gurin, 146
Gwa, 432–3, 467, 469, 471, 486

Habé Dynasty, 15
Hadeija, 57, 83
Hakluyt Society, 17
Harar, 338–9, 341, 345, 346
Hargeisa, 339, 343
Harmann's Farm, 139–42
Harmatan, 38
Hausa Constabulary. *See* Constabulary (Units and Formations Index)
Hausaland, 15
Hausas, origin of, 14; praise of by Willcocks, 59; recruiting of, 14, 31, 33
Health, pamphlet on, 34
Helo Island, 30
Ho, 481
Holland, 17
Hpontha, 453–4
Htittaw, 392, 437
Htizwe, 382, 392, 431, 449
Hut Tax War, 23, 33

Ibadan, 11, 17, 26–27, 33, 41, 44, 315, 318–21, 480
Ibi, 42, 112
Ibibio, 44
Ibo, characteristics of, 16
Igarra, operations, 41
Igbo-Bini, 41
Ikom, 106, 112–14, 118
Ilella, 46
Ilesha, 41
Illo, 30, 32, 51
Imo, River, 44
Indaw, 415
Indawgyi Lake, 417, 423–4; casualties evacuated from, 424
Inspector-General. *See* W.A.F.F., H.Q. Staff (Units and Formations Index)
Irrawaddy River, 379, 432
Isamankow, Battle of, 6
Ishan, 50
Ivory Coast, 21

Japanese: characteristics of troops, 378; their view of the African soldier, 470; comments on their methods of coast defence, 466–7; replacements, flow of, 377, 429
Jebba, 11, 32, 33
Jebuode, 16, 26, 33, 41
Jehad, 15, 28, 46
Jelib, 335–6
Jenne (Djenne), 13
Jibrella, 42, 45
Jiggers, 140
Jijiga, 339, 341
Jimma, 349–50, 356, 358–9
Joliba, 10
Jollofs (Wollofs), 11, 12
Jong, 21, 24
Juba River, 333, 335–6, 339, 485; crossing of, 335–7

Kaballa, 43
Kabba, 29
Kachia, 49
Kaddera, River, 33
Kaduna, 35, 106, 318–9, 321–2, 324, 477, 479, 482
Kaiama, 29, 33
Kaiema, 22
Kailahun (Kanrelahun), 23, 84, 88
Kake, 123
Kaladan: village, 387, 399, 400, 406, 433, 436; valley, 379, 381–2, 385, 389, 392–5, 399, 401, 405–6, 432, 435–7, 439, 443, 485
Kalapanzin, 379, 382, 398, 400, 402, 405, 431, 439, 440, 469
Kamaing, 425–6
Kambia, 21, 24
Kamina, 97–100, 103
Kangaw, 432, 450, 453–4, 456, 467
Kano, 11, 14, 15, 45–47, 318, 321, 324, 477, 480
Kano-Sokoto Expedition, 44–45, 96
Kanrelahun (Kailahun), 23, 84, 88
Kanuri, 14–16
Kanzauk, 382, 389, 391–3, 431, 436, 444, 447, 451, 467
Karene, 23
Kartucol, 241–6
Kasse, 23
Katsena, 9, 14, 46, 48, 57
Katsira, 477
Kaw, 454–7
Kawdu, 454
Kebbawa, 47
Keffi, 45
Kele, River, actions at, 147–9, 161, 163
Kentu, 112, 135
Kenya, frontier district, 329, 331; topography and climate, 329, 333
Kerneo Bilali, 22
Keta, 99
Khra, River, 102–3
Kiang, 59
Kibata, action of, 183–7
Kikarung Hill, affair of, 178
Kikende, 221
Kilba, operations, 48
Kilimanjaro, mountain, 177
Kilwa (Kisiwani), 182, 205, 207, 212–13
Kimbabwe, 193, 195
Kindaung, 402–3, 442
Kindaunggyi, 466–9
Kintampo, 50, 58, 95, 318, 320
Kismayu, 329, 333, 335, 337
Kissi, 23–24, 43, 50, 84; operations, 78–79
Kitoho Hill, action of, 180
Koinadugu, 23
Kokofu, engagement at, 55–58
Kolan, 460, 462
Kolmaka, 169
Koncha, 157
Konno, 21
Konongo, 136
Kontagora, 35, 42, 48, 96
Koranko, 21–22
Krachi, 98, 100, 103
Kreinggyaung, 387, 396–7
Kribi, 105, 127, 136, 140, 168

Kudaung Island, 430–1
Kumasi, 9, 10, 25–26, 35, 40, 43, 51, 81, 95, 98, 318, 320, 478
Kunde, 154
Kunywa, 456, 463, 465
Kusseri, 136
Kussu (*see* Mende), 12
Kwahu, 9
Kwale, 44, 50
Kwellu, 24
Kweshi, 457–8
Kwissa, 55–56
Kyaukpandu, 454–5, 461
Kyaukpyu, 431
Kyauktaw, 382, 385, 387, 389, 391–2, 395–7, 402, 436–8, 444
Kyingri, 396, 399, 433, 436–7, 439
Kyusanlai Pass, 425
Kyweguseik, 453–4, 456

Lagos, 315, 319, 322, 475, 479–81, 483; colony, 10; Hausas, 7, 17, 26
Lamurudu, 16
Lamy, Fort, 108, 121
Lapai, 30, 32
Largo, 21
Leaba, 33
Lechmenti, 359
Ledo, 379, 415
Lemro River, 439, 443, 447, 453
Leopard Society, 85
Letmauk, 457–9, 461, 464–6, 469
Letmauk Chaung, 463
Letpan, 433, 467
Liberia, 9, 43
Lili, River, 107
Limba, 21, 23
Lindi, 207, 212–13. *See also under* Columns (Units and Formations Index)
Lisoka, 130
Liwale, 204, 207, 213
Liwinda Ravine, 214–15
Lokoja, 8, 28–29, 32–33, 35, 46
Lome, 97, 99
Lomie, 143
Long Juju, 41, 63
Lukuledi Valley, 207, 235–8, 240
Lum, 132

Mabanta, 43
Mabungo, 337–8
Mafub, 171
Mafwe, 24–25
Mahamuni, 391–2
Mahenge Plateau, 183, 204, 213
Mahiwa, 225–34
Maiduguri, 48, 106–7
Maka, 122–30
Makonde Plateau, 217–40
Makurdi, 480
Makyaze, 444
Malaghea, 21
Mali, 12
Malinkes. *See* Mandingos
Malongwe, 182
Mamfe. *See* Ossidinge
Mampong, 81
Mamprussi, 13–14, 98
Mandara Mountains, 105, 107
Manding, 12
Mandingos, 10, 13, 21
Mangeles, 166–8
Mano, River, 21
Mansa Musa, 12–13
Maradi, 46
Marchand incident (F), 29
Marda Pass: topography, 341; capture of, 343–6, 485
Massasi, 204–7
Matem, 149
Maungdaw, 380, 382–3, 431
Mawarenye, 219
Mawlu, 415, 417, 420, 423
Mayu: Peninsula, 381–2, 431, 436, 439, 444, 485; River, 389, 392, 439, 440
Mazegyaung-Hkamwe, 402–3
Mbemkuru, River, 207, 220–1
Mbila, River, actions of, 148, 161, 163
Mbombomya, 213–14
Mbonjo, 122–3
Mbureku, 139, 141–2
Mdsik, 126–7
Me Chaung, 456–7, 463, 465
Mecca, 12, 46
Medals, grant of West African, African G.S. and African D.C.M., 49
Medina, 59
Medo, action, 242–5
Mekene, 318, 320
Meko, 4
Melle, Mellestine, 11, 13
Melong, 139–43
Mende, 7, 11, 12, 21–25, 85
Mgeta River, 180–1, 193
Mgwembe, action of, 193–7
Miang, 123
Mihambia, 213
Minbu, 432–3
Minbya, 430, 432, 453
Mizawa, 393, 395, 398–9, 400
Mkindu, 193–8
Mkpani, 44
Mkwera, 239–40
Mogadishu, 329, 335–6, 338–9, 341
Mogaung, 381, 416–17, 425
Molugwe, 107
Mombasa, 176, 329, 331
Monsi Hills, 55–56
Montols, 48
Mora, 107, 136–7, 156, 158, 172
Morocco, 13
Morogoro, 177, 199, 200, 203
Moshi, 10, 13, 14, 43, 100
Mowdok, 382, 393, 398, 404, 406–7, 433, 435
Moyambu, 43
Mpundu, 123, 127, 129
Mremba Hill, 230, 239
Mtumbei Hills, 187
Munaya, 113–14, 117
Mungo River, 123, 127
Munshi, 35, 82
Museums: Nigeria Regimental, 47; Ghana Regimental, 26

Muyuka, 123, 127, 129
Myebon, 430–2, 444, 467
Myitkyina, 379, 413, 416–17, 427
Myohaung, 389, 392, 406, 430, 432, 436–9, 443–5, 449–51, 467, 477; approach to, 444–7; battle of, 447–50; pursuit from, 453–4

Nafada, 107
Nahungo, 220
Nairobi, 326, 331, 333
Namupa Mission, 225–33
Naragauk Chaung, 443
Narungombe, Battle of, 209–13
Navarro, 84
Ndupe, 149, 161, 163
Neghelli, 339, 350
Nengedi, River, 222–3
Ngaundere, 105, 108
Ngoa, 172
Ngulamakong, 168
Ngwe, actions of, 147–9, 161
Ngwembe, action of, 193–7
Nigeria, disturbances: the Woman's War (1929), 321; in same area (1957), 481
Nikki, 19, 20
Nile Valley, 14–16, 28
Nkan, 171–2
Nkessa, 181
Nkongsamba, 105, 133, 139–45
Nkonjok, 150, 166
Nkoranza, 26, 81
Nlohe Bridge, 131–2
Northern Territories, Gold Coast, 13, 18, 21, 26, 40, 43, 51, 84
Nsanakang, action of, 112–16, 231
Nsanarati, 112–14, 116–17
Ntem, River, 172, 174
Nun River operation, 44
Nupe, 14, 28–29
Nyamtam, 124
Nyangao, Battle of, 226–35
Nyassa, Lake, 182–3
Nyengedi, action of, 222–5
Nyong, River, 105, 126–7, 155, 168–9

Obagbana, 88
Obassa, 59
Obokum, 44, 112, 114–15, 135
Obuassi, 55, 57
Odumassi, 43, 81
Ofinsu, 58
Oguta, 50
Okemue, 95
Okigwi, 57, 323
Okpoto, 48
Omo River, 356, 485; northern crossing, 357–8; southern crossing, 358–9
Onitsha, 51, 481
Osai Tutu, 52
Ossidinge, 112–14, 116, 131, 135
Owa operations, 83
Owerri, 50–51

Pagoda Hill, 389, 391, 393–5, 400
Paletwa, 385–6, 399, 431, 436
Panguma, 23, 43
Patani, actions, 28
Paundok Chaung, 443, 450
Pekki, 56
Penja, 145
Pepo, 24
Pi Chaung, 387, 389, 391, 394, 396, 398, 401, 433, 435–6
Pisani, 87
Pleiad, The, 19
Polo, 84
Port Harcourt, 480–1
Port Loko, 21, 23
Porto Novo, 19
Portuguese, 17
Prahsu, 25, 55–56
Prome, 379, 433, 467, 469, 471, 486
Protectorates: Lagos, 16, 17; Niger Coast, 8, 34; Northern Nigeria, 8; Oil Rivers, 8, 16, 34; Sierra Leone, 18, 22; Yorubaland, 26
Puge, River, 149

Quinella, 40
Quorra (Kworra), 10

Ramadaung Pass, 389, 401, 437 *n.*
Ramree Island, 431, 469
Rangoon, 376, 433, 471
Rawia, 49, 96
Razabil, 440
Rifle, Short Magazine Lee-Enfield, 49
Rio del Rey, 8, 118
Rio Muni, 105, 127, 145–6, 164, 169, 172, 174
Robin Tree Expedition, 28
Ronietta, 23–25
Rotifunk, 23–25
Rusha, River, 181
Rufiji River, 181, 183, 187, 193, 197, 199, 200, 204, 207
Ruponda, 221, 238, 240
Ruvu, River, 181
Ru-Ywa, 432, 454, 458–60, 462, 465, 467

Sahara, 9, 20
Saingdin Chaung, 399, 402, 441
Sakbajeme, 147, 161, 164
Saki, 41
Salaga, 50
Sallikeni, 43
Samory, 16, 21, 26
Sanaga River, 105, 126
Sandoway, 432–3, 467, 469, 471, 486
Sanga, River, 105, 120
Sangmelima, 169
Sangu River, 383, 407
Satiru, 82, 83, 96
Say, 19
Sekondi, 11, 17, 40, 81
Selborne Committee, 34, 37, 40, 45
Semolika, 48
Sende, 149, 163
Senegal, 5, 11, 15, 19, 77
Seychelles Islands, 26
Shari, River, 42
Shashamana, 350
Shaukchon, 461–3, 465–6
Sherbro, 12, 23–24
Shua, 14–16

Sierra Leone, 363, 365; disturbances (1955), 479, (1957), 481
Sikassiko, 50
Skarcies, River, 21
Slave Trade, 17, 18
Society of Merchants, 7
Soddu, 350, 355–6, 358
So-Dibanga, 147
Sofa, 21–23, 26
Sokoto, 9, 14–16, 19, 44–46, 51, 82
Somaliland, British, 85, 328, 331, 341; Italian, 329, 331–2, 360
Sonwa, 36
Southcol Route, 437 *n.*, 439
Stoebels Farm, 142
Strada Imperiale, 339
Sudan, 329, 363
Susa, 122–3
Susu, 12, 21

Tabora, 199, 200, 201
Takoradi, 363, 481
Takum, 112, 135
Tamale, 11, 14, 318, 320, 478, 481
Tamandu, 432–3, 454, 456–8, 460–2, 465–7, 485
Tambi, 21
Tambu, 21
Tana River, 329, 333, 347
Tanlwe Chaung, 464, 467–8
Tanga, 182
Taung Bazar, 383, 398, 402–3, 406, 437, 440
Taungbro, 383
Taungdaung, 391
Taungup, 379, 433, 464–7, 469
Tchara, 46
Tchiberi, 46
Teasani, 88
Teinnyo, 391, 443–5
Tejani, sect of, 45
Tembikunda, 10
Tepe, 108, 111
Teshi, 474, 482, 484
Thandada, 431, 438, 469
Thayettabin, 387, 391, 393–4, 437–8, 444
Themawa, 387, 399, 401
Thingyittaw Pagoda, 445, 447
Tibati, 154
Tigris, River, 13
Timbuktu, 11, 13
Timini, 7, 10, 12, 22, 23
Tingere affair, 154
Tinma, 399, 437–8
Tinto, 135
Togblekove, 100
Togoland, 9, 20; disturbances in, 481
Training, 323–4, 365–6, 371; R.W.A.F.F. Schools, 474, 482, 484
Tribal campaigns: Argungu, 68; Aro, 63–66, 96; Asaba Hinterland, 76; Bida, 61; Bende-Onitsha Hinterland, 80; Bornu, 66; Chibuk, 92–93; Dakakerri, 77–78; Eket, 74; Hadeija, 90–91; Igarra, 67–68; Irgungu Escort, 42; Irua, 69; Ishan, 62; Kaduna Surveys, 60; Kano-Sokoto, 69–72; Kilba, 77–78; Kissi, 78–79; Kontagora, 61; Kwale, 77; Kwale-Ishan, 79–80; Mkpani, 75; Munshi (1900), 60, (1906), 91–92; Niger Cross River, 86; Northern Hinterland, 86; Northern Ibibio, 76; Nun River, 74; Obokum, 77; Ogwashi-Oku, 93–94, Okpoto, 75–76; Onitsha Hinterland, 69; Owa, 92; Owerri (River Imo), 77; Satiru, 89–90; Sokoto-Burmi, 73–74; Sonkwala, 93
Tripoli, 15
'Tropical Dependency' (Lady Lugard), 14
Tschipadara River, 224
Tsevie, 100
Tumbru, 383
Tunnels Area, 383, 402, 431

Uganda Railway, 329
Uluguru Mountains, 177–8
Umoru, 46
Uri operations, 41

Victoria Cross, 45, 54
Volta River, 9, 13, 18, 87, 97, 478

Wa, 26, 50
Wacheke, 155
Wadara, 350–1; battle of, 351–4; 485; pursuit from, 354–5
Wagdugu, 18
Waiima, 21
Walagan, 391, 394–5
Wase, 48
Waziri, 45
Wendeh, 21
Wesso, 127
West Africa, situation in June 1940, 363; headquarters, 364, 366, 373; new units to be formed, 365
'West African Way', 381, 383, 391, 406
'Westdown', 439, 443–4
'White City', 415–17, 418–21, 423
Widemenge, 168
Wulade, 81, 83

Yabasi, 124–5
Yadaung, 389, 401
Yadu, 22
Yan Chaung, 454–5
Yangbassa, 33
Yapoma Bridge, 125
Yarbutenda, 19
Yaunde, 105, 143, 147, 151, 156, 164–6, 168, 175
Yavello, 350
Yegi, 478
Yeji, 50, 87
Yendi, 14, 48, 108
Yerghum, 49
Yola, 11, 35, 42, 46, 323
Yonni, 21
Yoruba, 14, 16, 31, 33, 35, 59
Yorubaland, 5, 10, 16

Zamfara, 14
Zaria, 318, 320–1, 323, 477, 483
Zungeru, 33

UNITS, FORMATIONS, ETC.

African Colonial Forces, 371, 471, 475, 477, 483, 485
Anti-Tank Regiments:
21st, 437
22nd, 453, 459, 464–5 *n*.

British and Indian Formations in Burma:
11th Army Group, 377, 411
14th Army, 377, 411, 429, 431, 433
IV Corps, 377, 381
XV Corps, 377, 380–3, 387, 389, 391–2, 401–2, 429, 432–3, 439, 441, 444, 458, 466, 469, 485
2nd (British) Division, 380
36th (British) Division, 382, 426–7
70th (British) Division, 411
3rd Commando Brigade, 377
3rd (Indian) Division. *See* 'Chindits'
4th (Indian) Division, 328
5th (Indian) Division, 382–3
7th (Indian) Division, 382–3
25th (Indian) Division, 383, 431–2, 439, 453–4
26th (Indian) Division, 382–3, 411, 431, 433, 467
4th (Indian) Brigade, 467–8
74th (Indian) Brigade, 432, 456, 460
Burma Rifles, 414

Carroll's Horse, 32
'Chindits': first expedition, 376, 411; second expedition, 411–27; strongholds, 413; results achieved, 427
Formations:
14th Brigade, 413, 415–17, 421, 423–4
16th Brigade, 413, 415–17
23rd Brigade, 413
77th Brigade, 413, 415–17, 419–21
111th Brigade, 413, 415–18, 424
3rd (W.A.) Brigade, 411, 413–14, 417–21, 423–5, 432
Columns:
No. 1, Linforce, 214, 221, 236, 240
No. 2, Linforce, 221, 236, 240
No. 3, Linforce, 213, 222, 233, 234, 239
No. 4, Linforce, 213, 222, 233, 234, 239
Constabulary:
Gold Coast, 18, 25, 26, 35, 40, 51, 53, 54, 56, 59
Hausa, 15
Hausas, Glover's, 25
Lagos, 5, 27, 51, 53, 56, 59
Niger Coast, 8, 33, 34
Royal Niger Company, 8, 16, 27–34

East Africa Formations:
11th (E.A.) Division, 331, 335, 341, 349–50, 355–6
12th (E.A.) Division, 331–2, 335, 339, 350
21st (E.A.) Brigade, 331, 350, 355
22nd (E.A.) Brigade, 331, 335, 337–8, 341, 347, 349–50, 355–6, 358, 444, 464–5, 467–9
23rd (N.) Brigade,[1] 331, 335, 336–9, 341, 343, 347, 349–50, 356–7, 359
24th (G.C.) Brigade,[1] 331–2, 335–7, 339, 350–1, 355
25th (E.A.) Brigade, 350
East African Armoured Car Regiment, 329, 338, 341, 352, 357
East African Scout Battalion, 385, 387, 389, 391–4, 399
European Reserve Force, 322; Engineer cadre, 322; Lagos Defence Force, 322; Cadre re-formed at Jos, 482

Fifth Indian Light Infantry, 157

Gambia Company, 320, 325
Gambia Regiment, 1st Battalion, 385–7, 391, 393–4, 399, 400, 406–7, 437–8, 444–5, 481
Gold Coast Regiment, 322, 475
1st Battalion, 325, 332, 336–7, 351–5, 441, 454, 459
2nd Battalion, 325, 336–7, 352–4, 459
3rd Battalion, 332, 336–7, 339, 351–5, 441, 454, 459, 474
4th Battalion, 365
5th Battalion, 387, 389, 393–8, 402–3, 435, 437, 445, 450
7th Battalion, 387, 389, 393–7, 435
8th Battalion, 387, 389, 392, 394–9, 401–3, 436, 445
Batteries, 332, 337, 352, 355, 400
Engineers, 352

Hausa Constabulary. *See* Constabulary
'Holdforce', 437, 439
'Hubforce', 399, 407

Indian Mountain Artillery, 433, 447
30th Regiment, 450, 455, 458, 460, 477
50th Regiment, 445
Italian formations:
21st (Colonial) Division, 349
22nd (Colonial) Division, 349
23rd (Colonial) Division, 349, 360
24th (Colonial) Division, 349, 351
25th (Colonial) Division, 349
26th (Colonial) Division, 349, 360
101st (Colonial) Division, 335, 349
102nd (Colonial) Division, 335

Japanese Formations and Units:
15th Division, 383

[1] These Brigades were renamed 1st and 2nd (W.A.) Brigades on their return to West Africa in 1941.

18th Division, 377, 415
31st Division, 377, 383
33rd Division, 377, 383
53rd Division, 417
54th Division, 377, 432, 450, 460, 466–7
55th Division, 377, 432, 450
56th Division, 377
24th Independent Brigade, 416, 419
54th Reconnaissance Regiment, 466
55th Divisional Cavalry, 389, 395–400, 407, 436, 443
111th Regiment, 391, 395–6, 398, 400, 403, 407, 436, 460, 466–7
121st Regiment, 432, 466
143rd Regiment, 395, 399, 436
144th Regiment, 395, 407
154th Regiment, 467
213th Regiment, 385
Honjo's detachment, 395

K.A.R. (King's African Rifles) Battalions:
1/2, 234
2/2, 183, 197, 214
3/2, 234
1/3, 211
3/3, 200, 211

Lagos Defence Force, 322
Lagos Battalion. *See under* W.A.F.F.
Linforce, 213, 221–5, 227, 231, 233, 238

Nigerian Marine, 105, 151
Nigerian Police, 104
Nigeria Regiment, 316, becomes 'Queen's Own' in 1956, 480. *See also* under W.A.F.F.
1st Battalion, 320, 322, 325, 332, 338, 343, 345–7, 357–8, 360, 441, 443, 449–50, 457–9, 463–4, 466, 471, 473, 475, 479–80
2nd Battalion, 320, 322, 325, 337, 339, 341, 343, 346–7, 350, 358–9, 441–3, 449–50, 457–8, 463–5, 475, 479–80
3rd Battalion, 320–1, 325, 338, 343, 345–6, 357–8, 360, 441–3, 449–50, 457–9, 463–6, 475, 480
4th Battalion, 315, 320–2, 325, 382, 385–6, 389, 391, 393–4, 396–7, 399, 401–4, 435–6, 444–5
5th Battalion, 322, 325, 447, 449, 455–7, 460–4, 474, 480
6th Battalion, 322, 417–18, 423, 425–6
7th Battalion, 419–21, 423, 426
9th Battalion, 445, 449, 455–6, 458, 460–3, 466 *n.*, 468–9
10th Battalion, 445, 447, 454–6, 458, 462, 465–6
12th Battalion, 416, 418–19, 423, 426–7
Light Batteries, 338, 343, 346–7, 357, 386, 400, 456; conversion to Reconnaissance Squadron, 482
Engineers, 338, 341, 357–8, 400–1

Pathans, 40th, 185

Punjab Regiment, 7th/16th Battalion, 393, 395, 398–9, 406–7, 454

Reconnaissance Units:
81st (W.A.) Regiment, 382, 385, 391–2, 402–3, 433, 436–7, 439, 444, 447, 453, 483
82nd (W.A.) Regiment, 444, 447, 449, 453, 456–8, 460, 466
Squadrons re-formed, Nigeria and Gold Coast, 482–3, 476
Royal African Colonial Corps, 6
Royal Niger Company Forces, 8, 14
R.W.A.F.F. Schools, 474, 482, 484

Senegalese Tirailleurs, 11, 121
Sierra Leone Regiment, 1st Battalion, 320, 325, 385–6, 389, 391, 393–4, 397, 399–403, 407, 435, 438–9, 444, 474, 479, 481, 483. *See also under* W.A.F.F.
Somaliland Camel Corps, 328
South African Formations:
1st Division, 331, 333
1st Brigade, 331–3, 335, 337, 341–2, 347
Artillery, 343, 345–7, 352, 357
Engineers, 333, 338, 347
South East Asia Command, 376–7, 432
Special Force. *See* Chapter 11, 'Chindits'

Tripura Rifles, 406–7

West African Formations:
81st Division, 374, 377, 381–3, 393, 395, 398, 402, 411, 431–2, 439, 443–5, 447, 450, 469, 473, 485
82nd Division, 374, 431–3, 439, 444–5, 454, 464, 466–7, 471, 473, 485
1st Brigade,[1] 373, 440–2, 444, 447, 449–50, 453–4, 456–60, 463–6, 469, 471, 473–4, 485
2nd Brigade,[1] 373, 440–4, 447, 450, 453–4, 456–60, 462–5, 467–9, 485
3rd Brigade. *See* 'Chindits'
4th Brigade, 440, 442, 443–4, 447, 449–50, 453–4, 456–8, 460–5, 468–9, 485
5th Brigade, 382, 387, 389, 391–7, 399–404, 435–9, 444–5, 447, 450
6th Brigade, 382, 385–7, 391–404, 407, 433, 436–8, 444–5, 447
Light Batteries, 394, 397, 399, 465
West African Frontier Force: Administration, composition, etc., 5, 14, 19, 31–34, 36–39, 49, 51, 59, 83, 87, 88, 167, 175, 253; Headquarters Staff, 31, 38, 49, 51, 70, 87, 88
Period 1897–1916:
Gambia Company, 11, 40, 42, 139, 147, 161–7
Gold Coast Regiment, 6, 10, 13, 97–103, 123, 127, 139, 140–2, 147, 161–7
Lagos Battalion, 5, 17, 41, 44, 95
Nigeria Regiment (Northern and Southern), 31–37, 44–48, 53–94, 106–75
Sierra Leone Battalion, 7, 11, 40, 43, 85, 99, 123, 127, 139, 140–2, 147, 161
Period 1916–19, East African Campaign:

[1] Served in East Africa, 1940–1, as 23 and 24 Brigades respectively. See Chapter 8.

Gambia Company, 212, 226, 230–31, 233–4
Gold Coast Regiment, 176, 177, 180, 181, 184, 185, 187, 197, 207, 209–11, 214, 216, 220
Nigeria Brigade: 188, 189, 197, 212–16, 223–8, 241
1st Battalion, 193, 201, 217, 226–30, 231, 233, 239
2nd Battalion, 193, 200, 217, 220, 226, 239
3rd Battalion, 193, 195, 200, 216, 223, 233, 239
4th Battalion, 193, 195, 199–201, 212, 216, 226, 227–9, 239
Both periods:
W.A.F.F. Artillery, 85, 176, 266–82
W.A.F.F., Mounted Infantry, 110, 146, 157–8, 258–66
West African Regiment, 24, 53, 56, 119, 124, 126, 137, 141, 169
West India Regiment, 6, 22, 26, 157
West Yorkshire Regiment, 26